Bill Frisell,
Beautiful Dreamer

Bill Frisell, Beautiful Dreamer

The Guitarist Who Changed the Sound of American Music

Philip Watson

First published in the UK and USA in 2022
by Faber & Faber Ltd
Bloomsbury House
74–77 Great Russell Street
London WC1B 3DA

Published in the USA in 2022.

Typeset by Faber & Faber Ltd
Printed and bound by CPI Group (UK) Ltd, Croydon, CR0 4YY

A CIP record for this book
is available from the British Library

ISBN 978–0–571–36166–3

2 4 6 8 10 9 7 5 3 1

'Now I will do nothing but listen,
To accrue what I hear into this song, to let sounds contribute toward it . . .
I hear all sounds running together, combined, fused or following,
Sounds of the city and sounds out of the city, sounds of the day and night . . .'

WALT WHITMAN, 'SONG OF MYSELF', LEAVES OF GRASS

'You can only go as far forward as you have gone back.'

RAHSAAN ROLAND KIRK

Contents

1. The Searcher   1
2. Billy the Kid   10
3. Once Upon a Time in the West   26
4. A Portrait of the Guitarist as a Young Man   40
5. Raised by Deer   57
6. Is That You?   75
7. Trioism   96
8. The Rambler   113
   COUNTERPOINT I:
9. Hal Willner Listens to *Lookout for Hope*   134
10. Once Upon a Time in the East Village   140
11. Song of Myself   160
12. Have a Little Faith   173
   COUNTERPOINT II:
13. The Bad Plus Listens to *Where in the World?*   190
14. Change Gonna Come   199
   COUNTERPOINT III:
15. Justin Vernon Listens to *This Land*   219
16. The Sounds I Saw   227
   COUNTERPOINT IV:
17. Jim Woodring Listens to *With Dave Holland and Elvin Jones*   250
18. Roots   258
   COUNTERPOINT V:
19. Sam Amidon Listens to *Good Dog, Happy Man*   279
20. Frislandia   286
   COUNTERPOINT VI:
21. Martin Hayes and Dennis Cahill Listen to *The Willies*   301

22. Like Dreamers Do   309
23. Across the Universe   323
    COUNTERPOINT VII:
24. Paul Simon Listens to *The Intercontinentals*   335
25. Six Hundred and Eight   341
    COUNTERPOINT VIII:
26. Gavin Bryars Listens to *History, Mystery*   360
27. History, Mystery   368
28. The Composer   386
    COUNTERPOINT IX:
29. Van Dyke Parks Listens to *Big Sur*   396
30. The Quiet American   403
    COUNTERPOINT X:
31. Gus Van Sant Listens to *When You Wish Upon a Star*   419
32. Music Is   424
    COUNTERPOINT XI:
33. Rhiannon Giddens Listens to *HARMONY*   440
33⅓. Becoming Bill Frisell   448

Acknowledgements   453
List of Images   457
Notes   461
Index   523

1: The Searcher

Bill Frisell has a dream. It's a real dream, one that he had thirty years ago now but that has stayed with him. A dream that occasionally comes back to him during waking hours, yet only partially, mutably, like a sequence of fading and distorting Polaroids.

In it, Frisell enters a large mansion and climbs a series of winding stairs that take him higher and higher. The building is rambling, ornate, American Gothic; it is dark and shadowy, and feels strangely claustrophobic.

At the top of the house, at the end of a long wood-panelled corridor, he scales a ladder that leads him up, through a gap in the ceiling, to a dimly lit attic lined with mahogany shelves, tall bookcases and curious artefacts – it's a cocoon-like space, a private library, perhaps.

Seated around a heavy central table are three 'nice little people' dressed in dark brown hooded robes. The 'miniature monks' tell Frisell they are going to show him 'stuff, the real stuff, how things really are'. They are going to share special truths, secret quiddities that very few come to know. One of them takes from a shelf a small wooden box containing cubes of different colours. He invites Frisell to open it. 'This is the true essence of colour, what colour really looks like,' he tells him.

Frisell looks at a red so bright and intense that it hurts his eyes: 'It was a red like I'd never seen, like it was psychedelic or something, or lit from within.' He has the same experience with blue and green: 'It was like I'd been blind and was seeing colour for the first time.'

Another 'monk' then turns to Frisell and says, 'We know you're a musician, so we'd like you to hear what real music sounds like.'

The sound that streams into the room is so pure and physical that it feels like a rod passing through his head. 'It was like an arrow shot between my eyes or a rocket ship travelling through my brain,' he explains. It's every piece of music he has imagined or heard, coexisting

1

and playing simultaneously. Yet what could be cacophony coalesces into the most harmonious, beautiful and perfect music. Then suddenly, of course, Bill Frisell wakes up.

'It was the most amazing thing I've ever heard, though it would be impossible to describe,' he tells me. He cannot recall what the melody was, be sure there even was one, or what type of music was being played: 'It was like one of those super-elaborate Chinese carved ivory [puzzle] balls – you don't know how they do it, but the further and further you look inside, the more and more layers you discover. I sort of remember the sound of strings – like a thousand violins playing independent parts. But it wasn't really a particular instrument, or instruments. And it wasn't a drone, because you could hear every little bit. It just included everything. It was all one thing. It was one sound.'

His memory of the dream may be elusive, yet its meaning and significance to Bill Frisell seem more clear. On one level, the dream represents the ideal (and myth) of artistic perfection, the apogee of creative struggle and endeavour, the liminal, mysterious forces at work in music and the arts. On another, it symbolises Bill Frisell's search.

'I could never, in any way, achieve anything remotely close to what I heard in the dream,' he says. 'But I got a glimpse of something to strive for, something real and concrete, something that I feel I actually heard. Something I know is there. I'm always reaching out for things that are just a little bit beyond my grasp, different things that sort of float by a little outside my focus. Sometimes I reach out, and they disappear. But that's what keeps me going, every day, every time I play.'

Frisell says he has experienced the sound, fleetingly, when playing in concert. 'There have been a few moments, just for a split second, when things have really lifted off, when I've just totally lost who's playing what, and I've had a tiny flash or reflection of that sound. I've barely seen it; it's like I'm on a high-speed train. But it's pretty awesome to even think that it might be there, to be reminded that maybe there's a way to get to all this stuff. Maybe that's what the beam or rod [of sound] means. It's about paying more attention, right? About staying clear, and making sure you somehow stay on target. It's about there being no reason why music can't be all together in one place.'

It may seem fanciful, romantic even, to allude to the power of such a dreamworld in the music of Bill Frisell. Yet he is not the first musician to have experienced such a striking epiphany. The inimitable jazz original Rahsaan Roland Kirk said that the extraordinary innovation of playing more than one horn at the same time came directly from a dream. 'The idea came from a whole lot of different dreams that I was having,' he once said. 'I'd be so frustrated after I'd practised, day in and day out. And I'd lay down and have these dreams; I'd hear different instruments simultaneously . . . one of the dreams . . . showed me playing two instruments simultaneously. So after that I set out to find the instruments that I heard in my dreams, by looking in antique shops and different types of music shops and things.'

From Paul McCartney to Keith Richards, Johnny Cash to Jimi Hendrix, Wagner to Ravel, Stravinsky and Berlioz, countless musicians and composers have said songs and compositions have come partially or fully formed to them in dreams. Jazz pianist Dave Brubeck even claimed to have found religion through a reverie of music. After hearing in a dream an entire composition and orchestration of the prayer 'Our Father' for a mass he had been commissioned to write, he was reportedly so moved by the revelation that he joined the Catholic Church.

The influence of Frisell's dream continues to resonate. He has written compositions with oneiric titles such as 'Like Dreamers Do', 'Dream On' and 'Shutter, Dream'. Then there are the albums *Beautiful Dreamers*, which includes a gently oblique version of Stephen Foster's 1864 parlour song 'Beautiful Dreamer', and *Blues Dream*, a suite of songs that stretches and expands across many American musical forms, and is widely considered to be one of his finest works. Beautiful Dreamers also became the name of one of Frisell's most consistently creative groups, a trio with Eyvind Kang on viola and Rudy Royston on drums.

Those who've worked closely with Frisell recognise the dream, and the search, as being important and revealing.

'Yeah, yeah, yeah, that sounds exactly what Bill is like,' says drummer Kenny Wollesen, when I describe The Frisell Dream to him. 'Because he has these ears that just capture everything. I mean, it's amazing, man; crazy. It's all going into his brain, and it makes me realise that there's a lot more going on than what I'm hearing.'

Eyvind Kang sees the dream as a kind of enlightenment. 'A dream like that is not just another wild dream; it represents a polarity, a dialectic with the practical side of Bill's world – all the extreme travelling and the brutal stuff to do with the making of the gigs,' he says. 'That dream, and other things, have hinted to me over the years that, from time to time, he's kind of operating on a sublime and visionary level.'

Cartoonist and animator Jim Woodring, who has illustrated two of Frisell's album covers, also takes a knowingly mystical line on The Frisell Dream: 'It's about something transcendental he can't remember, but that he knows is there. He's been to the mountain; he's heard it. Jesus, that's a great story. It's like a chapter from the Bible: "Bill's Revelations".'

•
•

The abiding impact of Frisell's dream is at the heart of his singular vision and exploratory drive – forces that over a period of forty-five years, forty-one albums as leader, appearances on more than three hundred recordings, and innumerable tours and live performances have established him as one of the most important, pioneering and panoramic musicians at work today.

Frisell has been lauded in the *New York Times* as 'the most significant and widely imitated guitarist to emerge in jazz since the beginning of the 1980s'. He has been called 'the musing poet of the jazz guitar' and 'the most distinctive stylist in contemporary jazz'. He has topped jazz charts, played major concert halls and festivals around the world, received prestigious grants and awards, and influential American jazz magazine *DownBeat* has acclaimed him as 'Best Guitarist' no less than fifteen times in its annual critics' poll.

Frisell has worked with many jazz luminaries, including venerated elder statesmen Charles Lloyd, Ron Carter and McCoy Tyner, venturesome free spirits Tim Berne, Andrew Cyrille and Julius Hemphill, and fellow guitar greats Jim Hall, John Scofield and Pat Metheny. He is the active embodiment of Metheny's memorable maxim that 'jazz is more of a verb than a noun'.

For almost thirty years Frisell was also part of a peerless trio led by one of the most important musicians in modern jazz: drummer Paul Motian. Motian established a working unit with Frisell and saxophonist Joe Lovano in the mid-1980s that would come to be regarded as the *ne plus ultra* of group interaction and improvisation.

'I'm fine with being described as "a jazz guitarist", and I respect that, and there's certainly plenty to do within that form,' says Frisell. 'It's just that when I think about some of the people who've inspired me – Thelonious Monk and Sonny Rollins and Miles Davis – for me, jazz is not so much a style as a way of thinking, a process of transforming what's around you. What bothers me is when the word is used to describe some music that excludes something else; it's like there are these rules that keep people apart. I'm just trying not to shut anything out.'

That open and adventurous approach is a major part of the wider appeal of Bill Frisell's music. His reach and dedicated following stretch far beyond the freeform yet sometimes introspective borders of jazz into a musical world shaped and inspired by a multifarious range of forms, from bluegrass to pop, Americana to avant-garde, blues to West African, folk to film music, ambient to alt-rock, country to classical. By bringing and blending all these styles into his playing, Frisell has changed the sound of jazz, the sound of the guitar, and the sound of American music.

Other guitarists have, to varying degrees, fused jazz with elements of rock (Larry Coryell), prog (Allan Holdsworth), metal (Vernon Reid), R&B (John Scofield), funk (James Blood Ulmer), soul (George Benson), pop (Les Paul), country (Lenny Breau), classical (Ralph Towner) and the avant-garde (Elliott Sharp).

5

The process has worked vice versa too in the jazz-tinged flamenco of Paco de Lucía; the Latin rock of Carlos Santana; the experimental soundscapes of Robert Fripp; the alt-rock explorations of Thurston Moore; the later albums of 'country gentleman' Chet Atkins; the extended solos of the Grateful Dead's Jerry Garcia; Hendrix.

Yet no one before Bill Frisell has so successfully and seamlessly synthesised so many disparate musical elements into one highly individual sound. Frisell has looked past and beyond taxonomy to work in a new realm that thrillingly ignores categories and constraints. You can hear it in his music, across the breadth of his compositions and contrasting groups – the infinite sounds of his impossibly beautiful dream.

Bill Frisell's music reaches out, like an open hand. It embraces, and it renders the idea of genre in music, however useful as a shorthand or handle, redundant. Genre becomes the least interesting and meaningful way of thinking about his music.

'Frisell plays guitar like Miles Davis played trumpet: in the hands of such radical thinkers, their instruments simply become different animals,' read a preview in the *New Yorker*. By creating music that is free-moving yet deep-rooted, Frisell has forged something entirely distinctive and of itself, a sound that, even after one note, is instantly, irrefutably, unmistakably his and his alone.

He has an ability to connect to forms outside jazz, and to the music of the American past, without, crucially, sounding kitsch or ersatz. It is a rare and particular artistry: a respect for musical antecedents that never succumbs to mimicry or, worst of all, sentimentality. No nostalgia. Frisell always seems to be reimagining and reworking, to be filtering the music through his own highly developed musical personality.

'The older I get, the more I keep looking back trying to figure out where I come from, and why,' he says. 'And the more I look back, the more information it gives me to move forward.'

•
•
•

Frisell is a shy, modest, contradictory, gentle giant of a man. His tall frame and bespectacled face led critic Gene Santoro to dub him 'the Clark Kent of the electric guitar'. 'Soft-spoken and self-effacing in conversation, he apparently breathes in lungfuls of raw fire when he straps on his guitar,' wrote Santoro in *Spin* magazine. 'His music is not what is typically called jazz, though it turns on improvisation; it's not rock 'n' roll; and it sure ain't that tired dinosaur called fusion. In one of the biggest leaps of imagination since the Yardbirds and Jimi Hendrix, Frisell . . . slams his hovering split-toned ax into shapes of things to come.'

Add a spare yet evocative playing technique that values space, shape and structure; a playful and irreverent slant – though never to the point of parody or pastiche; and a very musical approach to the infinite opportunities afforded by an array of pedals and effects – and the layers of meaning and possibility in his music become even greater.

Frisell has also explored the interplay between music and the visual arts. He has written abstract compositions in response to the work of German painter Gerhard Richter, created wonderfully slapstick scores for the silent films of Buster Keaton and crafted offbeat soundtracks for television specials by *The Far Side* cartoonist Gary Larson.

By turns, some of them quick and disorientating, Frisell's music can be graceful, melancholic, fluid, warm, haunting, violent, unsettling and heartbreaking. It is like a journey through the landscape of the American West: mythic, expansive, cinematic and, yes, dreamlike.

It is a free-spirited approach that has proven at once quietly revolutionary and vastly transformative. 'Bill Frisell's influence on what is now a few generations of guitarists is incalculable: his eclecticism, economy of means, and judicious use of effects have become a stylistic blueprint of sorts,' wrote Steve Futterman in the *New Yorker* in 2018.

By steadfastly following his own path Frisell has become the most unlikely of guitar heroes, an unexpected agent of change who has inspired others to endlessly expand their view of what jazz and music can be. As the British poet Michael Horovitz once said, Frisell is the 'maestro of all guitar possibilities'. He has altered and expanded the vocabulary of his instrument – and the language of jazz.

Musicians today working broadly within, or informed by, jazz may take this remodelling as read: the twenty-first-century millennial mix is wide open and genre-blind. But it wasn't always like this.

'Bill is like nothing else – there's jazz guitar up until Bill Frisell, and then there's [jazz guitar] after Bill Frisell,' drummer Dave King of the Bad Plus has said. 'You have to somehow deal with Bill Frisell, as far as I'm concerned. I think he's one of those voices in jazz history . . . that changed the game, and everybody knows it.'

By celebrating the connections between American and other musical forms, by finding what lies at the heart of them, and then, like his music-al heroes, transforming them into music at once faithful and original, old and new, urban and rural, black and white, Frisell has also subtly reconfigured and reconstituted what it means to be a modern American musician, and to play American music.

Frisell's desire to integrate is not lost on trumpeter Ron Miles. 'America has this race issue because it's so diverse, and each generation has sought a way to look at it, and find a solution through it, through sound,' he says. 'Bill is one of those guys who has found a way to deal with that issue, in a way that resonates with a lot of different people and a lot of different communities. So in that regard, I think he is a historically important American musician.'

Frisell has dissolved differences and broken down borders. In divisive times, he has been a unifying force. While some have sought to exclude, he has stood squarely for inclusion, for a broader church. Where some see contradiction, he hears harmony. He has reasserted a timeless value, an idea that represents America at its best: *e pluribus unum*. Contain multitudes.

•
•

Frisell's widescreen vision of music, his versatility and pluralism, have made him one of the most highly respected and sought-after players in contemporary music. If Frisell finds a connection to, or inspiration in a musician or project, there appears to be no context, no setting, that he will not risk putting himself into. It seems wilful, fearless, a restless restatement of the search.

Justin Vernon of Bon Iver may have been voted by the *Guardian* in 2018 as one of the 'most influential artists in music today', but the most influential musician on Vernon himself is Bill Frisell, so much so that Vernon has a tattoo of the title of one of Frisell's songs, 'That Was Then', across the top of his back. 'I don't think there's anybody else that I could say was a bigger influence on us – by which I mean my group of friends that are all still playing music – than Bill. He's our touchstone,' he says.

Lucinda Williams is no mean picker herself, but her 'favourite guitarist in the whole world', the musician she considers the 'best living contemporary guitar player' is Bill Frisell. 'I keep thinking, "How am I going to make another album *without* Bill Frisell?"' she has said.

'He is one of America's most unique musicians . . . a great American voice,' wrote Elvis Costello. Marianne Faithfull considers Frisell 'a genius'. 'I feel completely covered playing with him – like a full tapestry of sound has been hung behind me,' she says.

Others who have worked with and hailed Frisell include a diverse group that ranges from Paul Simon to Gus Van Sant, songwriter/arranger Van Dyke Parks to leading contemporary composer Gavin Bryars; free-folk innovator Sam Amidon to downtown experimentalist John Zorn; Irish fiddle virtuoso Martin Hayes to American roots singer-songwriter Rhiannon Giddens.

It can seem as if there is hardly anyone who knows about music who doesn't love Bill Frisell. He is, to quote saxophonist Paul Desmond's encomium to Jim Hall, 'the favourite guitarist of many people who agree on little else in music'.

Everybody digs Bill Frisell. This is the story of why.

Bill Frisell is driving around Denver, showing me the city he grew up in. It is early March 2017 and cold outside; Frisell is wearing an olive-green hooded fleece and a thick grey and ochre houndstooth woollen jacket. Tuning the radio of the hire car to Denver's jazz station, KUVO, he hits upon the *Morning Beat* with Victor Cooper. 'He went to the same school as me, East High, and when I was sixteen, he was the second singer we had in the Soul Merchants, our kind of R&B funk band,' says Frisell, smiling.

Frisell turns into Larimer Street, where we're stopping for brunch at hip downtown café Snooze. 'This area has been drastically cleaned up, but in the sixties it was skid row, where all the bums and the pawn shops were,' he continues. 'In the pawn shops it was just guitars, guitars, guitars, and my friend Karle Seydel and I used to get the bus down here – and just look at them. Then Karle actually got a guitar from a downtown store called Wells Music. Soon after that, I got my first electric guitar from a place near here on California Street called Happy Logan Music. It was 1965 and I was fourteen. I paid for it with money from my paper route.'

More than forty years after he left Denver, Frisell still has a strong emotional attachment to the city. He seems to savour strolling down familiar streets – for him Denver represents a childhood of mostly happy memories, of support, safety and opportunity. Perhaps because he has led the peripatetic life of a gigging musician, Denver also symbolises stability. He is not sentimental about the place, and knows full well the stark reality of the civil rights struggles Denver faced in the 1960s. Yet he retains a certain idealism about his early years. Even now he finds revisiting Denver, and looking back to his time there, comforting and nurturing.

'I think there have been some filters going on over the years, because I know it definitely wasn't like that, but my perception of it now is that it *was* idyllic,' he says. 'It's almost like I've concocted some kind of utopian and completely fictionalised memory of the place, almost like a dream,' he adds. 'In fact, I still have dreams about Denver. I'll drive down some of the streets I lived in, and walk through some of the houses I lived in, and those dreams always give me the most wonderful kind of feeling. And I think I draw on that.'

•
•

William Richard Frisell was born in Baltimore, Maryland, on 18 March 1951, but his family moved to Denver just a few months afterwards. His father, also known as Bill, was a biochemist and educator, and had been offered an assistant professorship at the University of Colorado School of Medicine. That July, Bill Sr, Bill's mother Jane, and their four-month-old baby, whom they called 'Billy', travelled 1,700 miles west. 'They got a 1951 Plymouth, brand new,' Frisell told Ethan Iverson for his blog *Do the Math.* 'We drove and left a trail of dirty diapers all the way across the country.'

In a short memoir written fifty-one years later, Jane Frisell related, 'We started out with Billy in the back seat, in a cardboard box we were using as a carrier. It really wasn't as bad as it sounds. We had covered the outside and inside with white butcher paper and had put a small pillow inside . . . We also expected the motion of the car to soothe him to sleep. How wrong we were!'

The Frisell family moved into a modest apartment in a complex on Locust Street, on the then eastern edge of the city. Shortly afterwards they found a small single-storey brick house nearby at 949 Krameria Street in the Montclair neighbourhood. 'It seemed like our "dream house" – just the cosy kind we liked,' Bill's mother enthused in her memoir, seemingly aware of 'the typical fifties suburban life' she was now living.

That life was dramatically ruptured in January 1952 when baby Billy almost died. Suffering from chronic diarrhoea and unable to retain foods or liquids, the ten-month-old was rushed to hospital on the advice of a paediatrician named Dr Robinson. By the time they left Krameria Street though, Bill was already, according to Jane, 'limp in my arms'.

He was immediately put on an IV and the parents sent home. 'Hospital policy wouldn't allow us to stay, and we went away, terrified,' wrote Jane. Visits were also not permitted. Over the next five days, however, Bill slowly recovered, and his parents were allowed to see him. 'It turned out I was completely dehydrated and it was very, very touch and go,' Bill recalls. 'I don't know exactly what it was, but I think I got some kind of infection, like an intestinal thing.'

'We were thankful ever after for Dr Robinson,' wrote Jane in her memoir. 'We always believed that, because of his quick concern and action, he saved Billy's life.'

Bill's parents met in Baltimore in 1946: Jane worked as an assistant in one of the labs at Johns Hopkins University, where Bill Sr was teaching and conducting postdoctoral research. Their first date was to an orchestral concert that was part of a series to which Bill had subscribed.

'My father was interested in her, but he was so shy he couldn't get to the point where he could ask her to go out,' explains Bill's younger brother Bob, laughing. 'So he actually had his friend, a colleague, do it for him: "Bill really wants to . . ."'

They married two years later. In 1949 Bill was awarded an American-Scandinavian Foundation fellowship to study for a year at Uppsala University in Sweden with Theodor Svedberg and Arne Tiselius: two distinguished biochemists who had both won the Nobel Prize in Chemistry.

Bill's father had a direct family connection to Sweden. He was born Wilhelm Richard Frisell on 27 April 1920 in the small city of Two Harbors in northeastern Minnesota, on the shores of Lake Superior – a half-hour's drive northeast along Highway 61 from Duluth, birthplace of Bob Dylan. Bill Frisell's paternal grandparents, Olof and Thyra, had met in Two Harbors and married a month before Bill Sr was born. Both were from Sweden. Olof – or Ole, as he was known – was the youngest of seven and moved with his parents in 1910, aged fourteen, from the hamlet of Eda Glasbruk in the far west of Sweden, just a mile from the border with Norway, on what is also now the Route 61 road.

Thyra Falk was one of fourteen children and from Gräsmark, around twenty miles east of Eda Glasbruk. In 1913, aged sixteen, she emigrated to Two Harbors – through Ellis Island, as had Ole; around 1.2 million Swedish immigrants arrived in the US between 1885 and 1915. Ole worked on the railway that had been built along the North Shore from Duluth; later he was general manager of a department store in Two Harbors. Bill Sr was Thyra and Ole's only son and Swedish was the language of life at home; he spoke hardly any English until he went to school aged five.

Frisell's grandparents were sturdy, stoic, hard-working, and Lutheran by birth, if not always by practice. They were family-oriented, fun-loving and enjoyed the great outdoors. In 1928 Ole built a cedarwood log cabin on forty acres of land he had bought near Two Harbors. 'We would visit Two Harbors almost every summer and I have strong memories of going out fishing on the lake in a little motorboat or rowboat with my father and grandfather,' says Bill. 'But it's the cabin I remember the most – it had one small room, a little bedroom and kitchen, a well and an outhouse at the back. It was right in the middle of the woods, and it was an amazing place for me to go as a kid.'

Music was an important part of family and community life. Ole played violin, cornet and euphonium; Bill Sr was encouraged to learn tuba and double bass – he played the latter in the town band. Thyra loved to sing, especially Swedish folk songs; she used to lull her grandchildren, Billy and Bobby, to sleep, when they visited.

Education was also a priority and Bill Sr excelled at school; in 1938 he won a full scholarship to study chemistry at St Olaf College in Northfield, Minnesota, around thirty-five miles south of Minneapolis. 'My father was a straight-A student, but I never got the feeling that his parents were real strict disciplinarians or anything – it was just something in him,' says Frisell. 'He had some kind of internal drive to be super-perfect with whatever he was doing, and his handwriting was all super-neat and careful. He was incredible.'

Bill Sr was included in the 1941 edition of *Who's Who Among Students in American Universities and Colleges.* 'Selection is not based on scholarship alone, but rather on a well-rounded college life, placing extracurricular activities on a level with scholarship,' the book states. 'The qualifications considered are character, leadership, scholarship, and potentialities.' Bill Sr was a member of St Olaf's Honors Society, Science Club, German Club, concert band and orchestra. Graduating with the highest honours, he was accepted for a masters at Johns Hopkins. He worked at the US Government's wartime Office of Scientific Research and Development during 1943–44, and was awarded a doctorate in biochemistry at Johns Hopkins in early 1946, the year he met Jane.

'My father would take me into his lab and start talking about his work, and I knew it was something related to bacteria – and I should know more, even now – but it was just so beyond what I could under-stand,' says Frisell. 'It seemed so foreign to me, like another language. I do remember noticing how fired up he was about it all, how he just tried as hard as he could the whole way. He was meticulous, and I'm aware I've got some of that obsessiveness myself. I'm sure he's influenced my persistence and stubbornness, too. I can see now that biochemistry for him is what music is for me.'

Margaret Jane Fleagle was born on 6 July 1920 in Colonial Park, on the western edge of Baltimore County, Maryland. Her German-American family had worked hard and done well; Jane grew up in a large, three-storey, wooden-framed clapboard property with covered porches and gabled dormer windows. She was the youngest of four children; she had one sister, Mary, and two brothers, Robert and Benjamin; Benjamin was born in 1914 but lived for just nine days. Jane's father was also called Ben-jamin – 'There has been an "Uncle Ben" in every generation of our family for two hundred years,' Frisell's second cousin Matt Fleagle once declared.

Benjamin Fleagle, Bill's maternal grandfather, was born in Taneytown in northern Maryland as one of nine children, and grew up on a small farm in Mayberry, about three miles east of Taneytown (just a few miles down the road is a small community called Frizzellburg). He was a teacher and educator, serving as principal of Hampstead High School, twenty-five miles northwest of Baltimore, then head of the English department of Baltimore City College. He also worked at Johns Hopkins, and at the university in Columbia, on the outskirts of the city. Jane's father was, by most accounts, strict, stern, conservative and church-going – he was an active member of the Baltimore Presbyterian Church board and a Sunday school superintendent.

'He was tall, had thick white hair, always wore a suit, and I remember him as kind of stiff and uptight – he didn't talk much,' says Bill. 'But when he got to church every week he would really let loose. He'd sing the hymns so loudly that he would drown out all the others, or he'd try to sort of harmonise the melodies, or he'd carry on after everyone else in the church had finished. I just remember being so embarrassed; I can hear it in my mind even now.'

Frisell jokes there was another branch to the extended Fleagle family tree: 'I once came across a group called the Fleagle Gang, who were famous bank robbers that terrorised the country in the early twentieth century. I don't know if I'm related to them,' he deadpans, 'but that's pretty good.'

Bill's maternal grandmother, Frances ('Fanny') Guthrie was born in West Virginia. She was the fifth of eight children and grew up on a large farm near the town of Romney, the state's oldest settlement. The Guthries can trace their American roots back to around 1700, mostly to New England and Pennsylvania, and before that to the county of Angus in Scotland. Like the Fleagles, they were members of the Presbyterian Church; Jane's grandfather, William, was said to be 'a man of unbending integrity' – yet also one of 'generous impulses, open-hearted and frank'.

'Our grandfather was conservative, but my mother's mother was actually quite liberal,' says Bob Frisell. 'So it was sort of a mixed marriage.'

While there is no known link to the Woody Guthrie line of the extended family – all that was happening around a thousand miles west in Oklahoma – Fanny had a keen interest in music, studying piano at a conservatory in Baltimore before she married Benjamin. It's likely that she also had some feel for local Appalachian folk music, especially its songs and ballads. If so, it was a passion she passed on to her daughter.

'My mother used to sing and whistle when she was working around the house, and she knew hundreds of old standard songs . . . the words and everything,' Bill has said. 'Years and years later when I became interested in . . . trying to learn some of these old songs, I was surprised to realise that she knew all of them.'

Jane's parents moved to Catonsville, just to the west of Baltimore, in 1946. In the 1950s and 1960s, the Frisells would try to visit Jane's family every summer. 'I can't imagine this now, but when I was six, my brother and I would take the trolley car [from Catonsville] to downtown Baltimore by ourselves,' Frisell told the Baltimore *City Paper*. 'I remember all those rowhouses with the marble steps. I remember it being so hot that the tar on the street was bubbling up.'

Bill's mother inherited her father's love of education and literature, and her mother's liberal approach to life and the arts. But she shared one overriding characteristic with her husband: shyness. 'Shy is actually a mild way to put it,' says Frisell. 'I don't know if it was being repressed in some way, or whether my parents were just naturally withdrawn or inward-looking, or it was the religious thing, or a certain fearfulness, or something . . . but they were both *very* shy.'

Bill Sr's work as a prominent scientist and educator forced him to overcome such a potentially debilitating trait. 'I feel like that's happened with me and music,' says Frisell. 'I'm shy, but the music has always given me a way; it's brought me out of that feeling of being locked in or just terrified.'

Perhaps Bill Sr's shyness was, in part, a Swedish attribute. In his book *Shrinking Violets: A Field Guide to Shyness*, British author and academic Joe Moran suggests certain cultures may simply be more prone to diffidence and modesty: 'Nordic people have a reputation for shyness – a product, perhaps of a Calvinist Protestant tradition that shunned brazenness and ostentation, the freezing temperatures that necessitated taciturnity when outdoors, and the ethnic homogeneity which meant that shared experiences and feelings needed only to be implied rather than said out loud.'

Moran also quotes Susan Sontag, who lived in Stockholm at the end of the 1960s. 'Talking apparently never ceases to be a problem for the Swedes: a lean across an abyss,' she wrote. 'Conversations are always in danger of running out of gas, both from the imperative of secretiveness and from the positive lure of silence. Silence is the Swedish national vice.'

Bob Frisell agrees, yet sees its effectiveness. 'I remember one evening when I was around seven years old, Bill and I and our parents were on the couch watching television, and the cartoons were about to come on – and my dad turned the channel to some boring Walter Cronkite news programme. I actually had a temper tantrum, and I tore up the newspaper. My father didn't say a word,' laughs Bob. 'He just sat there calmly, and let me rant and rave, until I realised that the channel would *not* be turned to the cartoons, and I gave up. He was firm, and that was it. He just did the job without saying anything.'

Moran points out that the Swedish word for shyness, *blyg*, carries 'positive associations, suggesting someone who is unassuming and willing to listen to others'. He also draws reference to Swedish-speaking Finnish author and illustrator Tove Jansson, creator of the much loved *Moomin* books: 'Jansson's lesson is not that shy people should come out of their shells; it is that they should learn to become non-neurotic introverts. Moomins may sulk and skulk fleetingly, but most of the time they are neither needy nor neurotic. Their response to a problem is to think deeply and then make something – a hut, a painting, a poem, a boat carved out of bark – as a way of whittling meaning out of a terrifying world.'

Bill's paternal grandfather built a hut in the woods. Bill's father painted his entire life. Bill made music.

●
●

Bill Frisell is standing outside 834 Cook Street. The third Frisell family home in Denver was small but nearer downtown, and even closer to the

School of Medicine; Bill's father used to walk to work.

'We moved here in 1955, around the time we got our first television – I can clearly remember the evening my father brought this strange box into the house, and it being a big deal,' Frisell says. 'When I was around four or five, I'd watch cartoons on that black-and-white TV in this house every day, and I sort of became addicted. I'd watch *The Mickey Mouse Club* and at the end of the show the host, a guy named Jimmie Dodd, would come on to say goodbye, or sometimes to deliver some message, and all the kids with their Mouseketeer ears on would gather round, and he would play his guitar and they'd sing a song.

'Jimmie Dodd's guitar had a drawing of Mickey Mouse's head on it, with two big round ears on the body up by the neck. It was called a "Mousegetar" and I thought it was just so cool. It was this beautiful, fascinating object that seemed to have the power to bring everyone together. So I took a piece of cardboard, drew out the shape of a guitar, cut it out and put rubber bands on it for strings. That was my first guitar.'

This was the post-war era of boundless American power and prosperity, of national optimism and space-age vision, of no less than the galvanising potential of the American Dream made real. There was another very different and divided America, of course, especially if you were African American and living in the South, but the Frisell family in Denver benefited fully from this revolution. They were almost a 1950s American archetype: of the baby boom, high employment, rising wages and suburban expansion; of the consumerism of new cars, televisions, washing machines and vacuum cleaners; and of radios, and increasingly record players, that started playing a new music which would transform everything – youth culture, society, language, sex, rigid segregation, the country itself.

The chief instrument of that change, the one swaying suggestively between the sneer of Elvis's lip and the swivel of his hips, the one slung provocatively between the spreadeagled legs of Chuck Berry, the one adding an off-beat appeal to bespectacled Buddy Holly, was the electric guitar. In a country that was still politically, socially and culturally conservative, the electric guitar symbolised freedom, modernity, mischief and rebellion.

With more and more technologically advanced models being produced by manufacturers such as Gibson, Gretsch and Fender (the Fender Telecaster was 'born' the same year as Bill Frisell, in 1951), electric guitars were suddenly increasingly available and affordable. Democratic, populist and versatile, they were the instruments of a new music and a new generation. It was little wonder that they appealed to the young Bill Frisell, even – or especially – in distant suburban Denver.

'From a really, really little kid I remember always being fascinated with it [the electric guitar] . . . then growing up during that time it just seemed sort of normal – so many people had guitars,' Frisell has said. 'There was a time it was almost like sports or something. People would play baseball and then they would play guitar.'

Walking along Cook Street, Frisell points to a house across the road, towards the junction with 9th Avenue. 'That second-to-last house over there, that was where my friend George Kawamoto lived,' he says. 'He could make knives from pieces of metal and wood and stuff, and he was just a huge hero of mine. I used to really look up to him. When I was about ten or eleven, George got a guitar, and another kid I played with had a guitar in his house, and I just started noodling around on them, and I connected with it. But George was the guy who made me want to play the guitar.'

He'd had a positive impact on Frisell a few years earlier too. 'There was a little girl called Bea Davis, who lived next to George and that I didn't like, and one time I got into a fight with her,' confesses Frisell. 'I was only six, but it was my early juvenile delinquent phase, or something, and I thought I was being cool. George Kawamoto beat the shit out of me. Taught me a lesson: you're not supposed to beat up girls. I'm glad I got that straight back then.'

After many requests, Frisell's mother bought Bill his own small Japanese transistor radio. 'I can remember that radio even now, because I was just in love with the sounds that were coming out of it,' he says. 'It was a very powerful thing; I could almost taste the music. I would go to sleep with it.'

The sounds of surf music were the first to make serious waves in Bill Frisell's world – significantly, guitar-led instrumental surf music – despite the fact that Denver boasted a vibrant sixties acoustic folk music scene, and was around a thousand miles from the nearest ocean.

But what Colorado did have, wonderfully and perversely, was its own popular homegrown sixties surf group: the Astronauts. The five-piece band was based in Boulder, twenty-five miles northwest of Denver, a liberal college town in the foothills of the Rockies. In 1963 the Astronauts had a minor hit with 'Baja', a bright, catchy, Fender reverb-soaked surf-rock instrumental written by Lee Hazlewood. More than fifty years later, Frisell would pay tribute to its enduring influence by recording the song on an album called *Guitar in the Space Age!*

'The first stuff that ever got me fired up was surf music – the Ventures, the Astronauts, the Beach Boys . . . [that] awareness of guitars and how cool they must be to play,' Frisell told the Minneapolis *Star Tribune*. '[That was] the tipping point for me becoming obsessed with music as a kid.' Frisell would buy surf magazines and pore over photographs of surfers, as sporting daredevils and pop-cultural pioneers; 'I'd fantasise about buying a surfboard – not even to surf, but just to have it, just to look at it,' he told me.

The first record he bought with his own money was the Beach Boys' single 'Surfer Girl', also released in the summer of 1963. Frisell was attracted not just to the twangy guitar riffs, but to the song's swaying melody and swooning vocal harmonies: 'I didn't know what was going on, but I knew it was the most beautiful sound I'd ever heard.'

The B-side of that 45 was 'Little Deuce Coupe'. As a classic child of the early sixties, Frisell was a serious fan of performance engines, custom cars and hot rods (cartoons, rockets, dinosaurs, monsters, science fiction and outer space also rocked his world around this age). He was once asked, 'What musical/performing/visual artists turned your world upside down as a teenager?' Frisell replied, 'Ed "Big Daddy" Roth, Bob Dylan, Miles Davis.' In that order. Roth was a Southern Californian cartoonist, illustrator and custom car designer, builder and provocateur who created the hot-rod anti-hero Rat Fink. 'I had this fantasy about being a drag racer or race-car driver, but then I also loved guitars, and I remember one day it kind of shifted in my mind that I wanted to play guitar instead of being a racer,' says Frisell. 'I was in the alley and my mother was taking the trash out, or something – and I said to her, "I've decided I would rather play the guitar than be a race-car driver." And she was like, "Oh Billy, that's just wonderful."'

That Christmas 1963, Bill got his very first guitar: a cheap $20 archtop.

•
•

The guitar wasn't his first instrument, however. When Frisell was nine and in fourth grade at Teller Elementary School, he was asked whether he wanted to play an instrument. He chose, or more accurately his father chose for him, the clarinet.

'He thought it was a good instrument, and I remember he was excited and enthusiastic about the idea of me playing it,' says Frisell. 'My brother Bob was encouraged in the same way, on the trumpet, and he had a lot of musical ability. He sort of had a natural ear for music. It's just that he didn't stick with it the same way I did.'

Frisell would continue with the clarinet for the next ten years, playing the instrument through school and college, and being urged by his parents to work hard and practise diligently and daily. He had a series of supportive teachers who quickly recognised his talent and commitment: Jack Frederiksen at Teller, who was also a composer and working musician; Charles Fields at Gove Junior High School; and the director of the East High School band, Vincent Tagliavore.

Frisell joined the Denver Youth Musicians' marching and concert band, quickly progressing from the beginners' band, through intermediate, to lead clarinettist in the Gold Sash Band. 'It was a big deal to get into that band,' he says. It meant, for example, travelling to New

York, aged thirteen, to play at the huge 'Peace Through Understanding' 1964 World's Fair in Flushing Meadows Park in Queens. Frisell would play in the band until he was seventeen.

The director of the Gold Sash Band, Jack Stevens, was also a clarinet player, and an important early influence on Frisell: 'Jack was strict, and everything had to be just really regimented and organised; it was almost a military process. But he was an amazing teacher, he had a plan, and it was through him that I really began to learn the fundamentals of music. And to make progress, especially when it came to rhythm and time. That marching thing – left, right, left, right, left, right – had to get into me and affect me in some way.'

Frisell has also described playing in the band as his 'most character-building experience': 'You had to show up exactly on time, and then march in a dead straight line, while playing music and wearing a really uncomfortable uniform. One of the first parades I took part in was at the 1960 Denver Stock Show, and it was in January and freezing – so cold I couldn't move my fingers. And you couldn't break the line – whatever. If there were big piles of cow shit on the ground, you just had to splat right through them.'

Stevens became Frisell's private teacher, encouraging him at twelve to take up tenor saxophone. Later, when Frisell was sixteen and showing signs of becoming an exceptional musician – he had started playing in woodwind quintets and chamber groups and become first chair clarinet in the Colorado All-State Orchestra for high-school students – Stevens passed him on to study with Richard Joiner, the principal clarinettist with the Denver Symphony Orchestra. That involved playing Debussy's *Première Rhapsodie* and the Mozart *Clarinet Concerto*.

But Frisell's heart was not really in it. Six weeks or so after he was given that first acoustic guitar, and a little more than a month before his thirteenth birthday, the Beatles appeared on *The Ed Sullivan Show*. Frisell's world, like that of many kids his age at the time, changed fundamentally and for ever: '[The Beatles were] absolutely gigantic – about as gigantic as you can get. It's at the very beginning of me wanting to do this stuff.

Then they come along and it was like, *"Oh my God!"* It's so huge for me. It's about as big a thing in my life, an event, as you could possibly imagine. It got me playing music, really.'

Maybe it's hard, almost sixty years on, to fully appreciate the unprecedented hysteria surrounding the Beatles' first appearances in America: the outrageous success and crazy sales figures; the madness and the screaming and the fainting.

An estimated seventy-three million people, almost forty per cent of the American population, watched the Beatles on *The Ed Sullivan Show* on 9 February 1964; it was the largest ever television audience at that time. And every American kid who saw them heard that indelible early Beatles sound, at once oddly familiar and radically new. 'It was absolutely shocking, devastating. It was so strong, that sound,' Frisell told *Jazziz* magazine. 'When I first heard "I Want to Hold Your Hand", the harmony and power of all of them together was just . . . I'd never heard anything like it.' E Street Band guitarist and actor Steven Van Zandt, who was thirteen at the time, summed up the impact in the *New Yorker*: 'For those of us who were already the freaks and misfits and outcasts of the future, it was literally as shocking as a flying saucer landing in Central Park.'

Bill Frisell may have been no nascent 'freak', but his shyness made him something of a social misfit and outsider. He didn't like high school and was not an academic achiever. 'I was sort of just a B student; I wasn't enough of a rebel to totally flunk out of the whole thing,' he says. He wasn't naturally communicative or outgoing either. 'I flunked speech class in school,' Frisell explained to *Premier Guitar* magazine. 'Just to be alone and standing up in front of people and making statements . . . I've never been comfortable with that.'

Pop and rock music were the salve, and the guitar was the solution. Soon Frisell was trading his cheap archtop for a proper classical guitar and saving hard for his first electric. He started taking guitar lessons from Bob Marcus at the Denver Folklore Center (DFC), a now legendary 'rustic and rough-hewn' instrument, guitar and record shop-cum-performance space that opened in 1962. The DFC quickly became the focus of hippie, folkie and Beatnik life in the city: Judy Collins would regularly play at the store when she returned to Denver from performing in the folk clubs of Greenwich Village alongside Bob Dylan. Denver may have been an isolated backwater in the mid-sixties, yet the DFC was a tiny window into a wider American world that was radically in flux. It was equal parts meeting place, hangout and alternative community centre; many had gathered there in November 1963 during the days following the assassination of John F. Kennedy.

'A few other things happened in 1964,' Frisell has written. 'Muhammad Ali (Cassius Clay) beat Sonny Liston. The Civil Rights Act was signed. Nelson Mandela was sentenced to life in prison. John Coltrane recorded *A Love Supreme*. Martin Luther King won the Nobel Peace Prize. The times they are a changin'. I turned thirteen and decided I had to get an electric guitar and try to play it.'

People also gathered at the DFC to listen to music. Frisell was being swept up in the British Invasion, not just by the Beatles, but through Rolling Stones' singles such as 'Not Fade Away' and 'It's All Over Now', Manfred Mann's 'Got My Mojo Working' and 'Do Wah Diddy Diddy', and Herman's Hermits' 'I'm into Something Good' – the Manchester beat-band's August 1965 gig at Denver University football stadium was the first live concert Frisell attended.

It was also at the DFC that he began to listen to the American artists that inspired those British groups: Buddy Holly, Bobby Womack, Paul Butterfield, Mike Bloomfield, Mississippi John Hurt, Otis Spann, Junior Wells, Buddy Guy, Muddy Waters and Elizabeth Cotten. Frisell was still just thirteen, however, and he is the first to admit that he didn't make such a key connection – arriving at American music, particularly the blues, backwards – until a few years later.

•
•

The following June, Frisell went to Happy Logan Music and bought that first electric guitar: a Fender Mustang with a Deluxe amp. '"Happy"

Logan himself showed me the guitar, and even though I hadn't saved up enough money from my paper route, he let me have it,' says Frisell. 'I think the guitar was $215 and the amp $165.'

Shortly after, he was forming his first band, the Weeds, with school friends Greg Jones on drums and Tony Eberhart on hollow-body guitar; Frisell claims they were all entirely innocent of the name's dope-related associations. By this time the Frisell family had moved just up the road to a much larger house on East 7th Avenue that had a sizeable basement where the trio could rehearse. They played tunes, mostly by the Beatles, Stones and Byrds, at private parties and in friends' basements.

'When I first started playing guitar, it was like a completely different side of my brain was working,' Frisell told *Jazziz*. 'Clarinet was a real intellectual process. I read well, read music . . . But when I started guitar, I just sort of did it all on my own. It was weird. I couldn't read music on the guitar, but I could figure out stuff from records.' This is the genesis of the advanced Frisell approach to music, a combination of structure and freedom, composition and improvisation, rule and rebellion, of an all-embracing aesthetic that champions seemingly contrasting collisions and coalitions.

'If you took away those experiences in that marching band, then whatever my music is, it wouldn't be anywhere; it's just so much a part of it,' says Frisell. 'My greatest joy is to be soaring, flying, right? But you can't do that unless you have the ground to take off from. If it's not there, then you're just floundering around, lost. It just doesn't work. Even rebelling against those things – that has so much to do with what I love about music. It's the joy of realising you can push up against these structures, or just go ahead anyway and juxtapose one musical element against another.

'I think I learned something from that time in my life, having all that rigidity and structure, and wanting to break out of it somehow. There was the marching-band thing going on, and then there was the total freedom of playing guitar with my friends. And then I realised: wow, what if you could have both, have it all be in the same place?'

Bill Frisell and I are in Hooked on Colfax, a café, bakery, community space and 'chill hangout' on East Colfax Avenue, part of the near fifty-mile main drag that slices east–west through metropolitan Denver. Once described by *Playboy* as 'the longest, wickedest street in America', it's been cleaned up quite a bit since then and, as we sit drinking *cortados* from organic locally roasted coffee, the neighbourhood seems the epitome of the new twenty-first-century city: hip, modern, dynamic and forward-thinking.

East Colfax Avenue is less than a mile north of Bill's former family home on well-to-do East 7th Avenue – a large house to which the Frisells moved in 1964 – and just a few doors down from the Bluebird Theater. Now a celebrated Denver music venue, the Bluebird was a cinema in the sixties where teenage Frisell went most Saturday nights.

'We've talked about how my idea of growing up around here is still quite idyllic,' Bill says, 'but it doesn't take me too long to recall a different kind of experience, one that involves darkness, and a lot of pain, a lot of fear. Yes, I grew up in a safe neighbourhood with trees and houses with front lawns. I used to cycle everywhere, I had a paper route, I was a junior deacon at my parents' church. It was kind of like *Leave it to Beaver*.' But Bill also recalls that he was 'pretty painfully shy. I remember a feeling of being afraid and sort of trapped. I had to fight all the time against closing myself off.'

This duality of light and shade, high optimism and a more stark view of the world, existed on a number of levels for Frisell. One of which, of course, was his awkward introversion, and how music could be its catharsis – and antithesis, his social life. Friends, and friends of friends, would come over to jam in his parent's basement, and a year after forming the Weeds, Bill traded his Mustang for a flashier and more flexible second-hand Fender Jaguar and banded together with a few fellow teenagers to start a new five-piece group. With Frisell and Tony Eberhart again on guitars, plus Jack Hubble on vocals and harmonica, Paul Vanbuskirk on bass, and Bill Kraus on drums, they were called the Publik, then Market Street Trolley. The band played such popular hits as 'I'll Feel a Whole Lot Better' by the Byrds, 'You Really Got Me' by the Kinks, and 'House of the Rising Sun' by the Animals. In 1966 the group won a Battle of the Bands contest at the Clayton College for Boys on the other side of Denver's City Park.

Rather than being defined by formal marching and concert bands, and the clarinet – 'talk about the most uncool instrument you could be playing' – Frisell was playing guitar, playing in groups, having a social life, being taken outside of himself. His school, East High, was a significant part of that evolution. Located a few blocks from where we are sitting, the imposing red-brick public school had a strong academic record and reputation; in Bill's junior year, in 1968, it was ranked as one of America's top ten schools. The school's ambitious standards, however, didn't rub off too much on Frisell. He was even temporarily suspended when he was seventeen for smoking on school grounds.

Still, East High offered alternative learning opportunities, both social and musical. Located at the intersection of two distinct Denver communities – the mostly working-class African American and Latino neighbourhoods to the east and north; and a predominantly white middle-class area to the south – the school had always managed to achieve a remarkable degree of integration.

'It was like a beacon of political progressiveness,' says Ron Miles, who attended East High in the late seventies, and has worked in various Frisell bands since 1993. 'There was a kind of easier racial interaction at the school, and having friends from different races and stuff was like [Miles claps his hands] . . . yeah, of course. East seemed to be a place where racial turmoil was worked out without any kind of crazy violence.'

East High had an active and well-funded music department that encouraged both individual advancement and participation in the school's orchestra, concert and jazz bands, ensembles and choirs. There were theory classes, small group sessions and extracurricular activities. This suited Frisell just fine: all he really wanted to do, other than smoke cigarettes, was to play music.

As with racial and social differences, musical distinctions were largely disregarded. 'There were a lot of vocal groups, Temptations-type bands. I ended up playing in soul bands, and that seemed close to the blues,' Frisell told critic Josef Woodard. 'Some of the guys in Earth, Wind & Fire – Philip Bailey, Larry Dunn, Andrew Woolfolk – were at East High. We were in rival groups, but we played in the school band together and had jam sessions.'

Some of these groups required shrinking, self-conscious teenage Frisell to don dark glasses, a shiny silver suit, and attempt loosely choreographed dance routines. He even played in 'soul bands backing up singers doing their James Brown things. It must've been pretty strange to see me on stage playing "Say it Loud – I'm Black and I'm Proud".'

Frisell was living through a period of both immense social change – sexual liberation, the rise of the women's movement, the counterculture, Woodstock – and political unrest: the struggle for civil rights, Black Power, street protests and nationwide riots, Vietnam. In Denver there were confrontations between the police and the city's African American and Mexican-Hispanic communities. Forced 'desegregation bussing' of students from 1969 onwards led to fierce opposition among white parents; arsonists destroyed a third of the city's school buses.

Frisell was also affected by one of the most cataclysmic events of the decade: the assassination of Martin Luther King in April 1968. Four years earlier, Reverend King had spoken at the church where Frisell was a junior deacon, Montview Boulevard Presbyterian; Bill and his family had attended.

Frisell remembers the assassination well. 'I was playing clarinet with my concert band in the main auditorium at East High, and almost the whole school was there,' he says. 'But in the middle of the [evening] concert the principal came in and said, "Children, I'm sorry, I've got some really bad news: Martin Luther King has just been killed." The whole place erupted. I remember running home from school, guys chasing me with sticks and baseball bats. I got hit on the arm; it was mayhem.'

Riots and violence erupted across the US. In Denver, schools were closed and there were marches, memorials and rallies; nineteen stores were looted, fifty-two fires started, and one hundred vehicles damaged. But there was no major civil unrest. Denver wasn't Watts. But it wasn't exactly Wyoming either.

It sounds almost wilfully naïve, even utopian, but Frisell says East High gave him a sense of harmony, a model, a way of working; it advanced the idea that music can transcend division and overcome conflict. 'Even though I knew there was all this darkness and tension in the world, within my area of music there was this feeling that we were coming out of it somehow and making some kind of progress,' he says. 'It was like, "I know that shit is messed up, but we're figuring it out and working through this together." That feeling has never really left me: music gives me a structure to think about how the world could possibly be.'

•
•

East High also had a lasting impact on Frisell through Vincent Tagliavore – associate director of instrumental music, director of the school concert band, and organiser of the music for school theatre productions and talent shows.

One of the acts for the talent show of autumn 1967 was a dance routine, performed by four girls, to Wes Montgomery's 'Bumpin' on Sunset'; the radio-friendly Montgomery original, from his LP *Tequila*, had been released as a single the year before. The laidback Latin-jazz track had a cool and breezy West Coast feel, stylishly propelled by guitarist Montgomery's softly seductive three-octave melodic lines. '[The girls] were going to use the record, but the band director [Mr Tagliavore] thought it would sound cheesy,' Frisell told *DownBeat* in 2004. 'He knew I played guitar and . . . gave me the album. I went home and learned the song [by

29

ear]. I thought, "Oh, so this is jazz." Which I had never been exposed to up to that point.'

Luckily, 'Bumpin' on Sunset' is not 'Giant Steps'; it's a simple enough melody based on one A-minor chord throughout. Frisell enlisted school friends Bob Chamberlain and Mike Ringler on bass and drums, and when they played the music for the dance routine, 'the whole school went nuts'.

For Frisell, the track had everything he was looking for, but hadn't known existed. It had the catchiness of pop and the Californian shimmer of surf rock; the rhythmic pulse of Latin and R&B and the warmth of soul; and the harmonic sophistication and improvisatory freedom of jazz. It also had the easy-going sound of Montgomery's famous hollow-body Gibson L-5: full of light and space, yet punctuated with powerful block chords and the occasional thrilling attack.

'Everything changed from that moment on,' Frisell continued in *DownBeat*. 'That opened the door to jazz for me. Wes had hooked me.'

In Wes Montgomery, Frisell had found a role model whose journey into guitar playing and jazz closely echoed his own. 'Charlie Christian was my inspiration,' Montgomery says in the liner notes to *Tequila*, about his own discovery of a love of jazz. 'I heard his "Solo Flight" [with Benny Goodman in 1943] and something about it made an impression. When you hear something that sounds good, you want to hear it again over . . . And when it still sounds good, you want to make something like it . . . So I bought a guitar and started teaching myself.'

Frisell listened repeatedly and played along to the rest of the *Tequila* album. There was the fifties mambo-meets-rock 'n' roll instrumental title track; 'Insensatez (How Insensitive)', a bossa nova classic composed by Antônio Carlos Jobim; and Burt Bacharach and Hal David's 'What the World Needs Now Is Love', which Frisell still plays to this day.

He decided to seek out other Wes Montgomery albums, other jazz records. First stop was his local Woolworths: 'It was incredible what was in there. There were Riverside records and Fantasy records and tons of Blue Note records – all 79 cents each. I bought as many as I could afford.

I got *The Wes Montgomery Trio* record, which turned out to be his first album under his own name. Unbelievable.'

Frisell's young world was becoming more interesting, more complex. Rather than being moved by styles such as surf music, or groups such as the Beatles or the Byrds, Frisell began to focus more on the individual, on each player's own distinctive 'absolutely one-of-a-kind' sound, on jazz's essential and exceptional quality of personal freedom of expression. He started listening to jazz guitarists such as Kenny Burrell, Grant Green and Barney Kessel, and other instrumentalists, particularly saxophonist Sonny Rollins. He noticed connections: *Tequila* bass player Ron Carter also appeared on several of his Kenny Burrell albums, so he began to seek out records featuring Carter in the list of personnel.

That, in turn, led him to such giants of the music as Wayne Shorter and Miles Davis – to such epochal Davis albums as *Miles Smiles* and *Miles in the Sky*, and the live recording *My Funny Valentine*. The latter remains, if he's pushed, Frisell's all-time favourite album, with the Rodgers and Hart title ballad his number-one 'particular performance of a particular song'. 'It's one of those records that I keep coming back to and that still sounds totally . . . it always has sounded extremely beautiful to me,' he says. 'But at the same time it continues to be completely mysterious. Like on "My Funny Valentine" . . . it doesn't seem humanly possible Miles and the band could play on that level. I still haven't been able to figure out how they were doing it, and I don't think I'll ever understand it.'

In the summer of 1968 Frisell went with his father to his first jazz concert: a touring Newport Jazz Festival show at the open-air Red Rocks amphitheatre ten miles west of Denver. In one evening Frisell got to see, among others, Thelonious Monk, Dionne Warwick (performing several hits written for her by Bacharach and David), and a quartet led by vibra-phonist Gary Burton – featuring Larry Coryell, Steve Swallow and Bob Moses – who were breaking new ground in the borderlands between jazz, country and rock. 'That Gary Burton group was another one of those mind-expanding moments; they blew my brains out,' he says. 'Larry Coryell somehow seemed connected to both jazz and the rock 'n' roll guitar music I'd been playing, but he was also stretching the music out in all directions. I had never heard anything like it. I didn't understand it at all, but it hit me in a very emotional way.'

Wes Montgomery was also advertised in the Newport Festival line-up at Red Rocks. 'All I could think was, "Oh, boy, Wes Montgomery is playing, Wes Montgomery is playing,"' says Frisell. But he never got to see him live. Aged only forty-five, Montgomery died of a heart attack a month before the show.

•
•

At the same time that Frisell was beginning to discover a love of jazz, he was continuing to be exposed to many other forms of music. This was a time of unprecedented change in American popular music and Frisell was in the right place at the right time to experience it.

Denver in the late sixties was certainly remote. Framed by the theatrical backdrop of the Rocky Mountains and the slow, flat, endless slide of the Great Plains, the city was little more than a speck in the monumental landscape of the American West. It had a music scene that was more wedded to the revival of acoustic folk music than to the arrival of new electric pop. This was an era still in thrall to the radical post-Beatnik protest songs of Pete Seeger, Woody Guthrie, Joan Baez, Josh White and Denver's own Judy Collins. And to Dylan, of course. Rebel music that reflected the turbulent times.

Yet Denver also had a vibrant FM radio culture that connected listeners to the latest American and British trends. Frisell would go to Woolworths, Walgreens and the Denver Folklore Center and come back with LPs by, for example, Paul Butterfield, Mississippi John Hurt, Cream, Marianne Faithfull and Frank Zappa and the Mothers of Invention. He would play along with them, try to figure out the chords, learn the solos.

'There is a spirit here in Denver and Colorado that's born out of geographic isolation and that creates a sense of community, a sense of being outsiders who can embrace diverse styles and create something independent,' says Megan Friedel, a former curator at the History Colorado museum in Denver. 'Unlike the New York Greenwich Village folk scene of the 1960s or the Seattle grunge scene of the 1980s and nineties, we didn't have the luxury in Denver of focusing on one genre.'

Denver was also big enough to be visited by the major artists of the day – it became a regular stopover for acts travelling between Chicago and San Francisco or Los Angeles. Frisell had already attended some further concerts with his father, such as an evening of Indian classical music with Ravi Shankar, but as he got older started to go to gigs with his friends. He saw bands and musicians as diverse as Buffalo Springfield, Chuck Berry, Bob Dylan and James Brown. During 1967 alone Frisell also came into contact with San Francisco Sound bands such as psychedelic rockers Big Brother and the Holding Company (which, at that time, included Janis Joplin), funky R&B band Sons of Champlin, and heavy metal pioneers Blue Cheer. Frisell even got to see the Jimi Hendrix Experience – twice: first at a concert in the sports hall of Regis College on St Valentine's Day 1968, with support from English psychedelic jazz-rockers The Soft Machine (as they were then called); and again, less than seven months later, as Hendrix hysteria continued to grow, at nine-thousand-capacity Red Rocks.

He could have seen Hendrix for a third time at the riotous 1969 Denver Pop Festival: it was an event attended by an estimated fifty thousand people that turned out to be the trio's final gig. But for Frisell, it seems, twice was enough. He went to the festival on the other two days, catching acts such as Creedence Clearwater Revival, Tim Buckley, Johnny Winter, Frank Zappa, Poco, and Big Mama Thornton. New local hard rock band Zephyr were also on the bill; the group featured seventeen-year-old Denver guitar sensation Tommy Bolin, who would later play with both Billy Cobham and Deep Purple.

'From age twelve to sixteen or seventeen, I raced through tons of music; it was just pouring in,' Frisell once told *Vintage Guitar* magazine. 'In a short period of time, there was a massive amount of information.' It was information that, at this early stage, he didn't feel a need to differentiate between or categorise; there was little idea in Frisell's musical mind of placing one style above another. The same couldn't be said for his playing, however, where the guitar was beginning to gain more precedence. He continued to play clarinet, and occasionally tenor saxophone, with the Gold Sash marching band, but he left in the summer of 1968 before his final year at East High. When Vincent Tagliavore secured Frisell a place on the prestigious 'national music camp' at Interlochen Arts Academy in Michigan during the summer of 1967, Frisell recalls being largely ungrateful and unimpressed. 'By that time, I was already leaning . . . my heart was in the guitar, but . . . that was a hard summer, because I couldn't bring my guitar, and it seemed like an eternity not to be able to play it for two months,' he says. 'I just remember how good it felt when I got home and I got my hands back on it.'

The following year Frisell gained one of only a hundred places in the national McDonald's All-American High School Band, participating in the Rose Parade in Pasadena, California, and the Thanksgiving Day Parade in New York. But, again, he was something of a reluctant participant. He just wanted to play guitar with his friends.

The trio that had performed 'Bumpin' on Sunset' in the East High talent show eventually grew into a group called the Soul Merchants; vocals were added by Chauncey Blakely, then Victor Cooper, and there was a horn section of Ken Wright on trumpet, Rick Yamamoto on alto saxophone, and Keary Nitta on tenor saxophone, who was one of Frisell's best friends. The student band was popular, playing songs by James Brown and the Temptations for school dances and fraternity parties.

Frisell was no showman. 'I never got into the physical thing,' he has said. 'Getting down on my knees, playing with my teeth . . . the guys in the band told me, "You can't just stand there, you gotta move around."' He did, however, have one major musical advantage over most of his bandmates: the support of his parents. A love of music was part of Frisell family life and, while Bill's father may no longer have been playing the tuba or double bass, Jane would sing songs around the house such as Stephen Foster's 'Beautiful Dreamer' and Jerome Kern and Oscar Hammerstein's 'All the Things You Are'.

When Frisell was eleven his parents bought a Hammond organ. Two years later, when the family moved up the road to the larger house at 3401 E 7th Avenue, the Frisells also purchased a piano – there was even room for a baby grand. Frisell began to colonise the basement, as a den, record room and practice and rehearsal space; he even began to sleep down there. 'I spent a lot of time playing music with my friends in that basement,' says Frisell. 'My parents could sometimes be overly strict and protective, especially when I was getting to be a teenager – but not when it came to music. Because of their love of music, my parents allowed my friends to come over and just make a bunch of noise. They made it safe for me to do what I'm doing now. My father was into music, so the idea of me doing that, as a career, even back then, was not so crazy to him. I just feel so lucky. They backed me up, and I owe a lot to my parents for that.'

Frisell's wife, Carole d'Inverno, agrees, but says Bill's parents also expected a certain level of commitment. 'They were very supportive, but they also expected him to study and take music seriously,' she says. 'They were insistent; they expected him to deliver.'

It is another Frisellian teenage duality: his parents may have been personally reserved and socially conservative, yet they were also cultur-ally liberal and politically progressive. Frisell admits that as a teenager he began to pull away and distance himself (hence his retreat into the basement), and to rebel, or at least non-conform. Yet, to his parents, he certainly wasn't, as Dylan warned in 'The Times They Are a-Changin'', 'beyond your command'; more often than not they supported him, and Frisell reciprocated.

'Bill was one of the first in his large Denver school to let his hair grow long,' wrote Jane Frisell in 1978. Bill's brother Bob soon followed suit. 'I still can't understand why the question of hair length became such a vital issue in those days. My intelligence told me that it really didn't matter in the least. The thing that was important was what was inside my sons – in their hearts and minds. And their hearts and minds were OK.'

Bill and Bob stubbornly resisted all requests to shorten their hair – apart from when their paternal grandfather, Ole, died, aged seventy-three in July 1969. 'They willingly allowed one of my friends to cut their hair the night before the funeral,' wrote Jane. 'I know this was a tremendous sacrifice for them and a real act of love, and I'll always remember it with gratitude.'

•
•

In early 1969, in his senior year at high school, Frisell traded his guitar again – this time for a very different instrument, a Univox archtop, a copy of Wes Montgomery's guitar. He knew that he had reached the stage where he required lessons, so he asked around and Dale Bruning was recommended to him. Bruning is a fine guitarist from Pennsylvania who in the late 1950s studied with influential teacher Dennis Sandole, an important early mentor to John Coltrane. In 1964, aged twenty-nine, Bruning had moved with his young family to Denver, quickly gaining a reputation as a gifted jazz player and inspirational private teacher.

'At first I couldn't play anything – I would just be noodling around on some sort of blues scale – but then I remember Dale asking me if I'd heard of Charlie Parker,' says Frisell. 'And I think I said, "Oh, is he a guitar player?" After that he introduced me to Dizzy Gillespie and Oscar Peterson, to standards such as "Stella by Starlight" and newer songs such as Johnny Mandel's "The Shadow of Your Smile".'

Bruning gave Frisell saxophonist Lennie Niehaus's books on jazz styles and techniques, as well as instruction on harmony, articulation, soloing and melodic phrasing. His two worlds were coming together: a theoretical foundation and practical facility on the clarinet and saxophone combined with his passion for the possibilities of the guitar. Mind and heart.

'Bill was tall, wore glasses, had lots of hair, and was very quiet and reticent – he might've been one of the first teenage students that I'd had,' says Bruning. 'But the one thing that stood out about Bill, in a huge way, was his talent. Any assignment that I gave him, I could be sure the following week, when he would return, that he would be well prepared and eager for the next instalment. He just wanted to learn anything and everything that he could about jazz and the guitar. And because of that, and the promise he was showing, I felt a kind of responsibility. I wanted him to listen to the historic innovators of the music, because that's what Dennis Sandole had shown me.'

Two of those pioneering progressives were pianist Bill Evans and guitarist Jim Hall. On Bruning's recommendation, Frisell bought the 1966 Evans/Hall duo album *Intermodulation*. 'The first time I heard Wes Montgomery, it was like having your head blown off,' Frisell has said. 'This [Jim Hall's playing] was more subtle. But then I listened to the thing again, and I listened again, and it didn't take long before it absolutely flipped me out.'

Hall connected not just to Bill Evans, but to other major contemporary jazz figures such as Sonny Rollins, Art Farmer and Jimmy Giuffre. Frisell became fascinated with the way Jim Hall could adapt to different contexts, relate to and harmonise with them, become an instant orchestrator of the group sound. He began to see the guitar in a completely new way, like 'a legitimate instrument, not just a poppy thing'.

'It was at a very crucial time in my life,' Frisell told Denver *Westword* magazine. 'I don't know if I'd really be playing now if it wasn't for Dale; I can't overstate the importance of him in my life. He opened the door on this gigantic world of music that I really knew nothing about. He also just gave me confidence. I knew I wanted to do it, but that was the beginning of me thinking about it in a really serious way. He gave me a way to believe in it. It was like this was real music. And that I could maybe do it.'

•
•

Towards the end of summer 1969 Frisell's parents moved to suburban South Orange, New Jersey; Bill Sr had been offered a position as professor and head of the department of biochemistry in the New Jersey Medical School in nearby Newark. This gave Frisell a place to stay within striking distance of New York City. In August, he went for the first time to the famous Village Vanguard jazz club in Greenwich Village, once described by *New Yorker* jazz critic Whitney Balliett as 'the Parnassus of jazz'. He took his friend from Denver, drummer Mike Ringler, and together they saw the Gary Burton Quartet. Burton's album *Country Roads & Other Places* had recently been released; the LP features further fascinating syntheses of jazz, country, rock and even classical. This was the new form of 'fusion' at its most quietly radical. It was also for Frisell vastly influential; in Burton's late sixties music lie some of the seeds of Frisell's subsequent adventures in Americana.

Determined on music as a future career, eighteen-year-old Frisell applied to study clarinet at the renowned Eastman School of Music in Rochester, New York. He was guided again by Ron Carter; the bass player and cellist had graduated from the college a decade earlier, having played in the Eastman Philharmonia and gigged around the city in jazz groups. By the late sixties, Eastman had introduced additional 'jazz studies' courses, one of the few music colleges in America to do so.

Frisell's application was rejected, however. Instead of a performance degree, he was offered a music education major, which he turned down. He applied to study as a music major at Colorado State College (as the University of Northern Colorado was known at that time) in Greeley, a city of around forty thousand people fifty miles north of Denver. He was accepted and received a scholarship. Frisell's parents bought him a 1961 red Volvo 544.

Frisell majored in clarinet, and played tenor saxophone and guitar in the university's big bands. He was soon making an impression. While the jazz programme at the college was still in its infancy, Colorado State did enter bands and smaller ensembles at collegiate jazz festivals and Frisell was quickly recruited to the number-one jazz band, even as a freshman.

During his time at the college Frisell would win the 'outstanding soloist' award at festivals in both Salt Lake City, Utah and Champaign-Urbana, Illinois – on guitar. Dale Bruning's tuition was clearly paying off. The judges at the festivals included such jazz luminaries as Quincy Jones, Oliver Nelson, Cannonball Adderley, Benny Carter and Gary Burton.

He was recruited into new college bands too, most significantly a jazz-rock group called Joshua, which trumpeter, fellow student and good friend Bob Gillis helped put together. The band also included Keary Nitta from the Soul Merchants on tenor saxophone, Lyle Waller on trombone, John Sherberg on electric piano and vocals, Alan Aluisi on drums, and Fred Hamilton on bass.

'Bill had a different sound even back then,' says Gillis. 'Not just the distinct sound of his guitar, but he already had an individual voice. There was a logic and structure to his solos, and a sort of different sense of time. There was also an economy to his playing; he played fewer notes and fewer chords, but somehow they had more impact. He made every note matter.'

4: A Portrait of the Guitarist as a Young Man

For four years, from 1969 onwards, Bill Frisell continued to have regular guitar lessons with Dale Bruning. He would make the hour's drive from Greeley to Denver once a week in his red Volvo – often alongside tenor player Keary Nitta, or sometimes with trumpeter Bob Gillis. One of the pair would wait in the room next to Bruning's music studio while the other was having his lesson. On the way back, they would compare notes – not just on what they had learned, but on Bruning's first-hand accounts of some of the musicians they were listening to: Dizzy Gillespie, Erroll Garner, Percy Heath and Jim Hall.

Bruning kept expanding Frisell's musical education, introducing him to figures outside of jazz. 'When I studied with [Dennis] Sandole, we listened to and looked at all of Bartók's [six] string quartets. So, in turn, I was trying to share that with Bill,' says Bruning. 'I wanted him to be aware of such things as harmony, rhythm and orchestration in the music of Charles Ives, Leonard Bernstein, Poulenc, impressionists like Ravel and Debussy, and certainly somebody like Béla Bartók. And, just like when I first began teaching him, Bill was like a sponge.'

Bruning concluded that his young protégé needed a far better guitar than his second-rate Univox copy. The year before Frisell began lessons with him, Bruning had taken delivery of a new customised Gibson ES-175, one of the most famous guitars in jazz. A hollow-body archtop played by such jazz masters as Jim Hall, Joe Pass, Pat Metheny, Herb Ellis, Kenny Burrell and even, on occasions, Wes Montgomery, the instrument is prized for its warm, clean, rich tone, and for its versatility. Elvis's guitarist, Scotty Moore, played an ES-295 (essentially a 175 with decorative gold lacquer) on Presley's 1954 Sun singles, earning it the badge of 'the guitar that changed the world'.

Bruning found an older, early fifties ES-175 that he liked better, so he sold the newer model to Frisell. 'It was a big deal; he was passing this along,' Frisell told *Fretboard Journal* magazine. 'I think he sold it to me for $450.' The cost today would be around $3,300; Frisell sold the Univox and his parents made up the shortfall. 'It was a heavy thing, the best guitar I ever owned . . . I had a real guitar; I played it non-stop. I just lived with this guitar. Everywhere I went, this was my only instrument. This guitar came at the point where I decided that music was going to be my life.'

.
.

While he was at the University of Northern Colorado, Frisell was taught by one of the great, if criminally unsung, jazz guitarists of the 1950s and 1960s – Johnny Smith. While there was no dedicated guitar programme, Smith had been hired for one semester to teach a class that was open to any student interested in learning the instrument.

Smith had spent most of the fifties in New York, playing regularly at Birdland, though since 1958 he'd been living in conservative Colorado Springs. He had moved west after his wife died and he was left as the sole carer of their four-year-old daughter; Smith's mother and two of his brothers lived in the city. Johnny Smith opened a music store in the city and he helped design guitars for companies such as Gibson and Guild. He also continued to record albums for the Roost and Verve labels.

Thinking back on Smith's UNC class, Frisell told *Jazz Times* magazine in 2014, 'It was as if the course just happened to have this master teaching it. I signed up for that class, but after a few weeks it was too much for everyone else – they didn't want to be learning scales and inversions and all this stuff. Everybody dropped out, except me. It pretty much ended up being a private lesson with Johnny Smith.'

Frisell admits now, however, that he didn't fully appreciate the opportunity he was being given. Increasingly under the influence of the progressive playing of Jim Hall, and leaning more towards the contemporary sounds of Thelonious Monk, Ornette Coleman and Sonny

Rollins, Frisell too easily dismissed Smith as a schmaltzy relic of the uncool past. 'I wanted to be a modern avant-garde bebop jazz cat,' Frisell once wrote, only half-jokingly.

Smith was best known for his 1952 hit single 'Moonlight in Vermont', a cover version of the popular ballad that to nineteen-year-old Frisell must have seemed the epitome of all that was soft and syrupy in jazz. Yet Smith had also written the instrumental 'Walk, Don't Run', which had subsequently become a hit for Frisell's beloved band the Ventures and a song he had played himself. Smith had recorded compelling solo versions too of traditional American folk songs such as 'Black is the Colour (of My True Love's Hair)' and 'Shenandoah' (the latter would become something of a Frisell standard). He had a quiet finesse, harmonic richness, ringing clarity of tone, and a commanding gift for revealing the internal dynamics of a song that would later become hallmarks of the advanced Frisell sound and style. 'Johnny Smith will always be the poet laureate of the archtop guitar,' journalist and musician Chip Stern has written.

'I didn't realise what was right there in front of me,' says Frisell. 'I had the utmost respect for him as a guitarist, and everything he told me to do I took very seriously. But I wasn't as open as I should have been. I was seeing him as a little bit corny, sort of almost easy-listening. It's embarrassing how stupid I was.'

Frisell was full of self-doubt and insecurity at the time about his playing and the possibility of forging any kind of career in music, let alone as a jazz guitarist. Johnny Smith provided crucial support at a crucial time. 'He was so encouraging to me,' says Frisell. 'He was one of the guys who took me aside and said, "You've really got something going." He gave me so much.'

Buddy Baker, head of the jazz programme at UNC, instilled similar confidence in Frisell. Baker was a gifted trombonist and experienced musician, and an influential early advocate of university jazz studies. He remained a dedicated player too, even turning up at student jam sessions. 'One day I was so discouraged and I was thinking about quitting music;

I didn't think I could do it, I was seriously bummed out,' Frisell remembers. 'And then, out of nowhere, walking down the hallway, Buddy Baker appeared before me, and he said, "You know, you've got it, you can be a real musician, keep at it." He said that right at the moment when I needed to hear it the most. Saved my ass.'

During Frisell's two years at UNC he mostly immersed himself in music, studying conscientiously and rehearsing and playing gigs with various student bands in Greeley, and in Boulder, sixty miles to the south, near Denver. He carried his guitar wherever he went. Frisell also listened to a lot of records, often with Bob Gillis, with whom he shared the basement apartment of a UNC frat house; they played albums not just by jazz stars of the day such as Miles Davis, Gary Burton and Carla Bley, but also the new folk-rock records of Bob Dylan and Crosby, Stills, Nash and Young, among others.

Gary Burton was to have a rather more direct impact on Frisell in April 1971. Coming to the university as a snazzily dressed guest soloist for the inaugural UNC/Greeley Jazz Festival, Burton not only played a concert with the UNC big band, with Frisell on tenor saxophone, but he also gave a talk to the music students. Burton described the time in his late teens at Boston's Berklee School of Music when he felt he had to decide between the piano, the instrument he was majoring in, and the vibraphone, the instrument he was passionate about.

'He said just this simple thing,' Frisell recalls. '"If you are going to play an instrument, you have to commit to it solely, because to try to play one instrument well is more than enough to worry about. Focus. Put all your energy into one thing." It was around the time that I was thinking of going to Berklee, and I had known for a while that the guitar, not the clarinet or saxophone, was where my heart was, so I said to myself, "I'm just going to play guitar." I took Gary Burton's advice. I pretty much right away went out and sold my clarinet and sax.'

Although Frisell remained shy and soft-spoken, he expressed his newfound independence and freedom by growing his thick brown hair down to the shoulders of his treasured green corduroy jacket. He sported a moustache, mostly unconvincingly, and smoked a lot of cigarettes, which he loved – and pot, especially when listening to records.

One time, he and Fred Hamilton, a fellow guitarist, drove to Boulder and bought some mescaline; on another occasion Frisell took acid with his close friend, saxophonist Keary Nitta. 'Both were pretty heavy and intense, and I had some extreme hallucinations with the mescaline, but I think it was too much for me, and I didn't want to deal with either again. I was just trying to see what it would do to playing or listening to the music, I guess.'

On the way to a competition in Salt Lake City in April 1971, Frisell's college band Joshua played a concert at a high school in Glenwood Springs, Colorado. Before the performance began, as was customary, everyone in the school hall was asked to stand for the Pledge of Allegiance. This was at the height of the time of protests against, and a growing opposition to, the war in Vietnam – especially to such controversies as the military draft lottery, to which Frisell was subjected in July 1970 (luckily for him, his birth date was not called). Opinion in the country was polarised and feelings were running high. 'We were on stage,' says Frisell. 'I did not stand up. And none of my friends did either.'

Some members of the high-school faculty were markedly critical of the students' actions and complained to the UNC president. The jazz faculty issued a new 'Dress and Conduct Code for UNC Jazz Ensembles', which listed such handy instructions as 'while en route on a trip: sport or dress slacks only – no blue jeans of any type' and 'hair must be less than shoulder length, clean, combed and well-groomed at all times'. The code also stated that 'anyone who cannot in good faith and honesty pledge allegiance and loyalty to this country and to this school will not perform anywhere with the jazz ensembles' and may face 'immediate dismissal'.

That June the UNC big band had been invited to perform, with Johnny Smith, at Montreux, the prestigious jazz festival by the shores of Lake Geneva in Switzerland. It was to have been Frisell's first trip abroad. Frisell, Gillis and Nitta resigned from the band, however, and stayed at home.

'It wasn't like I was really politically active, or anything,' says Frisell. 'I'd been to a few protest marches, but they seemed to turn more into parties, like another excuse for everybody to get high. But having your hair that long at that time in that little town of Greeley was a badge of pride. There were definitely a lot of really right-wing conservative people living there, and they called us freaks, and we called ourselves freaks and we gave each other the peace sign and felt we were part of a sister- and brotherhood, or something. There was this big controversy about whether we should or we shouldn't go [to Montreux]. But I wasn't gonna cut my hair just because they'd given us an ultimatum. It felt wrong. I didn't feel like I had done anything wrong. So I, and a few others, just said, "No."'

∶

By spring 1971 Frisell had decided to quit the course at UNC and apply to the most renowned jazz studies school in the country: the private Berklee College of Music in Boston. In 1962 Berklee had become the first higher education institution in America to offer a dedicated guitar degree. Frisell had almost gone to Berklee the year before; the 'outstanding soloist' award he had won at the 1970 National Collegiate Jazz Festival in Champaign-Urbana included a scholarship to the summer programme at the college. The prize, however, did not include room and board, and Frisell's funds and his parents' goodwill would not stretch that far. Not attending, though, only strengthened his desire and determination to study there.

Frisell's parents were concerned. It was one thing to be studying music at UNC on a respectable instrument such as the clarinet, and to be potentially leaving with a teaching qualification at worst. It was quite another for Frisell to be thinking of concentrating exclusively on the ubiquitous electric guitar, with all its disreputable pop, rock and jazz associations and excesses. Booze. Drugs. Sex. Violence. Altamont. It was as if Frisell, the firstborn, the eldest son, was about to run away with the rock 'n' roll circus. Bill Sr and Jane flew in from New Jersey.

'I remember my parents were . . . like, "Oh my God, what is our son doing?" So we had this meeting over at Dale's house, with me and my parents and Dale. They just wanted to talk to him and get his take on if I was really imagining things.'

Bruning remembers Bill Sr and Jane sitting in the small waiting room next to his music studio, looking worried but sincere. 'Not only did Bill's new focus on the guitar cause them some anxiety – that it could take him down some primrose path to destruction or something,' says Bruning, laughing gently. 'But they also asked me, more generally and very politely, "Do you really think that our son, Bill, has enough talent to be able to make his way in the world of music, because it's a very unstable and precarious kind of a pursuit, and you'd better have a lot of musical skills and wherewithal in order to do that?"

'Well, that just brought a smile to my face, because I could, without any hesitation, answer, "Absolutely, yes. He's got the talent, the enthusiasm, the determination, the willingness to spend a lot of time practising and to learn, an eagerness to play with others – Bill's got *all* that you would want to be successful in the world of music." And I didn't say that just to set their minds at ease; I said it because I really believed, with Bill, that was totally the case.'

Shortly afterwards, Bill was accepted at Berklee, majoring in guitar and composition, and in the autumn of 1971 Frisell drove his Volvo 544 to his parents' home in New Jersey (where the car ceremonially died), and then travelled on to Boston, Massachusetts, to enrol. He'd arrived at the perfect place for him to dedicate himself fully to the thing he loved doing most: playing the guitar. The world-famous school has the motto '*esse quam videri*' – 'to be, rather than to seem'. At last Frisell could 'be'.

He lasted one semester. Frisell left four months later, at the end of the year.

There were a number of reasons for his early departure, most of them related to the rapid and sometimes radical changes jazz was going through. It was the start of the so-called 'fusion decade', of jazz's new adventures in rock, soul, funk, R&B, even disco. Miles Davis had gone electric with *In a Silent Way* and *Bitches Brew*, and many in his orbit had plugged in and dropped out of the seismic sixties shift towards free jazz and the avant-garde. Tony Williams formed jazz-rock power trio Lifetime with John McLaughlin on guitar and Larry Young on organ. Herbie Hancock, with his Mwandishi sextet, began experimenting more and more with electric pianos, keyboards and synthesisers. The year Frisell went to Berklee saw debut albums from Joe Zawinul, Wayne Shorter and Miroslav Vitouš's Weather Report, a group that championed a startlingly new electric, ambient and rhythmic soundworld, and from John McLaughlin's Mahavishnu Orchestra, which added progressive rock and Indian classical music to the psychedelic mix.

It seems, at Berklee at least, Frisell was mostly impervious to these new directions. Perhaps he was freaked out by McLaughlin's double-neck guitar virtuosity and mega-watt amplification, put off by all that weight and speed and density. Or perhaps the seduction of the Jim Hall school of guitar playing, with all its light and grace and studied consideration, was just too great.

Frisell had seen Hall play in Denver, when he came to play a week at a small downtown bar on Colfax Avenue called the Senate Lounge. Hall played in a duo with Dale Bruning on bass, though the pair found plenty of room for guitar duets too. Frisell went several times and, through Bruning, got to meet Jim Hall. It left a big impression. He had the same guitar as Hall; the same small amp; the same fascination with economy, patience and implication – three things fusion most definitely was not. Frisell wanted *to be* Jim Hall. His was the higher calling, the model for how he wanted to sound. The other musicians that he'd been fired up by in his teens were simply child's play. The blinkers were on.

'At that time, I couldn't see anything but basically just Jim Hall, and the strands that went off of him . . . Charlie Parker, [jazz from] mid- to late forties to early sixties,' Frisell told Ethan Iverson. 'I just wanted to be a bebop guy, and I shut out everything else [all other music] that had led up to that point as kid's stuff. I didn't want to have anything to do with it. And any kind of rock and roll. I was kinda closed off.

'Some of that I got from Dale Bruning. I shouldn't blame him, but at the same time, he would make little comments, like in rock music the chords weren't right, or the harmony didn't move in the right way, or they were too simple, or it was too loud. So I definitely had tunnel vision about it.'

There were some aspects of Frisell's time at Berklee that were positive. Gary Burton had begun teaching there in 1971 – the start of the vibraphonist's long association with the college – and Frisell attended his classes and was in an ensemble led by Burton ('I think I barely played a note; I was like the invisible kid in the corner'). He went to the Jazz Workshop and Paul's Mall, legendary sixties and seventies Boston twin music rooms on Boylston Street. Frisell even got to see Herbie Hancock's Mwandishi band – at that time one of jazz's most electrifying groups, especially live, and especially in a room that held no more than 150 to 200 people. Yet it seems Frisell was mostly confused by such cutting-edge sounds. 'It was awesome,' he has said of the Mwandishi gig, 'but as far as being able to decipher it?'

Frisell didn't like the course, the college or the city. 'It didn't click. There were all these rock and roll guys, just out of high school, and . . . it was a drag. I didn't like Boston. The neighbourhood was intense. I was living in a small dorm with three other guys; one day I came back and my bunk-mate was with a hooker, going at it in my bed.'

Frisell moved back to his parents' house and regrouped. He felt encouraged by the fact that he'd followed his instincts, and didn't want to waste time getting swept up in something that wasn't him; he had more to lose, he argued, by actually staying at Berklee. 'I didn't feel like I had failed at all,' he told me. 'I felt certain that I was doing the right thing.'

Bill Sr and Frisell went to see Jim Hall play in a duo with Ron Carter at a tiny Manhattan club called the Guitar. Frisell had written to Hall asking him for private lessons, and his hero had agreed. Just as Bill and his father were arriving at the club they bumped into Hall getting out of a taxi; Frisell reintroduced himself, re-established the Dale Bruning connection, and helped Hall carry his gear into the club. Frisell's prospects were on the up again; he was re-energised and re-engaged.

· ·

Jim Hall lived in New York's Greenwich Village, on West 12th Street, for more than fifty years, and it was here, in an apartment that Hall shared with his wife Jane, that Frisell went for a series of eight weekly lessons in the spring of 1972.

This was quite a step up for Frisell, even from the elevated levels of instruction he had received from such educated players as Dale Bruning and Johnny Smith. Hall had played with, among many others, Bill Evans, Paul Desmond, Jimmy Giuffre, Bob Brookmeyer, Art Farmer, Ben Webster, Ella Fitzgerald, Lee Konitz, Ornette Coleman, Gunther Schuller and, perhaps most prominently, for periods in the early sixties, in a quartet led by Sonny Rollins. Hall had played jazz that ranged from cool to hot, standards to third stream, chamber to free, folk to blues. Pat Metheny has called him 'the father of modern jazz guitar'.

It again shows Frisell's fascinatingly dual nature – his shyness yet determination, his humility yet strength – that, at the age of just twenty (he would turn twenty-one in March 1972), he still possessed the single-mindedness and self-belief to seek out Jim Hall.

The truth was, of course, that he had found a kindred spirit, both personally and creatively, and even though Hall has said that he 'couldn't teach someone *how* to play the guitar or *how* to improvise if my life depended on it; I had no system', his impact on Frisell was fairly immediate.

'I went for that first lesson, and Jim was still a larger-than-life hero to me, but . . . the first thing we played was "Stella by Starlight", together, and what was so incredible was that, even in those first few moments, he made me feel like I knew how to . . . play somehow. He made me sound good. His playing was great, obviously, but it wasn't about him. Like with his own groups, or with Sonny Rollins or Art Farmer and so many others, he kinda put a spell on the music. Without dominating it, he was influencing and orchestrating the music from within in real subtle ways so that both of us sounded amazing.'

Hall talked about the ideas and inspirations he had drawn from some of his favourite guitar players, such as Charlie Christian, Freddie Green and early swing guitarist George Van Eps – new ways of harmonising scales and using different intervals and inversions, 'breaking apart the run-of-the-mill guitar voicings', breathing life into long strings of notes, and turning the guitar 'into a fluid, wind instrument kind of thing'. He offered Frisell lessons from Sonny Rollins's thematic solos, Bill Evans's chords, Jimmy Giuffre's 'compositional approach to performing jazz', Bach's violin sonatas and partitas, Bartók's string quartets, and the music of some of his other favourite composers, from Stravinsky to Schoenberg.

'It wasn't just about the guitar, [it was about] using the guitar as a means to get at whatever music you're hearing in your head, which could be a whole orchestra,' Frisell told *JazzTimes*. 'It's your imagination. So not just listening to guitar players, but listening to saxophone, piano, banjo and every other thing.'

Frisell told me that even today he is still thinking about those eight lessons; 'I haven't scratched the surface of all Jim's possibilities and permutations.'

Hall considered his primary goal was to help Frisell find a voice, his own voice. '[It's] kind of my philosophy about everything,' Hall also told *JazzTimes*. 'You know, I was hearing all these marvellous guitar players – Tal Farlow was a good friend, Jimmy Raney, Wes Montgomery. Finally I realised, if I practise every second for the rest of my life, I'll never be able to do that. So I said, "Dummy! Find yourself!"' Hall told his young student to 'find Bill Frisell'.

Frisell decided to return to Colorado to do just that – but it took him a good few years. A good few hard years.

His parents bought him a 1969 red Volkswagen Beetle, and he drove back to Greeley. Frisell lived with Bob Gillis, who was still studying at

UNC, and then moved to Denver, into a tiny single-room apartment in a corner of a run-down three-storey L-shaped block in the once-grand residential Capitol Hill district. The brick building was named 'Rob Roy', as it is today, but there was little that was epic or heroic about Frisell's life or accommodation at that time. 'It was not much bigger than a closet – just one room, at the back, around eight feet by twelve, with nooks for a kitchen and a bathroom, one window looking out on an alley, just barely enough room for a small single bed,' he says. 'But it only cost $70 a month [around $450 today].'

Frisell recommenced lessons with Dale Bruning and started looking for work, keen to prove to himself and his parents that he could survive as a musician, pay his way. He got back together with Gillis and his jazz-rock outfit Joshua; a little later the band morphed into a more straight-ahead acoustic jazz group called Portraits that played in a Denver venue called Global Village. Frisell worked briefly with the Edgewater Chamber Players, an enterprising ensemble consisting of five horns, a string quartet, guitar, bass and drums. He took part in a regular Sunday afternoon jam in a Mexican restaurant and played with bands at the Denver Folklore Center. Frisell also got a gig working a summer season in the Rocky Mountain resort of Grand Lake as part of 'a small big band' that mostly played Glenn Miller arrangements. Membership of the Bermuda Brass required the compulsory wearing of Bermuda shorts; 'embarrassing' is all Frisell will say on the subject.

Frisell even got to play in 'this Las Vegas kind of supper club' in Denver as part of the orchestra backing popular sixties singer-songwriter and poet Rod McKuen and impressionist and comedian Frank Gorshin. His abilities as a jazz player and accompanist became sufficiently developed that Dale Bruning began to invite Frisell to play in some of his regular Denver gigs.

Frisell supplemented his meagre income by recording a few local radio commercial jingles, and teaching at a guitar and instrument store called Gordon Close's Melody Music. The lessons didn't go well. 'I was teaching mostly little kids and . . . I hate to say it, but . . . my heart wasn't really in it,' he says. 'I was so out of touch, so into the jazz thing, the bebop thing, that a little girl would come in with her mom and I'd be telling her, "Man, you've got to check out Charlie Parker." I was so far off-base.'

Frisell did have two notable student successes, however. He taught a guitarist and singer called Chuck Hughes, who would go on to front highly respected and popular rockabilly group the Hillbilly Hellcats, a band that is still gigging today. He also gave lessons to eighteen-year-old guitarist Kenny Vaughan, whose father had taken him, aged twelve, to see Johnny Smith play at a bar in Denver, and who was already gigging regularly in Denver rock 'n' roll and country bands. Vaughan is now one of the most in-demand guitarists in country, rock and Americana, having toured with Marty Stuart and Lucinda Williams, and recorded with Jim Lauderdale and Emmylou Harris.

'Bill's a very sensitive, sort of quiet and introspective kind of individual, and back then he was very shy – he would take a long time to answer a question,' says Vaughan. 'My grasp of music theory and the fretboard wasn't very good, but he taught me essential things such as how to negotiate improvising over chord changes and how to comp behind a soloist properly. I only studied with him for a couple of months, but I hung on to his lessons, and I kept going back to look at them, long after he left Denver. I think the thing that I learned the most from Bill was the concept of economy, of picking the most important notes and getting rid of the ones you don't need.'

Vaughan says Frisell was the perfect teacher for him. 'He had that attitude that he was still searching himself, too,' notes Vaughan. 'He didn't really know what he wanted to do at that point in his life. I remember him telling me, "I don't want to be a regular jazz guitar player. But I don't want to be a rock 'n' roll guitar player" – which he clearly wasn't; I was.'

Frisell was in a musical no-man's-land. UNC couldn't give him what he was looking for, but neither, it seemed, could Berklee. He felt secure living back in Denver, yet was restless to expand beyond its horizons. New York offered endless opportunities, but Frisell lacked the nerve; 'I couldn't imagine going there and living by myself – it just seemed *way* too intimidating.' He had painted himself into a purist's corner. In appearance and outlook, he was self-confessedly 'a young old fogey . . . I was frustrated and I don't think I was just that happy, really,' he says.

He had no girlfriend; 'I wished that I did, but I didn't know how to . . . I don't know, I was paralysed, or something . . . and I couldn't read signals.' Music was the only thing in his life, and mostly he stayed at home in his tiny apartment and practised – unplugged, during the day, every day, for hours upon hours upon hours on end. He would occasionally take a break, walking downtown or in nearby Cheesman Park, and then go back and practise some more.

On one of these outings Frisell bumped into his first teacher and mentor, the clarinettist and director of the Gold Sash Band, Jack Stevens. 'My hair was really long, I looked like some lunatic, and I saw him on the street. I told him, "I think I just want to play guitar." He really got down – "You should get your teaching degree. You'll never amount to anything."'

Eventually, though, the practice paid off. 'I can remember a clear moment, looking out of the little window of that little apartment, out to the back alley – almost when I had lost all hope of making a living at it, or having any kind of success at it, or of anything ever happening – when I decided to make a commitment,' says Frisell. 'It wasn't a commitment to get a record contract or to make a bunch of money, or anything. It was: I'm going to play this instrument, no matter what. This is all I got, and even if I just sit in this room for the rest of my life doing it, I don't care, that's what I'm going to do.'

●
●

Denver in the early seventies may have been a small isolated city in the middle of the big Western nowhere, where racial tensions were sometimes as high as the inflation rate, Anti-Vietnam war protests continued, petrol was in short supply, and Colfax Avenue became better known as a thoroughfare for drugs, crime and prostitution. Yet the city had a music scene that was fertile, diverse and largely integrated. In a divisive decade, music seemed to bring people together.

'In Denver, you can't make a living as a musician unless you're playing different kinds of music,' says trumpeter and cornetist Ron Miles. 'There's just not enough of anything to go around, so there's an easy exchange of ideas and a lot of chances to play with musicians of different stripes. I think there is a Colorado sound, and it's one that champions melody, values diversity, and respects the different traditions of American music.'

During this period there were no rock concerts at Red Rocks. At a June 1971 event headlined by, of all groups, British progressive folk-rockers Jethro Tull, there was a full-scale riot. Fans without tickets stormed the open-air amphitheatre; Colorado police responded with tear gas dropped from a swooping helicopter. Rock concerts at Red Rocks were banned for the next five years.

There was, however, a strong sense of musical community. The folk scene remained active, there was a bluegrass revival, and many venues put on experimental and psychedelic rock. The famed Five Points district, the 'Harlem of the West', where Jack Kerouac and Denver-native Neal Cassady had hung out in the late forties, and Billie Holiday, Duke Ellington and Miles Davis played in the fifties, still had a number of lively jazz bars and clubs. There was also a general DIY aesthetic that created new bands, sounds and music spaces.

'Denver in the seventies was a Wonderland,' says Kenny Vaughan. 'It was a cow town, for sure, but it was a big cow town. I was making a living playing country music, I was in a jazz band, and I had a punk-rockish party band. And then nearby Boulder was sort of a spiritual development centre. There were a lot of people taking mushrooms and all kind of drugs, but in a positive mind-opening way. There were musicians who were up there studying Indian and psychedelic music, whatever.'

Eventually the 'real strong undercurrent of eclecticism', as drummer Rudy Royston, who grew up in Denver, describes it, had to filter into Frisell's thinking, even a little; it encouraged him to venture out of his corner, out of his self-made shell. It wasn't as if he had been listening solely to *Intermodulation* from 1966, or Sonny Rollins's 1962 comeback album *The Bridge*, or the Art Farmer Quartet's elegant 1963 LP *Interaction*, all of which just happened to feature Jim Hall (although Frisell did listen to them *a lot*).

He was also tuning in to Miles Davis's directions in music, to his seventies syntheses of electric jazz and ambient Afro-funk; to the visionary new music of Ornette Coleman, lyrically angular sounds he has 'always loved'; to Dave Holland's swingingly avant-garde 1973 album *Conference of the Birds*; and to the spare, spacious and adventurous playing of Montreal-born pianist Paul Bley – 'I wanted to play guitar like Paul Bley played piano. Started to get free-er,' Frisell has written.

In 1974 Frisell met Mike Miller. Another supremely gifted guitarist deserving of wider recognition, Miller had moved to Boulder from his native South Dakota. He was already something of a prodigy, having played in his father's jazz band at twelve and double bass in the Sioux Falls Symphony by fifteen. He quickly made an impact in Boulder, and in Denver, playing in all kinds of groups, from jazz to pop, blues to fusion, rock to garage bands, and occasionally playing bass with legendary Colorado guitar hero Tommy Bolin.

If Graham Greene is right and 'there is always one moment in childhood when the door opens and lets the future in', then that moment for Bill Frisell was when, at the advanced age of twenty-three, he saw Mike Miller play live for the first time. While they had already jammed together – 'we just played standards and stuff,' says Bill, 'but, man, could he ever *play*' – for Frisell that night in a club in Boulder was revelatory.

'He was playing the same guitar as mine, an ES-175, and with this same intelligence that I'd been trying to get to – by ear; he wasn't reading charts, he was hearing everything, hearing all the inner workings of a song,' says Frisell. 'But he was playing all kinds of tunes, from Stevie Wonder to Weather Report to some theme from a TV show – and playing them *loud*. I had never heard anybody play guitar like that and it just blew my mind, obliterated my whole idea that I had to only play soft. It really shook me up, shook me out of my whole deep Jim Hall obsession, and something snapped. I realised it wasn't 1957, it was 1974. And I had to reassess *everything*.'

Frisell began to realise that by too closely imitating Jim Hall he had closed off his own creativity, closed off himself. The lesson of some of the jazz musicians he most admired – Hall, Sonny Rollins, Thelonious Monk, Miles Davis, Ornette Coleman and Charlie Parker – was that they had overcome the anxiety of influence and not copied anyone. They had relentlessly pursued their own musical paths, taken what they knew and loved from their own lives and times, from the music that was around them, taken all that information and miraculously transformed it.

'It wasn't right to be pretending I was in a time zone I wasn't,' Frisell once told the *Washington Post*. 'And then the walls broke down and I tried to be more open and honest to all this other stuff in my own life and what I do.'

That meant letting in all the sounds that had led him to that point – the Beatles, the Ventures, Hendrix, Eric Clapton, Wes Montgomery, Pete Seeger, Buddy Guy, the Kinks, Aaron Copland, Bob Dylan, Henry Mancini, Stephen Foster, Sonny Rollins and, of course, Jim Hall – and allowing all the music that was in his head to come out, allowing himself to be who he was. 'If you don't play *yourself*, you're nothing,' Art Pepper writes rather more brutally and succinctly in his autobiography *Straight Life*. 'I decided that maybe *that* should be the example, the model. So I tried opening myself up, and a light went on,' says Frisell. 'And I've tried to keep that attitude ever since.'

5: Raised by Deer

August 2015, a hotel lobby in Antwerp, Belgium. I am interviewing Tony Scherr, bass player in many of Bill Frisell's myriad groups since the late nineties.

Unbeknownst to both of us, Frisell steps out of the hotel lift, heads totally the wrong way to the breakfast room, and comes across us, *in flagrante*, caught fully in the act of talking about him. Scherr spots him first, and as we both turn to look, Frisell freezes, bolt upright, in mock horror, then sneaks slowly, like a startled woodland creature, out of view behind some reception-area foliage. We can't see him, but we know he's there.

Scherr leans into my digital recorder, raising his voice up a notch. 'So yeah, there was this Czech woman, Barbara, in Munich,' he begins. 'I'll tell ya, she was about seven-and-a-half feet tall, glass eye, in *both* eyes, *two* wooden legs. She was fucking paradise.'

Frisell makes a dash for it, moving from lush indoor vegetation to the nearest solid marble pillar.

'We've been talking about how there's got to be some real dirt in this book, so OK, I'm gonna tell you where all the bodies are buried,' Scherr continues. 'Joey [Baron] almost bit his ear *entirely* off. If you look closely, you'll see the line where the bolts are holding it in. That's where [Mike] Tyson got it from. You think that was an original move? No, that was Joey clamped onto his left hip, and—' Scherr lets out a loud grunt that echoes around the shiny lobby, we both fall about laughing, and Frisell decides this is his chance to break cover and strike out across the open floor, hurriedly darting past us, heading for the hotel buffet. 'It was all over Barbara,' says Scherr, his voice following Frisell's path. 'The two of them had to go outside and settle it.'

Frisell is gone, but the improvised scene leaves a lasting impression, mostly because it seems to say so much about the man. Not just about Frisell's playful and often winningly childlike sense of humour. Nor about

Scherr's slapstick creation, his Frisellian alter-ego. It's fitting and memorable because it perfectly demonstrates the gap between expectation and reality: how Bill Frisell is not how he seems; how much of his personality remains ambiguous and hidden; how he is very often misunderstood. Scherr's comic exaggeration evinces more than is intended; it opens up a whole spectrum of possibilities.

Frisell is a complex and contradictory character not easily judged on first meeting, and who is often subject to a series of stark misconceptions. His reserve and remoteness are mistaken for a lack of resolve, and his reticence gives rise to a whole raft of misreadings – from rudeness to inarticulacy to a crippling deficiency of focus, intelligence and originality of thought. Other potential Frisell fallacies include the idea that his gentleness corresponds to weakness; his self-consciousness to a paucity of self-belief or self-expression; his humility and soft-spokenness to an absence of ambition and hard determination.

'We have this American expression: "Don't let the smooth taste fool ya,"' says Ron Miles. 'The first thing that's apparent with Bill is that he's very quiet and very mild-mannered and very self-effacing. But don't let the smooth taste fool ya, because underneath that, there's some other rougher stuff. It's the same with his music. The first thing that draws people in is, "Oh, it's so beautiful and melodic and pretty Americana-like, or something." But then you listen closer and you say to him, "That's some strange shit in there, sir!" There's some grungy stuff down there, some weird angles.'

Violinist Jenny Scheinman, who has worked with Frisell since 1998, agrees. 'I think Bill is often misunderstood as a soft person, as only kind and gentle and generous and good,' she writes in an email to me. 'He also has a temper, is easily wounded, likes to gossip, is interested in confrontation, is a passionate feminist, and is very, very tough. I've never seen him give up on something or someone. I think he is one of the strongest people I know.'

Still waters run dark and deep with Bill Frisell, so much so that he's often described as inscrutable, oblique and even, by cartoonist Jim

Woodring, as 'something of a spectral presence'. Frisell's particular personality can seem akin to Winston Churchill's famous observation about Russia: 'It is a riddle, wrapped in a mystery, inside an enigma; but perhaps there is a key.' One of those keys is Frisell's inherited and sometimes chronic shyness. Yet, as a human characteristic, it too is confusing, inconsistent and multilayered.

The most obvious paradox, of course, is why someone so inherently shy should explicitly choose a life that necessitates him being so glaringly exposed and in the public eye, both on stage and in the media. One answer, as Frisell has suggested, is that music is for him, in fact, a form of catharsis.

'The power of the music, and the attraction of being in it, are so strong that they totally outweigh any other thoughts I might have about being embarrassed, or standing in front of people, or something,' he says. 'Whatever my outward appearance on stage, when we start playing, and as soon as the music starts happening, that is the place, that's when it feels really good. I feel like I'm home. That's when I'm comfortable, you know. And that's where I've been lucky I think, all along, never to experience stage fright, or something. It's almost the opposite: I'm more frightened just in normal everyday life.'

The author and critic Francis Davis once asked Frisell if playing music was a way to channel emotions he might otherwise be hesitant to express. 'I think it's healthy,' Frisell replied. 'I can't imagine what I would be like if I didn't play. Certain things that come out that way – what would they . . . ? How would they be expressed if . . . ? It's frightening to think.'

Frisell's wife, the artist Carole d'Inverno, concurs. 'If he couldn't play, he would just shoot himself. It's that simple. Because I don't think Bill, who *is* shy and introverted and all those things, ever felt like he belonged anywhere. He was just this guy with these nerdy glasses. But when he started playing music – even at high school, and then later with some of these quirky and creative musicians, who were just their own wonky people – I think it helped him; he realised this was a place where he could be himself.'

For Frisell, music is a world of freedom, possibility and opportunity, a place of never-ending complexity and learning. It is at once a safe space, an infinite challenge, and a deep mode of expression. It is music that is, in the end, the ultimate Frisell alter-ego, so much so that by now the two are inseparable and indivisible. He once said that music 'sort of saved me somehow'.

The music producer and creative free spirit Hal Willner first met Frisell in 1980, shortly after Frisell had moved to New York. 'I actually had Bill play something for me, for the Nino Rota album I was working on, and he was almost *clinically* shy,' Willner told me. 'He really didn't talk. Hardly ever. Carole was sort of his . . . spokesman.'

'Bill is just reserved and cautious; he checks you out, takes his time, processes,' says d'Inverno. 'I'm more of a livewire. I jump in, even if it ends in a car wreck.'

Frisell sympathises. 'Back then I could barely speak; I was just morti-fied at the thought of doing an interview with someone, for a magazine or something,' he says. 'Or the idea of having to talk on the radio – that was just . . . *really* hard. I was, like . . . petrified.'

Frisell was little different with many of the more edgy and experimen-tal New York downtown and no-wave musicians with whom he started to make connections and play in the eighties, including John Zorn, Wayne Horvitz, Tim Berne, Vernon Reid, Arto Lindsay, Elliott Sharp and Bobby Previte. It led bass player Lindsey Horner, who was part of that number, to joke that, in person, Frisell was so timid and furtive that he must have been 'raised by deer'.

It was a label that stuck. And it led drummer Joey Baron, who met Frisell in that underground community and subsequently played in his first band, to extend the cervine metaphor further by nicknaming him 'Moose'. It was a more accurate reflection, in Baron's eyes, of Frisell's physical strength and size, his general slowness in speech and move-ment – and a recognition perhaps that, if provoked, he could sometimes become passive-aggressive around humans.

Frisell wouldn't be the first performer to exhibit such seemingly unmusician-like qualities, or to find ways of overcoming that shyness, on and off stage – even to the extent that his reserve can act as a prop or strategy, a protection and a defence.

'He's *not* shy. See, that's the thing: I think he likes that persona. It's *very* useful. It's *perfect*. He can hide in his shell. He can pretend,' says Claudia Engelhart, laughing. Engelhart has been Frisell's sound engineer, road manager and one-woman fixer on almost every tour Frisell has made around the world since 1989, and she knows him better than most. 'He's definitely more aggressive than a lot of people. He knows what he wants, all the time. He's very clear about that.'

Frisell is working inside the carapace of music: a place where he can be comfortable within his own skin; play out different versions of himself, and play out his dreams, all the things he feels he can't do in real life. It's a place where he can connect with people and not be afraid; take risks without anyone getting hurt; trust and give way to a benign and some-times miraculous force far greater than himself.

'That's what's so great about music – it's not so proprietary in terms of feelings; everyone can read what they want out of it,' says Joey Baron. 'Yeah, Bill really *speaks* through his instrument. I think it's his favourite language.'

Frisell agrees. 'Music is how I express myself, how I communicate with people, much more than verbally . . . where everything makes sense. It's just my voice. That's when I actually feel like I am talking. For me it's just been a way . . . like now, as I'm struggling to find words to express myself . . . I'm just sort of . . . stammering around, trying to construct a sentence. With music it just feels like it's a much more natural way for me to express who I am.'

●
●

The English novelist Jonathan Coe interviewed Frisell for *The Wire* at the end of the untalkative eighties and was so struck by his unique way with words that he felt it necessary to present, towards the beginning of his profile, 'some things you have to know about Frisell as Interviewee'.

'He speaks at the rate of about a word every five minutes . . . The traditional three dots aren't always enough to do justice to the length of his pauses: so now and again I've stretched it to six,' wrote Coe, only exaggerating slightly. 'Occasionally there'll be an even longer pause than usual. When this happens, you know that he's searching for some elusive word. You try to guess what it's going to be, but invariably he comes down on something completely different.'

It's almost as if, for Frisell, English is a second language, an alien, unsettling and somewhat bewildering place, a process of translation from thought to deed in which he sometimes simply cannot find the words. Or rather, he cannot decide which *ones* to choose. Because contrary to the notion that Frisell is opaque and inarticulate, he is actually extremely thoughtful and intelligent in conversation. 'He's a haltingly articulate speaker,' wrote Dan Ouellette in *DownBeat*.

If anything, *too many* ideas come into his head, often all at once. He is the opposite of a linear thinker, and often all the more original for it. He has a mind that operates on parallel and interlocking lines: as soon as he finds one path through an answer, another will emerge or connect, and he'll feel it necessary to explore that viewpoint too. They are like channels, radio waves or streams of consciousness flowing and occasionally coming together, sometimes interfering with each other, sometimes cutting one another off, sometimes leading to a degree of static. It's the reason that when you transcribe a Bill Frisell interview you are often left hanging by ellipses, a sentence not quite completed, a phrase or word that trails off and is abandoned, a linked idea or tangential thought newly pursued.

'Oh, boy, every time I make a statement I immediately think of something that contradicts it,' he once said to me, chuckling. 'I don't think I'm schizophrenic quite yet, but there's a lot of other voices [in my head] almost interrupting me, voices that are saying, "Well, yeah, that's true, but this could be true as well, and don't forget this, and don't forget that."

'The older I get, the more I seem to have accumulated stuff, *information*, and the harder it gets for me to stay focused on one thing. So I'll get halfway through an answer, and then I'll back up and start coming around at it from a different or opposite direction, and sometimes it takes me a while to get to the actual point of what I'm trying to say. Part of the nature of it is just in the thing itself: there are all these possibilities and paradoxes, all these other truths, and there's not just some . . . there's no one *answer*.'

If, in particular, he is asked to unpack some aspect of his music – which already puts him on shaky and uncomfortable ground, a territory he is suspicious of and mistrusts, as if something will inevitably get irredeemably lost in translation or reduced by explication – he will pause, think carefully and sometimes at length, search for the most truthful and creative response, and eventually embark upon the journey of an answer.

'I find Bill to be very precise and extremely articulate. Not a lot of people comment on that,' says Eyvind Kang. 'They think that he stumbles around words, or something, but there's craft, intuition and spontaneity to the way he speaks, and all kinds of interactions between the three. He's actually a wordsmith.'

It can be challenging, though, as Jonathan Coe and many others have discovered, if you're the one asking the questions. You have to adapt, revise your expectations, slow down to his pace, settle yourself, tune in, listen more actively, respect the silences, resist filling in or finishing off. 'The thing is that Bill knows he has this effect, and I think he quite enjoys it,' British concert promoter John Cumming told me. 'He enjoys the Pinter-esque pause.'

Frisell somehow calms and quietens you, like a psychiatrist or a sage. Perhaps it's his voice that does it: soft and slow; hesitant, uncertain, awkward, even fragile; yet ultimately warm and somehow winning. It used to be a little more lilting, by some accounts: 'the voice, say, of a man who makes his living talking consolingly to children on television, dressed in a clown suit,' wrote Tom Junod in *GQ*.

If you listen to Frisell on some YouTube interviews – or even on relatively solid ground, reading a poem by Carl Sandburg on jazz drummer Matt Wilson's fine 2017 album *Honey and Salt* – it sounds like he is verbally feeling his way in the dark. 'He talks as though he is almost but not quite thinking aloud,' wrote Francis Davis.

Improvising, if you like. Jonathan Coe back in 1989 was one of the first of many commentators to observe that, at times, Frisell talks very much like he solos. 'Just as he delights in dismantling the syntax of the orthodox guitar solo, so he has little time for the syntax of ordinary speech,' wrote Coe in *The Wire*. And just like one of his solos, there is a deep sense of economy. When he is relaxed in your company, some of his stories can be on the elaborate side, yet there is little circumlocution or logorrhoea.

There's a deep sense of space, too. 'Bill holds the silence for a little longer than you might expect,' says Irish fiddle player Martin Hayes about Frisell's approach to both composing and soloing. That charged silence is extended further in conversation, as if the clock is slowly melting and time has become elastic. It somehow makes his statements more meaningful; if you listen closely enough, there is a quiet and distilled wisdom.

He laughs easily, but he is not demonstrative; he is contained. Frisell would make a good poker player: hard to read and easy to underestimate, yet clever, focused, with strong powers of concentration. Except that he has none of the prerequisite killer instinct; he wouldn't want to win enough, to annihilate his opponents. At the end of the game, he would want to give you all your chips back.

•
•

Bill Frisell is a big man with a certain crumpled presence. He is six feet, one inch tall and around 180lbs, though in his forties, he once admitted, he just kept getting 'fatter and fatter'. He has mostly, though, kept his weight under control, keeping fit by being, at various times, a dedicated cyclist and committed walker. He took up cycling in his late thirties and fell hard for it in much the same way as he did for the guitar as a teenager, both as object, and agent of freedom and change. 'I got *way* into biking, like obsessively, and when I was home I used to ride my bike a lot, almost every day,' he tells me. 'It used to clear out my head in the most amazing way.'

After a fall on a racing bike in Italy in 1998, in which he was flung over the handlebars and injured his left hand, Frisell began walking more – with the same gusto, and with the same parallels to his music. 'I love walking; that's almost the first thing I'll do when I get home from playing,' he says. 'I probably should be practising my guitar, but I'll sometimes walk for hours and hours and hours. Not on any particular route or hiking trail. Just anywhere. It's such a great feeling to walk past the point you can see, and then just keep going. I love that feeling of almost being lost and there being no limit.'

For all his dexterity and skill with guitars and pedals, Frisell's body language, like many shy people, largely expresses discomfort. He carries an awkwardness, even gawkiness, and he sometimes crosses his hands across his body, or cups them around opposite elbows, as if he's hugging or protecting himself – or trying to make himself smaller.

'Mr Frisell, in his person and in his playing, is the refutation of all that is heroic and priapic about the guitar tradition, a goofy affront to every teenage boy who ever picked up the ax in the desperate hope of getting laid,' wrote one critic. Bill Frisell: full-on, all-out anti-guitar hero.

Coming from hardy hands-on American stock, however, Frisell is a man of surprising energy, endurance – and, as Jenny Scheinman has suggested, strength. Cellist Hank Roberts, who has known him since the mid-seventies, tells a story about Frisell at the Vermont Studio Center artist retreat. 'I was with Bill at the end of his time at the centre and there was a gentleman in a wheelchair who wanted to get up a flight of stairs,' says Roberts. 'So Bill just picked up the wheelchair – with the guy in it – and he got him up the stairs. I was impressed with the physical strength that he had to do that, and I think it comes from an earthiness, and maybe that good side of stubbornness, you know.'

Frisell is also generous physically in another unexpected way: he's a hugger. Before the Covid-19 pandemic, at least, he would do it with almost everyone he knew reasonably well, male or female, or with whom he worked, especially fellow musicians – and with me, from early on in our contact together. It's both a little clumsy – more of a teenage-boy hug than a man or bear hug – and yet, at the same time, deeply touching, another instance of Frisell's strength through vulnerability.

He's generous emotionally too, often disarmingly so. The pianist Cecil Taylor once said that 'the great artists, rather than just getting involved with discipline, get to understand love and allow the love to take shape', and that is what Frisell has done, and achieved.

'Bill is so incredibly sweet and big-hearted – and I don't say that in any dismissive or casual way,' singer-songwriter and producer Joe Henry tells me. Frisell has worked with Henry on several projects, including albums for Bonnie Raitt and Allen Toussaint. 'He is so invariably and authentically kind, and you can't miss it, and it surprised me. I just don't expect most people to be that sort of uniquely . . . available, emotionally and compassionately. And, of course, once you register that, you under-stand that that's what you're predominantly hearing in the music: a deep empathy and real compassion.'

Bill Frisell talks about the musicians he plays with as 'my best friends', even as 'family'; he unshakeably splits concert fees equally with his band members ('I've played on other things, so I know that's not always how other people do it,' says Ron Miles); and he often signs off handwritten notes, and his idiosyncratic emails, with an unabashed, 'Love, Bill' ('You know, that's just him!' laughs pianist Jason Moran).

'One of the keys to Bill's music is how it draws you into a space and can feel very private,' says journalist, poet and record producer David Breskin. 'There's something really compelling about that, a kind of intimate quality. It's the same with him as a person . . . he's not afraid of intimacy, even with men. Which, I think, is a beautiful thing. And it's not so common with musicians, and it's not usually so cool. Musicians usually have to be cooler.'

Even into his sixties, and not just in hotel lobbies, there remains some-thing wonderfully wide-eyed about Frisell's demeanour, some idea that he's out of place in society, and, for all his strengths, needs safeguarding somewhat.

'There was some quality with Bill – the boy in the city, that kind of rural quality he had in New York – which made me sort of want to help and take care of him,' says Breskin. 'That was not a feeling I ever had with other musicians in New York, like Joey Baron, Ronald Shannon Jackson or John Zorn; they seemed very street-smart and in control. There was a certain childlike quality – and there's such a key difference in art between being child*ish* and being child*like*, right? Childish work: no one needs to have time for that. But with Bill there's a feeling of childlike wonder or openness, of him retaining a sense of play, a certain kind of uncontaminated innocence.'

Frisell cries fairly easily and often: hearing for the first time bluegrass legend Ralph Stanley sing live; visiting Louis Armstrong's unassuming house-museum in Queens, New York; even at an onstage Q&A session in Denver after a screening of Australian film-maker and singer Emma Franz's 2017 film about Frisell, when he recognised his childhood babysitter in the audience.

'I feel things, you know – that's what makes things hard,' he explains, taking a long pause. 'I know that people are in pain. And I can . . . feel it. There is always going to be pain and joy and all that, and whatever is in your life is going to come through in the music; it flavours what you play. It's just naturally part of the music: you can repress it, or you can let it out; you can feel it, or not feel it; but it's got to be in there somewhere. But, I mean,' he adds, laughing. 'I don't think I'm at a point where I'm a danger to society, or anything.'

Frisell's laugh is more naughty chuckle than uproarious shriek, his clothes sometimes loose-fitting and frumpy, as if he's never left Middle America. 'With his boyish face, round glasses, and baggy jeans,' wrote critic Geoffrey Himes in 2002, 'the guitarist looks like a middle-aged Harry Potter.' Since then, though, Frisell has sort of perfected the hipunhip, conservative-with-a-twist look, a further country-in-the-city contradiction: tweed jackets in eye-catching tartans and plaids; top shirt-button done up, but no tie, like a would-be David Byrne or David Lynch; crazy socks, in all kinds of wacky colours and designs, the brighter and bolder the better; Adidas suede sneakers.

'One of the things that I've known about Bill for a long time is that he has this cowboy side to him, and I think that's reflected a lot in his style choices,' says Nels Cline, a guitarist who plays in the band Wilco. 'He has this sort of gentleman-farmer look. It's stylish, but it's definitely coming out of a country kind of thing. That's who he is, and that's what his music resonates with, I think.'

•
•

There is something of the Frank Capra about Bill Frisell: a kind of determined individuality; a tough idealism. And like various campaigning Capra characters, Frisell's personality can seem, on the surface at least, the very embodiment of the nice or good guy. It's what a lot of people instinctively say about him, even within an industry as ruthlessly commercial, competitive and unforgiving as music.

'I feel a little unqualified and out of my depth saying this, still being totally intimidated by Bill Frisell, but he's probably the nicest person I've ever met,' says jazz trumpeter and composer Dave Douglas, whose 2004 album *Strange Liberation* was conceived both as a collaboration with and tribute to Frisell. 'He was super-nice to work with, of course, as he always is, and we all know that that feeds his music; it's part of the mystery of what makes him so great.'

Cartoonist Jim Woodring sees something deeper in Frisell's apparent benevolence. 'I've had the chance to watch Bill over the years, and I feel confident in saying he's not in any way a phoney,' he says. 'The niceness that he projects, the positivity, the desire to do well, and the people he attracts to him, that's all the real deal, and that's goodness of a high order. He's not just a good musician, there's something heavily great about him and the things he does in this world.

'I would never say this in front of Bill, because no, he doesn't like hearing it. He just goes, *"Oh, man."* And sometimes it's hard to tell whether music is so good it's like a spiritual experience, or it really *is* a spiritual experience. But he and his music have a lot of power and magic. It's affected my world, changed the way I see it. It's made order out of chaos, I think you could say. It's just sort of cemented this feeling of goodness there, created a sense of . . . orchestrated appreciation.'

For all the success he has enjoyed, Frisell has retained an innate humility. There is certainly an ego present, and a functioning self-belief – even occasionally a mockingly knowing self-praise. I once asked him what traits he most disliked in himself. A long, super-elliptical Frisell interlude followed, which he finally broke by saying, straight-faced and *sotto voce*, 'Well, I think very highly of myself, you know.'

Maybe it can all start to sound much too good to be true, yet the source of such wholesome Frisellian goodness is a strong sense in him, and of the people he admires, of integrity. It's about trying to stay true to yourself, and to the music, the way he believes such figures as Sonny Rollins, Wayne Shorter, Ornette Coleman and Charles Ives have done and did.

'He's my great high example of incredible musical integrity,' Frisell said about Ives in 1993, shortly after he'd recorded two short excerpts from the composer's landmark work, *Three Places in New England*. 'He was never recognised; he just did it for the music and that [music] is still so wonderful that it terrifies me.'

Frisell is firmly of the belief that the only times he has run into difficulties in his career are when he has gone against his instincts, and allowed the driving force to be financial rather than creative.

'The thing that's *never* let me down is the music,' he says. 'If the reason I go for something, the number-one thing, is because I'm excited about the music, then that almost always works out, everything takes care of itself. But if I've ever done something and the motivating factor is . . . the money . . . or because it's convenient . . . or just because someone's asked me fifty times . . . then that's dangerous, that gets me into trouble.'

The source of that trouble can be anything from a commercial to a musical compromise. Frisell's music has been occasionally used in business and advertising settings, but he is careful to ascertain what is being sold. He has swiftly turned down lucrative offers – once for $80,000 for use in a thirty-second commercial – from agencies representing companies with which he has ethical issues.

'I can remember soon after we first moved to New York, it must have been 1980 or '81, and Bill was asked to do this tour with a commercial funk or fusion band, or whatever, and he just started agonising about it,' Carole d'Inverno tells me. 'He kept saying to me, "Do you realise that if I do this tour, we can buy a house?" And I remember we had a long talk and I said to him, "Oh yeah, you'll buy a house, but you'll also kill yourself, you'll die playing this music." And he just said, "Oh yeah, I guess you're right." So . . . however many times we've struggled financially, and shit goes up and down, he's never done it for the money, never done it for the fame, and never given a damn about any of that. It's just the way it is. And I think that was one of the things that attracted me to him in the first place.'

If this sounds idealistic, it's because it *is* idealistic. He believes in good more than God; 'I still deep down believe that somehow people are good and there's a way, like in the sixties, we can work our way out of this,' he told me in 2017.

Frisell was referring to what he regarded as the 'messed-up' state of President Trump's America – though his politics are more usually implied. He has played festivals in Israel for many years because he believes music is about crossing borders not building them, about dialogue and freedom of expression, and that playing a concert in a country is not the same as endorsing its government. His form of protest is often through song choice: he has ended live sets with a version of Burt Bacharach's 'What the World Needs Now is Love', Bob Dylan's 'Masters of War', or the civil rights anthem 'We Shall Overcome'.

Mostly he believes in the positive power of connections. It can be a little hard to pin down exactly what this force is, but what most people regard as random coincidences and reasonable chance, Frisell sees as deeply significant, as organised serendipity.

The connection can be a much-loved early guitar (the custom 1968 Gibson ES-175 passed on to him by Dale Bruning), sold by Frisell in Boston in the late seventies, resurfacing thirty-six years later at a vintage guitar shop just twelve miles from his then home in Seattle. Or a road numbered 61 that has a direct link both to his paternal grandfather's birthplace in Sweden and hometown in Minnesota. It could be a peripheral figure from his distant past turning up unexpectedly in the heart of his creative present. Hearing something on the radio. Bumping into someone in the street. 'The way his mind works is that he's got this complete architecture of connections,' says Carole d'Inverno. 'It not only gives him an extremely good memory, but it also provides him with a bigger picture, something more universal.'

'He's superstitious about the coincidental criss-crossing of all of our paths,' writes Jenny Scheinman. 'It's like he's weaving a big tapestry of his life and we're all in it . . . It's almost like a religion, his faith in the constantly unfolding coincidences of existence and the weaving together of our lives.'

It is the nearest Frisell comes to a life philosophy or belief system. 'This stuff drives me crazy, but it's not like some special thing that just happens to me,' Frisell explains. 'I mean, it's happening all the time to all of us, right? Maybe I'm just on the lookout for it, or something . . . I'm more prepared. Part of it is just recognising it, just seeing it.'

Frisell chooses to regard these happenstances as benevolent forces, to be receptive to them as opportunities: 'You see, it doesn't seem random to me – more like everything that's happening is a result of something. There's a unity; it's all connected. And that's just so much what happens with the music, so much about how it works – on a micro, macro and every level – with the musicians that you play with and the notes that you play. It's just like . . . this web, you know.'

Frisell works hard to stay fastened to these first principles, to the threads and tapestry that bind his love of music. He is extremely industrious. 'I kind of hesitate to blow it up too much – because he's really worked his ass off, and he's never given up on himself,' says Joey Baron.

'But I would say that Bill is a model of someone following and maintaining their vision. And you can hear it; it's all there in the music.'

Frisell's artistic vision stretches to Steinbeck. On a 'Bill's Favourites' section on his pre-2019 website, there was a long quotation from John Steinbeck's *East of Eden*, a passage dealing with little less than the essence of the creative spirit and a meaningful life.

> There is great tension in the world, tension toward a breaking point, and men are unhappy and confused.
>
> At such a time it seems natural and good to me to ask myself these questions. What do I believe in? What must I fight for and what must I fight against?
>
> . . . And this I believe: that the free, exploring mind of the individual human is the most valuable thing in the world. And this I would fight for: the freedom of the mind to take any direction it wishes, undirected. And this I must fight against: any idea, religion, or government which limits or destroys the individual. This is what I am and what I am about.

⦂

Famously uncompromising drummer Paul Motian once described Frisell as the most stubborn person he'd ever met. There can be a bad side to Frisell's obstinacy, and a bad side to Bill Frisell. If he doesn't want to do something, he will simply remain silent and refuse; nobody can persuade him. Or if he wants something done a certain way, he will persist, quietly, but persist and persist, all the same.

Both can be viewed as rich strains of artistic virtue and honesty. Or they can be seen as darker shades of the shy spectrum, a kind of 'social deafness' and 'low-heeled arrogance', to quote from Joe Moran's *Shrinking Violets*. Frisell is not good at confrontation, and not good at intervening, or communicating dissatisfaction. He waits, he holds back, he watches and observes.

'I hate to use this term, but there's this passive-aggressive thing that goes on a lot with Bill, and that drives me crazy sometimes,' laughs Claudia Engelhart. 'It'd be better if he just said out loud what he wants or doesn't want. But he doesn't do that.'

David Breskin agrees. 'Bill will find a way to get what he wants – not by acting, but by *not* acting, which is a classic definition of what people would call, psychodynamically, passive-aggressiveness,' he says. There is, Breskin suggests, a 'dark energy' to Bill Frisell that largely remains hidden. It surfaces sporadically on some of his records, however, especially in his early work. And it surfaces in his personal life.

You don't expect 'terminally polite' Bill Frisell to liberally employ the f-word, or to tell, according to jazz composer Mike Gibbs, 'the filthiest joke I've ever heard' (so filthy he declined to repeat it). Somehow, from Frisell's modest mouth, they all sound more startling and shocking. Frisell's 2018 interview with pianist and critic Ethan Iverson is sprinkled with expletives, including this salty description of an unnamed teacher Frisell studied with at Berklee College of Music in Boston in the mid-seventies, and who heavily criticised one of his early compositions: 'I didn't write anything for a long time after that. The fucking asshole prick bastard. Fuck you, whoever you are. I'd just like to say that now for the record.'

'Oh yeah, he swears all the time,' says Claudia Engelhart. 'Are you kidding? He has a bad mouth.'

Drummer Rudy Royston, who has been playing with Frisell since the mid-nineties, also recognises binary Bill. 'People like to think of him as a gentle sort of soul, but I'm not sure that's what it is. I think Bill is truly a person who is open to compassion, open to people's lives and perspectives, open to people's pain and open to their joy. And he's about playing music that relates to those things.

'But it's not like he's just that. I've seen him kind of go off on some people before, and it's just like, "*Whoa*, this dude is kinda mean." If you rub him the wrong way, it's like, wow, Bill can kinda be "*umph*".'

What ultimately save Frisell, however, and mostly override his doubtless many faults, are his wide-ranging intelligence and that offbeat sense of humour – and perhaps crucially the relationship between the two. As Joe Henry says, 'He holds a really quite unique balance, I think, between possessing a deep intellect and consciously preserving a bit of *naïveté*.'

Frisell's fluid intelligence means he is quick to humour and laughter, especially if there is some strangeness in the mix, some gentle absurdity, some opportunity for humorous self-deprecation. In an email sent to me in 2016, following several days of initial in-depth interviews for this book, Frisell couldn't resist lightening the load a little by again playing the knowingly slapstick joker.

He wrote: 'Next time I'll tell you about when I was on that chain gang in Louisiana (wrongly convicted of course . . . I swear it was self-defense), and the voodoo initiation ceremony, and hopping freight trains with the hobos, and the years I spent as a cowboy bronco buster in the rodeo, and, of course, the whole Playboy Mansion controversy fiasco . . . I'd like to set the record straight on that one!'

In the spring of 1975 Bill Frisell set out on a path back to the Berklee College of Music in Boston. Even though he hadn't enjoyed his time in the city a few years earlier, he decided that he was in a better frame of mind to resume his studies; that, at twenty-four, he was more mature and more musically open-minded. He knew the college, knew what he wanted, and he was quickly accepted.

Frisell settled on arranging and composition as his major, rather than guitar or performance. 'I wasn't interested in taking guitar lessons. I wanted to learn about music more in general,' he says. His parents agreed to support him – 'well, yeah, *again* – for the umpteenth time,' he adds. Studying at Berklee has never been cheap; undergraduate fees today, including room and board, total around $70,000 per year.

He left Denver with Mike Miller, the guitarist who had 'blown his mind' in that bar in Boulder a year earlier. Frisell and Miller had become friends, and they continued to jam together in private – 'We would play for hours and hours, get in a trance, or something, just playing tunes,' says Frisell. But they'd made a pact: *it's time to get outta town*. Packing up his VW Beetle, Frisell dropped Miller at his parents' home in Sioux Falls, South Dakota; from there Miller went west to Los Angeles, where he has lived ever since. Frisell drove on east to Boston.

Even though he was returning to the city, and he quickly found an apartment, Frisell's second stay at Berklee did not start well. 'I didn't know *anybody*, I was completely flipped out, I was just terrified,' he says. 'I was just sitting in there the first night, completely alone, completely freaked out, by myself, just crying my eyes out.'

The following day, however, he met bass player Kermit Driscoll, who would be a major figure in Frisell's musical life over the next twenty years. Driscoll was wearing a T-shirt emblazoned with the logo of a dive bar in Colby, Kansas, called the Rusty Bucket. 'I was like, oh wow, somebody else from out West, so we immediately started playing together,' says Frisell.

A few days later, on Mike Miller's recommendation, he went to see another (Mid)Westerner, guitarist Pat Metheny, play in a small bar called Club Zircon. In 1973, at the age of just nineteen, the prodigious Metheny had been invited by Gary Burton to teach at Berklee; Metheny was also working in Burton's band, for a time playing twelve-string electric alongside guitarist Mick Goodrick, and gigging around the city. He had formed his first group, a trio with drummer Bob Moses, who was also playing with Burton, and a relatively unknown twenty-three-year-old electric bass player from Florida named Jaco Pastorius. Coincidentally, Pastorius had taught Kermit Driscoll for one semester at the University of Miami a year earlier.

Frisell was astonished yet inspired by the experience of hearing Metheny. Not only had Metheny, who was three years younger than Frisell, begun to write a lot of his own music – compositions that would appear on his debut album, *Bright Size Life*, with the same trio the following year – but he was also translating on to the guitar many of the more progressive, free and abstract post-bop forms and ideas that Frisell himself had been thinking about. Metheny had even played in Paul Bley's band in New York during the previous summer.

'That messed me up. It was bad, bad; it was traumatic,' Bill has said. 'He was playing Paul Bley, and [Wayne Shorter's] "Nefertiti", and it was like, *fuuuuuuuuck*! He was just massacring it. In my mind there was this inkling of what could be, and he was just slaying it. He was there already.'

Despite feeling that Metheny was 'light years ahead of what I could ever do', Frisell asked him for a lesson. Metheny agreed, though the session at his small Boston apartment was not exactly didactic.

'There really wasn't much of a lesson; right away we were just playing together,' says Metheny. 'At that point he was a very different musician, and clearly coming from a deep Jim Hall thing. But I could also see right off that he was unique somehow, too.'

•

•

Frisell's main tutor at Berklee was the trumpeter, bandleader and legendary jazz educator Herb Pomeroy, who joined the teaching staff in 1955 and taught at the college for the next forty years. Pomeroy had a reputation for being strict and systematic, but his tuition was leavened by a great deal of natural grace and good humour (one of his musical heroes was Duke Ellington). He inculcated discipline and rigour, and was a teacher who seemed to get the best out of his students; he was ambitious for them.

'Herb Pomeroy was massively huge,' says Frisell. 'His classes were small, we did a great amount of work, and you couldn't get anything past him – not even one little mistake. He had rules, he was very precise, and he could hear and see music on another level. He got me thinking about some things that you would never think to do on the guitar.'

Frisell was also taught by Mike Gibbs, with whom he continues to have a musical relationship even today. An English jazz composer and arranger born in Southern Rhodesia (now Zimbabwe), Gibbs had been brought in by Gary Burton as a Berklee 'composer-in-residence'. Gibbs had studied and played trombone with Burton at Berklee from 1960–61, and written music for various Burton ensembles and projects, including his landmark 1967 proto-fusion LP *Duster*. Gibbs was also a vital force in various early seventies alliances of jazz, classical and rock – perhaps most heroically in his orchestrations for the Mahavishnu Orchestra's groundbreaking 1974 album *Apocalypse*. Gibbs was Gil Evans to Herb Pomeroy's Duke Ellington, and Frisell was a fan. 'I couldn't believe it!' Frisell has said. 'There he was . . . teaching. I took all his classes.'

Gibbs had studied in the early sixties with such leading-edge jazz and new-music composers as Gunther Schuller, George Russell and Iannis Xenakis, and even at one point with the 'dean of American composers', Aaron Copland. He was a career rule-breaker whose pedagogy stood in stark contrast to the more rigid diktats of other teachers at Berklee.

'In the harmony class, they'd have "avoid notes" – notes you weren't supposed to use over a particular chord,' Frisell told *Guitar Player* magazine. 'Naturally, those were the first ones I'd check out.'

In another class, Frisell was asked by a teacher to write a modal tune in the style of Miles Davis's 'So What' or John Coltrane's 'Impressions', but within certain parameters. 'I wrote this thing, and everything was according to what he had instructed, what the rules were, but it sounded like a folk song, or something,' says Frisell. 'And I brought it into the class and the guy said, "Are you kidding me? This is ridiculous. This is like *folk music*!" He could have used the same words but with a different emphasis and said, "*Wow*, that sounds like folk music." That would have been great, and I would've written a bunch of other stuff. But he just totally put it down, squashed the whole thing, and I just felt like a complete failure. I ended up not writing anything for a long time after that.' Frisell pauses and smiles. '*Asshole!*'

Gibbs offered a more modern, flexible and individual approach. 'When they first got to Berklee, students were too often told, "You can't do this and you can't do that,"' explains Gibbs. 'I looked at it a little differently. I said, "I want to know how you *can* do it."'

Frisell was so fired up by Gibbs's classes that he called him to ask if he could join his crack student band – even though he knew the composer already had a guitar player. 'It's one of the most aggressive things I've ever done,' he has said. 'It was a big deal for me to do that . . . But I thought, "I can't *not* do this . . ." [Mike] immediately said, "Great, come on board."'

Frisell's guitar tuition at Berklee was provided by one of the college's most consistently creative and inspirational teachers, Jon Damian. An artist and activist as well as a gifted guitarist, Damian invented the 'Rubbertellie', a standard Fender Telecaster, retuned and played like a cello or lap steel, which he would use for sound-art improvisations that combined music with painting and performance.

Frisell had lucked out again; Damian was the perfect tutor for him at that time. 'I wasn't even really looking for a guitar teacher; I was looking for something more . . . trying to figure out how to break things apart,' says Frisell. 'You know, he understood all the theory and harmony and all that, but he was more into these conceptual things, like asking me to play what I felt after he'd read me a poem, or just the two of us playing completely free and me trying to get comfortable with that.'

•
•

The classes at Berklee were only a part of the broad education that Boston offered music students in the mid-seventies. There was also an active music scene in the city, centred on small clubs that attracted big names from New York and beyond. Not only did Frisell get to hear Pat Metheny's first trio in Club Zircon and at a bar called Pooh's Pub, but in 1977 he also caught one of the very first gigs by the newly formed Pat Metheny Group, with Lyle Mays on keyboards, Mark Egan on electric bass, and Danny Gottlieb on drums.

At these venues, and also at the Jazz Workshop and Paul's Mall, Frisell was to witness some of the pivotal musicians of a fascinatingly fractured though creatively fertile decade: from McCoy Tyner's intensely muscular and majestic playing to Anthony Braxton's restless exploration of the limits of post-bop, free improvisation and modern composition; from David Sanborn's first fusions of jazz with funk, pop and R&B to Sonny Rollins's colossally inventive improvisational flights; from the 'beautiful power' of B. B. King to the 'radical-conservative' classicism of the Modern Jazz Quartet.

The college and the city's venues provided countless opportunities for students to jam, play and form bands. They were greatly assisted by the first samizdat volumes of *The Real Book*, a by now legendary, and in some circles infamous, anthology of unlicensed lead sheets for jazz standards first transcribed and collated in the early seventies by Berklee students of Gary Burton and Pat Metheny. Dozens of classic and contemporary jazz compositions were newly democratised and suddenly available – in Boston at least.

Initially Frisell's sights were set firmly on finding work in a band that would help support him financially. He had started playing in a guitar trio with Kermit Driscoll, and through him Frisell was asked to audition for a pop band called Boston Connection, in which Driscoll had started playing. Even though the bassist was just nineteen and five years younger than Frisell, he was already a savvy musician, having gigged and toured with rock and pop bands since the age of sixteen.

'I remember going to Bill's apartment, and he had an amp, a chair, a sleeping bag, and nothing else,' says Driscoll. 'He had no money at all, whatsoever.'

Frisell passed the audition, combed his straggly beard, and bought one of the band's signature three-piece flared-trouser orange polyester suits. Boston Connection was a tight six-piece comprising two singers, a Hammond organ player (who was also the group's leader), Bill, Kermit, and drummer Vinnie Colaiuta, who had recently graduated from Berklee. Colaiuta would go on to play with Frank Zappa, Joni Mitchell and Sting, and as a session drummer with hundreds of others, from Olivia Newton-John to Ray Charles, Leonard Cohen to Megadeath.

Bill, Kermit and Vinnie may have occasionally kidded themselves that they were in a version of the Tony Williams Lifetime, one of the great jazz fusion bands of the era, led by former Miles Davis drummer Williams, yet Boston Connection was a commercial covers band that played the Top Forty radio hits of the day – 'I remember playing "Feelings" a lot; I was not a big fan of that song,' says Frisell – and early disco tunes by the Bee Gees, O'Jays and Donna Summer.

'I remember one time we came back from a Boston Connection gig,' says Driscoll, 'and Bill went straight to the calendar on his wall, and he wrote down the exact amount he'd earned – $20 or whatever. There was one figure on it, from playing in a different band, of $4.50 – I remember that too, because I played that gig. Four-and-a-half dollars! And I asked Bill, "Why are you writing all this down?" And he said, "Well, I have to pay taxes on it." Is there anybody else you've ever met that, in those circumstances, would do something like that?'

Boston Connection may not have made Frisell's fortune, but the group led to Bill buying a very different type of guitar, a solid-bodied Gibson that would be his primary instrument for the next decade or more, and on which he would first begin to make a name. 'My ES-175 wasn't cutting it for the [Boston Connection] gig. I needed to play louder,' Frisell has written. 'On the bulletin board at Berklee there was an ad for a 1971 Gibson SG. I bought it for $200.'

The guitar body had been 'customised' with white house paint, which Frisell stripped off and revarnished. Shortly afterwards, a fellow student gave him a volume pedal – and Bill Frisell's sonic world was to change for ever. All the extensions of electronic sustain, echoing abstractions, enveloping expanses and warping soundscapes start here. All the infinite colours, shades, textures and dimensions within the Frisell sound, The Frisell Dream, owe something to the possibilities first opened up by a single pedal unit, a box on the floor.

Suddenly Frisell could breathe attack, control and dynamics into a guitar phrase in the same way he once did on clarinet and saxophone. But just like rock, metal, fusion and many other guitarists before him, he wanted more. 'I heard [Carlos] Santana play this incredible sustain sound that sounded like a trumpet,' he told critic Ted Panken. 'I was trying to play like a horn player; I wanted to sound like Miles Davis. So I got a distortion thing. And a wah-wah pedal. Then I was listening to pianists and admired how they could hold notes down and let them ring. Back then, there was a little cheap delay that had a cassette tape in it which sort of did . . . that piano-y sustained thing.'

•
•

There were three other crucial events during Frisell's time at Berklee that slowly nudged the door further open.

Firstly, he met cellist Hank Roberts, with whom he is still playing today. Roberts studied at Berklee during the summer of 1973, and had been gigging and working on and off in Boston and at the college since then. He played in Mike Gibbs's top-tier band, and worked as a vegetarian chef in the college café. Roberts was then, as he is now, a wide-ranging and wholly original voice on an uncommon instrument in jazz and improvisation, and Frisell was immediately attracted to working with him.

Another compellingly mercurial musician who had a powerful effect on Frisell was guitarist and vocalist Michael Gregory Jackson. A key member of the seventies New York avant-jazz loft scene, Jackson was an innovator who was also strongly drawn to blues, rock, folk and new-music forms. He played several gigs in Boston in the mid-seventies, mostly in lofts and small arts spaces, displaying equal levels of artistry and experimentation on acoustic and electric; on electric he made imaginative use of a volume pedal. 'He's another one of the ones that completely blew my mind,' says Frisell. 'He helped me find my way.'

A third progressive force was Toru 'Tiger' Okoshi. The trumpeter had moved to Boston from Japan in 1972 and graduated with honours from Berklee the year Frisell arrived. He was one of the most admired musicians at Berklee, a fiery soloist, talented composer and strong personality greatly respected by both Gary Burton and Mike Gibbs.

Okoshi formed a fusion band, Tiger's Baku, with Frisell at Berklee in 1976. Bill recommended Kermit Driscoll, and the quintet also comprised keyboard player Frank Wilkins and nineteen-year-old drumming sensation Tommy Campbell, who was the nephew of soul-jazz organ supremo Jimmy Smith. Tiger's Baku was an exclusive vehicle for Okoshi's smart compositions – tunes that were melodically striking, harmonically advanced, rhythmically dynamic, and that provided a good amount of room for individual expression. The leader was inspired by the music of Pat Metheny, not just in the way that it bridged so many styles but in that it was so singular, so much of itself.

The band landed a Monday night residency at Pooh's Pub, and for the next eighteen months this was *the* Berklee gig to attend – not just for college students and local musicians (even Metheny himself was a regular) but for many college tutors too (Mike Gibbs, in particular).

'We were sort of the superstars among the students,' says Frisell, in a rare lapse of modesty. 'The club was just mobbed every time we played there. It was packed.' It was something similar to Frisell's Wes Montgomery 'Bumpin' on Sunset' moment at high school. 'Suddenly I was . . . the hotshot guitar guy. That's the first time I remember someone telling me that they'd never heard any guitar sound like that.'

Kermit Driscoll says Tiger's Baku was 'a hell of a band; we were the cats.' Guitarist and fellow Berklee student Leni Stern agrees: 'Tiger is an amazing writer, and it seemed to me like a new type of music – beautiful melodies, complex changes, but electric and totally modern at the same time. Bill was rockin'. They were Boston's Weather Report.'

Tiger's Baku gave Frisell permission to be the musician he hungered to be, to sound more fully like himself: a guitarist who could marry the advanced intensity, intelligence and sophistication of post-bop jazz with all the immediate energy, excitement and potential of modern rock and pop. He had a jazz sensibility, a classic rock guitar, and a brave new world of special effects. The 'Jim Hall-meets-Jimi Hendrix' analogies were just around the corner.

'We had a very strong body of music, and I would play Tiger's tunes as well as I could, but I wasn't being told to hold back in any way,' says Frisell. 'I could do exactly what I wanted, go full-on, take it absolutely as far as my imagination could go within the song.'

Not that Frisell was given to excess, to shredding like some of the Boston guitar whizz-kids.

'Every other guitar player at Berklee at that time seemed to be learning to play as fast as possible – and they still are,' says Mike Gibbs. 'But Bill wasn't. It was *what* he played. With less notes. Even one note could grab your attention and fill the room with sound. Everything Bill played had a mark through it that caught your ear in a surprising way.'

●
●

In the summer of 1977 Frisell met Magdalena Thora, a twenty-five-year-old actress and musician, well known in her native West Germany, who had come to Berklee to study film scoring. She was passionate, bohemian, strong-willed and, with long blonde hair, strikingly beautiful. She also played jazz and blues guitar, which was increasingly becoming her first love.

Soon after she arrived at the college, Magdalena went to see Bill play with Tiger's Baku. She kept asking him for lessons, and eventually he reluctantly agreed, though he wouldn't charge. The lessons were to continue for almost a year, and Bill and Magdalena began hanging out together, driving around Boston in his Volkswagen Beetle, which reminded her of home. A closeness developed from there: it continued until Bill introduced her to one of his best friends, Mike Stern, and Bill went to live and work in Belgium. Magdalena married Mike three years later, eventually changing her name to Leni Stern, and shaping a career as one of jazz's most vital and respected guitarists, vocalists and cross-border connectors – especially to the music and musicians of West Africa.

'Bill was very quiet and modest-looking, and people would always underestimate him, but really he was quite a rebel, quite a revolutionary figure at the time,' says Leni. 'Not just in the way he played guitar, which blew *everybody's* mind. But also in the way he thought about the world, the way he would always support and side with me.

'There were only a handful of women guitar players at Berklee back then, and nobody wanted to hire a woman lead guitar player like me – to some men, we were like the *jokes* of the scene. So part of the reason Bill taught me so much, I think, is because he saw how disadvantaged I was. He encouraged me not only to develop my own sound and voice, but also to play gigs as much as possible, and to write my own music. Bill gave me the tools. He helped form me into the guitar player that I managed to become.'

Frisell completed his studies at Berklee in 1977 and was given the prestigious Harris Stanton award for 'Outstanding Guitarist of the Year'. Like many graduates before him, he hung around Boston for a while, but was beginning to think it was time to move on. Even though he had Tiger and Leni, he was also curious to put himself in creative situations that would force him to learn and develop.

An opportunity to do just that was provided by Belgian alto sax-ophonist Stéphane (more commonly, Steve) Houben, who had studied at Berklee during 1976 and 1977, and formed groups in which at different times both Bill and Mike Stern had briefly played. Houben was back in Belgium, leading and working in various bands, and teaching a jazz sem-inar he had set up with serialist composer Henri Pousseur at the music conservatory in Liège. Something of a jazz fixer and impresario, Houben began to invite American Berklee students, and even teachers, to join him. Musicians such as tenor player Greg Badolato, who taught saxo-phone at Berklee, guitarist John Thomas, and drummer Eddie Davidson travelled to Belgium in 1977. Houben formed a group called Solstice, and he recorded a lively post-bop debut album, on which, on one track, Chet Baker guested.

At the beginning of 1978 Houben travelled back to Berklee. He invited Frisell, Kermit Driscoll, Greg Badolato and drummer Vinnie Johnson to join him in Belgium. Forty-one-year-old Johnson was already something of a local Boston legend – he had played jazz with saxophone giant Cole-man Hawkins, blues with guitar great T-Bone Walker, and anything from funk and soul to psychedelic rock with various bands around the city.

'Steve was a really great alto player – he had his own sound, and he also played flute – and he was a smooth operator and real charismatic,' says Frisell. 'He picked players that he thought were the happening guys around town, and you know, he just had this European thing . . . and he kind of seduced us. He said he had connections in Belgium and he would sort of be our manager.'

Frisell was also attracted to playing with Kermit and the other musi-cians, and to travelling abroad (he had only been to Canada, once) – espe-cially to Europe. He sold almost everything he owned, including his VW Beetle and the Gibson ES-175, and bought a cheap one-way plane ticket.

.
.

Situated in the primarily French-speaking southeast of Belgium, Spa is a small, historic tourist town most famous for its natural springs (it is the origin of the term 'spa') and its nearby Formula One grand-prix circuit, set within the mountain forests of the Ardennes. But while it was conveniently close to the German and Dutch borders, Spa, in 1978, was not exactly London, Paris, Berlin or Amsterdam. It was not the jazz capital of Europe, of Belgium, or even of its own region of Wallonia.

Houben had arranged for the quartet to lodge for free in rooms above Spa's one jazz club, Chapati (pronounced, in Spa, as 'CHAP-a-tee'), housed in a four-hundred-year-old building in the town centre. The owner, Robert Delcour, was a friend of Houben's, an amateur trumpet player and an ardent fan of the music, running the club more for love than money. Delcour managed to attract an extraordinary roster of leading American jazz musicians to the tiny Belgian bar and club. While Frisell and Driscoll were there, they got to see Art Blakey and the Jazz Messengers, Betty Carter, the Art Ensemble of Chicago, Cedar Walton, Woody Shaw and Henry Threadgill. Mal Waldron recorded a live solo piano album, *Mingus Lives*, at the club in February 1979.

On the one hand, the set-up at Chapati was ideal: they could practise all day and then, every so often, as the resident 'house band', play at night, all night, if they liked, in the club. Attached was a restaurant, where they had meals. On the other hand, the living space was worse than basic. 'It was a disaster – more like a construction site, with piles of dirt and dust everywhere, and internal walls not finished,' said Frisell. 'We ended up on the floor in sleeping bags. That was maybe the first inkling that things weren't . . .'

The group eventually made the rooms habitable, and for Frisell, over the next year or so, Chapati actually proved invaluable; it was like a musical retreat or laboratory, a room of his own far away from everything he had known, with no distractions and few locals speaking English – somewhere he could continue to grow in confidence, grow into himself. 'It wasn't until I went to Belgium that I started to let my music come out, that I felt I could express something of my own,' says Frisell. 'We were just stuck in that situation, and we had a lot of downtime and very little new music, but right there I had this great band. I could try things and hear what the music sounded like.'

Kermit Driscoll was also an important part of the process, a key Frisell supporter from the moment they first started playing together. 'So many times while I was at Berklee I'd write a tune, and I'd be at a jam session and was shy about it – "Here, could we try this?" And I'd almost always get shut down; my belief in my own writing pretty much didn't exist,' says Frisell. 'But Kermit was always there. He was maybe the first guy to be like, "Wow, that's cool" when looking at my tunes – especially after we made the move to Belgium.'

Spa is a provincial and conservative town, the type of place that, even today and in summer, mostly closes after nine at night, but Chapati in the seventies was its alternative scene, its hippie hangout, its small slice of jazz-fuelled rebellion. 'There were quite a few of these bizarre but really interesting people hanging around the club,' says Frisell. 'One guy always wore black and a top hat, and he carried a coffin around with him.'

Jean-Jacques Bloemers, a Chapati regular during this time and now the respectable managing director of the tourist office in Spa, says something similar when I get talking to him. 'It was very dark inside and it wasn't for everybody,' he says. 'Not everybody was . . . well, welcome. It was a place only for serious music lovers, and serious drinkers.'

Chapati mostly worked out for the visiting Americans, especially for Driscoll, who was deeply serious and committed to both music and Belgian beer. Steve Houben fixed a few other local gigs, and organised for the musicians to teach at the Royal Conservatory in Liège, thirty miles away, which brought in some much needed funds.

Houben also arranged for the band, which he named Mauve Traffic, to record an album. He brought in Belgian keyboardist and composer Michel Herr, whom he had met at Berklee while Herr was on a scholarship at the college. In a small home studio near Liège, the sextet cut nine originals – four by Frisell, three by Houben, and one each by Driscoll and Magdalena Thora.

The album was released in 1979 and titled *Oh Boy . . .* , a Frisell tune on the record (and one of his catchphrases, then and now), and it's a classic slab of superannuated seventies American fusion that today Michel Herr describes as 'jazz-funk with muscle'. While the players are clearly first-rate, most aspects of the LP haven't weathered well – from the flashy drum fills to the heavy synth effects and even Frisell's guitar solos, which sound closer to soft rock than anything sparked by Hall or Hendrix.

Yet in Frisell's first compositions there is a hint of something more substantial and complex. While Houben's tunes are loose structures for often energetic soloing, Frisell's songs are written-through and arranged for the group as a whole – they progress through changes in mood, character and atmosphere, like chapters in a novel.

In November of that year, by which time Bill had already left Belgium, Houben also organised for Frisell and Driscoll to record five tracks in a Brussels studio with him, American pianist Dennis Luxion, Belgian drummer Bruno Castellucci – and Chet Baker; the album, which came out in 1980, was simply called *Chet Baker–Steve Houben*. Songs were chosen that Baker knew and suited his muted vocals and spare trumpet playing – slow-tempo numbers such as Sam Rivers's ballad 'Beatrice' and Jimmy Van Heusen and Eddie DeLange's stately 'Deep in a Dream'. Out of respect, no doubt, Frisell plays it safe and reverts to his sympathetic Jim Hall guitar persona. Baker sounds bruised and breathy, but during these long brutal years of heroin addiction there is still a devastating vulnerability and poignancy to his singing and playing that is acutely affecting.

'He was definitely pretty high at the dinner the night before, but I'm not sure he was [out of it] at the actual recording session,' Driscoll remembers. 'And he killed me. He fucking killed me. Just one note. There was so much *soul*. Man, it was like I'd never heard a trumpet in my life before.'

Overall, however, there was little for the visiting Americans to do. Houben says he 'didn't promise, you know, nirvana, or riches', but there was clearly a gap between expectation and reality. 'There was nothing. Nothing. *Nada. Rien du tout*,' says Driscoll, laughing. 'All I ever remember doing – and this was the best part – was playing in duo with Bill. All day long.'

Frisell agrees. 'We thought that we were going to play at all these European festivals, that we'd be touring and have a lot of work,' he says. 'It turned out that there wasn't quite as much going on. But there was something going on.'

Frisell is referring to the woman he met on his first morning in Spa, at Chapati, a twenty-two-year-old waitress, bartender and music lover called Carole d'Inverno.

Carole's parents were Italian. She grew up in Italy and Belgium, studied chemistry at the university in Liège, and worked at Chapati during the summers, mostly for the social life and live music. She was lively, fun, passionate, headstrong, and a hard worker – her Italian grandfather had walked more than a thousand miles from his poor mountain village in Lazio to Brussels in 1889 for work; he made and sold ice cream, eventually setting up a business in Spa. Her brother played guitar, and her father was a good pianist and loved jazz; in another life he might have been a musician.

The connection was immediate, especially after Carole saw Bill play at an impromptu jam session. 'I do remember that, very early on, before I even got to know her . . . we had hardly talked . . . but somehow she recognised something in what I'd played,' says Frisell. 'She said something like, "Well, that sounded like the real thing, something I haven't heard." And that made me feel good.'

Carole says that, for her, it was love at first sight: 'I was attracted to him, of course, and to his playing, but the more appealing part for me was his nature. You can tell, as soon as you meet Bill, that, OK, this is a nice guy, a good person to be with. I wasn't about to do the school of hard knocks; I had already done that enough, you know. With Bill . . . I just felt like completely safe. But for him, he had no clue. Because, you know, it's Bill. It's like, *whatever.*'

Frisell could not have been slower on the uptake. Everyone seemed to know that Carole was interested, except him – even after Steve Houben told him straight, 'I think she likes you, you know.' As previously with women, Bill was blind to the signals and suggestions.

Late one night, however, just a month or so after Frisell had arrived, Bill and Carole found themselves alone in the bar.

'So I had to literally sit on his lap,' says Carole. 'And I had never done that before. But it was kind of like, this is not going to happen if I don't make the first move.'

Frisell smiles at Carole's version. 'I mean, Carole says she had to sit on my lap, but it wasn't quite like that,' he says. 'It was more like she said, "OK, what's going on?" But yes, she definitely forced things along.'

•
•

Shortly after he arrived in Spa, Bill received a call at Chapati from Mike Gibbs. The composer had been asked by the Arts Council of Great Britain to put together a big band for a twelve-date concert-hall tour of England and Wales. The all-star orchestra, playing Gibbs's compositions, included such leading international players as American alto saxophonist Charlie Mariano and Canadian trumpeter and flugelhornist Kenny Wheeler, as well as German double bassist Eberhard Weber and British jazz-rock drummer John Marshall. The fine Belgian guitarist Philip Catherine was also lined up for the tour, but had to cancel.

Gibbs knew that, at Berklee, Frisell had played many of the original compositions and arrangements Gibbs had selected for the tour. He also knew that Bill was an excellent sight-reader, a quick learner and an exciting new talent. He asked Frisell to join the band.

'I already felt in awe of some of the musicians I was playing with in Belgium, especially some of the guitar players, like Philip Catherine himself, who would sometimes play at Chapati,' says Frisell. 'They seemed like the real deal, real European musicians who made records, and I just felt . . . kind of out of my depth.

'But the Mike Gibbs thing was a whole new level. Kenny Wheeler was like a god to me. I'd seen him play in Anthony Braxton's quartet in Boston, and everyone at Berklee had *Gnu High* [the 1976 album Wheeler recorded for ECM with Keith Jarrett, Dave Holland and Jack DeJohnette]. John Marshall had joined Soft Machine, a band I'd loved ever since I saw them open for Hendrix [in 1968] and first smoked marijuana. But what could I do? This was just an incredible opportunity for me to be able to play with these guys.'

In October 1978, aged twenty-seven, Frisell undertook his debut official tour anywhere with a band, 'the first kind of professional real gig I ever had'. Gibbs decided to include an interlude in the programme in which Frisell and Eberhard Weber would play an improvised duo, mostly led by Weber, the more experienced musician, on his custom, five-string, upright solid-body electric bass, with added pedal effects. The highly respected German double bassist had already worked with some of the leading American guitarists of their generation, including Pat Metheny, Ralph Towner and Mick Goodrick. He was, however, unusually impressed with Frisell.

'In these duos I was able to "force" Bill to react to any sound that I played. And he did!' Weber tells me. 'It wasn't just that, for example, he could play in octaves, or play only chords, or avoid the plucking sound of the guitar by opening up the tone with a volume pedal. With Bill it was more that he was a listener; he was somehow able to follow and respond to any idea, composed or improvised, expressed by a fellow musician. This person needs to be better known, I thought, and to be introduced to the wider jazz world.'

Weber had already recorded four LPs as leader for ECM, the game-changing German label founded in 1969 by producer and creative catalyst Manfred Eicher, and was due to make his next album in Germany in January. Gary Burton, with whom Weber had recorded two ECM records a few years earlier, was scheduled to join him. Weber asked Frisell to the session. Within just six months of arriving in Belgium, Frisell was about to record for one of the most respected labels in jazz, the home of many of his heroes and mentors, from Keith Jarrett to Dave Holland, Pat Metheny, John Abercrombie – and Gary Burton, the musician who not only perfectly embodied ECM's uncompromising excellence and rigorous aesthetic, but who had been a vital inspiration for Frisell since he was a teenager.

The session took place at the Tonstudio Bauer in Ludwigsburg, just north of Stuttgart, West Germany. Weber added two singers to the recording: American vocalist Bonnie Herman and English singer and lyricist Norma Winstone. Frisell was so shy and insecure about the session that he was fearful of using his pedal effects, so he simply brought his guitar. 'I was so green,' he says. 'I thought, "Oh wow, I'm going to go into the studio and they are going to make me sound like ECM, or something."'

In fact, he was 'so terrified' of the process, of playing with such established players and working with Manfred Eicher, a producer with a reputation for exacting standards, that the whole experience overwhelmed him. 'Even travelling and staying in the hotel, I didn't know what to do; I didn't even know how you checked into a hotel, or anything,' he told critic John Kelman. 'And I wasn't able to get much going; I was pretty inhibited during that recording.'

The album, *Fluid Rustle*, has its moments, as you might expect from improvisers of the quality of Weber and Burton. The ECM sound is characteristically rich and resonant, and there are some intriguing world music accents too: Weber plays tarang, a kind of Indian zither; Burton adds marimba; and Frisell, for the first and only time in his recording career, strums a balalaika, brought to the studio by Weber.

But this is far from being a classic, or even particularly happy, ECM recording. Weber's originals are weak, meandering and unmemorable, and Frisell is so far back in the mix as to be barely present – even his short and uncertain solo on the title track fails to make any mark. The album feels closer to etiolated new-age, ambient or film music, or the softer fringes of seventies prog, than to the lustrous chamber jazz Weber had triumphed with just a few years earlier. In Richard Cook and Brian Morton's *The Penguin Guide to Jazz Recordings*, *Fluid Rustle* is summed up in one word: 'enervating'.

'The recording turned out to be tough, because Manfred Eicher didn't like *anything* in the whole recording,' writes Weber. 'He hated my method of recording a female choir made up of only two singers, recording one voice after the other, and he was also not taken with an unknown guitar player who couldn't play fast improvised lines, like other guitarists. I could have sworn at the time that Bill had no chance at all of ever recording again for ECM.'

Frisell has similar memories of the session. 'I don't think I ruined the record, and I probably played something supportive and OK, but it certainly wasn't anything that changed the world – and Manfred was absolutely not impressed in the least with what I played,' says Frisell. 'I remember him coming out of the control room and saying to me something like, "Could you just try thinking about John Abercrombie?" He was trying to get me to play stronger. And I was very timid. I basically went away afterwards with my tail between my legs.'

In the autumn of 1978, Frisell, Driscoll, Johnson and Michel Herr went into a studio in Brussels for two days to record an LP for EMI Belgium. The result was *Good Buddies*, another album of originals that owes much to the prevailing shibboleths of seventies fusion, in particular the compositional ambitions, keyboard effects, funk rhythms and lush production values of Jaco Pastorius-era Weather Report.

Frisell allows his rock influences to express themselves more fully; he sounds like a completely different guitarist to the one (not) heard on *Fluid Rustle*. Vinnie Johnson also sings a kind of street rap at the end of one track. Perhaps most notable of all, however, is the record's questionable cover, a hyper-realistic image of a naked woman, in a state of shock, by Belgian painter Roland Delcol.

'It was just a fun and informal session, with some good tunes and good grooves, but I want to make clear that neither Bill nor I voted for that cover,' says Herr, laughing. 'We only discovered it after it was too late!'

That winter Frisell organised a series of live reel-to-reel tape recordings at Chapati of a trio with Kermit and Vinnie; the album was called *Triode* and seven of the nine tracks were written by Frisell. It is something of a minor revelation, a chance to experience more fully what others were hearing at the time, and what Eicher missed out on.

Certainly there is a lot that gets in the way, from Johnson's overly generous drumming to an almost six-minute track in which tape of other takes is irritatingly run backwards throughout – the Beatles' *Revolver* it most decidedly is not. But in this company, Frisell also feels freer to experiment, to range across a spectrum of sounds and styles, from blues to hard rock to fusion to free and straight-ahead jazz.

At the beginning of the short slow second track, 'What Do You Mean?', there he is, proto-Bill, playing himself, bringing all those sounds and more together into something of his own: that ringing, lyrical, mysterious, warping, all-encompassing, clear and complex sound of The Frisell Dream to come. It is Frisell, inchoate yet unmistakable. It's little wonder that, for certain hardcore completists, *Triode* has become much sought-after and now sells in Japan and on internet auctions for almost as many pounds as the number of copies that were pressed – 200 to 300.

'That music, that sound, that way of playing together felt like the first blueprint for what I've been doing ever since,' says Frisell. 'But yes, the recording was kind of basic. On one track you can hear [Chapati owner] Robert Delcour's dog, Baba, barking in the background.'

Frisell's further recordings while he was in Europe are somewhat more random. In June 1979, the Frisell–Driscoll–Johnson trio travelled to Prague in Czechoslovakia, still at that time part of the Eastern Bloc of communist countries, to record an LP over four days with Emil Viklický. Frisell knew the Czech pianist and keyboardist from Berklee. From 1977–78 Viklický had studied composition and arranging with Herb Pomeroy on a scholarship; Viklický wrote all the songs on the album.

The record was called *Okno*, which means '*Window*' in Czech, and it was released, in Czechoslovakia at least, the following year; extra tracks found their way in 1985 onto a second LP, *Dveře*, which translates as '*Door*'. Frisell's solos spark some interest, but this is determinedly Viklický's session, and jazz-fusion approaching its most humdrum and hemmed in.

Also in 1979 Bill appeared on one track of an LP by Guy Cabay, a Belgian vibraphonist, pianist, composer and vocalist, who was one of the teachers on the jazz course in Liège. Cabay also played alongside Frisell in a twelve-piece ensemble directed by Michel Herr called Act Big Band; Frisell contributed two compositions, which were later recorded.

Despite all these diverging musical directions, this was an important period of growth and transition for Frisell. He progressed from student to professional, practice room to recording studio, club gig to concert hall. Maybe he could only have achieved this away from all he knew in America; out of context, he had to find his own way. But by the summer of 1979, a little more than a year after arriving in the country, Frisell knew that Belgium, and Steve Houben, had given him as much – and often considerably less – as they could, and it was again time to move on.

And back. Back to America: to the place that cultivated his desire to play music in the first place; to the home of the music that still moved him above all others – jazz; and to its modern epicentre, New York.

Frisell did not, however, go alone. 'By then Carole and I had really connected, and . . . perhaps it was her experience seeing her father play, and listening to all that music, but . . . all along, more than anybody, she was the one who backed me up and believed in what I was doing,' says Frisell.

It was a brave decision for Carole to make – to move with Bill to another country and continent. 'It was a very big deal,' she says. 'But I think a part of me always wanted to get out and experience America – it was the place, after all, that I looked up to for such things as art, architecture and music. Art had been something I had always wanted to do, and I thought finally I could start slowly thinking about it and making things. I think we both wanted to move to New York, and that we could help each other to adapt and learn how to live there. We both felt that we needed each other to do it.'

Frisell agrees. 'I never could have moved to New York if it hadn't been for Carole. New York always seemed too big a deal; I was too afraid of it. But then again, we get to New York, and it's like, "Wow, what am I going to do now?"'

In December 1980 Bill Frisell received a phone call that would change his life and, over the next thirty years, lead to one of the longest, deepest and most important relationships he has experienced in music.

The call came while Bill and Carole were living in an apartment in Cliffside Park, New Jersey, and for Frisell the impact of the voice at the end of the line was almost like the beam of sound that travels through his brain in The Frisell Dream – a beautiful moment that alters and illuminates all around it.

The caller was Paul Motian, a drummer who had played briefly with Thelonious Monk, made his name in the pioneering Bill Evans Trio during the pianist's pivotal years between 1959 and 1964, and been a key member of Keith Jarrett's modern-thinking sixties and seventies groups. He had worked with musicians whom Frisell hugely admired, including Paul Bley, Carla Bley, Lee Konitz and even singer-songwriter Arlo Guthrie, son of Woody, who Motian had appeared alongside at Woodstock.

Since the early seventies Motian had focused increasingly on his own music and groups, some of which included guitarists – Sam Brown, for example, features on two tracks on Motian's remarkable 1973 debut as leader, *Conception Vessel*. The guitar was one of the drummer's great loves; it had been his first instrument as a child.

Frisell had been passionately following Motian since he first saw him in Denver in February 1969 as part of the strikingly visionary Charles Lloyd Quartet, with Ron McClure on bass and Keith Jarrett on piano. 'Paul had been part of my life since then, since high school,' says Frisell. 'To me he was sort of a hero, not just for his own playing, and the whole world of music that opened up and I discovered through it, but because he had this direct connection to people like Monk, Bill Evans, Lennie Tristano and Paul Bley. He was massively important to me. He pointed the way. His zone of music – that was where I wanted to be.'

When Frisell picked up the phone he had been looking at the album sleeve for *Conception Vessel*, borrowed from a library in New Jersey.

'I still think of it as a *bam* kind of moment, one of the biggest turning points, out of the blue – *that one phone call*!' says Frisell. 'Paul asking me if I wanted to come over to his place and play. For me, it was sort of like Miles Davis calling; I couldn't believe it.'

Carole says she can still recall that day clearly. 'He was sitting on the couch, and all I really remember him saying is, "OK, I will" – and his voice was like two octaves higher. Then he hangs up, and he's like ashen, all white, and I'm like, "What's wrong?" He goes, "*Ahhhhh . . .*" He couldn't even breathe, or talk, or even say who it was that had just called. He just went over to our stack of records, and he pulled out one by Paul Motian, the album that has that really intense close-up of his face on the cover [*Tribute*], and it was all he could do to just point at it. So yeah, that was definitely one of the most important calls of his life.'

The contact had come about via a recommendation from Pat Metheny. The drummer was approaching fifty and looking to further refresh himself and his music by forming a new band of younger next-generation New York players. He wanted to include a guitarist – or possibly two; Motian had recently played a gig in Boston with Michael Gregory Jackson – and he approached Metheny, but the guitarist had committed to touring for the next year and was unavailable.

Metheny had shown a strong interest in Frisell since his Boston days, occasionally mentioning him in interviews. He was also hearing positive reports about him in New York from his friend and former bandmate, drummer Bob Moses. 'Bill had come a long way in those few in-between years towards being the Bill we all know now,' Metheny tells me. 'He is really open to music in the widest and best sense, and that openness has made him naturally connect with an incredibly wide range of listeners and musicians. It seemed to me he would be a perfect fit for what I sensed Paul wanted to do.'

The following month Frisell went to Motian's apartment on Central Park West. 'I still remember, when he opened the door, just the energy,'

Frisell told Ethan Iverson. 'He had cargo pants on, a flannel shirt, and the door opens and it was kind of a speedy thing.' Also in the apartment was Marc Johnson, a twenty-six-year-old classically trained double bassist who had a strong, if sideways, connection to Motian: from 1978 to 1980 he had played, along with drummer Joe LaBarbera, in the final Bill Evans trio; Evans had died, aged fifty-one, just a few months earlier, in September 1980.

'That was heavy-duty,' says Frisell. 'I'd never met Marc; I'd never met Paul. Bill Evans had died . . . and they were talking about him. Then we started saying, "Well, let's play something." They said, "My Man's Gone Now." So I'm playing this song I associate with Bill Evans with these two guys who played with him. It was heavy for me. And I'm still trying to play that song.'

Motian asked Frisell to come back the following week. 'We got along really well,' the drummer said. 'There is this thing about some kind of magic happening between people that is very rare . . . everything grew from that.'

In the interim, however, Frisell was rushed to hospital in New Jersey for an emergency appendectomy. 'I'm in the hospital thinking, "Oh no, now I can't go back." I was so scared he wasn't going to call me again, but he said, "No, that's cool. When you feel better come back and we'll play some more."'

Frisell rehearsed with Motian almost every week for the next nine months. 'Getting that call, and going over to his apartment, gave me an amazing infusion of confidence,' Frisell has said. 'That was one of the first times that someone asked me to be myself. Paul wasn't just calling some random guitar player to fill the job of playing a certain way . . . I felt like he really wanted me and my personality, and I've always felt that playing with him it was really *my* music, even though he is the leader of the band. It feels as if it is totally wide open.'

Various other New York musicians, all in their twenties, came and went. Marc Johnson recommended Joe Lovano, with whom he had been playing in the Mel Lewis Jazz Orchestra at the Village Vanguard. Frisell also knew Lovano from Boston – not so much from Berklee, although the saxophonist had studied at the college in 1971, but more by daunting experience. 'It was always this thing of, playing a gig, and someone says "Lovano's in town", the door would open, and this big guy would come in,' Frisell told Ethan Iverson, remembering the time Lovano came to a Tiger's Baku gig. 'Joe stormed the bandstand. He'd just walk into a place and take over . . . just the confidence, just a badass. He came in on that band, and just blew everyone away, and then left. I still had never talked to him.'

After Marc Johnson left to tour with saxophonist Stan Getz, altoist Tim Berne suggested bass player Ed Schuller, son of composer, conductor and conceptualist Gunther Schuller; Ed had also played with Lovano. Finally, in this fabric of connections and permutations, Lovano recommended fellow saxophonist, clarinettist and flautist Billy Drewes, with whom he had played in the Woody Herman band.

'At the beginning we rehearsed a lot,' says Frisell, 'and a lot of times Paul would ask me to come before the start of the rehearsal, because I think it helped him to hear somebody else play his new songs. He would say, "Yeah, maybe play it slower, or play it faster." Or sometimes I'd add some chords, or something, and we'd try and work it out. He was at this point in his life where he had committed to doing his own thing, and it was inspiring for me to be around somebody who was *that* strong. I was like, "Wow, I wanna someday do that, too."'

Motian taped many of these often spirited sessions. Some have been made available in recent years by Motian's niece, visual artist Cindy McGuirl, who hosts the weekly two-hour radio show, *Uncle Paul's Jazz Closet*, on WRFR, a community station in Rockland, Maine. She has also published two invaluable volumes of Motian's compositions: 128 songs in all.

Paul Motian's music has a special sense of strength and freedom – Frisell would later describe it as 'conjuring this atmosphere that you can really move around in . . . like a structure without walls' – and listening to these tapes you immediately sense that Frisell has found a home, a place where he can develop into the guitarist he burns to be. In his solos are all the melodic references and harmonic extensions that come from his deep love and knowledge of Jim Hall, but also something that is darkly and even dangerously advanced – the beginning of Frisell's syncretic, symphonic and spellbinding guitar world that sounded like everything and nothing anybody had ever heard.

Even Motian's deceptively simple folk-like melodies feel more emphatic and alive, as if they are drawing in, like a magnetic Thelonious Monk tune, the rich and ample spaces around them, making them stronger and more supple. A lot of this implied heat and overt experimentation is being generated by Motian, from his drum kit, from the force of his personality.

In the autumn of 1981 Motian settled upon a quintet with Frisell, Schuller, Lovano and Drewes, and they started playing gigs, the first at a club called Ryles in Boston. 'It was magical,' Lovano recalled in 2004. 'Very creative. Very spontaneous.'

•
•

Paul Motian was born in Philadelphia in 1931 and raised in Providence, Rhode Island. He was the son of Armenian immigrants from Turkey; his grandmother, Yazgol DerMoushegian, had been killed by Turkish soldiers in the Armenian genocide of 1915. He named his publishing company Yazgol Music, in her honour.

Motian is pronounced 'MO-tee-an' by the family, and 'MO-shun' by the wider music community; Motian himself became accustomed to the latter, telling one writer, 'Someone once said to me, "It doesn't make any difference, as long as they know who you're talking about."'

Motian's nephew David McGuirl writes in a foreword to the Motian songbooks that 'Paul grew up poor and became something of a "juvenile delinquent" – he was arrested three times before the age of thirteen'. He was fascinated by the look and sound of the guitars he saw in cowboy films, but he was also drawn strongly to the drums and began taking lessons aged twelve. Music, he would later say, kept him 'both alive and out of jail'. At high school he played in marching and big bands and went to dances and concerts by local swing bands. He joined the navy in 1950, telling critic Ben Ratliff that he 'considered it a better option than being drafted into the army'. For the most part, he was right. He briefly attended the Navy School of Music in Washington, then joined the Seventh Fleet in the Mediterranean for two and a half years, playing in the admiral's band. He was discharged in 1954, moved to the East Village, studied at the Manhattan School of Music, and never left New York.

Motian and Manhattan were a perfect match for each other: streetwise, wise-cracking, romantic and tough. Most of all, Motian was attracted to the music – the ever-renewing creativity and diversity, the endless Promethean possibilities and punch.

Motian was short, wiry, candid and upfront, and over the next few years he hustled for gigs and manoeuvred himself close to the heart of the bop and post-bop New York jazz scene. He played not just with Monk and Tristano, but with saxophonists Coleman Hawkins, Stan Getz and Zoot Sims and innovative composers and arrangers such as Gil Evans and George Russell. It was in the Bill Evans trio, most notably with bassist Scott LaFaro, that he began to transition from sideman to associate. His contributions to the series of canonical Evans albums released in 1960 and 1961 – *Portrait in Jazz*, *Explorations*, and the live recordings *Sunday at the Village Vanguard* and *Waltz for Debby* – established him as one of jazz's most assertive yet sympathetic young drummers.

'In this group Motian created a highly interactive style of playing in which the phrasing became less closely related to the meter of the composition than to the phrasing implied by the other group members,' reads one rather dry summary of Motian's work with Evans. 'He also made effective use of varied textures and tone colours as elements of musical interest in themselves.'

Motian became a hugely versatile and in-demand drummer, playing with Jarrett and Bley, and for many others, ranging from jazz and blues singer and pianist Mose Allison to avant-garde trumpeter Don Cherry.

'Motian evolved into a drummer who could play free and time with the same amount of personality,' Ethan Iverson has written. He could swing. And swing out.

Encouraged by Keith Jarrett, from whom he bought the piano Jarrett had played throughout his childhood, Motian began to compose and advance his own music. He resolved to lead bands, not freelance solely within them. *Conception Vessel* was one of four albums he released on the new ECM label in the seventies, all with different moods and settings, but each with Motian's spare and seductive songs at their centre. Nine more would follow in the eighties. 'I was Bill Evans's drummer in the 1960s, Keith Jarrett's drummer in the 1970s,' he liked to say. 'And Paul Motian's drummer in the 1980s.'

At the end of 1981 the new Paul Motian quintet conducted a short tour of Europe, establishing a pattern that would continue for the next twenty years. Motian would mostly play small club dates and runs in New York, but make the majority of his income from touring two or three times a year in Europe, where audiences were larger and often more appreciative. 'I don't work in the States hardly at all,' he told *Jazziz* magazine in 1995. 'You know, I don't give a shit if my name ain't in the paper.'

Frisell had finally managed to obtain the work he felt Steve Houben had promised but that had never quite arrived. He was to visit many major European cities for the first time with Motian – Paris, Rome, Berlin, Vienna, Madrid and Stockholm.

At the end of the 1981 tour the group went into the Tonstudio Bauer in Ludwigsburg to record Motian's next LP for ECM. It was the same studio where, almost three years earlier, Frisell had recorded with Eberhard Weber and, he felt, sorely embarrassed himself. The upshot, released the following summer, was *Psalm*, a work in progress that often feels over-engineered and peculiarly over-produced. Yet it is an album that highlights not just Motian's intriguing and diverse new compositions, but also a group of raw and often rough-edged individualists closely attuned to his collective spirit and ideals.

The album gives Frisell plenty of space to swell, sustain and stretch out, to suggest an entirely new realm of liquid guitar colours that flow from twisted romanticism to turbulent avant-rock. Frisell even gets to play solo on the hauntingly lovely Motian ballad 'Etude', creating distant mournful echoes that feel like sounds lost in deep space or dark below ground.

So profoundly different is Frisell on this recording that producer Manfred Eicher must barely have believed his ears. 'Playing with Paul really made my credibility go way up,' says Frisell. 'I remember we played a small club in Munich on that first tour, and Manfred came, and he was so excited with Paul and the music and me and the whole thing. He was just fired up.'

Eberhard Weber suggested Frisell for a new group being put together by the leading European musician on ECM during the seventies, Norwegian saxophonist Jan Garbarek. Directly after the *Psalm* sessions, Frisell flew to Oslo to meet Garbarek and record a new album with him. 'When we were recording with Paul, Manfred started recommending me for other ECM gigs,' says Frisell. 'The whole time he was like, "Wow, we must do this, and we must do that."'

In one year Frisell had progressed from scratching a living in New York to being, as British concert promoter John Cumming put it, 'the geeky new kid on the block'. He was a favourite both of one of the most revered American drummers in modern jazz and the boss of a highly respected and increasingly influential European record label. Together with 'Juliet of the Spirits', the unaccompanied track he had recorded for Hal Willner's celebration of the music of Fellini film composer Nino Rota, 'Etude' stood as a Frisell calling card for a certain New York jazz and alternative music community.

Paul Motian, ever curious and often contrary, continued to stir the pot. Feeling that the two saxophonists were beginning to sound too similar, he substituted Billy Drewes for Jim Pepper, a fiery and full-blooded tenorist who Motian had first played with in Charlie Haden's Liberation Music Orchestra. More European tours followed. 'Spring, summer and fall – we played *everywhere* and toured like *crazy*,' says Lovano. 'There's hardly a place I go now in Europe that Bill and I didn't first play with Paul.'

Motian was to record his next two albums, *The Story of Maryam* and *Jack of Clubs*, in Milan for the enterprising Italian Soul Note label with this revised quintet during two of these tours in 1983 and 1984. *Jack of Clubs* features another slowly unfolding Frisell solo spot, the gently chiming and shimmering 'Lament', elegantly meditative music that sounds almost oriental.

On one European tour in early 1984, Motian had something of an epiphany. 'We were playing one night somewhere in Italy, and there was a piece of mine that called for the bass to lay out, and for a few minutes it was only Joe and Bill and I playing,' Motian told Ted Panken. 'At that moment I thought I could play my music with this trio . . . without having a quintet. Economics was involved, and I liked the idea of playing without a bass and just to give it a try.'

Frisell and Lovano felt the atmosphere change. 'For one extended moment, it just took off in a whole other direction that we hadn't touched before,' says Lovano. 'And after that, *that night* Paul said to me, "When we go back to New York, let's play at your loft, and let's play some trio. I have some new tunes."'

The result, recorded in July for ECM, again at the Tonstudio Bauer, was the no doubt ironically titled *It Should've Happened a Long Time Ago*. It was not just some of the finest music of the eighties, but the beginning of a trio that many regard as one of the most consistently creative, inspirational and exhilarating in jazz over the past forty years.

'That's the highest level of free group improvisation you can get,' saxophonist Joshua Redman has said about the trio. 'It's kind of like magic. The sense of three musicians becoming one . . . the degree to which they're listening and reacting to one another.'

Before the trinity could reach such dizzying heights, it had to adapt to the challenges of what was then a highly unconventional line-up. During another European tour before recording the album, *Motian and Frisell*, Ethan Iverson has written, 'realised that rather than play *more* to compensate for not having a bass, they should actually play *less*'. It was to be one of the trio's key philosophies and guiding principles. In 2011 Motian said, 'After many years, I realised that less is more. And as I get older, I think even more less adds up to even more.'

It Should've Happened a Long Time Ago is what transpires when three highly creative and imaginative musicians are set free, individually and collectively, within a secure yet flexible structure of infinite forms and shapes – a new dreamworld where 'everything can happen at once', and the music can be 'extraordinarily dense and complex' yet 'also absolutely clear and constant, absolutely distilled and direct'. It is Paul Motian as miniature monk.

It doesn't always work, and the three are clearly adjusting to the light and space. Frisell's first forays on several tracks, one again solo, into the further sonic layers and electric storms suggested by his new guitar-synthesiser are not always successful – sometimes they serve only to blur and blot out the essential humanity at the heart of Frisell's guitar sound.

But the group interaction and restraint, the freedom and control, the spontaneous harmonies and on-the-spot orchestration, and the way melody, tempo, harmony, dynamics and solos seem to pass seamlessly between the players are rarely less than astonishing. Lovano seems an entirely new and original saxophone voice on this album: tough, throaty and abstract in the more heated exchanges, but liberated on the ballads, his tender and poetic side rising gently to the surface.

In the title track, the album has one of Motian's most irresistible and affecting folk melodies, a refrain that stays with you long afterwards, and that Frisell is still playing almost forty years on. There is something rooted yet timeless about the song, a mysterious and melancholy air, a proud and heartfelt sense of respect: it's as if, somehow, Motian is channelling something of his past, personally, culturally, historically.

'The track feels holy to me, like a kind of communion with melody,' wrote journalist and musician Hank Shteamer, a senior editor at *Rolling*

Stone. 'There are solos, I guess, but there's really only one sound, and it's the sound of this swaying, haunting waltz, a tune that, once you've heard it, sounds like it's always been there.'

⋮

Joe Lovano sits back in his high wingback chair in the lounge of a hotel in Antwerp, Belgium, and the sentences tumble and flow out of him like one of his graceful solos. There is a gentleness to him, a calmness and courtesy, but he is a big, broad-shouldered man with a commanding presence, and not someone you interrupt lightly. The only other person I've interviewed who has a similar charge and authority is Martin Scorsese; maybe it's an Italian-American thing.

Joseph Salvatore Lovano was born into a Sicilian-American family in Cleveland, Ohio, at the tail end of 1952. His father, Tony (more usually, and respectfully, 'Big T'), was a barber by day and tenor saxophonist by night. He gave his son saxophone lessons from an early age. Lovano was playing alto at five and tenor by eleven; two years later he began sitting in with his father's bands. Aged fifteen he also started playing drums – like Frisell, who had invaluable experience playing clarinet in Denver marching bands, Lovano had a solid and deep grounding in rhythm and time. In the early seventies he studied at Berklee, where he also developed his skills on clarinet and flute, toured briefly with Welsh crooner Tom Jones, before working with a variety of post-bop, soul-jazz, swing and big bands.

As with Frisell, Paul Motian was his big break. 'For Bill and I to have a master musician like Paul embrace us in the way he did, with that amount of trust, and how he made us feel like it was actually *our* band, was a big, big, big contribution to us as musicians and eventual leaders,' says Lovano. 'I could hear and feel the three of us, and the music, continually developing and taking shape; man, it was like new music every time we played.'

Lovano would go on to become one of the great modern improvisers, leaders and composers in jazz, a Grammy Award-winning saxophonist who has worked with many contemporary greats in a fertile continuum that flows from bop to free, cool to avant-garde, duos to large ensembles, even Sinatra to Caruso. He has also taught at Berklee since 2001 and currently holds the Gary Burton Chair in Jazz Performance.

Lovano took the Motian model of structure, freedom and interaction as a core belief. 'Paul was a funny character, and he had, like, a real *wild* dimension of ups and downs in his energy, and he could be really aggressive,' he says. '"Mean Modeen" was one of his nicknames. And "Mr No". He would just say, "No!", you know. But he was also the sweetest cat in the world. He was the same as a musician. He would play from triple forte, *like a monster,* to triple piano in the same piece of music, even in the same *phrase.* He had all these dimensions and more in his playing.'

. .
. .

The Paul Motian Quintet recorded a third CD for Soul Note, *Misterioso,* in the summer of 1986. The album is as joyously unpredictable as its predecessors, encompassing plaintive ballads, power blow-outs and many points in between. Significantly, the album contains two tunes by Thelonious Monk, indications of Motian's subsequent passion for the compellingly off-centre compositions of the great pianist – as well as for other standard, Broadway and repertory songs. Frisell's spare, serrated, bluesy and playful solo on 'Misterioso' echoed that enthusiasm, hinting at the guitarist's many thrilling Monk interpretations to come.

For the next decade or so, however, from 1984 onwards, Motian focused mainly on the trio, occasionally augmenting it with players with whom he felt a special affinity and bond. In 1987 came *One Time Out,* the trio record chosen as a particular jewel by pianist Ethan Iverson in 'Counterpoint II', the listening session with the Bad Plus (see chapter 13). It is at times, especially on Motian's uptempo originals, a dark, dense and uncompromising record. Frisell sounds as buzzing, abrasive and metal-edged as he has ever done – only for the trio to then play a ballad, such as 'Portrait of T', Motian's ode to Lovano's father, with such beauty and poise that it can break your heart.

One of Thelonious Monk's earliest ballads, the yearning and lovely 'Monk's Mood', also features on the record, and Motian decided to make his next CD an album of Monk tunes alone. Newly signed to JMT, Motian was now able to record as a leader in New York and more easily bring in other players: pianist Geri Allen and tenor saxophonist Dewey Redman each play on two tracks.

Monk in Motian is a model of this kind of salute and celebration, a fascinating selection of some of Monk's more agile and unorthodox tunes – 'Ugly Beauty', 'Crepuscule with Nellie', 'Trinkle Tinkle' – given a decidedly contemporary edge and imagination. The harmonic foils, leaping intervals and melodic fragments Frisell fires behind Lovano's muscular solo on 'Justice (Evidence)' is little short of miraculous, and shows just how far both they, and the trio, have come.

'We had to have that foundation of Paul's songs, or Monk's, to know where we were, but after that we all wanted to see what was over the edge,' says Frisell. 'It was like flying or gliding, or something – you have to let yourself fall before the music can pick you up again somehow. We were all constantly jumping off into the unknown, and then at the same time we were constantly rescuing each other.'

The high levels of creativity continued over the following series of *On Broadway* albums, which explored and honoured Motian's love of the Great American Songbook. Motian felt close to the material: they were songs that he loved as a teenager and had played with musicians who were dear to him, particularly Bill Evans. There was nothing glib or gratuitous about his desire to document the thirty songs he selected for the albums; this was direct, honest, heartfelt music.

The leader brought in Charlie Haden, his great partner in the Keith Jarrett quartet, on bass, creating a trilogy that stands as one of the great modern paeans to jazz and popular standards. Everyone has their favourite – mine remains *Volume 2* – and many regard the third outing, with Lee Konitz on alto, as something of a minor masterpiece. *Volume 1* has many great collaborative moments too, and its own supporters; '[the trio] do not so much play the standards as *love them to death*,' wrote Tom Junod in *GQ*. A fourth album, released in 1990, with Marc Johnson on bass and simply called *Bill Evans*, also brilliantly surveyed the gently pensive compositions of the pianist himself.

Motian had hit upon a kind of postmodern formula: a forward-thinking unit with the ability to meaningfully look back; a reimagined jazz trio that challenged received notions of straight and free, high and low, reverence and irreverence; a perfect balance of energies that embraced paradox, pluralism and multiple meaning – and could play in any way.

The Paul Motian trio was like a tetrahedron, a triangular pyramid, a three-dimensional equilateral triangle with four faces – the fourth being that of the music itself. It was a force and a philosophy that remains a primary influence on Frisell to this day.

∴

The trio became a phenomenon live, taking up residency in such fabled venues as Visiones, a small club in the West Village, and the original Knitting Factory on East Houston Street, near to CBGB. 'We were one of the first groups to really put the Knitting Factory on the map,' claims Lovano. 'We actually had lines around the corner.'

The main goal and prize for any self-respecting New York jazz musician, then and now, however, is a week at the Village Vanguard. The small, storied and wedge-shaped basement room on 7th Avenue South first opened in 1935 and can, with some justification, style itself as 'the greatest jazz club in the world'. The splendidly Stygian space may only cram in an official capacity of 123 in one sitting, but those audiences have witnessed many of the greatest moments in jazz. The 1961 Bill Evans Trio recordings at the club, with Motian on drums and Scott LaFaro on bass, are a classic case in point.

Paul Motian first played at the Village Vanguard, in a group led by Lee

Konitz, on New Year's Eve, 1956; in the late fifties and early sixties he would often work at the club for up to nine weeks a year. As Frisell and Lovano's profile and standing rapidly increased in the eighties, initially as a result of their association with Motian, they too were offered runs at the club — as champions of their own groups.

The leader of the Paul Motian Trio had no such luck. The owner of the Vanguard, Max Gordon, was approached several times, by all three musicians, but he was reluctant; perhaps he simply considered Motian, his music, and his bass-less trio too unconventional — one time out too far. Perhaps he had a misconception about Motian as a person, as some-one difficult to deal with and not prepared to compromise.

'On the surface Paul could be sort of edgy or loud, and maybe he hurt some people's feelings every once in a while,' says Frisell. 'But he was just trying to stay true to himself. He had a path that he was on, real strong, and everything came from some sort of joy and love — he was excited and curious all the time about stuff, and he wouldn't let business get in the way of the music. And that is still so inspiring to me.'

When Gordon died in 1989, his widow Lorraine, another inimitable New York character, took over as manager of the club. Finally, in June 1993, Motian secured his week in the jazz city's spiritual home.

At the end of that run the trio went into a studio in New York and recorded *Trioism*, an album of Motian originals that felt as if it was a conscious act of deconstruction, an assault on the very nature, form and language of the trio. The outcome is Motian's music at its most compulsively complex, elusive and unstable. In the CD booklet there is a pencil rubbing of a triangle, with three circles at its points and at its centre the word 'other'.

The trio's week at the Vanguard was so surprisingly well received, by critics and club regulars alike, that it led to an annual engagement — even after Motian had formed a new ensemble of young players, the Electric Bebop Band, and Frisell and Lovano had begun to concentrate full-time on their own projects. There were fewer rehearsals, and eventually there were none; the trio created the music extempore, on the bandstand, often playing a new Motian composition for the first time live – it was often the same on record.

The run also resulted, two years later in June 1995, in Motian's own contribution to the long and venerated line of *Live at the Village Vanguard* recordings: *Sound of Love* and *You Took the Words Right Out of My Heart* represent the definitive statement of the trio as a live unit.

Frisell has described some of these Vanguard gigs as 'the highest musical moments' he has ever experienced. 'Paul definitely had some pathways into some stuff – every action he made, in every single moment, every note, was about always surprising himself,' says Frisell. 'His presence right next to you, and his aura, even if he had stopped drumming for part of a tune, were so powerful that it brought you into that zone, brought out things in your own playing. I would constantly amaze myself playing with Paul.'

Carole d'Inverno has similar memories. 'One night Paul and Bill locked into this long interaction together, and I just remember the architecture that they started building,' she says. 'It became this huge vertical structure . . . and then it just disappeared, as if, all the time, it had been resting on quicksand. I looked around and everybody in the club went, "Oh my God, this is *it*."'

⋮

In 2003 Paul Motian had quadruple-bypass heart surgery. He made the decision to stop touring and stay at home in New York; in interviews he talked about being 'burned out', of being tired of the travelling and the countless flights.

The annual residency at the Village Vanguard with the trio became, highly unusually, a two-week run, two sets a night, often three at weekends, usually at the end of August, beginning of September. It became an unmissable event in the New York jazz calendar, an essential occasion for fans, journalists and musicians alike. I saw the trio at the club several times during the nineties and noughties; you could often compile your very own fantasy supergroup from the players in the audience.

The trio recorded its first studio album in eleven years in 2004, *I Have the Room Above Her,* an ECM record as wistful and reflective as the Hammerstein and Kern song title suggests. Two years later the less memorable *Time and Time Again* was released on the same label; it was to be the final time the trio would appear on CD together.

In 2010 Frisell played on Motian's *The Windmills of Your Mind,* an album of mostly romantic popular songs and standards. It was the first time Frisell recorded with the young double bassist Thomas Morgan; vocalist Petra Haden, daughter of Charlie, also featured on the record. This notion of playing songs important to your youth would, over the next decade, be a vital influence on Frisell.

For Frisell, Paul Motian was like a cross between a tough uncle, hipster godfather and liberal patriarch, constantly encouraging him, always pushing him to believe in himself, unfailingly giving him the support and freedom to be his absolute best.

Frisell recorded a total of twenty-eight albums with Motian, mostly in groups led by the drummer, but also in ensembles headed by musicians such as Paul Bley, Leni Stern and Danish guitarist Jakob Bro, as well as in bands formed by Frisell himself. Even if this was all he had achieved during the thirty-year period he played with Motian, Frisell could be immensely proud of the remarkable range, originality, audacity and quality of the music.

Paul Motian died on 22 November 2011, aged eighty. Shortly afterwards Frisell wrote on his website: 'No words for what I am feeling now. Music is good. Paul Motian was a MUSICIAN. He taught me, brought me up. Pointed the way. Showed me things I never could have imagined. Led me to places of extraordinary beauty. Indescribable. Paul never let up for one second. Raising it up. Always. No compromise. Listen to the MUSIC. I am blessed to have known him.'

Carole d'Inverno is standing in front of a sheriff in the basement of a courthouse in Greenville, North Carolina. Beside her is Bill Frisell. Nearby are Bill's parents and his brother, Bob. The room is bare, officious, municipal. An American flag stands in the corner. Carole is nervous, confused, and she can barely understand a word the sheriff is saying.

It is August 1979, she is twenty-three, and Carole is about to get married.

The sheriff tells her to repeat after him, to say exactly the words he says. Which she does. But not just the words. The accent too. The slow and strange vowel sounds. The elongated extra syllables. The *drawl*.

More than thirty-five years later, sitting in the living room of his home in Seattle, Frisell recreates something of the scene – in a knowing stage-Southern accent.

Ah, Carole . . .
Ah, Carole . . .
Take you, Will-yam . . .
Take you, Will-yam . . .

'None of it was exactly romantic,' Carole says. 'A few days before, I had been just stomping around, and freaking out, and shouting, "I don't want to get married!" In fact, because of things I'd seen in my family and how they could have gone a lot better, I'd always said I was *never* going to get married. But then Bill said, "That's OK, this is America, we can always get divorced." And I thought, "Oh, you're right." He knew me. He knew that I needed to have an escape door. Very smart man.'

Tu be mah law-ah-ful hus-band . . .
Tu be mah . . .

Law-ah-ful hus-band . . .
Law-ah-ful hus-band . . .

'Greenville was where my parents had moved to while I was at Berklee,' says Frisell. 'The sheriff was this kind of big military-looking guy, with a cowboy hat and this real *heavy* Southern accent.'

From thees day fo-ward . . .
From thees day . . .
Fo-ward . . .
Fo-ward . . .

'And Carole at that time didn't really speak English that well, and she's scared, you know . . . we've gotta do this, or she's going to get kicked out of the country . . . and the guy's speaking English in a way she's never heard before . . .'

Fowah rich-ah, fowah poor-ah . . .
Fowah rich-ah . . .
Fowah poor-ah . . .
Fowah poor-ah . . .
In seek-ness and health . . .
In . . .

'This Italian woman from Belgium was speaking like she'd been born in the Appalachians, or something,' Frisell adds. 'I was laughing, and she was hitting me . . . in front of the sheriff. But anyway, we made it through.'

Until day-ath do us part . . .
Until day-ath . . .
Do us . . .
Do us . . .

Part . . .
Part . . .

●
●

When Bill and Carole had arrived at JFK in New York a month or
so earlier, Carole was taken aside, interrogated and very nearly refused
entry. At the last minute, she was granted a temporary six-week visa. The
couple flew to North Carolina. Bill's father had been appointed chair
of the biochemistry department at the new East Carolina University
Medical School in Greenville in 1976; he had also been made assistant
dean of graduate affairs. A lawyer recommended Bill and Carole get
married; it was the only way of guaranteeing that she could remain in
the country.

'Carole and I had started living together just a few months after we
began seeing each other – in a tiny space above Chapati that was little
bigger than a doorway,' says Frisell. 'But this was something else again. I
think Carole was just in total serious shock.' The couple bought a light
blue 1967 Volkswagen Beetle and, while the marriage arrangements were
being made, drove to Colorado. Bill wanted to show Carole where he
grew up, and to introduce her to some of his friends.

In the autumn, soon after they got married, Bill and Carole then drove
to Manhattan and tried to build a new life. They borrowed a friend's
place in TriBeCa for a month, a small apartment owned by vibes player
Bill Molenhof in a desolate block near the World Trade Center and West
Side Elevated Highway. They looked at accommodation in Brooklyn,
but couldn't find an affordable place with enough room for Bill to play
and practise. Bill went back across the Hudson to New Jersey, to where
his parents had moved at the end of the sixties, and to Hoboken, where
his brother Bob had lived, but still he and Carole had no luck.

'It just seemed like we were never going to find a place,' says Bill. 'I
can remember sitting on this bench in Weehawken [New Jersey] with
Carole, on the edge of the [Hudson] River, with that amazing view of

Manhattan all spread out in front of us . . . and just crying. I felt hopeless and completely defeated.'

The newly-weds eventually found an apartment in the solidly unfashionable New Jersey suburb of Guttenberg, just across the water from Manhattan's Upper West Side. It was along this densely populated stretch of northern New Jersey that Bill and Carole were to live for the next ten years. From their place in Guttenberg, they moved in late 1980 even further away from Manhattan, to the first floor of a house in Fairview. 'The house was owned by a super-racist prick asshole landlord,' says Frisell. 'Tiger Okoshi came to visit, and the guy saw him and told us he didn't want people like that in his house. We moved out as fast as we could.'

The following year they rented a flat above a 'particularly fragrant' fishmonger's in neighbouring Cliffside Park, and in 1985 the couple moved into an apartment in Hoboken – it was the largest of the four and even had two bedrooms, though it was on the fifth floor and a walk-up.

'These were neighbourhoods where you not only could actually find a parking space, but you also didn't feel like you were going to be jumped at night and killed for something,' says Carole. 'Bill couldn't deal with the threat of violence – it would freak him out – and in Jersey he didn't have to worry too much about walking down the street with his guitar and amp, or being constantly afraid of having his equipment stolen. Which, in other areas of New York at that time, was normal.'

In many ways Frisell was right to be nervous. In just a few decades New York had fallen from its primary position as E. B. White's 'capital of the world' to being dubbed 'Fear City'. Crime rates were high, as were incidences of poverty, heroin addiction, muggings, homelessness, abandoned buildings, arson and looting. Just a few years before, the city had almost gone bankrupt; budget cuts had led to a lack of public services, a significantly reduced police force, and lawlessness. In 1980 there were 1,814 murders in the city (in 2019 the figure was eighty-two per cent lower at 319). Many parts of the subway were considered unsafe, especially at night. Central Park was effectively a no-go area. Times Square was largely home to sex shops, prostitutes, hustlers, drug dealers, hardened criminals, vagrants, pickpockets and the mentally unstable.

'Not that Hoboken was very different when we lived there in the eighties, but for some reason Bill thought it was,' adds Carole. 'It was actually trashed-out – half of the city had either been burnt down or abandoned. It was pretty grim.'

It was hard for the Frisells to tell some of the more hardened New York musicians they knew or were to meet, especially those living in lofts, warehouses and squats on the Lower East Side, where they lived. Like, not even in Brooklyn. Like, *not actually in New York City*. 'Oh my God, if somebody asked for our phone number, and you gave them a number starting with 201 [the area code for New Jersey], they would be like, "Oh, you're the most uncool human beings on the planet!"' says Carole, laughing. 'But, you know, that's just New York bullshit.'

In fact, the year after the Frisells moved to Hoboken in early 1985, Joey Baron and his then wife Leslie Kamen were to relocate to exactly the same building. In spring 1987 close musical and personal friends Wayne Horvitz and Robin Holcomb followed. At one stage the three couples lived just a few floors apart.

Carole got work in a local kosher food factory making sausages at $2.70 an hour. Over the following years Carole found jobs in a paint factory and dry-cleaning store, and as a home-care nurse and bookkeeper. Through a contact of drummer David 'D.' Sharpe, Frisell worked briefly for an agency that mostly employed musicians – to clean stores and factories at night.

'None of that was a big deal, because we were young, and what the hell did we care?' says Carole. 'It wasn't like I was enjoying it, but it was just like, whatever – you work hard and you just buckle down and do what you've got to do.'

Frisell self-produced posters advertising his guitar-teaching services, which he put up on poles around Guttenberg. The response was close to zero. 'He'd illustrated it with one of his crazy drawings, some kind of weird-ass alien,' says Carole. 'I remember looking at it and thinking, hmm, that's not going to attract too many people!'

Serious professional gigs were hard to come by, and it did not help that Bill knew so few musicians in New York. Mostly Frisell played 'GB gigs' – 'general business' jobs such as weddings, bar mitzvahs and other private and corporate events. The sort of shows he was playing five years before in Boston. It must have felt at times like he was back at square one – except that the square was much larger and more intimidating.

There was worse: a stint in an Elvis covers band; and a regular Saturday night gig at a venue near LaGuardia Airport in Queens, playing pop music, five sets a night, with a group and singer. 'It would take him until Tuesday to get over it, because he was so depressed,' says Carole. 'And then by Thursday he would get into a depression again, because he had to go back to LaGuardia and play the next Saturday gig.'

During these early years in New Jersey and New York, the country was in a deep recession, the city unemployment rate hovered around nine per cent, and inflation peaked in 1980 at eighteen per cent. Bill and Carole worked odd jobs and struggled to get by. Their combined income for their first three years in America – most of it, Frisell readily acknowledges, earned by Carole – averaged less than $9,000 a year.

'It was hard for us, and tough to witness such visible hardship on the streets, and a couple of times I was ready to go back,' says Carole. 'But we had no money for the plane tickets!'

•
•

Things did, however, begin to look up. Through musicians Frisell had met in Boston, he started to get invited to private jam sessions and proper gigs. During 1980 he played in New York and Boston in a group led by English flautist and composer Nick Pike, whom Bill knew from Berklee; the band was rather fantastically called Flute Juice. The quartet included bassist Tim Landers and drummer Mike Clark, who had been a vital member of both Herbie Hancock's Headhunters and British jazz-prog rockers Brand X.

Frisell reconnected with Mike Gibbs, who was still teaching at Berklee but mostly living in New York and maintaining a stellar big band that would sometimes play at a club in the West Village called Seventh Avenue South. The drummer in the band was Bob Moses, whom Bill knew from his playing on records made by Gary Burton's late-sixties quartet, and from that first Pat Metheny gig he had attended in 1975.

Moses was another of Frisell's great role models – and subsequent supporters. Bob was excited by Bill's playing in the Gibbs orchestra. 'I can remember Moses checking me out and he was really flipped out when he heard me, like he'd never heard the guitar sound like that, or something,' says Frisell. 'He was like, "Wow, what is that sound? I thought there was a French horn in the band!"'

Playing Gibbs's clever compositions and sympathetic arrangements made Frisell appreciate just how much his multiple musical experiences had benefited him: 'It was all those years playing clarinet – in a woodwind quintet and really learning to listen, or in a full orchestra and feeling the acoustic phenomenon of instruments vibrating together, or in a marching band, where everybody's together, in the rhythm of the thing.

'And it was all the dynamic and harmonic guitar techniques I'd learned from Jim Hall, and then maybe adding some more modern effects. Or how you could play an electric instrument like the guitar, and really use it to open up the sound and find ways of letting all the music from my past come in, but also know how to make it blend with other instruments, which is just the most amazing feeling. I was playing the guitar using a sound you would get when it was really loud, but I could bring it back into the range of the natural dynamics of these acoustic instruments.

'Getting the chance to play with those guys in the Mike Gibbs band . . . like, I was just ecstatic, out of my mind. So I didn't want to just play electric guitar and play great, and just blast everybody away; I wasn't trying to show 'em what I could do. I just wanted to play *with* them.'

Moses began to introduce Frisell to some of New York's leading players, including avant-saxophonist Julius Hemphill, one of the co-founders (in St Louis, Missouri, in the late sixties) of the hugely influential multi-disciplinary Black Artists Group. In 1982 Frisell played on Bob Moses's

When Elephants Dream of Music, an album co-produced by Pat Metheny that was one of Frisell's first New York recordings. 'Bob Moses was a massive turning point,' Frisell has said. 'He heard something, and gave me a chance. [Playing with Moses] I really felt like I could be myself.'

D. Sharpe was also important to Frisell in the early eighties. Bill had known him only slightly in Boston, but he was aware of his work with the Carla Bley Band, Laurie Anderson, and Jonathan Richman's acoustic rock group the Modern Lovers. Bill went to see D. Sharpe play a date in New York; they started jamming and gigging together and quickly became close friends.

'Yeah, right away we connected, and D. Sharpe had a huge impact on me – he had his own thing, real strong, one of a kind,' says Frisell. 'We even exchanged lessons. I would teach him harmony and theory, and he'd give me drum lessons, ultra-simple stuff. But it made me that much more aware of what was going on the next time I played with a drummer.'

Sharpe also began introducing Bill to New York musicians and recommending him for gigs. It was D. Sharpe who told Hal Willner about Bill, which led in 1981 to Frisell recording the solo 'Juliet of the Spirits' track for Willner, his first American session under his own name, and one of his big New York breaks.

Frisell even continued to play with Sharpe after the drummer moved back to Boston. Sharpe formed a band, comprised of Bill, and sometimes Wayne Krantz on second guitar, Gary Valente on trombone, and either Steve Swallow or John Lockwood on bass, which played every Wednesday at the 1369 Jazz Club. Frisell used to drive up – a round trip of eight hours.

'The gig didn't pay any money, like $20, but the music was real good,' Frisell told interviewer Radhika Philip. 'And then one week someone in New York asked me to do another gig, it paid more money, and I didn't go up to Boston. And it was a drag; the music wasn't good and I felt terrible. It was just a little lesson. I should have just gone to Boston and played for $20.'

Bill's collaboration with D. Sharpe was to end a few years later, in January 1987, with the drummer's death from AIDS-related complications.

He was just a few days short of his fortieth birthday. The following year Bill dedicated the final track, 'Alien Prints', on the debut album of the Bill Frisell Band, *Lookout for Hope*, to Sharpe.

Frisell's connections led to other opportunities. After Mike Stern began playing with Miles Davis, following the trumpeter's return in 1980, Mike and Leni moved to Manhattan, and Bill and Mike began gigging together at Seventh Avenue South, and at another legendary New York jazz venue called 55 Grand, in SoHo – where Leni and Mike lived above the club.

As well as meeting Pat Metheny at Berklee, Frisell also knew Metheny's older brother, Mike, a fine flugelhorn and trumpet player who taught at the college from 1976–83. Mike had arranged to record his first album in a studio just north of Boston in February 1981 and asked Bill to take part; it was Frisell's debut US recording. The album was called *Blue Jay Sessions*, and it's a somewhat predictable and straight-ahead affair – although the leader displays a beautifully mellow and mellifluous tone on flugelhorn. It was also a far from ideal context for the nascent Frisell guitar sound and style. Here, he is fitting in, working to someone else's agenda, and it shows: he sounds peculiarly restricted and restrained.

The opposite was true for some of the impromptu sessions Frisell attended in Manhattan. Through drummer Charles Telerant, whom Bill knew at Berklee, Frisell took part in a series of jam sessions in 'dirt-cheap rehearsal spaces on the Lower East Side' organised by vocalist and pianist Julian Summerhill during the hot New York summer of 1981. 'We played completely free as an ensemble, inventing whole song structures together on the spot,' Summerhill has written. 'The only rule was that there were no rules, and even if there were, there was nobody about to enforce them.'

Summerhill recorded the improvised sessions live to stereo cassette, and in 2018 they were made available as a digital download on Bill Frisell's website. The music is of dubious merit and sound quality, but it's fascinating to hear Frisell given such a free rein. He employs a full range of avant-guitar screams, twangs, warps, loops, echoes and effects, and shows he has the chops to shred, skronk and fully rock out. Yet amid all the excess and experimentation, there is often an unmistakable Frisellian melodic line that lifts the sessions to another level.

Other private sessions led to more concrete opportunities. Through journalist and musician Chip Stern, who in July 1983 in *Musician* magazine would write the first major profile of Frisell, Bill was invited to play at Stern's Upper West Side apartment. 'He would have these kind of crazy jam sessions,' says Frisell. 'Chip would play drums, and sometimes it'd just be me and him, but often he'd call over some other people he knew.'

It was here that Frisell first played with multidirectional rock guitarist Robert Quine, who had worked with Richard Hell and the Voidoids, as well as Lou Reed and Brian Eno. The two became friends, Quine guiding Frisell to his first Fender Stratocaster, a reissue of a vintage 1957 model, and an effects pedal called the Electro-Harmonix 16-Second Digital Delay, one of the first devices to create digital loops, echoes, overdubs and changes in pitch and tempo. 'That delay pedal was a major moment,' says Frisell. 'I took to it immediately, and it really opened up a whole new world for me. It was like I'd been waiting for something like that to come along.'

Frisell jammed with Stern and bassist Jerome Harris, whom he knew from Boston. Frisell loved Harris's warm and fluid playing and in 1984 would ask him to play on *Rambler*, his second album as leader.

Stern invited Julius Hemphill to the sessions, and they too hit it off. Hemphill started calling Frisell for occasional gigs; in 1985, alongside fellow guitarist Nels Cline, Frisell was part of the Hemphill band that travelled to Europe for a five-week tour. 'Julius was another massive inspiration to me – as a completely original thinker and composer, as someone who'd invented his own way of doing things,' says Frisell.

There were an increasing number of regular gigs too. In 1982, through Mike Clark, the drummer with whom Frisell had played in Flute Juice, Bill joined an intrepid trio called Stone Tiger that also featured Clark's bandmate in Brand X, Welsh bassist Percy Jones. A supremely versatile player, Jones had gigged and recorded with English experimental rockers

Soft Machine, poetry-rock group the Liverpool Scene and on Brian Eno's mid-seventies adventures in ambient music. Stone Tiger caused quite an impact playing venues such as Kenny's Castaways, a mainly folk, rock, blues and punk club in Greenwich Village, and CBGB in the East Village, where Robert Quine had first made his name.

'Bill went from being, like, nobody to somebody in New York almost in a flash,' says Kermit Driscoll. 'Everybody loved him, and everybody wanted him. Because he made them sound good. And then he made them sound even better. He was like the number-one sideman and accompanist, so good at listening and reacting. I don't know how many times people told me, "When I play with Bill, different shit happens. And I play better!"'

Drummer and bandleader Chris Massey, who recruited Frisell for a studio recording in May 1981, agrees: 'Bill was wildly creative, had a great sound, even then, and was great fun to be around. He's an incredibly sweet person with an undeniable power underneath – kinda like a doughnut filled with Red Bull.'

•
•

It wasn't only American musicians who were beginning to recognise and admire Frisell's fresh approach to the guitar – his unique combination of sensitivity and strength, eclecticism and effects.

Doubtlessly inspired by the independent spirit of Paul Motian, in 1981 Frisell recorded four new songs he had written since returning to the US on a friend's reel-to-reel four-track tape machine – solo, with some overdubbing; twenty minutes of original music on a cassette tape.

One of the compositions was the deceptively simple and gently captivating ballad 'Throughout', a tune that would become something of a Frisell favourite. The work has, over the years, also intrigued other composers, including Gavin Bryars, Carla Bley and Mike Gibbs, all of whom have written arrangements of the piece. Frisell gave the cassette to Bob Moses, D. Sharpe and Chip Stern in New York, and he sent copies to

Eberhard Weber and Manfred Eicher in Germany. Weber was instantly inspired to rekindle the earlier rapport he had felt touring with Frisell in the Mike Gibbs ensemble. In 1981 Frisell returned to Europe to play two short duo tours with Weber.

'Eberhard didn't really have much of a plan, and I don't remember anything being composed – it was totally improvised,' says Frisell. 'We would show up, mostly at these small clubs, and just play free.'

Weber remembers the tours as an unqualified success. 'It was a different musical time and there was far more of this kind of improvisation than nowadays,' he writes. 'But Bill was able to enrich any section or space the music called for.'

At the end of the first tour, Weber sent The Frisell Tape to ECM label-mate Jan Garbarek, with whom he had been playing and recording. Garbarek had already worked with some of the pre-eminent guitarists of the era – Terje Rypdal, Ralph Towner, Bill Connors, Egberto Gismonti and John Abercrombie – but he was impressed. 'I was immediately attracted to Bill's playing, as I hadn't heard a guitar sound like that,' says Garbarek. 'He was *vastly* different from any of the guitarists I'd played with before. I couldn't even say, "Oh, he plays a little bit like so and so." Or whoever. No! He played like Bill, and that was very interesting to me.' Garbarek invited Frisell to record with him on his next ECM album, scheduled for the end of the year.

Eicher was similarly taken with the cassette and the ECM boss passed on The Frisell Tape to another trusted and longstanding musician on the label, Arild Andersen. The Norwegian bassist and composer had released five ECM albums as leader and was looking to put together a group for a one-off concert at the famous Molde Jazz Festival in Norway that August. Without Frisell even having spoken to Eicher, Andersen called Bill and offered him the gig; it was to be a quartet with English pianist John Taylor and American drummer Alphonse Mouzon.

'I only knew Arild from listening to those early ECM albums, so getting that call was a big deal,' says Frisell. 'I was excited about the gig, and flattered to be asked, but at that stage I hadn't even travelled that much, or played festivals, so I guess I was also a bit nervous.'

The event was recorded and released on ECM as *A Molde Concert* (in 2000 the album was reissued with twenty-six minutes of extra music, and tracks rearranged to 'restore the original dramaturgy of the performance'). Both versions are equally hard to love. This is often suffocatingly tricksy and pyrotechnical music that was the polar opposite of the open, interactive and pared-down playing Frisell was experiencing at the time in rehearsal with Paul Motian. It's only when you listen to what he does in the quieter passages, often *behind* Andersen and Taylor, that Frisell really begins to breathe.

One remarkable thing did happen, however, on that visit to Norway. 'The phone rings and Arild is talking to Manfred [Eicher], and Manfred asks how the rehearsal is going, and Arild says, "It's going great." And then he hands me the phone,' says Frisell, taking a pause. 'I hadn't spoken to Manfred in almost three years. But he says, "I know you're going to play with Paul [Motian], and record with Jan, so yes, I think . . . how would you like to do a solo record, something like the music on the tape?" And I was like, "Oh, man, this is insane!" Suddenly so many things were starting to happen – all at the same time.'

Two of those things were the Garbarek album *Paths, Prints*, recorded in December 1981 at the Talent Studio in Oslo, and Eberhard Weber's next record, *Later That Evening*, recorded in March 1982 at the Tonstudio Bauer in Ludwigsburg. Both were, of course, produced by Manfred Eicher.

Paths, Prints is by far the more successful album and the first intimations that this quartet – Garbarek, Weber, Frisell and Norwegian drummer Jon Christensen – would be one of the saxophonist's great, if relatively short-lived, groups. Garbarek, like Paul Motian, is committed to clarity and space, to allowing the music to develop organically, in its own way; there is also a dramatic kind of coiled and controlled tension. Frisell is the ideal foil for Garbarek's searching and skywards sounds on tenor and soprano, heightening the contrasts, enhancing the colours, emphasising the emotions.

'I will always treasure that album – thanks to Bill, and the others,' says Garbarek. 'Whether the music was raunchy or rhythmic or floating or ballad-like, or whatever, Bill would always find the right tone, find his voice. He would come up with something surprising but just right, a response that might be oblique, askew or off-centre, but that was beautiful and perfectly suited the circumstances. He never ceased to amaze me.'

This string of albums for ECM continued to significantly raise Frisell's profile on both sides of the Atlantic. With Paul Motian's *Psalm* also being produced during this period, Frisell recorded four albums in Europe for the label in just seven months; all were released by Eicher in 1982.

'It was only a few years earlier that I'd been sitting around in Greeley, Colorado, smoking pot with my friends, listening to some of those first seventies ECM records,' says Frisell. 'They made such an impact because, from the beginning, everything about ECM seemed different, better – the quality of the sound, the mysterious record covers, even the vinyl looked thicker. Manfred upped the standard.'

•
•

In August 1982 Frisell was to find out first-hand just how far Eicher was prepared to push his artists and maintain those personal standards. Back at the same Oslo recording studio, Talent, with the same engineer, Jan Erik Kongshaug, Frisell had been given two days to record his debut album, with one day to mix it.

This was the norm for the majority of jazz recordings. The most famous jazz album of all time, Miles Davis's *Kind of Blue,* was recorded over two separate dates in March and April 1959; John Coltrane's *A Love Supreme* took just four momentous hours one evening in December 1964.

It was also standard for Eicher and ECM. The label boss and creative force may have been on a mission to record the music he loved, to the highest possible level, but he wasn't about to compromise when it came to sparking spontaneity and creative tension. To achieve that, to slightly paraphrase Duke Ellington's famous mantra, 'they didn't need time, they needed a deadline'. Inspiration through limitation. Two or three days max.

The challenges for Bill Frisell coming into such a scenario were manifold. Despite his recent run of recording work with others, he was still relatively inexperienced in the studio – and had never before played a complete set of music, solo, in public. In front of *anybody*. Let alone the head of the most prestigious and influential jazz label in Europe. And let alone for a high-profile first album, of his own compositions, under his own name. Even today it seems an extraordinary notion: that the debut album of an almost unknown American guitarist should be totally solo, performed fully alone.

On the first day, for the first takes, Frisell felt the recording went well. 'I prepared the album, because, like, this is the biggest thing that ever happened in my life up to that point, and I had a whole bunch of stuff together that I wanted to do, such as using the studio to do overdubs,' he says. 'And I was really nervous, but I was working through the songs, and I almost couldn't believe that I was doing it, recording my own album for ECM – I was just feeling ecstatic, like I was in heaven. I was thinking, "Wow, this is great, the songs sound incredible." I had no inkling that anything was wrong.'

Towards the end of the day, as Frisell was recording the first of four parts for one of his compositions, an arrangement that involved Frisell playing both electric and acoustic guitars, Eicher stopped the session and told him to move on.

'Manfred lost patience with the process and he just wanted me to play something that sounded freer,' says Frisell. 'I've thought about this a lot since, and I don't think I was strong enough – to explain to him what I was doing, and to say, "Just hold your horses, let me finish what I'm doing, so you can hear how the whole thing's going to turn out."'

At breakfast the next morning, matters got a whole lot worse. Eicher told Frisell that they needed to talk, that he wasn't happy with the session, that maybe Frisell wasn't quite ready for the challenges of a solo recording.

'He didn't really like my acoustic guitar playing either,' says Frisell. 'He'd make reference to Ralph Towner and say, "You know, you're not really an acoustic guitar player. Ralph really knows how to get a *sound* out of an acoustic guitar." I didn't play acoustic for a number of years after that.'

Eicher's general advice to Frisell was to think of Keith Jarrett's spontaneous solo piano performances, to just play free. 'So I said, "Well, let me just try and do it", but he'd scared the shit out of me. I was in shock. And then the doubt came in, and I didn't really know what to do.'

Frisell suddenly felt very exposed and very alone. It was just him and his electric guitar reaching out over a widening abyss to Manfred and Jan Erik in the control booth beyond. 'I just started flailing . . . I was trying to grasp at anything, to find *something*, and Manfred was in there, saying, "No, no, that's not it." Which didn't exactly do much to build my confidence. I was in a panic, in deep trouble, and it wasn't working at all. He wasn't responding to anything, and the music kept going further and further down. That day just sort of unravelled. I don't even mean to blame Manfred, but it was pretty ego-crushing, pretty devastating.'

At one stage Eicher called English saxophonist and clarinettist John Surman into the studio (Surman happened to be holidaying nearby). 'I was a but unclear exactly what this was all connected to, but Manfred asked me to play over some of Bill's improvisations,' says Surman. 'I think he had an idea that he was going to use the music in a play or theatre production.' Matters were moving even further beyond Frisell's control. By the end of the day, Eicher had another plan: he knew Frisell was about to go on a two-week tour of Norway in a duo with bassist Arild Andersen, so he suggested to Frisell that they resume the recording after that – with Andersen present.

'I thought, "Well, that's a great idea." I mean, it was a way out. And Arild is this super-nice guy,' says Frisell. 'And then I was like, "Wait a minute, what have I got myself into?" I was sort of flipping out, because this wasn't my vision for the album at all; in fact, it had nothing really to do with it.'

Carole says that Frisell has always been unwaveringly ambitious and single-minded about his music, but not always adept at addressing the inevitable conflicts that sometimes arise. 'Oh, he's lethal – just so determined and doggone stubborn,' she says, laughing. 'But at the same time he's never been confrontational; he's not that personality at all.

'He's changed and gotten better, and compared to back then he has a lot more sway, but he won't always express his frustration or anger at certain situations. He's not going to show it to you if he's pissed. He'll fold his arms, and stand there, and say nothing, and just look at you. I'm fiery, but outside. Bill's fiery, but very much inside.'

Frisell and Andersen went into Talent Studio for a day, and the album was completed. Of the nine Frisell originals on the final record, four remained from the guitarist's solo work on the first day, and five feature Andersen. Frisell titled the album *In Line*, after one of the tracks; if you look up the phrase in a dictionary, two definitions are 'under control' and 'behaving properly or as required'.

'Arild was amazing – he played beautifully, the vibe between us was great, and he lifted things up,' Frisell says. 'In the end, I was thankful for him for being there.'

The album was released in Europe in April the following year and was not quite the disaster Frisell felt it was proving to be after the first day's recording. There are tracks, both with and without Andersen, that fail to really go anywhere. Yet you have to admire the guitarist's reach. 'The Beach', for example, is six minutes of dark, swirling, turbulent undercurrents that sound like the score to a horror movie; it's unlike anything else in the entire Frisell canon. The title track is similarly experimental: among the rapid harmonic clusters are dissonant sounds of cracked church bells, contorted gamelan and broken music boxes. *In Line* also contains one of Frisell's earliest yet finest compositions, 'Throughout', a beautiful ache of a song that strongly suggested the guitarist had the potential to develop into a composer of deft and oblique originality.

'If anybody was to ask me, "What's so great about music?"' says drummer Joey Baron, laughing, 'I'd say, "Here, listen to this!" and I'd play them "Throughout" from that first record. It's a *beautiful* song. I mean, it's just how Bill makes that combination of melody and harmony *work*, where the song takes you. Jazz snobs might not agree, but in terms of music, it speaks to your inside.

'When that happens, there's no filter about colour, age, gender, where you're from and what your identity is. None of that shit's important when you hear something like "Throughout". It just leaps right over all of those stupid walls. And when somebody can do that, it just makes the world a better place.'

The track has had a similarly powerful effect on singer Petra Haden. 'When I first heard it, I said, "This is my favourite song, *in the world*,"' she says, smiling. 'There was a point where I would listen to "Throughout" for hours – how he layered the sound, like I enjoy doing when I record my vocals. The music reminded me of that feeling of being in a dreamland.'

The record is the first comprehensive look into Frisell's emerging soundworld – there are country twangs, jazz harmonics, rock glissandos, folk acoustics, filmic intermissions, ambient abstractions and the orchestral overtones of violins, clarinets and horns. It's a more fascinating album than Frisell often acknowledges. 'I wanted to say something big or have a wide range of things,' he explained in *Guitar Player*. 'I wanted to play everything I possibly could, and I ended up with something less.' Yet somewhere within *In Line* are the opening scenes of the guitarist's elusive dream of music, the reverberations of an imaginative sound that would embrace all around it.

•
•

As well as recording ECM albums in Germany and Norway, and Paul Motian records for Soul Note in Milan, Europe was where Frisell mostly played and toured, far more so than in the US. The guitarist John Abercrombie used to say, 'I'm a commuter: I live in America, but I work in Europe.'

In 1983 alone there were three tours with the Paul Motian Quintet – in France, Italy and an arduous five-week trip around the continent. Frisell had also been recruited to the new Jan Garbarek Group and there were tours of Norway, Europe and an appearance at the Bergen Jazz Festival with the saxophonist and a string orchestra. During 1983 Frisell spent 154 days working away from home: fifty-one in the US, 103 in Europe.

'Europe has always been a better place to make a living, but it was especially so in the eighties,' says Frisell. 'Like most musicians I knew in New York, I'd go to Europe to play – and get paid. Maybe we didn't make much money on those first tours with Paul [Motian], but it was still way more than what we would make in the States. *Way* more.'

The time away could be challenging, however, for Carole and the early years of the marriage. 'At that time we could only communicate by phone once a week, because it was so expensive,' she says. 'So Bill being away so much put a strain on us. But I never really felt like we would split up. I was where I wanted to be, and with who I wanted to be. And I knew he was at the beginning of his journey, that he had something to say that was going to develop into something consequential later on. Also we made a pact: I hold down the fort; you keep your nose clean and your zipper zippered – no drugs, no messing around.'

Being a member of the Jan Garbarek Group gave Frisell a certain amount of standing and exposure in the US; the saxophonist had close associations with such respected American musicians as Keith Jarrett, Ralph Towner, Charlie Haden and George Russell. Garbarek had a small yet significant American audience, and in 1982 Frisell toured the US and Canada with the Norwegian's group. 'It wasn't even a big tour, really, but that was the first time I travelled around the States playing music,' says Frisell.

In March 1983 the new Garbarek group recorded a second album for ECM in Oslo, *Wayfarer* (in the interim Michael DiPasqua had replaced Jon Christensen on drums). The album contains some of the leader's loveliest melodies and most absorbing compositions, and Frisell seems suitably inspired, revelling in the group dynamics and interaction, flying in and out of Garbarek's swooping, spiralling and soaring improvisations.

Shortly afterwards in New York, however, at the end of an American tour, a conflict arose between an upcoming Garbarek tour of Europe and a commitment Frisell had already made to play a similar series of dates with Paul Motian. Manfred Eicher expected Bill to play with Jan; these were, after all, far more high-profile concerts in much larger venues.

'No one at ECM had cleared the dates with me, or asked me to do the tour with Jan; they just *assumed* I would do it,' says Frisell. 'I mean, it was great playing with Jan, and he was always amazing, and we had some success with that group, but again, I felt cornered. So the four of us [in Jan's band] had this big meeting, because they knew I was struggling with this, and I remember Eberhard gave me some advice. He said, "You know, sometimes you have to just do what you really believe in, what's right and best for you, even if you end up hurting other people." I listened to Eberhard, and I thought about it, and then I said, "OK, I'm sorry, but you're right, I'm going to do what's right and true for me . . . I'm going to play with Paul."'

Frisell had no doubts he had come to the right conclusion. 'It wasn't like a fifty-fifty decision, or something, because there was no way I was going to cancel a tour with Paul,' he says. 'Even though I knew I'd probably screwed my whole relationship with Manfred and ECM, Paul was where my heart was, what I was committed to. I'd put way more time in with Paul, and . . . you know, it was too heavy a thing to mess with.'

Garbarek says he was extremely sad to see Frisell leave. 'I was at a loss and didn't really know what to do when Bill left,' he says. 'I really thought we had something very special together, so . . . yeah, it was a hard time, really. A short while after that I decided to go with keyboard players, and since then I haven't really worked with guitarists.'

Manfred Eicher was much more disgruntled. 'This was before my solo record had come out in the States,' says Frisell, 'and Manfred basically said something like, "If you don't play with Jan, I don't know what's going to happen with your record." It was pressure, you know.' The US version of *In Line* did not appear until eight years later; it was released on CD with a different cover in 1991.

Eberhard Weber was nonplussed. 'It was a shock to me that Bill was quitting the band to play with Paul,' he writes. 'There were no arguments, no animosity, but touring with Jan's group, especially in Europe, would probably have doubled or tripled his income. It might also have allowed Bill and his wife to have moved to a nicer apartment. I seem to remember him telling me they were living above a particularly smelly fishmonger's in New Jersey!'

9: Hal Willner Listens to *Lookout for Hope*

Lookout for Hope: recorded New York City, March 1987;
producer Lee Townsend; released on ECM, February 1988;
Bill Frisell (electric and acoustic guitars, banjo),
Hank Roberts (cello, voice), Kermit Driscoll (bass), Joey Baron (drums);
all compositions by Frisell, except 'Hackensack' by Thelonious Monk

Hal Willner was one of modern music's most creative auteurs. A free-spirited producer who worked in music-recording, television, film and live performance, he is best known for his unique series of 'various artist concept records', many of which Bill Frisell contributed to. These defiantly cross-genre albums took inspiration from the music of, among others, Charles Mingus, Thelonious Monk, Kurt Weill and vintage Disney films.

Willner was like the genial host of a postmodern vaudeville. Some of his many projects included producing albums for Lou Reed, Marianne Faithfull, William Burroughs, Lucinda Williams, Laurie Anderson and Gavin Friday (again, Frisell guested on many of these records); and live concerts exploring the work of Tim Buckley, Neil Young and Randy Newman, as well as outlier writers Edgar Allan Poe, Marquis de Sade and Hunter S. Thompson. His film work included producing the music for Robert Altman's *Short Cuts* and *Kansas City*, and in 1981 he began selecting the music for comedy skits and sketches on celebrated television show *Saturday Night Live* – a relationship he maintained for almost forty years.

In 2004 Willner produced Bill Frisell's album *Unspeakable*, which won the first and only Grammy for both musician and producer. 'There are these few people in my life who create an atmosphere that allows me to do interesting things,' Frisell said in 2016. 'Hal is one of those people.

He creates these opportunities and invites me into them. He doesn't tell me what to do, so I have to figure it out.'

We met at his tiny studio in an art deco office building in the Hell's Kitchen district of Manhattan in April 2017. Willner was an inquisitive polymath and gentle provocateur, and his workspace resembled a bright and precocious child's bedroom: around him were shelves and boxes overflowing with his myriad obsessions and diversions – records, CDs, posters, figurines, a Popeye doll, a David Bowie puppet, photos of Lenny Bruce, a DVD of the British TV comedy series *Dad's Army*, and a ghoulish open-mouthed mask of Donald Trump.

PW: *I'm going to start by playing you Bill's three-minute version of [Thelonious Monk's] 'Hackensack'.*

HW: [As the track ends, laughing] Yep, one note and you know who it is. That . . . is . . . wild. Insane. I don't know any one other guitarist who can do that. I just think it comes from here [points to his heart].

When I think of Bill, or hear him, like now, I don't think of him as a guitarist, as 'guitarist Bill Frisell'. Ever. It's too limiting. Like [Marc] Ribot, he's a master musician who just happens to play guitar. I don't hear guitar with Bill; I hear this other thing.

And what is that?

It's the spiritual thing that I sometimes talk about. The second you hear that sound, he has you one hundred per cent. It's like jumping into an ocean. As soon as you hear the first notes, you're in that world; you're in a different part of the forest, you know.

A highly personal quality that takes you to another place?

Yes, that's what you're looking for, what makes him different to anything else. When I'm putting together any personnel, for an album or live show, I'm looking for that difference, and for differences between people. Like putting this real commercial guy next to this real avant-garde guy. Which was *always* an important element: a taste for the avant-garde.

Some of us aren't the ones who skipped the 'Revolution 9' track [on the Beatles' *White Album*].

I'm going to play you the title track. I noticed this recording is almost exactly thirty years old.

[As the track plays] Takes me back, back before Bill was in the [Village] Vanguard scene, when I was seeing him in places like the Limelight and the Knitting Factory. And it takes me right back to the Nino Rota album. I needed a solo guitarist, because of [limited] budget, and I was asking around, and Bill sent me a cassette – it was in this torn envelope, I remember – and, oh God, I actually had him sort of audition for me.

Bill was almost a total unknown back in 1980, wasn't he – especially compared to the other solo musicians on that album, such as Steve Lacy and Jaki Byard?

But that was never the issue for me with those records. I always wanted to have unknowns next to stars; that was what I was looking for. It was also Wynton and Branford Marsalis's first New York session. And John Zorn was basically unknown outside New York and Japan when he did the Monk record. That's hard to imagine now. That's how a lot of people got to hear Zorn for the first time.

And in turn the Nino Rota record was how John Zorn got to hear about Bill.

Yeah, and why not? I grew up on variety shows, and I thought that records like the triple *Woodstock* [original soundtrack] album were something that worked.

What did you hear on that tape Bill sent you that convinced you to try him out?

I heard this: it was great. And I heard this: it was perfect for the 'Juliet of the Spirits' track. I just knew if I could bring Bill in . . . he would elevate it.

You say something similar in Emma Franz's documentary on Bill, that in all the times you've worked with him 'he just makes everything better and takes it to a whole other level of complete heaven, [where] the angels join the session'. That's quite some compliment.

Yeah, if there's something missing with a track, or a problem, you just give it to Bill and . . . he makes everyone and everything sound great.

Like on the Marianne Faithfull record we did a few years later [in 1987]; Bill's playing was stunning and a large part of the reason why *Strange Weather* is now considered such a classic. We also did some live shows in New York with Marianne and Bill, in a band with Garth Hudson [of The Band] on accordion and Dr John on piano. It was the absolute highlight of that time.

And the following year we had Bill on the Disney record [*Stay Awake: Various Interpretations of Music from Vintage Disney Films*]. That record was sort of when the drugs were working, as they say. I felt like Cecil B. DeMille. It was Bill and Wayne Horvitz with [voiceover artist] Ken Nordine doing 'Hi Diddle Dee Dee (An Actor's Life for Me)'. And Yma Sumac, Betty Carter, The Replacements, Ringo [Starr], Tom Waits, Aaron Neville, and it was like *whooossshhh*. Then I put Bill all over the fucking album, and it just turned into this amazing thing.

I'm going to play you another track, another short one, 'Hangdog'. Though it's more a feature perhaps for Hank Roberts on cello.

[Track plays; as the looping tintinnabulary final section fades . . .] Holy God, that's another side we've always experimented with with Bill: the weirder side. It reminds me of an out-take from the Mingus record, 'Minor Intrusion', in which Bill wrote an arrangement just for the Harry Partch instruments, and it's so insane. [Instruments designed and built by Harry Partch, such as Cloud-Chamber Bowls, Chromelodeon II, Harmonic Canon and Surrogate Kithara, were used on *Weird Nightmare*.] A lot of Bill's contributions to the Mingus record were like the track you just played. It might not seem it, but there's still a melody, a hypnotic line, anchoring the music.

137

And a strange sense of time as well.

Yeah. That was Bill playing banjo, wasn't it? I wish Bill played acoustic more.

Do you think Bill's abilities as a composer and arranger have been overlooked?

That's why I've created projects with Bill, such as *The Kentucky Derby* [based on Hunter S. Thompson's influential gonzo article] and [Allen Ginsberg's beat poem] 'Kaddish', in which I've asked him not to play. *Don't* play. Just write, just conduct. People questioned me about that, but it brought out yet another side to Bill.

It was the same with *Unspeakable*; I thought, 'What haven't we done? Bill's been jazz and country and avant-garde and da-da-da-da . . . but what about funk?' A lot of non-African Americans have an interesting take on funk; some of my favourite funk has been made by white guys, in fact. Including, now, Bill. Because he listens to everything and I knew he would play his own version of funk, take it in a different direction. And it was successful. It won a Grammy that year; Bill's Grammy.

Maybe that helped move Bill into the larger picture. Or maybe it was just the constant working; he's prolific in a way that certain major work-aholics are. Like Zorn. Allen Ginsberg. Jim O'Rourke. And lots of others I know. It's what they do. They get up and work. They go to bed, then work.

But Bill's not quite like that, is he?

No, maybe not. Maybe not quite that bad [laughs]. You can still take him out.

What's he like, in your experience?

Well . . . I would say . . . you know his music? Well, he's like that. His playing is so him. It *is* him. It's just beautiful. Nothing competitive about him. And he's funny. He's just a magic man. He's probably the only person Zorn's never flipped out on, and Zorn goes ballistic on everybody.

Even musicians he's played with and known for years. But it's like . . . how could you get angry with Bill? *What?* I can't think of anybody else in this business who's like that, where nobody has a bad word to say about them. Who the fuck doesn't get on with Bill Frisell?

Let me play you one more track. This is 'Little Brother Bobby', the one the Bill Frisell Band played on [Willner's late-night jazz-and-beyond programme] Night Music.

Yep. Boy, I sure went for it in that show, huh? Some of the best music TV ever – the concept, the casting – and I'll never work in that business again [laughs]. Anyway . . . Jools Holland just fucking took the idea and ran with it to England, and he's still on. Even though it doesn't have the controlled chaos *Night Music* had. Like [country singer] Conway Twitty with [avant-garde art collective] The Residents.

Or that weirdness again. When you hear Bill and Ken Nordine doing 'Desolation Theme' [on *Stay Awake*], it's so weird, so fucking dark. Same with Bill's playing on the Bernard Herrmann *Twilight Zone* section on the [David] Sanborn record [*Another Hand*].

Or that solo piece I gave him on the sea shanties record [*Rogue's Gallery: Pirate Ballads, Sea Songs and Chanteys*], 'Spanish Ladies'. At the time I was obsessed with those Buddha Machines [small plastic boxes that generate loops of ambient and meditative music], so we got a bunch and put them around the studio. And Bill played off them, and, boy, it was just magic, beginning to end. That darkness is always, always in the mix with Bill; it's his home town.

●
●

Almost three years to the day after this listening session, in April 2020, Hal Willner died at home in New York of symptoms consistent with the coronavirus; he had just turned sixty-four. 'I mean, Hal – that was a massive shock,' Frisell told me. 'Like being hit with a baseball bat.'

10: Once Upon a Time in the East Village

In the autumn of 1982 Bill Frisell walked into SoHo Music Gallery on Wooster Street in Lower Manhattan, and his life was to change again.

In the seventies and eighties, New York City had hundreds of independent records shops. SoHo Music Gallery was one of the best, a special haven of all that was intriguing, curious, arcane and inspiring in alternative music. As a fan of the store once commented, if you were looking for 'the first Diamanda Galás twelve-inch single' or 'two obscure Aldous Huxley speeches made in New Mexico in the late fifties', then SoHo Music Gallery was the place to go.

Today upmarket Wooster Street is lined with high-end fashion emporiums, trendy cafés, snazzy restaurants and stylish model agencies. With its cobblestones and cast-iron buildings, the street has an 'old gritty feel' and is often used for film and photo shoots. Back in 1982 the grit was real. With the rents being mostly affordable, and the area's lofts and industrial spaces populated by artists of all kinds, it was a bohemian and cosmopolitan neighbourhood. Yale Evelev, now president of David Byrne's Luaka Bop records, worked at SoHo Music Gallery. Others who did stints there include alt-rock drummer Anton Fier, saxophonist-composer John Zorn, and avant-altoist Tim Berne, whom Frisell had met that summer through Paul Motian.

Frisell says, 'So I walked in, because I had heard this [King] Sunny Adé record on the radio, and I didn't really know his music, so I wanted to pick up one of his records. And I was looking through the bins, and Tim was in there, and he said, "Oh, here, if you're looking for that, you should ask . . . this is John Zorn.' And he introduced me.

'I was amazed that Zorn knew who I was. I think he'd heard Hal [Willner]'s Nino Rota album and that track I'd played on. Or maybe Wayne [Horvitz], who I hadn't actually met at that stage, had mentioned me . . . *"There's this guy out in New Jersey!"* I think he even knew I'd been rehearsing with Paul [Motian]. I mean, Zorn retains a lot of information.' Frisell pauses, laughing. 'But right away, he was like, "Oh wow, you're *that* guy."

'Then John immediately said, "Oh no, if you like King Sunny Adé, you gotta check out this Ebenezer Obey record." And I ended up buying LPs by both of them, and some other African albums that he recommended. I thought he was some kind of expert on African music, or something. Then I realised that he sort of knew every record in the whole store.'

Frisell's knowledge of Zorn was more sketchy. He knew that the twenty-nine-year-old New Yorker was a killer alto player influenced by such avant-garde innovators as Anthony Braxton and Oliver Lake; that he was a composer of fiercely experimental music; and that he'd been a vital force in the free-spirited downtown music and arts scene since the mid-seventies. 'But, to be honest,' says Frisell, 'I still didn't really quite know what Zorn *did*.'

Soon after, Frisell got the chance to find out – he went to see Zorn and his ensemble stage one of the composer's 'game pieces', '*Track & Field*', during a festival at leading rock venue Irving Plaza. These compositions were created for live collective 'controlled improvisation' – there was no sheet music, no conductor, no requisite instrumentation or number of musicians, no preconceived sequence of events, and no time limit. Instead, the participants improvised according to a set of rules, strategies and tactics that could change at any player's whim. Zorn's game pieces 'de-centred both the process of improvisation and the composition itself' – they were musical and visual, collaborative and competitive, and fun.

'I was like, "What the . . ."?' says Frisell. 'I mean, I'd listened to a lot of abstract and improvised music, but this was so different from anything I'd ever heard. I didn't know what was going on: there was obviously a structure, an architecture to the music, but the way things were coming at you within that – the speed, the juxtapositions, all the information – just blew my mind. It was music without any idiomatic references, more like freely improvised noise or *sounds*, and it was so new and startling and intriguing to me.'

The next time Frisell visited SoHo Music Gallery he told Zorn how much he had been affected by '*Track & Field*', and Zorn invited him to the next performance – to play. Zorn arranged for the musicians to meet the day before the gig at his small apartment in the East Village. Here he would introduce the game piece, explain its rules, and there'd be a short practice session, just to get the feel of the form and its possibilities.

It was here that Frisell first met many of the leading figures in what became known as the 'downtown scene', a frequently contested catch-all term that had been used to encapsulate the extreme variety of experimental and interdisciplinary music and art being created below 14th Street ever since Yoko Ono opened her Chambers Street loft as a performance space in 1960.

The performers at Zorn's that afternoon towards the end of 1982 included keyboardist, composer and genre-transgressor Wayne Horvitz, and pianist, singer-songwriter and broad surveyor of American folk music 'spun from many threads' Robin Holcomb; at the end of the seventies Horvitz and Holcomb had helped set up a legendary basement performance space in the West Village called Studio Henry. Also present were English guitarist, multi-instrumentalist, composer and improviser Fred Frith, co-founder of British underground art-rock group Henry Cow; no-wave guitarist, subversive pop singer, Brazilian music devotee and visual arts collaborator Arto Lindsay; and solo free improvising violinist Polly Bradfield. The pianist Anthony Coleman took part too, as did percussionist, sound artist and self-taught improvising vocalist David Moss.

As Gene Santoro wrote in an early profile of Zorn, 'eclectic is far too weak a word to describe his demanding yet playful sonic assaults', and the same could equally be said of the work of Zorn's downtown contemporaries. While experimental music and free improvisation were common compulsions and connections, and most of the group were in their late twenties and early thirties, their music was as individual as they were, and resisted easy categorisation.

Where else, for example, were radical Japanese drummer, composer, sampler and electronic adventurer Ikue Mori, and electroacoustic composer and pioneer of 'contemporary harp practices' Zeena Parkins going to fit in? Or guitarist Eugene Chadbourne, who around this time led an alternative rockabilly band named Shockabilly? Or composer, iconoclast and supremely different drummer Bobby Previte? Or kinetic altoist Tim Berne?

'I think through some kind of weird accident of music, or social history, it seemed like there were people from, what before and since, were fairly separate worlds – contemporary classical, avant-garde jazz and punk rock – which for a moment seemed to cross paths,' guitarist Marc Ribot has said; Ribot was to join John and Evan Lurie's archetypal downtown art-jazz-punk combo the Lounge Lizards in the mid-eighties. 'So you not only met, but played with, or wound up in bands with people who it wouldn't normally have been the case. And that was exciting.'

These musicians needed a home, and downtown provided them with one, both artistically and practically – many lived together in the same Lower Manhattan neighbourhoods, sometimes even in collectives in the same building. Apart, of course, from Frisell.

'When I first started to hear about Bill, he was described to me as two things: he'd studied jazz at the Berklee School of Music, and he lived in New Jersey – both of which were definite negatives to our sort of downtown New York weirdness,' says Horvitz, chuckling. Horvitz was to become one of Frisell's closest friends, during this period and beyond.

Robin Holcomb agrees. 'Yes, we'd heard that there was this great guitar player living in New Jersey, but at that time New Jersey just seemed like a world away to me – like that famous *New Yorker* cover with the drawing of the view from Manhattan, with Jersey and the rest of America way in the distance.'

'And then, when he became the ECM guy,' continues Horvitz. 'That was *another* thing. I also remember that Bobby Previte said to me, "Oh, Bill Frisell? He's really interesting. He plays orchestrally." And I was sort of like, "What the fuck does '*orchestrally*' mean?"'

Horvitz was to discover an answer to that question at Frisell's first Zorn session. 'He obviously was kind of a kick-ass guitarist, but he wasn't a lick or lead type of player, and he wasn't a straight-jazz chordal player – although his rhythmic sense was unbelievable,' says Horvitz. 'It was his harmonic sensibility, which was so rich and expansive and astounding. It was the way he was colouring the music all the time, the way his solos were so compositional, the way he used all the guitar's resources and sonic possibilities, the way he had a sense of tradition, of what's right, but was making choices that no one else ever made.'

Frisell's contribution to the performance of '*Track & Field*' went well, yet he was very much outside his comfort zone. 'I felt really super-shy and scared at first, because someone might tell me to do something and I *had* to do it, or I might even have to tell someone to stop doing something,' he says. 'And for me that, socially, was a big step – just stepping into all that with these really strong personalities.'

With his modest demeanour, college looks and jazz-school training, superficially he must have seemed the least likely downtowner in the history of alternative art.

'These people did *not* play weddings,' says Frisell, laughing. 'And they weren't playing jazz, or being asked to. Or working as sidemen or women. They were all just committed to doing their own thing. So even though they were all playing for Zorn, each one of them had their own world going on. And Zorn wanted that; his music allowed for that. He expected them to express their own individual ways of thinking about music.'

•
•

Frisell began to play more concerts with Zorn, mostly to small yet dedicated audiences in downtown clubs such as Roulette, 8BC and Chandelier, and in Zorn's own tiny East Village DIY clubhouse, the Saint. Much of the music reflected the prolific composer's hybrid, high-velocity, maximum-decibel and information-overloading aesthetic; it was maximalist, machine-gun and aggressively postmodern.

'Zorn's music was really difficult for me, and different, but also *healthy* – it kind of put a wrench in the works in a good way,' says Frisell. 'Up until then, my model for what to do with music was to take some material and develop it over a period of time, like Sonny Rollins or Ornette Coleman [did], maybe up to twenty minutes or so. With Zorn I had to come up with something that made some kind of sense – *every three seconds*. I was like, "*Whoa!*"'

Frisell hung on, thrilled by the ride. 'That whole slash-and-dice thing wasn't really my aesthetic, and it certainly wasn't Robin's aesthetic, or Bill's,' says Wayne Horvitz. 'But we were good foils for John – Bill especially. He could just say, "Do this, do this, do this" – and Bill could do all those things, and yet he always sounded like himself.'

In interviews with Zorn at the time, the composer could come across as abrasive and confrontational – as the critic Francis Davis pointed out, somewhat satirically, Zorn is German for 'anger'. Thirty years later, however, Zorn appeared to have significantly mellowed, at least in an audio recording for Emma Franz's 2017 documentary, *Bill Frisell: A Portrait*. Rather than Frisell being the square in the downtown circle, it seems it was Frisell who was doing Zorn and his associates the favour. 'This was a time at the beginning of a community when people really worked together, because they loved it, because there was something exciting happening,' said Zorn. 'It was always an incredible kick for the downtown scene that a musician of the stature of Bill Frisell was interested in working with us; that was a kind of validation in a way.

'Whenever Bill played, it just got better – it was always *better*. No matter what music it was, no matter who was performing, Bill's presence would *lift* everything up to his level. It was [as] if John Coltrane had come in and said, "Hey, you guys are doing something interesting – I want to be involved." And we were all like, "My God, if Bill wants to play with us, we must be doing something right."'

•
•

As well as the burgeoning reputation Frisell was beginning to enjoy through his association with such highly respected figures as Julius

Hemphill, Mike Gibbs and Bob Moses, his relationships with Paul Motian and John Zorn secured him considerable credibility, if not the largest of audiences and incomes.

Frisell also started to play regularly with Tim Berne, in duo, and in Berne's various bands, mostly in New York, but occasionally on short US and European tours. During 1983 and 1984 Berne and Frisell recorded an album together, *Theoretically*. It's a striking and surprising record, far more written-through than freely improvised, more about an overall mood and atmosphere than the undoubted strengths of the two individual voices.

In August 1984 Frisell got the chance to bring together these new and disparate influences, and forge his own personal future sounds. That opportunity – to record his own album, of his own compositions, in New York, with his own band – came from Manfred Eicher and ECM.

'I was like, wow, super-surprised, because I thought I had blown everything, burned all my bridges with Manfred,' says Frisell. 'But it sort of felt like a fresh start, recording my own new music with a bunch of new people. In a way, it felt like my real first album.'

Eicher suggested two hugely contrasting personalities for the record. First was the shy and self-deprecating London-based Canadian trumpet, cornet and flugelhorn player Kenny Wheeler, with whom Frisell had toured England and Wales in 1978 as part of the Mike Gibbs big band. Eicher's second recommendation was Al Foster, the fluid, extrovert and versatile American drummer who had been a key member of Miles Davis's seventies electric bands and comeback early eighties groups. 'And again, I was like, "Oh my God, are you kidding me?"' says Frisell. 'Kenny and Al Foster – that would be incredible. I sort of used that as a starting point, thinking, "What could I do?"'

Frisell was determined to integrate other elements into the recording. He had recently bought a new Roland guitar synthesiser, as well as various digital-delay and pitch-transposing pedals, and was eager to exploit 'a new array of sounds and techniques not possible on the conventional electric guitar'.

Frisell was also attracted to the sonorous low-end tones created by Bob Stewart on tuba, an instrument with a heritage in jazz that stretches back to its beginnings in New Orleans, before the music moved indoors and the string bass became more prevalent. In the seventies Stewart had helped liberate the tuba from its strictly rhythmic and harmonic functions, moving it from the second line to the front line, giving it a solo voice. Frisell particularly admired his work in groups led by free-flowing altoist Arthur Blythe – the way his rumbling timbre combined so effectively with the jaggedly soulful electric guitar of James Blood Ulmer and the resonant bass of Fred Hopkins. 'I hadn't met Bob Stewart, or anything, but there was something in his sound that got me going,' says Frisell.

Bill also brought in electric bassist Jerome Harris, whom he had first met in Boston and jammed with at Chip Stern's; Harris had played with Al Foster in Sonny Rollins's bands.

All the musicians agreed to the recording date, though Al Foster baulked at the fee. Frisell had been offered five thousand dollars by ECM for the session, and even though the album would be under his name, with all compositions and arrangements written by him, he had decided to split the fee equally.

'That was totally great, because like, *wow*, a total budget of five thousand dollars seemed like a lot of money to me,' says Frisell. 'But when I phoned Al and told him about the thousand, there was like this silence, and he seemed really insulted. It just seemed absurd to him, especially for a label with the stature of ECM. I was panicking. So I thought, "Well, wait, what if I just give him all of my money?" So I said to him, "Well, I could give you two thousand." And he said, "I don't know. Call me back." And this is like a week before we're meant to record the album.'

Frisell kept calling. A few days before the date, he phoned again. 'A woman answered the phone, maybe it was his daughter, I don't know, and I said, "It's Bill Frisell. Can I speak with Al?" And she said, "No. Al told me to tell you: he doesn't want to do it." Bam. Click.'

Bill called Paul Motian. 'I was completely flipping out and I was confiding in him, as a friend, because he knew I was all excited about the record, but also really scared because I was entering into something big with this completely new group,' says Frisell. 'It wasn't in my mind at all to ask him to play, because I knew he was committed to his own music, and turning down almost any kind of offer for anything else, especially sideman gigs. But, right away, he just said, "Oh, man, I'll play."'

The resulting album, *Rambler*, released by ECM both in Europe and the US the following year, is a fascinating snapshot of how far Frisell had developed, as a guitarist, improviser, composer and potential leader. The record received generally favourable reviews too at the time; 'Bill Frisell has built a little masterpiece here – not just a showcase for his own instrumental creativity (of which there is much in evidence), but a clever and poetic whole,' read a review in *Fanfare* magazine.

If the leader's guitar synthesiser can sometimes prove oddly bulldozing and overbearing, what does emerge is Frisell's ability as an already accomplished composer, a weaver of captivatingly sideways yet song-like melodies, the sort of tunes that stay with you. Squeezed into the middle of side two, for example, is one of Frisell's finest and most enduring songs, 'Strange Meeting', a seemingly simple though wholly enigmatic composition that would go on to become a Frisell standard.

•
•

In September 1984 Frisell went into the studio for the first time with John Zorn, for the initial recordings of *The Big Gundown*, Zorn's radical reworking of the music of Italian film composer Ennio Morricone.

Originally given the working title *Once Upon a Time in the East Village*, the album featured a roll call of leading figures in the downtown scene at that time – from Wayne Horvitz and Tim Berne to Anthony Coleman, Polly Bradfield and Bobby Previte, plus players such as turntablist Christian Marclay, harpist Carol Emanuel and bassist Melvin Gibbs. Special guests included gothic-rock vocalist Diamanda Galás and soul-jazz organist Big John Patton. In an inspired piece of Zorn casting, illustrious Belgian harmonica maestro Toots Thielemans provided the whistling on 'Poverty' from the Morricone score for *Once Upon a Time in America*. Zorn himself features on alto, piano, harpsichord, vocals, game calls and saw.

The record also found room for, as it reads in the liner notes, 'six of the most heralded guitarists in new music: Bill Frisell, Fred Frith, Jody Harris, Arto Lindsay, Robert Quine and Vernon Reid'. Frisell plays on two tracks: a darkly soulful version of 'Erotico' from Morricone's score for 1970 film *The Burglars* (the track also features Laura Biscotto on additional 'sexy Italian vocals'); and the menacingly playful and quick-fire title track, loosely based on the music Morricone wrote for 1966 spaghetti western *The Big Gundown*.

In a classic Frisellian criss-crossing of serendipity and coincidence, the liner notes state that the inspiration for the thunderous opening to the title track, the first cut on the album, came from a dream that Zorn had prior to recording: '[It was] the first dream in his life that was pure music. He woke in the middle of the night and wrote down the music he had heard, and it became the introduction not only to the song but also to the entire record.'

The guitarist's role is limited to little more than occasional stringy cowboy quivers, Hawaiian surf ripples and, on 'Erotico', seventies rock squeals. Yet Frisell's connection to such a watershed album again raised his profile and standing; in the *Penguin Guide to Jazz Recordings*, Richard Cook and Brian Morton describe it as 'utterly remarkable in every way and one of the essentials records of the eighties'.

Frisell's luck held with Zorn's next few recordings. Premièred at Roulette in November 1984, with Zorn as 'prompter', *Cobra* is a game piece that has become one of Zorn's best known and most successful compositions. Bill took part in the first two recordings of the piece, live in October 1985, and at the Radio City studios in New York in May 1986. A double album of both performances, *Cobra*, was released the following year; it was another hyper-fragmentary and highly influential record.

'Hearing *Cobra* pretty much crystallised how much advanced, interesting, innovative, thought-provoking and inspiring music was happening in downtown New York at that time,' says guitarist Nels Cline. 'Zorn was creating music in a way that was beyond what everybody else was doing or thinking about, and he had coalesced all these unique and stunning individuals into one ensemble.'

In August and September 1985 Frisell was at Radio City again with Zorn to record 'Godard', the composer's nineteen-minute *hommage* to French New Wave film director Jean-Luc Godard, whose speedy jump-cut editing and radical use of sound had been a primary influence. 'Godard' features an octet of Zorn on alto and clarinet (and 'French narration'), with Frisell, Coleman, Emanuel, Marclay and Previte, plus David Weinstein on keyboards and computer, and Luli Shioi on vocals. 'Godard' was Zorn's first 'file-card composition', a method in which the composer assembled musical ideas and images, inspired by his extensive research, on index cards, and then sorted and sequenced them into a narrative whole.

'Zorn created the music in an amazing way,' says Frisell. 'The file cards were almost like scenes from a movie organised how he wanted them. Then he gathered a bunch of really interesting musicians, and he'd have an idea for a section, or we'd improvise something, or I'd take a banjo and make up a melody. So within the structure, and amidst the noise and everything, more tonal and harmonic things also started to happen.

'He also liked this beautiful old real recording studio, up above Radio City Music Hall, which around that time was sort of, but not quite, in disrepair – it used sixteen-track tape, and sounded really great. Today you'd splice the music together digitally, with a computer and Pro Tools or something, but the room had a beautiful natural decay, so that, as the sound of one section was dying out, we'd immediately start the next. It was really something.'

The effect is like turning an avant-garde radio dial – an unfolding mosaic of snippets and shards, stark juxtapositions and abrupt transitions – and fascinating, for a while. Vastly superior in design and execution, however, was Zorn's next file-card soundscape: 'Spillane'. Named after popular American crime novelist Mickey Spillane, the composition appeared on the album of the same name in 1987. It was to be another breakthrough record – in terms of creativity and repute – for Zorn, and for many of the musicians that took part in the session.

Frisell appears on the twenty-five-minute title track, again created and arranged in the studio (Radio City, during June and August 1986), with Zorn using sound blocks triggered by 'some aspect of Spillane's work, his world, his characters, his ideology'. Some of the music was again scored for an eleven-piece ensemble, but, as Zorn explains in the liner notes, 'at other times I'll simply say something like . . . "Bill, go and improvise *My Gun Is Quick* [an early Spillane novel]".' The spirit of Jon Damian, Frisell's guitar teacher from a decade before at Berklee, was alive and well.

The track is a powerful statement of Zorn's supreme ability to evoke an entire world of sounds and pictures, collisions and collages. Frisell is stretched about as far as any Zorn collaborator has been, before or since. Among the screams, sirens, thunderclaps, phone dials, windscreen wipers, and gun shots, Frisell creates a thrilling array of guitar styles and languages, from swing to cocktail jazz, surf to space-age, country blues to rockabilly and noirish ambience. This is Frisell as compleat postmodern guitarist: he can go anywhere, reference anything, at any time, and still sound like himself.

In 1987 Zorn devised another dream project that had Frisell at its core: *News for Lulu*, an album of relatively unsung and overlooked bop tunes, first recorded in the fifties and sixties on the Blue Note label, interpreted by Zorn on alto, Frisell on guitar, and composer, scholar and Association for the Advancement of Creative Musicians (AACM) member George Lewis on trombone.

While Zorn confessed in the liner notes to *Spillane* that 'even though the jazz feeling is essential to me, it is not the tradition in which I feel I can make a significant statement', it is hard not to conclude that he was saying something about the state of jazz in the eighties, and the rise of a neo-classical/traditionalist/conservative movement spearheaded by virtuoso trumpeter Wynton Marsalis and leading critics Stanley Crouch and Albert Murray.

That prevailing view rejected a broad sweep of, as they saw them, corrupting and commercialising forces in favour of a credo that returned 'America's greatest music' to fundamentals such as swing, blues, tonality, harmony, mastery and craft. As Marsalis told me when I interviewed him in 1991, 'In my era I've come up between two camps – the avant-garde camp and the rock camp – and I'm a jazz musician.'

Zorn, Frisell and Lewis refuted Marsalis's orthodoxy by integrating avant-garde, rock and other influences into the greater whole. 'They approached the Blue Note material with a considered artistic agenda: to test its capacity for tolerance of outside techniques,' Bill Meyer wrote in the liner notes to the follow-up live album, *More News for Lulu*, released in 1992.

The electrifying result is music balanced between respect and reinvention, structure and freedom, sensitivity and bite – and that fully re-energised an established form. 'It's really music the way it should be played today – exciting, on the edge,' Zorn said in *DownBeat*. 'Bebop is not just running the changes the way Sonny Stitt or Bird did; there's no point to just copying that . . . It's tunes and changes and a certain tradition that needs to be updated to keep it alive.' Gustav Mahler said something similar eighty years or more earlier: 'Tradition is not worshipping ashes, it's preserving fire.'

●
●

This creatively alive and dynamic mid- to late-eighties period would set a pattern for a significant part of the rest of Frisell's working life: that of being, as Gary Giddins wrote in the *New Yorker*, 'a quiet, bespectacled, but musically charged presence on every kind of session' for an astonishing range of musicians 'who have little in common beyond their conspicuous individualism'.

It was Frisell replicating exactly the kind of alchemy he had experienced the very first time he played with Jim Hall in the spring of 1972: of not just sounding good himself, but of magically making others sound

The Frisell family home at 949 Krameria Street, Denver, 1951.

Baby 'Billy' with his parents, Bill and Jane, Krameria Street, 1952. The painting of a Baltimore street scene on the wall is by Frisell's father.

Three-year-old Bill, pliers in hand, in front of his parents' 1951 Plymouth; this photograph was used for the cover of Frisell's 1990 album *Is That You?*

ABOVE Bill and his paternal 'grandpa', Ole, Krameria Street, Christmas 1954.

LEFT Five-year-old Bill playing his grandfather's euphonium. He is sitting on a cobbler's bench he helped Ole build, and which he still has today. One of his father's paintings again hangs on the wall.

RIGHT Bill (*right*), thirteen, with his mother Jane and younger brother Bob outside the house at 3401 East 7th Avenue, Denver. Bill is holding 'Walk, Don't Run '64', a single by instrumental surf rockers the Ventures.

ABOVE A pivotal moment: clarinet in one hand; his first electric guitar, a brand new Fender Mustang, in the other. Bill and Bob in the garden at 3401 East 7th Ave, June 1965.

RIGHT Bill in his Gold Sash Band uniform, Denver, December 1965; he was first chair clarinet.

BELOW Fifteen-year-old Bill practising at home with his brother Bob.

Frisell's East High School graduation photo, Denver, 1969.

Frisell, Denver, Christmas 1972, during the 'hard years'.

LEFT Frisell (*back, left*) and Kermit Driscoll (*front, third from right*) sport pop band Boston Connection's orange polyester suits, Boston, 1976.

Smokin' Bill with (*left to right*) Vinnie Johnson, Kermit Driscoll and Michel Herr (the Good Buddies band), backstage, Belgium, late 1978.

LEFT The Mauve Traffic quintet: (*left to right*) Frisell, Kermit Driscoll, Steve Houben, Vinnie Johnson and Michel Herr, backstage, Belgium, late 1978.

RIGHT Carole and Bill on their wedding day, Greenville, North Carolina, August 1979.

Frisell in 1987 with his Gibson SG, the 'rock axe' he played from the mid-seventies to late eighties.

Frisell's first band: (*left to right*) Kermit Driscoll, Hank Roberts, Frisell and Joey Baron, New York, 1987.

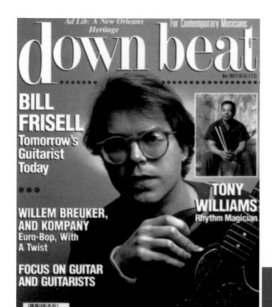

BILL FRISELL
Tomorrow's
Guitarist
Today

LEFT 'Tomorrow's Guitarist Today': Frisell's first *DownBeat* cover, May 1989.

BELOW

John Zorn's Naked City: (*left to right*) Wayne Horvitz, Zorn, Joey Baron, Frisell and Fred Frith, New York, 1990.

BELOW Frisell on stage with Naked City, Florence, Italy, 1990; he is directing his attentions at Zorn.

A portrait of Frisell by
cartoonist (and guitarist)
Gary Larson, 1997.

A 'psychological portrait' of Frisell by cartoonist Jim Woodring – part of his
artwork for Frisell's 2001 album *With Dave Holland and Elvin Jones*.

as good if not better. As Frisell says, of 'influencing and orchestrating the music from within in real subtle ways'.

Some of the eighties sessions were led by musicians connected to the downtown music in which Frisell was engaged. Wayne Horvitz released the compositionally and rhythmically rich *The President,* which owed more to rock and roots music than jazz – as did Robin Holcomb's compellingly original eponymous debut album, which, for all its folksy singer-songwriting, retains a strong sense of experimentation.

Hank Roberts made the quietly exploratory *Black Pastels,* which features the leader's tender vocals. Cornet, trumpet and flugelhorn player Herb Robertson produced the harmonically ambitious *Transparency,* with Tim Berne on alto, Lindsey Horner on bass and Joey Baron on drums. Berne also led a thrillingly frenetic quartet, with Frisell, Hank Roberts and drummer Alex Cline on *Fulton Street Maul,* which was closer to the uncompromising energy and electricity of heavy rock, trance and groove-based music than anything approximating to jazz.

On *Mumbo Jumbo,* a double album of free improvising trios assembled by Jim Staley, Frisell shows just how far he has embraced the downtown aesthetic. In a triad with Staley on trombone and Ikue Mori on drums and drum machine, Frisell clangs, clatters and distorts, playing close to his wildest and most *out.* 'I was connecting with a lot of people, and at some points it seemed to be happening very suddenly, almost simultaneously,' says Frisell.

The momentum kept up. In 1988 Frisell took part in two remarkable large ensemble recordings. He contributed gritty blues solos to Julius Hemphill's driving modern compositions on *Big Band;* and resonating rock-orchestral atmospheres to the beautifully textured writing of Mike Gibbs on *Big Music.* British producer John L. Walters wrote in the liner notes to the latter that he was 'looking for a missing link between [Gil Evans's] *Out of the Cool* and [Miles Davis's] *Bitches Brew;* between Charles Ives and Salif Keita'.

There were also albums of experimental eighties sounds that haven't weathered so well. Frisell guested on the engaging, self-titled 1986 debut of Lyle Mays, the pianist and innovative keyboardist who was coming to prominence in the Pat Metheny Group; some of the early digital synthesiser effects, however, create a sometimes syrupy and self-consciously romantic air.

Smash & Scatteration was a duo album with guitarist Vernon Reid, who had recently formed forward-thinking 'black-rock' group Living Colour. Produced by David Breskin, and released in 1985, it's a surprising and audacious record that 'straddles high tech (guitar synths, drum machines, MIDIs to keyboards) and low tech (banjos, acoustic guitars, nasty old electrics)', yet it's hard today to get past the weighty synth washes and surging electronic swirls.

Another project conceived and produced by Breskin was the vastly more rewarding Power Tools: Frisell with bassist Melvin Gibbs, who had played with Vernon Reid, John Zorn and, most prominently, in the Decoding Society, the radical 'free funk' ensemble led by the third arm of the triumvirate, legendary avant-garde drummer Ronald Shannon Jackson.

The trio made just one album, *Strange Meeting*, released on Island Records in 1987, and toured briefly in Europe the following year. The band played Outside In, a jazz and new music festival in the unlikely setting of Crawley, a commuter town near Gatwick Airport. It was one of the first times I'd seen Frisell live, and I emerged from the concert stunned and silenced. 'Frisell sparks the colours of a symphonic electric storm,' I wrote around that time in *The Wire*.

Despite being short-lived, the group's inspired convergence of strong and irresistible melodies, Frisell's rockier, noisier and more unfettered guitar and effects-driven instincts, Gibbs's warm and liquid bass playing, and Jackson's densely swinging polyrhythms have given Power Tools a bona fide cult status. 'That awesome and under-sung Power Tools album,' Greg Tate has written, '[is] in my humble opinion, the most paradigm-shifting power trio record since [the Jimi Hendrix live album] *Band of Gypsys*.'

More straight-ahead was *Clairvoyant*, a bright modern fusion record by guitarist Leni Stern and also her debut as leader. Frisell also plays on two all-star post-bop sessions, *Oshumare* and *Rah,* led by drummer Billy Hart. While it's significant that by 1985 Frisell had already been added to line-ups of some of the leading lights in seventies and eighties jazz, including Dave Holland, Dave Liebman, Branford Marsalis, Kenny Kirkland and Steve Coleman, his distorting solos and warping pedal effects gave the impression that he had been beamed in from the future.

Another fascinating Frisellian contrast was to be heard on one of the most lauded jazz records of the decade, Marc Johnson's *Bass Desires* – a quartet of Frisell; double bassist Johnson, whom Bill first met at that initial rehearsal at Paul Motian's apartment in 1981; drummer Peter Erskine, best known for his work in Weather Report; and John Scofield, a member of Miles Davis's group, and, with Pat Metheny, the most admired and talked about young guitarist in contemporary jazz.

The record, and its sequel, *Second Sight,* inhabit many moods: from hee-haw to hoedown, blues to post-bop, rock to reggae; from band originals to an exhilarating rendition of 'Resolution', the second section of John Coltrane's towering 1965 suite *A Love Supreme.* Scofield is a thrillingly inventive player, his bluesy tumbling improvisations fired by linear logic and speedy ideas; like Sonny Rollins, his solos have a great internal energy and drive. Frisell, on the other hand, is all ambiguous implication and edge, his harmonic extensions and expressionist colours lead you into a much darker and more dangerous netherworld; he is asymmetrical, digressive, deviating, multiple.

'Bill completely freaked me out; he sounded so foreign and alien, and I had no idea what the hell he was doing,' says trumpeter and educator Cuong Vu, one-time member of the Pat Metheny Group. 'Bill didn't sound like jazz at all to me; he was taking things to a totally different place. Bill's thing was just completely *weird* and whacked out, but at the same time there was something extremely compelling and *accessible* about it that pulled you right in. Bill was like chocolate-covered ants.'

Frisell's creative dissonance was also proving perfect for Hal Willner, and Bill continued to appear on several contrasting yet characteristically off-centre Willner projects. On *The Lion for Real* Frisell provides eerie bittersweet settings for Allen Ginsberg's jazz-poetry; for spirited Irish singer-songwriter Gavin Friday's debut *Each Man Kills the Thing He Loves*, he is part of an agile band that scurries from post-punk to dark cabaret and tortured love songs; and on Marianne Faithfull's brittle and brilliant *Strange Weather*, Frisell travels from twenties Berlin to fifties Nashville to twenty-first-century New York, sometimes all in the same song.

'As Bill was playing, gradually I began to realise what a genius he is,' says Faithfull. 'I've worked with a lot of different musicians, but playing with Bill is always going to be completely different to anyone else, not just because of his character – his sweetness and gentleness – but because he can play anything. I know he has a particular special style, which I love, but actually you can ask Bill to play any other kind of thing.'

There was even a major opportunity missed. In 1985 Tom Waits phoned the Frisell apartment; he was bringing together various musicians for a recording in New York. Waits had recently contributed a track to *Lost in the Stars*, Willner's celebration of the music of the great German-Jewish expressionist composer Kurt Weill. The producer had recommended two guitarists to Waits for his next project. One was Marc Ribot, who made the session; it was his first major-label recording, and the beginning of a series of crucial and career-changing collaborations with Waits. The other was Bill Frisell, who was on an extended tour of Europe with Paul Motian.

'So Tom talked to Carole and she told him, "Sorry, Bill is out of town and unavailable,"' says Frisell. 'Then she said to him that she knew someone else who would be great, and she recommended Quine.' Guitarist Robert Quine subsequently played on two tracks on the album. 'I got home and Carole said, "Yeah, some guy named Tom *White* called who had a very gruff-sounding voice." I thought that was hilarious. She didn't know who he was, but they had this great conversation. I was bummed I didn't get to record with him. That album was *Rain Dogs*.'

●
●

Frisell's association with John Zorn continued. In 1986 he was part of a thirteen-piece ensemble of downtown musicians that recorded one of Zorn's first film soundtracks, a score for Sheila McLaughlin's controversial *She Must Be Seeing Things* – 'the story of love and obsession between a lesbian film-maker and her lover, whose jealousy reaches near psychotic proportions'. Frisell plays soulful, if sometimes lopsided, blues guitar throughout.

He was also in two of the groups Zorn assembled to record music the composer had written for *Cynical Hysterie Hour*, four short films by Japanese cartoonist Kiriko Kubo. The animations proved ideal mediums for Zorn's mercurial methods: between the bells, barks, whistles, whoops and zaps, there were high-gear shifts in mood, style and tempo, including short clips of Frisell on down-home banjo and reverb-soaked surf guitar.

Far more renowned and revered, however, as well as sometimes slated, was Zorn's next conceptual art-music project: Naked City. Formed in May 1988 and comprising Zorn on alto, Frisell on guitar, Wayne Horvitz on keyboards, Fred Frith on bass, and Joey Baron on drums, plus Japanese experimental noise-rocker and primal screamer Yamatsuka Eye on vocals, Naked City was named after a 1945 book of graphic black-and-white images by fabled Lower East Side street photographer Weegee. Contrary to what many listeners believed at the time, the music Zorn wrote for Naked City was not at all random or chaotic. The dozens of quick-fire originals, and the select choice of reworked compositions by Ornette Coleman, John Barry, Henry Mancini and Claude Debussy, among others, may have whirled dizzyingly through different styles, but live sets and album recordings were carefully conceived, fully orchestrated and highly organised.

'The music was exciting and exhilarating, and fun, but it was also very, very intense, because for every thirty seconds of music there would be as many details as a serious classical piece or a long big-band chart,' says Joey Baron. 'Physically, for me, it was the most demanding thing I've ever done. There were cues in the music, and at times Zorn asked me to play as *loud* and as *fast* as I possibly could. John pushes people *right* to the edge, and then a little bit over. And it's not always comfortable. We each had moments where we were just fed up, because we were all doing things that we would *never* do, if left to our own devices. But it was an exercise in trust. We were all like, "Well, John's trusted in us to realise his vision of the music, and our responsibility is to repay it.'"

Naked City released five studio albums and one EP over a four-year period between the beginning of 1990 and end of 1993, and the twitchy kaleidoscope of styles and approaches is utterly astounding. Some critics and listeners found the music too scattershot and self-consciously posturing; it sometimes sounds like a manic mixtape compiled from the far reaches of Zorn's record collection. Yet Naked City brilliantly presaged our current age of excessive over-information, of split-second attention spans and random mix-and-match streaming, shuffling and channel surfing. 'You've got to realise speed is taking over the world,' Zorn said at the time.

You get the feeling that Frisell was selected by Zorn for Naked City precisely because, even then, and even within those diverse downtown circles, no other guitarist could have read his complex compositions that well, that fast, and have played in so many ways, in so many directions, so convincingly.

In return, for Frisell, Zorn was like a compulsive dare, a postmodern PhD, a confrontation with the outer extremes of his ability, taste and personality. Was this another adventure in, and intimation of, the dense and distilled sounds of The Frisell Dream?

'John got us all together. Naked City was one of those jackpot moments where all the right people hooked up at the right place, right time. I learned so much,' Frisell has said.

The band developed a cult reputation as an explosive and challenging live act that sometimes channelled Zorn's more disruptive inclinations and aesthetics. Provocation was taken a few stages further, for example, during an expanded Naked City concert in a suburban theatre in Paris in April 1992. With Arto Lindsay, Zorn conceived a music, spoken word and pornographic film 'opera' in celebration of the Marquis de Sade. The performance included the additional participation of American modern classical pianist Stephen Drury, versatile alt-metal vocalist and screamer Mike Patton, nearly naked Butoh dancer Keiko Konishi, and Lindsay himself reading erotic passages from de Sade's *The 120 Days of Sodom*. The Grand Guignol also involved two performance artists who joined the musicians on stage carrying various whips, chains and BDSM equipment. Frisell described the scene many years later in 2011, in a conversation with fellow guitarists Marc Ribot and Greg Leisz:

> **Frisell:** There was this dildo that was, like, three foot long, and Stephen Drury, he's concentrating, trying to play this incredibly complex [Charles Ives] piano music. And one of the dominatrices came over to him with this giant dildo and she's like . . . poking him. And then I'm playing, and one of the women is whipping me. And . . . there was this other woman. She took an SM57 microphone and she . . . you know . . . she pleasured herself with it [stunned silence, then laughter] . . . And the mic was turned up.
>
> **Ribot:** It was on! [more laughter]
>
> **Leisz:** What did it sound like?
>
> **Frisell:** Kind of a muffled sound.

'It's not that this is the only thing that makes a musician great, but Bill's one of these people who's just *instantly* recognisable,' says Mary Halvorson, who was born in 1980 and is probably the most original and acclaimed jazz guitarist of her generation. 'You know that sound and you know it's him. It's very expressive, and very emotional to me.'

Bill Frisell has what is widely known as, and most aspired to, in music: a *voice*. Every player will bring something unique to their instrument: a feel, a touch, a personality. But some musicians – a few – will do far more than that: they will transcend a particular vernacular, transcend the history and traditions of their instrument, transcend themselves. Composer, multi-instrumentalist and educator Anthony Braxton described the phenomenon like this: 'It's the ones who've put together their own language, their own syntax, their own way of being – these are the ones I'm interested in.'

Defining that voice and language, however, is more difficult, especially in someone as fully first-person as Frisell. He is one of those rare musicians who manages at all times to unequivocally sound only like himself, yet there is much about his sound that remains elusive and nebulous ('cloudy' is a word writers often employ when analysing his work). It's like he's speaking a foreign language you can understand but that causes you to miss things – all that is implied, understated or unsaid.

Frisell's sound operates in some kind of parallel reality, a world at once familiar and strange. There is something absorbingly abstract and elliptical about the way he communicates; it's like he expresses himself through figures of speech, most particularly, as Joni Mitchell once said of Wayne Shorter's playing, 'through metaphor'.

Wayne Horvitz once even went as far as denouncing such a literal search for definition and nomenclature in the music of Bill Frisell as 'an exercise in absurdity': 'What is amazing is that the guitar has been the defining instrument of the last fifty years, yet Bill has created his own distinct style in the face of – dare I say it? – too many guitar players.'

Critic Ben Ratliff recognised the wider challenge yet couldn't resist meeting it anyway. 'I mean "sound" as it has long functioned among jazz players, as a mystical term of art: as in, every musician finally needs a sound, a full and sensible embodiment of his [sic] artistic personality, such that it can be heard, at best, in a single note,' he wrote in his introduction to *Coltrane: The Story of a Sound*. 'Miles Davis's was fragile and pointed. Coleman Hawkins's was ripe and mellow and generous. John Coltrane's was large and dry, slightly undercooked, and urgent.'

So, what is Bill Frisell's sound? What are its qualities, and how might we possibly begin to put it into words?

Early attempts by critics to answer those questions seemed to coalesce around such concepts as 'rubbery', 'wobbly' and 'woozy'.

'Mr Frisell has extended the [Jim] Hall style by warping it – putting even wider leaps into smooth melodies, giving notes a countryish twang . . . floating a chord with a hint of electronic sustain,' wrote Jon Pareles in a 1987 review of Frisell's first appearance at the Village Vanguard, playing in a quartet led by Jim Hall himself. 'Together, they played whisper-quiet sets full of oblique lyricism.' *Warping. Oblique.*

The explanation of this sonic buckling and bending was rooted in something largely prosaic and mechanical. By this stage, Frisell had long swapped his (admittedly beloved) ES-175 for a very different type of Gibson: an SG, the solid and best-selling mahogany-bodied guitar that has been played by rockers ranging from George Harrison to Angus Young. Frisell's early seventies SG had a neck that was somewhat unsteady on its body – 'like a rubber band, pretty flexible,' Frisell told *Guitar Player* – which allowed him to add manual vibrato and chorusing by tugging it awkwardly back and forth. He could bring different notes in and out of tune – the guitar equivalent of 'touching your finger against the edge of an album while it spins on the turntable'. *Woozy.*

By 1997 journalists had assigned so many adjectives to the inscrutable Frisellian soundworld that Tom Junod, in a five-thousand-word feature on Frisell in American *GQ*, was able to cite a long roll call of interpretations. 'That sound – was it, as other writers have said, "bleary", "gnarled", "cinematic", "echoey" and "airbrushed"? Was it "oozing", "cloudy", "enveloping", "billowing", "mysterious", "melancholy", "giddy", "earthy", "frail", "pastoral", "metallic", "lilting" and "drizzly"? Well, sure – it was all those things, for if Bill's sound is anything, it's encompassing.' *Cloudy. Enveloping.*

Two years later music critic Tom Moon, in a piece titled 'The Language of the Guitar', took a far more visual and metaphorical approach. 'He slides and bends pitches as though careening around a racetrack,' wrote Moon. 'His downtempo pieces, which are beautifully plainspoken, suggest placid cornfields in fading light, or the muffled words of old-timers remembering when. In his hands, the guitar can be a buzz saw with a rusty blade, or a surgical needle, or a child laughing.'

The dilemma of how to best address and encapsulate Frisell's sound has remained the same ever since: where to stand on the spectrum between billowing clouds and a laughing child?

•
•

So what is the nature of the many mysteries that surround the Frisell sound? And are there some more concrete qualities that are a little easier to discern?

One perhaps is the 'hint of electronic sustain' that Jon Pareles detected in his *New York Times* review: the idea that Frisell seems to defy guitar gravity by making notes hang and glide in the air, like a bird of prey riding the thermals. It's like he breathes life into the guitar, makes it sound like a completely different instrument. The reason for this partly lies in the fact that he spent a decade playing two instruments other than the guitar: the clarinet and saxophone. Those instruments gave him the ability to sustain notes at will and for as long as he could hold them – then far longer still, once he'd learned the technique of circular breathing.

'Bill's phrasing is so interesting, because it's not only coming out of a guitar language, of all of his guitar heroes, like Hendrix,' trumpeter Dave Douglas told me, 'but you hear shades of what saxophone players do or trumpet players do – the bending of notes in unusual ways. Being able to put all that together in such a personal way is what makes a great artist.'

The sustain partly comes from Frisell's judicious use of effects: distortion boxes, loops and delays, compressions and echoes, and, of course, the volume pedal. But mostly, the sense of notes ringing out and having a life of their own – of them expanding and contracting, forming and fading – comes from Frisell's fingers and imagination alone. It's the reason he can achieve such results not just on electric guitar, but on acoustic as well.

Frisell once went to some lengths to explain his approach to guitar fingerings that 'allow notes to sustain simultaneously wherever possible' in a contribution to the first issue of John Zorn's *Arcana* series of musician essays on 'new music theory and practice'. Yet it largely remains a virtuosic ability, allied to a sensitivity of touch, that can leave his fellow guitarists agasp.

'It takes effort to bend one note into another,' Marc Ribot wrote in *BOMB* magazine. 'It takes enormous calculation to translate the pianistic harmonies Bill uses onto a six-stringed instrument. And every guitarist who has ever heard Frisell has wondered how he managed to get his guitar to produce notes that swelled in volume as they sustained, like a violinist or horn player, instead of steadily fading, like the notes on everyone else's guitar.'

That sense of breath in Frisell's sound, and the way he'll phrase a melody, have led some listeners to hear a strong vocal quality in his playing. It's something Frisell himself has increasingly recognised; when he plays music written by others, it often involves popular songs deeply imprinted with the mark of a particular artist with a particular lyric: Sam Cooke's 'A Change is Gonna Come', say, or Hank Williams's 'I'm So Lonesome I Could Cry'. It's as if Frisell is trying to mirror their vocal inflections and idiosyncrasies, capture the way the human voice can communicate the heart of a song, and bring the emotion to the surface by opening himself up.

'Sometimes my interpretation will spring from the words, even though I'm doing it instrumentally,' Frisell said in *JazzTimes*. 'Thinking about the words will bring this inner meaning to the thing when I play it and hopefully that will come out when someone is listening. I used to play this John Hiatt song, "Have a Little Faith in Me", and when I played it I was actually hearing his voice and words and I was trying to mimic that. Or when I played Aretha Franklin's "Chain of Fools", I totally tried to have my guitar be her voice.'

Because of this, the sound you often hear when Bill Frisell is playing is the sound of a melody, however true or twisted. It's like a version of the Joe Zawinul paradox, one of his guiding principles for the music of Weather Report: 'we always solo, we never solo'. Frisell never offers the grandstanding solo, the easy display of proficiency that generates a whooping applause. He is always playing and not playing the melody; the two are organically connected, so much so that you are often unsure where one ends and the other begins.

'It's not a stretch to put Bill in that category of musician who has transcended technique and innovation to just become so purely musical that only the song remains,' says singer-songwriter and producer Joe Henry. 'That's what you end up hearing: the song, the story, the movie that plays in your mind when you hear it.'

Frisell feels it is the melody that 'puts a tune in its own world', marks out its individuality and potential. 'Instead of discarding it, the melody stays in there and connects with your own voice,' Frisell said in 1998. 'Lately, I have been learning bluegrass tunes, and it amazes me how good bluegrass players will improvise around the shape of the melody . . . In the music of my favourite jazz players, I have always heard this approach. No matter how far Miles went, I could always hear that the melody was affecting what he was playing. Monk played the melody all the time.'

Frisell also tries to honour the architecture of a song, investigate its shape and structure; it's the reason he has played certain tunes again and again throughout his career – Henry Mancini and Johnny Mercer's 'Days of Wine and Roses', Thelonious Monk's 'Epistrophy', the nineteenth-century American folk song 'Shenandoah', Stephen Foster's 'Hard Times Come Again No More', 'Baba Drame' by Malian singer and guitarist Boubacar Traoré, and Lennon and McCartney's 'In My Life'.

It's the same with his own numerous compositions. Frisell wants to try to understand all the inner workings of a song, the nuances of its melody, the internal dynamics of its harmonies, the dimensions of its form and construction. Like great singers, he wants to internalise the song, play it from inside, feel that it is, as he once said, 'part of my bloodstream'. And then wholly make it his own, make it new.

'With his conception about melody and form, Bill's a real song player,' saxophonist Joe Lovano told the website *All About Jazz*. 'He can play the way he plays within any piece of music. A tune doesn't hold him back.'

.
.

The super-smart and many-sided guitarist Nels Cline tells a story about Bill Frisell trying out a new guitar in a music store in Seattle. 'The way I heard it is that it was a Saturday, late morning, so the store had probably just opened, and Bill was sitting in a corner playing a first-position C chord, and a first-position G chord, over and over again, really slowly on this guitar.

'And some hotshot guy – one of those annoying regular-customer guys that hang out in guitar stores – came up to him and said something to the effect of, "Oh yeah, man, that's cool, but hey, check this out!" And he took the guitar out of Bill's hands and started playing some kind of fancy crap. And Bill looked at him, and nodded, and smiled, and said, "Yeah, wow, that's great" – and got up and left.

'And the guys in the music store called the customer guy over and shouted at him, "Like, what the *fuck* is wrong with you? That was *Bill Frisell*!"'

Soprano saxophonist and composer Steve Lacy, who spent a lifetime exploring the music of Thelonious Monk, once said, 'you go through the complex to get to the simple', and another important attribute of the

Frisell sound is its deceptive simplicity. His guitar colours are the result of deep understanding and hard-won knowledge, and yet they have a vibrant clarity to them, as if the music has been distilled somehow and is naturally transparent, like water in a rock pool. It takes enormous skill and some daring to play as sparely and directly as Frisell does and yet retain all the subtleties, shades, implications and abstractions of a fuller form; 'expansive miniatures' is how violinist and singer Jenny Scheinman describes the interplay.

That process allows for another facet of Frisell's sound: its intrinsic sense of space. Partly this comes, as we have seen, from the way Frisell approaches speech and conversation: there are pauses, gaps, lacunae. It's the same with many musicians, especially improvisers: they play, and often aspire to play, like they talk.

'I think it . . . there's a natural . . . way I have of speaking . . . I hesitate and I think and I . . . it takes me a while to get . . . the thoughts formed in my mind and to get 'em to come out,' Frisell said, laughing, in 2010, in a video interview with website Big Think. 'And the same thing happens when I'm playing music. There's . . . I'm thinking and . . . there's . . . I'll hesitate or I'll . . . [five-second pause] . . . so there's a natural rhythm that I have that happens when I play. But then also, I mean, you can't just . . . the, the silence is . . . as important as the . . . you know, there's dark and light, and you can't see one or the other if . . . you know, they cancel each other out, so . . . I mean, if there's sound, there has to be . . . no sound, to go with it, before it will mean anything, I think, so.'

This is an archetypal Frisell response (and one that, rather unfairly, I've transcribed verbatim). But you can hear that, if it was put to music, it would sound very much like a Frisell composition or solo: a mix of statements, signals, suggestions . . . and space.

This sense of openness also derives from Frisell's economical approach to playing. Put simply, he uses far fewer notes than most instrumentalists, particularly other guitarists. Frisell maintains that he has never managed to develop the requisite technique to play pyrotechnically. He can play runs of fast notes when a melody demands or a stream of eighth notes to add dynamic contrast to a solo, but he is just not temperamentally, or even physically, manually, given to the showy, speedy or virtuosic: 'Sometimes I feel like whatever style I have is basically the inability to do something else,' he has often said.

'I like Charlie Parker, but I lean more to spaced-out stuff; it seems to fit with my bodily rhythms,' Frisell explained in *JazzTimes*. 'I discovered [early on] that by implying some notes, the sound became bigger rather than smaller. And I learned to leave enough space so that when you do play something it has more weight. That's something I've been working on ever since.'

Frisell often waits before he improvises; he is trying to make each note count and mean something, especially in relation to the music that has come before. There is an overarching sense of structure and connection, even when he is not playing.

'Bill's one of the few so-called jazz musicians I could name who I listen to every note he plays,' says Joe Henry. 'It's never for me a flurry that's just there to create expanse. I feel like every note and chord is so considered that it strikes my ears as conversation. It's just like someone's speaking voice, and that's a *completely* unique gift, I think. His sensibility is so unwaveringly sublime, and I can count on one hand how many musicians I think operate at that level, where just every choice they're making seems essential. Nothing about it, to my ear, seems gratuitous – he never just plays to take up space. He's only playing to amplify the drama of a moment.'

The pianist Jason Moran, who has played with Frisell in a variety of contexts, also uses a comparison from the world of art and line-making to describe the guitarist's soundworld. 'His approach is about making exactly the right etch into the plate,' Moran told me. 'In that way, he goes against the grain of how most guitarists play their instrument: his music is about economy, texture, and making each mark work. Bill is a genius at reducing the sound to one single note that has the power of three or four or more.'

Moran says he even gets the same sensation of space when Frisell plays more rapidly, more aggressively – when he 'shreds', to use the guitar vernacular. 'Bill shreds in a different way; it's a well-paced shred,' he says in the documentary *Bill Frisell: A Portrait*. 'But it also speaks volumes about what his sound is too, and his intention behind all the sounds he makes. It's an approach that's careful, and sensitive, and that I think separates him from the bunch – by a far distance.'

Frisell's dedication to using and respecting space in his music – for it being irreducibly part of his sound – goes further, however. Like Miles Davis, John Cage, Samuel Beckett and Mark Rothko, he is someone who seems to understand the profound presence and importance of silence – that music not only emerges from and returns to silence, but that it is shaped, charged and defined by it. 'Music is the silence between the notes,' Claude Debussy once famously declared.

In Thelonious Monk's music, silences are not simple caesuras; they are present, and part of the melody. It was Monk who said that 'what you don't play can be more important than what you do play'. It's a philosophy that has led many to see strong parallels in Frisell's sound, to him being described as 'the Thelonious Monk of the electric guitar'.

'There is a balance of powerfully oppositional forces, a sense of what I call "asymmetrical equilibrium", in both Monk's and Bill's music,' says David Breskin. 'It's there in the juxtaposition between melody and space, and between rough and smooth. There's a kind of beauty in Bill's playing, but, especially back then [in the eighties], there was also a kind of disorder, an anarchic feeling or danger in his playing, which I think Monk had too. Bill has that kind of idiosyncratic uniqueness that Monk had, that *voice*. He is of himself and only of himself, and there is a *world* in him. It's the difference between being a musician and being an artist.'

Dave Douglas also has a story about Bill Frisell. It involves Douglas driving home from a Frisell gig with his then nineteen-year-old stepson, a guitarist who is mostly 'into virtuosic instrumental metal players such as Yngwie Malmsteen'. 'I've been taking him to hear Bill since he was about eight years old, and he says, "Well, what . . . *Wow*. What . . . What the hell is Frisell *doing* up there?"

'And I go, "What do you mean?"

'And he says, "Well, it's so incredible, all the time, but he's hardly doing anything."' Douglas laughs. 'For me, that puts it perfectly; that's the whole point. I just said to him, "You nailed it! Yes. Correct. The secret's out."'

．
．

Those who feel a close connection to Frisell's music have a way of talking about his sound that is at once physical and visceral, tangible and intangible. One recurring idea is that his playing suggests solid bodies that are strong yet fragile, and are in constant motion.

'His music is very anchored and yet it can also feel like it's about to fall,' says Carole d'Inverno. 'It's like things are continually cantilevering.'

'When I think about Bill's sound, it's almost more like a *sculptural* thing, like a *shape* or a *feeling*,' says Mary Halvorson, accenting certain words in the way she might one of her inimitable solos. 'It's hard for me to put it into words, because it's very *complex*, and it feels like he's gotten to something that nobody else has gotten to. There's *a lot* of feeling and emotion expressed through his music, which I think *many, many* people connect with.'

Jason Moran agrees. 'Bill builds these forms that rise up, and then come tumbling down – and then are lain on their sides,' he says. 'He's like a Zen architect; he makes these structures that, as a player, you have multiple doors into.'

The same can be said for Frisell's listeners. For many, the Frisell sound is an echo and reverberation of his particular personality, its dimensions and complexities, its constructions and alleyways. Others talk about the honesty and humility in that sound, an integrity and generosity, a world of freedom and possibility.

'He's got a lot of layers,' says Claudia Engelhart, Frisell's tour sound engineer and perhaps the ultimate Frisell listener. 'Yeah, he has ego – he's a performer, he's on stage, and he loves it when people clap – but he's also the most humble person I know. He's very at one with who he is and what he's doing. And I think that's rare.'

Bill Frisell's sound, like the music in The Frisell Dream, creates a world that is powerfully direct and yet beautifully infinite. It's like Frisell is a facilitator, the guardian of a precious space that values participation above performance, group contribution above individual expression, and the dynamics of trust, change, progress and discovery above all else. It is music as a healing force, something larger than itself. Music, as Frisell has stated on a number of occasions, is good.

'He knows exactly what he wants out of his music,' Joey Baron told *Jazziz*, 'but the thing that's really great about it is that he lets people explore what they want to do with it first. That one little stage of letting the person do what they would do under their own judgement – that's really generous. He's willing to go down the road to explore where that takes you.'

It's as if Frisell is saying, 'This is my contribution, this is what I've written, and this is what I mean by this music.' But after that, he actively encourages band members to augment and amplify the music, to reshape and transform it in ways he could never have imagined; he wants and champions this as part of the process, as part of his fellow musicians taking some control, as part of the adventure, the mystery.

It works the same way when Frisell is collaborating with others, with their vision. That open-hearted generosity is there again: his sound makes the overall sound more spacious and boundless; he is there to support and advance, but also to open up unexpected horizons and new possibilities.

'He is so big-hearted, so invariably and authentically kind, and you can't miss it, but it surprised me,' says Joe Henry. 'I just don't expect most musicians to be that uniquely . . . emotionally available. And, of course, once you register that, you understand that what you're predominantly hearing in Bill's playing and sound, in his music, is a deep empathy and real compassion.'

•
•

At the end of a gig many years ago, a fan of Dave Holland's wonderfully vibrant and lyrical playing came up to him, pointed to his double bass, which was lying on its side on the stage, and proclaimed, 'Wow, your bass sounds wonderful, man.' Saying nothing, Holland bent down, cradled his ear to the instrument and, smiling, replied, 'Really? I can't hear anything.'

The song of Bill Frisell is ultimately, of course, not the sound of his guitar at all. It is the sound of his mind and body and intelligence and imagination; as Irish fiddle maestro Martin Hayes told me, 'Music doesn't come from your instrument; it comes from you.' The challenge is to move beyond the guitar, the song, the genre, even the music itself, and play thoughts and feelings and ideas – to play yourself, and then play beyond yourself.

'Bill has this huge vision for what music could be, what a melody could be, what rhythm could set things in motion in a lot of different ways,' says Tony Scherr. 'He's got a really . . . huge range of possibilities and expansive ideas. It's a world in itself, a world within a world.'

That vision was always there, it seems. 'He could open a gate that not everyone can,' says Steve Houben, who played with Frisell both in Berklee and Belgium in the late seventies. 'I don't want to talk too much about the philosophy of it, or mention chakras, but Bill not only has a wonderful intellect and imagination, he also has something that he can open that allows the music to flow through him. It's all there in the way he is and the way he sounds. And that's rare.'

And it remains there, whatever the circumstances. In 2014, during a concert at the SFJAZZ Center in San Francisco, Frisell was an hour into a set with his free-flowing quintet of violinist Jenny Scheinman, violist Eyvind Kang, cellist Hank Roberts and Rudy Royston on drums when the main power supply went out. Having already borrowed a Gibson acoustic guitar from his longstanding producer and manager Lee Townsend, who was in the audience, Frisell and his unplugged quartet played on, under the venue's emergency lighting, completing the concert to enthusiastic applause.

Claudia Engelhart was, of course, there – listening from a redundant soundboard. 'It was beautiful, and it sounded totally like him,' she says. 'That's how strong he is, how solid, and stubborn – there's no moving him, you know. That's where his power is, because he can transcend *any-thing* and *any* kind of music in *any* kind of situation. No matter what, it's always going to sound like Bill.'

Two days after Christmas 1985 Carole gave birth to a baby girl, Monica Jane. Bill was thirty-four, Carole twenty-nine. 'I can't really remember how we arrived at it, but, somehow, as soon as she was born,' says Bill, 'it was clear to both of us that Monica was to be her name.' Jane was Bill's mother's middle name, the one she came to be known by.

The family went back to their apartment in Hoboken, and a year or so later Robin Holcomb and Wayne Horvitz moved into the building with their daughter, Nica, who was just five months younger than Monica. The families became close and spent a good deal of time together.

'In some ways Monica being born didn't change things because Bill was working so hard – although, of course, he did try to stay at home more,' says Carole. 'But in other ways I think it was really empowering for him, as a man. It made him face up to an extra sense of responsibility and commitment, not just to Monica and to me, but also to his music. I think Monica, this new human being, really focused him, and pushed him much harder. He was like, OK, now I *have* to do this music – my music, my band, my guys.'

Frisell has admitted that Monica coming into the world was a crucial catalyst for change. 'It wasn't until the mid-eighties that I was able to commit to having my own band,' he said in *DownBeat*. 'I connect that with my daughter being born. There were years and years of looking forward to that, [then] her being born and the band being born at the same time. I had this feeling like I was growing up. And that was where, I guess, I gradually started gaining confidence in writing music.'

The next few years were to prove exceptionally busy for Frisell and, driven by an inbuilt sense of dedication and duty, and his belief in the value of hard work, he was to enjoy unprecedented opportunities and success.

But with that newfound attention and profile often came intense pressure, both external and internal. Frisell, an anxious and introspective soul, sometimes found it overwhelming and difficult to cope – to live up to the extremely high standards he had set himself as a player, composer, leader, husband, father and provider. His music and creativity may have fed off such stresses and tensions. His body and his health, however, would suffer.

•
•

To some extent the members of the Bill Frisell Band chose themselves. Two were fellow string players whom Frisell had first met and gigged with at Berklee a decade before: bassist Kermit Driscoll and cellist Hank Roberts.

Driscoll had played a pivotal role during Frisell's time in Belgium, especially as a champion of his early compositions. The two musicians had become great friends during their time in Spa, both meeting their future wives in Chapati. Driscoll had been encouraging Frisell to form his own band almost from the moment they first started playing together.

Frisell had strongly reconnected with Roberts after Hank had moved back to New York in 1981 and begun playing with Tim Berne and John Zorn. Roberts had also decided to rent in suburban New Jersey, and he and his wife Jane spent a lot of time with Bill and Carole. They had a young son, Jake, and a daughter, Mary, who was three months older than Monica.

Frisell was looking to play with musicians he was comfortable with, whom he fundamentally trusted, who were loyal friends, for whom, and from whom, he felt, as he admitted to Jonathan Coe in *The Wire* in 1989, a deep sense of love.

Another of those connections, both immediate and enduring, was to drummer Joey Baron, whom he had met more recently in New York, at the end of 1983. Both musicians were called for a large ensemble session led by pianist and composer Kenny Werner at the SoHo loft and home studio of pianist Fred Hersch.

'I kept hearing about this guy Joey Baron . . . it was sort of like Lovano [in Boston], like a word out on the street,' Frisell told Ethan Iverson. Baron had studied briefly at Berklee and mostly been living in Los Angeles, playing with musicians such as Carmen McRae, Teddy Edwards and Chet Baker. 'Lovano knew him, Billy Drewes knew him. Lot of people that I knew, knew Joey.'

The Werner recording was somewhat confused and chaotic (and was never released), with a lot of musicians crammed into a small space. 'Joey and I had just barely met, but there was this moment where I could see him across the room in the drum booth, all this stuff going on, trying to hear each other and just play something decent; this moment where he played a backbeat, just at the perfect moment, that just made everything gel together,' Frisell explained. 'We looked at each other across the room through the glass, and we just smiled at each other, and that was the moment.'

It was something like love-at-first-sound. 'Everybody experiences it – you're around someone and you just click,' says Baron. 'You think on the same wavelength, you share a common philosophy, and you don't have to talk about it, you just know. You just *know*. It's nothing really special, other than it's really special when it happens.'

Soon after, Bill and Joey got together one afternoon in Baron's down-town building to play, just the two of them. They played free, improvising for hours on end. And they did it many times over. 'Joey and I, we were really, really hooking up strong,' said Frisell.

Baron admits that when he moved to New York he was 'a little bit of a jazz snob', a drummer dedicated to a very definite style and approach. 'I wanted to play like . . . 4/4 . . . jazz . . . swinging type music, with an upright bass player, and playing repertoire, like songs that have a form. That's what made me want to play in the first place, to play with the greats in that idiom, and develop it as far as I could. Because that allowed the drums the most freedom I had ever heard in any genre.' He pauses. 'And then I met Bill.'

Frisell invited Baron to hear a band at Chandelier with Bill on guitar,

John Zorn on alto, Dave Hofstra on bass and Bobby Previte on drums. On one level, a conventional jazz quartet: saxophone, guitar, rhythm section. On another level, a powerhouse of improvising equals and experimenters hell-bent on deconstructing the very notion and hierarchy of a conventional group of any genre: downtown musicians as Schrödinger (jazz) cats.

'I went to the gig and halfway through this guy comes up and he says, "Hey, can I sit in?" And everybody was like real positive and said, "Sure!"' says Baron. 'Then he took out his guitar, and he started making a whole lot of . . . I didn't know what it was, but it didn't make sense to me, and I just got so *pissed*. Bill gave me a ride home, and I was just like really . . . *bugged*, and I said, "Man, who was that asshole that came in and *ruined* the set?" And Bill says, "Oh, you mean Arto [Lindsay]? He's one of my heroes!"'

Soon after Frisell played at Roulette in a duo with Ikue Mori on drums, drum machines and samples. 'That also *totally* screwed me up,' says Baron, laughing. 'Because, from my perspective, I couldn't see that she was doing *anything*. But gradually I began to re-examine things. I was never really a downtown musician, but I started to think, "Oh, wait a minute, something else is going on here."'

Frisell connected Baron to such players as Tim Berne, Hank Roberts, Herb Robertson and eventually John Zorn. Baron first recorded with Zorn in 1988 on *Spy vs Spy*, Zorn's exploration of the music of Ornette Coleman as seen through the prism of short, sharp 'hardcore miniatures', the form that he would develop further in Naked City, of which Baron would be a vital part.

•
•

In the spring of 1986 Frisell asked Hank Roberts to come over to his apartment. 'He told me he was going to start a band, and so I think he kind of wanted to do, like, a formal audition – not that he said that's what it was,' says Roberts, smiling. 'He brought out some tunes, and the two of us played them, and that was my audition. I actually have a tape recording of that session somewhere; you can hear Monica, with Carole, in the background.'

Over the next few months the quartet rehearsed, playing some standards, particularly tunes by Thelonious Monk, but mostly learning and developing Frisell's new compositions, music he had written specifically for these musicians and this band.

This was a major moment for Frisell and he was determined to bring together everything he'd learned playing and collaborating with others. 'I'm trying to distil all these different situations that I've played in, what I've learned from all these people, and hopefully some kind of interesting mixture comes out, without sounding too derivative,' said a self-effacing Frisell shortly before the band's debut album was released in March 1988.

Frisell was not looking to be a frontman, or seeking sidemen. He was looking for equals, musicians he could look up to, who would stretch and challenge him, who were in service to each other, to the group, to the one sound – but at the same time open to expanding the music in any direction, at any moment. It has been the Frisell group paradigm ever since.

'When Bill formed the band,' says Kermit Driscoll, 'he said to us – and this is really important, because it changed my life – "There are no limits. Whatever you learned playing your first polka gig, or in a country band, where they were throwing beer bottles and cans at you" . . . and I could remember those gigs; at the end of the night there would be broken beer bottles and blood all over the place . . . "or Charles Ives, or whatever. It's all OK. Don't think about jazz. Jazz is OK, too. But bring everything you've ever experienced to this band."'

Joey Baron's view of the philosophy of the group was similar. 'It was a very exciting band to be a part of – just so encouraging, and very interactive; we all had a common goal,' he says. 'There were no roles within the band *per se*, unless we chose them. Nothing was dictated. So there was a certain sense of, wow, I can bring what I've got, whatever's in my background, into this situation, and it won't be judged. Bill brought his music, but again nothing was explicit – some tunes had song forms, others were just melodies. For me personally, it was one of the most liberating musical experiences I've had.'

Like many musicians, Hank Roberts saw the group as a quasi-family unit. 'Bill was the leader, a strong leader, but also very open, and we were a band of four brothers, who were together, and there was absolutely no ego or anything like that,' says Roberts. 'We were just all like, "Man! This is my family, and I'm gonna give this *everything* I can. It's going to be one of my highest priorities."

'We got together and had dinner, and cooked together, and cried together, and hung out together, and helped each other; I mean, we were family. Same with Joey and his wife Leslie. We all hung out. And Kermit and Michelle, his wife. Maybe that's one of the things about Bill – that when you're with him, in his band, the concept of love is there. Not in a kind of flimsy way. It's more about a level of respect and caring about each other, you know, in a sincere way.'

Before he had finalised the band and its line-up, and started looking for gigs, Frisell had already demonstrated that care and respect in the most sympathetic yet direct way. Kermit Driscoll had always been a serious social drinker (almost the first words he said to Frisell when they met on Bill's second day at Berklee in 1975 were, 'Wanna go for a beer?'), and that propensity had continued in Belgium. 'Back then I was pretty much oblivious to it, because I was doing it too,' says Frisell. 'We were just young, and we'd wake up and have a beer, or something. It just seemed normal.'

That routine gradually began to spin out of control after Kermit moved to New York in 1980. Driscoll's drink problem was the reason that Jerome Harris had played bass on *Rambler*. 'I think his hesitation,' Driscoll admits, 'was that, "Goddam, I don't know if Kermit's going to be drunk or not," you know.'

Despite several candid conversations between the two men, the situation seemed to be getting worse. Finally, Frisell went to see Driscoll. He desperately wanted him to be in any future band he was putting together.

'Kermit had played a big part in me getting to this point,' says Frisell. 'He was like a cheerleader for me to do my own music, from early on, when I had no confidence at all. I owed him a lot.' But more than that, he wanted his friend to find a way to stop drinking.

Kermit Driscoll described the conversation to me in 2017:

KD: Bill told me, he said, like, 'You either stop drinking, or you'll never see me again.' Yeah. That's what made me stop.

PW: Wow, that's heavy. That's a strong thing to say to anyone.

KD: It's the best thing to say. It's the only thing to say . . . Everything else was bullshit . . . People helping you out; it doesn't help. What you think is help, is not. It takes somebody to be that honest. He said, 'I'm tired of seeing you killing yourself.'

PW: That's some intervention.

KD: No shit. No shit. Yeah. That's Bill Frisell. That's the kind of person he is.

PW: So for all those years [almost a decade] when you were playing in the band . . .

KD: . . . I was sober. Yeah, yeah. I never played a gig drunk with Bill. Or high. Or anything. I never drank on the tours, never. On the records, never. All those years. Completely straight . . . I was going to AA, and I was into the whole thing. For seven years I even led AA meetings as a volunteer at the [Bergen County] jail in Hackensack.'

•
•

At first, Frisell couldn't get gigs for his new project; it was a working band without any work. Then he managed to secure some dates in Boston, where he still had a good name and music venue owners were more willing to take a chance. The very first gig the Bill Frisell Band played was at the 1369 Jazz Club, where Frisell had been playing with D. Sharpe; other gigs at Ryles, where Paul Motian's band debuted, and the Middle East followed.

In New York Frisell met much greater resistance: he had no track record as a leader, and wasn't well known enough for established jazz clubs such as the Village Vanguard, Blue Note and Sweet Basil, or for noted rock venues such as CBGB or the Bottom Line; even some downtown spaces, which paid very little, seemed reluctant.

'Bill would strategise,' says Carole. 'He would think to himself, "Well, you know, if I play with so-and-so as a sideman, maybe I can get one set with my band at the same time, even if it's five in the morning." And if he did, often he would pay those guys and come back with no money for himself. But at least he would have had that one set. And then, pretty soon, people started hearing what he was trying to do.'

During 1986 the Bill Frisell Band played as many gigs as Frisell could organise, sometimes at Fat Tuesday's in Gramercy Park, and more frequently at West Village club Visiones, where he was already appearing with Paul Motian.

'I would go hear Bill at Visiones and other little New York clubs, and his music was *huge* for me,' says Dave Douglas. 'He was writing in a way that combined a lot of different elements, and that really opened up a canvas to me – a way of thinking about creating music for a group of improvisers, within the framework of form, that was clearly coming out of straight-ahead jazz, but going towards something else, something new. It was hard not to be blown away by it.'

Frisell felt the quartet was ready to record. Manfred Eicher agreed to an album being made for ECM, but wasn't committing to a date. Eventually production was entrusted to the label's US general manager, Lee Townsend. Townsend had been working for ECM since 1984, had overseen the American release of *Rambler*, and had developed a good relationship with Frisell. That partnership was to flourish: Townsend has produced almost all of Frisell's thirty-five or so subsequent albums as leader (and many others on which Frisell has collaborated) and, with his wife, Phyllis Oyama, runs Songtone, the company that, in a couple of permutations, has managed Bill's creative and business affairs since 1988.

In March 1987 the band went into the Power Station studios in Hell's Kitchen to record its debut album, *Lookout for Hope*. The album, released a year later, is a remarkable achievement, a summation and synthesis of Frisell's many deep and diverse influences up to that point, yet also feels, even today, startlingly original and new. It feels like the start of Frisell as serious agent of change.

Lookout for Hope is partly personal: the waltzing country reggae of 'Little Brother Bobby' is named for Frisell's younger sibling; the modern march of 'Melody for Jack' salutes Joey Baron's father, who had recently died. The album also has intimations of some of Frisell's primary infuences. There is the melodic clarity and compositional depth of the title track, which slides skilfully from backbeat to swing, rock to avant-garde, harmony to dissonance in a way that would have made Mike Gibbs proud. And in 'Remedios the Beauty', named after the enigmatic and ethereal anti-heroine in Gabriel García Márquez's novel *One Hundred Years of Solitude*, the dark, metal-edged carousel of sounds owes something to the compositional boldness of Tim Berne.

The record was, however, too capricious for some. In the *Penguin Guide to Jazz Recordings*, Cook and Morton concluded that *Lookout for Hope,* and its predecessor *Rambler,* 'suffer from a certain waywardness of focus and a lack of real drive and centre'. In *The Wire*, Steve Lake described the album as 'a mixed bag', and the group 'sometimes too cute for its own good', singling out 'Little Brother Bobby' as a case of a Frisell composition that 'fails to take up a position anywhere, a common complaint in the eighties'. Perhaps Frisell *was* trying to do too much with the album, to offer too much in one sitting. Yet, somehow the record coheres, primarily because of the remarkable levels of group interplay, affinity and understanding.

'One reason that album, and that band, had something special was because of Bill's immense talents, the level of skill involved,' says Hank Roberts. 'He plays what he hears, and he hears a lot; he's open to a wide range of music, and it sometimes seems he can play *anything*.

'But then there's also Bill's other more spiritual side, of being able to give, his unique kind of integrity, humility and humanity, which also created a tremendous amount of energy and empathy in the group. Yeah, Bill just carried some benevolent good vibes.'

Baron felt the force too. 'That's one of the greatest things that I've ever experienced – that sense of trust and generosity. Technically, it was Bill's band, but I don't think any of us realised that. We all thought it was *our* band.'

⋮

While Frisell was both committing to his own band and adapting to his new role as a father, a plethora of other opportunities continued to come his way.

Most high profile was a recording for ECM with one of Frisell's musical idols, Canadian pianist Paul Bley. As part of a new quartet brought together by Bley and producer Manfred Eicher, Frisell was teamed with Paul Motian and English saxophonist and clarinettist John Surman. The album was made at Rainbow Studio in Oslo in mid-January 1986, just two weeks or so after Monica was born.

There was no rehearsal and little discussion about the music; all that was required was that each musician brought some original compositions to the session. 'We'd go in the studio and everything is ready to go and we just started improvising and that's what you hear,' Frisell told *DownBeat*. 'The first notes you hear on that record are some of the very first notes we played together.'

The result, released in October that year, was *Fragments*, a remarkable achievement in the circumstances, and a testament to the mastery and empathy of each player. Frisell contributes one new tune, 'Monica Jane' (the title was suggested by Motian), a tender and wistful ballad that would become another Frisell favourite.

Frisell sounds at times, perhaps understandably in such company, timid and tentative; he was, after all, collaborating with a pianist who had played with Charlie Parker, Sonny Rollins *and* Ornette Coleman, as well as many other modern jazz legends. Yet on Surman's 'Line Down', the more allusive and meditative mood changes abruptly into something far darker, louder and free, Frisell firing thunderous bass notes and avant-rock screeches behind Surman's blazing baritone. And on Motian's elegant ballad 'For the Love of Sarah', played as a delicate duet between Frisell and Surman on bass clarinet, the interplay seems immediate and instinctive.

'The first thing you have to note about Frisell's playing is that he plays the electric guitar at the level of an acoustic instrument,' says Surman. 'It's easier to have a more intimate dialogue with someone who plays at that dynamic level, and Bill and I seemed to be able, with an eye on each other, to connect notes together, and create small themes in unison.'

Bley was so taken by the recording that he decided to reconvene the group as the Paul Bley Quartet for a five-and-a-half-week European tour in October the following year, to be followed by a return to Rainbow Studio to record a second album.

As Steve Lake captures in his insightful ECM liner notes to *Fragments,* Bley is a pianist greatly admired for his 'forcefully unemphatic' style, how he makes 'sense of improvisation as spontaneous composition', and both qualities were cornerstones of the tour. None of the music from *Fragments* was played again. In fact, each performance was almost entirely improvised; one musician would begin, and the music would develop organically, freely, in and out of time and tonality, from there.

The record, simply titled *The Paul Bley Quartet*, was recorded in Oslo in November 1987, and released in March of the following year. The contrast with its predecessor is startling; there are splinters of melodic lines and hints of harmonic ideas, a bluesy abstraction here and there, but the music mostly progresses through its many moods and movements naturally, as if by design, like colour patterns in a coral reef.

At times Frisell seems wholly liberated, positively unrestrained. On the aptly titled 'Heat', for example, Frisell releases a series of molten and climaxing shrieks, skronks, smudges and distortions that sound like Jimi

Hendrix channelling English free improviser Derek Bailey. It's a startling two-minute shred – still connected, however loosely, to an implied sense of tempo and tune – like few others in the Frisell catalogue.

⦙

Frisell tested himself in many other ways during this same period. In 1986 he was asked to play in a guitar duet with another of his musical heroes and mentors, Jim Hall. Frisell had bumped into Hall in Greenwich Village a couple of years after moving to New York. Even though it was a decade since Frisell had taken those eight lessons with him in 1972, Hall remembered him clearly. The following year, Bill sent him his debut album, *In Line*.

'It was suddenly like all this time had gone by, but he immediately called me and said, "Wow." He was really impressed with what I'd done,' said Frisell. 'He said, "You were taking lessons from me, and now I want to take lessons from you. Now I can learn from you."'

It is yet another example of the Frisell paradox, how underneath all the soft-spoken shyness there exists a steely strength and resolve, a wilful desire to place himself in creative situations that will confront and challenge him the most. A performance with one of his greatest influences and inspirations would certainly do just that.

'For me to play duo with Jim, that was a huge deal, just playing the music with him, and being on stage with him – it was such a beautiful and intense experience, and it blows my mind even now,' he says. 'The following year, he asked me to play a week with him at the Vanguard, in a quartet with Joey [Baron] and Steve LaSpina on bass – and that really was the opening door to getting my own gig at the club.'

In April 1989 Frisell featured for the first time on the cover of *Down-Beat*, America's leading 'jazz, blues and beyond' magazine. Shortly afterwards Max Gordon, founder and owner of the Village Vanguard, offered him a date in the hallowed basement room; sadly, Gordon was to die just a few weeks afterwards. Four months later, neatly bookending an extraordinary decade in which he'd progressed from New Jersey nobody to significant Manhattan somebody, Frisell had reached the pinnacle of New York jazz credibility: a week under his own name, as leader of his own band, at the world's most famous jazz club.

The club had its doubts, however. Lorraine Gordon, Max's widow, had taken over the running of the club. She and general manager Jed Eisenman had heard *Lookout for Hope* and also listened to the band's second album, the recently released and equally open-eared *Before We Were Born*. They were worried the music might be too edgy and esoteric, too downtown for a Vanguard audience expecting to hear something approaching Jim Hall or Pat Metheny. 'I didn't think we could get away with presenting Bill when he first played there; Max hired him and I thought, "This is gonna flop,"' Eisenman has said. 'The bebop people were not all that pleased. They still don't think Bill is coming out of Wes Montgomery.'

The week, however, was a great success, partly because Frisell and the quartet quickly adapted to the especially sympathetic acoustics of the space; they played the room. 'The Village Vanguard,' Frisell told author Barry Singer, 'is like playing inside this strange, beautiful old instrument that all these amazing people have played before you.' A few months later, Frisell was booked for a second run, in May 1990.

There were many other gigs, both in East Village *boîtes* and European concert halls, with musicians within the various circles he had moved into, from Paul Motian and Marc Johnson, to John Zorn and Tim Berne, and larger ensembles led by Mike Gibbs, Carla Bley and Charlie Haden. 'He was just like a sponge, wanting to be exposed to as many things as possible,' says David Breskin.

Against almost every aspect of his personal and musical nature, Frisell also continued to severely test himself by playing solo gigs. He had first played on his own in a small loft space on Boylston Street in Boston in 1983, mostly improvising and playing his own music; D. Sharpe had set up the gig. 'Talk about scared,' Frisell said a couple of years later. 'There was no reason to be scared; there weren't that many people there, and they were all friendly. But it was hard. I probably learned more in that one hour than I have in a long time . . . I did have crutches, like a rhythm machine and a Casio doing a drone. But it was challenging.'

The experience led Frisell to explore the possibilities of using other effects in solo performance: from digital delays and distortion boxes to drum machines and guitar synthesisers, as well as developing a repertoire that he felt worked in such a setting.

Over the next few years he played solo concerts in New York, mostly at Roulette, at the Great American Music Hall in San Francisco, and at various festivals in Europe. At the 1986 Vancouver International Jazz Festival in Canada, his solo performance was filmed and there is a four-minute clip showing an uncomfortable-looking Frisell overlaying melodic sketches, ringing harmonics and electronic echoes and quirks; at the beginning, while he sets up various reverbs and loops, he can mostly be seen frantically fiddling with knobs.

There were many other recordings, too. Frisell played a pivotal role on downtown drummer Bobby Previte's rhythmically rich and compositionally vivid *Claude's Late Morning*, and, with Hal Willner producing, provided banjo and assorted guitars to Dutch singer Mathilde Santing's *Out of This Dream*. He was reunited with Lyle Mays for the keyboardist's second solo record, the eighties fusion extravaganza *Street Dreams*, and again with John Zorn for *Rodan*, an album of improvisations 'directed and produced' by Zorn that spotlighted Sato Michihiro, a Japanese player of the Tsugaru-shamisen (a traditional three-string, long-neck, fretless banjo-like lute).

Frisell's downtown connections also brought him to *Todos Santos*, a collection of instrumental pieces written by Robin Holcomb featuring on three tracks a delicate new music duet of Frisell and Doug Wieselman on tenor and clarinet; and to *Greed*, the second album of Arto Lindsay and keyboardist Peter Scherer's cult art-funk-pop-samba group Ambitious Lovers. There was even music for catwalks – Frisell appeared on Seigen Ono's intrepid *Comme des Garçons*, which featured music originally commissioned by the luxury Japanese label of the same name for a 1987 fashion show.

In 1988 Frisell calculated he had performed in twenty-nine different configurations – in that twelve-month period alone. 'This was a time when Bill was so busy and doing so much – he was just unbelievable,' says Nels Cline. 'God, I can't even remember all the different things he was doing. I do remember seeing him periodically around this time, though, and he was literally ashen.'

That appearance may have been because, during this period, and into the early nineties, Bill Frisell became unwell. He began to break out in hives, or urticaria, a type of skin rash with red raised bumps and welts ranging in size from small spots to large blotches that would appear all over his body and itch, or sometimes burn or sting. 'It was like an allergic reaction, as a result of some kind of pressure that was coming from this deep muscle ache,' he says. And while he had hives, his joints would also be painful. 'When it was at its worst, any kind of activity . . . if I picked up something, my hand would swell up. If I went for a walk, my feet would swell up,' says Frisell.

He also suffered from a kind of chronic fatigue; there were discussions with doctors that he might have the Epstein–Barr virus. 'My strength and energy levels would come in and out in waves. First it was almost a whole year of this hell, and then it sort of went away. And then it would flare up again.'

All this was happening while, or possibly because, Frisell was maintaining a demanding work schedule. 'I was still doing the gigs, and going on tour, even in Europe, but I just felt so horrible, and sometimes it was really hard to make it through,' he says. 'I remember on stage with Naked City, I sat down for a whole tour, because I couldn't even stand up. Same thing happened at the Knitting Factory. But when it really hit me, I was on a tour of western Canada with Kermit and Joey, in Edmonton, I think, and I lay down on the floor and I literally couldn't get up. I just had to cancel the gigs and go home. Then in our apartment building in Hoboken, I sometimes couldn't walk up the stairs. It was just an incredibly difficult time physically . . . for quite a number of years.'

As with many such cases, clinicians could not find a direct trigger.

It seems likely there were multiple factors, including Frisell's immediate environment: Wayne Horvitz, living in the same apartment block in Hoboken as Frisell, began to exhibit similar symptoms of fatigue. 'The notion that it might have been something environmental is not all that wild a speculation in the midst of eighties industrial north New Jersey,' says Horvitz. 'I love New York, but at the time I was having a real hard time with the noise and the constant hassle. I also think, for Bill and I, the stress of just trying to balance everything with the kids and all the touring was a factor.'

Perhaps for Frisell the hives and fatigue were physical manifestations of some new inner unease, of how much his world and his place within it had been reordered, of quite how much he was responsible for, and how much he cared. It was complex, diligent and dogged Bill Frisell doing his best to move as morally and truthfully, both as a person and artist, as he could through the world. And meeting a resistance, possibly of his own making.

'It's really interesting,' says Carole. 'I think when Bill's in the music, and he's working with it, and he puts all his energy into it – that's what he lives for. It's his catharsis. But when he steps out of the music, then all the anxiety – I mean, he's extremely anxious, all the time – can come back. He'll feel that he's never going to be good enough, that he's never really going to figure it all out.'

Carole says that Bill has tried to determine what supports and sustains him through these periods. 'He grew up with his father's example, which was very much about being committed, and about following what his parents called the Golden Rule: "Do unto others as you would have them do unto you" – that you have to be always kind, that anger is not necessarily something that is useful. So I think he feels that if he acts like that, in as constantly positive way as he can, it cushions some of the anxiety. As does his connection to the web of people he's created around him, people he feels extremely close to, even if he's not with them physically. But at the same time that dark hole is always there. He's always circling it, and sometimes he falls in, and then he has to spiral up again.'

Frisell continued to try to find a medical solution to his problems. 'I went to all kinds of doctors, all kinds of quack doctors, and I was drinking, like, peroxide,' he says. 'I never did figure out what was going on. I don't know if it was the tension of having a kid, or something, and the feeling of . . . you know, wanting to do the right thing for Monica and stuff. I was also still sort of smoking, on and off, mostly on tour in Europe – I gave up in the summer of 1988 – so maybe that didn't help.

'And even though I was doing lots of things, I was still struggling with just trying to make a living. Playing with Paul Motian . . . there was never any doubt that was the right thing to do; I was committed to that, until the day he died. But sometimes I'd do other gigs where I wasn't completely happy about the music, or I'd got pulled by some money or offer or something, and my heart wasn't totally in it, and Carole will tell you, that's where it's a super-dangerous thing for me and I get in deep trouble.

'Really, what I wanted to do . . . was my own music.'

By the end of 1989 Bill Frisell, aged thirty-eight and seemingly on top of the world, was burnt out. It was time to make a change.

13: The Bad Plus Listens to *Where in the World?*

Where in the World?: recorded Woodstock, New York, October 1990 and
New York City, February 1991; producer Wayne Horvitz; released
on Elektra Nonesuch, October 1991; Bill Frisell (guitars, ukulele),
Hank Roberts (cello, jazz-a-phone fiddle), Kermit Driscoll
(basses), Joey Baron (drums); all compositions by Frisell.

Up until 2021 the Bad Plus was a jazz piano trio in much the same
way that Cream was a guitar rock band. Self-proclaimed as 'constantly
searching for rules to break and boundaries to cross, bridging genres and
techniques', the equilateral triangle of bassist Reid Anderson, pianist
Ethan Iverson and drummer David King came together in Minneapolis,
Minnesota, 'at the end of the twentieth century'. With a complex Venn
diagram of influences that included classical, indie rock, pop, prog, electronica, noise, heavy metal and punk – with a deep and wide-ranging
love of jazz at its intersecting centre – the Bad Plus brought a resolutely
collaborative and determinedly irreverent spirit to improvised music.

As firm fans of Bill Frisell's work, especially of the eighties and nineties, and of his playing over many years with drummer Paul Motian,
the Bad Plus also played a number of concerts with the guitarist at, for
example, the 2012 Newport Jazz Festival and, in 2017, the Village Vanguard in New York and Walker Art Center in Minneapolis.

While the trio never aspired to being a holy trinity, and at no time
resorted to Cream's legendary levels of band-member antagonism and
recrimination, they did subtract from the group at the end of 2017 when
Iverson departed. Highly versatile and respected pianist Orrin Evans held
the piano chair for the next three years or so; today the Bad Plus equation
is a core duo of Anderson and King, plus tenor saxophonist Chris Speed
and guitarist Ben Monder.

This listening session with the original trio took place in a hotel room in San Francisco in December 2015 during a four-night 'The Bad Plus Joshua Redman' residency at the SFJAZZ Center. If the later reported 'long-simmering internal tensions' between the band members were active at the time, they disguised them very successfully.

PW: I was thinking of playing you tracks from one of Bill's late eighties/early nineties albums.

Ethan Iverson: I had *Lookout for Hope*, and I loved it, but I have a feeling that Reid and Dave are the deeper listeners of this particular era of Bill.

Dave King: I am a hardcore guy for this period. I know every note of the records: the Buster Keaton records; *Have a Little Faith*; the Americana record, *This Land*; everything from *Rambler* through *Gone, Just Like a Train*.

Reid Anderson: Yeah, I'm a big fan of *Where in the World?* I think that's a really unique record.

PW: Let me play you something from that album, then. All the music on this album is composed by Bill, but . . . I'm particularly fond of this track, 'Beautiful E'.

DK: Yes. It's gorgeous.

[The slow, stately and somewhat mournful track plays.]

DK: That's a perfect example of the way Bill is always writing songs, of a band playing a song, without words. It tells an emotional story, and it's beautiful. He's not afraid to be simple, super-simple, but there are also these quirky idiosyncratic tags he puts on things; there's an element of Monk in Bill.

This came out when I was twenty, twenty-one, and it was super-inspiring. It really hit me. It helped me marry the idea of some pop and rock concepts I had with really highest-level jazz. It brought the song element into the improvising realm in a way that I didn't hear anyone else doing at the time.

191

Bill is a master improviser. There's no one like him – the way he effortlessly combines country, blues and Americana with the most modern touches imaginable, especially with those sixteen-second delay maniacal [pedal-effect] excursions you heard in those days. But a lot of his music is orchestrated, and everyone's thinking on that level. They're not just blowing vehicles; there's no solo on that track.

This music is human and personal, it's small-combo music, and that was manageable to me. Because I wanted to improvise and experiment, but I always wanted to be part of an ensemble that focused on *songs*, and didn't have to blow long periods. In that way, I believe the Bad Plus is a child of Bill Frisell.

RA: I was the same age [as Dave] when this record was released, and I was interested in improvising, and curious about jazz and the avant-garde, but what first caught my ear was the way Bill Frisell brought in this rock-guitar element – personally, that was inspiring.

But the more I listened to his music, and to this record specifically, the more I realised how compositional it was. I feel like it gave me permission to say, 'You can be an improviser, but it's OK, you don't have to be improvising all the time.'

PW: Ethan, you once wrote that 'Bill Frisell's music is vitally important to the Bad Plus'. Can you talk a little more about that?

EI: Well, I think Dave just said it, right? I mean, he nailed it. I didn't have the same kind of connection to this music as Dave and Reid, any more than I had a connection to Nirvana or Aphex Twin or some of the other stuff that the Bad Plus plays. But in terms of my own early exposure to Bill, the trio with Paul Motian and Joe Lovano was it, and the Paul Motian [eighties] quintet records too. There's DNA in the Bad Plus, and one significant part of it, from back then, was seeing the Motian trio at the Walker Art Center [in Minneapolis].

DK: In 1991. August 1991.

EI: Yeah, even though we hardly knew each other at that point, we saw each other at the show – one of the few times I believe the trio played in America besides New York. I was eighteen and my mind was melted, frankly. It was really a *phenomenal* show.

DK: It was insane. It was a celebration of Motian's sixtieth birthday.

EI: As great as the greatest avant-garde jazz records are, when you see masters playing that music live, when you actually feel the energy, the tension, the real visceral tension of avant-garde jazz in the room played by a trio with full commitment, that's something different. That's when you're talking about music that can change the inner systems of your body and stuff. It was just glorious.

PW: Shall I play you another track? This one's called 'Again'.
RA: I love this tune.

DK: Yeah.

[We listen to all 6 minutes 39 seconds of it, barely moving.]

RA: I was thinking, as we were listening to this, that one really striking thing about Bill Frisell is that he accesses more of an interior world, a window to an inner life, than most other musicians I know. That song is beautiful, and it's so patient, but the reason that track is so captivating is because of the dark places that he's willing to go. You can hear that in his sound. It's lovely, but it's also as if lovely isn't enough.

PW: Listeners seem to hear all kinds of qualities in Bill's sound, from inner melancholy to something more exterior and cinematic.
DK: I don't know any other guitar player who can even come close to that level of mastery of atmosphere. Really, I feel sorry for guitar players after Bill Frisell. Like Eddie Van Halen did in rock, Bill just completely changed everything, he was so ahead of the game.

I was also listening there to the cross-pollination of influences. Bill's got Joey Baron swinging his arse off on the drums, playing *jazz*, but he's also taking this totally ethereal compositional approach.

EI: Joey Baron's importance cannot be overstated. Not necessarily on that cut, but with Bill the way he played rock and played jazz on the drum set . . . it was so . . . full-on committed. So unrepentant. A whole couple of generations of musicians in this music came out of not just Bill's sound, but Joey Baron's sound, too.

DK: Yes, it was *unapologetic*. But then how do you marry Joey's sound with Kermit Driscoll slap-bassing every now and again? [He jumps up from his chair and makes a screeching sound, like a clutch missing a gear, and Reid and Ethan laugh.] And then there's Hank Roberts on cello, who's got that Americana thing going on, too.

So they're kindred spirits, all the way, but just the idea of thinking about music in that way, where you're able to put these influences together, and see it and hear it that way. It's almost like he sees it perfectly, and then he just lets it go. And everyone gets to do their thing. But he knows exactly how to make that work.

And I think that's another connection to what we have in this band, and what inspired us. That one member of the band could be coming from their own life experience entirely, but somehow something happens in the group that we hope is transcendental or magical on some level. I don't know, I'm just sitting here listening and being reminded of why I was so excited about this music in the first place. [Dave King is standing now, and he is wide-eyed and on fire.]

PW: I can see how much this music means to you, Dave, by the way you're talking about it, and the way you're moving.

DK: This is my shit! I *love* jazz, but what was so cool about these guys is that they also had all of that fuck-you punk attitude. These are fierce avant-garde musicians that, in the right space, are going to rip your fucking face off. As they did to us.

At the same time, there's nothing aggressive – they're like gentle creatures that are in complete command. It's got this other thing that I really related to – it's swinging. It's just impossible how deep Bill Frisell's groove is; it's like he's the most swinging guitar player ever.

That's a huge part [he claps hands] of our awakening as musicians who want to contribute as part of our generation. Bill was the door for me, because his music had all the stuff that I care about: it had elements of all of the history of jazz; it had elements of a deep blues history; and it also had the attitude of we can play pop, we can play rock, we can dismantle things, and we can fully embrace the avant-garde.

RA: One of the takeaways from Bill Frisell is that he is so generous. And that was also an important thing to encounter in terms of our development, because you're checking out all this jazz, which I think a lot of times is not generous music. It can be very dogmatic and ideological at times, like the music has to be a certain way. And when I hear Bill Frisell, I hear the opposite of that. He obviously has his own highly developed aesthetic, but it's applied with a very giving spirit.

DK: He knows how to let go, too. He has all these disparate connections to people and he's not afraid of what anyone might do, or how they might contribute – there's a trust in there.

RA: Bill Frisell is one of those musicians who's there to make the music sound better; he's not there to make Bill Frisell sound better.

PW: Let me play you the opening track, 'Unsung Heroes'.

DK: [after a few seconds] This. I bought this record, and I was like, this is so irreverent. So gently irreverent – that underscores everything these guys seem to do. It is also undeniably bluesy and . . . strange and haunting.

RA: And I think it's really important to mention that Bill Frisell was one of the early, and still one of the few, people that successfully integrated the rock influence into jazz.

DK: The influence of Hendrix on him can't be denied.

PW: *[As Frisell's keening guitar solo starts] You must have known that was going to happen.*

DK: But Jimi Hendrix would have had a backbeat. This is super-swinging.

RA: Also the melody just keeps going, throughout the track, while all this other stuff is happening underneath.

DK: It's also big-hearted, and these are like big-hearted cats. I don't feel it's cynical music.

PW: *There was certainly nothing cynical about the way Bill talked at that time about the musicians in this band. He told one interviewer that he really loved these guys.*

DK: Hey, man, I've played – what? – three gigs with him and I fell in love. I was so in love with him at Newport I didn't even know what to do with myself. I just wanted to jump in his lap and have him adopt me [he laughs]. Bill's a huge-hearted musician and when you're on stage with him, you just feel great. You feel like anything's possible. There's Bill; he's smiling . . .

RA: And he's not going to judge anything that comes his way.

DK: Yeah, man. And that makes *you* think on the next level as well.

EI: I just think Thelonious Monk is such a big influence on Bill, and this tune really shows that. I don't know who played much Monk on the guitar before Bill, but I think he sort of solved that equation.

RA: Is there a better version of Monk on any instrument than Bill Frisell playing Monk on guitar?

EI: Monk also played slow a lot.

DK: Yes, at the Newport show one thing occurred to me. You know how with guitar players you can use the word 'shred'? Well, Bill is the only guitar player in history who shreds without playing fast. [RA laughs.] And it's sort of like, *whaaaaa*, how does he do that?

So you hear Monk in his music, you hear Hendrix in it, and at the same time it sounds like he's landed from an alien space craft, or time-travelled. He's got the civil war thing going on, he's got parades, the Charles Ives and Copland influences – and elements of early Americana funeral music, which you can hear all over this shit. He's got a beautifully slick sense of humour as well; he knows when to wink.

EI: Another record we all know pretty well in this band – it's sort of the secret DNA of the Bad Plus – is an album by Marc Johnson called *Second Sight*.

PW: *The second* Bass Desires *album [released in 1987] – the one with Bill, John Scofield, Marc Johnson and Peter Erskine.*

EI: Yeah. And the first tune on that album . . .

DK: 'Crossing the Corpus Callosum'.

EI: . . . is nothing but guitar effects, really, especially from Bill. And it goes on a long time, it's a real journey. And, for sure, Bill is the wild card. You see, those other guys, they're all great, but there's something a *little* square about them, you know. Bill is the guy who's the devil. The guy who's going to push all three of those other performances into new spaces.

PW: *There were plenty of people at the time in New York who thought Bill, with his big glasses and apartment out in Hoboken, was the square. Or at least they did until two bars into the first tune. [EI laughs.]*

DK: Yes, but with all that ah-shucks shyness, which is very attractive, he was insanely confident as well, from the get-go.

I was sixteen or seventeen when those *Bass Desires* albums came out, and I love John Scofield – he's such a perfect example of a guitar player, a master guitar player. It's John fucking Scofield, man! That's like a guy who's going to kill you playing guitar. [He pauses.] And then Bill Frisell is also in the band! It's like he's another animal entirely that just happens to be holding a guitar.

EI: Yeah. It's sure Scofield had a few things to think about after he played with Bill Frisell [he laughs]. I think you should end by playing us something by Paul Motian. I feel that's the key to the Bad Plus and Bill Frisell on some level. Do you have the *One Time Out* album and 'The Storyteller' track?

PW: Yeah, actually I do.

DK: [As Frisell starts his solo] Now that's shredding! This is the most modern improvised music. Still. On all fronts. Three cats playing together, deep in history, and deep outside of it. It's swinging, and it's got all the big juice of all great avant-garde music.

EI: Listening to this reminded me of something that's very important to say about Bill Frisell, which is that when he plays these Motian melodies, and improvises on them, he always improvises on the melody. It's totally explicit. He did the same when he played with us at Newport.

If you blow on the melody, you immediately get a deeper context for your improvisation. And I think what really helped the Motian trio was that Bill was just relentlessly playing the melody through all the free stuff, through all the noise.

RA: Another important thing to say is that, when we talk about Bill Frisell, I don't think any of us think about him out of the context of group music.

EI: Right. Absolutely.

RA: We've been waving the flag for group music since the beginning of this band, and that's what we believe in, and have been fighting for, and still fight for every day. This isn't about Bill Frisell, this isn't about Paul Motian. OK, their names are on the records, but this is a collective group experience, a group aesthetic – the idea that only *these* guys make *this* music when they play together.

PW: And I guess the music we've been listening to was one model of that idea?

DK: In many ways, it was *the* model.

14: Change Gonna Come

In 1988 Bill Frisell left ECM, the German record company that had given him his initial major-label break, both as a sideman and leader.

It must have felt at times to Frisell in the eighties that he had somehow magically floated, like a musician in a painting by Marc Chagall, into an ECM record sleeve and merged with the vinyl within. In a few short years he had become an ECM artist, a musician seemingly so perfectly in tune with the label's reverberant sound and aesthetic of restraint that he had become known, in some critical circles and to Frisell's chagrin, as 'ECM's house guitarist'.

Frisell and ECM had enjoyed the symbiotic critical and commercial success of albums such as Paul Motian's *It Should've Happened a Long Time Ago* and Marc Johnson's *Bass Desires*. The influential label's uncompromising high standards gave Frisell both credibility and a platform, especially in Europe where he was earning most of his income.

Frisell also formed some important relationships through ECM, in addition to his key connection to Manfred Eicher. One was with Hans Wendl, who had been working at the Munich-based label since the mid-seventies as part of the small team, and as a very occasional producer, and was a close friend of Paul Motian; he still looks after Frisell's music publishing rights today. Frisell also met Thomas Stöwsand, who had been at ECM from its inception in 1970. He left in 1983 to establish his own concert booking agency, Saudades Tourneen. Saudades has organised Frisell's European tours for almost forty years.

Crucially, Frisell also became friends with Bob Hurwitz, who had managed ECM's US operations at Warner Bros Records before Lee Townsend took over in 1984. Hurwitz had left ECM to take up a position with Elektra Records running Nonesuch, a small and struggling label founded in 1964 that he was president of until 2017. Hurwitz built on Nonesuch's legacy of wilful eclecticism by signing Brazilian singer, composer and activist Caetano Veloso and Argentinian *nuevo tango* innovator Astor Piazzolla, and releasing records by American new music composers and performers such as Steve Reich, Philip Glass, John Adams, the Kronos Quartet and John Zorn – *The Big Gundown* and *Spillane* both appeared on Nonesuch.

Today, with an almost unrivalled catalogue that stretches from Björk to Randy Newman, Pat Metheny to Chris Thile, Laurie Anderson to Dawn Upshaw, Brad Mehldau to Rhiannon Giddens, and Wilco to Fleet Foxes and the Black Keys, Nonesuch is one of the world's most admired record labels – 'an oasis of artistic excitement' and 'a kind of American cultural institution'.

Frisell was strongly embedded within the ECM culture and felt enormous respect for, and keen loyalty towards, Manfred Eicher. Yet he was also aware that almost no other record label boss had Manfred's extraordinary level of creative control – Eicher chose the musicians he worked with, how and when he recorded them, and had final say on an album's mix, edit, cover, design and release.

As Frisell's reputation began to grow in the mid-eighties, he began to receive offers from other record company executives. One of these was Gramavision Records boss Jonathan Rose, who had founded the independent label in 1979 and signed leading-edge New York musicians such as Oliver Lake, Anthony Davis, Jamaaladeen Tacuma and Bobby Previte to the jazz label. Bob Moses was recording for Gramavision – as was John Scofield.

Gary Lucas, eighties guitarist with Captain Beefheart's final Magic Band and a Columbia Records producer, also sought out Frisell; it was Lucas who had unexpectedly brought Tim Berne to the major label in 1986 to record *Fulton Street Maul*. German producer and label boss Vera Brandes met with Bill in New York and when he toured Europe. Brandes was the concert promoter who had rescued Keith Jarrett's legendary Köln concert; at the time she was only seventeen. In 1987 she formed the jazz and world music label Intuition – Lounge Lizard John Lurie, trumpeter and sonic innovator Jon Hassell and Brazilian singer-songwriter Milton Nascimento had links to the label.

'It was amazing because I was at a point where I had barely started to do my own music, but yeah, there were a number of possibilities, and at the time people were definitely . . . coming to lots of my gigs . . . and courting me, in a way,' says Frisell. 'But Nonesuch, they were *really* hot to get me.'

While this was happening, Frisell's frustration with Eicher and ECM was mounting: 'I was doing more and more things with lots of different people, and some of them were musicians that I knew Manfred didn't really like so much. I was also wanting to try to record in different ways – like, *not* going into a studio for just two days. We were ready to make that first quartet record, and we had to keep waiting. And I was ready to do the next album, and things would be scheduled, then postponed. Things were already starting to get backed up, and I just felt that I was sort of trapped.'

In May 1988 Frisell made the decision to leave ECM. He had not been in active negotiations with other labels and had no firm offers; he simply felt that he had no other choice, even with a label as prestigious as ECM.

'It was basically like when I left my parents,' Frisell told *All About Jazz*. 'I loved my parents and they supported me, but there was a time when I had to reject my parents, go out on my own and grow up . . . I could've just stayed there and done whatever Manfred thought I should do, but I really felt like I needed to find my own voice.'

Frisell posted a letter to Eicher in Germany explaining his decision, and then telephoned Lee Townsend at his office in New York to let him know. There was a silence at the end of the line, and Townsend said he had to finish a meeting and would call Frisell back.

Lee Townsend explains: 'Fifteen minutes later I called him and I said, "You're not going to believe this, but two days ago I sent Manfred a letter saying exactly the same thing." I told him that I needed to commit myself to producing the breadth of music that I wanted to do, and that I had to take the leap. Bill's jaw dropped. My jaw dropped. Our jaws just dropped together.'

Both parties have since put the coincidence down to classic Frisellian synchronicity; Eicher was more sceptical at the time, suspecting anything from calculation to conspiracy. In the weeks and months that followed, however, Townsend and Wendl set up Tone Field Productions, a management and production company in Berkeley, California – and their first client was Bill Frisell. Soon afterwards, Frisell signed to Nonesuch, and by August he was recording his first album for the label, *Before We Were Born*.

•
•

In November 1989 Bill and Carole made another major adjustment to their lives: they moved from Hoboken to a city 2,400 miles away on the opposite side of the country – Seattle, Washington.

Bill, Carole and three-year-old Monica had first travelled to the laid-back yet rapidly expanding port city over the previous Christmas, when they had visited Wayne Horvitz and Robin Holcomb, who had themselves relocated to Seattle a few weeks earlier. Wayne and Robin had good friends in the city, and they'd moved for a better quality of life – for more space, safety, and for a potentially better education for their daughter, Nica. They had both seen some success in their creative careers, and had bought a small detached house in the quiet residential lakeside suburb of Mount Baker in the southeast of the city. Horvitz's health was also a consideration; he was still suffering from the chronic fatigue that was similarly ailing Frisell.

Bill has said that he distinctly remembers the first time he set foot in Seattle. 'I stepped off the plane out onto the jetway, and I thought, "What is that sweet smell?" After a moment, I realised it was just the air, just oxygen. That was my very first impression of the city.' That Christmas and New Year in Seattle 'sort of planted the seed', he says.

In June 1989 Frisell and the quartet were invited to the city's inaugural Earshot Jazz Festival, and it was another positive Seattle experience. The band was booked to play the large and historic downtown Nippon Kan

Theatre, an ambitious piece of programming for a musician who had never played in the city and had no proven audience outside downtown New York and some major European cities. The event, however, was a great success, both critically and commercially.

'Frisell is without a doubt the single most important new guitar stylist in jazz, a genius who is going to have the kind of influence on the instrument Jimi Hendrix and Wes Montgomery had before him,' wrote Paul de Barros in the *Seattle Times*. 'It was no shock when the packed house gave Frisell a standing ovation.'

It was 'an amazing Seattle debut', de Barros added, and Frisell certainly felt the local love. 'Coming all the way out here, with my own band, and the place was sold out – they really liked it and everything,' he says. 'It was really a great gig, and it was in a great room and . . . that was just a little taste of how Seattle could be that way, and I was like, "Wow, this is . . . pretty cool."'

The Frisells found a spacious three-bedroom detached house in the Rainier Beach area, in the far southeastern suburbs of the city; the house had views of Lake Washington and, importantly for Frisell, who still intended to work regularly in New York and Europe, quick and easy access to Seattle's international airport.

A week after they moved in, however, while Frisell was back in New York for a one-off gig, and Carole and Monica were out of the house, they were burgled; even Monica's Christmas presents were stolen from under their tree.

'It did make the transition harder, but that stuff is everywhere,' Frisell told the *Seattle Times* a few months later. 'Here, I can just walk out the door, and it's nice. Where we were before, if you wanted to get some fresh air, you had to drive for a couple of hours.'

Even so, the move was a brave one. While the need for change had certainly been accelerated by Frisell's continuing ill health, Seattle was a surprising choice. The city was in no way an established music centre in the way New Orleans, Nashville or Chicago were (although in 1989 the city was revelling in the early eruptions of grunge, a movement that would put Seattle firmly on the world music map). In terms of its distance from New York, the main engine of Frisell's work and the primary source of his creative connections, it was like moving, as the crow flies, from London to Timbuktu in Mali. 'Jazz is very social music; it's a lot about your contemporaries and how everybody feeds off each other,' Joe Lovano once said in *DownBeat*. Frisell was breaking those bonds, potentially exiling himself on the Upper Left Coast.

'Some people thought we were nuts, that we were retiring, or something – in our thirties!' says Carole. 'For a year or so we kept our apartment in Hoboken, because I think Bill had a fear that he would be disconnected from the scene. Which didn't happen. Because he was already so much in demand. And he was travelling so much anyway, so flying from Seattle didn't really affect him. In fact, I think he started to like the times he went back to New York; he could enjoy the city, because he wasn't living there full-time.

'But our main drive was family, about doing the right thing for our daughter. Putting her through a good public-school system, for example. It was also good for Bill too, though. I think he wanted to come here just to unplug. And to do his own thing. Being away from that intensity in New York allowed him to start feeding all the other sides of his music.'

Frisell has talked about coming to Seattle to 'hide out a little'. It was somewhere where he could 'just sit down and think'. A slower pace for a slower-paced man. 'I don't know if it's something about growing up in Colorado and being surrounded by all that open space – that can be an over-simplification, because open space is something you can create in your own mind,' he says. 'But getting out of New York, and having that space in Seattle, it was almost like it allowed me to open my eyes to other things.

'When Monica was two or three years old, we'd travel from New York to visit my parents, who had moved to North Carolina, and we'd all go out to these Sunday afternoon fiddle contests in the mountains. I went to a bunch of those things, and one was near Boone, very close to where [guitarist and folk singer] Doc Watson lived, and there was this woman – she had to be in her eighties – playing a fiddle, and doing this clogging-type dancing. I'd never heard or seen anything like it. I started realising that there was music outside of New York, music that was mysterious and new to me, and that was resonating somehow, really knocking me out.'

Not only did the yearly outbreaks of hives and painful joints start to recede and his energy levels return, but Frisell began to find the creative room to write more of his own compositions. He had no intention of severing his relationships with Paul Motian and John Zorn; those were connections and commitments for a lifetime. But he could be inspired by their example, of having the courage and confidence to follow your own path – however hard, whatever the consequences, and wherever it takes you.

⠸

The albums that Frisell released from the late eighties to the mid-nineties reflected this thirst for constant challenge and change, and his desire to further define and explore his own distinct voice. American music was in the process of being forever transformed.

His debut record for Elektra, *Before We Were Born* – released in April 1989 on the Musician label rather than on Nonesuch, in an attempt by Hurwitz to revive the company's dedicated jazz imprint – was preceded by discussions between Frisell and the label boss about the album's content and direction.

'I had all these ideas, like for different records,' Frisell told Jonathan Coe in *The Wire*. 'Like, I want to do a record with Arto Lindsay, and I want to do a record with John Zorn, and . . . he [Bob Hurwitz] said up to this point, he didn't feel I'd made a record that really showed what I did . . . He said that you had to listen to about ten different records to sort of . . . get the picture.' Hurwitz was keen for Frisell to bring together his disparate interests and influences and, continued Frisell, 'put them in one place, so that you could get just a more broad view of what it is I do'.

Rather than working with one all-seeing and all-hearing producer, as with Manfred Eicher, Frisell chose to collaborate with three different producers on separate sections of the album, which were then corralled by overall producer Lee Townsend into some kind of consolidated whole.

The four-part suite 'Some Song and Dance', a segment produced by Townsend himself, featured the Bill Frisell Band of Frisell, Roberts, Driscoll and Baron, plus a horn section of Julius Hemphill and Billy Drewes on alto saxophones and Doug Wieselman on baritone. In a medley that extends from Dixieland to free improvisation, via excursions such as swing, tango and the blues, Frisell was attempting to bring musicians who had moved and motivated him into his orbit. That circle had to include, of course, John Zorn, with whom the Bill Frisell Band joined forces on the thirteen-minute phantasmagoria 'Hard Plains Drifter'. Inspired by a sixties episode of *The Twilight Zone* called 'An Occurrence at Owl Creek Bridge', the classic jump-cut composition contained thirty-six highly contrasting sections.

The remainder of the album comprised three tracks produced by Arto Lindsay and Peter Scherer of Ambitious Lovers. Frisell had been a long-time admirer of Lindsay's love of unusual musical juxtapositions, and of his unorthodox, exploratory and largely self-taught guitar style. Lindsay was the guitarist Joey Baron had found so hard to comprehend when he first heard Arto sitting in at a gig Bill was playing with John Zorn and others at Chandelier in 1984. Four years later Baron was the drummer in the band for these three tracks – with Frisell and Lindsay on guitars, and Scherer on keyboards and drum programming.

The album's final track, 'Steady Girl', was a reworking of Frisell's tune 'Throughout' into a miniature two-minute avant-pop song; Lindsay provided the enigmatic lyrics (which are not always easy to discern) and the delicate, whispery, otherworldly vocals.

If all that, over the course of a hectic nearly fifty-minute record, sounds too much, then that's because it was. Although it's sometimes thrilling to hear Frisell sound so unleashed, *Before We Were Born* ends up being more like a Frisell sampler, a haphazard index of his influences and ideas at that time. What's missing is the leader's peerless gift for synthesis, the twist in the kaleidoscope that reveals a whole new unified pattern and picture.

Frisell tried again the following year with his fifth album as leader, *Is That You?*, recorded over a month in a studio in Seattle, with Wayne Horvitz producing, while Bill and Carole were house-sitting prior to their move to the city.

'We took the budget that we would have had for a weekend in a New York studio,' says Horvitz, who also provides keyboard, drum programming and 'momentary' bass sounds to the record, 'and we rented a studio here in Seattle and spent a month, you know, fooling around. It was like that thing you hear people doing when they make pop records – not that this was pop music – but that *process* . . . like, people coming in, and lots of overdubs, and building things layer by layer. Some days, nothing actually happened that we kept. But it was fun to experiment that much, to try different things with amps, mics, drum machines and guitar sounds.'

Frisell plays a variety of instruments on the album, from bass guitar to banjo, ukulele and even clarinet. He also features on acoustic guitar and a new electric – a custom instrument Frisell had bought from highly respected New York luthier Roger Sadowsky. The guitar had a Fender Stratocaster-type body and a Fender Telecaster-style neck pickup.

Frisell and Horvitz were joined in the studio by Joey Baron, and on three tracks by Dave Hofstra on bass and tuba. Kermit Driscoll and Hank Roberts stayed in New York; this was not a Bill Frisell Band record.

If Frisell was seeking to present a more unified and interconnected individual whole than he had in *Before We Were Born*, then *Is That You?* largely failed. There are certainly some highlights, on an album of mostly Frisell originals – almost through-composed chamber pieces that are characteristically diverse and abstract. 'Rag', for example, is a vehicle for the guitarist's exquisite solo acoustic work, an expressive counterpoint of darting and overdubbed lines that has flourishes of ragtime, classical and flamenco. 'No Man's Land' is filmic and opaque; it could be the soundtrack to a twisted and noirish Midwestern Coen Brothers movie.

Elsewhere, however, the keyboard, synth and drum-machine sounds and effects have a clanking and crunching industrial edge that has not dated well; they especially disrupt Frisell's otherwise faithful interpretation of Aretha Franklin's 'Chain of Fools'.

Frisell's new guitar sound has a rockier and more strident bite too, which upset those jazz fans still wedded to the notion of the guitarist as a latter-day Jim Hall or Wes Montgomery alone. During a trio tour of Europe with Driscoll and Baron in June 1990, many dozens of the audience at the famous 2,500-capacity Royal Festival Hall in London walked out in evident disgust.

'Wow, I really don't remember that,' Frisell says, when I ask him about the concert twenty-five years later. 'And sometimes, in a larger venue, with all the lights and monitors and whatever all else that's between you and the audience, it might be harder to get a sense of what they are feeling. But I'm not saying things like that don't happen. They *do*. Of course, I hope the audience is going to like what I'm doing. But . . . I have to like it first. I can't be thinking about or trying to figure out what they might like. That's impossible. A waste of time. If I stay true to what I love, and if things are going well, if the music is really happening, then hopefully the audience can come along with us, become a part of it, too. And, if not, "Oh well. Too bad. Nothing I can do about it."'

The full Bill Frisell Band toured extensively in Europe and the US later that year before going into a studio in Woodstock, New York, in October 1990 to record Frisell's next Nonesuch album, *Where in the World?* Although these four musicians had only played together intermittently, they were, more than four years after forming, a group decidedly coming into its own.

Joey Baron once recalled John Zorn hearing the band in 1988. 'He was fascinated about how we went to so many different places in one song, how we were free to shape the tune, but it still remained a tune – it wasn't just free improv,' Baron said. 'He arrived at that same place by composing, having things written out and pre-planned.'

Released in October 1991 *Where in the World?* was somewhat

overlooked and under-appreciated at the time (with sales figures of around 27,000, the album also sold ten thousand or so fewer copies than its two predecessors). In the first edition of the authoritative *Penguin Guide to Jazz*, published the following year, Cook and Morton concluded that the record was 'curiously self-absorbed', 'anything but interactive', and pervaded with a 'polymorphous New Age quality'.

Perhaps affected by the sense of space and time for reflection that the move to Seattle had given him, Frisell offers a series of ten ruminative, often spare, yet fiercely original and fully realised new compositions that seem to both look out and in. The record accommodates dark country, brooding blues and uneasy ambience – yet also, on 'Smilin' Jones', the sprightly folk sounds and rhythms of those North Carolina fiddle fairs Frisell was occasionally attending. 'Child at Heart' is at least five evocative and miraculously interconnected moods in one: eerie swing, slow blues, cello chamber piece, gutsy rock 'n' roll, and zappy fifties TV cop show theme.

Frisell also had another new custom electric guitar with which to experiment – a remarkable, headless, ergonomically designed and futuristic-looking instrument created by luthier Steve Klein – and he made good use of it, firing searing screeches, scratchy explosions and thunderous chords across much of the album.

'That band was just so much fun to play in, and something special, I think,' says Hank Roberts. 'I mean, look at Joey Baron: he was already an incredibly accomplished jazz artist, but Joey in that band was *exploding* – man, he just became this incredible *dynamo*, you know.

'And Kermit had that energy, too. He had this tremendous passion and emotion, and he was *really* supportive there with Bill, because Kermit could play anything that he heard too. Kermit was amazing; incredible ears. Maybe we were lucky because there was so much energy around the music, and around what Bill was putting together.'

That spirit and enthusiasm was to run out though, for Roberts at least, in 1991. Two years earlier Hank had left New Jersey and moved with his young family to Ithaca, in upstate New York. By the summer of 1991 he had had enough: of New York and of travelling, flying, and long European tours. He was also feeling, as Frisell was, a strong sense of responsibility. 'I was kinda going through a lot of personal challenges to try to be . . . a father and make a living in a crazy business,' says Roberts. 'It was, like, painful for me, and challenging for my wife Jane, being away from home so much. We had two kids – and we ended up having two more – so I just felt I needed to put my emphasis there.'

Roberts spent the next two decades in Ithaca, teaching, playing, composing, self-releasing records, and being a full-time husband and father. His relationship with Frisell was not over, though. 'Groups have their life-span and that quartet had its time,' says Roberts. 'Then, that was it.'

·
·

Roberts's departure gave Bill, who had recently turned forty, time to take stock. He wasn't interested in simply replacing Roberts with another cello player; Roberts was too individual a voice and Frisell's connection to him too deep. Rather, he wanted to accept the change and move on to new ground.

Even though Frisell's music was expressly written for four distinct voices, the band continued to work as a trio. In the autumn of 1991 they toured Europe again and Driscoll adapted to the new demands by switching to five-string fretless bass, figuring out how to play both his own parts, and those of Roberts. 'Kermit's doing this weird leapfrogging, sometimes playing two completely independent lines: one the bass-line, and the other harmonics,' said Frisell in *DownBeat*. 'It's really cool.'

The new Frisell power trio also started to compensate for the loss of Roberts, who often brought a certain atonal abandon and emotional intensity to the music, by playing freer: at first within the tunes, and later outside them, in more openly improvised passages. 'What's unbelievable to me about these guys [Kermit and Joey] is they know everything I ever wrote,' continued Frisell. 'So, literally milliseconds before we start playing [a tune], I decide what we're going to hit with, and it's just BAM! It's such a luxury not to have to figure out set-lists, to be completely spontaneous . . . Now it's gotten to some sort of spiritual level.'

There is enduring evidence of some of the heights the trio reached during their 1991 tour in *Live*. Recorded by Claudia Engelhart at an Encounters of New Music festival in the Andalusian city of Seville in Spain, the album contains eleven tracks that provide a full and vivid picture of Frisell's music up to that point. There are nine originals, stretching from *In Line* to *Where in the World?* – plus versions of Sonny Rollins's bop classic 'No Moe' and John Hiatt's love song 'Have a Little Faith in Me', both of which would appear on Frisell's next album, released in 1993.

In 2015, when I asked Frisell who was the living person he most admired, he replied, after a long Frisellian pause: 'Oh, man . . . I mean, there are a lot, but . . . Sonny Rollins. I've never met him, but I look to him as this beacon of how to stay true to . . . what your thing is. He has set a standard, at such a high level, over a whole lifetime. And he has that wisdom too. Playing that tune ['No Moe'] was sort of acknowledging him as one of my masters.'

Frisell first heard the Hiatt song on a cassette of the singer-songwriter's 1987 album *Bring the Family* given to him by singer Betty Berken; it was Berken who had told Bill and Carole about the apartment in Hoboken when she decided to move out. The album effortlessly elides elements of rock, country, R&B and soul, and proved another catalyst. 'It got me just listening to words and songs more than maybe I had been before,' says Frisell. 'John Hiatt's songs are perfectly crafted – real simple, and there's no excess.'

Live begins hesitantly, with Frisell announcing, in his most timid and sing-song voice: 'I can't really *see* you. But I can *hear* you. I can *feel* you . . . Thank you.' But from that moment on, the trio offers an object lesson in advanced group dynamics, in sensitive listening and supportive interaction. Frisell supplies some of his most engaging and timeless compositions – 'Throughout', 'Strange Meeting', 'Rag' – tunes that are strong enough in structure to be taken apart yet still retain their essential form. His guitar playing is equally adaptable, taking in soft country swing and full-blown heavy rock-out. It sounds like the trio is having a lot of fun; you can almost see the big broad smile that often beams from Joey Baron's face when he plays.

'I might even say that *Live* is the most important Bill Frisell album to me,' says guitarist Mary Halvorson. 'I can remember getting it when I was about nineteen, when I was just getting excited about music, and about discovering all kinds of music – and then putting it on repeat, *all* the time.

'With Bill, on this album in particular, everything seems so *natural*. It seems like he's discovered this thing that was just right in front of him, and it seems really true to *him;* it doesn't seem like he's trying really hard to be different or to find something. To me, he's completely comfortable in his language, and it's just so clear and expressive.'

●
●

After Hank Roberts left the band, Frisell began to experiment by adding new musicians to the trio, expressing his music through a wider range of voices.

The first of those players was Guy Klucevsek, a versatile and virtuoso new-music, jazz and free-improvising accordionist and composer whom Frisell had met through John Zorn. The second was clarinettist Don Byron, with whom Frisell first played on a Hal Willner project: *Weird Nightmare*, his multiple-artist 'meditation' on the life and work of Charles Mingus. Byron was a musician equally at home in jazz, classical, folk, klezmer and popular music settings. He was also, of course, playing Frisell's first instrument. Frisell had contributed to Byron's much lauded debut album, *Tuskegee Experiments*, released on Nonesuch in 1992.

The quintet of Frisell, Driscoll, Baron, Klucevsek and Byron came together in New York in March 1992 to record Frisell's next album, *Have a Little Faith*. The idea for the record was initially sparked by a conversation Frisell had with Bob Hurwitz, in which the Nonesuch boss suggested that Frisell record an album of some of his favourite American songs.

'I used the album as a canvas,' Frisell says. 'It was partly a tribute to the people that had inspired me, partly songs I just liked, and partly a way of showing something of how my mind works. The choice of music wasn't autobiographical; it was personal. It was an attempt to just open myself up more, and to help put everything I'd done before in some sort of context.

'It also helped to have Don – who could just play anything, right? – and Guy, who was incredible; he could figure anything out, any part or arrangement. And there was something about the way we all played with Kermit and Joey, just the chemical combination of those five people for that kind of density of music.'

The weight and substance to which Frisell refers is an absorbing selection of American music that spans 125 years. The earliest tune is 'Little Jenny Dow', a sweet Stephen Foster song from 1862 – reworked here, in part, as a far dirtier and more distorted blues-rock jam. There is also a jubilant version of the popular 'Washington Post March', written by the 'March King' John Philip Sousa in 1889. The album ends with a similarly concise rendition of the traditional folk song and nursery rhyme 'Billy Boy', played as a duet by Byron and Klucevsek.

Along the way Frisell presents arrangements of compositions by two quintessential masters of twentieth-century American music: a pair of short, stately and evocative excerpts from the reflective first movement of Charles Ives's modernist tour de force *Three Places in New England*; and an agile and inventive twenty-minute adaptation of the eight movements of *Billy the Kid*, the famous 'cowboy ballet' written by Aaron Copland in 1938. Frisell went to some lengths to ensure his arrangement of *Billy the Kid* was authentic, however much he then chose to reinterpret it. He located a copy of Copland's original score in the library at the Juilliard performing arts school in New York.

'Oh, man, just to get to see Aaron Copland's handwriting on the score, where he'd crossed out this, or added that . . . and then copy out the part I was looking for . . . that was so cool and an education in itself – you could really see the struggle,' he says. 'That was part of what doing that record was all about. I wasn't, like, trying to show off. It was more a selfish thing. It was an opportunity for me to enter into some music that I was interested in, and learn more about it.'

The rest of the album was rounded out by more contemporary, if equally disparate songs. As well the Rollins and Hiatt tunes, Frisell offers an airy, countryfied version of Bob Dylan's 'Just Like a Woman'. 'I've loved Dylan for almost as long as I can remember,' he says. 'My junior high school English teacher Mr Newcomb used to play us Bob Dylan songs in class, and even in 1963 was telling us that they were poetry. I probably heard Peter Paul and Mary sing his songs around the same time. From then on, Dylan has just been part of my life; he's in my blood. Everybody knows he writes great songs; there's *so* much to draw from. But what I also admire about Bob Dylan is that he doesn't ever seem to stop taking chances and exploring. As well as still writing new songs, he can find new things in his old songs – they never sound the same. Like Miles, he doesn't just settle into one routine.'

There was also a stripped-back reading of the Muddy Waters standard 'I Can't Be Satisfied', which Frisell first heard in the mid-sixties at the Denver Folklore Center, and a lovely and delicate version of romantic fifties popular song 'When I Fall in Love' played by a trio of Frisell, Byron and Klucevsek.

Perhaps most surprisingly of all, however, was Frisell's impressionistic ten-minute take of 'Live to Tell', the well-known power-pop ballad from Madonna's 1986 album *True Blue*, one of the best-selling records of all time.

'I had a night off on tour, in some freezing hotel room in Norway, and on the television was a movie with [Madonna's then husband] Sean Penn, and Christopher Walken – *At Close Range*,' Frisell once explained. 'I don't even know if it was a good movie, but when that song came on at the end, it just killed me. It's been hanging around in the back of my mind ever since. Because it's such a simple open tune, it really lends itself to different possibilities.'

Produced by Wayne Horvitz, with all arrangements by Frisell, *Have a*

Little Faith was at once an encapsulation and a manifesto. In one interview Frisell said, 'I'm thinking that this record might help fill out the total picture of what I do.'

That image, much like Frisell's view of his childhood and connection to Denver, was in part idealised, a reaffirmation of his personal and political values – the sound of inclusion, integration, infinite possibility and The Frisell Dream. 'The composers [on *Have a Little Faith*] hail from diverse eras and cultural backgrounds,' wrote David Ake in *Jazz Cultures*, which contains an in-depth study of the album. 'Nineteenth and twentieth centuries, male and female, black and white, North and South.'

There is a nostalgia at play, a yearning for a more innocent time. Yet there is a lot more going on. The colourised cover photograph of a group of healthy-looking, all-American, all-white children taking part in a running race in the small town of Vale, Oregon, in 1941 was taken just five months before the US entered the Second World War by one of the leading documentary photographers of the Great Depression, Russell Lee. Inside the CD booklet there is also a photograph of miners' houses near Birmingham, Alabama, shot in 1935 by Walker Evans. These images, chosen by Bob Hurwitz, were simultaneously alluring and disquieting, and may also have mirrored Frisell's feelings about the anxious and contradictory times in which he was living: while the early nineties had finally seen the end of the Cold War and the reunification of Germany, global security had also been ruptured by the Gulf War and the collapse of the Soviet Union.

These ambiguities carry through to Frisell's recontextualising of the songs. 'I'm not trying to rewrite the songs,' Frisell said. 'I've never done that with any material – "Oh, I'm going to write new chords, or put it in a different time signature." I try to get as far as I can into what I know to be the original version of the song, and it shows me all this stuff. And every time we do it, I find something else in it that I didn't know was there – some other harmony, some other way.'

Released in February the following year, *Have a Little Faith* is a groundbreaking album that would change Frisell's career, become one of his key recordings and further establish him as one of the most significant and consistently compelling musicians of his generation.

•
•

During 1992 Frisell continued to explore further group dynamics and sounds. For various concerts, he augmented the trio with a new horn section of Don Byron on clarinet and bass clarinet, Billy Drewes on alto saxophone, and multifaceted instrumentalist, singer and bandleader Curtis Fowlkes on trombone.

In October 1992, just seven months after recording *Have a Little Faith*, Frisell assembled this new sextet in New York for his next Nonesuch album: *This Land*. Conceived as a companion to its 'covers-album' predecessor, the new record comprised fourteen Frisell originals. Six of these had previously appeared on albums Frisell had both contributed to and recorded under his own name; this would be the start of a pattern for Frisell – revisiting tunes to which he had a deep and enduring connection, in different contexts and with different musicians.

Produced by Lee Townsend and released in March 1994, the album title, *This Land*, was partly inspired by Woody Guthrie's famous folk song – and 'alternative national anthem' – 'This Land is Your Land'. Frisell is again very deliberately accessing archetypal American themes and contradictions: the sense that community can exist while there is stark individualism; that there is poverty and exclusion, yet liberty and opportunity too.

The album allows for a great deal of group interaction and individual expression. The three improvisations by Fowlkes, Bryon and Frisell on the spooky, slow-motion, sci-fi-like ten-minute track 'Julius Hemphill' are pitched perfectly between tradition and innovation, between statement, space and surprise. Yet they are also elevated and enhanced by being so connected to a collective sound and structure. For all its wide open soundscapes, its roaming high prairies and endless great plains, *This Land* is a deeply compositional work, scrupulously organised and arranged.

The influence of Copland and Ives is particularly strong; these are modern, multilayered pieces full of colour and theatre. 'In some of the writing on that record, you can hear just how obsessed I was with . . . checking out their [Copland and Ives's] music, and trying to figure out how to adapt it,' he says. 'I was definitely hearing all those tones and harmonies, and they are there – just my little, naïve, simplified version of them.'

With *This Land* Frisell achieves something rare: he transcends his influences and creates a form at once distinctly American, utterly original, and yet wonderfully elusive.

.
.
.

The Bill Frisell Band, in its various configurations, kept gigging and touring for another year or so after *This Land* was released. Trio gigs, especially in Europe, became more and more intuitive and spontaneous; they went from no set-lists, to longer more open explorations of Frisell's music, to sometimes no songs at all. 'We'd been playing together so long that the music just kept getting stretched and stretched and stretched, like, really extreme,' says Frisell. 'I mean, people talk about that live in Seville album, but that was actually pretty conservative compared to the way things kept going, breaking apart just more and more, as time went on.'

The trio embarked on a final project, music Frisell had written in response to three silent films by Buster Keaton, which led to live performances staged with screenings of the movies, and two Nonesuch albums, released together at the beginning of 1995 (see chapter 16). The working unit of Frisell, Driscoll and Baron came to an end soon after that. Frisell had already formed another ensemble: a quartet with Fowlkes, Ron Miles on trumpet, and Eyvind Kang on violin and tuba, which had no bass or drums at all. He also felt that, after a decade, 'We had just run the course.'

Still, it was another big step into the unknown, after having had the security, spirit and intimacy of a longstanding unit. 'We were best friends

. . . and we all used the same language,' Frisell told *DownBeat*. 'Not having a totally working band was traumatic, liberating, and terrifying.'

Joey Baron had also begun to develop his own music in the early nineties, writing original material, forming his own trio, and releasing records under his own name. 'I had the urge to explore other areas and try some ideas of my own, so I thought, "I'm going to go with it, commit to that,"' he says. 'I didn't want to become a piece of furniture, like, "Oh yeah, Joey Baron – Bill Frisell's drummer." Ten years was a good amount of time, and Bill's music seemed to be changing, which is natural, everything changes, and I felt the direction that Bill was moving in . . . didn't really require *me*.'

Kermit Driscoll had no desire at all for the trio to end, and did not take its dissolution well. 'Playing with Bill [during those years] was the highlight of my life – it was just fucking perfect, like . . . nothing else in the world,' he told me in 2017. 'Hard act to follow. About six months later, I picked up a drink again. So fucking depressed. Still am. Still am.' Driscoll began to cry. 'It was just *too* good.'

COUNTERPOINT III
15: Justin Vernon Listens to *This Land*

This Land: recorded New York, October 1992; producer Lee
Townsend; released on Elektra Nonesuch, April 1994; Bill Frisell
(guitar); Don Byron (clarinet, bass clarinet); Billy Drewes (alto
saxophone); Curtis Fowlkes (trombone); Kermit Driscoll
(electric and acoustic bass); Joey Baron (drums); all
compositions by Frisell, except the short final solo
drum track, 'Tag', by Frisell and Baron.

Justin Vernon is an American singer-songwriter primarily known as
frontman and creative force of indie-folk band Bon Iver. He grew up in
Eau Claire, Wisconsin; his mother's family trace their roots to Norway.
Modest, reserved and industrious, he has said that he has 'this sort of
Scandinavian-American-Lutheran guilt-work complex'. As a teenager
Vernon was inspired by a wide range of music that included grunge,
prog rock, post-punk, country, folk, jazz, blues and gospel; a multi-
instrumentalist, he played baritone saxophone in his local marching band,
drums in the town's showband, and guitar in his school jazz ensemble.

Bon Iver's debut album, *For Emma, Forever Ago,* originally self-released
in 2007 when Vernon was 26, was written and recorded by Vernon,
alone, over three months during a harsh Wisconsin winter, in a timber
hunting cabin that his father had built in the woods. A record of 'rare,
quiet perfection', it is now widely considered a modern classic, and has
gone on to sell more than one and a half million copies worldwide. Since
then he has worked with Anaïs Mitchell, James Blake, Kanye West and
Taylor Swift.

We met in a swish hotel in Dublin, Ireland, in June 2017. Vernon
is tall, handsome, courteous and articulate, and I had heard that he is
a serious fan of Frisell's music; he has enthused that one of Frisell's gigs

at the Walker Art Center in Minneapolis is 'maybe the best concert I've ever seen' and that Frisell's 2001 album, *Blues Dream*, 'is probably my favourite record'. I was amazed, however, by the breadth and depth of his knowledge of Frisell's prolific work. Justin Vernon, it turns out, is not just an aficionado or admirer; he's a bona fide Bill Frisell scholar.

PW: From what I've read, Blues Dream *is an important record for you.*

JV: Very important. I was in my first semester at the University of Wisconsin–Eau Claire, and *Blues Dream* had been commissioned by the Walker Art Center. So my brother and my two best friends, and their dad, drove up from Eau Claire and saw the première. Life-changing experience.

In what way?

Everything that Bill Frisell touched at that point was kind of gold to me and my friends. I can remember walking out and having this very specific conversation about how, just as Duke Ellington had summed up American music for the first half of the twentieth century, so had Bill Frisell for the second half. *Blues Dream* runs the gamut of so much American music and transports you to so many different times and places. It was just so *compositional*.

That comparison to Ellington, for me, puts Frisell in the right class and category. I think he's *that* important. What I love is that, although Bill Frisell is not a household name, almost every musician who's serious knows who he is. Even though Ellington was much more popular in his era than Frisell is in his, Bill's influence and impact on music is maybe just as deep.

Maybe I should play you some tracks from Blues Dream, *then, though isn't* Quartet *another possibility?*

Quartet was the first Bill Frisell album I ever heard. I was in eighth grade, so I was twelve or thirteen years old, and I had gotten into John Zorn – I was listening to Naked City's first album all the time.

So I was in New Orleans, with my mom, at the Jazz and Heritage Festival, and I saw that Bill Frisell was playing, and I thought, 'Oh, that's the guitar player from this album that I really like.' We didn't go to see him play, but I bought *Quartet* and brought it home.

I can clearly remember when I first listened to it, in my parents' kitchen, with my best friend, Joe Westerlund – he's a drummer, we started our first band when we were twelve, and we're still playing together. And since that day, Bill has been just central to me.

After listening to *Quartet*, and then *This Land*, we decided that Mount Vernon would have a horn section. We had no idea what we were doing, but we thought [puts on a geeky muso voice, something like Garth in *Wayne's World*] 'You know, Frisell would do it like this.'

So definitely, I don't think harmonically, compositionally or mood-wise, there's anybody else that I could say was a bigger influence on us – by which I mean my group of friends that are all still playing music – than Bill. He's our touchstone.

[Vernon looks through other CDs that I've brought: *Have a Little Faith*, *Nashville* and *Gone, Just Like a Train*] I know all these records pretty well. I could talk about stuff on those, and the other two you've mentioned, for days without even hearing any of them [laughs].

But I had this album [he picks up *This Land*], as I say, and I lost it in high school, or something. So it's been maybe fifteen years or more since I last heard it.

Let's go with This Land, *then. Let me play you a track.*

Great. Yeah, do it. ['Strange Meeting' starts playing] God, it might be since the late nineties that I had this record. Who's in the band?

So, it's Bill Frisell with Kermit Driscoll on bass and Joey Baron on drums—

The *Live* album, with that trio that came out in '95, is another big record for me. That trio is unreal.

Live seems to be a particularly popular album with musicians.

Yeah, that and the *Naked City* record. Even some of my friends who are to the harder edge of music, they all come back to *Live* and *Naked City*. I can sit down with anybody from Eau Claire that is into music, and play them *Live* and they'll know it. Joey Baron was definitely Joe Westerlund's first major influence, other than, say, someone like Dave Abbruzzese [one of the drummers in Pearl Jam].

The rest of the group is Billy Drewes on alto, Curtis Fowlkes on trombone, and Don Byron on clarinets.

Don Byron – OK, great. And I've worshipped Kermit and Billy Drewes ever since this record, and *Blues Dream*. That Billy Drewes saxophone solo on the third track of *Blues Dream* ['Pretty Flowers Were Made for Blooming']: it's so painful, so expressive.

I get the feeling that you've gone pretty deep into these records, and into Bill's catalogue in general.

Yeah, I know it all, I think. There's a couple in the last couple of years that I've haven't caught up with. He keeps putting out records! But in the nineties and 2000s we were getting everything that came out, and seeing him whenever we could. When you have good music, it gives you strength and understanding. And Bill's music does that in spades. More than anybody's.

Lately it has been that live trio recording, but *Nashville* was it for four years, I wouldn't stop listening to that, then *Gone, Just Like a Train* was for two years. I always go back to *Blues Dream*, always, always.

And, of course, *Good Dog, Happy Man*, which is almost my favourite, because it's a perfect album. That's probably *the* one between my friends. Phil and Brad Cook, who were both in Mount Vernon with me, and I all have *Good Dog, Happy Man* tattoos: the name of our favourite track, 'That Was Then'. It's on the top of my back. [He shows me; it's written in black, all lower case.] I have tons of tattoos now, all sorts, mostly reminders of things, but I was twenty when I got that done, and it was my second or third tattoo.

There was something about how Frisell had gone through all this intense compositional study and musical learning, that he was at the highest level of music, and yet it was also so simple; he could bring the music back down to a simple rock beat, or something. And I think that combination was really inspiring to us.

The title of the song meant something to us, too: a reminder of that time. Although, we used to just call it 'Track 9'. In fact, we almost just had tattoos of 'Track 9'. It's like an exercise in nostalgia, which can be a little dangerous, I think, but it's also kind of a nod to our past and how important it was – always having that Frisell song on our bodies [laughs].

This one's the title track, 'This Land'. It has a slightly different feel to the previous song.

[The track plays; Vernon closes his eyes] This is the first time I think I've heard something that's as dissonant as Monk, but that feels like it wasn't just ripping Monk off. I've probably barked something like that to Bill once already [laughs].

You hear people go for dissonance, or seek more dissonance in their music, and it doesn't always work. But Bill's coming from this super-steady place melodically, which gives him the option to pull this off. Bill and Monk can create these chords that are un-static, moving, and have them also be just beautiful, just gorgeous.

Do you think there's something specifically American about Bill Frisell's music?

Yes, I do. Just think of the variety of American music and compositions even on the albums we've mentioned: jazz, blues, country, rock. That shows a great knowledge of American music, I think. Jazz is America's gift to the world, I guess, and he started very deep in that music, and in the downtown scene. But I always thought he was also very much an outsider, that he had other influences, other modes of American music, that throughout his career have kept coming back through. Bill broke the rules. And that made a huge mark on many people.

I've always responded powerfully to his writing on *Quartet*, a lot of which was inspired by, and music for, comics – Gary Larson's *The Far Side* – another great American art form. Track six on that record, 'Egg Radio', has been my favourite song for ever.

Bill's always had this ability to be respectful with his material, yet also playful, almost funny. It's not parody or pastiche, because it's so soulful and tasty. In a lot of his solos during this nineties era, especially when he was playing that headless Klein guitar and turning on the RAT [a legendary guitar distortion] pedal, you can see him with this kind of knowing, devilish smile. I love that.

Tell me about the record that Bill plays on that you re-released on your own label: Sarah Siskind's debut album from 2002, Covered. *How did you find your way to that record?*

Some of my favourite stuff of Bill's is when he plays on other people's records. I've listened to pretty much all of the [Paul] Motian trio albums; that's been some of my favourite stuff to listen to lately. My favourite sax player, Mike Lewis, who's in the band Bon Iver – his favourite saxophonist is Joe Lovano. So there are all these other kinds of connections, too. Mike's a big Frisell guy and we're all Frisell guys together.

I think I discovered the Sarah Siskind album on the internet. I was just looking up and ordering any CD that Frisell was on that I hadn't heard before. I think I went and got this weird Donald Rubinstein album, for instance. And the Siskind record is still a top ten all-time album for me, and still some of my favourite playing of Bill's.

And that's how I eventually met him, six or seven years back, at the Cedar Cultural Center in Minneapolis. I went to go see Sarah play, and Bill was playing with her, and I don't think it was particularly mind-blowing, but the three of us ended up playing Sarah's song 'Lovin's for Fools'. And he was very kind, very giving – just like his music. Even if sometimes he's not going to be so talkative, he lets you know that he appreciates you by being so gracious. He does that thing on stage, where he cups his hands and bows down a little.

Technically, I'd met him before that, when I was seventeen, when I went to go see him play at the same venue. I remember I was wearing a Tampa Bay Buccaneers jersey, or something weird [laughs], and I just barged into his room, with my 'Track 9' tattoo guys, our band guys. And Bill was like [mimics Bill's soft, singsong voice], 'Oh, OK.' Only time I've ever done that, still, to this day. Only time I've ever asked for a picture with somebody. It's on our mantelpiece at home.

Here's a final track, one of my favourites on the album, 'Julius Hemphill'.

Sweet. [Closing his eyes again, as Frisell starts his solo] Yeah! There's that RAT pedal [laughs].

[As the ten-minute track ends] Do you think Bill Frisell has changed the sound of the guitar?

Well, I mean, I play guitar. I got *The Guitar Artistry of Bill Frisell* on VHS when it came out. I've read Bill's chapter on how to make notes ring out and sustain in John Zorn's book, *Arcana*; it's amazing. But I don't really have dreams of being a guitar player, because Bill has done everything with the guitar that I'd ever want to do.

It's like he somehow developed both a new and an old approach to playing the guitar. It was never about appearing so different from everybody that came before. It was like he took everything before him, spread it all out, mixed it up, and moved it on.

And now how many people sound like Bill? Like that Norah Jones record, which Bill plays on [*Come Away with Me*; he guests on one track, 'The Long Day is Over']. Every other guitar solo on that album sounds like Bill Frisell – that soft, well-thought-out melodic thing. Before Bill became so influential, guitar solos seemed to be more about how well you could play, how technically interesting you could be. I think Bill gave people a licence to remember the melody.

It's just everything about his playing. Think of his use of simple delays, or his very early use of looping, which people are still doing. I'm still using a Line-6 [effects] pedal. But it's all based on Frisellian textures:

build a weird loop, or build a loop during a song and play it at the end, and get it all weird and stuff.

I don't think there's guitar playing, really, any more. Of course, there are some awesome guitar players, and some I really like, but I mean, honestly – I think he ruined it for everyone else. Bill Frisell changed everything.

16: The Sounds I Saw

In 1966, when Bill Frisell was fifteen, his parents invited some friends over for dinner at their home on East 7th Avenue in suburban Denver.

Bill Sr had met Florian Cajori at the University of Colorado School of Medicine; they were colleagues in the department of biochemistry until Florian retired in 1960. Cajori was almost thirty years older than Bill's father, but as well as a mutual passion for teaching and science, they shared an enthusiasm for trips to the nearby Rocky Mountains – Florian was an experienced hiker and mountain climber, and a collector of rare mineral specimens. Bill's parents had also become good friends with Florian's wife Marion, who had a love of music and education: she gave piano lessons, and when the Cajoris lived in Wayne, Philadelphia, she was one of the founding members of a new art school.

To that dinner the Cajoris also brought their son, Charles, an abstract-expressionist painter living in New York. Charles had been active in the city's downtown alternative art and social scene in the fifties, becoming close friends with artists Willem de Kooning and Franz Kline, and with experimental composer Morton Feldman. Charles was the same age as Bill Sr and Jane, and they had got to know him during his regular visits to Denver to see his parents.

'I remember when my parents had these dinners I would often feel uncomfortable,' says Frisell. 'My father and Charles's father would discuss something related to his biochemistry work, and I didn't know what they were talking about. My father's work was a mystery to me my whole life; I never could figure it out. But Charles was more like this Beatnik guy wearing jeans and tennis shoes, and he was someone who would tell me stories, about all this hip cool New York stuff, and who I could talk to and sort of hang out with.'

Charles Cajori had been a drummer at high school; soon afterwards he discovered a lifelong passion for jazz. 'Everything is rhythm,' he once said about his paintings. 'When I first became interested in art, about the same time I became interested in jazz . . . I felt a connection not only in the rhythm involved, which is continuous and non-climactic, but also the notion of improvisation. The rhythm is the control, I think.'

Cajori became a regular at such Greenwich Village jazz clubs as the Village Vanguard, Village Gate, Half Note, and especially the Five Spot, where he saw Thelonious Monk play many times, particularly during Monk's famed six-month residency at the club in 1957 in a quartet with saxophonist John Coltrane. Cajori's enthusiasm for the music inevitably seeped into his work. In a 1961 review of one of his shows, a critic wrote that Cajori was 'trying to strike the perfect balance between freedom and discipline, ambiguous flux and calm clear structure'.

'I remember he brought over this Monk album, *Criss-Cross* – I can still picture the cover – and he'd talk about seeing Monk play in New York,' says Frisell. 'I didn't have any idea who Monk was, but Charles was really the first person to talk to me about this stuff, this music, and I was sort of old enough to kind of get it.

'Charles would also describe going to the Vanguard to see Miles Davis. He would tell me stories about the band and the club, about Tony Williams starting to play with Miles when he was still a teenager, and about Charles being so close to the stage that he was sitting right underneath Tony's cymbal.'

After Bill's parents moved to New Jersey, Frisell lost contact with Charles. He would be reminded of him often, however, especially when he began to listen to Monk's compositions more carefully, and attempt to play some of them – and then himself move to New York. By the turn of the century, despite the fact that it had been more than thirty years since Frisell had last seen Cajori, his conversations with the artist often returned to him. In 2003 Frisell tracked him down; even though Cajori was now in his eighties, he was teaching at the New York Studio School in Greenwich Village, a mould-breaking art school that in 1964 he had helped establish.

'We sat on this bench in a park,' says Frisell, 'and it turned out he knew who I was, and he'd seen me play at the Vanguard with Paul Motian, but he hadn't actually connected that I was the son of his father's friend in Denver. But it was just incredible – sort of like being back with him at my parents' house. He was telling Carole and me all these stories about the fifties and sixties in New York, lots of stuff I didn't know.' Cajori revealed that he had created two large paintings – *Epistrophy I* and *II* – inspired by Thelonious Monk and his 1941 tune of the same name, co-written with drummer Kenny Clarke.

'Then there was just this one thing that Charles said, just a few simple words, and I'm pretty sure I have them almost exactly right,' continues Frisell. 'He was talking about spending his whole life just trying to paint, trying to find a line or angle or whatever it was he was looking for. He said, "After all this time, if there's one thing I'm certain of, it's that drawing is a worthy endeavour."

'That for me was, like, yes! There's something about that human impulse to draw that I really relate to, that gets close to what it is for me about playing the guitar and trying to make music. It's all coming from the same instinct – that same indescribable . . . link to your imagination. You draw a line and that suggests something that pulls you somewhere. It's exactly the same when you're composing or improvising; you just keep looking and . . . making up something to play. It gets down to the most simple thing. The worthy endeavour.'

Carole thinks Charles Cajori is some kind of role model for Frisell – 'In the way that he had a connection to Denver and had dedicated himself to his art,' she says. 'It was like he had got towards the end of his life and realised that he'd made the right choices.

'Bill's had a number of people around him during his life who were older – like Dale, like Paul – and who really just pointed the way. They said, "Yeah, you can do this. You can do it your way. You can be who you want to be."'

One of the things that Bill Frisell has always wanted to be is a musician open to exploring a keen interest in the visual world, and in investigating the potential interplay between music and the visual arts.

Perhaps the curiosity comes partly from his father's passion for painting. The walls of successive Frisell family homes were covered with his father's oils and watercolours, mostly landscapes, particularly after he retired and was living in North Carolina, and some urban scenes, from when Bill Sr and Jane were living in New Jersey. Frisell understood that a person of logic, rigour and science could also have a creative itch, and that this could accompany you throughout your life.

'My father just loved painting, and he certainly spent a lot of time doing it,' says Frisell. 'But he wasn't looking for any kind of recognition or anything, and he never sold any of his paintings – in fact, he gave many of them away to friends. I think he just did it purely for the sake of doing it.'

Frisell himself has always been a sketcher. When he was a kid, he drew monsters, dinosaurs, rocket ships and souped-up hot rods, and that desire to draw a line, with a pen, and then continue it, has extended into his adult life.

'When I met Bill, he was already doing all these strange drawings, and they've always been there; he's always been interested in it,' says Carole, who from the late nineties has worked as an artist, exhibiting widely. Her bold abstract drawings and paintings are large and diverse yet, like some of Frisell's compositions, they often display an intriguing economy of line, colour, shape and form. Monica too works in the visual arts, as a portrait and documentary photographer and videographer.

Carole experiences synaesthesia – the phenomenon in which the stimulation of one sense triggers an involuntary perception of another – especially between shapes and sounds, and between writing and visual images. 'There's a connection between music and the visual world,' she continues. 'It's almost like visual art is slowed-down music. It's an expression of the same thing, but on the other side of the spectrum. And I think that's why so many musicians are visual.'

I visited Bill and Carole in Seattle twice in 2015 and their home was creatively cluttered with a rich array of artworks and objects (a drawing by Cajori here, *commedia dell'arte* puppets there). Frisell's workspaces looked a little like Hal Willner's studio: they were packed with paintings, drawings, photographs, illustrations, cartoons, statues, busts, postcards, coloured pens, stickers and old transistor radios (he is a hoarder).

Before one of my first interview sessions with Bill, Carole showed me some of his 'strange drawings', and I was particularly struck by a pencil drawing of a fantastical and misshapen naked man, partly shaded jaundice yellow, with long thin arms, a beaky head and a red tongue. 'It's a self-portrait,' said Carole, laughing. 'Just so you know what you're letting yourself in for.'

There were many more sketches, mostly figurative line drawings in ink, done freely and quickly – they had an engagingly carefree and cartoonish sense of the playful, grotesque and absurd. The drawings were full of odd figures and creatures that seemed to spring from the darker corners of Frisell's imagination: bug-eyed and big-toothed man-boys; disturbed and menacing trolls; distorted, anxious-looking, guitar-wielding cowboys – much like Frisell's drawings for the CD artwork on his 2002 album *The Willies*.

'To me, his drawings look like how his music sounds,' says bass player Tony Scherr. 'Not in a superficial way – like, "Oh, they look silly", or something. It's more in the way that Bill can imagine a world within a world. Like a cartoon. Some of his songs are so original – they're not written at all to be like jazz standards, or like any other kind of music. They're just some world that Bill can imagine really clearly and give voice to.'

'I can't draw, but if I didn't play music, I'd probably do something like that,' Frisell told *DownBeat* in 2008. 'When I met [cartoonist] Jim Woodring and saw his art, I felt his drawing was a lot closer to what I'm trying to do with the music than a lot of musicians I know. It's the place you're trying to get to – to bring something to the surface that's not always visible or audible, something people feel in this reality that isn't always there.'

In an interview with the innovative banjo player Danny Barnes, Frisell described this quality and ambition in Woodring's art further: 'He's trying to find things . . . that you might see in a dream. I can relate to that. There are things I see in dreams, when you're half-awake or half-asleep or whatever, where I think, "Wow, if I could just get that to come out in a sound or get it to affect somebody that way . . .'''

Woodring is a cartoonist with a broad taste in music and a deep bond to Bill Frisell. 'I think our widest point of connection is that we both feel there are benign mysteries beneath all the terror, and that devoting your life to uncovering those was something worth doing,' he says. 'Bill's music is wonderful, and it's fun to listen to, but there's a dark humour there too. He likes strangeness. It's the same with all of the visual stuff he likes: he appreciates images that have a depth and an edge to them. I don't think he would ever be a *Garfield* fan, for example.'

•
•

Frisell's music has always, right from his earliest recordings, had a visual dimension to it, a sound that evokes images of inner and outer worlds far beyond the notes and compositions.

It is a quality that hasn't escaped critics. While some have been prepared to venture into Frisell's more shadowy and entangled interior world – 'the dark places' to which Reid Anderson of the Bad Plus referred – most writers and reviewers have stayed firmly above ground.

'One might say that a Bill Frisell gig takes the listener . . . through diverse, ever-changing terrains,' wrote one, Jeff Tamarkin. 'Climbing peaks, diving into valleys, crossing verdant fields, jumping off stark rocky cliffs – and sailing down a twisting, raging river.'

He has created a soundworld that has pulled jazz, a music more usually associated (in the US at least) with urban scenes such as New Orleans parades and basement New York clubs, into a rural and pastoral landscape that is poetic, epic and elegiac. It is how Bill Frisell began to change modern sounds in jazz and country and western music – and much more besides.

'One of the things I felt very strongly when I first started listening to Bill's music [in the eighties] was that it was much more visual than a lot of music I was hearing,' says writer and producer David Breskin. 'I remember talking really early to Bill and saying, "Your compositions: they're like film scores." I could so easily see how the music would work with film.'

In 1993 Frisell was presented with his first opportunity to put this theory to the test, when he was asked to compose music for Buster Keaton films. Commissioned by Arts at St Ann's, a performing arts organisation located in a large church in Brooklyn Heights in New York, Frisell wrote the scores for his then working trio of Kermit Driscoll and Joey Baron.

The silent films chosen by St Ann's were two of Keaton's energetic independent shorts from the early twenties: the twenty-one-minute *The High Sign*, in which Keaton plays a drifter who cons his way into working at an amusement-park shooting gallery; and the nineteen-minute *One Week*, the story of newlywed Buster and his bride's labours with a DIY house that can supposedly be built in a week.

Keaton's wildly inventive 1925 classic, *Go West*, was the third selection, a feature in which Buster plays a hapless character called Friendless, who decides to escape New York and head west to find his fortune. He ends up working on a cattle ranch, striking up a friendship with a cow called Brown Eyes, and steering a herd to Los Angeles.

The inspired experiment revealed the substance and versatility of both Keaton and Frisell – that Keaton was far more than a simple slapstick clown, and Frisell much more than a musician for all seasons. In fact, Frisell's all-encompassing music was the perfect choice for exploring the 'mirth and melancholy', the pratfalls and the pathos in Keaton's films. Frisell did not attempt to scrupulously synchronise the music; he was aiming for emotional rather than literal truth, for Keaton's humanity.

'I'd seen some Buster Keaton films when I was a kid, but I wasn't really that familiar with him when St Ann's approached me,' confesses Frisell. 'It was an education, and I learned so much, but it was hard, because, apart from what I was seeing him do on the screen, I had no input at all from anyone else, no rules I had to follow. It was just me and Buster Keaton. So it was basically a case of jumping in the water, and just flailing around, and trying to do something.'

The music premièred at a sell-out concert at St Ann's in May 1993, and was so well received that for the next couple of years the trio performed the music, accompanied by screenings of the films, whenever the staging allowed.

'The first time we did it, it was complete panic, basically,' Frisell told *JazzTimes*. 'I couldn't believe we made it through the whole thing; it was really intense. But then we did a tour in Europe, and there was a point where we knew the music well enough and our attention could really spread out into the film. It felt almost like Buster Keaton was another guy in the band.'

Frisell decided to record the music for his next Nonesuch album; there was enough material for two separate CDs. While the music, especially for *Go West*, stands on its own merit, it inevitably only told half of the story; a DVD of the films with the music was eventually released in 2009.

The music spans a spectrum that runs from woebegone ballads to swinging blues to bustling free improvisation, and captures many of the nuances and contradictions in Keaton's often subversive work. Frisell accesses the all-American story secreted within Keaton's films – perhaps Bill related to Buster as a fellow creative adventurer and improviser, or maybe as the shy, stubborn and soft-hearted outsider.

In February 1994 St Ann's commissioned music from Frisell for screenings of three further Keaton films: again, two early independent shorts, *Neighbors* and *Convict 13*, and one feature, *Sherlock Jr.* Some of the music for *Convict 13* appeared two years later on the album *Quartet*, the first record Frisell released after the trio came to an end.

Quartet was a pivotal album for Frisell. For one thing, it consolidated his commitment to composing music for film. Six of the thirteen tracks on the record were compositions originally written by Frisell for *Tales from the Far Side*, a twenty-two-minute animated television special created in

1994 by the cartoonist Gary Larson. The short film was a loose sequence of darkly humorous Larson vignettes, all staged during one desperately dark and stormy night, which featured many of the cartoonist's surreal, macabre and demented collection of monsters, aliens, anthropomorphic animals, UFOs, cavemen and zombie tourists. There was a Frankenstein cow, a malfunctioning plane with human-sized insects as passengers, an egg horror movie, the story of the lives of carrots (it doesn't end well; they get eaten alive) – and no dialogue, only spooky sound effects and Frisell's unsettling music.

'The Gary Larson thing was just the perfect next step after Buster Keaton, in terms of what I was comfortable with being able to handle,' says Frisell. 'There weren't any others giving instructions, like in a real full-on Hollywood movie, or something. The Buster Keaton music was just me and nobody else. With *The Far Side*, it was just me and Gary Larson.'

Frisell had met Larson in Seattle through guitarist Jim Hall. The cartoonist started playing guitar as a teenager in Tacoma, Washington, later developing a passionate interest in jazz, and taking lessons in New York with Remo Palmier, Herb Ellis and Jim Hall. When Hall played the Jazz Alley club in Seattle in 1991, he introduced Frisell to Larson.

The following year, when the Frisells moved to a more upscale Seattle residential neighbourhood, Hawthorn Hills, in the north of the city, they discovered that Larson lived nearby. Larson is just seven months older than Frisell, they have a mutual love of guitars and Jim Hall, and soon they were getting together at Larson's house to play, mostly standard songs.

'Gary's a great player: really dedicated, totally seriously into it, and plays every day – he practises more than I do!' says Frisell, laughing. 'When he was younger he played banjo, old-time banjo, *a lot*, and I can really hear that in his [guitar] playing. There's a way of strumming, this rhythm-guitar thing – like George Van Eps did, and Jim Hall was great at it; Freddie Green was the god of it – and it's becoming a fairly lost art. I can't do it, but it's really fun to play with somebody that knows how to – like Gary; he's got that thing going on.

'What was also nice for me, totally selfishly, was . . . we could just get together to *play*. Gary didn't want to do gigs or record, or something. He just wanted to be there, working on the music, and just playing. It was really pure music.'

Larson was similarly fascinated by Frisell and his creative process. 'The first time I saw him play live,' Larson told the *Seattle Times*, 'it conjured the image of a mad scientist toiling in a lab.'

For Tom Junod's 1997 *GQ* feature, Larson attempted to capture that concept: he drew a portrait of Frisell, holding his Klein guitar, a lead stretching from the instrument to a socket at his left temple lobe. Above is Frisell's scalped head, which reveals his brain as a madcap laboratory full of tubes, flasks, machines, an ice-cream cone, a jack-in-the-box and, high up, in a chair atop a ladder, a scientist in a lab coat and flippers feeding large black musical notes into a funnel.

Frisell recorded the original music for the assorted *Tales from the Far Side* with a band composed of Eyvind Kang on violin, Rob Burger on accordion and keyboards, and Tucker Martine on various looping, sound-manipulating and audio-processing devices.

Two years later, after Larson had retired his hugely successful *Far Side* cartoon strip in 1995, he created a longer animated sequel, the forty-five-minute *Tales from the Far Side II*. Once again Frisell wrote the music, but it was never broadcast in the US, only in the UK, on the BBC.

The *Quartet* album, recorded in San Francisco and released in April 1996, featured trombonist Curtis Fowlkes and twenty-three-year-old violinist and tuba player Eyvind Kang – a deeply inquiring musician as interested in philosophy, ethnomusicology, classical and Indian music and Laurie Anderson as he is in jazz and improvisation.

The foursome was completed by trumpeter Ron Miles, who had been strongly influenced by Frisell's work. Early on in his career, Ron had sent Bill a cassette of his music, which Bill liked, and they had stayed in touch, eventually playing together in Denver in 1993 in a concert that also featured Dale Bruning.

The new group's unusual instrumentation was closer to a modern chamber music quartet than a traditional jazz ensemble, and very consciously did not include a standard rhythm section. 'I wasn't sure if I could play without them [Joey and Kermit],' Frisell explained in *DownBeat* at the time. 'So I thought I'd do something completely different and form a new band without drums or bass. It's so different from the traditional guitar–bass–drum thing, even though Joey, Kermit and I never played like a typical jazz trio. This group, with the violin and brass, can play an orchestral range of sounds. It's gigantic.'

For the new quartet, Frisell re-orchestrated the music he had written for *Convict 13*, *Tales from the Far Side* and for Italian feature film *La Scuola*. He also reworked his short tune 'Twenty Years' from *Is That You?*, added two new compositions – and relied heavily on the structural, textural, interpretative and especially rhythmic skills of his collaborators to give the music a new life.

The music on the album fully matches its variety of visual inspirations and references, and often transcends them. Arrangements abound with colour, nuance, dissonance and mystery; themes roam freely and accommodate contrast. 'Much of what I do deals with opposites,' Frisell said. 'I like things to be delicate and spaced out, but I want the music to kick ass, too.'

Like Larson's and Keaton's films, the compositions are often whimsical and warped, yet they also hint at a landscape more lyrical, even mythic. The album is unafraid to venture into more dark, difficult and sombre corners too; at a *Quartet* concert I attended in London in July 1996 Frisell said of the music, with an impish smile on his face, 'We call it sad-core.'

Quartet is a suitably far-sighted record and it was another significant success for Frisell, critically and commercially. Reviewing the album in the *New York Times*, Peter Watrous enthused, '*Quartet* may be his masterpiece'. A few months later, in the *DownBeat* annual critics' poll, Frisell had climbed to the top spot in the guitar category, ahead of John Scofield, Kenny Burrell and John McLaughlin.

When Elvis Costello was asked by *Vanity Fair* in 2000 to name his

'500 albums essential to a happy life', out of the seventeen albums Frisell had released as leader up to that point, Costello chose *Quartet*. In the tough-minded *Penguin Guide*, Cook and Morton were unequivocal: 'This is an album,' they wrote, 'he was born to make.'

•
•

One of the most important and fruitful relationships Frisell has had with a visual artist is with the cartoonist Jim Woodring. In 1996 Monica was attending the same Seattle middle school as Jim and Mary Woodring's son, Max; the Frisells and the Woodrings met at a parents' evening, and sometime later CDs and comic books were exchanged.

Frisell's music was new to Woodring, but it made a strong and immediate impression on him. 'The first time I put on one of Bill's CDs,' he says, 'I was like, "Jesus Christ, this can't be *this* good."' As a comic-book fan, Frisell already knew Woodring's work and liked it. 'I thought, "That's good,"' continues Woodring. 'Maybe we can be friends here, you know.'"

They began meeting at Frisell's house. '"Let's just get together and jam," is how he put it,' says Woodring. Frisell would play lines and figures on the guitar, and Woodring would sketch lines and figures in his drawing book. Soon afterwards they began talking about how they might make the music and images work together. 'Bill would say to me, "Gee, it's too bad. Could you learn to play the trumpet, or something? Then we could collaborate." And then through the magic of his contagious genius, he made it happen.'

In 1997 Frisell asked Woodring to create the artwork for his new Nonesuch album *Gone, Just Like a Train*, a trio session with Viktor Krauss on bass and Jim Keltner on drums. The process was the same as for their 'jam' sessions – as Frisell wrote in his handwritten liner notes to the album: 'One day Jim Woodring and I got together. I was working on the music for this album – playing my guitar – and he was in the corner drawing the image you see on the front cover.'

There were, in fact, two cover images. The CD cover featured an archetypal Woodring landscape – precisely defined, primary-coloured, and at once seductive and unsettling – occupied by organic plant-like creatures and a tubular tunnel, the entrance of which is surrounded by holes in which you can see the proboscises of various animals. The slip-case has a drawing of one of Woodring's favourite subjects and symbols, frogs: this particular crossbreed is half-frog, leaning back casually on a rock, and, where its head should be, a half-gaping open aperture, like a giant mouth or sound amplifier.

Three years later Frisell asked Woodring to originate drawings to accompany another of his albums, also a trio record, with Dave Holland on bass and Elvin Jones on drums. Woodring created four drawings – this time in charcoal, and colourised in the CD booklet – triggered by the music.

Excited by the various connections and alliances they were forming, Frisell and Woodring decided to take the collaboration further and stage their interactions as multimedia performances. In 2002, at St Ann's in Brooklyn, the pair presented a seventy-minute work titled *Mysterio Simpatico* – various Woodring drawings and short animations were projected onto a large screen, while Frisell, trumpeter Ron Miles and violinist Jenny Scheinman played the guitarist's original accompanying music.

'The two artists have come to a similar place from different mediums, and want to show you what that place is,' read a review in the *New York Times*. 'It's a weird, carefully tended and, despite its trippy quality, an essentially naïve place.'

The article also noted that Frisell and Woodring 'don't talk about the similarities [between their work]; words might ruin the whole delicate exercise'. Frisell explained further to me: 'I seem to use the word "mystery" all the time, and I like the idea that things are not always what they seem. There's a whole bunch of different ways to look at Jim's images, and I've always thought that's what's happening with the music, too.'

Frisell and Woodring won a prestigious United States Artists Fellow-ship in 2006 to stage another sound-and-vision event, *Probability Cloud*.

Doubtless much to the duo's chagrin, the award explicitly stated that their work 'explores the themes of spirituality, the evolution of consciousness, and the contrast between horror and beauty'.

The world première took place in New York at the Carnegie Hall's contemporary performance space, Zankel Hall, with the music performed by an ensemble featuring Frisell, Ron Miles on cornet, Greg Tardy on clarinet and tenor saxophone, and Frisell's 858 'modern string quartet': violinist Jenny Scheinman, violist Eyvind Kang and cellist Hank Roberts. The Frisell-Woodring partnership had come a long way from a casual 'jam' in Bill's practice room at home in Seattle. Much of the music for *Probability Cloud* and *Mysterio Simpatico* was also re-orchestrated by Frisell for a touring octet, and appeared on Frisell's 2008 double CD, *History Mystery.*

Since 2006 Frisell and Woodring have continued to stage multimedia events in the US, and the interplay has become more spontaneous; the drawing as well as the music is now 'live'. One of the first such events was 'an intimate performance of live illustration and musical improvisation', ironically titled *Close Your Eyes*, held in Brooklyn as one of the opening concerts of New York's 2012 Crossing The Line arts festival; it also involved Eyvind Kang on viola.

'*That* was an amazing experience,' says Woodring. 'There was a passage in which Eyvind went off on this eight-minute Persian riff that just had everybody in the place spellbound. And Bill was playing along with it, and I was drawing arabesques and percussive shapes to it – and it was magical. I could hear the music bending to the images, and hear people in the audience going, "*Whoa!*", and it was really truly interactive. That was as close as I'll ever . . . it was like I was in Bill Frisell's band as a *player*. That *happened*.'

Frisell's pull towards creating music for visual images is redolent of Robert Frost's assertion 'that poetry is a fresh look and a fresh listen'. When he composes for visual images, Frisell may be more tied to external considerations such as content and context, yet the process also takes him to new creative spaces into which he might not otherwise have ventured.

'It's confining, in a way,' Frisell has said. 'But then, within the confines, I find that it helps me to sometimes generate things that I wouldn't
. . . think of when I'm just left completely free. So, for me, that is the
most attractive thing about film . . . or being inspired by paintings or
pictures – just that it will get me to another place. Just that one little
extra looking at a picture, or something: something might happen that
wouldn't happen otherwise.'

•

•

Frisell has also written music in response to two other contrasting visual
artists: the influential German abstract and photorealistic painter Gerhard
Richter, whose work regularly sets record prices at auction for paintings
by a living artist; and reclusive American photographer Mike Disfarmer,
whose celebrated portraits of everyday people in rural Arkansas only
became known many years after his death in 1959.

In 2001 David Breskin had the idea to combine three of his most
particular inspirations – art, literature and music – in an ambitious multimedia project focused on the work of Gerhard Richter. The artistic element involved Breskin approaching Richter with the idea of creating 'a
special kind of book . . . something substantially different . . . a work that
opened out, rather than closed down the art'. The book would coincide
with a major Richter retrospective at MoMA in New York, which would
tour to various US art galleries, including the San Francisco Museum
of Modern Art. SFMoMA was planning to stage its own accompanying
Richter event at the same time: the first American exhibition of *Abstract
Pictures, 1999 (858-1 to 8)*, a series of eight small paintings recently
added to its permanent collection. Breskin intended to focus on these
works, seven of which were oil on aluminium and one oil on linen. Aluminium is a medium that allows Richter to streak, scrape and drag paint
across its smooth surface with a homemade squeegee, creating a narrative
energy, rhythm and cohesion. The paintings prompt a wide variety of
interpretations, including shimmering land- and waterscapes.

For the literary perspective, Breskin commissioned poems and essays that celebrated and investigated Richter's work. The book included contributions from thirteen poets, including former US poet laureate Robert Hass and Pulitzer Prize winners Jorie Graham and Richard Howard.

The musical element entailed Breskin commissioning Frisell to write a suite of eight pieces of music for the eight Richter paintings, 'each piece having a 1:1 relationship to the painting, which serves as its "trigger"'. 'When I consider all the improvisers that I know or all the kinds of master musicians,' Breskin said in an interview included in the CD booklet, 'he [Frisell] has a relationship to the guitar when producing sound that is closer to Richter's relationship to producing abstract paintings than anyone else . . . What Richter does with paint in these abstractions, I think Frisell does by analog with music, with sound . . . He [Frisell] shapes it. He torques it. He inverts it . . . He modulates pitch. He changes tunings.' There were also potential connections, Breskin argued, between Frisell's synthesis of composition and improvisation, and Richter's 'spirit of controlled experimentation'. And between 'colour in painting and tone in music'.

Breskin arranged for Frisell to spend time alone with the works; Frisell took almost two hours looking at, thinking about, and responding to the eight paintings, and sketching some initial musical ideas. 'That was amazing, just spending that amount of time with those works,' says Frisell. 'I don't even know in the end really what relationship the music *actually* has to the paintings, but I just tried to open myself up to what they were, and what I was seeing in them, how I felt about them. Then the process that we used to record the music also helped.'

Breskin and Frisell had previously discussed recording a 'Bill Frisell with strings' album, and for the project Frisell decided to form a new quartet with violist Eyvind Kang, violinist Jenny Scheinman and cellist Hank Roberts, with whom Frisell had recently reconnected. It was Frisell's contemporary take on a classical string quartet: instead of a lead or second violin, Frisell featured on electric guitar, plus various effects and electronics.

The music was recorded in Seattle in July 2002. Breskin positioned high-quality prints of the paintings around the walls of the studio as further stimulation. Tracks were cut live, in a sequence that corresponded to the eight works, in one or two takes, without any overdubbing or editing. Three days were set aside for the recording, but Frisell only needed two.

'On most of my recordings I overdub, mix, obsess over it, go back and tweak things,' Frisell said in the *Richter 858* CD booklet. 'But I wanted this one to somehow represent this gesture of paint going across aluminium or canvas, and you just have to deal with it being there. I was thinking of my role as the guy with the squeegee . . . If a melody could be the equivalent of a photograph or a recognisable visual image, then what I was doing was kind of smearing the paint around . . . but there was always some underlying structure that was more carefully worked out.'

Even though Breskin suggests that the music should 'come from the Richter work, not [be] dependent on it', the music is highly site-specific: it is part composed, part improvised, sometimes lyrical, often dissonant, and highly expressive. The eight pieces are suffused with organic textures, layers and details, the compositions unfold much like the movement of paint across canvas; and they retain an overall sense of unity.

Breskin brought the tripartite structure together in 2002 in an oversized, lavishly produced, limited-edition $125 book, housed in a brushed aluminium slipcase, which also included a CD of Frisell's music. Three years later the music was made more commercially available by Canadian record label Songlines as an audiovisual CD-ROM. The paintings were also reproduced in the twenty-eight-page CD booklet.

In 2005 Frisell was given the opportunity to write music in response to the life and work of Mike Disfarmer, an untrained small-town 'outsider' photographer with a bizarre and intriguing story and a growing reputation as one of the leading American portrait photographers of the twentieth century.

Disfarmer was born Mike Meyer in Indiana. In 1892, aged eight, he moved with his family to Arkansas; by the age of thirty he had settled in the small and secluded mountain town of Heber Springs, where he set up a bare and basic portrait studio. For the next forty years or more he photographed members of the local community for small fees.

Taciturn, eccentric and a strict disciplinarian, Meyer legally changed his surname to Disfarmer in 1939, possibly to break from his family's Lutheran German-American agrarian roots. He died twenty years later alone and in obscurity. What he did leave behind, however, were around three thousand black-and-white photographs, portraits that shine a stark if penetrating light on life in an ordinary Depression-era American town. They are rigorous photographs with both an austere realism and a touching intimacy.

The idea for the audiovisual project came from Chuck Helm, the director of performing arts at the Wexner Center at Ohio State University, who sensed the misfit mystery of Disfarmer might appeal to Frisell. 'I knew nothing of Disfarmer,' explained Frisell, 'and of course was blown away when I saw his photos for the first time and started to learn a little about his life.'

Wanting to dig deeper, Frisell visited Heber Springs in 2006 to spend some time in the town, to 'smell the air, talk to some people, taste the food – so the music wouldn't be coming only from what I had seen or read in a book'. He was fascinated by Disfarmer as an artist unrecognised and misunderstood in his own time, as someone who uncompromisingly stayed true to his own aesthetic. 'I tried to picture what went on in Disfarmer's mind,' Frisell continued. 'How did he feel about the people in this town? What was he thinking? What did he see? We'll never know, but as I write the music, I'd like to imagine it coming from his point of view. The sound of him looking through the lens.'

The music was premièred at the Wexner, and the Walker Art Center in Minneapolis, in 2007; a trio of Frisell, Jenny Scheinman on violin and Greg Leisz on lap steel guitar played a suite of short narrative musical vignettes that evoked aspects of Disfarmer's life and work, while the photographer's portraits were projected onto screens either side of the stage.

In 2009 the music was released on the Nonesuch CD *Disfarmer*, with the trio augmented by Viktor Krauss on bass; the slipcase and booklet featured a range of Disfarmer's intimate and illuminating images (the portraits of children are especially affecting). The twenty-six tracks are mostly variations and improvisations on a handful of melodic themes – elegantly simple yet artfully structured folk forms that are as individual and universal as Disfarmer himself. A video on the making of the music, with a concert performance filmed in France, was produced in 2012.

•
•

While Bill Frisell's music has been regularly used in independent documentaries – on subjects that range from Finnish masculinity to Mississippi Delta barge-workers; from the life and work of New York Pop artist Ray Johnson to a profile of an isolated family in the Appalachian Mountains of Kentucky – it is feature film-makers who have long appreciated the ability of Frisell's vivid and evocative compositions to suggest mood, emotion and setting.

Hal Willner brought Frisell into the mix when he was putting together the soundtrack for the 2000 film *The Million Dollar Hotel*. Directed by Wim Wenders and starring Mel Gibson, the 'tragicomic romantic who-dunit', set in a dilapidated downtown Los Angeles hotel occupied by a group of dysfunctional misfits and miscreants, was 'based on a concept story' co-written by Bono of U2, one of the film's producers.

Willner enlisted an all-star cast for the recording of the original soundtrack, which included new music by U2, Jon Hassell and Daniel Lanois; Bill Frisell was part of a 'Million Dollar Hotel Band' that featured Hassell on trumpet, Lanois on guitars and vocals, Brian Eno on keyboards, Adam Dorn on 'beats, synthesisers and programming', Greg Cohen on bass, and Brian Blade on drums.

The Million Dollar Hotel, however, was a spectacular flop, both at the box office – according to online database IMDb, the film grossed only $106,000 worldwide – and critically: reviewer Jonathan Romney described it as 'a catastrophe . . . Wenders's own artistic suicide'. At a press conference to promote the film, even Mel Gibson admitted it was 'as boring as a dog's ass'.

Frisell's music played a greater role in two higher profile films: *Walk the Line* and *Finding Forrester*. The music for the 2005 Johnny Cash biopic was created by famed producer and musician T Bone Burnett, who produced the Grammy-winning soundtrack to the Coen Brothers' *O Brother, Where Art Thou?* The accompanying album mainly highlighted the vocals of the film's leads, Reese Witherspoon and Joaquin Phoenix, but the film also featured music by Bob Dylan, Sister Rosetta Tharpe, Mississippi John Hurt – and a recording from Frisell's 2000 solo album *Ghost Town*, a dreamy and delicate overdubbed segue of the title track and 'Poem for Eva'.

Finding Forrester was the second time Frisell had worked with Gus Van Sant. The director had asked Frisell and Wayne Horvitz to provide music for the end credits of his curious 1998 shot-for-shot colour remake of Alfred Hitchcock's *Psycho*; as Marion's car is towed from the swamp, Frisell's atmospheric guitar and effects both reference Bernard Herrmann's famously edgy film score and create an eerie soundscape of sadness, loss and deep unease.

For his 2000 film, about a young black writer who finds a mentor in a reclusive white author (played by Sean Connery), Van Sant used three existing Frisell tracks – 'Beautiful E', 'Coffaro's Theme', and 'Under a Golden Sky' from the recently released *Ghost Town*. Frisell also recorded a version, solo on guitar and loops, of Harold Arlen's signature song from *The Wizard of Oz*, 'Over the Rainbow'.

Frisell has composed full original scores for two films: *Tongzhi in Love*, a 2008 thirty-minute documentary by Oscar-winning director Ruby Yang about the challenges of being gay in modern China; and *All Hat*, a 2007 Canadian 'western comedy' feature film directed by Leonard Farlinger that went the way of *The Million Dollar Hotel* – it was, to borrow a titular line from the film, 'all hat, and no cattle'.

A CD of Frisell's soundtrack was released the following year on the EmArcy label; the thirty-one short themes, variations and interludes work well enough as scenic and narrative film devices, but *All Hat* fails to ever find momentum as a standalone album. It sounds like a zigzagging journey across the guitarist's roots and Americana heartland – it's like a sampler, a fun Friscellany.

•
•

Bill Morrison is an award-winning experimental film-maker who uses rare archival footage 'in which long-forgotten, and sometimes deteriorated, imagery is reframed'. While he often shoots his own footage, Morrison is best known for discovering decayed and neglected films, and investing them with a new narrative life and historical perspective. As the *Washington Post* declared, 'Out of the cinematic ruins, Morrison salvages art.'

Music has always been an integral part of Morrison's films, and he has collaborated with many contemporary composers and musicians, including Philip Glass, John Adams, Steve Reich, Gavin Bryars, Jóhann Jóhannsson and Michael Gordon, as well as alt-country band Lambchop and jazz musicians Dave Douglas and Vijay Iyer.

Frisell first met Morrison in the early nineties and a few years later Morrison made *The Film of Her*, a twelve-minute short in which he used Frisell's slow, mysterious and offbeat ballad 'The Way Home' from *Is That You?*

At the 2004 New York Guitar Festival, Frisell, bassist Tony Scherr and drummer Kenny Wollesen performed new music Frisell had been commissioned to write for the screening of five early silent films. The trio also played Frisell's compositions 'Again' and 'Tell Your Ma, Tell Your Pa' to accompany Morrison's *The Mesmerist* – a hallucinatory and sometimes disturbingly psychedelic sixteen-minute re-edit of a deteriorated nitrate print of *The Bells*, a 1926 silent film starring Lionel Barrymore and Boris Karloff.

Frisell and Morrison realised an ambition to collaborate on a longer feature film 'from the ground up' in 2011 – with *The Great Flood*, a non-narrative portrayal of the Mississippi River flood of 1927. Again using found footage, with minimal text and no spoken dialogue, Morrison and Frisell explored the enormous economic, social, political and cultural consequences of the flood. As well as leaving more than 700,000 people homeless and displaced, the inundation forced many African Americans, mostly sharecroppers from the Lower Mississippi, to relocate north as part of the so-called 'Great Migration'. In Chicago, to take one example of the effects of the flood on the history of American music, Delta blues gradually became urban, electrified and reimagined.

'The magnitude of the event, and the gigantic effect it had on the US and the world – that really blew my mind,' says Frisell. 'It's only one small aspect, but . . . what happened, with those musicians plugging in their instruments, their guitars . . . it meant things went from acoustic to electric; from country blues to rhythm and blues and rock 'n' roll.'

Morrison arranged for Frisell and the musicians playing the music for *The Great Flood* – Tony Scherr, Kenny Wollesen and Ron Miles – to accompany him on a field trip to the areas affected by the 1927 floods. In May 2011 Morrison and the Frisell quartet travelled to the Mississippi, and for a fortnight, as Frisell began to write and the band workshopped the music, they played gigs in various cities up and down the river.

'While I was just starting to write the music, it was bizarre, because coincidentally, the river was flooding again, to a huge degree, in some places as bad as it had been in 1927,' says Frisell. 'That added some real power to the subject and the music, some emotional weight, or something – especially when we were playing the piece live.'

The Great Flood is a seventy-five-minute confluence of Morrison's immersive black-and-white silent images and Frisell's shimmering blues and oozy roots music. The original score is at times meditative and mournful, yet Frisell also imbues the music with a sense of resilience, rebirth and redemption.

Frisell was keen that the quartet continued to develop, reinterpret and renew the score. 'There are set pieces and melodies,' he told me, 'but, just as it's the nature of a river to dry up or flood, or to change its course, I wanted the music to be alive and evolving all the time.' Performances of the work were held in concert halls and at festivals in the US and Europe from 2011 to 2014. While no album of the music was released – a shame, as *The Great Flood* contains some of Frisell's most powerful and affecting work for film – a DVD of a live performance in Seattle was produced in 2014.

Frisell and Morrison have worked on two further projects. In 2018 the duo created *Electricity*, a UK commission by the Museum of Science and Industry in Manchester that used British technical, educational and commercial films on electricity as part of an exhibition; Frisell's score was performed by his string quartet of Scheinman, Kang and Roberts.

The following year the two Bills began an association with The Tank Center for Sonic Arts, a remarkable sixty-five-foot-high Corten steel water tank in northwestern Colorado, built around 1940, which has been converted into a resonant performance space and adjacent recording studio. Frisell and Morrison have developed a work, premièred in August 2021, which 'tells the history of the Tank as a way of evoking the larger story of the American West'.

'With all these [visual] projects, it's a chance for me to go further into something new, to learn, and to explore my own feelings about a subject,' says Frisell. 'But I think the only reason I've been asked to do any of them is that the directors and programmers knew who I was, and they wanted what I do. A lot of the time I'm not really aggressively going after these opportunities. The music always seems to bring me to them.'

17: Jim Woodring Listens to *With Dave Holland and Elvin Jones*

With Dave Holland and Elvin Jones: recorded New York, spring 2000, and San Francisco, early 2001; producers Lee Townsend and Michael Shrieve; released on Nonesuch, October 2001; Bill Frisell (electric and acoustic guitars, loops); Dave Holland (bass), Elvin Jones (drums); all compositions by Frisell, except 'Moon River' by Henry Mancini and 'Hard Times' by Stephen Foster.

Jim Woodring is one of the world's great visionary cartoonists. Best known for the hallucinatory comics and illustrated autojournals in his magazine *JIM,* and for his wordless cartoon series depicting the misadventures of his anthropomorphic character Frank, he creates a phantasmagorical world of hybrid creatures that seem familiar, naïve and harmlessly mischievous, yet are often menacing and deadly. Born in 1952, Woodring is also an accomplished fine artist, graphic novelist and toy designer, and his artworks are often surreal and subversive, with a black humour at work. You can see why Frisell instantly took to them.

Woodring first began collaborating with Frisell on the artwork for the guitarist's 1998 album *Gone, Just Like a Train*. Frisell wrote in the liner notes: 'Some people may be surprised by the cover – it's quite different from my others – but [it] may be the first time where the cover art is so closely linked to the music.' In 2002 Frisell reciprocated by recording a short soundtrack to accompany Woodring's story about a playful elephant-like creature called *Trosper* – 'A children's book,' according to one review, 'that really shouldn't be read by children.'

I met Jim at his home on Vashon Island near Seattle, on a rainy Sunday afternoon in December 2015, to listen to the 2001 trio album Frisell recorded with Dave Holland on bass and Elvin Jones on drums, for which Woodring again provided the artwork.

'Talk about a big person,' Frisell has said of Holland. 'Hearing him with Miles [Davis] – when I really got deep into jazz music it was when he played with Miles. That's as big a thing as could be – someone who was in that world.' Recording with Jones, a member of John Coltrane's classic sixties quartet and one of the greatest drummers in jazz, was a monumental moment for Frisell. The session was facilitated by former Santana drummer Michael Shrieve. 'Michael got it in his head that I should play with Elvin,' Frisell has said. 'And I said, "Yeah, right. Like that's ever going to happen."'

Woodring is thoughtful, clever, serious (in a good way) and self-deprecating, and the vibe he created while I was with him was so congenial that it reminded me of a long-lost time as a teenager, sitting around playing records with a best friend. I had a strong urge to draw the curtains, turn off the lights, and spark up a joint.

PW: I'm interested in how you make the music visual. Can you tell me how you went about creating the artwork for this album? What was the process?

JW: [Looking at the CD] Well, I didn't have this finished record to work from; I had tapes, with track numbers, and no titles. So I didn't really know what I was listening to. And I didn't really know anything about the other two musicians.

All I knew was that it was an album by these three masters, who had never played as a trio before, and that Bill had said that it was a record he could not have made at an earlier point in his life. So I guess I was influenced by the fact that I knew that it meant a lot to Bill; I felt the album was something significant and heavy.

It struck me as being more cerebral than a lot of Bill's other music, a little more austere and formal. That wasn't a *bad* thing, because even though I'm not a musician, I've been able to tell when jazz is *fun* and when it's *serious*. And this struck me as being kind of *serious*.

Let me play you a track. It's a kind of a Frisell standard by now – 'Strange Meeting'.

[As the music is playing] Yes. The first drawing that I did, this red one, a kind of endlessly blossoming flower creature, was to this track. I can remember thinking that the music represented kind of a controlled flight – hemmed in, but not *oppressed* in any way; just having to work within parameters. It wasn't taking off and soaring; it was trying to get through something, to move forward through these archways.

It was like these three musicians got together and they created this thing, this creature, something that was moving, and marking the area it was moving through, and causing its environment to unfold and expand. That was how the music sounded to me.

These images are just snapshots – of sounds. They correspond to things I heard in the music. But this other picture here [he points to the purple drawing of a symmetrical anthropomorphic figure] is more of a portrait, of Bill, based on a drawing that I did.

Oh really?

Yes. Bill's competence musically seems just other-worldly – he's a great, great genius, in my opinion, of a particularly useful and totally construct-ive kind. If he's ever done anything malevolent, or bad, or underhanded, or heartless, I don't know about it. He inhabits this sphere of blessedness that, if you're in it, if you're in a car with him, that car's in the sphere, and you always find a parking spot, you know.

So this is a psychological portrait of Bill as kind of a reigning entity, somebody who came from another world to ours and turned out to have strange powers to bring . . . *bliss* to people.

Then I thought, 'What might that person be in his own world?' Would he be a potentate or a sage? So I did this drawing of this other-worldly creature with a lot of artistic and intellectual attributes. He's holding an embryo in one hand and the brain of a lamprey in the other. And he doesn't have eyes, but he has these tentacles which form loops, so it looks like he has eyes. So you don't quite know what you're looking at. It kind of forms a lacuna in your mind.

Here's another track, the first on the album, 'Outlaws'.

[We sit in silence listening to all eight minutes of it] Oh, boy. Yeah, *so* many things happen in this music. It's just like one half-second experience after another. Yet it seems uneasy to me. With a lot of this album, I can't tell if it's fighting or coming together.

Well, Bill probably told you that the trio didn't exactly have much time together. It was like 'this little jam session' for just a few hours in a studio in New York.

To me, it seems like there's *a lot* of understanding, but a lot of reaching at the same time. Which makes it so interesting. It's so strong. Yet it seems like there's a lot of tension. It's like they're after something that's really, really difficult to nail.

For this CD artwork, did you listen and draw at the same time?

Yes, I would sketch while listening to the music – just listen for something that sounded like something, and then I would try to draw that thing.

Like the picture on the back of the album, of this bulbous thing in what looks like an abandoned schoolroom. I remember that came from some little discordant *blap* in the music, followed by a pause, an emptiness, which made it seem portentous.

Did Bill or the record company give you any kind of brief?

Bill said, 'Do whatever you want.' But when I gave him the pictures, I said, 'OK, Bill, I know this is aggressively weird. And, again, pretty different from your other record covers. Don't accept them, if you don't like them.' I really did everything but beg him to turn me down. And he was going, 'No, no, it's great. I love it; it's perfect. I see what you're doing; this is good.' So I went along with it.

I wanted to do the three musicians as wind-up, post-war Japanese toys. Like, have them in their boxes, looking really cute on the cover, but when you see the actual toys inside, they are real kind of horrifying-looking. Bill was a mechanical squirrel with a guitar. Elvin was a kind of spooky-looking cat playing a drum set. I had just come up with these figures arbitrarily, but I think he or they [the record company], or both, thought it was too undignified, especially for Elvin. That was the official reason given.

Well, Bill said at the time that he was very nervous about the recording, about playing with such greats of the music, so . . . you might expect the cover art to be, well . . . more reverential? It's something of a surprise: that actual cover for that particular record.

Yes, it really is. And I think that's great. For me personally, that record packaging is one of my great artistic triumphs. Because those individual drawings capture for me the strange passages in their playing, which is what I like. I like it when they break the music and then they fix it, but for a while things look like they're really going awry.

When I think about certain records – Captain Beefheart's Trout Mask Replica, *for example, which I know is a favourite of yours, or Miles Davis's* Bitches Brew – *I think about the music and the covers almost simultaneously, as one. Was that quality any kind of an ambition or inspiration for you and this record?*

You're trying to get me to admit that . . . it's a failure. [There is a comedic pause. We both laugh.]

Absolutely not!

[In mock accusatory voice] Well, what else? I've just told you how good I think it is. Why do you keep trying to see if there's some . . . 'Were you even thinking about how this would become part of posterity? Did you recognise your responsibility? Did you know that you were possibly making millions of people angry and diminishing their ability to enjoy this record? Don't you realise that Bill is a nice guy, who will say yes to you, even when he knows you're going to torpedo his project?

Didn't you know what you were doing?' [There is more laughter, and a pause.]

Can you tell me about the cover image for the album?

Well, these are the three musicians, as I visualised them. The one in the foreground being Bill.

Oh, I didn't realise that.

Yeah. I didn't broadcast that notion at the time very much. I don't even think I told Bill that was the idea.

And which one is Elvin Jones?

Well . . . I think of the figure at the top of the hill, the spiky building thing, as being the drummer. I don't know why; there's no logical reason for it. [Laughing. Backtracking.] But I would *hate* for anybody to think that this was my idea of them. This is not really the three of them; it's just a landscape, you know.

If I just let my mind go and enjoy music in an abstract way, it conjures up places and landscapes that these figures accompany. I'm much more visual than I am aural – something has to sound the way something else looks for me to really get it.

When you're creating these images, how much are you responding to the music as abstract sounds, and how much are you influenced by it being very specifically the music of Bill Frisell?

Well, it's obviously nobody but Bill. It's like he's speaking to you in his voice. So no, I can't completely just listen to it as sound.

But I do think of it in terms of, 'What is Bill saying here? What's on *his* mind?' That's really what intrigues me, because I feel like he's got this language, and we understand that we like it, but we can't really – I can't really – know exactly what he's saying. I have to find meaning in it; it isn't evident to me. But it's obvious that he knows what he's talking about.

Here's another track, 'Justice and Honor'.

[As it ends] Does it sound to you like Bill's playing cowboy music?

Definitely. I think the song was even described by one critic as 'a kind of modern-day cowboy ballad'.

Isn't that weird [he laughs]?

Well, no more I guess than Elvin Jones playing with Pete Seeger, which he did once in the sixties . . . Has Bill ever talked to you about his process, about how he moves a sound, like a cowboy-ballad sound, say, from his head, his imagination, to the guitar and ultimately to a record? Has he talked about how he gets it out?

No, he hasn't, really. I've watched him do it – write, and come up with ideas. But he probably doesn't know how he does it himself – how he can sit down and write music, and then also stand up and make it up on the spot, too. They seem like two totally different skills to me.

He certainly has a knack [Woodring laughs]. And he works so god-damned hard at it. He has written tons of music. He has files and files of the stuff – some full of things he has written and done nothing with. Can you imagine the amount of music that guy is going to leave? Has left? It's *unreal*. It's a long shadow.

Yeah, he's not slouched.

[Laughing] He's not slouched! [He laughs again, more uproariously.]

In his liner notes to Gone, Just Like a Train, *Bill wrote about you, 'I feel a connection with him – kind of a common quest for something – that I've found in only a handful of musicians.' He writes that you 'bring up to the surface a world of things that are hidden and buried'. Have you any idea what those connections and that 'world of things' might be?*

[Pause] I think that we both have . . . well, it's a transcendental thing, you know – there aren't words for it.

I think it's probably something like a hopeful attitude. Because the evidence that there's terrible shit in the world, that the good things don't seem able to withstand the onslaughts of evil, is kind of overwhelming.

But there's also the belief that the good in the world really *is* strong and pure and more meaningful, and only temporarily defeated. And even though there's a lot that is frightening and mysterious, it is also benign – and can be enjoyed for its frightening and mysterious qualities, therefore.

I think it sounds silly to say this, because you could say the music's in him and it's just coming out, but it's like his soul is speaking. Something is emerging from the realm of discrete information through him.

It's a sense that there's more to all this than meets the eye, that there are forces behind. And that some of the best things in the world are expressions of these benign forces that we can't see directly, but the influence of which we perceive in an act of kindness, an act of artistic generosity, or in music – Bill's music.

Marc Ribot: I'm a fan of your Nashville and American music stuff – can I call it American music, for want of a better name?

Bill Frisell: Sure.

MR: What do you call it?

BF: Oh, I don't. But I guess that's what it is.

MR: When I listen to it, I always feel that you're hip to these strange correspondences between musics that are socially at opposite ends of the spectrum – for example, country music and R&B.

BF: Yeah, for me, those are totally the same music.

MR: This is something that musicians know, that sometimes I wonder if the fans know. I mean, musicians know it in a deep way. For example, that the Telecaster is the common main guitar of R&B and country music, or that 6/8 beats are common to both country and R&B ballads. It sounds nerdy when you say it, but . . . it seems that you've managed to find some of those hidden connections in what you've done.

BF: Yeah, going to Nashville and doing that record [*Nashville*] – I mean, I've always been interested in that – but it stepped up my interest. I got more fascinated with, not so much bluegrass or country music, but in looking at the music that was happening in the twenties and around the beginning of the century. I started hearing musicians like Blind Willie Johnson or Dock Boggs and Roscoe Holcomb. There are places in the music where you don't know if it's black or white. It really gets blurred.

MR: Absolutely.

BF: Or even Bill Monroe, the father of bluegrass music, which has become this totally white thing, sort of. But it's just not at all. I'd hear these momentary flashes where, man, it sounds exactly like some recording of Duke Ellington's band. Just for ten seconds, but it's exactly the feel, the whole way the instruments are interacting and everything.

MR: Is that what you look for when you're going into that music, the moments when its borders meld?

BF: Yeah, where it just transcends all that stuff that's been put on us by a record company or a writer or somebody analysing everything after the fact and then categorising it. Musicians don't do that when they're in the midst of playing; that stuff always comes later.

∴

From the mid-nineties onwards Bill Frisell began to make his enthusiasm for a broad range of American music more explicit.

Perhaps it all comes back, inevitably, to his childhood, to that exploding universe of music he heard in the sixties, and the big skies, high mountains and Great Plains above and beyond his suburban horizons. Or maybe it was the revelations Frisell experienced at those North Carolina fiddle fairs he visited with his parents in the late eighties. 'I was hearing these people play stuff that nobody was playing in New York,' he told banjo player Danny Barnes. 'Folks who had lived there their whole life were playing the heaviest music I'd ever heard!'

Perhaps he felt, too, that he'd arrived at a place in which he had the freedom to express himself more fully and completely.

'In the past few years, I've been obsessed with old blues and bluegrass – all this real simple, open-string guitar and banjo music,' Frisell said in *Guitar Player* in 1999. 'Earlier in my career, I was more interested in what Bill Evans played on the piano, or what Sonny Rollins played on the saxophone, or what some orchestra played. I was always trying to think of the guitar as a piano – *not* as a guitar.'

Frisell was simplifying, searching, going back to what first turned him on to music and playing the guitar; he was trying to understand himself and his musical identity. *The Rambler. This Land. Before We Were Born. Is That You*, Bill Frisell?

'It's a weird, exciting time for me,' he continued. 'I'm definitely moving away from the postmodern jazz direction I followed for years, but I don't really know *where* I'm going.'

•
•

In 1995 Nonesuch president Bob Hurwitz asked Frisell if, for his next album, he wanted to head south to Nashville and record with some Music City musicians. It was another example of Hurwitz's shrewd artist management; he knew Frisell would not be able to resist.

Nashville went against some of Frisell's more deeply ingrained musical instincts. 'I hated country music when I was growing up in Colorado,' Frisell told Francis Davis in the *Atlantic*. 'It was, like, the most uncool thing you could imagine.' Yet Frisell was also aware that country was part of his musical make-up. 'You heard it all the time,' he continued, 'and it was right there in so much of the jazz and pop music that I really liked – Dylan, Sonny Rollins's *Way Out West*, the things that Gary Burton did with Larry Coryell on guitar in the sixties. So going to Nashville didn't feel like that big of a jump.'

A jump, perhaps not – but a leap of faith nonetheless. This would be the first time Frisell was to record an album under his own name with musicians outside his own groups and immediate circle, and coming from an American tradition as far removed from advanced composition and arranging classes at Berklee, and Naked City gigs at the Knitting Factory, as it was possible to imagine. 'It was sort of like if I was going to India to play with some people,' Frisell said in *Jazziz*. 'I had no idea what was going to happen.'

He must have known that the Nashville idea might turn out to be a folly, an act of musical dilettantism, a mistake both creatively and commercially that could alienate both his core audience and any potential new listeners. How would those drawn to the more improvised and experimental aspects of Frisell's music – the 60,000 or so fans around the world, for example, who had bought his best-selling album up to that point, *Have a Little Faith* – respond to him releasing an album of American country music? And how would even the most open-eared roots music enthusiast react to having such a fearlessly groundbreaking jazz-and-beyond interloper in their midst?

Hurwitz and Frisell decided to bring in Wayne Horvitz as producer. Not only did Horvitz understand the multiplicity of Frisell's talent, but he also had a strong passion for country, blues, folk and singer-songwriting. 'I thought musically it was a no-brainer, just an obvious great idea,' says Horvitz. 'We all loved that music and Bill was so good at it. You listen to his own compositions and there's obviously a tremendous amount of country music and American harmony even in his more jazz-related tunes.'

Hurwitz put Frisell in contact with Kyle Lehning, a leading Nashville producer and record executive, who had worked closely with Kenny Rogers, George Jones and Randy Travis. Lehning could connect the guitarist to Nashville musicians who, as Frisell once explained, 'were young, open, and willing to try something totally haywire'.

Frisell and Horvitz flew to Nashville and met with Lehning. He took them to the *Grand Ole Opry*, where they saw singer and fiddler Alison Krauss and her popular bluegrass and country band Union Station; the great Bill Monroe; and country music legends Little Jimmy Dickens and Hank Snow, both of whom had been singing on the fabled radio concert stage for almost fifty years. 'We got to hear *all* those guys that one night,' says Frisell. 'Wow, it doesn't even seem real!'

Lehning introduced Frisell and Horvitz to banjo and guitar player Ron Block and mandolinist Adam Steffey – both members of Union Station (Block remains part of the group today). Lehning was pushing Frisell more towards progressive bluegrass players, because of the strong element of interpretation in their approach.

'Bluegrass and jazz are very compatible, because they're both very improvisational musics,' says dobro master Jerry Douglas, who would also contribute to the album (the dobro is a type of resonator guitar). 'You would think that in bluegrass we just play the melody, but the music's evolved to the point where we have large encyclopaedias of phrases and note choices and countermelodies and ways of turning things around. We always think of songs in those terms.'

Frisell went away, wrote and arranged music with Block and Steffey in mind, and selected other songs to record. He also asked along twenty-six-year-old bass player Viktor Krauss: the younger brother of Alison Krauss and a member of Lyle Lovett's group. Viktor had also played with Block and Steffey, and was a member of Jerry Douglas's band.

There were two mostly acoustic recording sessions for the album, a year or more apart: in September 1995 and October and November 1996. 'When I heard that vibrato he would get out of the guitar,' says Jerry Douglas, who played on the second session, 'I said, "Your sound, your tone, is a lot like Chet Atkins's tone was on the Louvin Brothers records. You're country, even if you don't know it!"'

Frisell knew of Atkins's playing, and admired his 'mind-blowing technique', but Douglas's favourable comparison encouraged Bill to also seek out some of Atkins's earlier work as a sideman. 'Jerry mentioned that Chet played with the Carter Sisters and Mother Maybelle, so I listened to some of that music,' says Frisell. 'Hearing his electric guitar in that acoustic environment – so beautiful.'

As with Frisell's previous release *Quartet*, there was no drummer, on either session – a conscious decision by Frisell and Horvitz designed to spotlight the melodic intricacies and harmonic interplays between the string instruments; the overall sound on the album is closer to chamber Americana or jazz Arcadia than country hoedown.

Rather than providing sheet music, Frisell sent tapes of the songs to the players in advance. The first time Frisell and the musicians played together was in the studio – famed Studio A at Sound Emporium in

Nashville. Frisell said he would 'play the tune, and they would learn it that way – they were frighteningly fast'.

Robin Holcomb contributed to the first session, singing three songs in her plaintive soprano and fluttering vibrato: 'One of These Days' from Neil Young's album *Harvest Moon*; 'Will Jesus Wash the Bloodstains from Your Hands', an anti-war song by bluegrass singer and pioneer Hazel Dickens; and 'The End of the World', a hit for country singer Skeeter Davis, which Frisell remembered hearing on the radio at home in Denver when he was eleven or twelve. 'It feels very natural collaborating with Bill; we fit well together and it's very intertwined, on a deep level,' says Holcomb. 'We can just be right in the zone of the song, stay very true to it, and it's always inspiring, but in very subtle, beautiful ways. There's a lot of push and pull of the rhythm of the melody, and it's different every time. It's like we're breathing a different kind of life into the song.'

Frisell contributed eleven new tunes, all previously unrecorded. They are mostly wholesome, plain-spoken, folk-like melodies – songs that contain little of Frisell's hallmark darkness or distortion. Even the titles seem carefully chosen to set and suit the mood: 'Gimme a Holler', 'Shucks', 'Dogwood Acres', and 'We're Not from Around Here'.

The album, simply titled *Nashville*, was released in April 1997, and – with its unorthodox marriage of jazz harmonies, rhythms and improvisation with country themes, instrumentation and interpretation – it divided reviewers almost immediately.

Most critics, from *Jazziz* to the *Journal of Country Music*, seemed to sense *Nashville* was an honest and heartfelt expression of Frisell's affection for this music, and not some ersatz imitation, and praised the album accordingly. The record even went on, somewhat controversially, to win Jazz Album of the Year in the *DownBeat* annual critics' poll. Some writers, however, felt the record was oddly polite and overly respectful – not nearly 'haywire' enough, in fact. '[*Nashville*] tends to tread a tad too cautiously,' ran the review in *The Wire*. 'Frisell almost sounds intimidated by the virtuosity of the band. He takes a back-seat role for much of the record, and when he does solo he's frustratingly tentative.' Cook and Morton in the

Penguin Guide were more damning: 'A weak and watery collage . . . perhaps the most one-dimensional record Frisell has ever made.'

Even though the record did well – it sold almost 80,000 copies and remains one of Frisell's best-selling albums – some jazz fans seemed severely disgruntled by the record, and remain so. After Frisell was voted the top guitarist in the *DownBeat* annual critics' poll in 2013, one reader was moved to respond: 'That's such a crock. He's a country & western/ wedding band player. He is not a jazz player.'

'The criticism was that I was selling out, playing it safe,' Frisell told *Jazzwise* magazine. 'They perceived it that I was trying to go commercial, to make money. They perceived it that the music was not as challenging as it was before. For me, it was just the opposite! For me, it was going out on a limb, taking a chance . . .' Frisell has asserted over the years that, in fact, *Nashville* was one of the riskiest career moves he has ever made, and one of his biggest creative steps. 'For me to go to Nashville, and play with guys I didn't know, was much more dangerous and edgy and adventurous than going to the Knitting Factory and playing a bunch of noise with people who I had been doing that with,' he told Radhika Philip.

Reflecting on the album a few years after its release, Frisell concluded in the *Seattle Times*, 'People want to put you in a box. It's a journey for me. You know, you have to go somewhere to get somewhere.'

•
•

In December 1996 Frisell returned to Seattle after recording his next album, the remarkable *Gone, Just Like a Train*.

'I was super-high off of that amazing, uplifting experience,' he says. 'But almost as soon as I got home, I got a phone call from my parents with some bad news.' Bill Sr had been diagnosed with pancreatic cancer, and was seriously ill. 'My father had been told it was terminal. I was in total shock.'

That Christmas Bill, Carole and Monica flew to North Carolina to see Bill Sr for what was to be the last time. 'He cried when he saw Monica, knowing he'd not have the chance to see her grow up,' says Frisell; Monica was about to turn eleven. 'That's the only time I ever remember seeing my father cry.'

Frisell played Carnegie Hall for the first time in January 1997 with the American Composers Orchestra, conducted by Dennis Russell Davies; he wrote a letter to his father telling him about the experience. 'It was close to the end, and he was weak and in bad shape by then, but I thanked him for the support and encouragement he had always given me,' says Frisell. 'My mother told me afterwards that she had read it to him.' Six weeks after Frisell had been told about his father's illness, and a week after the concert at Carnegie Hall, Bill's father died in Chapel Hill, North Carolina; he was seventy-six.

Bill received the news late at night on the phone from his mother; perhaps inevitably, he was working – Frisell was in a studio in New York recording *The Sound of Summer Running* with Marc Johnson, Pat Metheny and Joey Baron. Bill and Joey were due to fly to San Francisco to play two concerts that had been organised far in advance. Frisell was torn, but in the end his mother encouraged him to proceed with the performances; he was also conscious of honouring his father's example, which, as Carole said, 'was very much about being committed'. Immediately after the concerts, he flew to North Carolina for the funeral.

Bill Sr had retired as professor emeritus at the East Carolina University (ECU) School of Medicine in Greenville ten years earlier, and had remained as chair of the department of biochemistry until 1990. There is still, more than thirty years later, a page dedicated to Wilhelm Frisell on the ECU website, with a summary of his career, and illustrations of two of the paintings he donated to the department. The eulogy reads, 'Dr Frisell led with knowledge, kindness, humour and an artistic flair . . . He is remembered as a mentor who only ever asked us to strive for excellence in our teaching and our science.'

Carole says it was only after Bill's father died that she and Bill discovered there was a microorganism called the Frisellium named after him. 'That was the thing about Bill's father: he was *very* modest. Bill's like that too; you don't see any of the trophies or awards he's been given around the house. They're all in a box somewhere.'

Frisell confesses that, as the years have gone by since his father died, he has become aware of how, curiously, he feels more and more connected to him, and how much he has become like him. 'I'm noticing that as I get older, I'm just turning into him,' he says, smiling. 'Not just physically, like catching my reflection, or something. I remember being in Chicago a couple of years after he died, right where all the amazing glass buildings are, and suddenly I saw my father walking towards me. That really flipped me out.'

Frisell says he also relates to his father's intense dedication. 'Even though chemistry was my worst subject at school, I can see his drive, and how hard he worked, how he tried the best he could the whole way. But also that he never really felt he was a success. I think I've got some of that. Like when I realised that I wanted to play guitar, I knew I just had to practise and practise, but then I also felt that it was never quite good enough. The farthest thing from my mind at the time was that it had anything to do with my father. But now I think what a presence he was, and how it's maybe all coming from the same place.'

David Breskin spent some time with Frisell soon after he received the news of his father's death. At one point David gave Bill a telegram that the drummer Ronald Shannon Jackson had sent to him when Breskin's father died in 1981. It reads, 'Winter always turns to spring.' The Buddhist saying became the title of one Frisell's compositions, recorded on his 2000 solo album, *Ghost Town*, and 2020 trio album, *Valentine*. Frisell has carried that faded, now forty-year-old telegram with him ever since, in a leather wallet alongside his passport.

In 2004 Breskin published a collection of poems titled *Escape Velocity*, the opening work of which was 'The Guitarist', and dedicated to Bill. It is a poignant and perceptive poem that looks back to that fragile time in January 1997 before Bill left to go 'home to the old home where his father died'. The poem is laid out in couplets, like guitar strings or musical staves, and it scans like a slow ballad, with lots of air and space and easy rhythm. The last lines are:

> *. . . The guitarist carries his axe*
>
> *with him at all times, into the forest*
> *of funeral, into the Douglas fir*
>
> *and weeping willow, live oak, sycamore,*
> *because in the end your chops are all*
>
> *you have against the skirling tone-deaf world:*
> *hammer, pluck, chord, gouge, pedal, ring, sustain.*

•
•

After Nashville there was no turning back. An entire world of American vernacular music was starting to open up to Frisell, and he wanted to go deeper and wider. He was at the entrance to Greil Marcus's famous 'invisible republic', the 'old weird America' that had supported and seeped into much of the music that followed.

It was also no coincidence that a lot of this early music featured guitar players. Frisell explored some of the great originators and pathfinders of sounds that encompassed folk-blues singer and 'king of the twelve-string guitar' Lead Belly; ragtime blues bravura fingerpicker Blind Blake; and gospel blues singer and slide-guitarist Blind Willie Johnson – his sound 'kind of rips your spine out', Frisell told *Fretboard Journal* magazine. He embraced old-time music – singer and banjo player Dock Boggs; early country – singer-songwriter Jimmie Rodgers; and country-folk – the Carter Family. 'Maybelle Carter has been a big influence on me,' Frisell has said. 'Actually, she's a big influence on most non-classical guitar players, whether they know it or not, with that way of playing melody and rhythm simultaneously.'

Frisell also investigated Appalachian folk – singer and banjo player

Roscoe Holcomb; and country – the 'Hillbilly Shakespeare' Hank Williams. 'I think I listened more to Hank Williams in the last two or three years than I did in my whole life,' Frisell said in 2000. Bluegrass also featured strongly, especially Bill Monroe and singer and banjo player Ralph Stanley. The first time Frisell heard Dr Stanley's high tenor 'old-time mountain voice', at once frail and strong, was at a banjo festival in Seattle. 'Tears just started pouring out of my eyes,' he says. 'It was like I was hearing *something* – something real. I don't know what it was, but then I was thinking that all that family history in Virginia on my mother's side is not so far from where he [Stanley] came from, where that sound – there's a sound he has – comes from.'

Frisell explained his relationship to these American musics to Marc Ribot in *BOMB*: 'I was fascinated with the notes and the rhythms. But it's also about figuring out where I come from, looking at my own roots . . . The idea started growing on me to try to figure it out . . . it felt like I needed to patch up the foundations.' In Frisell's mind, these foundations had to support something new. 'I love looking back,' Frisell told *Jazziz*, 'but somehow, looking back is a way to get into the future for me, too.'

From *Nashville* Frisell progressed to back-to-back album releases that stand as two of the many high points of his recording career.

The first, released just nine months after *Nashville* in January 1998, was *Gone, Just Like a Train*; the album saw Frisell return to a more stripped-back guitar-trio format – one of his own musical roots – with Viktor Krauss on bass and Jim Keltner on drums.

Frisell was determined to work with Krauss again, as he felt the bassist had been crucial to the *Nashville* sessions. 'He turned out to be the magic glue that held everything together,' wrote Frisell in his handwritten liner notes to the new album. 'Viktor is classically trained, [has] played lots of bluegrass, and he *loves* AC/DC.'

Frisell had first met Keltner a few years earlier when Jim had called in to a recording studio in Los Angeles to see English drummer Ginger Baker; the legendary Cream co-founder was making a trio album with Charlie Haden on bass and Frisell on guitar.

Often referred to as the 'leading session drummer in America', Keltner is a highly respected and sought-after musician, a quiet master who has played with some of the biggest names in popular music – from John Lennon to Bob Dylan, Eric Clapton to Ry Cooder, Dolly Parton to Barbra Streisand, and Brian Wilson to Randy Newman. He had also been the drummer on John Hiatt's *Bring the Family*, the album that had made such a strong impression on Frisell in the late eighties. As Frisell wrote in his liner notes, 'There may be some people on the planet who don't know his name, but there's probably not many who haven't heard him play.'

Frisell told me, 'The simplification, the cliché is that, say . . . Paul Motian plays free jazz – abstract, colouristic, textural – and Jim Keltner is a studio guy who plays really heavy groove. And that's true for both of those guys, but, man, I could just as easily turn the names around. Of course, Jim's got that beat, that great feel that he has. But he can also play spontaneous, textural and extreme – in the most fantastic and beautiful way.'

If the leader sometimes sounded curiously restrained on *Nashville*, on this new album – on songs and solos that echo and expand with elements of jazz and country blues, rockabilly and reggae, country and metal, surf rock and tango – Frisell's playing could not be more contrastingly unleashed and out-front. The music evokes journeys, landscapes and scenes, yet there is also much hinted at and implied, much that is hard to exactly place and locate. It is music that mesmerises and beguiles, an album that, as one critic wrote, 'defies almost every rock power trio and jazz trio precedent'. It went on to become one of Frisell's most popular albums.

As did its follow-up, the quietly timeless and revelatory *Good Dog, Happy Man*. Recorded in the same Los Angeles studio (O'Henry Sound in Burbank), and produced by Lee Townsend, the album featured the core unit of Frisell, Krauss and Keltner, augmented by Wayne Horvitz on piano and Hammond B3 organ, and Greg Leisz on various guitars (including pedal steel, lap steel and dobro) and mandolin.

The inclusion of Leisz was a significant development for Frisell. An understated yet remarkably versatile musician whose skill and sensitivity have made him a vital contributor to countless recordings by k. d. lang, Joni Mitchell, Emmylou Harris, Fiona Apple and Beck, Leisz mines deeply into traditional folk, country, blues and bluegrass forms, as well as being influenced by jazz electric guitar pioneer Charlie Christian. It would become a close musical partnership that endures to this day.

Frisell says he felt an instant connection to Leisz. 'I didn't know *anything* at all about Greg – who he was or what he'd done,' says Frisell. 'But we talked, and it turned out we did have mutual . . . he knew Jim Keltner, for example, and it was just the way he thought about music, the atmosphere that I felt from him. It's just something that I'm attracted to in a person, an instinct that I trust. And it's weird . . . What is it? Kismet? I had the same feeling with Greg as I did when I first spoke to Eyvind [Kang] in Seattle or Ron [Miles] in Denver: I sort of knew I was going to play with him even before I heard him play.'

Frisell invited Leisz to the *Good Dog* sessions, but the pedal steel player was nervous. 'Before I met Bill, I listened to a lot more jazz than I played,' Leisz told *DownBeat*. 'I'd work up a tune like [thirties jazz standard] "All of Me" or [John Coltrane's] "Naima" just to hear how it might sound on the pedal steel, but I was never in a jazz band . . . Playing with Bill brought me into that world full-on.'

Frisell brought eleven new songs to the recording – tunes of unerring beauty, deceptive simplicity and folk-like restraint – that also showed his increasing confidence as a composer. There is a kind of easy grace to the songs and recording, a sense that the music takes, and exists in, its own time. It is age-old and cutting-edge. It is focused and concentrated. It is *sui generis* and pure Frisell Dream: extraordinarily dense and complex, yet absolutely distilled and direct.

While most critics thrilled to these ideas and to the infinite new possibilities they opened up, it was easy to see why the album might also have lost Frisell some listeners, in the jazz and avant worlds at least. There was the occasional dissonant blur, harmonic sophistication and looping-effects squiggle, just to stop the music getting all too pretty, but where was the edgy experimentation – and where were the *solos*?

The album, however, attracted a far greater audience than it alienated, possibly because there were simply so many ways into this new music.

Perhaps Ry Cooder helped. Frisell had been introduced to Cooder by Jim Keltner, and the guitarists bonded over a mutual love of Johnny Smith. After Frisell had told Cooder that he had been taught, almost thirty years earlier, by Smith in Colorado, Cooder suggested they play 'Shenandoah' – the popular nineteenth-century folk song was one of Cooder's favourite Johnny Smith recordings. It was also one of Frisell's, and their version has much of the poignancy and pathos of Smith's reading, and is an undoubted highlight of the record. Since he recorded it on *Good Dog*, 'Shenandoah' has become an integral part of the Frisell repertoire, a tune he plays often, especially solo.

Good Dog became, during the time when albums were physically and digitally purchased rather than streamed, Frisell's best-selling record, topping almost 100,000 copies.

•
•

Throughout the nineties, Bill Frisell also featured on many of the decade's more notable, and even landmark albums – and a giddying number of other sessions – not as leader but as close collaborator.

Frisell seemed to find sustenance in the challenge of being thrown into new contexts and configurations. They were sessions he could relax into and simply enjoy. 'It's a lot easier when it's somebody else's thing,' he said in 1998. 'I don't have to worry about whether it's going to work or not – all I have to do is play.'

Frisell appeared on several duo records, perhaps the most high profile of which was *Songs We Know*, lyrical and intimate interpretations of jazz and Great American Songbook standards recorded with masterly pianist Fred Hersch and released on Nonesuch in 1998. Another significant if very different duet was with the great double bass player Gary Peacock; their sequence of intriguing and largely improvised exchanges appeared on the 1994 album *Just So Happens*.

Deep Dead Blue was recorded with Elvis Costello live in London in 1995 – seven songs, mostly penned by Costello, which last less than half an hour, on an album that almost feels like a bootleg, but that nonetheless again showed what a wonderfully spare and ingeniously supportive accompanist Frisell is to singers. With unsung classically trained jazz violin innovator Michael White, a mentor to Eyvind Kang, Frisell released *Motion Pictures*, an album of standards recorded in one day that fascinated, yet failed to totally convince. Sometimes you feel Frisell simply needed longer to fully cultivate the common ground.

The same might have been true, on paper at least, for the trio led by drummer Ginger Baker – except that players of the versatility of Frisell, legendary double bassist Charlie Haden, and Baker himself were more than able to adapt and compensate. The unlikely triumvirate recorded two albums for Atlantic: *Going Back Home*, a 'kind of jam session' set up in 1994 by Chip Stern; and 1996's *Falling Off the Roof*. Baker's busy, bustling, more-is-more approach occasionally overwhelms the mood and material, but there are many surprising peaks and turns, some great grooves and even the occasional Frisell rock-out.

'[In 1968] while I was still in high school, I went to see Cream play in Denver,' Frisell told *Rolling Stone*. 'So [Ginger's sound] was deep down in my DNA. Like, nobody sounded like that. It wasn't how the drums were tuned, or anything, but it was that touch, and the way he placed the beat; the feel of it was so extraordinary. If you had told me then that someday I would actually be playing with him, I would never have believed you.'

In between sessions for *Falling Off the Roof* Frisell went into the Power Station studio in New York at the beginning of 1996 as part of something akin to a jazz supergroup: trumpeter and flugelhornist Kenny Wheeler, alto saxophonist Lee Konitz, and double bassist Dave Holland. The result, released by ECM the following year, is one of the most acclaimed albums of the nineties: *Angel Song*.

While the four musicians had various connections – Frisell had played with Wheeler on *Rambler*, with Konitz on Paul Motian's *On Broadway Volume 3*, and with Holland on Billy Hart's album *Oshumare*

– this was the first time they had collaborated as a quartet. The degree to which they work together, loosely yet with great strength, across a suite of nine eloquent Wheeler compositions, is astonishing. The album is a favourite among many musicians; for London-based songwriter, producer and guitarist Dave Okumu, *Angel Song* is even a kind of artistic lodestar.

'It feels to me that all four musicians are completely in service to these compositions, and bringing their unique voices and their imaginations to them, but with a real humility and grace,' says Okumu. 'Those ideas and values tap into some of my core beliefs about music. There is a sensitivity and generosity to that recording that I'm constantly trying to make part of my practice. And whenever Bill's involved, I feel . . . love, that he just brings an enormous amount of love to what he's doing. And that's really, really important to me, too.'

No less star-studded were two further quartet dates, with Joey Baron and Marc Johnson. On Baron's *Down Home* from October 1997, the drummer brought together Frisell, brilliant alto player Arthur Blythe, and Ron Carter – the illustrious double bassist whose playing, for Frisell, was its own cynosure: Carter plays on the very first album that twitched Frisell's ears towards the sounds of jazz, Wes Montgomery's *Tequila*. *Down Home* is a bluesy, groovy, soul-jazz skip and stroll through eight breezy Baron originals. In keeping with the record's throwback vibe, and with Frisell's early school-band experiences, he even plays funk rhythm guitar, however idiosyncratically, on a couple of tracks.

A few months later Baron also appeared on Marc Johnson's *The Sound of Summer Running*, with Frisell and Pat Metheny – this was the first time the guitarists had recorded together. The album revisited the dynamic twin-guitar territory Johnson had marked out with Frisell and John Scofield in *Bass Desires* a decade or more earlier, though this is more resolutely Johnson's jazz album and Americana aesthetic – a record rich in melody, lyricism, diversity and beauty.

Those are four words that can equally be applied to Frisell's contribution to *Dialogues*, a Jim Hall trio plus guests album released in 1995.

This was the first time Frisell had recorded with his guitar mentor, and Hall marked the occasion by writing two tunes for Bill: the countryfied 'Simple Things' and the playful 'Frisell Frazzle'. They sound like two old friends wisecracking with each other.

There were three small group dates that were also significant. *Play* was a 1999 Mike Stern album of originals similarly dedicated to two of his 'favourite musicians who just happen to be guitarists' – Frisell and John Scofield; Bill appears on four blues- and fusion-shaped tracks, one of which is called 'Frizz'. Ron Miles's eclectic *Woman's Day*, released in 1997, contains the leader's gently elegant trumpet work, and some surprising heavy-rock shredding by Frisell. This was also the first time Frisell recorded with another musician who would become an integral member of many of his future ensembles: drummer Rudy Royston.

Clarinettist Don Byron's fine 1999 Blue Note album *Romance with the Unseen* features imaginative readings of compositions by Ellington, Herbie Hancock and Lennon and McCartney, as well as the leader's spry and sometimes sorrowful originals – on 'Basquiat', a salute to the New York artist Jean-Michel Basquiat, who died in 1988 aged twenty-seven, Frisell's ringing tones and eerie effects significantly magnify the sombre mood.

That was not all: there were other records with John Zorn, Ron Carter, alto saxophonist David Sanborn, guitarists John Scofield and Arto Lindsay, drummer Jerry Granelli, singer-songwriter Donald Rubinstein (the CD art contains a Frisell line drawing), Brazilian guitarist and singer-songwriter Vinicius Cantuária, and Frisell's guitar teacher at Berklee, Jon Damian. There was also a Hal Willner production of *Naked Lunch*, in which William Burroughs read 'some of the most shocking sections' of his notorious 1959 novel, accompanied by music from Frisell, Wayne Horvitz and Eyvind Kang.

In 1995 Frisell appeared, alongside Joey Baron, with members of the Los Angeles Philharmonic, conducted by Esa-Pekka Salonen, in the première of composer Steve Mackey's *Deal*, a one-movement 'concerto for improvising electric guitar and drums with orchestra' written specifically for Frisell. Two years later the performance was reprised by the San Francisco Contemporary Music Players, and at Carnegie Hall with the American Composers Orchestra.

In Argentina, a singer-songwriter named Gabriela wrote Spanish lyrics to Frisell's 1985 song 'Rambler'; it led to two quietly beautiful and largely overlooked Lee Townsend-produced Gabriela albums with Frisell, *Detrás del Sol* and *Viento Rojo*, which featured Gabriela's tender folk-like originals and her lyrics for further Frisell tunes. A third record, *El Viaje*, was released in 2006.

There was even sufficient interest in the mysteries of Frisell's advanced guitar technique to warrant the release in 1997 of an hour-long instruction video: *The Guitar Artistry of Bill Frisell*.

•
•

In the autumn of 1999 Frisell released *The Sweetest Punch*, his arrangements of songs written by Elvis Costello and Burt Bacharach. The album was an instrumental companion to the Grammy-winning Costello/Bacharach record *Painted from Memory*; PolyGram's original intention was to release both projects simultaneously, a sweet one-two that would potentially give the music a broad pop-to-jazz appeal. With that in mind, Frisell was sent music and lyric sheets – and a tape of Bacharach playing the piano with Costello singing the twelve new tunes – immediately after they were written, and asked to compose and record the music in quick succession.

'It was intimidating,' Frisell said in *Jazziz*. 'I was thinking, "How am I going to do justice to this?" It was such an honour to be asked. I felt like they were trusting me . . . I wanted to be respectful of the music; I didn't want to mess it up. But I also didn't want to kiss up to them either.'

Costello knew Frisell's work not just from their live duo set in London a few years earlier – they had first met recording the title track for *Weird Nightmare*, Hal Willner's 1992 celebration of the music and spirit of Charles Mingus. Frisell had long been a fan of Bacharach's music – ever since 1968, in fact, when he heard Dionne Warwick at the Newport Jazz Festival show at the Red Rocks amphitheatre. As well as being drawn to the harmonic sophistication of Bacharach's songs, he was fascinated by the deceptive simplicity of his melodies. '[They] unravel so freely,' he told *DownBeat*. 'The way a phrase will continue longer than it's supposed to before the chord changes reminds me of Ornette [Coleman] or some old blues guy. There's a logic to it, but the music is really tricky and difficult to play.'

Frisell recorded the music in New York with a crack septet composed of a horn section of Ron Miles, Curtis Fowlkes, Bill Drewes and Don Byron, plus Viktor Krauss on bass and Brian Blade on drums, and additional vocals on three tracks by Cassandra Wilson and Costello himself.

'Record company machinations and other forces', explained Josef Woodard in *Jazziz*, delayed the album, however, meaning *The Sweetest Punch* landed more as playful afterthought than killer accompaniment. Some critics really didn't like the pop-jazz confection at all. 'As a piece, the record gets boring, and doesn't reward a direct listen,' wrote John Corbett in *DownBeat*. 'It could even function as Muzak.' If the record was simply too easy on the ear for some, 'underneath,' as Costello said at the time, 'there are all these pretty complicated mechanics going on' – odd and unusual time signatures, harmonic shifts, melodic counterpoints and changes in tempo. Frisell emphasised these nuances and details; he saturated the colours, heightened the mood, made Bacharach's tunes sound closer to compositions than songs.

At the beginning of October Frisell began 'his most extensive US tour yet', twenty-two concerts in twenty cities. He also completed a series of dates playing unaccompanied, after which he recorded his first solo album, *Ghost Town*, and formed another group designed to aid his further adventures in American roots music – the Willies.

In November Frisell premièred a large-scale work that built upon his experiences on *The Sweetest Punch*. The suite was titled *Blues Dream* and commissioned by the Walker Art Center in Minneapolis as a kind of mid-career retrospective – 'a musical statement that would encompass

Frisell's increasingly diverse range of interests and styles: the sweeping pastoralism of lost Americana; a cinematic sense of orchestration; Nashville country and bluegrass; the raw qualities of distortion, tape loops and electronics; skilful yet unconventional writing for horns; and, of course, the melodic and improvisational jazz guitar mastery for which he first gained attention.'

In December 1999 *DownBeat* pronounced Frisell's nineties albums 'the best recorded output of the decade'. Critic John Ephland wrote, 'Every time you turn around, Frisell is doing something else that amazes with a level of creativity, burgeoning wondrous spirit, and incredible collaborative energy.'

By the end of the nineties Bill Frisell was in an enviable position. He had a strong working relationship with Bob Hurwitz and Nonesuch. His records were selling better than ever, and he had more offers of recordings with people from across the world of music than he could possibly manage or fulfil. He had also built a close understanding with his manager and regular producer, Lee Townsend. It may have been regarded in music industry circles as unusual for one person to perform dual roles, but it seemed to work for Frisell.

'It started with *Nashville* and *Gone, Just Like a Train*,' says Townsend. 'But with *Good Dog, Happy Man*, then *Ghost Town*, and the release of the music from *Blues Dream*, there is a triumvirate of records during which Bill's musical sound became more overt and direct. It wasn't any kind of transformative moment, but there was this gradual watershed development of him just being more and more confident in his musical vision. He was able to express, in an unfettered way, all of the musical interests that he wanted to mine.'

Frisell had gathered a group of musicians around him who shared his open ideas and approach, and whom he could bring together in various permutations. He could play dates in New York (twice annually at the Village Vanguard, for example, with his own groups and with Paul Motian), concerts in the US, and tour Europe two or three times a year.

Bill Frisell had built himself a highly successful career, financially and artistically. As *Jazzwise* magazine wrote in 2002, 'Frisell, at least for now, is an artist who can pretty well do what he wants. "It's like my dreams are coming true," he says.'

19: Sam Amidon Listens to *Good Dog, Happy Man*

Good Dog, Happy Man: recorded Burbank, California, 1998; producer Lee Townsend; released on Nonesuch, May 1999; Bill Frisell (guitars, loops, music boxes); Greg Leisz (pedal steel, Dobro, lap steel, Weissenborn, National steel guitar, mandolin); Wayne Horvitz (organ, piano, samples); Viktor Krauss (bass); Jim Keltner (drums and percussion); all compositions by Frisell, except 'Shenandoah' (trad).

'Part preservationist, part visionary', Sam Amidon is a very modern kind of folk musician. He takes a wide range of traditional songs – from American field recordings and Irish fiddle tunes to hymns, spirituals, chain-gang laments and murder ballads – 'extracts their essence', and reimagines and reinterprets them. He also records his own offbeat and idiosyncratic songs – original music that similarly feels at once old and new.

Amidon was born in 1981 in Brattleboro, Vermont. He started learning fiddle at the age of three, and at seven met pianist Thomas Bartlett; they became best friends and fellow musical adventurers. In their teens they formed a folk band that played Thomas's original songs and his 'wild arrangements' of traditional fiddle tunes. Amidon's father gave him a copy of Miles Davis's *Bitches Brew* when Sam was thirteen, and he started to explore jazz, especially avant-garde jazz of the sixties. He also found his way to Bill Frisell. Amidon once said, 'It's like, Miles Davis, an Irish fiddler named Tommy Peoples, and Bill Frisell – those were my gurus as a kid.'

When he was eighteen Amidon moved to New York, where he began to focus more on singing, banjo and acoustic guitar. He also continued to work with Bartlett, collaborate with composer Nico Muhly, and to release his own records – one of which, *But This Chicken Proved False-hearted*, released in 2007, he gave to Frisell at one of the guitarist's gigs.

'Out of the blue, quite a while later, Bill wrote me an email, and he told me he'd been listening to the CD I'd given him, and one of my earlier experimental albums, and watching some weird surreal videos I'd made – and that blew my mind, just to know he'd connected in some way with them,' says Amidon. 'All I ever wanted in life was, like, for Frisell to dig my music. But then the last sentence was "I hope we can play sometime." I could have died.'

In 2011 Amidon and Frisell performed as a duo. Since then they have performed together in various line-ups, festivals, radio studios and one-off concerts; Frisell also appeared on Amidon's 2014 album, *Lily-O*. 'Sam makes these old tunes his own, staying true, but transforming them, from the inside out, bringing them into the present,' Frisell has said. 'He is an inspiration to me.'

We met in a Dublin hotel in 2015 while Amidon was on tour supporting singer-songwriter Sharon Van Etten. Looking like an archetypal modern folk artist – shaggy hair, trainers, jeans and buffalo check shirt; a younger, hipper, more relaxed version of Frisell's 'country-in-the-city' vibe – he spoke quickly and had a lot to say. It was almost as if he couldn't quite get the ideas out fast enough.

PW: The first time I met you, in London, at a Bill Frisell concert suitably enough, you told me that Good Dog, Happy Man *changed your life. Can you explain how and in what way?*

SA: I was around eighteen when I first heard that album, and Thomas [Bartlett] and I had this shared vision about what we wanted to do as musicians – we had a kind of Platonic ideal about what the perfect album would be. *Good Dog, Happy Man* was both that vision and ideal. In fact, it was way beyond what we had imagined.

Thomas and I loved the New England [folk] music we grew up with, but we were searching for more sounds and ideas, listening to whatever other music we could get our hands on. It's like we had these weird ears from being so deep into this one style of music; they had only developed so far. We were trying to reach out beyond.

Slowly, certain things started to catch my ear and grab my imagination – Jimi Hendrix, Steve Reich, Yo La Tengo and Latin Playboys, a side project of Los Lobos. I also started to listen to a lot of jazz: Miles Davis, of course, and Sonny Rollins, Monk, but also pianist Abdullah Ibrahim. Then I really got into free jazz – Albert Ayler, Sun Ra, Ornette Coleman, late Coltrane – and that music made sense to me. Like the fiddle and folk music we were playing, it was visceral, intense, sound-based and often had simple melodies and a strange beauty.

This specific aesthetic started to develop in our minds for our own music. We liked the melodies and modal forms we found in Irish and New England music; we liked the beautifully open harmonies of minimalist music, and of jazz, but we didn't want a million chord changes; and we wanted our music to be rhythm-based, have riffs and grooves, like the kind of dance music we played, but not be like funk or jam music. And then we also didn't want the music to be connected to one particular style or genre.

Wow. It sounds like you were asking for quite a lot!
Yeah, it was very weird. And a bit random.

Let me play you 'Shenandoah'; this was the first time he'd recorded it.
[Track plays; I pass Amidon the CD] Great to hear that again. Beautiful. It's just, like, Bill and Ry Cooder singing the song. And it has this incredible expansiveness. I'd never noticed before that the track is dedicated to Johnny Smith. Not that I would have known who that was back then. And if I had, I probably would have dismissed him anyway.

Even though we were only fifteen or sixteen, Thomas and I were also very definite about the things we *didn't* like. Like the Rolling Stones. To us they just sounded weird, like English people playing American blues. Why not just listen to the originals? Electric keyboards; they just sounded dumb and dated and annoying. Jazz guitar was also off limits. That kind of soft jazz guitar sound was just the definition of cheesiness to us.

I remember being in my local CD store and they had Bill Frisell's *Gone, Just Like a Train* on display; it had just been released. I was a big comic-book nerd and I recognised that the cover was drawn by Jim Woodring – I was a huge fan, and I was like, "Dude, that's awesome, that looks cool, I should buy this." So I asked the guy behind the counter, 'Who's Bill Frisell?' And he said, 'Oh, he's a jazz guitarist.' And I was like, 'Oops, I can't buy it. Off limits. I'm not gonna like it.' [He laughs.]

So how did you subsequently connect to Good Dog*?*

Thomas went to see Bill Frisell and the *Good Dog* band play, and he sent me an email saying, 'It's amazing, it's not jazz, it's not jazz guitar; in fact, you can't tell the background of any of the players, or what kind of music they come from. So we're OK, you're going to be OK, like, it's safe!' Then he sent me some tracks from the album on a MiniDisc. And that was it.

That's a good cue for me to play you another track. Is there one you'd like to hear?

Sure, yeah, how about 'Roscoe'? That was on the disc. I've always liked that track. [The music plays] Fantastic. That's killin', man. It was named for Roscoe Holcomb, I guess, because he'd clearly been listening to a lot of Holcomb's music, and there's another track on the album called 'Monroe', after, again I'm assuming, Bill Monroe – but the crucial thing for us was that this wasn't Appalachian or bluegrass or country music. It was more improvised, more enveloping; it was something else, something different. It was a masterpiece of a genre we didn't know existed. The quality that was so life-changing for me was that on *Good Dog*, like most of my favourite albums, like *Bitches Brew*, Bill [and Miles] created an invented world, an imaginary genre and universe completely unto themselves.

Great artists, master musicians, present such a complete aesthetic world that you can only imagine them and the people they're playing with doing it. Bill's music is like a novel that creates a fully realised world inhabited by different characters.

What was it like for you seeing Bill play live for the first time?

I went to see him play as much as I could after I moved to New York, especially at the Vanguard. That's when you get the full power of the effects and loops. And all the different tones and colours, all the subtle voicings. The biggest thing for me was his sense of control, his sonic power as an *electric* guitarist.

Now that you know him a little, do you think he's the same on stage as he is in person?

Yeah, it's funny watching him play. Sometimes I close my eyes, even when I'm on stage with him, because I always feel that he looks like somebody who's in the middle of a dream – or the classic nightmare, really, in which you wake up and you're a physics lecturer in front of a hall of university students, but you know nothing about physics . . . and you're not wearing any trousers [we both laugh out loud].

Bill's like that on stage. It's like he's just woken up, and he's holding a guitar, and he's in front of an audience, and he's like [gently mimics Bill's voice] 'Oh shit, what am I . . . ? What should I . . . ? Oh, I'll try that . . . Oh, did that work? I guess so. So . . .'

Even though it's quite long, around nine minutes, let me play you 'Cold, Cold Ground'.

Let's hear it. [During the track] Yeah, the melodies have so much space in them. The music is so open and there's just so much room to enjoy what's going on. The track passes through many different phases – like this long section, what's even happening now?

[As the Hammond B3 organ surges in] Wayne Horvitz! That's an amazing sound. And Viktor Krauss. Greg Leisz! And Jim Keltner, one of the great drummers of all time, right? He's a deceptively simple player who doesn't call attention to himself. Like Bill. You know, everybody's amazing on this album.

It was very magical to me – the way the musicians played together like they were all part of this total unified vision of the music, like some of the pure wild colours and textures in Hendrix's music. I used to call this album *Acoustic Ladyland*!

What was it like the first time you played with Bill?

I remember one of the first times was in 2011 and we were going to play some of my folk material. And what blew my mind was that he had painstakingly written out charts of the songs, with my guitar parts. Which the musicians I usually play with never do. They play almost totally by ear. And first of all I was like, 'You don't need to do that. You're Frisell, dude – it's just two chords, you can just shred along.'

Then I realised that Bill is a profoundly structural player. His music might have all these colours and atmospheres, but it's not a bunch of random guitar stuff; he always plays from the structure of the song. He's a post-Thelonious Monk musician, in that sense. Monk didn't just take wild solos. He played from the melody, played it over and over again but in weird, upside-down and strange little ways. That's what Bill does.

Then when he's feeling comfortable in a situation, once he's figured out the structure, it's total freedom, you know. And that's my favourite feeling. I'm almost scared to say this out loud, because I don't want him to, like, read it and then not do it, but I like those unleashed moments when the distortion pedal goes down and the fire in his playing comes out.

There are certainly some listeners who would like to hear Bill play more often like that, with less restraint and control.

I always want to hear him shred. But I also know that it's only going to happen when it's right, and ready to happen. I'm not one of those fans for whom Frisell's music ended in 1992, when he stopped playing that snarling, reverby Gibson guitar, or something.

Here's a final track, the last on the album – 'Poem for Eva'.

[Track plays] I just love that major scale running down over and over again. So good. This was a big one for me, because the music was so simple, yet so beautiful and so deep at the same time.

I've tried, in my humble way, to take inspiration from that track, and from this whole album. The structure is so simple harmonically – it's incredibly spare. But, at the same time, the music is actually jam-packed and dense with delights and stories; it feels rich and full of content. New things are constantly shifting between the musicians, with the melody, the rhythm, the arrangement and the whole atmosphere.

Some albums are a thousand times more produced than this and take, like, nine months to complete, and when you listen to them it's like you're hearing an object or a sculpture. *Good Dog* is like listening to a garden that's still growing and changing in time.

How important do you think Bill Frisell is as a musician?

He's hugely important and iconic. Frisell is somebody who has spanned and synthesised the traditions of so much American music – jazz, blues, folk, country, bluegrass, rock, pop and so on – but who's also stayed completely individual.

A lot of these American musics may have started out close to each other, but along the way they got separated out and ghettoised. Bill Frisell came along and folded them all back in.

In Gothic thirteenth-century St Canice's Cathedral in the medieval city of Kilkenny in Ireland, a spotlight falls on master fiddle player Martin Hayes. It is the grand finale of the 2014 international Kilkenny Arts Festival, and Hayes is standing on a large stage at the far end of the soaring interior. Around him are high limestone arches, black marble columns, vibrant stained-glass windows – and some of the country's finest ancient tombstones. On stage, things are somewhat more alive: Hayes is surrounded by popular contemporary Irish-American supergroup The Gloaming, of which he and pianist Thomas Bartlett are a vital part, and by Sam Amidon, American clarinettist Doug Wieselman, percussive dancer Nic Gareiss, members of Berlin-based contemporary chamber orchestra s t a r g a z e and former US poet laureate Billy Collins.

Bill Frisell is also there somewhere, hidden at the back. He has spent the past five days at the enterprising festival as one of its 'artists-in-residence': Frisell has played solo, headlined his own concert, and been part of the s t a r g a z e ensemble that performed Terry Riley's groundbreaking minimalist work *In C*.

'This has been a festival about making connections – the aesthetic is a sense of feeling and possibility,' Martin Hayes tells the capacity audience, towards the end of a performance that has involved everyone on stage. 'I can't really say what it is we're playing. It's certainly music. But it's difficult to categorise, because it doesn't have a genre. It's its own genre. Except that, in a way, we're tired of genre, and what that means.' Hayes pauses. 'Hopefully there'll be no genre left by the time we've finished.'

•
•

Bill Frisell's music has always, right from the beginning, raised critical questions about definition and classification, about the very nature of genre. What is it that Frisell is playing, and how might we begin to describe it?

The most common descriptor, of course, is that Frisell is a jazz guitarist. 'I don't know if it matters that you call it jazz, but it's definitely jazz to me,' says Nels Cline. 'Even though I'm certainly one of the most impure and probably poorly trained of musicians, I can hear the improvisatory coherence and vision of Bill's music, the way he plays with great harmonic awareness of what that jazz vocabulary and syntax entails.'

Marc Ribot agrees. 'Essentially I'm a rock player who has been playing jazz for a long time and has a huge affection for jazz . . . some types of jazz,' he explains. 'But Bill has succeeded in playing jazz – on jazz's terms. He actually plays *jazz* and, while he can do a lot of things, he embodies those values. There's something just very basic about his understanding of time – something existential that happens before you get into figuring out how to play notes.'

Ron Miles positions Frisell firmly in the jazz pantheon: 'I think Bill is truly one of the greatest musicians to ever play this music, and I say that without qualification – not, like, in the post-1950 era, just period. I place him in the company of masters such as Duke Ellington and Thelonious Monk; his playing is so personal, and he is important enough to our generation that knowing his approach is essential to being a contemporary jazz musician – it's just one of the languages you would know.'

Miles, however, has a corollary. 'I think the question about whether Bill plays jazz depends on how reductive you want that word to be,' he continues. 'Because it's true that, when you hear Bill play with a conventional jazz rhythm section, I don't know that it really works, that it really shows off his gifts. He needs a certain type of musician to complement him, someone who understands the wider universe that he's carved out for himself.'

Frisell's own position on The Jazz Question is . . . mostly that he'd rather not have the conversation. If he is wedded to anything, it is to the Keith Jarrett doctrine – that, as the improvising and classical pianist once told the great oral historian Studs Terkel, 'What jazz signifies to me is the freedom to be yourself.'

Except that, understandably perhaps, the question is a common line of enquiry. The subject arose in a 2002 interview with Francis Davis: '"Oh, boy," Frisell said when I put that question to him, though he must have known it was coming. Jazz, he finally said, "is still the best way of describing . . . the mechanics of what I do." He said, "If I have a pedal steel guitar in my group, someone can say, 'Oh, then it must be country music.' But that's just on the surface."'

Frisell said something similar to *DownBeat* in the interview that saluted *Nashville* winning the magazine's 1988 Jazz Album of the Year. 'My inspiration comes from all over the map,' he said, '[But] deep in my heart, no matter what anyone calls it, no matter what the rules are, I approach my music from a jazz sensibility.'

'That word [jazz] has so many . . .' Frisell once said to me, pausing. 'It will mean a million different things to a million different people. To me, jazz means the musicians who've inspired me and still inspire me, who I've learned from and still learn from. For me, it's not copying them, or anything like that, or imitating something that was created long ago . . . but trying to imagine what they would be thinking if they were in the same situation as me now. When I first started to listen to and play jazz, it was a place where anything was possible. These musicians weren't following any rules about what the music was supposed to be. They took all of the information that was around them, and they used this process to transfer their experience into music, to find their own thing. That's part of the struggle. That's what I'm trying to do.'

There are two main strands to Frisell's response: the ideas of tradition and process.

Frisell told interviewer Radhika Philip that he feels deeply connected to and respectful of the jazz tradition and its contribution and consciousness – what the music means musically, culturally, socially and politically: 'There's a tradition in the music that for me is sacred. I mean, there are people who I am very serious about.' He mentions again his artistic standard-bearers: Rollins, Monk and Davis. 'I acknowledge the body of music that these masters are feeding me, you know . . . I'm trying to keep what they were doing in mind . . . A part of the music was to move with the head, and I'm trying to think that way.'

Jason Moran also sees Frisell as firmly part of a tradition. 'I do think it matters that we say Bill plays jazz, because there is an empathy that he has for what the music means to our culture, and then what it means to his culture,' the pianist says. 'It's important for me to acknowledge, and I think it's important for him to acknowledge, that the root of the music, and the circumstances that created it, are not separate, you know. They are together. So I think, considering the history of what jazz has done, for the world, it's important to put Bill as a part of it.'

The second concept Frisell touches upon is the idea that jazz is fundamentally a widely applicable process, rather than a rigidly individual style. Other musicians who have worked broadly within the form have made similar observations: Pat Metheny once expanded on his idea that jazz is more a verb than a noun by adding, 'It's a process, a way of thinking, not a result'; 'Music isn't a style; it's an idea,' declared Ornette Coleman.

It's the notion that jazz is a transformative art, that it can bring distinctly different alchemies and perspectives – rhythms, melodies, harmonies, emotions, moods, meanings and contradictions – to almost any piece of music in any genre; that, in the right hands, it can reframe and make new. 'The process can be applied to anything – country songs, arias, anything,' Sonny Rollins once said in *Jazz Times*. 'This is what makes jazz the greatest music in the world. It's a force of nature; it has no boundaries. You can jazz anything up; you can improvise on anything.'

For all this, Frisell is also aware of jazz's identity crisis: that many musicians actively reject the word and challenge its use, arguing that it limits, and even attempts to reduce them creatively, commercially and culturally, that it is a linguistic anachronism. 'I guess I don't even know what jazz is supposed to be any more,' Frisell told me.

'The term jazz, in a sense, perhaps is its own worst enemy,' Herbie

Hancock once said, and it can often seem that the word fails to fully articulate the sense that jazz has always been a generous and malleable music – that it has always reached out beyond race, culture and nation, and beyond doctrine and dogma. Jazz has always been a hybrid music as complex as its history.

'So many other kinds of music have rubbed off on jazz in the decades since [1960] that a definition based on the assumption that jazz is somehow autonomous no longer seems realistic, let alone wise,' Francis Davis has written in the *Atlantic*.

'I find the word "jazz" actually difficult to deal with . . . and I try to use it as little as possible,' pianist, composer, educator and writer Vijay Iyer once stated. 'Jazz is a term used to limit people, and . . . most of the musicians I admire have rejected the term, so I don't really see why I should use it. Charlie Parker, John Coltrane, Miles Davis and Duke Ellington had no use for the word.'

There are many other musicians who might be added to Iyer's roster. Anthony Braxton said in 1982 that, 'I've never understood what people are talking about when they say jazz, because they've frozen the music and applied definitions in a way that never really satisfied the composite reality of the music.'

The Art Ensemble of Chicago eschewed 'jazz' in favour of their motto 'Great Black Music – Ancient to Modern'. In more recent years trumpeter and writer Nicholas Payton has suggested that jazz be replaced with the term 'Black American Music'; others have preferred 'America's classical music'. Pianist Jon Batiste makes the argument for what he calls 'social music', a more open, inclusive and democratic form.

'Stretch music' is the term trumpeter Christian Scott aTunde Adjuah employs, a 'genre-blind musical form that attempts to stretch jazz's rhythmic, melodic and harmonic conventions to encompass as many other musical forms, languages and cultures as possible'.

•
•

Bill Frisell and I are back in Hooked on Colfax, the café on East Colfax Avenue in Denver; it has become our stop-off for coffees and snacks as we tour areas of the city in which Bill grew up.

'Sorry to interrupt, I'm a huge fan, great to meet you.'

'Oh, oh . . .'

'I've seen you play a million times, but I just recognised your voice, and I'm like . . .'

'Oh, yeah . . .'

The hipster in his early thirties, with the curly hair, generous beard and check shirt, standing politely at our table is, we discover, Yan Westerlund, drummer with the band Mipso, who are playing that night a few doors down at the Bluebird Theater.

We get talking and I ask him what sort of music Mipso plays.

'Oh yeah, it's a folk-Americana kind of a thing. We're based out of Durham, North Carolina, and in that area it just seems like any Appalachian music really does well. There are so many festivals.'

'Yeah, my brother lives in Chapel Hill,' says Bill.

'No kidding. My brother does, too.' Bill and Yan both break out into a friendly laugh.

'I grew up here, and then my parents . . . eventually they ended up in North Carolina.'

'No kidding.'

It turns out that Westerlund is originally from Eau Claire, Wisconsin, and went to the same school as Justin Vernon. There must be something in the water that chemically connects the community of musicians in Eau Claire to the music of Bill Frisell; either that, or this is Frisellian serendipity at the next level.

Westerlund tells us that Kenny Wollesen, who has been a pivotal member of many of Frisell's groups since 1999, is one of his favourite drummers. 'Yeah, I think about Kenny most days,' he says, smiling. 'And about Dave King [the drummer in the Bad Plus]. He's a crazy guy; I love him. I've had conversations with Dave about you, Bill, yeah. You and the Bad Plus were like my childhood heroes.'

Westerlund is joined by his bandmate, guitarist and vocalist Joseph Terrell, who is in his late twenties; photographs with Bill are taken.

'Are you playing in town tonight?' Terrell asks Frisell.

'No, just passing through.'

'Well, come and join us on the gig,' says Terrell, enthusiastically. Bill demurs, shyly, and says nothing. 'No, really. That's an official band invitation.'

Frisell doesn't sit in on the concert – he is committed to completing our tour of Denver, and has an early flight to New York the next day. Yet, in a very subtle Frisellian sort of a way, he seems genuinely flattered to be asked – that whatever category his music may or may not fit into, it is open enough to appeal to a group of Appalachian 'folk-Americana' musicians almost forty years his junior. 'I feel as if a small victory has been made if someone from another area gets to hear my music,' he once told *All About Jazz*.

'We'll leave you guys to it . . . but, Bill, you know, think about it,' Terrell says, as he and Westerlund head back to the venue for a soundcheck.

'Oh, yeah . . . wow . . .' replies Frisell. 'Nice to meet you. Have a great gig.'

•
•

The other genre that has come to be closely associated with Bill Frisell is country music, an often catch-all classification that seems warm-hearted enough to be able to wrap its arms around, as far as Frisell is concerned, allied American vernacular musics such as old-time, blues, bluegrass, string-band, cowboy songs, western swing, soul, rock and rockabilly. 'Bill Frisell is always an American folk musician,' Elvis Costello has written. 'That is, he works with all the music made by American folk.'

Frisell wasn't the first, by a long way, to fuse country with jazz. Back in 1930 Louis Armstrong played trumpet on 'Blue Yodel No. 9', a country blues written and performed by 'the Father of Country Music' Jimmie Rodgers; forty years later Satchmo reprised the song with Johnny Cash. 'Jazz is only what you are,' he once said.

Armstrong's musical cross-pollination was reciprocated in 1936 when the 'King of Western Swing', Bob Wills, recorded one of Satchmo's signature tunes, 'Basin Street Blues'. Wills's version, with his band of Texas Playboys, may sound far cleaner and straighter than Armstrong's radical original, but throughout the thirties and forties Wills successfully integrated elements of jazz, blues, rags and stomps into his sprightly country sound.

In the early forties, so legend has it, bebop innovator Charlie Parker played 'Home on the Range' (Frisell once recorded the song with Gary Peacock) with a country and western band in a Dallas roadhouse. 'He moved Texas roustabouts, cowboys, and rough women when he . . . played [the song] straightforwardly, as a dirge,' wrote American academic and cultural historian Alfred Appel Jr in his book *Jazz Modernism*.

The two major statements in the two decades that followed – about how the melodic strength, harmonic texture and emotional depth of country music might be applied to jazz – are Sonny Rollins's 1957 album *Way Out West* and Gary Burton's *Tennessee Firebird* from 1966.

Way Out West featured Rollins's joyous versions of two thirties tunes: the western song 'Wagon Wheels'; and 'I'm an Old Cowhand', a humorous tune written by Johnny Mercer and made popular by Bing Crosby. There was nothing kitsch or comical, however, about Rollins's playing or intention. 'Maybe other people looked down on it [country music],' he once told *Jazz Times*. 'But I'm a big music guy. I like music; it doesn't matter what kind.'

Vibraphonist Gary Burton recorded *Tennessee Firebird* in Nashville – RCA announced the album as 'Jazz and Nashville: a Thrilling New Blend' – using pre-eminent Music City players such as guitarist Chet Atkins and harmonica player Charlie McCoy. The record includes Burton originals and two Bob Dylan songs, but mostly features versions of country classics by Bob Wills, Hank Williams and Smokey Rogers – music that could easily be put together in the studio by musicians who mainly did not read music.

In the nineties the term Americana began to emerge as a musical genre, becoming, as Giovanni Russonello wrote in a critical essay in the *New*

York Times, 'a nickname for . . . weather-beaten, rural-sounding music . . . warm, twangy stuff, full of finger-plucked guitars and gnarled voices'.

Soon the ragbag term, brimming with sepia-toned nostalgia, pastoral sentimentality and a feel-good, if false, sense of national identity – one predominantly applied, as Russonello pointed out, to musicians who were white, male and older – began to be readily applied to Frisell, a white middle-aged male guitar player whose music reached back to much of Americana's most cherished heartlands.

Because his music was also located, however, in a form – jazz – which was largely excluded from Americana (curiously so for a genre that sought to widen definitions of American roots music); because Frisell's music also stood equally for traditions of innovation and experimentation; and because his connection to American music also embraced Aaron Copland, Muddy Waters, Bob Dylan, John Hiatt, Burt Bacharach and Madonna, a new compound term was required.

In *Jazziz* in 2002 Frisell was 'a purveyor of something called "new Americana"'. By 2007, in the same magazine, Frisell was billed as 'the ultimate fusion artist' and profiled under the headline 'Fusion Americana'. Four years later critic Kevin Whitehead had coined another neologism: 'Bill Frisell's Pan-Americana'. And in 2013 Jazz at Lincoln Center in New York appointed Frisell as guest curator for a series of concerts that explored 'the intersections of rock, country, jazz and blues'; its title was *Roots of Americana*.

'The fearless and adaptable guitarist Bill Frisell . . . is primarily associated with two of jazz's border towns, each of which he helped put on the map,' wrote Gary Giddins in the *New Yorker* in 2009. Those two interzones were 'Jazz Americana' and 'Minefield America', the latter being, somewhat more enigmatically, 'a forbidding territory of ascetic, chess-like improvisations – multidirectional interactions in which every note counts, every modulation is eventful, and intense concentration is a prerequisite for player and listener alike'.

Frisell was asked about Americana as a genre in 2013. 'I feel like anyone who's listening closely can hear similarities between bluegrass and bebop, or country music and R&B,' he replied. 'For me, all that stuff is coming from the same place. That label, "Americana" – it always bothers me when people use the names to limit what people think the music is. In my imagination, the music is all happening simultaneously . . . To me, "Americana" is Louis Armstrong and Duke Ellington and Bill Monroe and Elvis Presley – it's everything, all together.'

•
•

Bill Frisell used to have a map on his website showing a phantom island called Frisland. Sent to Frisell by film-maker Bill Morrison, the map was one of many of the North Atlantic drawn between the 1560s and 1660s that detailed the island; it was also referred to as Frischlant, Friesland, Fixland, Frislanda and Frislandia.

Variously located near Iceland, Greenland, the Faroe Islands, and even as far afield as Labrador and Scotland, the myth of Frisland was eventually exposed, and the island eliminated from maps, by later more extensive voyages. It is believed Frisland was an 'Italian fabrication' invented in the sixteenth century by a descendant of Venetian explorers and brothers Nicolò and Antonio Zeno.

In a similar way, writers who venture into the wide world of Frisell's music, and then struggle to find their bearings, have decided that the guitarist is fully 'deserving of his own genre' and devised their own phantom classifications – most usually 'friz'. Even Bill's genial Denver guitar teacher, Dale Bruning, has got in on the act: 'Bill Music' is his simple shorthand.

Sometimes it seems that it's a lot easier to say what Frisell's music is not. For one, it is not about a set of codes and doctrines, policed by some higher authority or keeper of the flame.

'With all kinds of music – jazz, country, bluegrass, Irish music,' Frisell told me in Kilkenny, 'there are always these people who decide on some sort of set of rules that everybody has to agree to. I spent quite a lot of time when I was younger just being in one of those zones – a bebop zone – and I don't want to go back.'

Over the years Frisell has resisted explicitly criticising the neoclassical movement in jazz, which was born during his years in New York in the eighties, continued to grow in the nineties and beyond, and that has argued precisely that jazz requires a new and definitive manifesto.

Frisell did, however, make his position clear in an interview with Seattle's *Earshot Jazz* in 2005. 'It seems that in the last few years, priorities have become mixed up and turned into this thing,' he said. 'OK, jazz is this and to do it correctly, you have to wear a suit, look a certain way, and have to follow all these rules and stay within certain parameters. That's just not what it's about for me.'

Frisell's music is also not concerned with musical rankings and genre gradations; it is open and egalitarian. 'To say that some kind of orchestral classical music is on a higher level than jazz music, or that jazz music is on a higher level than folk music or blues is wrong,' Frisell told Radhika Philip. 'I don't like to put music in that sort of hierarchy.'

He gave drummer Kenny Wollesen as an example. 'Kenny doesn't do that at all . . . He understands this really broad spectrum of music, and doesn't judge it. So when we're in the midst of playing, the music can travel to all these places. And it's not a joke; he's serious about it. He's not playing up or down.'

Some would argue, as Frisell himself has suggested, that there is more than enough to do, a lifetime's work, in fact, within one's own area of music. Other musicians might also be suspicious of fusing their playing with other genres, arguing that too often something is compromised, diluted or lost, that not all unions are equal or even desirable. If you blend instrumental jazz with easy-listening pop and R&B, for example, does it not unavoidably lead to the vapidity of smooth jazz?

Bill Frisell has, however, largely avoided such pitfalls by remaining adaptable and adventurous, by approaching any collaboration with empathy and respect, and by being able to combine his various musical enthusiasms into one singular sound and vision.

'Because Bill has an incredible and amazing set of ears, he's been able to work past the boundaries that one sets up in one's mind about music,' says Hank Roberts. 'He's curious, and he's able to hear and get in touch with all kinds of music.'

Pat Metheny concurs; he admires the way Frisell has resolutely followed his own path, how he mixes and matches yet stays essentially true to himself. 'Like every other major musician who has ever stuck his neck out to create something new and fresh, I couldn't say that Bill is *universally* loved,' Metheny told me. 'I have spent more than a few evenings defending him to diehards of a certain ilk.

'But one of the many things I have always admired about Bill is that he always finds his own space in the panorama of possible roles in this music, on both a micro and a macro level. He defines himself in his own terms. Along the way, he has also continued to mess with the traditional way of approaching things in sometimes unfamiliar ways. To conservative gatekeepers, that means trouble. Bill is a musical progressive in all the best ways.'

Frisell may not see himself as any kind of pathfinder or groundbreaker, more as simply an artist trying to follow the music and be true to himself. There are also many other musicians who have pursued a similarly panoramic approach and successfully brought diverse elements into their work: David Bowie, Philip Glass, Kendrick Lamar, Robert Glasper, Lana Del Ray, Jonny Greenwood, Bob Dylan, the Byrds, Taylor Swift, the Beastie Boys, Joni Mitchell, Frank Zappa, Talking Heads, John Zorn and Pauline Oliveros, to name just fifteen.

Yet it's hard to think of anyone in the contemporary era who has so comprehensively and successfully integrated as many different types of music as has Frisell. 'I get so tired of people trying to divide up music into categories,' Frisell wrote in a foreword to a book of interviews with Charlie Haden. 'Names. Folk, jazz, country, hillbilly, classical, rock. Whatever. It's a waste of energy. Charlie sat on Mother Maybelle Carter's knee when he was a kid, and played with Ornette Coleman. He was pure music. All together. He played everything.'

For the past forty-five years or more, Frisell has been living proof that the old classifications don't work any more, that his music represents a 'polite assault on the very idea of genre in music'. He is so much more than being one type of musician, one type of player and personality.

'That's the magic that you find in a great musician,' says Eyvind Kang. 'I've studied Indian music, and there's this Sanskrit word for it, "*bhava*". It means "being" or "presence" – but it's multilayered. You bring things to it from your unconscious, from your dream-life, things that are psychological or psychoanalytical, and then also other things that we can't be aware of. You will find *bhava* with Bill, for sure.'

Categories and their amalgams do not contain Bill Frisell. In a tribute to Aretha Franklin in the *Paris Review* following her death in 2018, Brian Cullman wrote, 'Her playing is thirty per cent jazz, fifty per cent gospel, and seventy-five per cent just plain Aretha. And if those numbers don't add up, that's just the way it goes. Aretha was bigger than math.'

Singer-songwriter, guitarist and producer Joe Henry agrees. 'I've never had the temptation or need to label Bill's music as jazz or anything,' he says. 'He's kind of transcended to that place where . . . it's not that genres don't apply, but it's just . . . Bill, you know. People only refer to him as a "jazz guitarist" because they don't know what else to call his deep, nuanced and complex instrumental music.'

Genre can, of course, be useful as a signpost or a handle. It can also help to emphasise specific and often hard-won aspects of a music's history, culture, vocabulary, politics and practice – music's strong sense of identity, of belonging to a community, however global. Yet, at the same time, as well as acknowledging that identity and respecting those traditions, Frisell has rendered genre an aesthetic anachronism, an inhibitor, a historicised restraint and control that serves neither musician nor listener. Genre is fixed; music is fluid. Genre is generalisation; music is individual, a personal vision.

Frislandia is a polyglot place of learning, a space that respects the irreducible mysteries, ambiguities and complexities of music, that is interested in the margins and what exists beyond them, that is ever-changing and moving forward, ever-expanding and striving for the universal, something higher. It may have been dismissed as a fantasy island a long time ago, but Frisell has single-handedly revived and restored it, reimagining it as a new world in which no classifications exist, in which everything is just music and accepted as such.

The English journalist and author Richard Williams recognised it way back in 1989 in a review of *Before We Were Born*: 'The most exciting music around just now has no name,' he asserted. It may have been a radical idea in the eighties, but Frisell's music – then and now – has always championed such a philosophy, and it is thinking that has proven hugely influential. Once you've heard that all-encompassing sound, it's sometimes hard to adapt to a narrower bandwidth.

'His impact on the landscape of creative music, not just guitar music, is incalculable,' says Nels Cline, in the *Bill Frisell: A Portrait* documentary. 'There was a time in the eighties, but certainly in the early nineties, where Bill's influence seemed very widespread, and I was hearing lots of guitar players . . . at whom I could point my finger and say, "Ah, I hear Bill in you." But they're everywhere [now].'

Fellow guitarist Mary Halvorson says the same was true when she studied at the New School in New York in the early 2000s. 'I heard a million guitarists copying Bill; he was one of *the* people,' she says. 'I think he's really paved a way, not just for guitarists but for all musicians – that idea, for example, of taking things from jazz, while not being married to jazz. Bill was an early model for that, for me and many others – for taking things from a million different places and synthesising them, for making music that doesn't have to be just one thing.'

Free yourself, be honest, and play who you are: that, ultimately, is the Frisell model, the national motto of Frislandia.

•
•

Bill Frisell is in his music room in Seattle, a sanctum stuffed with racks of guitars, sheet music, speakers, pedals, leads, books, notebooks, pens, correspondence, files, magazines, LPs, old radios and a framed photograph of Johnny Cash. It is also where he keeps his many hundreds of CDs.

'What kinds of music do they cover?' I ask, sort of casually, but Bill is ahead of me, hands up, eager to explain.

'Yeah, I know, look at them,' he replies, laughing, and pointing shame-facedly towards the shelves. 'There's the jazz section, there's the classical section, there's the country section, there's rock, and whatever. Look how neatly I've organised things! Man, I'm just a total hypocrite.'

21: Martin Hayes and Dennis Cahill Listen to
The Willies

The Willies: recorded Seattle, May 2000 and March 2001; producer Lee
Townsend; released on Nonesuch, June 2002; Bill Frisell (guitars, loops),
Danny Barnes (banjo, guitar, bass, harmonica, pump organ), Keith Lowe
(bass); compositions by Frisell, plus a selection of traditional tunes by,
among others, Hank Williams, Lead Belly and A. P. Carter.

Martin Hayes and Dennis Cahill are two of the most creative and revered
figures in Irish traditional music.

Hayes is a fiddle virtuoso born in 1962 in East County Clare in Ireland. While he received little formal training – 'I'm a complete guerrilla
performer from the side of a mountain,' he once joked – he was a child
prodigy, winning six All-Ireland fiddle championships by the time he was
nineteen.

Acoustic guitarist Cahill was born in 1954 in Chicago; his parents
were Irish-speaking immigrants from the Dingle Peninsula in County
Kerry. He began playing the guitar aged nine, and studied at the prestigious Chicago Music College. He later went on to study classical guitar.
Cahill has become vastly respected as a creative and sympathetic master
of colour, accent, rhythm and restraint.

Hayes moved to Chicago in 1985 and the pair met shortly afterwards.
They formed a band called Midnight Court that fused Irish folk and
rock, with Hayes playing electric fiddle and Cahill Fender Telecaster. The
pair began performing as a duo in the early nineties, and their concerts
around the world have become celebrated for their vitality, versatility
and expressiveness. Hayes and Cahill are also members of highly successful Irish-American supergroup The Gloaming, and of the Martin Hayes
Quartet, an Irish-music-meets-jazz and chamber music ensemble with
Doug Wieselman on bass clarinet and Liz Knowles on viola and violin.

Frisell met Hayes in Seattle when the fiddler moved to the city in the nineties. Their connection was mostly social and one of mutual admiration until 2007, when Frisell joined Hayes and Cahill for a short tour of Ireland. The trio also played together in various line-ups at the 2014 Kilkenny Festival.

Our listening session took place in the living room of my house in Cork, Ireland, while Hayes and Cahill were in the middle of a national tour. We'd agreed to listen to *The Willies*, Frisell's 2002 'modern take on bluegrass and country blues'. Cahill was the quieter of the two; he is witty, soft-spoken and somewhat internal. Hayes is more easily eloquent and outwardly confident – bright, impassioned, a musician's musician.

PW: Can you remember the first time you heard Bill Frisell's music?

DC: Yes, it was *Stay Awake* [Hal Willner's 1988 album of multi-artist interpretations of songs written for old Disney films]. There are a lot of great guitarists on that album – John Scofield, Marc Ribot and Bonnie Raitt, for example – but Bill Frisell really stuck out.

It was amazing how he could play so simply, with so much space, and yet get such a powerful effect. I'd never heard anything quite like it. It was something like a pianist might play: his choice of notes, and his way of bringing out exactly what he wanted. He's also brilliant at being able to eliminate the excess and the clichés, and to just get to the point.

After that, I started buying more and more of his albums, and I was fascinated by them. And quite baffled, because whatever he played, whatever genre he was in, it seemed to fit; he always sounded like Bill Frisell. He would always make the *whole thing* sound good. To me, he thinks more like a musician than a guitar player.

PW: Martin?

MH: I don't exactly remember, but I know that one important record for me was *Angel Song* [the Kenny Wheeler CD released on ECM in 1997]. The opening song on that album ['Nicolette'] has this lovely short intro by Bill – it's no more than thirty seconds, but it's very melodic and very *moody*.

One of the first things I noticed about Bill's music was his capacity to create this ambience and *feeling*. It seemed like everything emanated from, and was driven by that feeling. And that was what I myself was attempting to do around that time.

PW: *Let me play you the opening track on* The Willies, *'Sittin' on Top of the World'.*

MH: That was great. Lovely. What Bill Frisell is doing is taking all these threads of American music – like blues, jazz, rock 'n' roll, country, bluegrass, old timey – and tying them together again.

The American music story is incredible, by any standards, especially in the twentieth century. There was such an outburst of music; there's been no other country that has created so many different styles in such a short space of time. And it just seems like Bill feels free to graze through all of them, and to find ways in which many elements can harmoniously sit together. But it's distilled too; there's nothing showy or more than is needed.

PW: *What do you think, Dennis, as the actual American in the room?*

DC: [Cahill laughs] The thing I really like about Bill is that he finds and plays these old country tunes – because he's realised they have beautiful melodies and are really well written. A lot of people are much too hip to want to admit that they like this stuff; it's all a bit hokey to them. But it's not.

I worked country bands, just to make a living, and I played with a lot of old guys who played the *Grand Ole Opry*. And these guys played the stuff serious; this wasn't like a big joke to them. If you started laughing, they'd probably hit you. [We all laugh.] I love Bill's opening section [to the track]. This is a pretty happy tune, but it's also kind of serious too. It's like, OK, don't get *too* happy about stuff. 'Yeah, I'm sitting on top of the world – but I'm not sure I like it.' [Cahill chuckles] He can make a song go through different moods, and there's often that sort of humour in there.

PW: What was it like when you played with Bill?

MH: We were a bit intimidated. But we learned a lot. It was very interesting for us to just live with that amount of spontaneity. Every single night was different, and every single night Bill was different more than I was different. In the middle of a tune, he would do an interesting and beautiful thing – and he would feel no compulsion whatsoever to repeat it ever again. I found it fascinating that he would just let it go. I thought he had a lot of courage.

It also taught me that the more you can stretch into other people's worlds, into their sense of understanding in the music, the deeper you get to know your own thing. It's not about *acquiring* the music of other genres; it's about experiencing another world view, in music. Being adjacent to, or inside the room of Bill's music just opened up a free flow of things. His practice is one of keeping the spigot open. And that's something I think, ever since, Dennis and I have tried to internalise, to stay as open as *we* can, too. Let the music go, you know.

DC: Some people feel the need to try to control something that's not controllable. That's where the rules come in, the way music has to be judged somehow – especially when it gets into music institutions, on such things as technique and your ability to perform. But that doesn't really have a lot to do with feel and mood, and the actual musical quality that comes out.

One teacher I had would always tell me, 'OK, your arm doesn't have the proper angle.' And I'm thinking, 'Yeah, that's like the least of my worries.' [We all laugh.] 'I take your point. But I'm not really worried what my angles are; this isn't geometry.'

PW: Here's another track, a Frisell original, 'I Want to Go Home'.

MH: Gorgeous. This is like a country song.

DC: You only have to listen to his version of [Hank Williams's] 'I'm So Lonesome I Could Cry' to know how much he likes country music. The vibe he gets on that song is not maudlin in any way; it's just so *sad* [Cahill laughs]. And I think it's great. It's absolutely spectacular.

Bill plays acoustic on half of that track, and I just love the incredible *texture* he gets from the instrument. He gets all these flavours and sounds, all these percussive and swelling effects, out of a straight-up acoustic guitar, which is . . . really difficult. It's just the control he has.

MH: That melody though reminds me of [he pauses] the theme music to *Father Ted*. [I burst out laughing.] Did you not notice?

PW: No, I can't say I did.

MH: Yeah, there are a few snippets in there. I'm sure Bill's never heard of *Father Ted*, but I think he probably would really like it.

PW: You could be right.

MH: I think he would like it *a lot* actually. [We all laugh.]

PW: Here's a traditional song you'll both likely know ['Cluck Old Hen' plays].

MH: The one thing you can say for certain is, you *always* know it's Bill Frisell playing. Whatever the song. Bill is like a piece of artwork that you can hang on any wall – and it works.

DC: There's a particular attack on the guitar – that real *snap*, that little *cut* – which you can hear; he gets the notes to form *really* fast, and it's a *sound*. Bill Frisell's sound. It just is *there* [he laughs]!

It's like he comes from this tradition way back. Bill's like the old blues players, or some of the real old rockers – they didn't have the amplification do the work; they created the sound with their hands. It's a real physical thing. He's still controlling the guitar; it's not the pedals, boxes and amps he's plugged into. I like his version of this song too. Again, it's happy–sad.

PW: 'My old hen's a good old hen/She lays eggs for the railroad men.'

DC: Yeah, he gets a lot out of the song emotionally. It's an interesting choice. You'd never think of doing it, but then when you hear Bill play it, you realise, boy, it has a great melody.

PW: Here's another Frisell original, 'I Know You Care'. [The track opens with twangy discordant sounds, like a faulty music box, and segues into a sort of up-tempo hoedown, fit for dancing. There is also a low drone, like a didgeridoo.]

DC: You often get a visual image in your head when you listen to Bill. That opening reminds me of looking at somebody with a bad hangover. [We all laugh.] *'Oh my head!'*

MH: I think you can hear something of Bill's artwork on the album in the music. [Looking at the CD slipcase] There's a cartoon quality to it; it's humorous and a bit playful.

PW: What sort of influence do you think Bill Frisell has had on you and other musicians?

MH: I think he has walked into so many different worlds, he has interacted with so many different musicians, and he has planted a lot of seeds that have affected a lot of things in a very quiet and subtle way. It's not overt. It's not like there's been a number-one Bill Frisell hit and the world followed it. It's not like that. He has opened some doors, I think, for people. He would've given licence to certain music impulses for all of us, I think – that feeling that your genre is not a limitation, and it's not something that you need to be wedded to *endlessly*.

You can feel free to do the simple thing. You can feel free to almost have that . . . musical naïvety and vulnerability that Bill sometimes brings – that almost childlike quality. And I mean that in the very best sense of the word, of course. It's an aesthetic that a good number of us have opened ourselves up to. We feel a kind of a . . . communion with Bill, in that respect.

DC: I had a friend in Chicago, a guitar player, known him for forty years, and he came up to me recently and he says, 'You ever heard of this Frisell guy?' And I looked at him, and I said, 'It's about time.' [We all laugh.] Yeah, finally, he caught on.

MH: Yeah, I know one or two people who haven't liked Bill's music, and I've jokingly said to them, 'That's a major blockage in your life.' [He laughs] There's no reason *not* to like Bill Frisell's music. There's no *conceivable* reason why anyone couldn't enjoy it.

PW: Well, for the sake of journalistic balance, I feel I should at least try to suggest some reasons. I know some people don't like Bill's music because they feel it's all too polite and controlled. They'd also like him to be more unfettered and unrestrained as a guitarist.

MH: I don't think he's restrained at all. There's loads of unrestrained notes being played everywhere in his music.

DC: What do they want? For Bill to be like a jazz-fusion guitarist playing at five thousand miles an hour? I remember when I was in music school, one guitarist I studied with said, 'I'll tell you two things: it's really, really hard to play fast – and it's really, really hard to play slow.' He isn't being restrained; he's just playing to get out the mood he wants.

MH: If playing a melody is considered restraint, I'm with the Bill Frisell world, OK. There are loads and loads and loads of people doing the other thing. There's only one Bill Frisell, however.

PW: Let me play you one last track, not from this album, but from Gone, Just Like a Train *– 'Verona'.*

DC: Oh, yeah.

MH: Yeah.

PW: You've been playing this song in concert, haven't you?

MH. Yeah, sometimes. [The track plays] That's a lovely end, isn't it? We played it with Bill at the festival in Kilkenny; it was Thomas Bartlett's idea. He said, 'Well, Sam [Amidon] and I used to play this when we were kids.' And I said, 'Hah! Yes, of course, let's do it.' Because I knew the song too. But then, I think we played it quite differently.

DC: We slowed it down a lot. There's a lot of space in the song – it has a very flexible melody line, and you can bend it into almost anything you want. Which is the mark of a really good tune.

MH: It's such a *beautiful* melody. You know what? We played it last night. Other than 'Verona', we played a whole night of Irish melodies, and people were coming up to me afterwards going, 'Who wrote that again?' 'Who's that guy?' 'Bill Fr . . . ?' 'What? Who?' [Hayes laughs.] And I was like, 'Bill Frisell.' 'Can you spell that?' 'Sure. It's B . . . I . . . L . . .'

22: Like Dreamers Do

It's a sharp bright afternoon in March 2017 and I'm in the West Village with Bill Frisell to visit 'one of the last redoubts of Old New York', a narrow, cluttered shop in a tall red-brick tenement called Carmine Street Guitars.

Inside, between the old wooden floors and pressed-tin ceiling, are racks of gleaming guitars in all styles, shapes and sizes. There are displays of the store's own leather guitar straps, gig-bags and T-shirts, and around us the accumulation of almost thirty years of trading, at this location at least – guitar cases, strings, stands, accessories, magazines and instruction books. It's like a shrine to the six-string, a fretboardist's full-on fantasy.

On a wall near the cash register there are framed photographs of some of Carmine's more famous customers: Bob Dylan, Lou Reed, Patti Smith, Richard Thompson, Marc Ribot, Nels Cline, Robert Quine – and Frisell himself. In Bill's photo, he is playing his custom-made Telecaster-style guitar, handbuilt by the shop's proprietor, Rick Kelly; on it he has written, 'Howdy, Rick. Thank you so much for this killer guitar.'

We head to the workshop at the back of the store, where we find luthier Kelly and his apprentice and friend Cindy Hulej busy working. There are hugs for Bill, introductions for me.

'We play Bill's music all the time in here, you know,' Kelly tells me.

'Oh, really?'

'Yeah, are you kidding? We must have more of Bill's CDs than . . . well, anyone else!'

Frisell lets out one of his low chuckles and a long modest, '*Oooh, maaan.*'

He took delivery of his prized Rick Kelly guitar in 2010; the body is made, like all Kelly guitars, from timber reclaimed from local historic buildings such as the Chelsea Hotel, McSorley's Old Ale House and even a Serbian Orthodox cathedral – some of the wood is nearly two hundred years old. The timber for Frisell's guitar came from a loft in the nearby Bowery owned by film director, actor, guitarist (and Rick Kelly aficionado) Jim Jarmusch; the old white pinewood beams were replaced during a renovation.

Kelly calls these planks 'the bones of old New York City' and he uses them to build instruments that he and his devotees claim are more stable, seasoned and sonically superior. 'Believe me, you can feel and hear the difference,' he says, and Bill nods and smiles in agreement. Each guitar takes about a week to make and most cost around $2,500 (many of Kelly's customers insist he should be selling them for twice as much); he has a waiting list of around two years.

We talk about a forthcoming documentary on the shop by Canadian film-maker Ron Mann. In it, various musicians drop by the store over a typical week to shoot the breeze and strum some guitar, including Frisell, who offers a lovely shimmering version of the Beach Boys' 'Surfer Girl', the first single he ever bought. 'Yeah!' says Kelly, as the last note resounds around the shop. 'I'm going to charge a lot more for this guitar now. This one just went up in price. It's got Bill Frisell in there!'

•
•

Up until 1999 Frisell had mostly been a serial one-guitar man, much like some of the players who had strongly influenced him.

Wes Montgomery played a hollow-body Gibson L-5 throughout most of his career; Jim Hall used a similar Gibson, the ES-175, for almost thirty years, before swapping it for a D'Aquisto archtop, which he then played for the next twenty. John Scofield has remained loyal to one chief 'workhorse' – a 1981 Ibanez AS-200 that he bought new and has played ever since.

'Yeah, there are a lot of guys like Jim and John – everything they play goes into that one guitar,' says Frisell. 'And there's something incredible, amazing and great about that. Ron Carter's been playing the same [double] bass since 1959, or something. That's his bass that he plays – every time that he plays. On *all* those albums [Carter has appeared on more than 2,200 recordings].'

'And why are you not like that?' I ask.

'I don't know. I just lost control,' he replies, again releasing that child-like chuckle.

Frisell's single guitar from the mid-seventies to the late eighties was his Gibson SG, the rock axe with the somewhat relaxed neck that facilitated all those manual vibrato and chorusing effects. There was a brief romance with the custom electric from Roger Sadowsky, and a couple of beautiful acoustics built by Seattle luthier Steve Andersen, one of which was a gift from Gary Larson.

There was even, in 1989, a guitar journey back to the future. That September, after the Frisells had spent a month in Seattle, they decided to drive to Denver and then fly on back to New York. They ended up on Larimer Street, where there were still a few pawn shops selling second-hand guitars.

'So we go into one I remember being in when I was a kid, and there's a bunch of guitars, and then there's this [Fender] Jaguar hanging there,' he says. 'And I'm like, "*Oh my God.*" It was just like my old guitar, the one I had when I was a kid in high school. *And* it was, like, $350 – though Carole talked them down to three hundred, I think. It's worth at least ten times that now.'

Frisell is all too aware that this kind of recondite guitar-speak can render him not just engagingly nerdy but full-on 'guitarded'. Yet the enthusiasm that emanates from him when he talks about All Things Six-String is palpable and infectious; he rarely seems quite so *animated*. You can sense that Frisell has remained enamoured with the guitar, both artistically and technologically, and as a personal memory box, for almost sixty years.

Frisell invested a lot of time and effort into getting the 1964 Jaguar to play well; original parts were repaired and the neck replaced. At one stage it looked like the guitar was too far gone and couldn't be salvaged, and Frisell decided to sell it – only to buy the instrument back from the purchaser a few months later. 'I kind of flipped out, because that Jaguar had something about it,' he says. 'It was definitely a problem guitar, but I was just too attached to it, and I had to hold on to it.'

While Frisell flirted with the Fender throughout the nineties, his main commitment during that decade of many changes was to his weird and wonderful headless Steve Klein – the guitar with the body that looks more like an oversized artist's palette, and seems as if it might be more at home aboard the starship *Enterprise* or on a Scorpions stadium stage than in a basement jazz club.

'Steve was another kind of genius – a total original builder, just one guy, making guitars in his barn in California,' says Frisell. 'I fell in love with that guitar – everything was balanced and just right, and it had a lot of wood in it, which would resonate, and I liked that. But at the end of the nineties, I needed to have the Klein adjusted and redone, so I sent it back, and it ended up taking a long time. That's when the floodgates opened. I don't cheat on my wife; we've been married almost forty years [he was speaking to me in 2017]. But with the guitars, I'm like . . . what's the word? I'm very promiscuous. I sleep around.'

That guitar abandon was evident on Frisell's next Nonesuch release, *Ghost Town*, a solo record on which he plays seven different guitars, including the Klein and Jaguar, a Gibson Johnny Smith, plus bass and six-string banjo. He prepared for the challenge of returning to a studio alone – the first time he would do so since the ordeal of *In Line* with Manfred Eicher in 1982 – by playing a series of four solo dates in the US in October 1999.

Marc Ribot once described solo gigs as 'a mixture of terror and power', and it's true they are not Frisell's natural arena or inclination. Solo, there is too much exposure and intensity, too much risk of self-indulgence – too much of a conversation with yourself. Frisell couldn't resist, however: another challenge had been set, and he would meet it.

The concerts went well, but when it came to the recording, it was a different story. 'During the concerts, I got really loose and comfortable, and I wasn't really conscious of when there was an electronic buzz, or something,' Frisell told *Guitar Player*. 'But when I got in the studio, I freaked out. The first day, I couldn't even play. Every little movement bugged me – "Oh no, my shirt is rubbing against the guitar!"'

Luckily producer Lee Townsend had booked a full five days at Mobius Music in San Francisco – more studio time than even for Frisell's band albums – and by the end of the sessions Bill was seemingly so relaxed that he was improvising entire tracks on the spot.

Released in March 2000 *Ghost Town* featured mostly new songs, plus a variation on a theme written for Gary Larson's *Tales from the Far Side*, and interpretations of songs by A. P. Carter, Hank Williams, and John McLaughlin – his catchy acoustic blues 'Follow Your Heart'.

It is a rare opportunity to hear him up close and 'completely naked', to see where he was musically, and to discover what kind of personal statement he would make if he was left completely to his own devices. It was a summation, and a return – to one of his own musical roots: Bill Frisell alone in a room with a guitar.

There is plenty of layering and overdubbing on the album, as well as lots of, as critic Josef Woodard put it, 'dreamy looping and effects-with-a-cause' – so Frisell wasn't quite stripped bare; he was communing with various versions of himself. Yet mostly *Ghost Town* is the pure sound of Frisell, in all his panoptic guitar glory.

There is a kind of poetic reflectiveness to the record, a plaintive unease that is accentuated by Frisell's choice of material – 'I'm So Lonesome I Could Cry' and 'My Man's Gone Now', for example. Just when you think the programme of songs might be getting all too soft, spare and pretty, Frisell injects something surreal and unsettling into the mix. *Ghost Town* is populated with all kinds of spirits and surprises.

It is also inhabited with the characters that occupy the album's artwork, which features five *faux-naïf*, playfully figurative and darkly beguiling paintings by Seattle artist Claude Utley, with whom Frisell had become friends. The year after *Ghost Town* was released Frisell decided to combine two of his primary passions – guitars and the visual arts – by commissioning Utley to paint another new instrument he had recently acquired, a custom Telecaster-style guitar built by Seattle luthier Mike Lull, which used the neck from his '64 Jaguar. The result is a guitar which has many of the same colourful, cartoon-like and somewhat disconcerting figures, animals and creatures of Utley's paintings, rendered in acrylic, on both the body and back plate.

In addition, Frisell owns two guitars with 'custom artwork' by painter and sculptor Terry Turrell, who also lives in Seattle. 'Terry is one of my best friends, and our house is filled with his art, so I just had this fantasy about what would happen if he painted one of my guitars,' Frisell told me in 2015. 'And, I mean, the result was incredible.' That guitar was a Fender Jazzmaster, assembled by luthier J. W. Black, which Turrell densely illustrated in oil, enamel and collage with spirited primitivist-style figures, animals and portraits of people dear to Frisell, both personally and musically – Carole and Monica, as well as Roscoe Holcomb, Robert Johnson and Charlie Parker. A heavily modified Telecaster with a series of naïvely graphic figurative line drawings followed.

Frisell plays the former in Emma Franz's documentary, though at one point he has to stop. 'I'm drooling on my guitar,' he says, wiping his mouth. 'Did you get that? *Oh, man.*' He pauses. 'I just love it so much!' And Bill Frisell beams the biggest, broadest smile, like a kid playing with his favourite birthday toy.

•
•

After the intimacy and economy of his solo album, Frisell faced a new challenge: writing again for a larger ensemble, a septet. The result, *Blues Dream,* was another Frisell companion piece – it complemented its predecessor by further showing how far he had developed, especially compositionally.

Released at the beginning of 2001, the album featured his new working quartet – Greg Leisz on pedal, lap, resonator and various other guitars; Canadian bassist and frequent Leisz collaborator David Piltch (they were both members of k. d. lang's band); and Kenny Wollesen – the drummer and percussionist had worked with close Frisell associates John Zorn, Marc Ribot and Leni Stern, as well as recording with Tom Waits and Sean Lennon, playing in klezmer bands, and being a member of Steven Bernstein's subversive pop-jazz group Sexmob. Frisell then added a horn section similar to the one he had employed on *This Land* and *Quartet,* and featuring much the same personnel: Ron Miles on trumpet, Billy Drewes on alto and Curtis Fowlkes on trombone.

Frisell presented his musicians with a suite of eighteen new compositions, some linked and reprised, which made ample use of their collective skills and wide horizons. To say that you can hear elements such as folk, jazz, R&B, new music, pop, old-time, bluegrass, country and, yes, blues in the mix may be axiomatic, and possibly even reductive, by this stage in Frisell's body of work. Yet it is how he distils and distributes those forces into a coherent conceptual whole, suffused with thematic vignettes and narrative asides, which truly elevates the work. *Blues Dream* has the power and drive of a pioneering film or theatre piece: you recognise the territory, yet it takes you somewhere new.

'It's a brilliant work, a wondrous musical portrait of a melting pot or tossed salad or whatever metaphor you prefer for the multiracial, multicultural place America has never, in sad reality, managed to become,' wrote critic Gene Santoro.

The music is highly personal too: Frisell transports himself back to Denver high-school dances in 'Soul Merchant'; and he titles two tunes eponymously for musicians to whom he feels deeply connected – Ron Carter and Greg Leisz. The latter is significant in that Frisell and Leisz had quickly formed a close bond. On 'Outlaws', for example, Leisz achieves something similar to the support Frisell offers singers: he supplies counterpoint, texture, echoes and extensions. There is suddenly a whole new focus and depth of field. The music *moves* more.

'I once talked to David Piltch about Bill and Greg,' says Joe Henry, 'and he said, "You have to understand that when you get them together, there's a synergy that happens: you're not just connecting two people – you're plugging into an entire orchestra." There's a third voice that gets conjured into the room, like when two great harmony singers are singing together. They are both part of it, and it is equally available to each of them. They also have an ability to add something to the music – yet actually create *more* space. Like, how do you do that?'

The search for new and expanded guitar sounds also continued. On *Blues Dream* and his next record, Frisell again changed tack, using another guitar he had bought during the Klein hiatus: a new hollow-body electric, a Gibson ES-446, which he had extensively customised.

'When I began playing these other guitars, I started noticing all this other stuff that I liked,' says Frisell. 'There's a lot that happens in a guitar, all kinds of weird things that could be seen as sort of negative, a flaw or idiosyncrasy that you might have to compensate for, or even fight against. But then I started to like what those idiosyncrasies were doing to the sound; they made it all a little bit more unpredictable.'

If so, the ES-446 was the perfect guitar for *With Dave Holland and Elvin Jones*; Frisell had not played with drum legend Jones before (he confessed beforehand to 'freaking out just thinking about it'), and there was no time for a rehearsal. The two days allocated to record the trio album in New York were also truncated due to a misunderstanding. 'Elvin got the schedule mixed up – he thought the second day was the first day,' Frisell has explained. 'So [when] he finally got there, we played a little bit, and then the next day we played a little bit more. But it was really just this little moment – just this little jam session.'

The recording had been initiated by Michael Shrieve, whom Frisell knew from Seattle. Shrieve had met Elvin Jones when he was a teenager in the sixties and was working with him on a drum concerto, and writing a biography, which remains unpublished. When the album was recorded at the end of 2000 Jones was seventy-three; he would die little more than three years later. Bill had played with Dave Holland on Kenny Wheeler's *Angel Song* and knew that the English bassist had worked with Jones, so the session was set up.

Released in October 2001, *With Dave Holland and Elvin Jones* received some favourable reviews, possibly because it is largely held together by the strength of Frisell's songs; as well as popular standards 'Moon River' and 'Hard Times', Frisell selected ten originals from his back catalogue. The project, however, was more like a controlled experiment – one that incontrovertibly proved just how far from this classic jazz trio format, with its well-worn head–solos–head structure, Frisell and his music had come.

. .

July 1999: Bill Frisell is on stage at the Barbican Centre in London with yet another new group, the Willies: Eyvind Kang on violin, Danny Barnes on banjo and fiddle, Keith Lowe on bass and Chris Leighton on drums. He is opening for a genuine modern jazz supergroup: John Scofield, Joe Lovano, Dave Holland and Al Foster (it's the first time he has seen Foster since the drummer backed out of the *Rambler* recording). Frisell shuffles to the microphone and looks shamefaced yet mischievous. 'Yeah, I'm sorry, I didn't realise,' he begins, slowly. 'I didn't know "willy" was a slang term in England. I mean, "the willies" . . . it means something different back home. So I've decided to change the name of the band. From now on, we're going to be known simply as "Penis".'

The Willies came into being as a result of Frisell hearing Danny Barnes play two years earlier at the Tractor Tavern, a folk, roots and alt-country venue near his home in Seattle. He liked the vibe of the place so much that he named a track on *Blues Dream* after the club, and later would play there himself. 'I went to hear [bluegrass singer and guitarist] Del McCoury . . . and Danny opened the show,' Frisell has said. 'It flipped me out to hear him, because he was the real deal.'

Raised in a small town in central Texas, Barnes is widely considered to be one of the finest banjo players in America. He was co-founder and main singer-songwriter of the Bad Livers, a celebrated acoustic trio formed in Austin in 1990 that honoured and transcended many of Barnes's musical interests, especially bluegrass and punk, and ranged in style from old-time to metal. He also played guitar and resonator guitar in the band.

Frisell was so struck by Barnes's playing that he again decided to follow his instincts and actively forge a connection. He hadn't had an official lesson on a string instrument for twenty-five years – not since his weekly sessions with Jim Hall in New York in 1972 – yet Frisell knew Barnes had recently moved to the Seattle area, and he tracked him down. 'He had this wealth of knowledge that I wanted to find out about,' Frisell told Richard Williams in the *Guardian*. 'He didn't know who I was, or anything, so it started out just as guitar lessons with him. Gradually we began playing together more.'

Frisell met Keith Lowe through Wayne Horvitz. The Seattle bass player had begun working in various Horvitz ensembles; he'd also toured with Fiona Apple, and in funk and rock groups.

In 2001 Frisell decided to document the music he had been making with Barnes and Lowe over the previous four years (he judged that the songs worked best stripped back to a trio setting) by recording his next album for Nonesuch in Seattle, at the Flora Avenue Studio run by engineer, producer and musician Tucker Martine, who had worked on several Wayne Horvitz albums.

The record was titled, of course, *The Willies* and released on Nonesuch in June 2002; it was Frisell's eighth album as leader in just five years. Of the sixteen tracks, six were new compositions; the rest were mostly interpretations of songs by A. P. Carter, Hank Williams and Lead Belly, and of traditional tunes such as 'Cluck Old Hen' and 'Blackberry Blossom' that Frisell had learned from Barnes. 'I realised that jazz players have the facility to take the weirdness of old-time songs even further,' Barnes told *No Depression* magazine.

Frisell plays his Gibson ES-446, but he also employs several acoustics, including, naturally enough, a new guitar, a Collings D1 flat-top, similar to one owned by Barnes.

The album is another major highlight of this remarkable period of Frisell's career. It has the easy charm and relaxed appeal of listening in to 'three-way conversations between back-porch pickers', as Richard Williams put it. Yet there is also a lot going on: these are dialogues full of fascinating details and occasional nods towards harmonic complexity, even dissonance. Somehow Frisell had again dreamed up a world of old and new music that has a compelling sense of clarity and cohesion.

•
•

There were several other group configurations during this period, and from 1999 another new Frisell trio, with Kenny Wollesen on drums and Tony Scherr on bass; the three musicians are still playing as a unit today.

Scherr grew up mostly playing rock guitar and came to jazz relatively late. An electric and double bassist and singer-songwriter of great agility, Scherr had worked in New York in the nineties with friskily experimental downtown groups such as the Lounge Lizards and Sexmob – he once described the latter as 'a combination of Louis Armstrong and Led Zeppelin'. By the time Frisell met him, he and Wollesen had also developed their own rhythm-section sound.

The first time the trio played together was in May 1999, before one of Frisell's annual runs at the Village Vanguard. 'It was incredible from the first moment we played,' Frisell has said. 'We got together to do a rehearsal and we started playing for about three minutes, and it felt like we'd already been playing together for years.' The more they gigged, the stronger that understanding became. 'They just know everything I've ever done – we don't have to figure out anything at all; we just start playing and I can do whatever I want,' Frisell said three years later. 'That's the first band I've had that can do that since Joey and Kermit.'

Frisell's ongoing adventures in the world of guitars continued. In 2003 he bought a 1974 Fender Telecaster, an iteration of the world's first commercially successful, mass-produced solid-body electric guitar. Originally issued as the Broadcaster in 1950 and renamed the Telecaster in 1951, the guitar was affordable, versatile and practical; rather than the neck being artfully dovetailed to the body, it was simply bolted on.

Frisell had owned Telecasters before. He'd bought one in the early eighties and used it, among other guitars, on *Is That You?* In the mid-nineties he acquired a 1966 Tele; it's played briefly on *Blues Dream*. Together with the custom Tele-style guitar built for him by Mike Lull, however, the 1974 model would be the beginning of Frisell's enduring love affair with the Telecaster, in all its manifestations.

It was a serious switch that fellow guitarist Marc Ribot, who also plays Teles (as well as several other guitars, including a 1963 Fender Jaguar), sees as critical. 'It's hard for a non-guitarist to get the depth of moving to the Telecaster, but it's a huge thing,' he says. 'It's very austere – the least gimmicky and the most direct instrument possible. It's a board with strings on it, basically, and pickups. There's no place to hide with a Telecaster. It's kind of the equivalent for a guitarist of what checking into a convent is for a woman.

'It's a technical challenge to do all that amazing stuff that Bill does on a Telecaster. I mean, man, that's even more impressive. It's like saying, "Yeah, OK, you can do that – but can you do it on a Telecaster?" And Bill absolutely can. It's also a move to the guitar that is right at the centre of American music. It's the secret language that speaks across the racial divide.'

⠿

There is another scene in Emma Franz's film on Frisell, in which she asks him what is in the closet of his music room at home in Seattle. 'So I have to open the closet?' he replies, deadpan. 'Oh, boy.' Shortly afterwards, he opens the door to the storage room and looks in. 'Yeah, I was hesitant to show you this, because . . . there's a lot of guitars in here.' Frisell is soft-voiced and sheepish, like a child being caught out; it's as if he's done something extremely naughty. He waits at the threshold. 'Erm. Oh dear, what should I do?'

I'd persuaded him to do the same for me in 2015, and he eventually dived into the room, and pulled out some beautiful glossy instruments in battered old cases, and I asked him how many he had.

'Well . . . right now . . . there's all kinds of different . . . there's a couple of banjos . . . a mandolin . . . some of them are . . . ukuleles. And then there's been all the ones that I've got and sold or traded, or something. But . . . I think . . . it's somewhere in the vicinity of . . . forty? There's plenty of people that have way more than that. So that gets me off the hook from feeling *too* guilty.'

When I meet up with Frisell a couple of years later and the subject comes up again, he confesses that he recently had to catalogue all his string instruments for insurance purposes.

'The total was more than forty, wasn't it?' I say to him, smiling.

'Yeah.' A Frisellian pause follows. I wait.

'Sixty-three.'

'Wow. I mean, I think I understand it, because these are the things, after all, that you create your music on. But is there also a certain level of obsessiveness there too?'

'Yeah, there is. OK, I admit it,' Frisell says, laughing. 'I mean . . . it's stupid, you know. I can't play all of them at the same time. And yes, sometimes I wish I could get back to that thing of . . . just having one guitar.'

'Is it something about them as objects too?'

'Yeah. I'm definitely seduced by that. I can remember when I took my first guitar home and opened the case, and even the smell of it, the *smell* of it. And then there are lots of other people that are also like me, so it's dangerous. I don't know what that is . . . but there's definitely a hoarding instinct that I have, and they do have some kind of power over me.

'They are all different, and do different things, and they all have weird things about them. Even two Telecasters can be completely different; for me, there are these tiny variations and super-fine increments – in overtones, or in the way notes ring. Or if I play a chord and there's some kind of halo over it in a certain way. Or the harmony will speak in a different way; there's a slightly different tension I'll hit.'

Frisell knows that the sound and music he creates comes from inside him, but he is fascinated by the way these guitars work as conduits, how they aid and amplify that process.

'They act like magic wands,' he says. 'It's like that thing about reaching for something . . . OK, this guitar took a leap towards something, and then another one triggered a memory, and that guitar drew out certain things. I think the reason that I have so many of them is that they . . . start communicating with each other in some kind of way. It's like things are resonating from them; they're telling me things.

'I mean, I'm not like a collector; I don't hang them on the wall. I've recorded or done gigs, or something, with every guitar I have. And if one of these guitars causes me to hear or play something different, or write a tune, or if I record an album with it, or anything, it makes it feel like it's worth it . . . and there's no price on that.'

Frisell's enthralling eclecticism continued into the new century through further encounters with a wide world of music, including African, Brazilian, funk, soul, dance beats and samples, and ambient blues.

In 2000 his new trio with Tony Scherr and Kenny Wollesen played Bumbershoot, the mammoth four-day music and arts festival staged in Seattle over the September Labor Day weekend. The Malian singer, guitarist and bluesman Boubacar Traoré also performed at the festival, and he and band member Sidiki Camara, one of Mali's leading contemporary percussionists, came to Frisell's concert. Afterwards Frisell was introduced to the musicians, and a connection was made, even though Bill speaks no French (even after his year in Spa) and certainly none of their native language, Bambara, and they had very little English.

Frisell had long had an interest in music from Africa, but he was not familiar with Traoré or Camara. One of the festival organisers, who was helping with interpreting, said, 'Oh, you gotta hear these guys play,' and Bill and Carole were invited to a dinner the next day.

After the meal, Traoré took out his guitar. 'The very first time I heard him play he was sitting just inches away, and it was just the most amazing experience,' Frisell told NPR. 'Sidiki was playing with him too. He didn't even have his calabash. It was at the dinner table; he just had a plate and a pencil, or something. He was basically just banging on the table, but it was like the most incredible music.'

Although he was right beside Traoré, Frisell couldn't work out how he was making such sounds; he was convinced the instrument had to be tuned differently. 'There was only one guitar and they said, "OK, why don't you play it?" So Boubacar gives me the guitar and I thought, "Well, I'm not going to be able to play *that*." But, of course, it was just in normal tuning. So that was kind of a mind-blowing little moment there. That was the beginning of this fascination with Boubacar's music.'

Frisell didn't know what song to choose, so Camara simply said, 'Just play.' Then someone who knew Frisell's music suggested 'Wildwood Flower', the American folk song recorded in the twenties by the Carter Family; Frisell's poignant acoustic interpretation of the tune had appeared on his solo album *Ghost Town* earlier that year. Frisell played the song, with Camara again providing improvised percussion, using a salad bowl, chopsticks, the table and his hands.

Frisell was so struck by the experience, and his feeling that playing with Camara was 'meant to be' – the percussionist loved the melody and rhythm of 'Wildwood Flower' so much that he later wrote lyrics to it in Bambara – that soon after he decided to drive down to California to catch one of Traoré's concerts as part of his American tour. He got to spend more time with both Boubacar and Sidiki; Traoré taught him one of his best-known songs, 'Baba Drame'.

Frisell absorbed himself more and more in Traoré's music – 'Boubacar is the Elvis of Mali, an important musician,' Frisell enthused in *Down-Beat* – and kept in touch with both players. When Traoré returned to the US to perform again the following year, he stayed in Seattle with Bill and Carole at their new home on Bainbridge Island; Carole acted as interpreter.

The two guitarists jammed together and tried to find a common language. Gradually, Frisell started to unravel some of the mysteries of Traoré's guitar playing and music. 'I felt like he gave me the key to understanding,' Frisell has said. 'Not that I really understood the music, but I could see, technically, a little of what he was doing.' Frisell noticed that Traoré often played in octaves – 'but not in a bebop kind of way, like Wes Montgomery,' he told *DownBeat*. 'It's in a more open-position chords way. A lot of the melodies he's playing [are] in octaves with one note ringing into another like a rich harp-like sound. The notes are all ringing together with overtones.'

Camara had played with many of the greats of Malian music, including Oumou Sangaré and Toumani Diabaté, but had left Mali in the nineties and was living in Brussels. In 2001 Frisell toured Europe with his New Quartet of Greg Leisz, David Piltch and Kenny Wollesen, and he invited Camara to join the band for a concert in the Belgian capital, and for several more in nearby cities. 'He showed up, and he hadn't met the other guys, and [we] hadn't had any rehearsal, or anything,' Frisell has said. 'Maybe he'd heard some of the music, but it was just sort of an instant hook-up.'

There were other musicians Frisell had been bonding with from beyond the borders of America. In 1998 Hans Wendl asked him to contribute to *Tucumã*, an album he was producing in New York for Vinicius Cantuária. The master modern bossa nova singer and guitarist had moved to New York in 1994 and begun playing with such downtown and often Latin-leaning linchpins as Arto Lindsay, David Byrne and Laurie Anderson.

Frisell didn't actually play with Cantuária on the tracks he overdubbed in the studio, and his participation on three songs on the Brazilian's next record, *Vinicius*, which was produced by Lee Townsend, was recorded remotely. But, again, he felt a musical sixth sense. 'The first time, he was there [in the studio], so we met and . . . that's kind of when I knew, with him, the feeling was so . . . there was just this vibe, and it felt so natural,' Frisell has said. 'He also is an incredible drummer – I mean, he played drums with Caetano Veloso – so there's this really grounded thing. But then there are his melodies that are just sort of floating in the air, too. So that was another guy where I thought, "Man, I hope I get a chance to play with him sometime."'

Frisell met Greek-Macedonian oud and bouzouki player and singer Christos Govetas in Dusty Strings, a music store in Seattle, at the end of the nineties; Govetas was trying out an oud and Frisell stood listening to him, not really knowing what he was playing, but again, 'I just sat there and was mesmerised.'

Govetas is another maestro, mostly of Balkan folk music; after he moved to the US in 1978, aged sixteen, he began playing in various Greek rebetiko, Turkish classical and Arabic music groups. 'He had heard some of my music,' Frisell told the *Pure Music* webzine, 'so we started

talking about, "Oh, it would be great if we could get together and play."
But then . . . time kept going by.'

An opportunity to bring together these three intercontinental forces
finally arose in October 2001 when the Seattle jazz festival Earshot
approached him to stage a triple bill of concerts. Rather than work with
any of his new groups or existing configurations, the festival suggested
Frisell perform with musicians he had never played with before.

He played two duo concerts: one with drummer Jack DeJohnette, the
second with Vinicius Cantuária. A third event saw the debut of his Intercontinental Quartet with Camara, Cantuária and Govetas. The group
played 'Baba Drame', 'Corcovado' by Antônio Carlos Jobim, and ended
the set with 'Wildwood Flower'. Frisell had also written a few new songs
for the quartet, some of them inspired by melodies, rhythms and techniques he had learned from Boubacar Traoré. One song, 'Boubacar', was
actually dedicated to him.

The quartet played a few further concerts in the US and Europe the
following year; at the Barbican Centre in London Frisell added celebrated
Malian guitarist Djelimady Tounkara and English folk singer and fiddle
player Eliza Carthy.

Soon after, Frisell brought the quartet to Seattle to record his next
Nonesuch album, *The Intercontinentals*; Lee Townsend produced and
Tucker Martine was the engineer. Looking to add further string colours
and textures, he also asked Greg Leisz and violinist Jenny Scheinman to
join the session; neither had played with the quartet or heard the music
before the recording.

Scheinman is a violinist, singer and songwriter who grew up playing
folk music with her family in a remote part of northern California. She
moved to the San Francisco Bay Area in her early twenties, where she met
Lee Townsend; in 1998 he asked her to play alongside Frisell on Gabriela's album *Viento Rojo*. Since then she has been a regular member of
many of Frisell's groups, as well as releasing a number of highly original
albums as leader.

'Bill and I just had a connection immediately,' Scheinman has said.

'We both really love songs and melodies . . . playing unison with Bill is such a pleasure. He's just constantly learning, and he's so . . . you could call it "stubbornly curious" about new ideas. And [for] things that don't initially work, he just really goes after it. He's been a model for bravery in art.'

The Intercontinentals was released in April 2003 and featured nine new Frisell compositions. The album is something like a contemporary quilt: multilayered, communal and rooted in various historical traditions. Frisell creates an open patchwork of blocks of different fabrics, to which his collaborators add and integrate various cloths, colours, textures and features. Up close it seems detailed, even dense; stand back and you'll see Frisell has sewn it all into one artistic and harmonious whole. It won him his first Grammy nomination, not in any of the jazz categories, but for Best Contemporary World Music Album.

'Bill always seems to be exploring new ground,' Greg Leisz told *Down-Beat*. 'This seems like a natural progression in his own career in terms of seeking interaction with the musical universe . . . He's not moving into world music. It's more like he's gotten off the continent.'

•
•

Frisell brought together four more diverse sonic landscapes for his next record, *Unspeakable*, and sparked yet another twist and surprise.

The album was a long-awaited full-length collaboration with producer Hal Willner, with whom Frisell had continued to work on one-off projects, and it featured, in various combinations and as an ensemble: Frisell's core trio of Tony Scherr and Kenny Wollesen; the string section he had formed for his music for Gerhard Richter's 858 paintings – Jenny Scheinman, Eyvind Kang and Hank Roberts; a new horn section led and arranged by Steven Bernstein of Sexmob, with his bandmate Briggan Krauss on baritone saxophone, and Curtis Fowlkes on trombone; and various other soundscapes and effects provided by Adam Dorn on synthesiser and Willner himself on turntables and samples.

This being a Willner extravaganza, percussionist Don Alias, who had played with Miles Davis, Joni Mitchell and Carla Bley, was also added to six of the tracks, and engineer Eric Liljestrand is credited as co-writing five more.

As Willner explains in 'Counterpoint I', his idea for the album, released in August 2004, was to nudge Frisell into making a funk record, and there are certainly beats, bass-lines and guitar riffs firmly in that vein. In places *Unspeakable* even sounds similar to seventies Miles Davis, the heavy electric years when he was partly channelling Sly Stone, James Brown and Jimi Hendrix. There are also strong echoes of soul – both sixties Stax and seventies symphonic – and the soul-jazz stylings of guitarist Wes Montgomery, especially his Creed Taylor-produced mid-sixties albums with horns and strings.

Wollesen is a dream drummer for this kind of groove – steady, solid and swinging. 'It was fun and rewarding, and a cool record to do,' he says. 'And interesting to record too, because it wasn't like a studio jam, or something; it was organised almost like a construction or collage.'

That structure is supported by samples – of electronic sounds, bass drones, Nordic folk songs, 'pagan flutes', religious and tribal chants, speeded-up vocals and more – on obscure vinyl records that Willner had rescued from deletion at the sound library of TV network NBC.

Willner's sampled sounds inject a certain weirdness and waywardness into the mood of the record, amplifying the wistfulness of some tracks and the darkly surreal and unsettlingly psychedelic dreamworld of others. It is a production *tour de force*; the album won the Grammy in 2004 for Best Contemporary Jazz Album, for both Willner and Frisell.

•
•

Other significant events helped shape this mid-2000s period.

The first was an invitation for Frisell to act as musical director of an ambitious new arts festival in the Ruhr region of Germany called the Ruhr Triennale. Between 2003 and 2005 Frisell programmed and performed in a series of concerts, staged in former industrial sites and buildings, with some of his favourite singer-songwriters. He would provide the 'house band', and Lee Townsend produced.

There were many highlights: Elvis Costello sang lyrics to songs by Charles Mingus; Loudon Wainwright III offered a tribute to one of his idols, Hank Williams; Vic Chesnutt interpreted the elegant pop tunes of Hoagy Carmichael; and Marc Ribot played political anthems from the American Civil War. There were evenings of country music and gospel songs. Other singers Frisell invited included Suzanne Vega, Rickie Lee Jones, Van Dyke Parks, Ron Sexsmith, Carrie Rodriguez and Buddy Miller.

Another vocalist who took part in the festival was Petra Haden. The pair had first met in 1999 when Petra, who is daughter of the late bass player Charlie Haden, and triplet sister of bassist Rachel and cellist Tanya, was playing a duo concert in Seattle with an avant-accordionist and singer named Miss Murgatroid. Haden had been a vocalist and violinist in a wide variety of bands, from indie rock to punk-pop and alt-country, and released a mainly a cappella solo album, *Imaginaryland.*

'Paul Motian was always talking about Petra, and telling me how great she and her sisters were,' says Frisell. 'So Carole and I went to the concert, and she came off stage, and we walked towards each other – I guess she knew who I was, or something – and it was almost like everyone else in the room cleared away. It was like I had that feeling, that I knew her already.'

Frisell was feeling that instinct again, his ESP about certain musicians. 'It doesn't always . . . I don't want to try to even think of the times when it hasn't worked out . . . but with someone like Petra, it was already all in my head what it might be. And then when we played together for the first time . . . *bam,* the first note and it's like, "*Whoa!* How can this be happening?"'

Frisell and Haden began playing duo concerts and in 2003 released a CD together, *Petra Haden and Bill Frisell.* It's an album as unadorned as its title: a dozen favourite songs – chosen by the pair for their melodic pull, and rendered simple, spare and beautifully sensitive – ranging from

'Moon River' to Tom Waits's 'I Don't Want to Grow Up'. 'It's just so easy to work with Bill,' says Haden. 'He's very open to ideas, and he always gives people space, in a very natural way, to do their thing.'

In 2004 Frisell had an album expressly written for and dedicated to him by trumpeter Dave Douglas; the genesis of the record was, suitably enough, in a dream.

'The working quintet I had at the time was playing this tune I'd written called "The Frisell Dream",' says Douglas. 'I had this dream that I was at a Bill Frisell gig, with Joey, Kermit and Hank, I think, and they were playing this strange but beautiful song, which I didn't recognise, and I woke up and wrote it down, almost the whole thing. That was the piece. So, it sort of made sense to make our next record with Bill as our very special guest, and one of my biggest heroes.'

Strange Liberation was recorded in New York with Douglas, Frisell and a crack band of Chris Potter on tenor saxophone and bass clarinet, Uri Caine on Fender Rhodes, James Genus on bass, and Clarence Penn on drums. The record abounds with stirring solos, especially by Frisell and Potter, and open, ambitious and keenly melodic compositions that strongly suggest both structure and freedom. Douglas says he was trying to honour Frisell's considerable influence on him as a composer. 'He really opened up a canvas to me – a way of thinking about creating music for a group of improvisers, and within the framework of form, making something new,' he says. 'I learned a couple of other things from Bill too: never overwrite and always serve the players in the band.'

•
•

In 2005 Frisell returned to the art of the trio, releasing one of his most instantly appealing and perennially popular records: the double live album *East/West*. *East* was recorded during four days at the Village Vanguard in 2003 with Frisell, Scherr and Wollesen; *West* was from a similar run in 2004 at a club called Yoshi's in Oakland, California, with bassist Viktor Krauss replacing Scherr.

The album presented a collection of originals, standards, traditional tunes – and Frisell's further investigations into popular song, including such enduring classics as 'I Heard it Through the Grapevine'. There are also, on additional tracks from the concerts that were released as the digital download album *Further East/Further West*, sixties songs that seem, for Frisell, to speak to the post-9/11 Iraq-war moment: Dylan's 'Masters of War' and Bacharach's 'What the World Needs Now Is Love'.

At the Vanguard, perhaps unexpectedly, he begins to play the Barbra Streisand signature tune 'People' – only for a woman in the audience to break out laughing. Frisell stops and pauses, and you can hear him say, in a somewhat irked voice, 'Do you think I'm joking, or what?'

A few years later, Frisell told critic Jim Macnie, 'I don't want anyone to think I'm making fun of those tunes. It's just that I'm now really comfortable with stuff that I thought was a little corny years ago. Being a jazz guy and having to be super-hip . . . man, it takes years to shake that off and just be honest. I knew I had to be true to the music I really loved, like letting in . . . stuff from my childhood.'

These albums are pure unadulterated Bill: there are passages augmented by random effects and controlled loops, yet little in the way between artist, music and audience. Frisell is at his most expressive, joyous, inventive and unpredictable; the music on these albums is among the most alive and affecting he has recorded.

Out east at the Vanguard Frisell is more in general jazz mode; he plays a 1956 Gibson ES-125 archtop, another new acquisition, a hollow-body 'entry-level' model popular in the fifties with jazz, swing, rockabilly and blues guitarists. At Yoshi's he plugs in his '74 Telecaster and rocks out more; the tracks are longer, freer, even in places louder – you can almost hear the music expanding out into the larger club space.

The two bass players have similar levels of elasticity and command, yet differing styles: Krauss has a big, fat, resonant roots-rock tone; Scherr a round and agile sound that swings into many different territories. '[With Viktor] you can lean on him so hard, he really is a "bass" bass player,' Frisell said in *Jazzwise*. 'He doesn't want to solo; he just wants to lay the stuff down with that huge sound he gets. Tony? Boy, I learn so much from him. He's younger than me, but the amount of music he knows is overwhelming. Anything I go for, he already knows.'

Frisell's next Nonesuch album, released in September 2006, was a record made with two of his musical heroes: *Bill Frisell, Ron Carter, Paul Motian*. 'For a long, long time I had a dream about getting Ron and Paul together,' Frisell said in the *Village Voice*, when the trio played their first live dates at New York's Blue Note club the following year. 'They hadn't really played much [together, but] they're both so important for me, in my musical life.'

Frisell had been playing with Motian for a quarter of a century; his connection to Carter went back even further, to those very first jazz records he heard when he was sixteen. Ron Carter led him to Miles Davis, and the first time he saw Carter play live was in 1971 in a duo with Jim Hall. He was so central to Frisell's sense of musical integrity and worth that he had even, of course, named a track after him.

The choice of material, and on a subsequent EP of four additional tracks, reflected that lineage: 'Eighty-One' and 'Mood' were two Carter compositions, written and recorded with Miles Davis on his landmark 1965 album *ESP*. There were also two Monk tunes, 'Misterioso' and 'Raise Four', some standards, Jimmy Davis's country-pop classic 'You Are My Sunshine', and a selection of tunes by Frisell and Motian.

It was, however, a very different trio album to the ones Frisell made on *East/West*. Just a day and a half of recording had been scheduled at Avatar Studios in New York, and Carter, for one, was looking to keep things firmly within prescribed limits.

'One of my loves of Bill Frisell is how he plays with no metre but with some metre at the same time,' Carter said in a public interview in 2010. 'He just kind of floats around the beat sometimes. And Paul Motian . . . does that very well [too]. I like it when they do that. But I explained to them . . . we all met there [in the studio] at 10.45 a.m. So I told Paul, and I told Bill, starting at eleven o'clock, don't play any clouds, don't play any smoke, don't play any steam. Let's just play some good old-fashioned time.'

That approach may partly explain why the record fails to generate any heat. It is fun to luxuriate in the warm, rich natural sound of Carter's bass, and to hear Frisell make a fairly straight-ahead jazz record, but too often these tracks meander and fizzle out. It is only on the slower-tempo numbers, such as Motian's tender 'Introduction' and Hank Williams's heartbreaking 'I'm So Lonesome I Could Cry', that you really feel the interactive and interpretative power of these three masters.

Frisell's next project, *Floratone*, was something else again, born out of a decision by Frisell and Matt Chamberlain to get together in a studio to jam. Chamberlain is one of the most versatile session drummers in America, having recorded or toured with musicians ranging from David Bowie to Kenny Rogers, Brad Mehldau to Hans Zimmer. The duo had long talked about working on a project with Lee Townsend and Tucker Martine, and in 2005 a plan was put in place: Frisell and Chamberlain would jam in the studio; Townsend and Martine would record, edit, manipulate, structure and programme. Further layers and collages were then added: the bass of Viktor Krauss; multitracked horn and string parts written and arranged by Frisell for Ron Miles and Eyvind Kang; further loops; and guitar and drum overdubs.

It is certainly Frisell's most studio-centric project. 'Most of my own music is more of a documentation of a band or some composition that I write,' he told *Premier Guitar*. 'The germ or the seed of *Floratone* comes from this wide-open improvising with Matt Chamberlain and myself – it's a completely spontaneous thing. We'd go in the studio for a day or two, and put hours of stuff on tape, and then . . . just let Tucker and Lee go wherever they want to, and it's wild to hear what comes back.'

This was a chance for the producers to creatively studio-construct something similar to Miles Davis's *In a Silent Way* or, at a stretch, the Beatles' *Sgt Pepper's*, with Townsend as Teo Macero and Martine as, well, George Martin. The experimental spirit of Hal Willner might also have been hovering somewhere nearby. It worked: Martine received a Grammy nomination for 'Best Engineered Album, Non-Classical'. The quartet also went on to produce a second record in a broadly similar vein,

Floratone II, again with contributions from Miles and Kang, plus bass from Mike Elizondo and keyboards by Jon Brion.

The albums are a swampy and spacey trip to a soundworld where jazz, blues, dub, country, rock, funk, trip-hop and psychedelia seem to simply coexist. The atmosphere is often hypnotic and hallucinatory, and the overall sound, as Townsend described to me, is 'both very clear and a little gritty' – and best appreciated extremely loud.

Townsend calls the four-way *Floratone* collaborations 'a laboratory experiment', and it represents another new genre to add to the long checklist that can be applied to Frisell's work: 'By the end,' Townsend has said, 'it was some kind of weird futuristic roots music.'

24: Paul Simon Listens to *The Intercontinentals*

The Intercontinentals: recorded Seattle, May 2002;
producer Lee Townsend; released on Nonesuch, April 2003;
Bill Frisell (electric and acoustic guitars, loops, bass), Greg Leisz
(slide guitars, pedal steel guitar), Vinicius Cantuária (electric and
acoustic guitars, vocals, drums, percussion), Christos Govetas
(oud, vocals, bouzouki), Jenny Scheinman (violin),
Sidiki Camara (calabash, djembe, congas, percussion, vocals);
compositions by Frisell, plus by Boubacar Traoré, Gilberto Gil,
Christos Govetas and Vinicius Cantuária.

Paul Simon has written some of the best-loved and most enduring pop songs of the modern era – sixties number-one singles, recorded with Art Garfunkel, such as 'The Sound of Silence', 'Mrs Robinson' and 'Bridge over Troubled Water', and, after the duo split in 1970, 'Mother and Child Reunion', 'Slip Slidin' Away' and '50 Ways to Leave Your Lover'.

In 1986 Simon released *Graceland*. Made primarily in Johannesburg with South African musicians, including choral group Ladysmith Black Mambazo, the album is estimated to have sold sixteen million copies worldwide. '*Graceland* was a bridge between cultures, genres and continents,' wrote singer-songwriter and journalist Andrew Leahey, 'not to mention a global launching pad for the musicians whose popularity had been suppressed under apartheid.'

Four years later came *The Rhythm of the Saints*, a record mainly influenced by the music of Latin America, in particular Brazil. Of the two albums Simon once said, 'I learned how to collaborate with players from other cultures. Some didn't speak English or speak in musical terms that I was familiar with. I learned to pay attention and listen. Music is about listening.'

Born in 1941, Simon has always maintained a gift for music that is rigorous, restless and quietly intrepid, and in 2005 he asked Frisell to contribute to a track on his album *Surprise*; Brian Eno also adds electronics to the tune, and 'sonic landscapes' to the album. Subsequently Simon and Frisell played duo live on a 2017 episode of *The Late Show with Stephen Colbert*; the following year Frisell appeared, as did Joe Lovano and Wynton Marsalis, on Simon's record *In the Blue Light*.

In Emma Franz's film, Simon describes himself as a fan of Frisell's work for many reasons, '. . . but mostly it's his sense of tone, the way he mixes colour, and the different forms of music that he combines; it's a unique kind of Americana that's really Bill Frisell.'

I met Paul Simon in Dublin, Ireland, in 2015; he was in town to play a concert with Sting, as part of a fourteen-month global arena tour. His suite in the luxe InterContinental hotel was the size of a large apartment; the living room in which we conducted the listening session must have been forty feet long. Simon is friendly, warm and courteous; he spoke gently, yet was a still and powerful presence, a thoughtful and intelligent man of strong opinions.

The choice of music to play Simon for this session seemed self-evident, and not just because of the name of the hotel in which he was staying: *The Intercontinentals*, Bill Frisell's 'world music album'.

PW: I had an idea to begin by simply playing you a track from one of Bill's albums, to let the music pose the questions and speak for itself.

PS: Well, that's a good idea. ['Baba Drame' plays] Well, my first reaction was that it sounded like music from Mali and I liked it. [The song was written by Boubacar Traoré.] But, you know, I'm not uncommon in how much I like music from Mali. A lot of musicians do, particularly guitarists.

So Bill and Mali is a potentially good combination. He's got great, great ears, and he has a wonderful modal and harmonic sense, like when he moves into that kind of chordal Americana, which maybe suits the seeming openness of the scale they like to play in Mali. He is one of the few people I know who's really good at those sounds, from wherever he takes them. He really makes them beautiful. And obviously he loves them. And, I mean, I happen to love them too.

And my next thought about that combination was, 'Well, we'll see . . .' [I laugh.] Because with this kind of music you're really not quite sure what you've created. You're not doing the music of Mali, or Brazil, or Greece; you're making up some kind of hybrid. And the really big task is to balance these instruments and where they want to go naturally. Like, can the percussionist – who's playing that big gourd, the calabash, right? – go to places other than Mali? Because those type of [West African] instruments don't always sound great when you put them with other music. They sound *clicky*.

Bill's really put a lot of spices into that stew. And I'm not exactly sure how they all work together. [Looking at the CD booklet] He's added a bouzouki, another stringed instrument, into the mix of the lap steel, violin, and Bill on [electric] guitar. And he's saying, 'OK, well, does the Greek ear relate to the music of Mali and of me?' That's a good question. And given good musicians, it's going to produce an interesting answer.

Is there a trick, do you think, to making these disparate elements work together?

Well, it's not a trick. But it's easy to get it wrong. Most of the time it is less than the sum of its parts. But what's amazing is that when it's right, it's something really special.

I think one of the issues about putting together a group of musicians from different countries is . . . you want to be very respectful of everybody. But it's a delicate balance, because you don't want to be *too* respectful, and keep withdrawing, and saying to the others, 'No, no, you please.'

I mean, if you're buying the album, you're buying it for Bill Frisell. It's his album, Bill chose all of these people, this artistic mix of sounds, so you want to hear him finish his idea, if he has a good one, and part of his job in this particular project is to be an editor. Without hurting anybody's feelings. I can tell people in my band, 'Don't play there.' And everybody knows there's nothing personal in it, or that there's anything wrong.

Making it work is also subjective. I just put together sounds that I like, and my personal experience with all this started very early. Like, for 'Cecilia', well, we just played rhythms and taped them on a home recorder, and the machine had a wrong switch on, or some kind of malfunction, which made the whole track play as if it were in triplets [Simon sings the famous rhythm]. That's what made the track swing so much. Anyway, so I heard that, and I liked it, and I made a loop of it, and then I played the song against it.

And that's what Bill does, I think. He likes a sound, it touches him, he plays with it, and sometimes that magic, whatever that is, occurs. Because sometimes what he does is really, you know, on the money.

Like the album he made with Dave Holland and Elvin Jones. I was aware of Bill's music, but that was my real introduction into it, the first time that I really listened to it. And it was my favourite album *for weeks*. I thought that it was just great. When he makes his music, it's absolutely *his*, you know.

I also like the one with the Mexican title and kind of cover . . . I'm sorry, I've forgotten what it's called.

Lágrimas Mexicanas *[Mexican Tears]?*
Yes. I really like that album a lot.

That's a duo record with Brazilian guitarist and singer Vinicius Cantuária, and he's on this next track, written by Bill; it's called 'Good Old People'.
[Track plays] Well, that's delightful. I enjoyed that a lot.

Can you tell me how Bill came to play with you on the Surprise *album?*
I just admired him, and I wanted to work with him. He played on 'Everything About it is a Love Song', and, well, that's one of the songs I like the most on that album. That was *mostly* a good song.

You know, Bill and I only met this one time, and it wasn't like we had a lot of time together, but I do remember one of the things he said to me. He said, 'Well, I'm trying, and I hear it, but I don't know if I actually captured it.'

But the truth is . . . his sense of sound is exquisite. I guess a lot of the space was already filled on that track, so there's not a lot of him on there, but as soon as he came in the studio and turned his amps on . . . it sounded just like Bill Frisell. It was just one guitar; and his sound was there immediately. And he has a lot of different sounds that are beautiful.

From the perspective of somebody who's a guitarist and who loves the guitar, I think he's just a really great, great guitarist. As a player, I'm crazy about him, and as a guy, he's great. I mean, I just don't know enough jazz improvisation to have an opinion on that. And my problem with a certain kind of jazz is, like, there are too many notes. But the thing is, Bill's a smart guy. He's a good creator of sounds, and a good editor of them. That's what I like about him as a player.

I thought you might be interested to hear this: it's a Gilberto Gil song called 'Procissão' [Procession]. [There is a long pause after the track finishes] The track didn't really do it for you, Paul?

Oh . . . I wasn't thinking that way. First of all, I noticed Bill's use of loops and the way it created a very interesting rhythmic pattern, which one of the other instruments then picked up and started to play. I'm not saying this in some, like, professorial way. I can't really analyse it. I think it was cool. My ears said to me, 'Whoa, I really liked that.'

Then I was thinking about these different cultures and their relationships to the drone. And I was wondering which way it was going to go – towards a kind of microtonal scale or something closer to western country open-fiddle strings.

So that's what I was listening to. And I stayed with it for a while, and it was an interesting conversation. About drones. I mean, for me; I don't even know if that's what Bill meant. It doesn't matter whether it was. His work is deep, so it can produce all kinds of reactions that he may not have specifically intended. Then I heard Bill in the background playing some kind of interesting chords against the drone, and they were very Bill, those chords. So I waited to see if he was going to build off those chords, but he didn't; he gave them up to somebody else.

Shall I play you another track?

Yeah, sure. I'm enjoying it, I'm enjoying it. Why don't you play me your favourite track from the album?

Well, OK. I like this track a lot; it's called 'We Are Everywhere'. There are vocals on it, but no lyrics, and it's the longest track on the album, but anyway . . .

[The seven-minute tracks plays] That's a lovely piece. Parts of it were very beautiful. And this is just a first listen to this album. I always play his records much more than once. My favourites, I listen to all the time. Then I let some time go by, and I play them again. And I always hear more and more sounds: the sound he speaks in, and how he contrasts that with other sounds, and how he takes you to all the sounds and places that he's interested in.

Well, Bill has this idea that he's always searching for something, for a sound just beyond his reach.

Yes, I can hear that. And I identify with it, trying to hear the thing that's just beyond what you can hear. It's like . . . a combination of a pleasure and an irritant. So that's where he goes; he goes there. To try to find the sounds that he loves. That's his job and his passion, and I'm personally very happy that he's doing it.

And I would think it would continue. Because that just seems to be who he is, and the kind of music that he likes to play. He'll keep developing, with all these trios and quartets and sextets and groups that he has. They're really beautiful.

But then maybe he'll surprise us all one day. Maybe Bill Frisell will write a symphony, or something.

25: Six Hundred and Eight

In June 2014 Bill Frisell visited his daughter Monica at the Vermont Studio Center. Located in the historic village of Johnson in remote northern Vermont, near the Canadian border, the centre runs the largest international arts residency programme in the US, and is a kind of creative community paradise – a thirty-acre campus of studios and gallery spaces set among scenic forests and mountains.

Monica was working at the centre for a year as a visual arts coordinator, focusing on her photography and video art in her spare time. Bill came for a few days during a break in touring, mostly to collaborate with Monica. She would record Bill playing various atmospheric tones, patterns and effects that sounded like gently abstract film scores. The pair then edited, mixed and structured the music into tracks that Monica integrated into a series of stop-motion animations.

'The last day I was there . . . that day was really amazing,' says Frisell. 'I'd created some music, and Monica had made some videos, and I was just so happy – like, wow, me and my daughter together doing this stuff.'

Monica remembers it vividly. 'That day was incredible, because we made this song that was awesome, and it just felt like it was really fun, and I was like . . . I don't know, I can't explain it – it was him and me having our time.'

Around nine o'clock in the evening, as the light was fading, Monica and Bill decided to play table tennis; there was a table under a large awning behind the sculpture studio that had spotlights. Around them were sculptures, including an oversized deer made of iron, and nearby a fire pit – this was a popular gathering spot at night, but there was a party elsewhere on the campus.

'Again, it's just me and my daughter, and I'm thinking, this is *great*,' says Bill. 'So we start playing, and we played a game, and then it just seemed like, well, we don't need to do that. Why don't we just hit the ball back and forth and see how far we can go?'

It seems Frisell's impulse is to collaborate, even when faced with a competitive sport. 'We did that for a little bit, and then I said, "Well, let's see if we can get to 100, right?" So then we started going . . . 25, 26, 27, 28, "*Oh shit.*" And then . . . you know, 17, 18, 19, "*Oh fuck.*" And 50, 51, 52 . . . 63. . . and I start thinking, "Oh, getting closer . . ." And then, "*Cussshhh*, no, fuck," you know.

'And then my arm starts getting tired, and it's like an hour later, and it's kind of dark all around us, and I'm like, "Man, we've got to be able to get to 100 . . ." 89, 90 . . . 91, 92 . . . "*Oh, fuck.* So let's start all over again."

'We kept doing it. And then, finally, we sort of got into this thing . . . 100, 101, 102 . . . we're in this thing, and . . . it was incredible . . . 199, 200, 201 [Frisell starts tapping his foot, metronomically] and it just kept going . . . and it was just in this zone, where we weren't thinking, we were just in this rhythm . . . and every once in a while it would kind of go off and we'd get back on track . . . 250, 251 . . . 300 . . . 400 . . . 500 . . . and then it was 600 . . . and then I thought, "Fuck! We're going to make it to a thousand." And as soon as I thought that . . . *Bam*. But it was 608. We made it to 608!'

Monica says they carried on for a short while afterwards, and tried to match their score, but they knew they wouldn't achieve anywhere near it; in fact, they couldn't get past 50 again. 'It was just this moment of total connection, of totally being present, like nothing else was going on,' she says. 'Maybe it was something to do with everything that had happened that day: the way we'd totally worked together on the videos – an artistic connection that I guess we hadn't felt before. But it was a pretty powerful thing: just the ball and my dad and me.'

Frisell gets quite emotional even talking about it. 'So that was like one of the best days of my whole life,' he says. 'It's up there with the feeling I had when Monica rode a bike on her own for the first time . . . I'm sort of holding her and then suddenly she just [he makes a *whoosh* sound] took off all by herself, racing down the sidewalk, like "Holy shit, she did it. *Go Monica!*"

'But it was also a total lesson. Every time you start thinking about, or you become aware of what it is you're doing, it just screws it all up. But still, for ten minutes or more, from 100 to 608 . . . that was just incredible.'

•
•

Bill Frisell is in Jim Woodring's house, looking at his drawings, talking about the creative process and his need to stay naïve. 'It seems like the best things I do are the things I do *before* I figure out what they actually are,' he says, in a clip from Emma Franz's film. 'Something'll come out, something'll appear to me, I'll get *at* something when I'm more in a state,' he starts laughing, 'of *not* knowing what I'm doing.'

Frisell has talked about this aspect of his work, and especially how it applies to the way he plays and performs on stage, on a few occasions, but he is often reluctant to articulate it, as if the very act of describing and defining the practice contaminates it somehow – by irrevocably limiting and reducing it, by breaking the spell.

One interviewer, Eric Nemeyer, put it to Frisell that 'the greatest obstacle to discovery is the illusion of knowledge'.

'It's clear to me that I don't know much about anything,' he replied. 'To me, it's important to do the work. You can really get yourself bogged down in being too self-critical, or thinking that you're really happening. You have to be critical to a point, and good enough to a point. But you have to just get deep into what you're doing.

'That to me is the best feeling – those moments when I'm trying to write or when I'm on a gig playing. When the stuff is really happening, you're immersed in it and you're not thinking about whether it's bad or good; you're just inside of it. There are moments when you just forget all that stuff and you just get lost in the process of doing it. Or, if you're on a gig, and everything is happening – as soon as you have the realisation that it *is* happening, it usually crashes down.'

At one point Frisell and I discuss Gunther Schuller's close if contested analysis of Sonny Rollins's staggering solos on the eleven-minute 'Blue 7' from his 1957 album *Saxophone Colossus*. Rollins later admitted being taken aback by the influential essay – 'because I didn't know what I was doing!' he explained. 'It made me self-conscious about playing. It took me a while to get over that. It's almost superstitious, where you don't want to investigate too much [for fear of] losing your soul. It's something very personal. People like Gunther Schuller are analytical, which is fine, but I'm a little bit more of a primitive!'

'I can totally relate to that,' Frisell says. 'If we can stay in this kind of innocent state, there are so many things that we do that are *way* more advanced than if we're micro-thinking about it. I mean, I want to be at the point where I'm at the edge of, or just beyond what I understand. I'm trying to keep it there, and it's harder when everyone's telling you what it is.'

I suggest to him that writers and artists sometimes talk about allowing things to come from the back of the brain rather than the front: that's where the good stuff often is.

'Yeah,' he replies, 'that's *exactly* the same for me.'

This gets to the heart of who Bill Frisell is as an artist, particularly when he is on stage, when he is at once at his most exposed and vulnerable – and his most present and himself.

In truth, this is where he lives most of the time, what his regular musical life looks like, and has looked like for fifty years. The albums are high-profile punctuation marks along the way, vital documents of a particular time and group and set of tunes. But Frisell is a musician who, in his busiest years, travels for 250 days and plays 200 gigs. As Duke Ellington said, 'The road is my home.'

'You make up your mind how you want to be,' Wayne Shorter once remarked about a musician's stage persona. 'Because the way you are does affect what comes out of your horn. You produce barriers of shyness, barriers of lack of confidence or barriers of over-confidence. You have to get your own balance together.'

What or who is Bill Frisell when he is playing? And what is he trying to say?

∴

In the early days, as agile and adept as the music might have been, Frisell was not always a comfortable watch.

The first few times I saw him play in the eighties, with Paul Motian, Power Tools, Paul Bley, and his own quartet, he was almost an anti-presence – you almost felt that physically he didn't quite want to be there. There was something almost stooped or hunched about him, and he would often, as one *DownBeat* critic noted in 1989, 'cradle his guitar as if he's protecting it, trying to hold in its sound'. There were the geeky glasses and the modest clothes, the introversion and the higher-pitched voice. You could see how the 'Clark Kent of the electric guitar' sobriquet was just waiting to be written.

'When I first saw him perform in New York [in the eighties], it was kind of hard to even watch Bill on stage,' says Phyllis Oyama, who runs Songtone with Lee Townsend. 'But I think he's grown into being comfortable in public. Now he's just himself, and he has this amazing sort of awkward charm.'

Like many shy people who perform in public, the discomfort was not the result of any internal terror or stage fright. In fact, playing concerts, doing the thing that he loves, absorbing himself in a world of music and infinite possibility, with people whom he trusts and who can offer unlimited support and inspiration, even seems to free and relax him, certainly more so than in real life.

'I might be nervous if I'm going to play with someone I don't know,' he says. 'But almost without fail, if I immerse myself in the music, it always works out. The music takes over, and that's the one place in my life where everything really makes sense and I'm *not* scared. Stage fright and stuff like that . . . as long as I'm in the music, everything's cool.'

Occasionally, however, his pose and persona have looked somewhat

345

worried, as if the creativity was not entirely sublimating the anxiety. 'He never looks ecstatic on stage,' Tom Junod wrote in *GQ* in 1997. 'Instead, he looks . . . concerned. Or befuddled. Or – if he's smiling – really, genuinely *pleased*.'

Over the years, that disquiet seems to have largely dissipated, and the big grins and beaming smiles have solidly taken over. But still, Frisell sometimes looks sort of bemused, even slightly embarrassed, as if he cannot quite believe what is happening to him and the music he is creating.

There is also the unfortunate fact, for some, that Frisell has always faced (and directed those smiles at) his fellow band members, not the audience. 'The idea of, like, standing in front of the band, and facing the audience, is just completely absurd to me,' he says. 'I can't even *imagine* doing that. It's just ridiculous. The idea of me walking to the front of the stage . . . and sort of saying, "Check out what I can do," and having the band behind me backing me up . . . is just so far from what I'm trying to do.'

Frisell wants his attention to be fully focused on the musicians with whom he is playing; he is in a heightened state of alertness. His stage position usually reflects that: centre left, facing inwards to the band. This sometimes means, depending on the venue, that certain sections of the audience can see very little of what he is doing. 'I'm making the music for people to hear, but sometimes I almost have my back to the audience. Some people get upset about that. They want to be watching my hands and fingers, or something.'

For Frisell, the music and the guitar are conduits of intense concentration. 'The way my mind works, I find . . . see the way I'm talking now . . . it's just like . . . so many things are going through my mind and . . . distracting me and . . . I'll forget one thing, I start to say one thing and I'll forget it,' he says. 'And, you know, that can happen in the music. But when I put the guitar in my hands, it seems to . . . it's like plugging myself into the world. Everything becomes much clearer and closer somehow – like, what I hear, the sound in my imagination. I can focus and my attention is able to stay . . . right on. When I'm playing music, that happens more than at any other time in my life. Music is the place where there's the least amount of interference.'

The idea that Frisell is not totally psychically there when he plays, that he is a different version of himself, is not completely outlandish, because most of the time he is trying to get out of the way. 'Even when the playing is going well, there could be a million things going through my head,' he says. 'Like, my seat assignment on the airplane, or I left my wallet somewhere, or I lost my credit card, or . . . my leg hurts, or I've got to go to the bathroom, or . . . wait a minute, did I just play this A-section once or twice?

'But when it's *really* going, there's nothing going through my head; I'm just *playing*. Sometimes I can trick myself, by not looking at my hands . . . or looking at the other guys in the band *a lot*. But I want to be in this place where I'm *not* thinking, where I can take my attention away from myself and just let the music *go*. And when everybody's doing that, it's the most amazing feeling.'

The 'Ameri-chicana' singer-songwriter and fiddle player Carrie Rodriguez, who has played in various Frisell bands, says, 'I've never really met anyone who has that ability to shut out everything else except for that moment in music. In some of our concerts I've noticed that my sense of time completely vanishes; it's really special, and it's really Bill.'

∙
∙

Frisell was once asked by Danny Barnes what frustrates him most about playing music, and he instantly replied, as he has done on a number of occasions, that it is the travelling. 'I don't like sitting on a plane,' he told Barnes in *Fretboard Journal*. 'I was in New York . . . I went to Florida, and then it took me three planes, like twelve hours, to get home [to Seattle]. And I was home for about sixteen hours, and then I got on another plane . . . to San Francisco, and then San Francisco to Tokyo. And that was all within three days. I got cheap tickets, there's no oxygen, all my bodily fluids and my kidneys are screaming, "What's happening?", all my skin is flaking off my face, I can't go to sleep, I'm puking . . . [laughing]. I don't like that part.'

If you look at some of Frisell's five-week European tour schedules, with their dates and flights almost every day, and the fact that every other year or so he plays in Japan, South America, Southeast Asia and Australasia, it can seem exhausting, especially for someone who is no longer in their twenties.

Travelling also takes Frisell away from his family. When I spent time with Carole in 2015, she said to me, laughing, that the secret of her and Bill's then thirty-six-year union was that they'd actually only been married for half that time; the other half Bill was away on tour. 'That's a joke,' she continued. 'But, yes, it can be difficult. The re-entry and the leaving are always extremely stressful. For both of us. Even to this day. I'll have been by myself [Monica first left home, to study in New York, in her late teens], and got used to my own rhythms, and it's like, "Who the hell are you to change everything?" And for Bill, he's coming off the road, and he's on such a creative high, and then reality hits. He's back with me, and I'm not so impressed, I'm not a *fan*.' Carole breaks out in a big laugh. 'And then, when he leaves again, he's absolutely stressed out, because he has to get the music and everything together for the next tour.'

It is either feast or famine, continual readjustment and recalibration. 'But then again I think that we both have a halfway decent grasp on the bigger picture,' Carole said. 'We understood we were going to have lives that were at times parallel. And we remember that there is something outside of us, bigger than us: a commitment to each other, and what we do. I can't stress that enough, you know.'

Carole says it was hardest when Monica was young: 'We couldn't share the little things or the milestones together, and it was tough for Bill to miss out on her growing up. Sometimes he was shocked at how much Monica had grown in just the four weeks or so that he'd been away on tour. But then, I remember when she was a baby, I would hand Monica, in dirty diapers, to Bill as soon as he got home. Nothing like a diaper change to bring you back to the everyday!'

During her childhood Monica couldn't watch cartoons, television programmes or films in which the father died. 'Bill always seemed to be leaving to go on tour: he goes, he comes back, he goes, he comes back – it was traumatising,' she says. 'It was really hard to understand, because it always felt like his band and the music came first. It sounds selfish when I say it now, but it was like, "Oh, for God's sake, *what about us?*"'

For Monica's thirtieth birthday, Carole gave her a journal she kept during the first year of her daughter's life. In one of the last entries, Carole details how difficult it was for baby Monica when Bill came back from being away. 'It makes me cry just thinking about it,' says Monica, 'but he was finally going to be home for four weeks, and he had been trying to put me to bed. But I didn't know who Bill was, and I was scared of him, and he could just never get me to go to sleep. So my mom always had to be the one to do it. And then, after trying night after night, he was finally able to put me to sleep, and Carole describes Bill as being so proud and excited.'

Monica says that one of her earliest memories of family life, from when she was four or five, is also more positive. 'I can remember Bill telling me that there's this silk thread that's connected to his heart, to my heart, and to my mum's heart, and that the three of us will always be connected, no matter where we are. As I've gotten older, I've not only begun to understand that it must have been difficult for him too, but also to appreciate the way he's so dedicated to his craft and beliefs. I'm very grateful to have that as a model in my life. But then my mum . . . she's fucking incredible. She holds us together somehow. She's the base, the rock.'

Leni Stern, who has been married to fellow guitarist Mike Stern for more than forty years, says it's difficult to balance the life of the road and of home. 'Some partners of musicians can't deal with the solitude and the constant separation, and relationships can fall apart,' she says. 'But it's perfect that Bill should be with Carole, a painter who needs solitude as well.'

Carole d'Inverno agrees: 'Spending so much time alone has taught me about myself and how to be by myself. It allowed me time to think, on

349

my own, about what I wanted. But to be clear,' she adds, smiling, 'even after all this time it can get hard, so I reserve the right to lose it and scream down the phone once every tour. It's my birthright!'

The sentence that follows Frisell's description to Danny Barnes of the physical effects and demands of travelling is, 'But then I get to play,' and this is the enormous overriding compensation for him of being away. 'He doesn't *hate* touring – that's all we *do*, all we've been doing together since 1989,' says Claudia Engelhart. 'Yeah, travel is *gruelling;* it's *hell,* it's *horrible.* And he does, he whines about it *all* the time. We all whine about it. It's hard work. But it's also where he's free to play whatever he wants to play, and where he can develop his music.'

Frisell's constant touring allows him to take the music he has written to an entirely new dimension. It's like his compositions are starting points for further exploration: the versions audiences hear live are often very different to the ones recorded earlier for the albums.

'The music can change two or three times *drastically* before the record even comes out,' says Tony Scherr. 'That's kind of the opposite of how most other people promote their music, and it sometimes goes against people's expectations. All that matters to Bill is how he's playing the music that night.'

Claudia Engelhart agrees: 'That's why I can't listen to the records; they feel so controlled and so . . . it's like the music just hasn't been let out of the box yet.'

This is part of the reason why some dedicated Frisell fans, however much they admire the conceptual ambition and rigorous craft of the albums, greatly prefer to experience the music live. They believe this is the sound of Frisell at his most liberated and unguarded, where he expresses himself more completely, where the multilayered picture of Frisell's art most fully emerges.

'Live performance offers the chance to fully apprehend,' critic and musician Tom Moon has written, 'the ways the taciturn Frisell makes the guitar talk – in woeful moans and pristine plucked notes that exhibit their own personality quirks, in music that starts with the same glib licks loved by millions and somehow wrings enduring, universal truths from them.'

•
•

'Have you noticed at gigs that people don't applaud after a Bill Frisell solo?' Ron Miles asks. 'It's one of the early lessons I learnt: it's a jazz solo, right? So you get applause and stuff after it's finished. But then, after a while, I began to realise that people wouldn't do that with Bill – because they never knew that he actually took a solo; they just thought the song had kept on going, that the tune had never stopped being played. And I was like, "There we go. *That's* what we're trying to get to."'

If, as Ted Gioia has written, 'a jazz improvisation is, in a very real sense, a character study or a Rorschach test', then Bill Frisell's solos are a clear reflection of the way he functions – his patterns and thought processes on the bandstand. They reveal that he is a deep listener, generous collaborator, and that he approaches music with a certain humility, that he is in service to the songs, rather than vice versa.

'I've heard stories of Monk playing the same song over and over and over and over again – and I totally get that,' he says. 'Especially with something new. I have to just get it so far in there that I'm not thinking about it.'

After he has internalised the song – one of his own compositions or a tune he has added to his repertoire – and made it second nature, ingrained, almost automatic, Frisell is then looking for it to reveal new perspectives to him, to take him to another place. 'It's almost like reflections start coming off the song,' he says. 'It'll start to show me other harmonies or possibilities. It's like I begin to see things around the song, something I didn't see before – it starts to sprout branches in an organic way – and that's an amazing feeling.

'Of course, you want the song to become your own, to become some unique, amazing thing. But it's not an intellectual decision, of changing it for the sake of changing it. It's like you want to be so far in the music that it just starts . . . it changes itself. It's not me doing it. The further and further you get into it, the song will start to go, "OK, now I'm going to let you try this, and now I'm going to let you try that." It's like it's teaching you, or something.'

Frisell is fascinated by the way improvising can reveal new internal connections in a song; he is searching for extensions and dimensions of melody, harmony, rhythm, texture and mood – new ways of telling the story. Almost everything he plays comes from the song, usually from somewhere near its heart. It is not so much Gunther Schuller's thematic or motivic improvising; it's soloing of deep structure.

'He hears a long way into the music,' says Ron Miles. 'He's not only hearing where he is, but he has a sense about where the music's going, or where it *could* go. It's like he starts a phrase and he can see the line and the grid.'

Drummer Rudy Royston sees it like a building. 'When we play a song, it's like we walk into a huge house,' he says. 'It's a different design to other houses, so we go into every room and we explore it in full, but we don't leave it.'

He explains that the house is often designed by Catalan modernist Antoni Gaudí. 'It's like, "This is a nice house, but what's wrong with that door? Is it a bit crooked?"' He starts laughing. '"And doesn't that wall have a little curve to it? Or doesn't this room have some weird corners? Aren't things just a little distorted?" Yeah, that's Bill's house.'

In March 2017 I saw Frisell play at the Village Vanguard with bassist Thomas Morgan and avant-garde drummer Andrew Cyrille. At one point the trio performed the most standard of standard jazz ballads, 'Body and Soul', a song that at first was barely hinted at, then stated, simply, and over the course of the next ten minutes or so, considered, examined, deconstructed, extended, reassembled and resolved. It was a masterclass in modern jazz music.

Between sets, Frisell told me he felt he could play any kind of music with Morgan, but he had thought long and hard about what material to perform with Cyrille, a venerated seventy-seven-year-old master who often favoured more open interpretations of melody, structure and time. Frisell had been part of the Andrew Cyrille Quartet that the year before had released an absorbing album on ECM; its unequivocal title was *The Declaration of Musical Independence*.

In the end, though, Frisell had decided to stick to a regular set of originals and standards. 'I didn't really know how free to make it,' he said, smiling. 'But we can still play *tunes*, right?'

•
•

The other fundamental facet of the Frisell live experience – unless he is playing solo – is his close and crucial relationship with the musicians in his many bands; at any one time he can have four or five different ensembles at play.

'Bill challenges and pushes himself *constantly*,' Claudia Engelhart told me in 2015. 'He's putting himself on the line *all* the time. I'm like, "This band is really great – why don't we just stick with it and tour with this one for a while?" But I don't think he can. And that's what keeps it *happening*. That's why it's fresh – all the time. That's why I've worked with him for twenty-six years. The music's constantly *moving*.'

Part of the impulse for playing with a wide range of groups, Frisell says, relates to The Frisell Dream: 'That sound was all-inclusive, it was all one thing. So part of the hunger for playing with different people is that I want to find out – it's like I have to try to know everything.'

Once he has chosen the musicians with whom he wants to work, Frisell will often give them detailed handwritten charts. He can be fastidious, and often hands his musicians not just their own parts but the whole score to a piece, so they can again improvise structurally rather than specifically. Depending on the group, there might also be a set-list and tour book of tunes, but he will often change both, sometimes at the last minute, or abandon them altogether. 'It's good to have a framework, that little assurance, but it varies a lot, and I like to veer off from the set-lists too,' he says. 'Sometimes I'll intentionally go in a different direction to the one the band are expecting – just to throw them off and keep the music on the edge, or something. I'm that calculating!'

Eyvind Kang says he's experienced this unpredictability on a number of occasions, especially when he was playing in the *Beautiful Dreamers* trio with Rudy Royston. 'He gave us a new piece to play on tour and I was like, "Oh my God, this is Varèse. We've got to get serious here. How are we going to do this?"' The short hypnotic piece, composed by the boldly innovative French-born American twentieth-century composer Edgard Varèse, was the song 'Un Grand Sommeil Noir' (roughly, 'A Big Black Sleep').

'So we played it, and it was like it could have been "Shenandoah", or something,' Kang continues. 'It was just completely natural to him. And then a couple of nights later, he'd give us [John Coltrane's quick-changing and harmonically challenging] "Moment's Notice", and I'd think, "OK, here we go again."'

There is no, or very little, discussion with the band about the nature or direction of the music, however, or how he expects it to be played. He is not looking to instruct, impose or dictate. Frisell wants his musicians to have the freedom to be themselves and contribute openly; he is trusting that the relationships he has built up with the players will bring their own rewards; and he is hoping that their connection to the music will create something extra, a musical conversation beyond anything he could have imagined.

'They're like my best friends,' he told *All About Jazz*, when asked about members of his bands. 'With the trios, we don't really talk about any-thing, or figure anything out, or rehearse, or anything. Everybody just sort of knows all the music and we just start playing and even though it's usually songs, it's one of the most free situations I've ever played.'

'We just play and it just works,' Frisell has explained. 'There's just this constant current of electricity going around amongst everyone, and what anybody does at any time, just with the slightest change in a note or something, it'll impact the whole thing. And that's just the best feeling in the world, you know, when it just sort of happens on its own.'

Frisell has sometimes talked about the musicians with whom he plays being *his* teachers. Discussing a gig with his trio of Tony Scherr and Kenny Wollesen in 2008, he said in *DownBeat*, 'In so many areas I want to go into, it's like they know twenty thousand [times] more than I do.

'Last night, as an encore, we played this Ron Carter song, "Mood". Tony knows twenty different versions, and any other song I'd ask him to play . . . When I discovered Roscoe Holcomb, Kenny went, "I got that record when I was twelve." I've put myself in this amazing situation where they can challenge me. But at the same time they respect me. They just play, and they're not intimidating . . . they blow my mind.'

Frisell can equally, however, show his displeasure, if he feels a band member is not meeting the challenge of the music. Quite a few of the Frisell community of musicians that I spoke to mentioned 'The Look'.

'No one in the audience might get it, and it's very quiet and subtle,' says Hank Roberts. 'But there's a bit of urgency in it as well, a certain kind of smile you get if things aren't going the right way. It's like, "Oh, man, oh, boy. *Busted!*"' Roberts starts laughing. 'If you can *hang* with him afterwards, it'll all come out; everything can be discussed. But at the time it's hard to be on the other end of that.'

Kermit Driscoll agrees. 'He'd even play a bass note and then look over at me, as if to say, "*Come on!*" He wasn't hearing what he wanted to hear from me, and he was fucking serious . . . he was as mean as Buddy Rich.'

'Just with a look?'

'Just with a look, yeah. Even though people think Bill's this light feathery guy who can just barely respond to anything . . . oh, man, he knows what he wants!'

Duke Ellington once said that 'listening is the most important thing in music', and that central to his philosophy and success was the idea that he was 'the world's greatest listener'. If so – according at least to those who should know, his bandmates – Frisell comes a close second.

'Bill listens more than others, and he hears everything,' says Kenny Wollesen. 'He actually hears all the little details, everything that's happening . . . it's crazy, supernatural – nothing goes past him. So it's fun playing with Bill because all the sounds are available to you; it's all part of the gestalt.'

•
•

That same night in 2017 at the Village Vanguard with Thomas Morgan and Andrew Cyrille, perhaps buoyed up by the fact this was the first time he had played in a trio with both remarkable musicians, and possibly because it was the last night of a two-week run at the club, Frisell not only introduced the band, but also, in his own inimitable way, started speaking somewhat to the packed house, even telling them at the end of the set, as if prompted, 'Oh yeah, we've got some CDs [for sale] at the bar.'

At one point he approached the microphone and left a heavily pregnant pause to float out into the room. 'You've never heard me talk before, have you?' he eventually said, smiling. 'I can do it. I *can* do it.'

The final part of the Frisell live dialogue is, of course, with his listeners. 'I feel really lucky that I have an audience that seems willing to just go with it and see where it takes them,' he says. 'There's a lot of power in what happens with people, as far as helping you get to, or keeping you from, that zone in the music where things start to happen. I'm hoping the audience becomes a part of the music, too.'

Frisell is aware that he can ask a lot of his public. Yet he has always been unapologetic in staying stubbornly true to himself as an artist, in inspiring himself first before he can inspire others. 'You've got to go for it all the way,' he once told *Musician* magazine, 'and then hope the audience has enough of an open mind to deal with it.'

Sometimes, of course, they don't, and anyone who has attended Frisell gigs on a regular basis has stories of audience indifference, disappointment, dismay – and even walk-outs. 'I can't say it doesn't affect me,' he says. 'But each concert is different and there are so many variables. In a smaller space, or a club, you can really feel people listening, and if there's some guy in the first row talking – or even snoring – and who's oblivious to what's going on, that can be a distraction, mess things up for the band *and* the audience. I just try my best to focus on what the band is doing, zero in on that. But just one person [in the audience] can throw everything off.'

In July 2004 Frisell played a club in Rome with Petra Haden; they had recently recorded their duo album, but it had not yet been released. 'It was very intimate and intense, just the two of us on stage,' says Frisell.

Haden remembers the night well. 'Wow, that was so weird,' she says. 'Because I was *so* in the moment of singing . . . it was the Stevie Wonder song "I Believe" . . . I *love* Stevie Wonder, and that song means *so* much to me, and I was just trying to sing it my best, from my heart. And then all of a sudden I heard this guy shouting, "What *is* this? This is not jazz! What are you doing? This is not jazz. This is bullshit . . ." And he just seemed to go on and on.'

Claudia Engelhart was there too. 'So Bill stopped playing,' she says. 'And he went to the microphone, and it's rare, very rare that he would do that, and he goes, "*Fuck* you." Loud. And long. *Fuuuuuucccccck. Yooooou!* And the guy starts answering back and Bill is angry and he says, "Why don't you just go home? *Fuck* you." Loud again. Yeah, I was shocked, man. But it was fantastic.'

Petra says the audience let out a collective gasp. 'It took me, and everyone, including the guy, by surprise,' she says. 'I've had to deal with hecklers, and even had things thrown at me, but I was upset, and a little sad. Then the audience started clapping. And eventually . . . the guy just left.'

Frisell was never going to be the kind of band leader who announces song titles, but on stage over the years he has begun to engage and experiment more with his public. 'I was still kind of inhibited, but then . . . I couldn't really see anybody out there, and I'm in that sort of comfortable space on stage with my friends, and I'd just go up to the microphone with no idea what I was going to say,' he says. 'It was almost like the music: nothing was pre-planned.'

At times that lack of forethought led to false starts, announcements that didn't go anywhere.

At the start a 2002 performance of *Mysterio Simpatico*, which is available as a download on Frisell's website, he comes to the microphone at the 1,200-capacity Meany Hall in Seattle. There is applause, the customary long pause, Frisell thanks the audience, and then says, 'Erm . . . I *just can't* do it; I was gonna explain what we were gonna do . . . but now that I'm up here . . . in front of you all, I *just can't* do it. So you'll just have to . . . figure it out for yourselves.'

On other occasions, especially with the trio of Kermit Driscoll and Joey Baron, the improvised approach might cause Frisell to be more confessional or comedic, albeit in a slightly surreal and disconcerting way. There were sometimes even jokes – or, rather, anti-jokes, uttered haltingly, yet with a certain certain droll whimsy and comic timing.

'I remember one time we were in between songs, tuning up, trying to think about what to play next, or something,' says Driscoll. 'And Bill told this joke, which he was great at, and I can't tell it the way that he told it . . . because I can't possibly speak that slowly. But the whole thing was something like, "OK, there's this turtle, and he's walking along the street in New York, and out of nowhere this snail just beats the shit out of him. So the cops come, and they say, 'Well, what happened?' And the turtle replies, 'I don't know. It all happened so fast.'" [Driscoll laughs out loud.] That's like the perfect Bill Frisell joke.'

There was also the performance art, albeit a long way from Yoko Ono or Marina Abramović. In the early nineties, in Bergen in Norway, at the end of a long European tour with Driscoll and Baron, Frisell started talking to the audience – but he was distracted.

'I said to them, "Man, I'm just getting sick of this long hair, you know,"' he says. 'So I called to Claudia to come down on stage, and she had a little Swiss Army knife, and I'm sitting in this chair, and she starts hacking away at my hair. This is in the middle of the gig. Kermit and Joey start playing "The Girl from Ipanema", like background music, a soft bossa nova. And then eventually she finishes, she gets a round of applause, she goes back to the sound-desk, and I went back to play some more.'

Even though audiences seemed to enjoy the non-musical aspects of his performances, Frisell says that it got to a point where he felt he was taking them too far. 'I thought, "Wait, I gotta stop doing this,"' he says. 'The comedy routines, the on-the-couch psychiatrist thing, the haircut, saying all kinds of weird stuff to the audience . . . "Man, this is like getting in the way of the music. I gotta just shut up, and play."'

Wayne Horvitz says he remains a firm fan of rambling Frisell. 'Bill's quiet, obviously, and he can be reticent, but I think there's sort of a mischievousness in that too,' he says. 'When he's on stage, and he goes to the mic, and he pauses . . . and then he's really funny . . . I mean, he totally knows what he's doing, and people find it extremely charming in this day and age. In its own way, it's his shtick. It's the thing he's found that works. It's sort of like his anti-stage personality *is* his stage personality. You don't hang around at a party and have Bill . . . Bill doesn't crack you up. But on stage, he's hilarious. I guess it comes back to that thing: it's kind of where he's really alive.'

26: Gavin Bryars Listens to *History, Mystery*

History, Mystery: recorded Washington, DC, Hanover, New Hampshire
and Boston, November 2006 and Seattle, May 2007; producer
Lee Townsend; released on Nonesuch, May 2008; Bill Frisell (electric
and acoustic guitars, loops), Ron Miles (cornet), Greg Tardy (tenor
saxophone, clarinet), Jenny Scheinman (violin), Eyvind Kang (viola),
Hank Roberts (cello), Tony Scherr (bass), Kenny Wollesen (drums);
compositions by Frisell, plus by Boubacar Traoré, Sam Cooke,
Thelonious Monk and Lee Konitz.

Gavin Bryars is one of the world's leading modern composers. Drawing inspiration from a dizzying range of disciplines, subjects and ideas, he is both extremely prolific and exceptionally difficult to pin down.

Born in East Yorkshire in 1943, he taught himself to play jazz double bass and in the early sixties started gigging and improvising with guitarist Derek Bailey and drummer Tony Oxley. A few years later Bryars began to focus increasingly on composition and new music, spending time studying and collaborating in the US with John Cage, and in the UK with English experimental music composers Cornelius Cardew and John White.

His first major works are perhaps his best known. *The Sinking of the Titanic*, written in 1969, was partly inspired by the story of the ship's band continuing to perform as the liner went down; the music was remixed in 1995 by Aphex Twin, and in 2012 Bill Morrison created film projections to accompany the work. *Jesus' Blood Never Failed Me Yet*, from 1971, is a composition in which Bryars added orchestration to the looped voice of an elderly homeless man singing on a London street; in 1993 the music was recorded with additional vocals by Tom Waits.

Bryars has written numerous other works, including five operas, three string quartets and several concertos (one, a jazz bass concerto, for

Charlie Haden); much of his chamber music is composed for his own ensembles. He has also written a significant body of vocal, choral and early music works, as well as music for theatre and dance, and in collaboration with artists.

Bryars dedicated his 1986 chamber piece 'Sub Rosa' to Bill Frisell; on hearing the work, Frisell said, 'It was what I wished I could do in my own writing.' Four years later Frisell recorded Bryars's composition 'After the Requiem' with the composer for the ECM New Series album of the same name.

We met at his home in the middle of a picturesque historic village in Leicestershire. Bryars is thoughtful and quick-witted, and I sensed that he enjoys going against the grain – he can also be straightforward and direct. He listened to the tracks – eyes closed, arms across his stomach – with great stillness and intensity.

PW: Do you remember when you first heard Bill Frisell's music?

GB: It was 'Juliet of the Spirits' on the *Amarcord* [*Nino Rota*] album. It's a really very elegant, very slow, very . . . careful, mellow and beautiful [solo] version of that song. I like that album a lot, because of Bill's track, and Carla Bley's arrangement of '8½'. Bill intrigued me, and I was thinking of writing something for him. But I hadn't really worked with a guitarist before.

I studied a bit of classical guitar at school. And I wrote a piece for Derek Bailey, 'The Squirrel and the Ricketty-Racketty Bridge' [it's on Bailey's 1971 album *Solo Guitar*], in which he played two guitars, lying flat, simultaneously, hammering the fretboard like it was kind of a piano. And Derek was the guitarist on the first [1975] recording of *Jesus' Blood Never Failed Me Yet.*

Then Manfred Eicher gave you In Line?

Yes. When I first recorded for ECM at the beginning of 1986, I had meetings with Manfred [at the ECM offices] in Munich, and I came away with a bagful of LPs and CDs, and one of them was *In Line.*

I loved that album: the sound, the music, Bill's playing – particularly on the track 'Throughout'. I used to be nervous about flying and I would play that track through my headphones on take-off; it was exactly the right length [nearly seven minutes] until the first drink arrived!

What was it about 'Throughout'? I assume it was meditative, soothing or relaxing in some way?

It was all those things. But I also love the intelligence of the song's harmonic sequence, and the way it goes round and round, and comes back on itself, and yet its arrival is always quite surprising. I love the elegance of that.

Then you transcribed the guitar solo?

Yes. And I wrote a score, 'Sub Rosa', which, instead of the chords repeating, I had each one played once – so my chords last a lot longer than Bill's [the piece is ten minutes long] – and all the various things he played on each particular chord, I put together within a single phrase. And so it was like an index of his piece in a way: this is what he does in chord one; this is what he does in chord two . . .

It was scored for your ensemble at the time, wasn't it, and for the contrasting tonal qualities of the particular players and instruments?

For that piece it was double bass, piano, violin, clarinet, vibraphone and recorder. The score moves slowly in parallel parts – the recorder and vibes play together, as do the clarinet and violin, and they are very widely stretched – the violin plays high harmonics and the clarinet is really low in its range; sometimes there's around three octaves between the parts.

The vibraphone was mostly played with a bow, along the edge of the bars, rather than hit with mallets, which provided these long sustained notes with hardly any attack – rather like the way Bill plays the guitar. The first time we played it was later in 1986 at the Flanders Festival in [Ghent] Belgium.

Shortly afterwards you met Bill for the first time, and you played him a tape of the performance?

Bill was on a short tour of Britain in Paul Motian's trio with Joe Lovano, and I was running the music department at Leicester Poly, and I got them to do an afternoon workshop for the students before the gig. They played a little, and talked about how they put the music together, and then answered some questions, like, 'How come you don't have a bass player?' [He laughs.] And I remember I got to carry Paul Motian's sizzle cymbal, the one that has that greatest sound on 'My Foolish Heart' on the [1961] Village Vanguard recordings with Bill Evans. It's a kind of sacred object for me, like carrying the Holy Grail.

Anyway, they do the gig, and afterwards I take them to my favourite local Indian restaurant, Curry Fever. I played the music for Bill through the headphones on my Walkman. He was shaking his head and his eyes were wide open, and when it had finished he said, 'Oh, wow. It's like some crazy dream.' It was like he knew the music, and it was still coherent to him, but it had been jumbled up and randomised. It sort of gave him a completely different vision of what the piece could be.

That's my cue to play you 'Throughout'; I've located ten different versions.

Oh wow. Gosh. [I quickly run through them – they are detailed in Notes – and Bryars chooses a duo track with Jim Hall, from the 2008 album *Hemispheres*. It plays.] That's quite astonishing. It's a really satisfying piece, even though it's absolutely nothing like the original that I know. It's rather like a dream itself: the music's all there, but in a really strange kind of hybrid way. I was struggling to place it, and then suddenly it clicked. Incredibly beautiful, incredibly beautiful. That's a kind of mastery: it's transformed, it's something else completely. And Jim Hall – I never knew him, but I always loved his playing.

What was your impression of Bill when you met him?

Oh, I found him immensely likeable. There seemed to be no side to him;

he had a sort of childlike quality, the way he would speak very slowly and say things like, 'Oh, man . . . that's so . . . great.' You can't interrupt him; you've just gotta hang on. He's one of the most genuine people I know, and he seemed to me to be completely artistically honest.

Let me play you a track from History, Mystery. *This is called 'Probability Cloud'.*

Very beautiful, very simple. Terrific. I love it. It's essentially just three or four chords, and the time signature is straightforward 12/8, but there's an intricacy to the way the rhythms are emphasised and displaced – they're not landing four-square all the time – and in the way the lines work and the textures interweave.

It reminded me a lot of Kurt Weill. It has that Weimar, slightly sinister, bittersweet quality to it. It's like something from *The Threepenny Opera* or [*Rise and Fall of the City of*] *Mahagonny*.

One of the great things about Bill is that he's always confounding expectations. You'll think, 'OK, now *that's* Bill Frisell, I have him sorted.' And then he'll turn up playing banjo, or cowboy music, or Buster Keaton. Suddenly you're hearing a whole different side to him. He can't be typecast.

A few years after 'Sub Rosa', you wrote another piece [partly] dedicated to Bill, which in 1990 you recorded for ECM, but this time with his participation.

Yes, 'After the Requiem'. When I was writing that piece, I made notes about different guitar sounds and approaches that I wanted, based on various of Bill's albums I'd been listening to. So I'd write 'BWB' for *Before We Were Born*, or 'LFH' for *Lookout for Hope* – although I didn't tell Bill all that.

The other instruments on that piece are two violas and cello, and I wanted to have this kind of surrogate bowed sound, which Bill had developed through his non-attack way of playing on certain of his album tracks. It's very grainy, but it blends well with a viola. Viola and guitar, cello and guitar – they all intermesh, which is why the nucleus of my ensemble now comprises viola, electric guitar, cello and bass.

I remember that I only finished the [sixteen-minute] piece at eleven o'clock in the morning of the recording in Oslo! I gave Bill a handwritten part and he just went along with it; it wasn't a problem for him.

What was Bill's input to the playing of the piece – was there room for interpretation?

Completely. I encouraged him to really be as free as he wanted to be. While we were recording, it was also, to the day, the twentieth anniversary of the death of Jimi Hendrix, so that was definitely in the air and, either deliberately or by coincidence, I think it led Bill to get into using certain feedback and distortion effects on the guitar.

There's also a section, towards the end, which for the guitar is improvised, and he starts very slowly . . . the first couple of chords, hardly anything; he just touches one note. And then he starts going. Eventually, it leads up to this kind of climax; it's like pure opera. Even though I'd written chord symbols for him, he didn't play changes, or anything like bebop. He played a kind of long sustained operatic aria, and it was unbelievably beautiful. Bill's a very special musician and he plays with a nuance, touch and acuity I've found in very few players.

Here's another track from History, Mystery, *'Lazy Robinson'. The music was written to be performed with projected animations by Jim Woodring. I'll show you some of the images that accompany this track as it plays.*

[As he's listening, and watching on my tablet] They're like strange hybrids. It's like seeing an animal that's a combination of two animals, and I always find that very disturbing. It's the cabinet of curiosities idea.

The music is in 12/8 again, and it's a simple chord sequence, and it just goes round and round again, but what really works is the way, little by little, everybody joins in, with rather wild unrelated stuff and it becomes sort of chaotic. It's anchored, but it's also a really sweet and slightly mad piece.

I like the fact that Bill will take on all sorts of curious and unlikely projects; it's a sign of his openness. He wants to do things which stretch him in different ways, which take him outside of himself. That's the reason I love collaborating with people, on a ballet or opera, or with fine artists. It means you're constantly being fed ideas, and you have to think again, and adjust your position. I think that's a very healthy thing.

Let me play you a Monk tune from the album, 'Jackie-ing'; it's short, less than three minutes, and was recorded live.

[Laughing] It's sort of treated like a *Tom and Jerry* piece, like very fast cartoon music. It's terrific. Very funny. I mean, this shows that Bill can play jazz. He plays in the company of jazz musicians, and he improvises and has a jazz inflection to his playing. But that doesn't necessarily make him a jazz musician. To call Bill a 'jazz guitarist' is to describe just one part of what he does – maybe like a twelfth, if that.

How do you rate Bill as a composer?

Well, I admire the way he alludes to all kinds of American genres within his music. He's a far better American composer than John Adams. Adams is Americana; he's almost like the new Leonard Bernstein.

But Bill is all that and much more besides. I think he understands these different American genres, from the inside. He's not copying; he's not doing a parody or pastiche. He has a sense of the essence of this music; he takes the heart, and then he makes it his own.

Here's a final track, 'Struggle'.

Lovely. Again it's quite a simple form, just one basic riff all the way through, but there's this almost hymn-like passage at one point, and it moves through all sorts of different territories. It's very beautiful. Very beautiful. It's a kind of a rich mix: both disarmingly simple and really quite complicated.

Do you see any connection between the man and the music?

Well, on the surface both seem much simpler than they actually are. You might think, 'Oh, this is kind of a slow-moving guy; there's that very careful and considered way he has of doing things.' But Bill is an astonishingly complex person, and his music goes a long way beyond what you might think.

If someone and their music are the same, then one of the two is redundant. When I stopped playing jazz, one of my objections was that the person and the music were the same expression, the one thing. It's rather like a painter continuously standing next to their painting in a gallery. It seems to me you have to get free of it at some point.

And what you get from Bill is the great range of things that must be going through his mind and his spirit, and which even those closest to him will never get to know. There are all kinds of hidden resonances and depths. There are dark things, and something rather mournful or elegiac. And then you also get an incredible simplicity and beauty. With Bill's music, you always get an edge.

In June 2008 Bill Frisell's mother Jane died in Chapel Hill, North Carolina; she was eighty-seven.

When his brother Bob called to say their mother was critically ill and only had a little time left, Frisell was on tour overseas, in Israel, and about to play a string of North American dates. He quickly cancelled five concerts – apart from when he missed a couple of gigs in Canada because of his mystery illness, this is the only time in his forty-year career on the road that he has done so.

Bill flew to North Carolina, where he met Carole and Monica, and he was with his mother when she died at home on the 22nd. A week later, again honouring the support his parents had given to his life in music, he was back playing three dates, in a trio with Tony Scherr and Rudy Royston – albeit in venues relatively nearby in Virginia, West Virginia and Alabama. Less than three weeks later, he fulfilled an engagement in Italy, playing a run of seven straight nights at the Umbria Jazz Festival with Tony Scherr and Kenny Wollesen.

'We thought Bill might need to take some time off,' says Phyllis Oyama. 'But he actually wanted to go out to play. He said it allowed him to process everything better.'

Bill says that the last five years of his mother's life were challenging: 'Especially after my father passed away, my mother became less and less social and even more withdrawn. She also had to have a lot of intestinal surgery. She broke her back in a fall at home, and she was not in good shape, so . . .'

Bill's brother Bob lived next door to their mother and became her full-time carer. 'It was pretty intense, but being a caregiver with my mother . . . it's something I feel pretty strongly about,' says Bob. 'Towards the end, her house was more like a hospital, but it gave me . . . well, not a cause exactly, but it was great that I never had to put her away in a home.'

Over the past forty years, Bob has enjoyed a remarkable diversity of study and employment. He has a degree in early childhood education, and began postgraduate studies in special education. In the seventies he studied at the New York School for Circus Arts, and at one stage was going to become a professional clown. He has worked in jobs ranging from lift operator to golf pro, and until recently he was employed on the information desk at his local hospital. In his spare time, Bob has written poetry, been a sculptor and played decent harmonica. 'Whereas I just fixated on this one thing,' says Bill, 'Bobby has had a tendency to move round a lot more.'

Jane also pursued a number of passions and interests after the family left Denver. When she was in her mid-fifties she gained a general arts degree at Upsala College in New Jersey. She studied subjects such as English and psychology, and her own writing was greatly encouraged.

'She wrote a whole stack of poetry and remembrances, and what she called "made-up stories" . . . they were short stories – some were eventually published in magazines and local papers,' says Bob. 'For my mother, the seventies were good times. She had these really marvellous teachers and her writing was blossoming.' Jane continued to write, publish and take creative writing classes after she and Bill Sr moved to North Carolina in 1976, but she was also plagued intermittently, over the last thirty years or more of her life, with depression.

One of the catalysts occurred when Frisell was around fifteen. 'My mother's parents came to visit us in Denver, and my grandmother had a massive stroke,' he says. 'One minute she was in the house with my mother and OK, and the next . . . she was totally incapacitated; you couldn't understand anything she was saying. Basically, her mind was just wiped out.' Bob says Jane was extremely close to her mother, Frances: 'My mother was extremely sensitive, and our grandmother's stroke caused her to have . . . I guess you would call it a nervous breakdown. I have some photographs of her from that time, and she looks . . . just very unhappy.'

As a teenager, Bill thinks he was largely unaware of how traumatic his grandmother's condition was for his mother. 'My father was still real busy working all the time, and then I'm pulling away from my parents – off riding my bike, and playing music, and smoking cigarettes, and distancing myself from them and all these rules they had that I didn't want to be dealing with.

'And I think she was having a really hard time. It was the beginning of some other dark phase for her . . . the way she dealt with stuff . . . she would sort of close down. And when I think back, I wasn't really there for her at all.'

Jane was prescribed and, Bill says, then over-prescribed various anti-depressants. There was also a history of mental illness in her extended family. 'Some people on that side of the family were definitely super-inward,' he says. 'I don't know if it was the religious thing, or the very, very shy thing, but they seemed withdrawn or repressed in some way.'

Bill has many happy memories of his mother, however, and since Jane died he has begun to reappraise her role and influence in his childhood.

'I guess my father was the ideas guy, or something – the idea that I should play the clarinet, for example,' he says. 'Or he would say, "OK, at the weekend we're going to go up in the mountains and go on a picnic." That was my time with my father. But other than that, he wasn't around much. He was at work all day, then we'd have dinner together, and then he would go off and do something else.

'All the rest of the time, all the basic stuff – like going to school, or going to my clarinet lesson, or buying my clothes – it was my mother who was the one who would take me. When I was a young kid, she would just seem like this . . . beautiful person, and when I think about it, a lot of my memories from that time, especially my musical memories, involve my mother. She bought me that transistor radio. She was with me when I bought my first electric guitar. She was the one I told when I decided I didn't want to be a race car driver – I wanted to be a guitar player.

'I'm not naïve – I know there are a lot of people who just want to block out their childhood as some horror story,' he says. 'And for me, you know, it wasn't all great, but . . . definitely . . . I had a pretty idyllic and nurturing environment, and a lot of that came from her.'

Margaret Jane was married to Wilhelm Richard for almost fifty years, and she is buried next to her husband in a plot in the Chapel Hill Memorial Cemetery. Surrounded by neatly maintained lawns, there is a modest granite marker in the ground simply inscribed with the name 'Frisell'.

•
•

A month before his mother's death, Frisell released his twenty-eighth album as leader: the double CD *History, Mystery*.

Featuring an octet that incorporated the 858 strings of Jenny Scheinman, Eyvind Kang and Hank Roberts, a horn duo of Ron Miles on cornet and Greg Tardy on tenor saxophone and clarinet, and Frisell's by now regular rhythm section of Tony Scherr and Kenny Wollesen, *History, Mystery* is primarily a live album – a document of a short 2006 US tour in which the ensemble played Frisell's arrangements of music he had originally composed to accompany live projections of drawings and animations by Jim Woodring.

'[The music] happened over a long period of time,' Frisell has said. 'I mean, the writing of the music was over a few years. It wasn't just, like, stuck together at the last minute, which a lot of times is what I do. [He laughs.] Also, all the people I had played with a lot . . . in all these different combinations . . . for this thing, it was sort of sticking it all together.'

Throughout the ninety-minute, thirty-track, two-disc suite, which is narratively titled 'Part One' and 'Part Two', the music operates in an imagined world in which there always seems sufficient space for an infinite variety of styles to naturally cohabit – including swinging jazz, artful chamber orchestrations, sweet soul, desert blues, reverby rock and a slow waltz.

Nominated for a Grammy for Best Jazz Instrumental Album, *History, Mystery* is an expansive and enigmatic work of great intelligence. With its introductions, reprises and fragmentary interludes the album feels cinematic, a soundtrack of remembrances of things past, present and possibly future.

'To me *History, Mystery* is one of Bill's quintessential albums,' says Eyvind Kang. 'I compare it to the films of Charlie Kaufman. The way you have memories. They mix together. Then something emerges out of them. Bill has tunes running through his head that he associates with certain times and places, even calendar dates. There are also memories of other music embedded within his pieces. It's like a collage of memory, I guess.'

Later in 2008 Frisell realised another personal ambition by releasing an album with Jim Hall. The pair had played together live on a number of occasions, and Frisell had contributed to a couple of tracks on Hall's 1995 album *Dialogues.* The new album, *Hemispheres,* however, was the first time seventy-six-year-old guitar master Hall and his one-time protégé Frisell would record a full album, side by side, with joint billing. Comprising twenty tracks over two CDs – the first a duo recording, the second a quartet session with Scott Colley on bass and Joey Baron on drums – the album captures the intimate sound of two consummate guitarists at ease and enjoying themselves.

As with Hall's two previous CDs, the album was released on crowd-funding record label ArtistShare, and the choice of material, and line of approach, are both straight-ahead and surprisingly deviating. There are several jazz standards, plus originals by both guitarists, including a reading of Hall's ballad 'All Across the City', which Frisell first heard almost forty years earlier on the 1966 Bill Evans/Jim Hall duo album *Intermodulation,* recommended to teenage Bill by his guitar teacher Dale Bruning. Hall's composition was one of the tunes, Frisell explained at the time of *Hemispheres'* release, 'that inspired me to just want to spend my life playing music'.

There is also a strikingly spare rendering of Dylan's 'Masters of War' and an exploratory and sometimes dissonant fifteen-minute free improvisation titled 'Migration'. The duo album in particular ebbs and flows with fascinating exchanges, and with Frisell's shifting current of mercurial loops, dreamy soundscapes and psychedelic effects.

In 2009 a DVD of Frisell playing solo was released in the US; the studio-style performance had been recorded five years earlier as part of a series for the Bravo television network in Canada. *Solos* features Frisell on a Fender Telecaster Relic (a new guitar 'pre-aged' or 'antiqued' to make it look old) playing a selection of originals and covers; the ten songs are interspersed with short interviews with Frisell, and some 'behind-the-scenes footage' that reveals this was quite a high-budget production. Frisell dresses for the occasion in black leather jacket, black shirt, black baggy jeans and black Converse high-tops. He is also wearing small, round, thin-rimmed John Lennon glasses, and appears heavier than he does in photographs and videos from the years that follow.

'Yeah, sometime after that recording I stopped eating sugar and bread,' he explains. 'Carole and Monica had discovered they were really allergic to gluten, so we were all fairly strict about cutting out bread and pasta and carbohydrates and stuff. I ended up losing almost twenty pounds. I'm kind of back on some of it [gluten] now, but since then I've felt *way* better.'

The direction of the film is mostly distracting, the brief chats with Frisell far from revealing, and at the beginning, by way of excruciating introduction, he says, 'I'm Bill Frisell . . . and I play the guitar.' There are, however, for players and aficionados at least, lots of close-ups of fingers and fretboard, and there is nothing mannered or contrived about his playing throughout; *Solos* is an outstanding account of pure mature Frisell. Surrounded by pedals and digital effects, he often starts out or segues between songs barely hinting at a melodic phrase or harmonic progression. The film is a document of the delicate and patient art of the slow reveal.

Frisell ended the decade with a centrepiece event at the London Jazz Festival in collaboration with another of his former teachers and mentors, Mike Gibbs. In a concert at the Barbican in November with the BBC Symphony Orchestra, Gibbs conducted Frisell, Joey Baron and the orchestra in the première of *Collage for a Day* – a specially commissioned hour-long programme that featured Gibbs's subtly shaded arrangements of a selection of Frisell compositions such as 'Again', 'Rag' and 'The Lone Ranger', as well as Gibbs's own gorgeous ballad 'Sweet Rain' and a reading of the Benny Goodman classic 'Benny's Bugle'.

'It's really a dream come true to be able to do this,' Frisell said on the night. 'So much of the way I think about music has come from my association [with Mike] . . . the way I think about harmony and the way the notes fit together . . . He's inspired me for so long, but it's a mystery to me what he does with music.'

•
•

In the autumn of 2009 Frisell ended his twenty-one-year relationship with Nonesuch and Bob Hurwitz. To outsiders, it seemed like a strange and surprising move; the special alchemy between artist and label, and the way Frisell's shape-shifting music had been so actively supported and skilfully presented, had often helped turn the twenty-one albums Frisell had released on Nonesuch to various grades of silver and gold.

Frisell's main frustration, however, was similar to the one he had felt in the eighties with Manfred Eicher and ECM: that the label was not releasing his music as quickly as he wanted. *Disfarmer*, for example, which proved to be his final album as leader for Nonesuch, was recorded in Seattle in February 2008 and Nashville in May of the same year, but not released until July 2009. The company filled the gap in February 2009 by releasing a smartly programmed compilation, *The Best of Bill Frisell Vol 1: Folk Songs* (there never were any subsequent volumes), a retrospective of the more rootsy side of his work over the previous twenty years.

Frisell had not deviated, however, from his strong belief that his music worked best if he recorded what he wanted, when he wanted; the challenge for a record company was to keep up with his many concurrent projects and prolific work rate. *Blues Dream* and *With Dave Holland and Elvin Jones* had both sold in excess of 60,000 copies, but as the noughties progressed the music industry was also facing the challenge of dramatically falling CD sales and revenues; consumers were rapidly switching to digital downloads and illegal file sharing.

Bob Hurwitz no doubt judged that he was managing Frisell's music as efficiently and effectively as he could, bearing in mind market conditions and the fact that he didn't want to saturate Frisell's admittedly dedicated audience by releasing too many records – the idea that, for listeners at least, less quantity might mean more quality.

'Bill's a very restless creative soul,' says Lee Townsend. 'It's reflected in his music, and even in the number of guitars he owns – he's just constantly, relentlessly searching. He's also restless with his output, and that doesn't always match with a record company's idea of the most market-friendly path for a career. When Bill was at Nonesuch, their approach was: you shouldn't put out a record more than once every year and a half to two [years]. But ultimately that just didn't fit with Bill's creative flow.'

Frisell says that, unlike his move away from ECM, the split was generally civil and good-natured. 'It wasn't like any big thing – we didn't have a fight, I'm totally on good terms [with Nonesuch],' Frisell told *All About Jazz* in 2011. 'I guess it's part of the nature of the times, but they just couldn't get the stuff out as fast as I was making it.'

Frisell had formed a fluid and highly flexible new trio in 2008 with Eyvind Kang on viola and Rudy Royston on drums, and he had been developing a repertoire of compositions for the group, plus an idiosyncratic selection of songs that stretched from 'Keep on the Sunny Side', popularised in the twenties by the Carter Family, to John Coltrane's testing '26-2', sixties pop classic 'Goin' Out of My Head' and Stephen Foster's 1864 parlour song 'Beautiful Dreamer', the title of which, in the plural, would provide the name for the threesome.

In the spring of 2010 Frisell signed a new deal with Savoy, a company with an impressive jazz pedigree that reached back to Miles Davis's first recordings in the mid-forties, as well as significant early albums by sixties avant-gardists such as Paul Bley, Sun Ra and Archie Shepp.

Recorded at Fantasy Studios in Berkeley, California, in March and April of 2010, his first album for the label, *Beautiful Dreamers,* was released just four months afterwards. While there was an immediate decline in the quality of the overall CD presentation and design, there was no change in Frisell's commitment to compositional ambition and group empathy.

Ten of the sixteen tracks were new Frisell originals, including the joyously skewed jump blues 'Winslow Homer', a commission by Wynton Marsalis and the Jazz at Lincoln Center Orchestra for a concert exploring the 'shared history of cross-influences' between jazz and painting; the piece was named after the famous nineteenth-century American landscape and seascape painter. The remainder were songs the trio had been playing live.

Beautiful Dreamers is a further landmark recording in another fertile period of Frisell's work, an album of extraordinary freedom, control, restraint and understanding. Some of the melodies are almost like simple, if angular, folk forms, yet there is a sense that this trio of multivalent equals can take the music to an infinite number of moods, from whimsy to hoedown; it is a Frisell trio that strongly recalls his work with Paul Motian. In fact, after Motian died in 2011, the trio started playing several of the drummer's tunes.

'The whole bass-less trio thing is a challenge that I responded to by doing that part myself with the pizzicato and the lower octaves,' says Kang. 'But at the same time I didn't want to use that as a crutch. The music is very multilayered: yeah, it's very friendly, but there are some teeth there too at the same time – it welcomes you in, and almost kind of pushes you away. I think it's the most open that I've played with Bill.'

Compared to some of his output at the time, the album features a more pared-down Frisell sound; he relies less on effects and more on the direct and unadulterated sound of fingers on Telecaster strings. Frisell says that his change of heart towards his use of looping, delay, distortion, compressor, pitch transposer, reverb and volume pedals came about a few years earlier, almost by accident.

'I was on tour with Paul [Motian], and the airline lost all my pedals and stuff, and I had to do the gig with just my guitar plugged into the amp,' he explains. 'And I was like, "Wait a minute, why have I been carrying all this stuff around?" I didn't need it. In a way, it felt like I had *more* control, with just the power and the strength that I was using, with my hands on the instrument.

'When I hear some of my early recordings, it actually kind of makes me uncomfortable. I'm hearing this *whirrrrrrrrr* sound . . . all the time. Part of it was probably being too shy to just play the fucking note.'

Frisell's approach since then has been to vary his use of effects. Once he'd freed himself from them, he could again begin to appreciate their infinite possibilities, the way they could both express sounds that he was hearing in his head and open up a surprising new rhythm, unpredictable atmosphere, or chance compositional idea that he might never have imagined – or dreamed of.

'I think my use of the pedals is always in flux,' he says. 'But it's interesting how, having experienced some of those effects, the sounds are still clear in my head, and I can, even after I've stopped using them, sometimes . . . somehow . . . through the will of my imagination, also make them happen. It's like I can hold on to the sounds even when they're not available to me.'

His eschewal of effects has not stopped some listeners and players from retaining an intense fascination in them; there is a five-minute video on YouTube of Frisell demonstrating his pedals that has been watched more than 420,000 times.

It is a phenomenon of which Frisell is well aware. 'A lot of times people talk about my equipment and particularly my use of electronics,' he told *Guitar Player*, 'and sometimes I get a little tired of the emphasis of the presumed importance of all that stuff, because about ninety per cent of the time I'm just playing a Telecaster into an amp.'

•
•

At the end of September 2010 Frisell made his first visit to the Vermont Studio Center (VSC); he has been four times since. Carole had visited the year before, but on this occasion she and Bill were accepted for simultaneous month-long residencies – they were given individual studio spaces and a private room in shared housing.

Frisell had played a concert near New York and Bill and Carole made the six-hour journey north by car, driving along the Hudson River and into the peak autumn foliage of the Green Mountain State, a painterly palette of vibrant reds, yellows, oranges and golds. The centre had hosted a wide range of visual artists and writers, but it had never before offered a residency to a musician.

Having toured with various of his ensembles almost incessantly that year – there had been two visits to Europe, and four weeks at the Village Vanguard alone – this was a rare opportunity for Bill and Carole to spend time living and working together. It was also the first time he would enjoy such an extended period of creative freedom for more than thirty years, since his time living alone in Denver in the early seventies or during his downtime while in Belgium.

Frisell had resolved to write new music specifically for Jenny Scheinman, Eyvind Kang and Hank Roberts. Since he had brought the players together for the Richter project in 2002, the trio had appeared as 'the 858 Strings' on *Unspeakable*, and more recently toured extensively with Frisell in Europe and the US. It was a group, a kind of alternative string quartet, that Frisell simply couldn't let go.

'I've got that wrench in the works [of the quartet], which is me playing electric guitar,' he told the *San Francisco Classical Voice* website, chuckling. 'Like when I was a kid, when I was in high school playing clarinet in the school band . . . we would play pranks on the conductor. Me and my friends in the clarinet section, we'd play stuff backwards, shift our instruments around. And that sort of planted this seed of a little bit of mischief or subversion. I'm making it sound like it's a joke, or something, and I don't mean to do that, but I love putting the guitar into all these different contexts.'

Frisell interacted with other artists at the centre – one painted a portrait of him, another sculpted a bust of him in clay – but every day Frisell would take his guitar into his white studio space, empty apart from a table and chair, and sit down with blank manuscript paper.

'I just wrote, wrote, wrote, wrote music,' he has said. 'My normal life: I'm travelling, I'm just running from one thing to another, and there's like these little tiny increments of time when I can concentrate. But [at the VSC] I had days on end, where whatever idea came in my head I could keep following it . . . I had piles of music, and I pinned it all up on the wall and looked at it, and then things started to just come alive.'

At the end of VSC residencies, artists are encouraged to open their workshops and exhibit; Frisell hung fifty pages of compositions around his studio walls.

The experience had a powerful effect on Frisell. In the digisleeve CD of the resulting album, *Sign of Life*, there are quotes, from such unlikely American bedfellows as John Cage and children's television personality Fred Rogers, on the blessings of being 'hushed and silent' and the 'invisible gift of a silent minute to think about those who have helped you become who you are today'.

In 2014, during his fourth stay at the VSC, he said, 'Maybe I'm just naïve, or something, but Vermont just seems like one of the few places left that, it seems to me, on a very surface level, hasn't screwed itself up quite as bad as a lot of other places in this country. It's just so beautiful . . . It feels like kind of [a] lifesaver to me.'

Towards the end of Frisell's residency, the 858 Strings came to the VSC for a couple of days, during which they rehearsed the new work and performed an informal concert for the staff and fifty resident artists. From there, via a concert in San Francisco, the quartet went into Fantasy Studios.

Sign of Life is an album of seventeen Frisell originals, many of which have the feel of short thematic sketches (nine of the tracks are under three minutes), written expressly with the strengths and personalities of the quartet in mind. 'I have these long ongoing relationships with Hank, Eyvind and Jenny, and they're like this incredible safety net that allows me to take chances,' Frisell told me in 2015 before a performance by the quartet at Ronnie Scott's jazz club in London (858 is a string quartet that can also swing). 'They're open to anything I want to do, and we trust each other, and there's no judging. It's not like I'm writing music for the Emerson String Quartet, or something; I don't even have to have everything fully realised before I show the music to them.'

There are no fixed individual parts for the players, as there would be in a formal string quartet. All four musicians see the same full score and can adapt and affect the music organically at will – Roberts playing the melody line, for example, and Scheinman the bass part; or Kang suddenly suggesting a new harmonic or rhythmic possibility that Frisell plays against or improvises upon. Roles are elastic and equal, and the music unfinished; some things are discussed and agreed upon, but mostly the music is a form of spontaneous group orchestration.

Kang says he has thought deeply about the relationship between composition and improvisation, especially in Frisell's work. 'Ultimately, I wouldn't describe Bill's music as either composition or improvisation, because it's both,' he has said. 'It seems like we know what we're doing. *We don't know what we're doing.* We never have known . . . we just go with him. We know when *not* to know. Which is often. Actually, it's all the time.'

If all this sounds exciting on paper, Frisell and the quartet don't quite realise the undoubted potential of such an approach on this CD. While the music is often powerfully evocative, it sometimes sounds underdeveloped and even incidental, as if it were background music for film. Live, Frisell developed a quartet repertoire that also took in 'Cluck Old Hen', Monk's 'Skippy', and Lennon and McCartney's 'Strawberry Fields Forever'. *Sign of Life* would have benefited from some of that heightened variety.

•
•

Frisell turned sixty in March 2011. Even though he was still spending many nights away from home, and not seeing Carole and Monica as much as he would have liked, the residency at the VSC had reminded him of the enormous value of taking time away from recording and the road. Frisell would try to build dedicated periods of respite and retreat into his schedule from this stage on.

His life in music could not have been in a better place. Not only did he have a new record company that was wholly committed to releasing the breadth and wealth of his work, but he also had at least six work-ing ensembles, countless other group configurations, occasional solo performances, his own digital live download series, a continuing collab-oration with film-maker Bill Morrison, and the priceless experience of thirty years' playing with Paul Motian.

Frisell also continued to receive more offers of live and recording dates than he could possibly meet. Over the previous few years alone he had played major concerts with such jazz greats as Ron Carter, McCoy Tyner, Jason Moran, Brad Mehldau, Charlie Haden, Ornette Coleman, Jim Hall, Lee Konitz and Jack DeJohnette. He had worked in duos and trios with Danny Barnes and Vinicius Cantuária, and also with Iraqi-American oud player Rahim AlHaj, Indian tabla master Zakir Hussain and in Ireland with Martin Hayes and Dennis Cahill.

Frisell had played one-off concerts in a church in Nashville with the city's chamber orchestra, and at Carnegie Hall as a member of the band for Gavin Friday's fiftieth birthday celebration – among the musicians on stage with Friday that night were U2, Lou Reed, Rufus Wainwright, Lady Gaga, Courtney Love, and Shane MacGowan of the Pogues, who at one point grabbed Frisell's guitar and played it loudly, upside down. There had also been a short European tour of the reformed Bass Desires band, and a benefit concert for Kermit Driscoll, who was suffering from the serious ill effects of longterm late-stage Lyme's disease.

In addition to contributing to albums by members of his immedi-ate musical circle, including Wayne Horvitz, Hank Roberts, Jenny Scheinman, Carrie Rodriguez, Hal Willner and Viktor Krauss, Frisell had recorded with a broad spectrum of other musicians, stretching from American drone metal and experimental rock band Earth to Italian singer and guitarist Gianmaria Testa and Danish jazz-guitar minimalist Jakob Bro. He had also appeared on significant releases by Paul Simon, Lucinda Williams, Bonnie Raitt, Loudon Wainwright III and Rickie Lee Jones.

'I've been beyond overwhelmed,' he confessed to *DownBeat* shortly after his birthday. 'My life is really the music . . . I just have to play, and I haven't figured out any other way than just travelling all over the place.

It's also like I feel blessed. So when I have the opportunity to do these things . . . I just want to try and get in as much as I can.'

The next project to which Frisell committed was *All We Are Saying . . .*, an album of the music of John Lennon. Recorded at Fantasy Studios with Lee Townsend producing, the CD had its origins in a European tour six years earlier.

Frisell had assembled another new configuration, a trio with Jenny Scheinman on violin and Greg Leisz on pedal steel and acoustic guitar, and the first concert of the tour was at the Cité de la Musique in Paris. Coinciding with the show was the opening of a new exhibition at the complex's museum, *John Lennon, Unfinished Music*, which traced Lennon's 'musical, artistic and humanist journey', had extensive material on loan from Yoko Ono, and marked the twenty-fifth anniversary of his death. To accompany the exhibition, the concert organisers asked Frisell if he would consider presenting an evening of Lennon songs; he didn't hesitate.

'I don't even know if I'd be playing guitar if it wasn't for the Beatles, you know, and John Lennon,' he said in a promotional video for *All We Are Saying . . .* 'This music – it's such a deep and important part of my life.'

In an interview several years later in 2014, before another concert of Lennon's music, Frisell also explained, 'To go back and look at [Lennon and the Beatles] through this lens of my whole life playing [their music], it's just incredible. The music is so rich that I could just keep playing it and playing it. It just keeps revealing more and more.'

Frisell, Scheinman and Leisz arrived in Paris a day before the concert to rehearse; Frisell had chosen Beatles songs in which Lennon had been the primary songwriter – 'Please, Please Me' and 'Revolution', for example – and from his ten-year solo career, including 'Beautiful Boy' and 'Number 9 Dream'.

Frisell had an opportunity to visit the museum; the exhibition literature detailed how Lennon was fond of asserting 'I am like a chameleon', and how as a singer, songwriter, activist, artist, author, poet and painter, he 'abolished the borders between artistic disciplines by making his life a permanent happening'.

The reawakening of his interest in the life and music of John Lennon, and the subsequent success of the Paris performance, had a strong effect on Frisell. At the next concert, at Usher Hall in Edinburgh, he and the trio decided to abandon the selection of tunes he had prepared for the tour, and play the Lennon songs. 'It felt so good that we decided to play this music for the rest of the [sixteen-date] tour,' Frisell writes in the liner notes to *All We Are Saying* . . . 'After Paris, it was never announced, or advertised that we would be doing this. We never told the audience. It was far out checking out their reaction when, after two or three songs, they started realising what was happening.'

While some in the audience at Usher Hall were less than impressed with Frisell's Beatlemania and exited early, most responded positively. 'By importing unexpected sounds, the trio cast new light on familiar material,' wrote David Peschek in the *Guardian*. 'These new treatments of songs, even to this resolute Beatles refusenik, are powerfully resonant; more ethereal than the earthly body from which it took its form.'

The tour ended at the Barbican in London and the ninety-minute concert was one of the first to be released in Frisell's live download series. It is fascinating to hear how the Lennon songs have been extensively developed over the dates – most of the additional songs are Beatles-era selections, including 'Julia', 'Come Together' and 'Across the Universe', and mostly they emerge slowly and obliquely from the leader's extempore segues and introductions. The programme flows between a tender and sensitive reading of 'In My Life' to a slowly building twelve-minute exploration of 'You've Got to Hide Your Love Away' and a dark and heavy free-your-mind rock-out on 'Revolution'.

Frisell put away the Lennon project until 2010, when Oakland club Yoshi's asked him to showcase a different group and repertoire each night of a short residency. Frisell added Tony Scherr and Kenny Wollesen to the trio, and his loose approximation of a John Lennon tribute band was born.

All We Are Saying . . . was recorded at the end of June the following year and released just three months later; Savoy was certainly helping to maintain Frisell's high productivity. Before the sessions, Frisell researched Lennon's life further and decided on a more equal balance of Beatles and solo material – additional Lennon songs included 'Imagine', 'Woman' and, as a final track, 'Give Peace a Chance', the lyrics of which provided the album title. He also played a recently acquired 1963 red Fender Stratocaster on some of the session, just for that extra ring of authenticity.

Frisell and Townsend's idea was to play the sixteen selections faithfully and at a similar length as (and sometimes even shorter than) the originals. Frisell was not interested in radically reworking, reinventing or deconstructing the songs, or even in 'jazzing them up', in adding to the long line of musicians – from Count Basie to Brad Mehldau, Ramsey Lewis to George Benson and Wes Montgomery – who have consciously attempted to make them *swing*. He and the band played the songs in the same way they might approach a Hank Williams, Stephen Foster or Sam Cooke tune – from somewhere honest and truthful, from deep inside.

'[Lennon's music] is just solid and good and unique, everything is there,' Frisell continues in the promo video. 'The only stamp I'm putting on it is just that we're playing it. I'm playing with my closest friends, we all have our own really super-personal deep long relationship with this music. And I figure I don't have to sit there and rethink what he already did.' As Frisell writes in the CD notes: 'There was nothing we really needed to do to prepare for this. We've been preparing our whole lives.'

For some critics this wasn't enough: Frisell's replications were simply too careful, conservative and 'cursed with ghastly good taste'. The complaint was mostly that they didn't add anything significant to these already ubiquitous and over-familiar tunes, that they lacked Frisell's customary sideways slant and creative audacity. In a rebuke that would resurface periodically over the next few years, some accused Frisell's interpretations of amounting to little more than a 'surrender to nostalgia'.

It's true that some tracks on the album are perhaps a little too polite. Yet many others are wholly revelatory: 'Give Peace a Chance' is an ambient experiment in tone and texture; the seven-minute 'Mother' a study in slowcore guitar dynamics, from guttural to chiming; 'Julia' a lovely lilting lament; and 'Across the Universe' a gently meditative invocation. *All We Are Saying* . . . tells its story subtly, cleverly, respectfully; there is a quiet magic to the record.

Frisell felt that mystery and wonderment during the recording. 'You listen for five seconds and then the songs just latch on to you; you can't shake them off,' he has said. 'There really is something transcendent about the music; it transcends all. So much of it is so personal to him, but it's also so universal at the same time. We all know what John Lennon's talking about.'

In April 2012 Frisell took another dedicated break from his hectic touring and recording schedule, spending some time alone on an 860-acre wilderness in California.

He had been invited by the Monterey Jazz Festival to stay at the Glen Deven Ranch in Big Sur, a mountainous oasis of woodlands, ridges, canyons and creeks located above Highway 1 on the spectacular Central Coast. The idea was that Frisell would write new music to première at the festival later that year. It was a commission that was hard for him to resist. Frisell flew to San Francisco on Easter Sunday and drove to Big Sur, arriving in the early hours of the morning; it was pitch-black, foggy and raining heavily.

'When morning came, it blew my mind,' Frisell said in the *Wall Street Journal*. 'You're surrounded by redwood forest, and there's a trail that you can walk to the bluff's end, where the land drops off and you see the whole panorama of the coast and the Pacific Ocean.'

Frisell stayed in a small guest cottage on the ranch. For the next ten days he saw no one other than the ranch's caretaker and had very little contact with the outside world. The cottage had no phone, television, computer, internet or mobile phone coverage; one night, after a violent storm, it didn't even have electricity. 'I was looking at a donkey one day,' Frisell recalled. 'I said something to the donkey, and I realised it was the first word I'd said in five days.'

He went on long walks, took in the beauty around him, and at night read *East of Eden*, John Steinbeck's epic 1952 opus set in the nearby Salinas Valley, and *Big Sur*, the 1962 Jack Kerouac novel about an author's retreat to a remote cabin in search of solitude and sobriety. Frisell was aware that other artists had been drawn to this coastline for a greater sense of spiritual communion and creative clarity – writers such as Henry Miller and Hunter S. Thompson, and photographers Ansel Adams and

Edward Weston. Musicians, from the Beach Boys to John Adams, had also made the trip; the saxophonist Charles Lloyd sought refuge in Big Sur in 1970 – and stayed for the next sixteen years.

During his time on the estate Frisell wrote a collection of nineteen new songs. He would take a notebook with him on his hikes and tried to allow the music to flow out of him, naturally and unconditionally, in a stream of consciousness. 'I didn't have any schedule; I never even looked at the clock,' he told the *Monterey County Weekly*. 'There was no pressure. It allowed this internal space to happen that's almost impossible to find these days. I don't know where the music comes from – it's just melodies floating around inside me.'

In a similar way to how he prepared the music for Bill Morrison's *The Great Flood*, in September Frisell brought the ensemble that would be playing at the Monterey Jazz Festival to the Glen Deven Ranch, to rehearse the music and experience first hand the landscape that had partly informed it. The quintet that played at Monterey was a hybrid of two of Frisell's recent groups, the 858 Quartet and the Beautiful Dreamers trio: Frisell plus Jenny Scheinman, Eyvind Kang, Hank Roberts and Rudy Royston – strings with drums. The following March the ensemble went into Fantasy Studios in Berkeley to record the music with Lee Townsend.

Big Sur was released on Sony's reactivated OKeh label in June 2013. Despite Savoy's best efforts over the previous two and a half years, Frisell had been made an offer by a major label that, in terms of reward and resources, was impossible for Savoy to match, and difficult for Frisell to refuse. In addition, OKeh's A&R and marketing consultant, Wulf Müller, was a longstanding enthusiast of Frisell's work; the pair had known each other for more than thirty years, having met in Vienna in the early eighties.

An album of interlocking narratives and themes, with, as Frisell described to me, 'the same melodies appearing in different places – but played in different keys, harmonies, rhythms and tempos', *Big Sur* is one of Frisell's most successful records of his later period. The overall effect is a sonic pattern that is both particular, often to place and experience, and poetically panoramic: the song sequence has a shimmering sense of space, of land and air and sea. 'I once listened to *Big Sur* as I was driving down the coast to LA,' says Phyllis Oyama. 'It was like watching a movie with my ears.'

The album also captures a remarkable range of moods and emotions – from anxious to elated, sorrowful to jovial – and of Frisellian free musical associations, including surf rock, country waltz, western swing, Appalachian dance, surreal film soundtrack and the music of Neil Young. They are all played, as the song 'Sing Together Like a Family' suggests, with a kind of collective kindred spirit.

While he was at the ranch, Oyama received word from an organisation that said it was imperative they spoke to Frisell straight away. She told them Frisell could not be contacted, but the caller was insistent, and finally a message was passed on to him.

'I was told it was like an interview, that they needed to ask me some questions, but it was all sort of top secret, or something,' says Frisell. 'And I was *pissed*. I had sworn that I wouldn't be doing things like that – that this time, in that place, was absolutely sacred to me. So anyway, I go somewhere [where there's mobile phone reception], and the phone rings, and I'm like, "OK [he sighs], you know, I'll talk to you." And then they mention this new grant, and describe the whole thing . . . and I'm getting more and more pissed, because I felt like they were wasting my time, asking me what I thought about the idea. My anger is building up. And just I was about to hang up the phone, they said, "And congratulations – we've decided to give the grant to you." And I didn't know *what* to say. It was a shock.'

The grant was one of the inaugural annual awards of the Doris Duke Charitable Foundation, 'an investment in twenty-one exemplary artists in contemporary dance, jazz and theatre who have demonstrated their artistic vitality and commitment to their field'.

There is no application process; recipients are chosen by peer panels, and then notified, out of the blue. As well as Frisell, musicians receiving awards in 2012 included Don Byron, pianist Vijay Iyer, drummer John

Hollenbeck and composer and vocalist Meredith Monk. Each received $275,000.

•
•

This was a particularly fruitful period for Frisell's work as a composer. As well as the music for *Big Sur*, he had written the seventy-five-minute score for *The Great Flood*, the music-and-film piece that he toured extensively.

In 2011 Frisell was approached by Hal Willner to compose music for a recording of *The Kentucky Derby is Decadent and Depraved* – a word-for-word dramatisation of Hunter S. Thompson's picaresque and highly influential 1970 magazine feature on America's most famous horse race.

Willner recruited an intriguing cast to play the characters in the story, including Hollywood actor Tim Robbins as Thompson, legendary New Orleans singer and pianist Dr John as boozy Derby regular Jimbo, jazz singer and actress Annie Ross as the louche motel desk clerk, and Thompson's collaborator on the story, British illustrator Ralph Steadman – as himself. The producer's idea for Frisell was that he would write the background music for, and interludes between, the readings, and assemble a group for the recording – but no more than that. 'I've worked with Bill for so many years on so many projects . . . that each time I like to give him a new challenge,' Willner said in *Jazz Times*. 'So this time I said, "What if you don't play at all? Just be the composer."'

Frisell absorbed himself in Thompson's life and work, and Willner gave him a recording of Robbins reading the text, which the actor takes in gallops and spurts, his gruff boozy smudge of a drawl a fine impersonation of Thompson's.

'After all that, there's a point when I start writing music, when it's just me talking to the music,' Frisell said in the same article. 'I can't force it; whenever I have some strong preconceived idea or I'm forced into some corner, it doesn't work. So I try to surround myself with the person and let the music come out.'

Frisell's septet for the recording was similar to the ensembles he had brought together for *History, Mystery* and *Unspeakable*: the 858 Strings, plus a horn section – Ron Miles on trumpet, Doug Wieselman on woodwinds and Curtis Fowlkes on trombone – and Kenny Wollesen on drums and percussion; there was no bass.

The score is incidental yet adds significantly to the often discordant and dyspeptic mood of the piece. There is a sense of occasion and celebration – especially in the short 'Entr'acte', a swinging avant-Dixieland romp, and in the sometimes playful rhythms and wry asides – yet also a creeping, ominous and all-enveloping sense of corruption.

Shortly after the *Kentucky Derby* recording Willner asked Frisell to compose, but again not to play, the music for a second spoken-word project: a reading of Allen Ginsberg's famed 1961 poem '*Kaddish*', a lament for his mentally ill mother and a meditation on his estrangement from Judaism that is a key Beat Generation work. The poem is in part about love, mortality and memory, and there were parallels and resonances for Frisell: Ginsberg completed '*Kaddish*' three years after the death of his mother Naomi; Frisell was composing the music three years after the passing of his own mother Jane. Paul Motian also died in November 2011, around the time he began to write the score.

'I'd read Allen Ginsberg's poetry on and off back in college, but it was in the course of this project that I really got into it,' Frisell said at the time. 'There were so many things going on, so many things lining up in my life. Paul – that was huge. The poem helped me . . . it gave me support.'

The première took place at the Park Avenue Armory in New York in February 2012. Willner and actress Chloe Webb read the poem, Ralph Steadman created accompanying visuals and illustrations, and Webb some short films, which were projected on a large screen at the rear of the stage. Frisell wrote music for and conducted an octet – the *Kentucky Derby* group, plus Robin Holcomb on piano and vocals. The seventy-five-minute piece was reprised the following year as part of the festivities for the new SFJAZZ Center in San Francisco – Frisell had been appointed as one of the new facility's inaugural artistic directors.

The music for '*Kaddish*' has never been released, but Frisell has given some sense of its spare but achingly affecting atmosphere on two tracks: an eponymous composition on drummer Andrew Cyrille's 2016 ECM album *The Declaration of Musical Independence*; and 'Hour Glass' on Frisell's 2020 trio album *Valentine*.

Frisell was asked to write a third piece in 2012, again not to be performed by him – or, in this instance, even by one of his ensembles.

Brooklyn Rider is an energetic American contemporary classical string quartet that has worked closely with Philip Glass and collaborated with musicians such as Martin Hayes, banjo virtuoso Béla Fleck and leading jazz saxophonist Joshua Redman. For the ensemble's album *Brooklyn Rider Almanac*, the quartet commissioned fourteen short compositions from composers including Vijay Iyer, Ethan Iverson, Wilco drummer Glenn Kotche and Frisell. Each work was to be inspired by an 'artistic muse' of the past fifty years; Frisell chose John Steinbeck. His piece is the final track on the CD, composed in two parts, and is a gentle, floating, if slightly unsettling folk-like chamber piece, played beautifully by the quartet. There is a strong sense of solitude and contemplation; the composition could easily have been a bonus track for *Big Sur*.

.
.

'I think that many of us guitarists tend to be overlooked as composers,' Nels Cline says, 'because we're always supposed to be so damn interesting as soloists, like we're some kind of virtuosi. So people might miss that there's some great writing in there too. Like with Bill.'

Right from the early stages of Frisell's long career, composing has been a fundamental part of who he is as a musician. It is the reason he decided to focus on composition and arranging at Berklee, electing to study with Herb Pomeroy and Mike Gibbs. It explains why, when Frisell made his tape of four original songs in 1981, he received such encouraging and enthusiastic responses from, among others, Carla Bley, Steve Swallow, Eberhard Weber and Manfred Eicher. It also accounts for why Frisell's debut recording as leader, *In Line*, was an album of nine originals – and why, when Gavin Bryars heard one of those compositions, 'Throughout', he was so captivated by the elegance of its form that he reshaped the tune into a modern chamber piece.

'You know, I'm a guitar player, right? And for a long time . . . I've spent a lot of time trying to be a composer too,' he says, smiling. 'I've talked about how the guitar is like a magic wand or a translation device, and composing is another way of documenting what's inside my brain. I'm trying to formulate these pictures, to bring to life that [inner] world.'

The saxophonist Steve Lacy once said 'improvisation is a way of finding music that can't be found by composing – and composing is a way of finding music you can't improvise', and Frisell has often experienced that creative dynamic. For him, though, playing often feels intuitive and like his natural voice; composing, on the other hand, can feel forced.

'When I'm writing, it sometimes feels like slow-motion, and I'm still struggling with trying to break the barrier between what's in my imagination and getting it down on paper. The amount of time it takes for a melody to get from my brain to the page is just long enough for me to start to doubt it.

'So, one of the most important things I've figured out is to try not to judge what I'm writing – in the moment, to *never* decide whether it's good or bad. What's most important is that I just *write* . . . just let it out, whatever it is, and then I can go back later and decide whether it's any good. Because that judging . . . all that does is keep you from getting to the music.'

If there has been some kind of obstacle or obstruction between Frisell and his muse as a composer, then it has rarely seemed evident. Reviewing *Before We Were Born* in 1989 critic Gene Santoro wrote of the album of Frisell originals, 'What sets Frisell apart from other post-fusion axeslingers is his insistence on composition as something more than an excuse for ever faster and flashier solos. His quirkily humorous melodies, his unpredictable herky-jerky rhythms, his faith in sheer space, echo Thelonious Monk.'

Four of Frisell's drawings of 'distorted, anxious-looking, guitar-wielding cowboys/man-boys'. The top two were used on the cover of Frisell's 2002 album *The Willies*.

Frisell with his Telecaster-style guitar featuring 'custom artwork' by painter Claude Utley, Seattle, May 2002.

Frisell with Jenny Scheinman and Greg Leisz, Columbus, Ohio, March 2007, during the first performances of Frisell's music for *Disfarmer*.

Trioism: Frisell, Paul Motian, Joe Lovano, New York, April 2007.

Frisell and Jim Hall during the recording of *Hemispheres*, New York, September 2007.

(*Left to right*) Ron Miles, Tony Scherr, Kenny Wollesen and Frisell play Frisell's music for Bill Morrison's film *The Great Flood*, Seattle, March 2013.

The *Beautiful Dreamers* trio: (*left to right*) Eyvind Kang, Frisell, Rudy Royston, SFJAZZ Center, San Francisco, September 2013.

TOP Good Dog, Happy Man: Frisell in his music room in Seattle, 2014,
with two Collings guitars and Monica's dog Lucy.

BOTTOM Frisell with Paul Simon on *The Late Show with Stephen Colbert*,
New York, May 2017.

Frisell, plus pedals and effects units, during the recording of *Music IS*,
Flora studios, Portland, Oregon, August 2017.

OPPOSITE PAGE
TOP Frisell's wife Carole d'Inverno, photographed by his daughter Monica,
Brooklyn, New York, 2019.

BOTTOM Self-portrait by Monica Frisell, *Truth or Consequences*,
New Mexico, 2020.

Frisell in Carole's studio in Brooklyn, New York,
during the pandemic, December 2020.
The Telecaster body has artwork by Seattle painter Terry Turrell.

By the nineties, most listeners to Frisell's music had come to appreciate that his playing and composing were one and the same. There is humour, vigour and freedom in his compositions, yet sometimes a sense of longing, darkness and depth too – a mysterious undertow. Frisell's music is often elusive, as if it's alive and ever-evolving, and never quite appears as it seems. He will juxtapose major and minor modes, play with unconventional harmonies and rhythms, introduce 'wrong' notes, place elements off-kilter, and offer a surprising twist or an unexpected resolution.

'I don't know how that happens,' he once said in *Jazziz* of such tendencies, 'but when I'm sitting there by myself, I'm drawn to certain places. As a melody starts to take shape, I'll want to pull it just a little bit further than where it's starting to go.'

Just like with his sound, it is an approach that creates music that is wholly distinctive and highly specific to Frisell.

'I put Bill in the same category of composers as Monk and Coltrane . . . Ornette [Coleman] maybe,' says trumpeter, composer and educator Cuong Vu. 'What they compose is so crucial to how they play – including what they play, and who they play with – and the way they play is also so crucial to the way that they compose. The thing that puts Bill up in the next level is that he's *so* radically different to everyone else. His music is just too uniquely different.'

Dave Douglas places Frisell in the highest ranks of American music. 'He is one of the truly great American composers and musicians,' wrote the trumpeter in the liner notes to his album *Strange Liberation,* 'emerging from a tradition of those like Charles Ives, Aaron Copland, Thelonious Monk and Julius Hemphill, whose work manifests the warmth and breadth of this country.'

●
●

Frisell's writing method has always been to work with pencil on music paper. He has tried to compose on a computer and tablet, but he finds they get in the way – 'It's taken me so long to get to the minimal intuitive level that I'm at,' he says, 'that I just want to stay with the paper.'

He used to compose on the road, but began to prefer to write in his music room at home, and more recently he has found inspiration and industry in extended stays at places such as the Vermont Studio Center. His favourite time to compose is in the morning, especially after he has just woken up and his mind is clear. When a composition seems completed, Frisell dates it, then later thinks of a title.

He is unsure, though, where the music comes from, and sometimes doubts its source. Is the melody actually the whisper of a song he heard his mother sing at home in Denver when he was three, a jumbled remembrance of a folk medley he heard at a North Carolina fiddle fair in the eighties, or part of a pop tune he heard on the radio just the day before?

Mostly he is attempting to get out of the way, trying to channel a force beyond and bigger than himself. The songwriter Nick Cave once advised, 'You are not the "Great Creator" of your songs, you are simply their servant . . . [the songs] are not inside you, unable to get out; rather, they are outside of you, unable to get in.' And Frisell says he identifies with such a notion – and with Bob Dylan's description of one of his more productive songwriting periods: 'They [the songs] came from out of the blue . . . they seemed to float downstream with the current.'

'It's like fishing,' Frisell told *All About Jazz*. 'I'm floating through this big ocean of notes . . . and just kind of grabbing at them and writing them down.'

Frisell explains that the musical ideas often arrive very quickly. 'When I'm writing, it could start with something small, like a gesture, or part of a line, or something,' he says. 'But sometimes a whole phrase, or a whole melody, or a whole song will suddenly appear.' If he feels the music has some originality and potential, Frisell will stick with it and see where it takes him. 'If I keep playing or singing it, and working with it for long enough, it's amazing what the idea will generate. It's the same feeling I have when I'm learning a song – if I absorb it deeply enough, I will start to see these refractions. In a similar way, with composing, these other layers and variations will start to happen, and it just keeps growing.'

Even though many leading composers have praised Frisell's contribution to the canon of modern American music, he remains modest about his achievements. 'I mean, compared to somebody who really knows how to write, and who spends all their time doing it, anything I've done is all so embarrassingly elementary,' he says. 'I'm serious – I'm really such a baby beginner at this stuff.

'But still, next to that ecstatic, amazing feeling I get when I'm with a band and we're playing and it's awesome, composing, when it's going well, and I just get off into it, and three hours have gone by and I don't even know where I've been, and piles of stuff have accumulated – that's it, that's the other great feeling.'

29: Van Dyke Parks Listens to *Big Sur*

Big Sur: recorded Berkeley, California, March 2013; producer
Lee Townsend; released on OKeh, June 2013; Bill Frisell (guitar),
Jenny Scheinman (violin), Eyvind Kang (viola), Hank Roberts
(cello), Rudy Royston (drums); all compositions by Frisell.

Van Dyke Parks is something of a pop provocateur. A songwriter, arranger, producer and multi-instrumentalist, he is best known for his work with Brian Wilson, in particular his contribution as lyricist to the legendary if ill-fated concept album *Smile*. Wilson saw *Smile* as a 'teenage symphony to God'; Parks viewed it more as an experimental and kaleidoscopic pop portrait of America.

Parks was born in Mississippi in 1943. Moving to Los Angeles in 1962, he immersed himself in the burgeoning West Coast pop and rock scene, working briefly in bands such as the Byrds and Frank Zappa's Mothers of Invention and playing on and producing sessions with songwriters such as Randy Newman, Harry Nilsson, Ry Cooder and Tim Buckley.

A champion of the 'counter-counterculture', Parks released his debut solo album in 1967, the fantastically ambitious and adventurous *Song Cycle*, an orchestral pop record that integrated elements of bluegrass, ragtime and show tunes. Since then he has released seven more highly original albums, scored music for countless film and television productions, written a series of children's books and collaborated with a wide variety of musicians, including Joanna Newsom, U2, Rufus Wainwright, Fiona Apple, Scissor Sisters and dubstep/EDM star Skrillex.

Frisell and Parks first met in 2001 at a multiple-artist live celebration of maverick film-maker, artist and polymath Harry Smith, who collected the formative *Anthology of American Folk Music* recordings. Two years later Frisell invited Parks to perform with him and Loudon Wainwright

III at the Century of Song concerts as part of the Ruhr Triennale. The pair has also guested on albums by Laurie Anderson, Joe Henry, Jesse Harris and Vic Chesnutt, who said working with Parks was 'like recording with Mark Twain, Erik Satie, Timothy Leary and Booker T'.

I met Parks at his home in Pasadena, California, in 2015. He is like an intellectually offbeat and immensely likeable college professor: eloquent, ebullient and fun. Before the listening session, Parks sent me several entertaining emails. One included the line 'Frizz has enuff sizzle to drive me thru drizzle'; in another he confessed, 'In truth, Philip, I'm no jazz or pop music aficionado (though complicit in the latter) – yet I sure know talent when I hear it.'

PW: When did you first become aware of Bill Frisell?

VDP: I first met Bill through the introduction of Hal Willner, who is something of . . . I think impresario is too big a word, but . . . he puts things together. He's a musical *macher* of transgenres, and that would be, of course, where Bill would easily fit in – as do I. The Harry Smith concert and the event in the Ruhr Valley – that was my immersion into Bill Frisell, the start of my informed appreciation of him.

Let me play you some of Bill's music. Here's the opening track on Big Sur*; it's called 'The Music of Glen Deven Ranch'.*

[Commenting, as the track plays] You hear Bill, with the depth of his very well-considered control of echo, and the general pliability and transparency that electronics can offer. But you also hear a deliberate application of *secco* strings – that is, high and dry, and bringing intermittent rhythms to the track, so they enunciate the harmonic environment, but also bring a physicality to the music with their anecdotal skill.

Bill's a unique talent – you get a sense with his music that it is what the Latin people used to call *sui generis*, of his own kind or making. Each work that he's created is like a good novella; it's a world unto itself. And yet I also see a similarity in his music to [early swing guitarist] George Van Eps.

That's interesting, because I know Bill is an admirer of Van Eps's playing, as was one of Bill's great mentors, Jim Hall.

Yes, as well as musicality and extemporaneous flair, they both have a charming chamber sensibility – not too big, not an attempt to muralise their environments, but still very fine work, in miniature, and very inviting. It's the details and definitions within the music, whether they're intended or accidental, which bring such pleasure to the ear.

The strings bring a great dialogue too – up front, in the face, very confidential, yet so economically applied. It leaves me with the impression that this arrangement is a performable event, and that to me is an extra dividend – when you think, 'Hey, man, this could actually take place.' That is the litmus test of an arrangement – when it can stand on its own damn two feet, without having to be within the confines of an album for sale.

The music has a sense of hypnotica – it reproduces a hypnotic event – and of meditation, and inertia. Some people think that inertia in music means 'comatose'. It doesn't. In contrast to exposition – music that varies and goes somewhere – inertia is the ability to create a sense of place, and not move from it. That's a big discipline, and a very interesting musical challenge, and I think that this is very successful.

It reminds me of the old adage, 'Don't just do something; stand there.' [I laugh.] That's what Bill has done with this piece, and that's why I like it.

This track's called 'Going to California'.

[As the track plays] That octave duplication at the beginning suggests an arid atmosphere and terrain. It adheres to the title very well. And I like the way Bill has decided to give the cello and guitar, rather than a bass, that position at the bottom of the arrangement, the opportunity to anchor the music.

There are also a few . . . yeah, harmonic detours that are deceptive – that is, they are unexpected. And he adds a furbelow or some kind of a decoration at the end of the coda to bring a little romance into the horizon. Very well done.

Bill's music on this album reminds me of some of the things you've said about how your own work is perceived – how you've found yourself caught in a musical no-man's-land.

Yeah. I'm not legitimate enough for highbrow music, 'cause I lie down with the dogs, and yet, doggone it I'm not a rocker, 'cause I work with premeditated intent. Yet this idea – as with Bill's prolific musical portfolio, and the music of Burt Bacharach, say – that people can't quite pin down where you come from, and what the music is . . . it's really very pleasurable. It's the idea that I'm not really at home in either camp, but I'm at home between them.

Let's look at the nature of jazz as a category, for example – because it *is* a category, or as my son-in-law once said to me, a 'gen-ra' [genre, said with a hard 'g' sound; I laugh]. It's a category that a lot of people hide in and think that they're going to get some status from, or that will justify their extremities. Often you come away from a jazz boîte highly disappointed, because it's a field of music that invites arrogance or the excessive application of ability.

Bill, on the other hand, like the emergent and enduring forces in any music, approaches these definitions with a sense of tolerance and inquiry. Jazz is, if nothing else, an entirely elastic field of music that is forever being transformed by new perspectives.

And I've seen that Bill has often gotten in trouble with the hauteur of people who think that they know definitively what jazz is; he has contested their proprietary expectations about what music should be.

I once met a man who knew Satchmo in his youth in New Orleans. And I heard from that man, Jack Nocentelli was his name, that the origin of the word jazz, like to 'jazz' somebody, was to be short on charity – 'Don't jazz me!' But Bill knows nobody can prove the etymology of that word; nobody can define what jazz means.

What Bill has done in his work, if I could be bold enough to opine, is to come up with an idea in music that engages the listener – and might even piss them off – with what is known, and yet brings something highly personal to it.

Bill's willing to work without a net, and that's really hard. Because what does a performer fear? I don't fear empty seats. I fear an *emptying* seat. But every artist must be willing to do that – to lose an audience – to really matter.

Randy Newman was once asked what music he likes, and he said, 'Oh, I'm a goat; I eat everything.' I like that idea. And I bet Bill does too. I like having a diet that is . . . eclectic! To me, eclecticism is the gift of an informed person.

Here's another track, 'The Big One'; it's something of a surf instrumental.

[As the track plays] All right, very interesting. Yeah, that . . . [he goes over to the piano, finds the key to the tune, and starts singing] 'I'm so tired. Tired of waiting. Tired of waiting for you.' I remember the Kinks used that positioning in that song, where it goes from G to F.

But to me this is so refreshing because of the depth in the music, the unapologetic dryness of the strings, and because Bill's chosen not to have any solos; it's totally charmed. [As the track ends] Yeah, *ta-da-dum* – old radio ending. That's nice and friendly. That's very good.

What was it like working with Bill?

Well, it seems to me, when he's working, he's happiest, and there's a sense of celebration in that. But, you know . . . he talks too damn much [Van Dyke laughs, heartily]. That's what I resent about Bill [he is still smiling]: you can never tell what he expects of you, and you're kind of left to your own devices – to do what he wants.

But, to answer your question . . . to be of value in the arts, one must have the advantage and the character of uncertainty. And I think there's no doubt that, in his demeanour, Bill has that.

He represents, in all his work, that ability of self-reinvention. And because that's become his signature, the people who approach him, like

Hal, or who are approached by him, like me, sense that, and that creates an immediate comfort – an invitation to collaborate. But that doesn't mean everyone on the board is a king. It takes a principal character to ignite that kind of a force. And Bill does that; he's known for it. It takes one flamingo to rise to get the pink cloud that we had hoped for.

This track is called 'Hawks'.

[Again after a few seconds and repeated bars] You get it immediately . . . hawks . . . still in flight. It sounds like a banjo run amok. Bill's messing with that ho-hum, aw-shucks, back-porch kind of musical cliché. And now Copland-esque. Highly economical. Makes John Adams sound like he's taking up too much space.

The strings give the piece a buoyancy . . . allowing him half-time, slow-mo reflections on the activity above. It celebrates minor seconds. There's a quality, in this piece, of what the Brazilians call *desafinado* – slightly out of tune . . . intentionally out of tune – to produce a pleasurable event in the ear. It's, you know, naughty but nice. [As the distorted guitar comes in] And there's some gaucherie in his work too. It's not like he's trying to be handsome all the time. He's not trying to be photogenic.

Here's a final track; this is called 'Highway 1'.

[As the music plays] I like the slow crawl . . . up a winding road. That's a brilliant violin comment there. Very *légère* – light and easy. Nothing over-projected. It's very beautiful.

This piece proves that Bill has a cinematic ability, that his compositions can be highly visual. Having lived in Big Sur, I'd say this music perfectly illustrates the album title; it encapsulates the hermitical qualities of the place.

It feels supremely American music to me, too. Do you have any thoughts on Bill Frisell as an essentially American artist?

Well, the problem with great American artists is that a great many are dismissed in their own country; they are often pariahs who find refuge abroad.

But, if any expectation of longevity is a precondition, I would say that Bill is a great American artist; I think his work will defy the present tense, and endure. And you can take that from a man who had a class with Aaron Copland. He gave me an A, and patted me on the ass as I left the room.

So Bill is, and will be, a great American artist. It'll be shown.

30: The Quiet American

At the end of 2014 Frisell again managed to engineer some valuable family time away from his numerous work commitments.

Monica was coming to the end of her year working at the Vermont Studio Center, and Bill and Carole returned to the artists' retreat for three weeks to spend time with her, and to work on their own projects. The family also devised a plan to drive from the far Atlantic Northeast of the US home to Seattle in the Pacific Northwest. It would be another of the Frisells' Great American Road Trips. Monica packed her car full of her possessions and equipment, and her dog, Lucy. The Frisells also invited on the journey Dana Gentile, an artist and farmer from New York State, with whom they had become friendly during their time together at the centre. Carole and Bill hired a second car. 'I love these drives, and Monica has it in her blood,' says Frisell. 'She's done it so many times, back and forth across the country.'

Monica has an ongoing three-to-five-year photography project, *Portrait of US*, in which she is travelling around America in a pickup truck with her partner Adam (and Lucy), towing a cargo trailer converted into a small mobile darkroom studio and living space. She says she is 'trying to understand my country more' by 'recording stories and creating portraits' of people she meets along the way. The enterprise is part art practice, part nomadic adventure and part anthropology documentary.

Carole's paintings and drawings have a similar relationship to her adopted country. 'My work is primarily focused on developing an abstract and personal visual language related to American history,' she has written, in an artist statement. 'To prepare for a new series, I extensively research a place, a time period, an event. From the information gathered I develop . . . a kind of visual storytelling.' Several of her more recent shows have been titled *Transumanza*, a word that, as one writer noted, 'loosely translated from Italian means "crossing the land"'.

For three weeks, over Christmas and the New Year, the foursome drove southwest to Nashville, then due west, across the heart of the country, to the Grand Canyon, Las Vegas and Death Valley, and finally north, through California, Oregon and Washington to Seattle. Forests, lakes, mountains, rivers, valleys, grasslands, plains, prairies, deserts, canyons and oceans. Bill calculated they covered, all told, with occasional diversions, five thousand miles.

In an email to me shortly after he arrived back home, Frisell wrote, 'Whew. Crazy country. Saw all kinds of ugly beautiful inspiring depressing funny sad bad good stuff.'

In many ways, the trip was a perfect symbol of a period in which Frisell had more than ever engaged with archetypal American themes. As well as releasing *The Kentucky Derby* and *Big Sur* in quick succession, in October 2014 Frisell launched his second album for OKeh, *Guitar in the Space Age!*

A collection of songs that he had been touring extensively in advance of the album, the CD served a similar function to that of the John Lennon project: it was a way for Frisell to revisit music that had made a powerful impact on him as a teenager, to look at some of those tunes through the prism of the intervening fifty years, and to attempt to learn something new.

His selection was mostly sixties guitar and pop music, including the first single Frisell ever bought – the Beach Boys' 1963 hit 'Surfer Girl', written, sung and produced by Brian Wilson. It also took in surf-rock instrumentals such as the Chantays' propulsive 'Pipeline' and Lee Hazlewood's irresistible 'Baja', the song that catapulted Colorado's finest, the Astronauts, to national fame.

Elsewhere, there were songs from the late fifties that Frisell first tried to learn on his Fender Mustang and Jaguar guitars, such as Duane Eddy's twanging rockabilly standard 'Rebel Rouser', and Link Wray's revolutionary and unruly 'Rumble', the only instrumental banned from radio in the US. Other songs in the *Space Age* set looked to the British music that had forcefully entered Frisell's universe – English songwriter and producer Joe Meek's futuristic space-pop instrumental 'Telstar', for example, recorded in 1962 by the Tornados and the first record by a British rock group to reach number one in the US. Two of the tunes, Jimmy Bryant's 'Bryant's Boogie' and Speedy West's 'Reflections from the Moon', were more recent additions to the Frisell catalogue – and in part a spark for the project.

Chuck Helm, who instigated and co-commissioned the music for *Disfarmer*, had introduced Frisell to the virtuoso country-jazz instrumentals of pioneering pedal steel guitarist Speedy West and his musical partner, early Telecaster hero Jimmy Bryant. After Bill began to play regularly with Greg Leisz in the late nineties, Helm suggested the pair present an evening of the music of West and Bryant; he saw similarities in their openness and empathy.

Frisell's initial reaction was, 'You're crazy! It's too fast!' He also once said, 'That Jimmy Bryant and Speedy West stuff – they must be jacked up on more than caffeine.' Leisz proposed they take the tunes at a gentler tempo, and eventually in 2011 Frisell and Leisz premièred their interpretations of the music of the 'Flaming Guitars' at the Wexner; the evening was aptly titled *Not So Fast.*

'There are all these seeds that have been planted for what this project is going to be,' Frisell said in a promotional video for the album. 'And it started out just me thinking about all this guitar music that inspired me as a kid.'

Frisell may have somewhat prosaically referred to the album in one interview as a 'research project', but in truth it was much more personal, even autobiographical. If *Have a Little Faith*, his wondrous 1992 survey of the diverse music that had inspired and influenced him up to that point, is like a memoir, *Guitar in the Space Age!* is Frisell's *Bildungsroman*.

On one level, he was recollecting a childhood full of fear of an atomic armageddon and the darkness of the political unrest and high-velocity social revolutions of the sixties. Yet Frisell was also recalling a period of new frontiers and unbridled optimism; of a liberating, space-age, sky's-the-limit future; of landing on the Moon, and returning safely. 'There was sort of this idea about how far can we take our imaginations,' Frisell continues in the video. 'And that seemed to be connected with science and discovering new things. It was about that feeling of possibility, and that fed directly into what was happening with the music at that time . . . I've tried to hold on to that.'

Designed with suitably cosmic imagery, graphics and typography, the CD featured a double-guitar-led quartet with Greg Leisz, plus a rhythm section of Tony Scherr and Kenny Wollesen, and also included two simple, floaty, if slightly unsettling Frisell originals that perfectly captured the contradictory mood.

Frisell's approach to the reading of the album's dozen other tunes was similar to *All We Are Saying . . .* 'We weren't trying to beat the originals,' he says. 'I just wanted it to feel true or real. We tried to do "The Wind Cries Mary", but it was somehow too heavy to attempt. Then I realised Hendrix was on the whole record: we wouldn't have played the songs the way we played them, if he hadn't come along.' The Jimi Hendrix ballad was, however, played occasionally at gigs.

Some critics – and not just those whose childhoods arrived long after Frisell's and outside America – found it easy to resist these songs' magnetic pull and formative influence. There were further charges that Frisell was again simply slipping into vanity project and cosy nostalgia. In the *Seattle Times* Paul de Barros wrote, 'Frisell gets so enraptured with the dreamy, shimmering sound of reverb that he sometimes forgets to give listeners much of a story. The result, with a few notable exceptions, is very high-level Muzak.'

It is true that, like the Lennon project, there are no radical reworkings or reconstructions of these songs – although they are not always as polished and in-the-pocket as some have suggested. The group render the inimitable riffs and languorous rhythms of Ray Davies's 'Tired of Waiting for You' accurately enough, for example, yet, during a six-minute exploration, also take the song into an entirely new sphere – somewhere psychedelic, freeform and out of this world.

There are many moments like this, passages in which Frisell gives these tunes an incremental lushness, both sonically and texturally, or a discreet embellishment, distortion and extension. The freshness comes from the music being played with the most subtle kind of jazz sensibility. It is the art of suggestion and implication, the modest gesture that makes the greater impact.

•
•

In some ways Frisell, now approaching his mid-sixties, had good cause to look back.

Some remembrances were positive. In June 2013 he played for the first time with a musician who had been another important influence in his youth: venerated saxophonist, jazz visionary and 1960s hipster Charles Lloyd. The seventy-five-year-old tenor player and flautist had been asked to curate an 'Invitation Series' of shows at the Montreal International Jazz Festival, one of which was a duo with Frisell.

Frisell was in equal parts nervous and elated. The engagement would transport him back more than forty-five years to the first *DownBeat* magazine Frisell bought as a teenager in 1967, which had Lloyd on the cover, and to one of the first live jazz events he experienced a year or so afterwards – a concert in Denver by the Charles Lloyd Quartet.

'Charles had sent me some music, but we didn't really have much of a rehearsal,' says Frisell. 'So I arrived at the hotel [in Montreal], and I phoned him, and he said, "Why don't you just come to my room, so we can talk about what we're going to do." And when I got there, the first thing he said to me was, "I look forward to singing with you tonight."'

Frisell recalls the line vividly, because not only did it instantly put him at ease, but he also felt Lloyd was a kindred spirit. 'I realised we were on the same wavelength, that it wasn't about a contest or anything like that. It just set the tone and said in a few words what music is really about.'

Lloyd introduced the evening with the incantation, 'We are dreamers . . . but we live in the *now*,' and the concert was a great success – pianist

Jason Moran, a member of Lloyd's New Quartet with whom Frisell had played several times before, also joined the duo for much of the set.

Following the Montreal appearance Frisell began to play more regularly with Lloyd, as a 'friend' or featured guest. 'It's kind of weird getting to be this age; it's like all these circles keep coming back around,' he said before a concert with Lloyd in November 2013. 'I just can't even believe I'm getting to do some of these things. It's like I woke up in some unbelievable dream.'

In 2015 Frisell introduced Lloyd to Greg Leisz. 'Charles talked about growing up in Memphis, and how he loved the sound of the slide guitar and wanted to reconnect to those sounds he was hearing as a kid,' Frisell has said. 'He asked if I'd heard slide players and I told him, "Man, this guy Greg is my total brother; we've been playing together for many years."'

At the beginning of 2015 Lloyd signed to the legendary Blue Note label, and a recording with Frisell and Lloyd's star rhythm section of bassist Reuben Rogers and drummer Eric Harland was arranged for April. Greg Leisz was invited to sit in on the session, and play a gig with the band; soon afterwards the saxophonist was forming a new group, Charles Lloyd and the Marvels.

I Long to See You, released in 2016, was an entrancing collection of ten songs, ranging from folk, traditional and anti-war tunes such as 'Shenandoah', 'Abide with Me', and 'Last Night I Had the Strangest Dream', to three Lloyd originals, including album highlight, the exploratory, meditative, sixteen-minute 'Barche Lamsel', named after a Buddhist prayer. There were also guest vocal appearances by Norah Jones and Willie Nelson.

'This record, it's deceptive,' Lloyd said around the time of the release. 'It sounds like we're playing some spirituals and some little songs like [Mexican folk tune] "La Llorona". But what we're really doing is using all the benefits of what has been rich in our lives, and what has been the cumulative benefits living this experience, to bring something forth that takes the individuality and transposes it in universality.'

In 2018 Lloyd and the Marvels released *Vanished Gardens*, an album that featured roots-rock singer-songwriter Lucinda Williams. The year before, on the day of Donald Trump's inauguration as forty-fifth president of the United States, the ensemble had announced itself by releasing a single of a compelling eight-minute live performance of 'Masters of War', Williams's enraged vocals suiting the menacing mood of the Dylan song. Three years later came *Tone Poem*, a more loose-limbed and jazz-leaning instrumental record that alongside three Lloyd originals featured tunes by Monk, Ornette Coleman and guitarist Gábor Szabó, who played with the saxophonist in groundbreaking groups in the sixties.

In an interview in 2017 Lloyd was asked about some of the guitarists he has admired over the years. '[There was] Wes Montgomery . . . he influenced Gábor Szabó,' replied Lloyd. 'But Gábor also had his own thing, and he influenced a lot of subsequent guitarists I've played with, such as John Abercrombie. Now I'm playing with Bill Frisell, who is the master for me.'

In January 2015 Frisell experienced another childhood throwback when he performed in the very space in which he not only learned that Martin Luther King had been assassinated, but he also had the life-changing revelation of playing Wes Montgomery's 'Bumpin' on Sunset': his school auditorium at East High in Denver. It was the first time he had been back since he graduated in 1969.

'I'm stunned,' Frisell said on the night, in front of an audience of more than nine hundred. 'I can't believe this is happening. I used to have dreams like this. Really weird dreams too. I really don't know what to say. Actually, it was back then I figured out I couldn't say any words, so I just tried to play my guitar, and that's what I should do right now.'

Frisell and the band played a set that included 'Surfer Girl', 'Baja', 'Pipeline', and, of course, 'Bumpin' on Sunset'. Afterwards he met some of his old school friends and bandmates, and even discovered that one of his first unrequited childhood infatuations had attended the concert – 'this girl named Linda Hart, who I was in love with, although I don't think she knew it.'

Other recollections around this time were more poignant and painful.

In December 2013 his great friend and mentor Jim Hall died of heart failure in his sleep in his apartment in Greenwich Village; he was eighty-three. While Hall had experienced some health problems in his later years, he had been working up until the end of his life, appearing at Jazz at Lincoln Center just the month before. A three-night 'Playing for Jim Hall' tribute was held at the Blue Note club in Greenwich Village the following April, which featured Frisell and several generations of Hall guitar devotees, including John Abercrombie, Nels Cline and Julian Lage.

Seven months later Charlie Haden died at the age of seventy-six, from the effects of post-polio syndrome (Haden had contracted a form of polio when he was fifteen) and from the complications of liver disease. In 2016 critic Josef Woodard published a collection of interviews he had conducted with the bassist, titled *Conversations with Charlie Haden*. In his foreword, Frisell thought back to albums he had recorded with Haden in the nineties for Paul Motian, David Sanborn, John Scofield and Ginger Baker, to gigs with the Liberation Music Orchestra in New York in the eighties, and to one of the 'first so-called jazz albums' he bought – Keith Jarrett's 1968 live trio recording with Haden and Motian, *Somewhere Before*. 'They played a Bob Dylan song on that record ['My Back Pages'] . . . and a whole lot of other stuff [ballads, a free improvisation, two rags],' Frisell wrote. 'Maybe this was some kind of blueprint for everything I've done since . . . I try to imagine the world if Charlie hadn't been there. I can't. Not my world. That's for sure. Thank you, Charlie Haden.'

Earlier, in June 2013, one of Frisell's first teachers, jazz guitarist Johnny Smith, had died at the age of ninety, following a fall at his home in Colorado Springs. Frisell may have admitted to sorely undervaluing Smith during his classes with him in 1970, but he had attempted to remedy his error in the intervening years, listening to his music more and more, and integrating tunes that Smith had skilfully interpreted – especially 'Shenandoah' – into his repertoire. Frisell later discovered that one of the songs that first stirred a passion in him for guitar music, the classic surf-rock instrumental 'Walk, Don't Run' by the Ventures, was originally written and recorded by Smith in 1954.

'Every time one of these giants leaves us, we feel more weight – the responsibility is on us now,' says Frisell. 'But the way music gets passed around, through time and space and generations, is the most extraordinary thing. The music is solid evidence that these people are still here. I find so much comfort in that.'

Frisell had an opportunity to further honour Smith's legacy in 2018. He had met and played with Mary Halvorson and, as well as a mutual admiration for each other's work, they had discovered a shared love of the advanced guitar style of Johnny Smith. When John Zorn heard about the connection – he too was a Johnny Smith aficionado – he suggested the two guitarists record a duet album of ballads associated with Smith. Halvorson transcribed and arranged some of Smith's recordings of the songs, and she and Frisell opted to play guitars that had been designed by Johnny Smith – a 1970 Guild and a 1962 Gibson respectively (the Gibson was another gift to Frisell from Gary Larson).

The Maid with the Flaxen Hair was recorded and mixed in April 2018 in customary Zorn style: in New York, in a single day, and released on his independent not-for-profit Tzadik label three months later. The CD is bookended by 'Moonlight in Vermont' and (the one non-ballad) 'Walk, Don't Run', and captures much of the warmth, artistry and harmonic adventure in Smith's playing – if sometimes filtered and warped through a more contemporary sensibility.

For one of the ten tracks, 'Black is the Colour (of My True Love's Hair)', Frisell could even directly reference Smith's arrangement for solo guitar – remarkably, he still had the handwritten sheet he'd copied from Smith's chart during the time he was studying at the University of Northern Colorado, which Halvorson plays note for note.

'As time goes on, the more I listen, the more I learn, the farther we go, deeper and deeper,' Frisell writes in the liner notes to the CD. 'I am astounded and humbled by the connections, the way music is passed around and brings us together.'

•
•

Frisell had remained in regular contact with John Zorn after the composer brought Naked City to a close in 1993; the band was unexpectedly if very briefly reunited a decade later for two dates in Europe, in Amsterdam and Warsaw, with Mike Patton on vocals.

That same year, 2003, Zorn released *Masada Guitars*, an album celebrating the composer's Masada project – a songbook of more than six hundred (in 2003, there were a mere 208) mostly short compositions, written in line with a few basic rules, and intended as a further Zorn commitment to, and evocation of, modern radical Jewish music and culture.

'The idea is to put Ornette Coleman and the Jewish scales together,' Zorn once said – though the results are often far more expansive, and can be played by any number of ensembles, or, in the case of *Masada Guitars*, by solo performers: the twenty-one mostly acoustic tracks are divided between Frisell, Marc Ribot and blues, jazz, klezmer and classical guitarist Tim Sparks. The contrast between the three guitarists is fascinating: Sparks is full of brightness and colour, Ribot often sounds more dark and direct, and Frisell plays the gently graceful if maverick melodist.

A decade further on Frisell recorded a full solo guitar album, *Silent Comedy*, for Zorn. A project that Zorn had nurtured in Frisell for many years, the idea was that the guitarist would simply turn up at a studio and play – not prearranged melodies or songs, but extempore sounds and improvisations. In the same way that *In Line* is a reflection of the supportive if often fraught experience Frisell had with Manfred Eicher, and *Ghost Town* an expression of the longstanding professional understanding and personal friendship between Frisell and Lee Townsend, *Silent Comedy* is a statement of Zorn's ability to cajole and challenge Frisell – to give him a creative arena in which he could reveal new dimensions to his playing.

'I went in without any preparation or preconceptions,' Frisell told

Guitar Player. 'I just wanted to do something really spontaneous in the moment and not obsess over it. We recorded, mixed, sequenced and titled everything within just a few hours.'

A fifty-minute album of eleven improvisations recorded in one take 'in real time, with no overdubbing', with Frisell on an 'aged' Nash Telecaster-style guitar and a wide array of pedals, the album does have the occasional twanged phrase, lush chord and repeated rhythmic pattern. Yet mostly *Silent Comedy* is a sonic guitar-and-effects adventure in dissonance, distortion and disturbance – an opportunity for Frisell to journey into the more murky corners of his guitar persona. The almost nine minutes of 'John Goldfarb, Please Come Home!', for example, contain a series of visceral bursts of scraping skronk and Naked City-like noise that is no doubt as unlistenable to those Frisell fans drawn primarily to his roots and Americana work as *Nashville* was to more dyed-in-the-wool jazz-heads. The album is as atonal, out-there and avant-garde as anything he has recorded.

The CD became a stock riposte, in some quarters at least, to the accusation that, during this late period of his work, Frisell had become too comfortable and complacent: *'Aha! But have you heard* Silent Comedy?' As Zorn claims, with some justification, 'You will never think of Bill Frisell in the same way again – revelatory and absolutely riveting!'

In supreme contrast, the year before, in 2012, Frisell had embarked upon a longer-term project with John Zorn, as one-third of a new chamber music ensemble: the Gnostic Trio. Featuring harpist Carol Emanuel, whom Frisell, through Zorn, had first met and played with in New York in the eighties, and Kenny Wollesen on vibraphone, bells and chimes, the trio was formed by Zorn to demonstrate yet another aspect of his protean personality.

'Inspired by early music, Debussy, the minimalism of Reich, Riley and Glass, and esoteric spiritual traditions from around the world', the first album of Zorn's new trio startled and surprised in equal measure – largely due to its resolute dedication to ravishing arpeggios, seductive counterpoint, modal lyricism, hypnotic rhythms and gentle interplay and improvisation. The music also played to many of Frisell's inherent strengths: sensitivity, melodicism and a tender touch.

The Gnostic Preludes: Music of Splendor is intimate and meditative music to escape and surrender to: songs that invite tranquil contemplation, and that crucially float just the right side of poetic to prevent them falling into any dreaded new age swamp. It is an inspired Zornian dream of music, enlightenment through harmony.

All the music is composed, arranged and conducted by Zorn, as it has been on the eight albums that have appeared over the following decade. As well as drawing upon Gnostic beliefs and the Masada songbook, the records have found inspiration in a wide variety of themes: the Romantic works of English poet, artist and visionary William Blake; biblical canticle the Song of Solomon; the character Scout in *To Kill a Mockingbird;* and the life and music of Zorn's close friend and mentor Lou Reed, who died in 2013. The Reed tribute, titled *Transmigration of the Magus,* features a double trio: there is a second harpist, Bridget Kibbey, a second vibes player, Al Lipowski, and organist John Medeski.

'Zorn is a great guy, totally amazing, and he's very egalitarian with his musicians – everybody shares everything,' says Wollesen. 'But he's also a really strong person and leader, and he's very clear about what he wants . . . so it can be fucking intense. With the Gnostic Trio, it is written music, but it's also improvised. And Zorn is also changing it in the studio as the music is going down. So it's also really spontaneous, too.'

In early 2019 Zorn established a new acoustic guitar trio with three highly gifted players: Frisell, prodigious jazz talent Julian Lage and classical virtuoso Gyan Riley, son of minimalist composer Terry Riley. The trio has released four suites of Zorn's music – *Nove Cantici Per Francesco d'Assisi, Virtue, Teresa de Ávila* and *Parables* – that often bear comparison to the transcendental beauty of the Gnostic recordings, if approached with a greater degree of flourish and flair.

In 2017 Tzadik also released *The Brill Building, Book Two, Featuring Bill Frisell,* an album by alt-rock/pop/outsider musician, arranger and producer Kramer celebrating the highly successful popular music songwriting teams that were resident in the Brill Building in Manhattan, especially in the late fifties and the sixties. With wispy and heavily processed vocals and backing on bass, drum computers and other instruments by Kramer, Frisell works through such recast classics as 'America' by Paul Simon and 'Solitary Man' by Neil Diamond. The results are best described as whimsical, mostly in a good way.

· · ·

Marc Ribot once said in a conversation with Frisell that 'musicians swim backwards up the stream' – they are searching for reflections in the past that might illuminate and inform new ways into the future.

In 2016 Frisell continued his personal retrospective with the release of *When You Wish Upon a Star*, an album of his arrangements of film scores from the 1950s and 1960s by such alchemical masters of the art as Bernard Herrmann, Ennio Morricone, Nino Rota, Elmer Bernstein and John Barry. Frisell also selected themes from American television series of the period, such as *Bonanza* and *The Roy Rogers Show*.

The music had a direct personal significance for Frisell. 'The Shadow of Your Smile', from 1965 film *The Sandpiper*, was one of the first songs he learned from Dale Bruning, while other scores connected him to his febrile eighties years in New York, when he was working with John Zorn on *The Big Gundown* and on Hal Willner's exploration of music from Disney films, *Stay Awake*. The latter record closes with a version, sung by Ringo Starr, of 'When You Wish Upon a Star', to which Frisell contributes.

'The music I chose for this [album] is so much a part of the fabric of what my musical imagination is,' Frisell explained in the *Wall Street Journal*. 'I remember when I first got my driver's licence and the very, very rare occasion I had a date with a girl and I got to drive my parents' car to downtown Denver to go to see a James Bond movie. That's resonating with the music [written by John Barry]. It gives you a lot more to hold on to than just the notes.'

Quite a few of the tunes alluded to the wistful and inexplicable power of dreams: the 'one life for yourself, and one for your dreams' in Barry's 'You Only Live Twice'; the 'dream-maker, you old heartbreaker, wherever you're goin', I'm goin' your way' in 'Moon River'; and 'When You Wish Upon a Star' . . . 'your dreams come true'.

Frisell assembled another new group for the project: Eyvind Kang on viola, Thomas Morgan on bass, Rudy Royston on drums and percussion, and Petra Haden on vocals. Haden was a clear and obvious choice: three years earlier she had released her own album of film music, *Petra Goes to the Movies*, on which, on a couple of tracks, Frisell had guested.

Frisell's idea for the album was again that he and the ensemble would play these songs faithfully, both musically and personally; they would be filtered through the story and memory of the music, films and television programmes, and the often momentous times in which they appeared. 'It's like having cataracts surgery and suddenly being able to see clearly,' Frisell said about playing these vintage tunes. 'I'm talking about decades of experience and then looking back at something and seeing all this complexity in it. It's like, "Oh, I didn't realise that was there."'

The record also included a suitably surreal and startling version of a Frisell original, 'Tales from the Far Side', and generated many good reviews. The record was nominated, as *Guitar in the Space Age!* had been the year before, for the Grammy for Best Contemporary Instrumental Album.

For some reviewers and commentators though, *When You Wish Upon a Star*, coming at the end of a rapid sequence of backward-looking albums, represented three strikes and you're out. While there had long been objections, especially among fans who prized Frisell's eighties New York records, that he was becoming too cautious and controlled, that he had lost the metaphorical dirt under his fingernails, the three retrospective records seemed to focus and harden such criticisms, even among long-standing admirers of Frisell's music.

Commenting on *All We Are Saying* . . . in *DownBeat*, John Corbett wrote, 'I'm afraid I don't get much from this CD . . . not that it's bad, but it lacks the great creative spark that made me love Frisell in the first place.' In an article in the *Atlantic,* David A. Graham commented that *Guitar in the Space Age!* was 'a little too perfect for the NPR [National Public Radio] crowd: middle-aged, kinda eclectic, but not very adventurous . . . The man can have his nostalgia, but please: make some weird, jarring music sometime soon, too.'

Perhaps most vociferous of all was ardent Frisell enthusiast, prolific blogger and Bandcamp reviewer Dave Sumner, who, in a post provocatively titled 'From now on all Bill Frisell decisions get run past me first', roundly dismissed *When You Wish Upon a Star.* 'I don't want forgettable music, especially not from Frisell,' he wrote. 'I want a return to the days when a new Frisell recording was a reason to celebrate, because it meant the potential for something brand spanking new that the world has never before heard.'

Even those close to Frisell express reservations with aspects of his work in the 2010s.

'Sometimes I feel like he's just relaxing, and not *pushing,*' says Claudia Engelhart. 'Paul Motian would push him; that's why that band was so unbelievable. Now he's playing these surf tunes, and they're good, they're really good – it's all cute and fun and everything – but, honestly, it's not pushing him musically. Maybe he doesn't want to play like that any more and that's his own choice. I mean, what he does is beautiful; there's nobody better to play a song than Bill. He's *master* of the song. But I feel like he's kind of just sitting back and just not really driving [his music] as hard as we know he can. To me, it's contained.'

David Breskin agrees. 'You can cut through the fabric of everything Bill's been doing more recently – his playing, the melodies – and there's beauty attached to it, absolutely,' he says. 'But there are a lot of people I know, including musicians who love Bill *to death,* who just wish there was more risk and danger in his projects, that it wasn't so comfortable.'

Breskin says he and others miss the friction and heat in Frisell's music. 'There are lots of listeners who would cut off the top digit of their left finger to hear that dark energy and anarchic spirit – they *loved* that quality in Bill's playing, probably more than he came to love that quality himself.'

417

I put some of these criticisms to Frisell; I tell him there are lovers of his music who believe he has become too safe and hemmed-in, that they would like him to be more unfettered and unrestrained.

'Well, I mean,' he replies, slowly, 'I can't . . . there's nothing I can do about it. It's just what I am. I know there are some people who want me to play something like what I played before . . . there have always been people that are attached to Naked City, or whatever, because they think that was . . . more risky and on the edge. Even if I play music that to me is the most heart-wrenching, excruciating expression of something, somebody will still say, "Well, that was, you know, too restrained." All I can say is, I'm trying my best, trying my hardest all the time to get it as high as I can.'

Frisell says he is reluctant to complain about any censure he receives because he feels so extremely fortunate. 'I'm about as lucky and as successful as I could possibly imagine,' he says. 'I went to see Louis Armstrong's House Museum, right? It's just unbelievable to think . . . I mean, I just started crying . . . Louis Armstrong, maybe the greatest musician of the last two hundred years, and he lived in this very modest little house out in Queens. Same with Wes Montgomery, the guy who completely changed and obliterated the whole history of the guitar – I saw a picture of the house in Indianapolis that he owned when he died.

'And then here I am, living in this house [he points at his and Carole's large, detached, five-bedroom family home in an affluent suburb of Seattle], and I think . . . if I start complaining that someone doesn't understand what I'm playing, that they don't get what's really going on . . . [There is a long pause.]

'What?' I ask. 'In the greater scheme of things you can live with it?'

'Yeah.' Another of those Frisellian schoolboy smiles beams across his face. 'And fuck them anyway!'

31: Gus Van Sant Listens to *When You Wish Upon a Star*

When You Wish Upon a Star: recorded Portland, Oregon, September 2015; producer Lee Townsend; released on OKeh, January 2016; Bill Frisell (electric and acoustic guitar), Petra Haden (voice), Eyvind Kang (viola), Thomas Morgan (bass), Rudy Royston (drums); compositions by Elmer Bernstein, John Barry, Bernard Herrmann, Ennio Morricone, Nino Rota, and Bill Frisell, among others.

Gus Van Sant is the director of some of the most acclaimed and category-defying films of the last forty years: highly original independent features such as *Elephant*, his chronicle of the Columbine High School massacre; innovative lowlife crime drama *Drugstore Cowboy*; and ambitious and anarchic road movie *My Private Idaho*.

Unusually, however, Van Sant has also found success with more popular mainstream audience-pleasers, including *Milk*, his biopic of San Francisco gay rights activist Harvey Milk, and the powerful emotional dramas *Good Will Hunting* and *Finding Forrester* – the Hal Willner-produced soundtrack to the latter included four tracks by Bill Frisell.

As well as being a screenwriter, producer, painter, photographer and novelist, Van Sant has shown a deep passion for music – and not just as an integral element in his films. Born in Louisville in 1952, he played drums and guitar as a teenager, and made a number of 'primitive home recordings', mostly on guitar, during the early eighties, some of which were later released on the albums *Gus Van Sant* and *18 Songs About Golf*.

Moving to Portland, he formed a 'deadpan punk' band named Destroy All Blondes, and in 1985 wrote the music for *The Elvis of Letters*, a collaboration with William Burroughs. In the nineties, Van Sant made music videos for, among others, David Bowie, k. d. lang, Elton John and Red Hot Chili Peppers.

We met at Van Sant's stylish, light-saturated, mid-century modern home high in the Hollywood Hills neighbourhood of Los Angeles. He was reserved and somewhat reticent as an interviewee – until, like Frisell, he began speaking about guitars and guitar playing. His personal collection stretches to such classics as a Fender Telecaster and Stratocaster, both built in 1971, a 1959 hollow-body Gibson and two vintage wooden-bodied National resonator guitars from 1929.

While he was clearly in the midst of a busy schedule, Van Sant remained relaxed and casual throughout. He was wearing a T-shirt and jeans, and he kicked off his slip-on shoes, perched his feet on the coffee table, leaned back on his oversized sofa, and listened intently.

PW: How did you first come across Bill Frisell?

GVS: Well, I was really into Cream in my teens, and my real introduction to Bill, the music that made the biggest impact on me, was a [1994] Ginger Baker record, *Going Back Home*. I got to know Bill's playing really well on that album, but I think I could also tell that this wasn't really the sort of music that he normally played.

It reminded me of another guitarist I was really interested in, Phil Upchurch, a jazz and blues player from Chicago who appeared on that psychedelic rock album that Muddy Waters made at the end of the sixties, *Electric Mud*. Phil Upchurch plays heavy rock on that record, and I thought it was the craziest guitar sound, and I loved it so much. I liked the fact that Upchurch was basically a jazz guitarist playing in a style and idiom that was unusual to him, and that reminded me of Bill with Ginger Baker. It pulled something new out of him.

I realised that Bill was in Seattle, and that was also interesting to me – the self-imposed escape-from-New York kind of thing, and that he's maintained it over many years. I was in the city with James Grauerholz, William Burroughs's business manager; he was going to visit Hal Willner, who was recording a track with Bill for a Burroughs recording of *Naked Lunch*. I knew Hal, but I really went along with James just to meet Bill.

Let me play you a track: here's 'Psycho, Pts 1 and 2'.

Cool. [The track plays] It makes me think of the time when Bill did the music for the end credits of [Van Sant's 1998 remake of Hitchcock's] *Psycho*. I loved the way he referenced Bernard Herrmann's score *and* used all kinds of Line-6 looping on that track ['Weepy Donuts', recorded with Wayne Horvitz]. It reminded me of some of the prepared guitar work of Fred Frith.

Can you say what it is that drew you to working with Bill?

As well as his more overt rock style of playing, it was actually the *restraint*. Especially compared to the other more kind of flashy guitar players who I admire, such as Clapton, Jimmy Page and John McLaughlin – I mean, McLaughlin's just so nuts that maybe you could never learn how to play or think like him – or jazz players like Pat Metheny, Mick Goodrick, Pat Martino and Charlie Christian. In fact, almost every other guitarist I know is more flashy than Bill.

I like the fact that there's a reserved quality to Bill's playing that . . . isn't always reserved. I enjoy that contrast between the reserved and the, say, more 'indulged' side of his playing. That comes across in his sound, which I also really like. A lot of the time, there's a kind of unique simplicity to it – a very direct sound, like a bell, especially on a Telecaster. He's gone to that Bill Frisell sound a lot, as have a lot of other guitarists. But then again, I like it when he's not creating that sound, when it's the opposite, when he's more rough and distorted.

I'm getting the impression that you have more than a casual interest in guitars and guitar playing.

Yeah, I'm always playing them, always doodling around, but you can only play one guitar at a time, and it's weird when you start realising, 'Oh, I haven't played this one in a year or more.'

Does Bill know about your collection?

Well, he and his wife Carole came over to my house after he had played a show in Portland. And yes, I had some guitars around – guitars that I really like. I was telling him a bit about them and their particular qualities, and he just said gently, 'Well, I think each and every guitar has a different sound.' And it made me realise, in the nicest possible way, I'm not really a guitarist; I've only played *my* guitars. Whereas Bill – he really knows *a lot* about a lot of guitars.

Here's another track.

[Music ends] 'To Kill a Mockingbird'?

Yes, Elmer Bernstein.

There's definitely some Aaron Copland in Bill – not just in these recordings, but in general. Hard to say, though, how much is in his musical blood and how much he's been influenced by what he's heard. But, I mean, John McLaughlin never sounded like this!

There's also a sense of an American heartland in this track; I can really hear and see that it's located somewhere in the South [Harper Lee's novel is set in the fictional town of Maycomb, Alabama].

Here's the one Frisell original on this album – 'Tales from the Far Side'.

[Track plays] Is this the thing Bill did for Gary Larson? Yeah, I think I've seen parts of it on YouTube. Cool. [There is a pause.]

How have you found working with Bill . . . as a person?

Well, he's very quiet – as I am – and, you know, sort of elliptical in his thought processes – as I am. So we get on. We talked quite a bit though when we were recording that track 'Over the Rainbow' for *Finding Forrester* – and he struck me as a deep thinker. And that, if you were rushing things, or not prepared to allow him the time to really get at something, it would be very easy to miss that quality in Bill.

Let me play you a final track.

Music from *The Godfather*, right?

Yes, Nino Rota.

There is something wonderfully weird about Bill's music too. I remember in 1995, shortly after I met him, I was asked to do a commercial for Levi's 501s, and I could really do whatever I wanted. The commercial featured four teenage boys on a road trip in the West [Van Sant later reworked the footage into a four-minute film, *Four Boys in a Volvo*], and I thought Bill's music would be ideal. We went up to Seattle to record something, and I was thinking of a sort of Ry Cooder slide-guitar soundtrack, but Bill [and Wayne Horvitz] made it much more dissonant, unsettling and mysterious, much more experimental, and it worked so much better.

I like Bill's level of experimentation, the way he can deconstruct a song like this [Nino Rota piece]. I went to see him play at a fundraiser in Seattle one time and he even played a version of 'Please Don't Eat the Daisies', the old Doris Day song. The way Bill approached it, it sounded familiar and strange and beautiful, again like this, and it wasn't until he announced the song that you really knew what it was.

I remember him saying to the audience, in that slow deadpan Bill sort of way, 'Does it help when I tell you the name of the song? Or should I tell you before I play it? Or should I not tell you at all?' I looked around and everyone in the crowd seemed to have a different answer. And everyone was laughing.

Around lunchtime in the lobby of a cinema in a swish shopping complex in Austin, Texas, I spot Bill Frisell sitting on a large studded leather sofa signing copies of a poster for the film *Bill Frisell: A Portrait*.

Even though he is in the middle of a two-week run at the Village Vanguard in New York, Frisell has flown to Austin for the day to attend a world première screening of the documentary as part of 2017's South by Southwest, the mammoth music, film and interactive media festival that runs for nine days in March.

As the film – produced, directed, filmed, edited and seemingly largely self-financed by Australian film-maker and jazz singer Emma Franz – begins, it soon becomes clear that she has foregone a linear approach to her subject in favour a more impressionistic survey. The story is not told via voiceover or narrator, but through revealing interviews and behind-the-scenes footage with Frisell, the observations and anecdotes of collaborators, and a series of compelling live performances. The intimate documentary is, as a critic for the *Hollywood Reporter* later writes, 'less a biography than a hangout film'.

Skilfully and smartly edited, the documentary is not without charm and humour too, largely due to Frisell's winningly bashful demeanour and deadpan sense of humour. There is an amusing scene, for example, in which Franz is filming Frisell on the streets of Greenwich Village and bystanders begin to turn and stare, trying to work out who the celebrity is in their midst. 'Little do they know,' says Frisell, smiling, 'I'm one of them.'

After the screening I ask Frisell how it felt to spend two hours gazing at himself on the big screen. 'Yeah, it was difficult . . . embarrassing . . . having to watch and listen to myself for that long,' he replies. 'It was like looking at the inside of my brain.'

Frisell uses the latter line in the documentary itself, talking with Mike Gibbs; Franz filmed rehearsals with Frisell, Gibbs and the BBC

Symphony Orchestra before the *Collage for a Day* concert at the Barbican in London in 2009. Discussing Gibbs's deft and insightful orchestration of his original compositions, Frisell remarks, 'It just feels like the inside of my brain. Or what I wish was the inside of my brain.'

He is clearly moved by watching two contributors to the film who have since died. 'It was pretty heavy – seeing Jim [Hall] at home in his apartment on West 12th Street,' says Frisell. 'She [Emma Franz] was also there at the Vanguard that last night with Paul [Motian, in September 2010]. She captured the final notes we ever played together as a trio.'

When I spoke to Franz a little while after the SXSW première, she said, 'To me, one of the major takeaways from the film is Bill's idea that if you do something that really works and is really great, you have to immediately forget about it – otherwise it's a recipe for not having something else good happen.

'Although he's got a very distinct style that's always going to come through, Bill is a shining example of someone who just actively tries never to repeat himself. He keeps pushing and challenging himself by working with different people, having different line-ups, playing different guitars. Bill's always wanting to learn, always trying to be fresh.'

●
●

In an attempt to remain just that – fresh – Frisell took a six-month sabbatical in 2016. He was jaded and exhausted, not by his prodigious commitment to the music and his many ensembles, but by obligations and necessities such as media interviews and constant travelling. 'If I don't stop, something's going to stop me,' he told me, a few months before the break began in March.

Carole would be at home in Seattle too, working in her studio at the house, and Monica was living in Olympia, sixty miles to the south, where she was completing a degree in photography – the family could spend time together again. Frisell still had some money put aside from the Doris Duke Artist Award, and some other savings, which he and

Carole hoped would help soften the significant loss of income from not playing live and touring, especially during the summer festival season in Europe.

Frisell had various plans for the half-year. One was to do more walking, an activity he felt he never had enough time for when he was at home, because he was always too busy preparing for the next trip or project. What he primarily planned to focus on though was his own music, revisiting compositions he hadn't played for many years, reworking and possibly re-orchestrating them for current ensembles and future projects.

'These three kind of tribute albums I've done are great,' he told me in 2015, referring to the Lennon, *Space Age!* guitar and film-score releases. 'They're inspiring, I'm learning, and I get so much out of them. They're very seductive too; I could go on for ever with more and more of them. And I'm so attracted to learning new songs.

'But, you know, I also decided . . . I should check out myself again a little bit, too,' he adds, laughing. 'I know it sounds weird, but . . . I would really like to try to learn some of my own music. I've probably played "The Days of Wine of Roses" and "Shenandoah" more than I've played any of my own songs. I keep coming back to those two tunes, and others, and the more I play them, the more I see in them – sometimes stuff that I never knew was there. But I haven't done that with my own music, and it seems like maybe I should try.'

It didn't quite work out that way, of course. Bill did spend much more time than he would have otherwise with Carole and Monica. He went for walks, some of them long ones. And he returned to and reassessed some of his previous work, to see if any of his tunes stood the test of time. Those re-examinations, especially of his compositions on *Blues Dream*, would lead to newly revisited songs from his past being included on Frisell's next three records. The offers of work, however, kept coming – not to play or record, but to compose, something Frisell found hard to resist. He took on three commissions to compose original music for feature films, although, through no fault of his own, very little came of the scores.

426

Change in the Air is a drama about a mysterious young woman who moves to a quiet American suburb; it was released in 2018, poorly reviewed, and quickly disappeared. Frisell recorded original music too with Pearl Jam guitarist Stone Gossard for *Andy Irons: Kissed by God*, a documentary about American three-time world champion surfer Irons and his struggles with 'bipolar disorder and opioid addiction'; the film was released two years later, but Frisell and Gossard's music was not used. He also wrote music, which he recorded with Jenny Scheinman, for a film by Yaron Zilberman, the Israeli-American director of *A Late Quartet*; the movie about American realist painter Thomas Eakins did not, however, progress past the development stage.

Far more positive was an inaugural $25,000 composition commission from FreshGrass, an American foundation dedicated to promoting 'innovative grassroots music'. The grant allowed Frisell to write new material, but he also chose to rework some existing compositions, and craft new arrangements of tunes from the Great American Songbook – ranging from Stephen Foster's 'Hard Times' to Billy Strayhorn's 'Lush Life' and Pete Seeger's 'Where Have All the Flowers Gone?'

Frisell premièred the commission in San Francisco in November 2016, after his sabbatical had ended, and he gathered a new group for the project: Petra Haden on vocals, Hank Roberts on cello and vocals, and Luke Bergman on acoustic guitar, baritone guitar, bass and vocals.

Bergman, a versatile guitarist whom Frisell had begun playing with in Seattle, is a multi-instrumentalist and vocalist who thrives in many different contexts, from acoustic folk to free jazz. 'He's another one of these guys where he's full of surprises,' Frisell has said. 'There's a lot of layers, a lot of depth.' He had also appeared with Bergman in concerts and events at the University of Washington School of Music in Seattle, where Bergman was an artist-in-residence and Frisell had been made an affiliate professor.

Unusually for Frisell, the new ensemble involved the majority of the members contributing to the music as vocalists. As well as Haden and Bergman, Roberts has always integrated singing into his music, and into

Frisell's – he adds vocal harmonies, for example, to many Frisell compositions on *Lookout for Hope*. Frisell, in fact, would be the only non-vocalist in the band – resolutely so; he once told a radio interviewer that he 'hoped one day to work up enough nerve to sing in the shower'.

It was only at the last minute, when the quartet was in rehearsal, that Frisell recognised the extra potential. 'I thought, "Oh, wait a minute, they're all vocalists, so let's try that too,"' he says. 'And as soon as they started, they super-spontaneously found these parts, and there was this sound, and it was exciting for me to have my guitar play amongst them. I wasn't expecting that at the beginning.'

The music Frisell presented in San Francisco was a curious yet compelling commingling of jazz, folksong, traditional tunes, standards, pop vocal dynamics and new-music polyphony. The following year the quartet played a series of further concerts: by this stage Frisell had named the group HARMONY – the all-capital letters apparently mirroring the qualities of unity and equality inherent in the definition of the word.

•
•

One major change that Frisell's six-month leave brought about was a resolution in Bill and Carole to leave Seattle. Seattle still offered an extraordinarily beautiful natural setting, and a certain liberal and progressive vibe, but the Frisells felt the city had become too corporate, too much about money, big business and voracious property speculation. 'All the interesting independent people are being squeezed out,' Bill explained to me.

Bill and Carole considered Los Angeles, Santa Fe and even Denver; a relocation to Europe was also contemplated. In the end, Brooklyn won out: it was close to the majority of Bill's work in Manhattan, more convenient for tours of Europe, and provided a reconnection to the remarkable cultural life of New York City.

Monica was also moving east, to New Rochelle, just north of New York, to take up a part-time position at New York University, helping to run a recreational arts programme for people living with early Alzheimer's and memory-related dementia. In 2017 the Frisells settled in the quiet Brooklyn neighbourhood of Ditmas Park.

In May Frisell released *Small Town*, a document of the live duo recordings he had made with bassist Thomas Morgan at the Village Vanguard the year before. Surprisingly, the record was released on ECM; OKeh's Wulf Müller had a long and constructive relationship with Manfred Eicher, and Frisell had recently appeared on ECM sessions for drummer Andrew Cyrille and Italian pianist Stefano Bollani. This would, however, be his first album as leader (or co-leader with Morgan, to be more accurate) for the German label since 1988's *Lookout for Hope*.

In some ways the Eicher connection was apposite; the interplay between guitar and double bass had distant echoes of Frisell's 1983 debut *In Line*, an ECM release to which bassist Arild Andersen contributed.

Frisell's relationship to Morgan had been growing steadily since he first played with him in a rehearsal led by Joey Baron in 2002, when Morgan was just twenty and still a preternaturally gifted student at the Manhattan School of Music. After Morgan began working regularly with Paul Motian in the mid-2000s, Frisell and Morgan appeared on Motian's final session as leader, *The Windmills of Your Mind*. In the 2010s, they also worked together on albums led by Danish guitarist Jakob Bro.

Frisell's appreciation of Morgan's resonant and responsive playing is fulsome. 'Thomas is almost like a time-traveller,' he says. 'He sees ahead of the music and seems to react to what I'm playing even before I've played it. He anticipates, in the moment, and that makes me feel weightless and that I can really take off.

'At the same time, it's very intense. It feels like my hand is physically connected to his instrument, and there's nothing that I can play – harmonically, rhythmically, whatever – that would throw him off. Even if I play a wrong note, he makes it sound good. It's the most amazing conversation, but I don't like to analyse it or break it down too much, because I could jinx it.'

In an almost seventy-minute set, which was also issued as a double LP,

Frisell and Morgan present an album of eight exploratory tracks that, to a certain degree, like its three predecessors, looked back. There are readings of the Carter Family's Appalachian folk standard 'Wildwood Flower', a song Frisell played solo on 2000's *Ghost Town,* as well as two further tunes from Frisell's youth – Fats Domino's rock 'n' roll classic 'What a Party' and John Barry's orchestral-pop movie masterpiece 'Goldfinger'.

They are interpretations, however, that feel entirely new, perhaps because they are heard so up-close, in intimate detail and delicate texture, played by intuitive and empathetic partners who share a rare bond and understanding. The title track, 'Small Town', first heard as a one-minute solo acoustic interlude on *Disfarmer,* is reborn as a cinematic country blues that strongly evokes the pain and poignancy of that album's enigmatic central character. There is also something highly personal in the eleven-minute opening track, 'It Should've Happened a Long Time Ago', a moving threnody to Paul Motian, and a song Frisell played countless times with the drummer in that very Village Vanguard basement room. The *New Yorker* lauded *Small Town* as 'a quiet masterpiece, its intimate interplay an example of the seismic power that occurs when two exceptional musicians truly listen to each other'.

In November 2018 Frisell appeared on a further ECM album led by drummer Andrew Cyrille, in a trio with another illustrious elder of the jazz avant-garde, trumpeter Wadada Leo Smith. While *Lebroba* is at once a study in sensitive restraint and abstract interplay, it also offered further refutation that Frisell had forever lost some of his edge; the track 'TGD' is an often fierce free group improvisation. A second Andrew Cyrille Quartet CD, *The News,* was also released on the German label in August 2021, its air of tender contemplation, uneasy blues and elastic time, on music recorded two years earlier, eerily presaging the pandemic days to come.

There was another bonus for Frisell fans of ECM's austere aesthetic and pristine sound in 2019. The label had recorded four sets of Frisell– Morgan duos over two nights at the Vanguard, and had enough material for the release of a second volume, *Epistrophy*; the title came both from the inclusion of the famous Monk tune on the album, and from the painting *Epistrophy I,* by Frisell's friend Charles Cajori, which graced the cover. The duo again played tunes by Paul Motian and John Barry, and ventured into the traditional folk song 'Red River Valley' and the Drifters' R&B classic 'Save the Last Dance for Me'. There was also a lonely-hearted ache of romance, in particular on the ballads 'In the Wee Small Hours of the Morning', a Sinatra signature song, and Billy Strayhorn's haunting and demanding 'Lush Life'.

'It took me years and years before I even had the nerve to play it,' Frisell told me, about the latter composition. 'When I started I struggled, but then I just couldn't shake it off. I think at one point I played "Lush Life" almost every day for a year. There's just so much to explore in that one song; it's endless.'

●
●

Perhaps instinctively, Frisell and Lee Townsend knew that his next studio album had to break new ground, and in 2017 Frisell decided to record a solo album – entirely of his own compositions. Whereas his previous solo record, *Ghost Town,* from seventeen years earlier, had included interpretations of songs by A. P. Carter, Hank Williams, John McLaughlin, George Gershwin and Victor Young, this new project would shine a light exclusively on Frisell the composer, via some new songs, and through investigations of his back catalogue – the results of 'learning his own music' again. It would be Frisell on Frisell. Sort of like *Silent Comedy* – with tunes.

Frisell prepared for the recording in the same way he had for *Ghost Town*: directly before going into the studio, Tucker Martine's Flora facility in Portland, he played a series of six solo concerts – this time in New York at a residency at John Zorn's Lower East Side performance space the Stone. 'My plan for making this recording was *not* to have a plan,' Frisell said when the album, *Music IS*, was released the following March. At the Stone he experimented by performing new compositions, and songs he hadn't played for a long time (in public at least) – tunes that almost felt like someone else had written them. 'I didn't want to play what I knew was going to work,' he continued. 'I tried to keep myself on the edge of not knowing what I was doing all week.'

Frisell endeavoured to maintain that spirit in the studio by not having a predetermined selection of songs. 'I brought this big pile of music and started from somewhere, just picked something, and then let whatever I started with generate what I did next,' he explained. 'I didn't want to try to recreate something I'd worked out. I wanted the studio to be where it was coming together for the very first time.'

The choice of songs, and the guitars on which Frisell played them – including a 1958 Gretsch Anniversary model and 1966 Fender Jazz-master – was decided in the studio, in the moment. He would sometimes record a song 'naked': the solid electric sound of a guitar through an amp. On other occasions Frisell would decide to orchestrate the tune, through the use of loops and effects, or by overdubs and overlays of counter-point, rhythmic patterns and improvisation. One track, the one-minute freeform 'Think About it', was recorded with the amp placed at the back of an old upright piano, next to its strings.

Frisell titled the album *Music IS* (again with emphatic capitals, on the second word) after one of his musical mottos, a simple phrase he first heard from banjoist Danny Barnes and that he used in his eulogy for Paul Motian: 'music is good'. Frisell has said that in a volatile and uncertain world, the maxim is one of the things on which he feels he can rely: 'It's so perfect. Everything I need to know is that phrase "music is good". I almost called the album that, but then I thought that might be too literal. It's good to leave it open.'

There are sixteen tracks on the record: five new compositions, including 'Change in the Air', a theme from the music Frisell wrote for the film; and eleven reimaginings of previous work. Some of the reinterpreted tunes, such as 'Monica Jane' and 'Ron Carter', are familiar, but most are surprise snapshots from Frisell's past, stretching back as far as his earliest recordings – the compositions 'In Line' and 'Rambler'. The latter tune is presented in two takes: a longer eerie and echoing effects-layered exploration; and an alternate version, with Frisell on electric guitar alone that, in less than three minutes, expresses much that makes the album so captivating and rewarding – melodic beauty, harmonic depth, sensitivity of touch, the suggestion of myriad musical selves.

Another original tune, 'Pretty Stars Were Made to Shine', a short skipping country theme that Frisell wrote for *Blues Dream*, had an unexpected link back even further, to a nineteenth-century American folk song – a Frisellian coincidence and universal connection pointed out by a staff member at one of the shows at the Stone.

'This guy [Don De Tora] said, "Oh yeah, I really like your version of 'Jesse James,'" Frisell explained in *Premier Guitar*. 'And I'm thinking, "What're you talking about?" Because I thought I had written the song. He said, "I have a version of Ry Cooder doing that song – 'Jesse James'." And I listened to it and I thought, "Oh my God, it's the same melody that I thought I wrote." Then I looked at it further and I realised it's this old folk song.'

Frisell thinks he may have heard a version of the tune when he was ten; American folk and pop group the Kingston Trio recorded 'Jesse James' in 1961. 'But when I wrote it down, what I wrote down was slightly different,' he added. 'I sit there and I write all this stuff and I'm not sure where it's coming from. It's like . . . am I remembering it? Or am I making it up?'

Later in 2017 Frisell received two distinguished awards. In a ceremony and concert at the Berklee College of Music in October, he was presented with an honorary doctorate; Frisell had come long way from 'barely playing a note' and being 'the invisible kid in the corner' during Gary Burton's classes at Berklee in 1971 – and dropping out after one semester. As British jazz guitarist Dan Waldman, who studied at the college in the mid-nineties, said in 2020: at Berklee, 'Bill Frisell is the patron saint'.

The following month Frisell was inducted into the Colorado Music Hall of Fame. In a concert in Denver, Bill was honoured along with Ron Miles, jazz vocalist Dianne Reeves, and Philip Bailey, Andrew Woolfolk and Larry Dunn of Earth, Wind & Fire. Frisell's alma mater, East High

School, received a 'special non-performer award for their long history of musical alumni'.

In 2018 Frisell seemed to be back working harder than ever, promoting *Music IS*, touring extensively with four of his own ensembles and with Charles Lloyd's Marvels, recording and guesting on albums with musicians as diverse as Paul Simon, Mary Halvorson and indie-folk guitarist William Tyler, and providing music for a Broadway revival of George Bernard Shaw's *Saint Joan*.

He even set himself the challenge of playing a ten-date tour of Europe – solo. It was a far cry from Frisell's first excruciating unaccompanied gig in Boston in 1983, when, 'I was just so terrified to sit there and try to play alone. It was like torture, or something. I swore I would never do it again.' Thirty-five years later, after the first solo concert in Berlin, Frisell wrote in an email to me, 'It was good. Trying not to think. Just start going. So far it's working. Don't want to get too cocky. But. Not thinking is good. The music always knows what to do.'

The following year Frisell signed to one of the most storied labels in jazz, Blue Note. The famous Blue Note roster of artists had been significantly bolstered and revived following the appointment of musician and producer Don Was as president in 2012, and Frisell followed Charles Lloyd to the label, as did musicians and bands ranging from Wayne Shorter and Van Morrison to Aaron Neville, Ron Miles, Kandace Springs and GoGo Penguin.

'I love the way that Bill annihilates the concept of genre,' Was said, when the move to Blue Note was announced. 'He's a versatile conversationalist who speaks many languages – and makes it all work.'

In October 2019 Frisell released the first album under his own name for Blue Note: *HARMONY*, a document of some of the repertoire he had been developing with his new quartet of the same name. The record includes three short new pieces, with Petra Haden adding wordless vocals – her spare and unaffected voice having an instrumental quality that blends deftly with Frisell's softly sustained notes and chords – and five further reappraisals of songs from deep within the Frisell archives, including 'God's Wing'd Horse' from the *Buddy Miller Majestic Silver Strings* album, and 'Deep Dead Blue', with lyrics by Elvis Costello.

While some critics found the music too flawless, wistful and clean, many listeners discerned Frisell's gentle push towards the more political. In 2015 he had been one of the 'artists, musicians, and cultural leaders of America' to openly endorse Bernie Sanders as Democratic nominee for President, and *HARMONY* contains an unhurried and disquieting version of Pete Seeger's folk lament 'Where Have All the Flowers Gone?'; live the group performed further protest songs such as 'We Shall Overcome' and 'This Land is Your Land'.

'Well, it's not a blatant [political] thing,' he says. 'I would never just come out and say, "Yeah, this is the anti-fascist quartet", or whatever. But I can't help thinking about these things, and these songs say something to me. I think music is something good, and it's something people need, and I'm just trying to put something beautiful out there somehow, I guess. Playing these songs is helping me, so I hope it can help other people.'

⋮

As well as many appearances in the US and four tours of Europe in 2019, Frisell also embarked on visits to Southeast Asia, Australia and Japan. In March the following year, however, as he was about to leave for Europe to tour as special guest with a trio led by saxophonist Chris Potter, the Covid-19 global pandemic began to increasingly disrupt and devastate – and Frisell's concerts for the foreseeable future were cancelled.

Frisell stayed at home with Carole in Brooklyn and, like most of the population of New York, watched in horror as the city and surrounding metropolitan districts became the worst-affected area in the US, and the pandemic surged exponentially into the deadliest disaster in the history of the city.

By September 2020 there were almost a quarter of a million confirmed cases in New York, and nearly 24,000 deaths. Two among that number were Lee Konitz and Hal Willner.

Hal's death hit Frisell especially hard. 'I'm stunned . . . and in shock,' Frisell wrote to me by email, the day after Willner's death was announced. 'Just talked to him a couple of weeks ago. I didn't know he was sick. It's almost impossible for me to imagine the world without him in it.'

For Frisell, as for most people, the lockdown was an enormous change in circumstances, and an intense challenge. Even though he had organised periods away from touring in the past, the sojourns were always fixed and finite; he knew at the end he would resume playing – alongside musicians with whom he had built up long and close creative and personal relationships. Without that connection, there was the risk that Frisell's generalised anxiety about the state of the world and his creative place within it might resurface.

'Well, I know I'm really lucky,' he told me three months into the pandemic. 'We have this great house, and I'm surrounded by my guitars and music and stuff, and there are trees and space – we are pretty far out into Brooklyn. But I guess almost everyone is feeling this kind of mass depression, and every day it's hard, you know, to get up and really get at it.

'I've spent almost my entire life in music interacting with other people – there's not more than a few days go by when I don't play with someone, right? Even before I started playing the clarinet when I was nine years old, we'd have music classes at school and everybody would play a tambourine or a triangle or something. And before that, when I was a toddler, I would hear my mother singing around the house. This is the longest I've ever gone without having any of that kind of connection . . . so it's rough, you know.'

What Frisell did manage to maintain was his deep and instinctive attachment to the guitar. 'What I've found is how much the guitar has saved me. Again. It's always saved me, and I'll start playing and I'll just keep on playing for hours and hours and hours, every day. Sometimes it'll just be one song, playing it over and over and over again, all day, finding different things in it.

'That's been an amazing feeling. Playing the guitar with no real reason, apart from the love of playing – because there's no schedule, no deadlines, nothing to prepare; no work, really – and realising that I love this thing. It sort of reminds me of the feeling back when I was living in Denver in the seventies.'

Frisell also found sufficient inspiration to compose, allowing the music to emerge as unconsciously as he could; in dark times, the music might again act as catharsis. By the end of June 2020 alone he had seventy new compositions in his music notebooks, forty of which he felt were near completion.

'Almost every day, I'll grab the guitar and just let my ear . . . just the first thing, that first instant, wherever my hand lands and whatever comes out – that's all you need,' he says. 'I'll write that sound down and then . . . I can hear the next sound, or the next phrase or melody coming. Maybe I might throw that first sound away, but it's the thing that set me on the path to something. Usually the tunes fit on one page, and some of them are short, more like miniatures or études. And they're not all necessarily good. But having this time, enough time so that the music isn't forced, I've been able to write some things which I can't explain.'

By the beginning of April, Frisell was taking part in livestream concerts. The first was an online music festival and fundraiser in support of fellow New York musicians being adversely affected by Covid-19. Frisell's solo concert, beamed to the world from a room in his house in Ditmas Park, didn't go smoothly. Technical problems caused the livestream to crash, and a full performance was only made possible after a two-hour delay. Public comments on the site expressed frustration yet mostly support – especially for Frisell's newly grown white 'Corona-beard', as one described it. 'Bill's beard broke my modem,' wrote another.

Those donors who lasted the course were treated to a delicate, reflective and somewhat mournful solo performance, with each song chosen for the unprecedented moment; the hour or so set included 'Someone To to Watch Over Me', 'New York, New York', 'I'm So Lonesome I Could Cry' and concluded with an effects-enhanced version of 'We Shall Overcome'. The week-long festival raised almost $60,000.

In May Frisell performed a second at-home concert, this time for the Blue Note jazz club in Greenwich Village; the set included two songs that for Frisell again had a powerful resonance with the tragedy of the ongoing pandemic: 'As Tears Go By', for Marianne Faithfull, who had tested positive for Covid-19 and spent three weeks in hospital in London; and 'Kaddish', for Hal Willner.

On a far less serious note was: the cushion. Part of the fascination of these at-home concerts is, of course, extra-musical: the public gets to see an artist's private space. In Bill and Carole's living room were African masks and ethnic art, and on the far wall a photograph of Monica. There was also, perched on an armchair, a black cushion with colourful lettering. Because the livestream was broadcast in mirror-image, it was hard at first to make out the words. After a while, however, it was clear: the letters spelt out 'FUCK TRUMP'.

Frisell played further ticketed livestream events, some broadcast direct from New York clubs such as the Village Vanguard, where he played in a trio with Thomas Morgan and Rudy Royston. The gigs provided some welcome income for Frisell (as did the rise in his monthly listener figures on Spotify, which topped five hundred thousand for the first time at the beginning of 2021), and all had their creative moments – if you could get past the weirdness of watching musicians perform in black face masks and the deafening sound of no applause after a song or set had finished.

'I'm thankful to be doing these online concerts, and to be able to play with others – it's all we've got right now,' Frisell told me. 'And I know that people watching get some kind of sense of being in the club. But, boy . . . it's not what I signed up for.'

What Frisell has always been committed to, of course, is releasing albums, and his second album for Blue Note, *Valentine*, had been recorded at Flora with Martine and Townsend in the autumn of 2019, before the pandemic took hold. The album was released by Blue Note in August 2020 and it is a document of Frisell's widely toured yet previously unrecorded trio with Morgan and Royston, a unit that has built up a great deal of belief and mutual trust.

'It's like when you're dreaming and you're on the edge of a cliff, and you know on a certain level that it's a dream, so you can just jump off,' Frisell says in the liner notes to the album. 'With this music we could do that.' The album is another intriguing selection of old, new, borrowed and blue. Compositions such as 'Where Do We Go?' from *Blues Dream* and 'Levees' from *The Great Flood* were mined from Frisell's past and recast. There are new tunes too, including the distinctly Monk-like blues of the title track; 'can't shake that guy off somehow,' Frisell once said, with droll amusement. Other songs are borrowed from Sonny Rollins – the thirties western song 'Wagon Wheels', which the saxophonist recorded on *Way Out West* – and from Billy Strayhorn: his captivating 'prayer to nature', 'A Flower is a Lovesome Thing'.

Valentine's cover image, and four further images in the CD booklet, were, for the first time, strong organic and geometric abstract paintings by Carole d'Inverno – and the album was almost universally well received, the review in *DownBeat* being fairly typical: 'Even though the selections on *Valentine* hail from a range of styles – Afropop, country-western, Brill Building pop, atmospheric electronica – the performances represent jazz playing at its most sublime. And music seldom gets more "together" than that.'

Two slow, stately songs were particularly highlighted in the reviews, perhaps in recognition of the pandemic times: Frisell's 'Winter Always Turns to Spring', the words in the telegram given to Frisell by David Breskin shortly after Bill's father died; and 'We Shall Overcome', the gospel song that became an anthem of the civil rights movement.

'I've been playing "We Shall Overcome" for the last few years quite a bit, but that song has been around my whole life,' says Frisell. 'It's always been relevant to something that's going on in the world, and I'm not sure that's going to stop in my lifetime. I mean, it's not like I'm trying to preach, or anything, but I play it, and I believe it, and it feels good just to keep that song going.'

33: Rhiannon Giddens Listens to *HARMONY*

HARMONY: recorded Portland, Oregon, August 2018; producer Lee Townsend; released on Blue Note, October 2019; Bill Frisell (guitar), Petra Haden (voice), Hank Roberts (cello, voice), Luke Bergman (acoustic guitar, baritone guitar, bass, voice); compositions by Frisell, plus by Stephen Foster, Charlie Haden, Alan Jay Lerner, Billy Strayhorn and Pete Seeger.

Singer-songwriter, banjoist and fiddle player Rhiannon Giddens is a uniquely powerful force in modern American roots music. Credited with 'systematically dismantling the myth of a homogenous Appalachia', the North Carolina native has deftly woven elements such as old-time, bluegrass, folk, country, blues, gospel and jazz into her capacious and captivating music. Add her background in opera and art-song, and a burgeoning interest in tracing American music's tangled links back to Africa, Europe, Latin America and the Arab world, and Giddens has emerged as a peerless once-in-a-generation musician, a vital new voice.

She was born in Greensboro in 1977 to a black mother and white father; it was a rare interracial marriage for the time and place, and somewhat controversial (her father was disinherited).

In the early 2000s, following opera studies at the renowned Oberlin Conservatory in Ohio, Giddens returned home and fell increasingly in love with old-time music. She took up the banjo and fiddle, became a caller (or prompter) at local contra dances, and began to explore the vibrant Scottish and Celtic connections to Appalachian music. She also developed a deep interest in the often hidden history of black musicians' involvement in early American folk forms.

In 2005 Giddens co-founded the Carolina Chocolate Drops, a group 'dedicated to reviving and extending the tradition of the African

American string bands of the 1920s and 1930s'. She began to gain wider recognition as a solo artist in 2013 after her electrifying performance at a T Bone Burnett-produced concert in New York celebrating the music of the Greenwich Village folk scene of the sixties. Two years later Burnett produced her debut solo album, *Tomorrow is My Turn*, on the Nonesuch label. 'She has a pretty profound gift,' Burnett said at the time. 'I've been doing this for fifty years, and I haven't seen anything like it.'

Giddens has also appeared in popular US musical drama TV series *Nashville,* she hosts a podcast on opera's most famous arias, and is artistic director of cellist Yo-Yo Ma's cross-cultural music and arts organisation Silkroad.

While Giddens has homes in Greenville and Nashville, she lives for most of the year in Limerick in Ireland, where her two children attend school (up until 2017 Giddens was married to Irish musician Michael Laffan) – and where we met, masked and socially distanced, during the pandemic. Giddens is tall, smart, passionate and hospitable (she even baked fresh scones for the occasion).

PW: I'm just going to play you a track and we can take it from there.

RG: OK. Great. ['Hard Times' plays] Now that's a song that I've heard . . . [almost sotto voce] many times.

I imagine.

But still, I like that version. I like the harmonies, and the singing style. But I was really listening to what Bill is doing on the guitar. I find his playing kind of harp-like; an accompaniment that also has its own personality. He's saying things, but in a way that doesn't pull from the singer.

Bill's playing is very minimal, and I like that, yet there are hints of a lot of different styles. 'Hard Times' is a minstrel song, written by Stephen Foster [in 1854], and I can even hear Bill give a little nod to that, too. I don't know how much research he does into these tunes, or whether he goes back and looks at the original sheet music, but *I* would hear that

441

it comes from that source, and from the idea that minstrelsy is proto-American music anyway.

Maybe he hears that too, and he did it on purpose, or maybe he's just playing what occurs to him. But it sounds like Bill approaches covers in the same way I do. You don't *try* to make the song different. You find your way in, you find the centre of the song, and then you express that centre. You do what you need to do to support that central vision of the song – and then you just do it like you do it!

How much of Bill Frisell's music do you know?

Honestly? I don't really know his music at all.

Excellent. This could be interesting!

Well, I know that he's a cool guitarist, and our paths have briefly crossed a couple of times. We both played on Allen Toussaint's final album, *American Tunes* [from 2016; Giddens sings two Duke Ellington songs]. And we bumped into each other at the Big Ears Festival in Knoxville [Tennessee; in 2019]. Bill introduced himself again; it was just a moment. He was shy. Extremely shy.

But I do remember Francesco [Turrisi, the Italian multi-instrumentalist who is her musical and relationship partner] once saying to me, 'You should do something with Bill Frisell, because you both do the same thing. He's just doing it on a guitar.'

I wouldn't presume to say I share much with Bill, but I think Francesco meant that we both take all these American influences – a bit of this, and a bit of that – and try to make them work together. It never feels like he's saying, 'OK, I'm going to play jazz now' – or folk, or whatever. It's about finding the path through, and not being afraid to use everything that you can. Because they all come from the same source.

So, yeah, I keep hearing how great Bill Frisell is, and I've always thought that I should be listening to more of his music.

Well, that's the reason I'm here! Here's another track, a Frisell original ['Lonesome' plays].

Well, that track's not so interesting to me, but I really like the choices that he makes and the attempt to transcend the [puts on ironic voice] 'This Is A Guitar' idea.

Being a guitarist can be really difficult in American music, because it's very hard to find unusual or idiomatic players any more; as soon as some-body gets popular, everybody wants to do what they do. It's the same with vocals – a lot of people want to be Alison Krauss, and they'll never be Alison Krauss, but gosh, darn it, they try.

When you listen to those first folk recordings, those guitars were frickin' wackadoodle. They were playing crazy stuff – sometimes in com-pletely different keys to each other [laughs] – and it was just a more fluid kind of thing.

So Bill on that track is going somewhere else with his playing, which I really like, and it's kind of what I try to do. He's much more skilful; he's a real actual instrumentalist. Whereas I just play banjo, and it's kind of its own thing – it's my sound. I'm a very minimal player, because I have to be. Whereas the players I admire might be able to play a million notes, but they choose not to. Maybe with Bill it's partly his age, and on earlier recordings he was different?

No, he's more like you, actually; he's never been a pyrotechnical player.

Well, I have the feeling that Bill is looking for the right path through the music, and if the notes aren't on that path, he doesn't play them. And I love that; that's my philosophy. The opposite makes me run away [laughs].

Let's see the effect this next track has on you ['Where Have All the Flowers Gone?' plays].

Now that's an interesting choice, and it grew on me a bit, but it's hard because I know that song quite well. I grew up in Greensboro with hippie parents who used to play the versions by Pete Seeger, and Peter, Paul and Mary, all the time. And I know Peggy Seeger [Pete's half-sister] quite well, too; I've taken lessons with her and she's been kind of a mentor of mine.

I love Pete, but it's a cheesy song and you wonder what Bill's statement is here. I'm fascinated with the idea of taking an old song and doing something different with it that's not the way, at all, it was intended. And Bill slowing it down like that is a very strong choice, and I'd much prefer a strong choice to a weak one. But you're only through the first verse, and it ends. For me, when a song is saying something, you don't denude it of that statement.

But, even if I don't like Bill's version that much, I love all the harmonic movement; that's a given. I especially like that chord change on the line [she sings the lyric 'when will they ever learn']. So I like the universe, the soundworld that it's in.

You mentioned growing up in North Carolina, and you may not be aware that your home state has played an important role in Bill's life. [I tell Rhiannon about his parents moving there in the seventies, Bill and Carole getting married in Greenville – and the impact on him of attending local fiddle contests.]

I'm not surprised. It's what happens when you've been learning music, and you like it, and it's great, and you're getting skilled at it – and then you run into people who make music because it is culturally connected to them, it's something their grandparents and great-grandparents did before them. If that's not your personal story, seeing somebody like that in that space is very magical. It can be like nothing you've ever heard.

The same thing happened to me, even though I'm *from* North Carolina and my [paternal] uncle and grandfather played bluegrass – like, it's a part of my DNA. I wanted to be an opera singer. That was it. I was one hundred per cent Western art music – dead European white guys. That was my focus.

Then I came back to Greensboro and started discovering what was right under my nose – contra dancing and old-time music. And when

you find *that*, when you listen to that music from the twenties and thirties, that's all you need, baby. That's, like, *it*.

I just jumped in and everything seemed up for grabs. It's the big beautiful soup that was American music before the [1927] Bristol [recording]
sessions, hillbilly music, race records, the recording industry, and the
intent to segregate the music.

I know Bill is pulling from all these things too, and when you start listening to this old shit, and you find the freedom that generation had, it's
gonna *shake you up*. It's an important journey that not everybody takes.

*Well, I do think you and Bill share a certain aesthetic: you both believe in the
idea that music is an expression of that freedom, certainly beyond boundaries
and categories.*

Yes, I think a lot of people are . . . tied up, and in a box, and are really
happy to stay that way. The first question that everybody frickin' asks
me is, 'What kind of music do you play?' And it drives me nuts; I'm just
like, 'Well, *why do you care*?' Other than, yeah, it's acoustic music, and
mostly American music – I don't play fifteenth-century Icelandic sagas,
for example. Very broad strokes.

Because I just don't hear the differences some people talk about. I
don't hear the difference between Sister Rosetta Tharpe and Bill Haley,
between the jazz of this and the blues of that and the rock and roll of that
again. To me, they're just different flavours of the same stuff.

I was interested in something you said in a profile in the New Yorker *– that
you play 'black, non-black music'.*

Yes, it's the idea that this music – old-time, bluegrass, folk, whatever
you want to call it – isn't considered black music, even though it is. As
a mixed-race person, old-time music is as much mine as anybody's, but
at one time I felt like it wasn't. And that's really messed up, on so many
levels.

The main thing is trying to get people to understand that black people
were integral to this music, that their involvement is deep and goes back

445

a long way. People don't consider where the music came from, and what it is now. Whose music it is. Because there's such ignorance of our history in general.

Well, I've talked to many white musicians who play jazz—
I'm sure you have. There are a lot of them [laughs].

And I was wondering if, therefore, they, including Bill Frisell, play 'white, non-white music'?
Right. Sure. If you want to play music that has cultural connections, then you *have* to understand it, historically and politically. That's all there is to it. There's a context for all music – like, Verdi's music is very political at times – and you have to dig into it, and realise what your place is in it.

You have to respect what other folk went through playing the music. You have to respect the elders who are still alive, their knowledge, and the fact that people are gonna have opinions about you playing the music.

You have to understand that so many of these types of American music came out of the formation of the African American character – that creolisation that occurred when Africans set foot in the New World. Jazz, blues and string-band music – they were all innovated in the black culture, in the black side of things.

It's not to say that white people don't have a purchase and creative capital in this; they do. Everybody has a stake in the game. But you have to acknowledge what came before, and that's the step some people can't get to. But if you can, then you're free. That's when you know where you truly sit in the music.

Here's a final track, from a different album, one Bill Frisell released in 2002 called The Willies *['Cluck Old Hen' plays].*
Hell yeah, like, rock it! I mean, who hasn't done that with 'Cluck Old Hen'? That's a rockin' tune [slaps her hands on her thighs], like so many of those old-time tunes, and I love it when people approach it that way. That tune wants to be like that. So much so that I kind of wanted to hear

somebody come up on top with [mimics a heavy metal screamer] really hard rock vocals. That would be, like, frickin' great.

Last question. Bill has a saying, one he first heard from the banjo player on that track, Danny Barnes: 'Music is good.' Would you agree?

Yes, I believe that, but I say it differently. I say: music is innocent. It's what you do with it that's the issue.

It can certainly be used as an instrument of evil. When those fiddle festivals and conventions that Bill attended first came into being in the twenties, the co-creators of that music, the blacks, were outlawed; they couldn't play. Even though in a lot of these places, the best fiddlers were black, right? It was a way of using music to find some mythical white culture that could trace its roots back to Britain and Ireland alone.

But I think it's harder to do that, because I don't think music wants to be used that way. We create music out of that part of us that's connected to something that unites *and* is much bigger than us. Like those shapes birds make when there are thousands of them flying together; the murmuration of starlings.

So yeah, I agree with Bill: music can also, very easily, be used as an instrument of good. One of the ways that we come together is through music. And if we hadn't, if different cultures hadn't talked to each other through music, we wouldn't have old-time or bluegrass or blues or jazz or rock and roll.

It's never inherently the music's fault; it's always a device or a division, like genre, that some people use to control it, and divide us. But the core of music – that always wants to bring people together.

In the summer of 1972, shortly after Frisell had returned to Colorado and was briefly living in Greeley again, Bill Evans played a week at the Senate Lounge in Denver. He appeared at the small downtown bar and club with Eddie Gómez on double bass and Marty Morell on drums – a trio that, over the previous three years, had grown into one of Evans's strongest and most stable units.

Frisell went every night, making the two-hour round trip. He knew the venue well – it was where he had seen his guitar teacher Dale Bruning play and where he had first heard Jim Hall perform live – and he knew it was a sympathetic space in which to hear the lyrical melodicism, harmonic invention and poetic touch of the revered pianist, the 'quiet fire' that had drawn Miles Davis so powerfully to Evans. 'Night after night . . . I was just having these religious experiences,' Frisell has said. 'I couldn't believe what they were playing . . . to me, it was just this heavenly music.'

On the last night of the run, Frisell and his friends left the club at one in the morning, only to turn a corner and discover Evans stranded. 'He was out in the middle of the street, under a streetlight . . . just standing there by himself, kind of freaked out,' Frisell told Ethan Iverson. 'We go up to him and we're like, "Mr Evans, we've been here every night, and the music is just like from another world." He's like, "Fuck, I lost my ride, can you give me one?" So I get to give him a ride to his hotel, but in the meantime we're saying, "The music was just great," and he was like, "Awwwww, man, this whole week I just haven't been able to play anything." He was so bummed.'

Frisell was incredulous at Evans's response – in another interview, he describes the pianist protesting that he 'couldn't play shit' – but it provided him with an invaluable lesson. 'It was like another bomb going off in my head,' he continued. 'I thought, prior to that, if I really practised hard and I get all these things together, then every night is going to be just like when I hear Bill Evans. It's going to be ecstasy every time I play, you know. For me it was the realisation that you never get there. You have to just keep plugging away and trying to get close.'

•
•

At one point during our interviews, I ask Frisell what is the most important lesson that life has taught him?

He laughs, and there is an even more protracted Frisellian pause than usual. 'Well, maybe,' he begins slowly, tentatively, 'it's that you always have to be questioning things, that there's no one answer . . . because I don't think it's really good to be certain about anything.'

Even about music?

'Yes, life and music. It's like . . . any time you think you might have figured something out, or you've arrived at a place where everything's OK, as soon as you're there . . . it's gonna turn itself around or upside down, contradict itself.

'That's what music has shown me: that it's not about a goal, or anything. You have to feel good about being in the process rather than . . . expecting some ultimate reward. Just to be in it, and enjoy being in it, and doing the best you can: that's the whole idea. There's always something to discover or that will be revealed. It's infinite; there's as much in front of me that I haven't done as there ever was.'

Bob Dylan once said that an artist needs to be 'constantly in a state of becoming'. Frisell maintains that position by preserving a conscious naïvety and certain unknowingness; he is propelled by a perpetual state of possibility, mystery and learning. Frisell is a quiet disciple of Ry Cooder's doctrine that 'you should go into every musical situation like you're a student'.

'When I pick it up, it doesn't feel very different from the very first time I touched a guitar,' Frisell told *All About Jazz* in 2011. 'You grab hold of this thing, and you think, "Man, what am I gonna do?" You're sort of imagining this thing, and you're trying to get it, and you just go for it somehow, but you can *never* get it. It's just this gigantic world of music that's floating around – not just in my head, but it's out there. When I get going playing, I'm just grabbing at all these things, but from moment to moment, it changes.'

If, as Steven Poole has written, 'all art aspires to something it cannot achieve', Frisell is an advanced musical adventurer, ceaselessly striving for the music in The Frisell Dream, the extraordinary sounds that exist just beyond himself. Frisell's music is the beautiful sound of that unending struggle.

'Yes, for those of us who have that kind of personality, the work is never *done*,' says John Surman, when I discuss the meaning of Frisell's dream with him. 'Part of the process is that you climb up the slope, you get to the top, and then as you look out, you see there's a further peak beyond. There's always another peak to climb. That's the part that makes you realise you never really get to where you want to get, or where you could get to. You step ahead, you learn things, and you accomplish certain things, but there's always something that keeps driving you forward, always something out there that we're looking for – the meaning of life, the meaning of music.

'But listen, Philip, give Bill a message from me, will you? "Dream on."' And Surman lets out a warm and enthusiastic laugh.

:

Swallow Hill Music is an association founded in Denver in 1979 that grew out of the Denver Folklore Center (DFC), the music store, record shop, performance space and alternative hangout owned by the 'dean of Colorado's folk music scene', Harry Tuft; the DFC was where Frisell had his first guitar lessons aged thirteen, and where he jammed with various folk and roots musicians in his early twenties.

The non-profit organisation has a music school, community outreach programmes, and it stages occasional concerts – in April 2019 Frisell was invited to play with his HARMONY quartet at the city's First Baptist

Church, just a couple of miles from both East High School and the final Frisell Denver home on East 7th Avenue.

A few days before the performance, this is how Frisell marked the occasion on his website:

'I grew up in Denver in the fifties. By the early sixties I had fallen in love with the guitar. It didn't take long to find my way to Harry Tuft's extraordinary Denver Folklore Center. I can't begin to tell you what an impact that place had on me and so many others.

'It was there I took some of my very first lessons with Bob Marcus. Baby steps. I knew a little about Peter, Paul and Mary. Bob told me about Mississippi John Hurt and Paul Butterfield.

'I can't believe it. Here I am now, more than fifty years later, about to play at Swallow Hill with my group HARMONY. It's likely we might play some of the same songs I began learning way back then.

'So many seeds planted. Still growing. Trying to get it together. Just getting started.'

Acknowledgements

While the germ of this book has been forming, somewhere in my head at least, for the past thirty-five years or more – ever since I first met Bill Frisell, and heard him play live, in the eighties – it is American music journalist Stanley Booth who supplied one of its crucial sparks.

In a scene at the beginning of *The True Adventures of the Rolling Stones*, Booth's revelatory insider's account of the group and its 1969 American tour, the writer is asked by Mick Jagger, 'What would your book be about?' By way of an answer Booth tells Jagger about a story he had written on the great blues singer and guitarist Furry Lewis, who had supported his playing for more than forty years by working as a Memphis street sweeper. Booth added, 'You write, I told him, about things that move your heart.'

That line came to me during an initial discussion with Bill Frisell about this book. 'But what will you write about?' he asked, with genuine modesty and amazement. 'I mean, there haven't been any fights, or anything. And all I've done is stay married to the same woman for the past thirty-five years.'

In response, I repeated the Boothian doctrine (leaving out my own personal addendum of 'and you keep your critical faculties about you'), told him that there was more than enough to write about in his music alone, sugar-coated it with my desire to be stretched as a writer in the same way I thought he had consistently challenged himself as a musician, and, well, the result lies in your hands.

My first and major debt of gratitude, therefore, is to Bill Frisell himself, who approached this lengthy project in much the same way, as many musicians told me, he does any collaboration: with generosity, patience and an open heart.

On countless occasions Bill's commitment to the book, and his good humour, went way beyond what any biographer might reasonably expect of their subject. Bill brought to our many meetings the gifts of rigorous intelligence, admirable honesty, philosophical depth, dark humour and, as his wife Carole says, 'an extremely good memory'. Interviewing Bill also changed me in the same way that his music has: it made me a better listener.

Frisell's life-enhancing 'architecture of connections' led me to many musicians, friends and associates who themselves display many of the qualities I see in Bill. There are too many to list here, but again and again those leading busy and demanding lives were often prepared to talk to me for many hours, and on more than one occasion.

If Julian Barnes is right, as he suggests in his novel *Flaubert's Parrot*, that the biographical trawling net always sorts and throws back a significant amount of its catch, then my apologies to those interviewees who gave their time and are not quoted more fully. Without those conversations, however, there would be no sea, no boat, no net, no catch, no book, and no Bill in all his diversity and complexity. So, I thank each and every one of them.

I would also like to acknowledge some of the many journalists who have written so perceptively on Bill Frisell, and from whom I have drawn both insight and inspiration; the list is long, but includes Nate Chinen, Francis Davis, Gary Giddins, Geoffrey Himes, Ethan Iverson, Martin Johnson, Tom Junod, John Kelman, Howard Mandel, Bill Milkowski, Tom Moon, Brian Morton, Dan Ouellette, Ted Panken, Andy Robson, Gene Santoro, Hank Shteamer, Chip Stern, Richard Williams and Josef Woodard.

Early sections and drafts of the book were read by Sandra Laville, Jessamy Calkin, Angus MacKinnon and Nuala Goodman; many others have also provided invaluable assistance, advice, friendship and encouragement.

A *Beautiful Dreamer* award ceremony would give gold gongs to Brian Aaker, Elaine Ahern, Roger Balch, Tom Bromley, Janice Brooks, Jemma Churchill, Bernard Clarke, Laura Connelly, Lynda Cullen, David Cutler, everyone at Faber, Gavin Friday, Brent Gibbons, Carole Heshmati,

Paddy Higgisson, Ashley Kahn, Wolfram Knauer, Martin Lane, Lisa Light, Douglas McCabe, Cindy McGuirl, Carol and Seamus O'Cleireacain, Sean O'Neill, Dan Papps, Robert Percy, Ian Preece, Francesca Ryan, Tim Scott Hunter, Nathaniel Volfango, Paul Waugh, and Robert Whyte and the Nine Fine Irishmen.

Some special mentions: artist Ann Hamilton for generous use of the cover image; writer Amelia Etherton for her supreme editorial skills and direction; and the late music writer Richard Cook for many other significant sparks and stimulations.

Phyllis Oyama and Lee Townsend at Songtone, Bill Frisell's management and production company, deserve their own *Beautiful Dreamer* outstanding achievement awards; without their unwavering belief and support some of this book would not have been possible.

Much the same could be said for Bill Frisell's close family – his wife, Carole d'Inverno, daughter Monica and brother Bob – who showed me enormous kindness and trust.

Just when I was starting to think that I might be writing for an audience of one, two people came along who completely got *Beautiful Dreamer*, and instantly understood its value and potential: my brilliant agent David Godwin and visionary editor Alexa von Hirschberg.

Finally, the lifetime achievement awards: to my late parents, Joan and Ron, and my dad in particular – a very large part of reason I became a journalist in the first place; and to Jacqueline O'Driscoll, my first reader, astute adviser and ultimate champion, to whom this book is dedicated, with much love.

Plate Section One

p1

The Frisell family home at 949 Krameria Street, Denver, 1951. Courtesy of Bob Frisell.

Baby 'Billy' with his parents, Bill and Jane, Krameria Street, 1952. The painting of a Baltimore street scene on the wall is by Frisell's father. Courtesy of Bob Frisell.

Three-year-old Bill, pliers in hand, in front of his parents' 1951 Plymouth; this photograph was used for the cover of Frisell's 1990 album *Is That You?* Courtesy of Bill Frisell.

p2

Bill and his paternal 'grandpa', Ole, Krameria Street, Christmas 1954. Courtesy of Bill Frisell.

Five-year-old Bill playing his grandfather's euphonium. He is sitting on a cobbler's bench he helped Ole build, and which he still has today. One of his father's paintings again hangs on the wall. Courtesy of Bill Frisell.

Bill (*right*), thirteen, with his mother Jane and younger brother Bob outside the house at 3401 East 7th Avenue, Denver. Bill is holding 'Walk, Don't Run '64', a single by instrumental surf rockers the Ventures. Courtesy of Bob Frisell.

p3

A pivotal moment: clarinet in one hand; his first electric guitar, a brand new Fender Mustang, in the other. Bill and Bob in the garden at 3401 East 7th Ave, June 1965. Courtesy of Bill Frisell.

Bill in his Gold Sash Band uniform, Denver, December 1965; he was first chair clarinet. Courtesy of Bill Frisell.

Fifteen-year-old Bill practising at home with his brother Bob. Courtesy of Bill Frisell.

p4

Frisell's East High School graduation photo, Denver, 1969. Courtesy of Bill
Frisell.

Frisell, Denver, Christmas 1972, during the 'hard years'. Courtesy of Bob
Gillis.

Frisell (*back, left*) and Kermit Driscoll (*front, third from right*) sport pop band
Boston Connection's orange polyester suits, Boston, 1976. Courtesy of
Kermit Driscoll.

p5

Smokin' Bill with (*left to right*) Vinnie Johnson, Kermit Driscoll and Michel
Herr (the Good Buddies band), backstage, Belgium, late 1978. Courtesy of
the Michel Herr collection.

The Mauve Traffic quintet: (*left to right*) Frisell, Kermit Driscoll, Steve
Houben, Vinnie Johnson and Michel Herr, backstage, Belgium, late 1978.
Courtesy of the Michel Herr collection.

Carole and Bill on their wedding day, Greenville, North Carolina, August
1979. Courtesy of Bob Frisell.

p6

Frisell in 1987 with his Gibson SG, the 'rock axe' he played from the mid-
seventies to late eighties. Photograph by Robyn Stoutenburg courtesy of
ECM Records.

Frisell's first band: (left to right) Kermit Driscoll, Hank Roberts, Frisell and
Joey Baron, New York, 1987. Photograph by Robyn Stoutenburg courtesy
of ECM Records.

p7

'Tomorrow's Guitarist Today': Frisell's first DownBeat cover, May 1989.
Courtesy of *DownBeat* magazine.

John Zorn's Naked City: (*left to right*) Wayne Horvitz, Zorn, Joey Baron,
Frisell and Fred Frith, New York, 1990. Portrait by ©1990 Timothy
Greenfield-Sanders.

Frisell on stage with Naked City, Florence, Italy, 1990; he is directing his
attentions at Zorn. Photographer unknown.

p8

A portrait of Frisell by cartoonist (and guitarist) Gary Larson, 1997. *Copyright © 1997 FarWorks, Inc. All rights reserved. Used with permission.*

A 'psychological portrait' of Frisell by cartoonist Jim Woodring – part of his artwork for Frisell's 2001 album With Dave Holland and Elvin Jones. Drawing by Jim Woodring copyright © 2001. All rights reserved. Used with permission.

Plate Section Two

p1

Four of Frisell's drawings of 'distorted, anxious-looking, guitar-wielding cowboys/man-boys'. The top two were used on the cover of Frisell's 2002 album *The Willies*. Courtesy of Bill Frisell.

p2

Frisell with his Telecaster-style guitar featuring 'custom artwork' by painter Claude Utley, Seattle, May 2002. Photograph by Michael Wilson copyright © 2002. All rights reserved. Used with permission.

Frisell with Jenny Scheinman and Greg Leisz, Columbus, Ohio, March 2007, during the first performances of Frisell's music for *Disfarmer*. Photograph by Michael Wilson copyright © 2007. All rights reserved. Used with permission.

p3

Trioism: Frisell, Paul Motian, Joe Lovano, New York, April 2007. Photograph by John Abbott copyright © 2007. All rights reserved. Used with permission.

Frisell and Jim Hall during the recording of *Hemispheres*, New York, September 2007. Photograph by David Korchin copyright © 2007. All rights reserved. Used with permission.

p4

(*Left to right*) Ron Miles, Tony Scherr, Kenny Wollesen and Frisell play Frisell's music for Bill Morrison's film *The Great Flood*, Seattle, March 2013. Photograph by Daniel Sheehan copyright © 2013. All rights reserved. Used with permission.

The *Beautiful Dreamers* trio: (*left to right*) Eyvind Kang, Frisell, Rudy Royston, SFJAZZ Center, San Francisco, September 2013. Photograph by Monica Jane Frisell copyright © 2013. All rights reserved. Used with permission.

p5

Good Dog, Happy Man: Frisell in his music room in Seattle, 2014, with two Collings guitars and Monica's dog Lucy. Photograph by Monica Jane Frisell copyright © 2014. All rights reserved. Used with permission.

Frisell with Paul Simon on *The Late Show with Stephen Colbert*, New York, May 2017. CBS Photo Archive/Scott Kowalchyk via Getty Images.

p6

Frisell, plus pedals and effects units, during the recording of *Music IS*, Flora studios, Portland, Oregon, August 2017. Photograph by Monica Jane Frisell copyright © 2017. All rights reserved. Used with permission.

p7

Frisell's wife Carole d'Inverno photographed by his daughter Monica, Brooklyn, New York, 2019. Photograph by Monica Jane Frisell copyright © 2019. All rights reserved. Used with permission.

Self-portrait by Monica Frisell, *Truth or Consequences*, New Mexico, 2020. Photograph by Monica Jane Frisell copyright © 2020. All rights reserved. Used with permission.

p8

Frisell in Carole's studio in Brooklyn, New York during the pandemic, December 2020. The Telecaster body has artwork by Seattle painter Terry Turrell. Photograph by Carole d'Inverno copyright © 2020. All rights reserved. Used with permission.

All direct quotes attributed to Bill Frisell, unless otherwise stated, are from interviews with the author: Seattle, 19–20 February and 2–4 December 2015; London, 20 October 2015; Denver, 3 March 2017; and New York, 17 March 2017.

Epigraphs

'*Now I will do nothing but listen*': Walt Whitman, section 26 of 'Song of Myself', in *Edward Weston: Leaves of Grass* (Paddington Press, 1976), p25.
'*You can only go as far forward as*': Rahsaan Roland Kirk, quoted by drummer Ralph Peterson Jr, in 'Smoking the Opposition', an interview with the author, *The Wire*, December 1990.

1. The Searcher

The idea came from a whole lot of different: Rahsaan Roland Kirk, in 1960s footage featured in the 2014 documentary *The Case of the Three-Sided Dream*, written and directed by Adam Kahan.
The Brubeck epiphany is detailed in *Flights of the Soul: Visions, Heavenly Journeys and Peak Experiences in the Biblical World* (William B. Eerdmans, 2011) by John J. Pilch, p84.
Yeah, yeah, yeah, that sounds exactly what: Kenny Wollesen, author interview, Antwerp, Belgium, 16 August 2015.
A dream like that is not just another wild: Eyvind Kang, author interview, Seattle, 15 February 2015.
It's about something transcendental he can't: Jim Woodring, author interview, Seattle, 14 February 2015.
the most significant and widely imitated guitarist: Mike Zwerin, in 'Bill Frisell Lets the Human Spirit Do the Work', the *New York Times/International Herald Tribune*, 20 June 1998.
the musing poet of the jazz guitar: Ivan Hewett, in 'Glimpses of Magic in the Landscape', the *Daily Telegraph*, 23 November 2009.
the most distinctive stylist in contemporary jazz: attributed to the *New Yorker* in

the press kit for Frisell's 1998 album *Gone, Just Like a Train*.

jazz is more of a verb than a noun: Pat Metheny, in 'Pat Metheny Group: Jazz and Hip Hop Now Live Here', by Tim Blangger, the *Morning Call* (Allentown, Pennsylvania), 27 January 1995.

I'm fine with being described as: Bill Frisell, author interview by phone, 18 October 2012.

Frisell plays guitar like Miles Davis played: preview in 'Goings On About Town', the *New Yorker*, 14 July 1997.

The older I get, the more I keep looking back: Bill Frisell, author interview by phone, 18 October 2012.

the Clark Kent of the electric guitar: Gene Santoro, review of *Lookout for Hope*, *Spin*, May 1988.

Bill Frisell's influence on what is now: Steve Futterman, in 'Goings On About Town', the *New Yorker*, 24/31 December 2018.

maestro of all guitar possibilities: Michael Horovitz, in a review of Marianne Faithfull and Bill Frisell at the Queen Elizabeth Hall, London, *Jazzwise*, September 2013.

Bill is like nothing else – there's jazz guitar: Dave King, in 'A Voice in Jazz History that Changed the Game', an interview by Chuck Helm for *Fourth Wall*, an online magazine of the Walker Arts Center, Minneapolis, 27 September 2017.

America has this race issue because it's: Ron Miles, author interview, Denver, 4 March 2017.

one of the 'most influential artists in music today': Ben Beaumont-Thomas, in 'Bon Iver, Frank Ocean and . . . Shania Twain? Here are the Most Influential Artists in Music Today', the *Guardian*, 1 March 2018.

I don't think there's anybody else that: Justin Vernon, author interview, Dublin, 4 June 2017.

favourite guitarist in the whole world: Lucinda Williams, in Emma Franz's film *Bill Frisell: A Portrait* (2017).

I keep thinking, 'How am I going to make': Lucinda Williams, in 'Perspective of Time, Age Lifts Lucinda Williams' New Album', by Glenn Gamboa, the *Columbus Dispatch*, 17 April 2016.

He is one of America's most unique musicians: Elvis Costello, in liner notes to *The Best of Bill Frisell Vol 1: Folk Songs* (Nonesuch, 2009).

I feel completely covered playing with him: Marianne Faithfull, author interview by phone, 19 July 2016.

the favourite guitarist of many people: Paul Desmond on Jim Hall, quoted in

Jazz and its Discontents: A Francis Davis Reader (Da Capo Press, 2004), pp230–231.

2: Billy the Kid

They got a 1951 Plymouth, brand new: Bill Frisell, in 'Interview with Bill Frisell', by Ethan Iverson, January 2018, published on Ethan Iverson's blog *Do the Math*, 1 July 2018.

We started out with Billy in the back seat: Jane Frisell, from a private collection of her essays and recollections, courtesy of Bob Frisell.

My father was interested in her: Bob Frisell, author interview by phone, 6/7 February 2017.

In 1928 Ole built a cedarwood log cabin: he would go there with friends and relatives to hunt, mostly for deer; remarkably it is still there, though in need of extensive restoration.

Her German-American family had worked hard: Fleagle is most likely an Americanised spelling of the southern German surname Flügel or Fluegel.

There has been an 'Uncle Ben' in every generation: Matt Fleagle on the fleaglefamily.wordpress.com blog, 14 July 2015.

'a man of unbending integrity': from *The Guthrie Family*, a private history, courtesy of Bill Frisell.

Our grandfather was conservative: Bob Frisell, author interview by phone, 6/7 February 2017.

My mother used to sing and whistle: Bill Frisell, in 'Bill Frisell Interview', by Dan Kern, on the blog *Six String Soul*, 1 September 2004.

I can't imagine this now: Bill Frisell, in 'Wide Open Spaces', by Geoffrey Himes, the Baltimore *City Paper*, 10 September 2002.

Nordic people have a reputation for shyness: Joe Moran, in *Shrinking Violets: A Field Guide to Shyness* (Profile Books, 2016), pp69–70.

Talking apparently never ceases to be a problem: Susan Sontag, in 'A Letter from Sweden', p26 (quoted in Moran, p99, ibid).

I remember one evening: Bob Frisell, author interview by phone, 6/7 February 2017.

positive associations, suggesting someone who is: Joe Moran, in *Shrinking Violets: A Field Guide to Shyness* (Profile Books, 2016), p99.

Jansson's lesson is not that shy people should: ibid, p189.

Bill's father painted his entire life: he produced many hundreds of landscapes, often with birch trees, some urban scenes, in oils and watercolours.

From a really, really little kid I remember: Bill Frisell, in 'Interview with Bill
    Frisell', by Anita Malhotra, on her *Artsmania* blog, posted 17 June 2014.
a liberal college town in the foothills of the Rockies: later in the sixties Boulder
    would become a magnet for hippies and lovers of alternative lifestyles.
The first stuff that ever got me fired up: Bill Frisell, in 'Bill Frisell's Beach Blanket
    Guitar', by Britt Robson, the Minneapolis *Star Tribune*, 2 July 2014.
I didn't know what was going on, but I knew: Bill Frisell, in 'Bill Frisell,
    Reclaiming the Elation', by Geoffrey Himes, *DownBeat*, November 2014.
Ed 'Big Daddy' Roth, Bob Dylan, Miles Davis: Bill Frisell, in '8-Ball: Bill Frisell',
    a Q&A posted on the Walker Art Center, Minneapolis website, walkerart.
    org, 1 April 2005.
most character-building experience: Bill Frisell, ibid.
[The Beatles were] absolutely gigantic: Bill Frisell, in 'The {vurb} Interview with
    Bill Frisell', by Greg Nesteroff, the *Nelson Star* (British Columbia), 13 June
    2012. In the liner notes to *All We Are Saying*, Frisell's 2011 album of songs
    by John Lennon, he writes: '1964. I saw an article in *Time* magazine about
    a group called the Beatles. Wow! Look at their hair! And those suits, and
    boots, and stuff . . . Then I heard the MUSIC. Man alive! That was IT.'
It was absolutely shocking, devastating: Bill Frisell, in 'Lennon Songs', by Bob
    Weinberg, *Jazziz*, fall 2009.
For those of us who were already the freaks: Steven Van Zandt, in 'Let Them Eat
    Rock', by John Seabrook, the *New Yorker*, 28 May 2018.
I flunked speech class in school: Bill Frisell, in 'Bill Frisell: Made to Shine', by
    Nick Millevoi, *Premier Guitar*, May 2018.
rustic and rough-hewn: Paul Malkoski, in *The Denver Folk Music Tradition*
    (History Press, 2012), p33.
Judy Collins would regularly play: Collins had also been a student at East High
    School; she graduated in 1957.
Denver may have been an isolated backwater: even the Beatles failed to sell out
    the famous 9,000-seat Red Rocks Amphitheatre just outside the city in
    August 1964; it was the only venue on their debut twenty-six-date tour of
    the US and Canada to do so.
A few other things happened in 1964: Bill Frisell, in his liner notes to *All We Are
    Saying* (Savoy Jazz, 2011).
Manfred Mann's . . . 'Do Wah Diddy Diddy': went to number one in the US
    charts in October 1964. The song was first recorded the year before, as 'Do-
    Wah-Diddy', by African American vocal group the Exciters.
I think the guitar was $215 and the amp $165: Frisell paid 'Happy' Logan

a few dollars every week until the outstanding amount was cleared; 'Somewhere I still have the little notebook in which I'd write down every payment,' he says.

When I first started playing guitar: Bill Frisell, in 'On the Road to Bill Frisell', by William Stephenson, *Jazziz*, May 1997.

3. Once Upon a Time in the West

It was kind of like Leave it to Beaver: a reference to the late fifties/early sixties feelgood American TV sitcom about a goofy yet wholesome boy and his archetypal suburban family.

second-hand Fender Jaguar: the sunburst finish had been scraped off and Frisell later had the body painted white.

East High's 'strong academic record' and 'ambitious standards': alumni include silent film star Harold Lloyd; Hattie McDaniel, the first African American to win an Oscar; Beatnik hipster and muse Neal Cassady; bestselling novelist Sidney Sheldon; and screen actors Pam Grier and Don Cheadle.

It was like a beacon of political progressiveness: Ron Miles, author interview, Denver, 4 March 2017. Miles moved with his family to Denver when he was eleven and still lives in the Park Hill neighbourhood of the city, just off Colfax Avenue. He and Frisell are close; Miles has Bill's grandfather's cornet hanging on the wall of his music room at home.

There were a lot of vocal groups, Temptations-type: Bill Frisell, in 'ECM's Lyrical "House Guitarist"', by Josef Woodard, *Guitar Player*, April 1985.

soul bands backing up singers: Bill Frisell, in 'The Clark Kent of the Electric Guitar', by Gene Santoro, in *Dancing in Your Head* (Oxford University Press, 1994), p271.

Frisell was living through a period of . . . political unrest: this was also the era of the Cold War and the threat of nuclear armageddon. A thousand public buildings across Denver were designated nuclear fallout shelters and the city boasted the nation's first model homes featuring built-in nuclear shelters.

In Denver, schools were closed: including East High, whose students, according to a report in the *Denver Post* the day following Martin Luther King's assassination, were 'thirty-six per cent Negro'.

Tequila: featured Montgomery with a consummate trio of Ron Carter on bass, Ray Barretto on congas and Grady Tate on drums. Production was similarly impeccable: the silky string arrangements were by German composer Claus Ogerman, then at the peak of his creative powers; the session was recorded by Rudy Van Gelder at his storied studio in Englewood Cliffs, New Jersey; and producer for the Verve label was the legendary Creed Taylor.

[The girls] were going to use the record: Bill Frisell, in 'Bill Frisell on Wes Montgomery', as told to Dan Ouellette, *DownBeat*, July 2004.

Everything changed from that moment on: ibid.

Charlie Christian was my inspiration: Wes Montgomery, quoted in Burt Korall's liner notes to *Tequila* (Verve, 1966).

He decided to seek out other Wes Montgomery albums . . . First stop was his local Woolworths: in other interviews, Frisell has said the department store was Walgreens, and the albums were 89 cents each.

I got The Wes Montgomery Trio *record*: the 1959 album, which is subtitled *A Dynamic New Sound*, features Melvin Rhyne on organ and Paul Parker on drums, and includes swinging straight-ahead interpretations of jazz standards such as Thelonious Monk's 'Round Midnight', Duke Ellington and Billy Strayhorn's 'Satin Doll', and Jerome Kern's 'Yesterdays'.

the live recording My Funny Valentine: as well as Davis and Carter, the Miles Davis group consisted of George Coleman on tenor saxophone, Herbie Hancock on piano, and nineteen-year-old Tony Williams on drums; the concert at the prestigious Philharmonic Hall of New York's Lincoln Center was staged partly in memory of John F. Kennedy and held on 12 February 1964. Three days earlier the Beatles had appeared on *The Ed Sullivan Show*; on the same night, little more than half a mile or so away, the band was playing Carnegie Hall.

There is a spirit here in Denver and Colorado: Megan Friedel, author interview, Denver, 9 March 2017.

From age twelve to sixteen or seventeen, I raced: Bill Frisell, in 'An Uncategorizable Guitarist Returns to His Roots', by Dan Forte, *Vintage Guitar*, December 2014.

I never got into the physical thing: Bill Frisell, in 'The Axman Cometh: Bill Frisell Turns Jazz Guitar Inside Out', by Joseph Hooper, the *New York Observer*, 27 October 1997.

my parents allowed my friends to come over: 'Some of my friends had to struggle a lot more with their parents,' says Frisell. 'They had to sneak out of their houses to go play music.'

They were very supportive, but they also: Carole d'Inverno, author interview, Seattle, 18 February 2015.

Bill was one of the first in his large Denver school: Jane Frisell, in her essay 'Prance in a Black Robe', dated 24 April 1978 (courtesy of Bob Frisell).

466

Bill was tall, wore glasses, had lots of hair: Dale Bruning, author interview by phone, 15 December 2014. Bruning continued to teach, on all instruments, in the Denver area for the next fifty years; he estimates he has taught more than 1,800 students.

The first time I heard Wes Montgomery: Bill Frisell, in 'Extended Lesson: Bill Frisell interviews Jim Hall', *Fretboard Journal* (winter 2008/January 2009) and in 'Bill Frisell and Jim Hall: Free Stylists', by Evan Haga, *JazzTimes*, April 2009.

a legitimate instrument, not just a poppy thing: Bill Frisell, in 'ECM's Lyrical "House Guitarist"', by Josef Woodard, *Guitar Player*, April 1985.

It was at a very crucial time in my life: Bill Frisell, in 'Jazz Guitarist Dale Bruning Looks Back on His Love of Music and Teaching', by Jon Solomon, Denver *Westword*, 20 March 2012, and in a subsequent *Westword* blog, 23 March 2012.

together they saw the Gary Burton Quartet: Frisell remembers the line-up with Burton as David Pritchard on guitar, Steve Swallow on double and electric bass, and Bill Goodwin on drums.

Bill had a different sound even back then: Bob Gillis, author interview, Lakewood, Denver, 8 March 2017.

4. A Portrait of the Guitarist as a Young Man

When I studied with [Dennis] Sandole: Dale Bruning, author interview by phone, 15 December 2014.

the guitar that changed the world: quoted in *Rockabilly: The Twang Heard 'Round the World: The Illustrated History*, by Greil Marcus, Peter Guralnick, Luc Sante and Robert Gordon (Voyageur Press, 2011), p40. Versions of the Gibson ES-175 have also been played by guitarists ranging from free improviser Derek Bailey to rockers Steve Howe of Yes and Buck Dharma of Blue Öyster Cult, BB King to Andy Summers and The Edge.

It was a big deal, he was passing this along: Bill Frisell, in 'Lost & Found: Bill Frisell's ES-175', by Jason Verlinde, *Fretboard Journal*, April 2014.

It was a heavy thing, the best guitar I ever owned: Bill Frisell, ibid.

Smith had spent most of the fifties in New York...: for more on Johnny Smith's life and musical times, see 'Guitar Legend Johnny Smith Alive and Well in Colorado Springs', by Bob Campbell, the *Colorado Springs Independent*, 15 March 2001 (available online).

Johnny Smith had a music store: Colorado Springs is south of Denver and 130 miles from Greeley. At weekends Smith played in a bar called Shaner's in downtown Denver with Dale Bruning, who switched to acoustic bass for the gigs, and drummer Derryl Goes, director of the number-one jazz band at UNC, the ensemble in which Frisell was playing.

It was as if the course just happened to have: Bill Frisell, as told to Evan Haga, in 'Bill Frisell Remembers Johnny Smith', on *JazzTimes.com*, posted 6 April 2014.

I wanted to be a modern avant-garde bebop: Bill Frisell, in the liner notes to *The Maid with the Flaxen Hair: A Tribute to Johnny Smith*, Mary Halvorson with Bill Frisell (Tzadik, 2018).

Johnny Smith will always be the poet laureate: Chip Stern, in 'Johnny Smith, Four Appreciations', on chipstern.com.

Frisell was full of self-doubt and insecurity: like Frisell, Smith was by most accounts extremely modest, reserved and self-effacing – he once made the erroneous claim that 'I never considered myself a jazz guitar player, just a guitar player'.

He was so encouraging to me: Bill Frisell, as told to Evan Haga, in 'Bill Frisell Remembers Johnny Smith', on *JazzTimes.com*, posted 6 April 2014.

Baker was a gifted trombonist and experienced musician: he had played in bands led by Woody Herman and Stan Kenton, and was principal trombonist with the Greeley Philharmonic Orchestra.

One day I was so discouraged and I was thinking about: Bill Frisell, email to author, 30 April 2018.

We were on stage. I did not stand up: Bill Frisell, ibid.

Some members of the high-school faculty were markedly critical: However, Frisell's parents, as his mother Jane was to later write, 'were proud that Bill was strong enough to put himself on the line and take the consequences'.

Dress and Conduct Code for UNC Jazz Ensembles: as quoted in 'Letter Chastizes UNC Jazz Ensemble', in the *Mirror*, the student newspaper of the University of Northern Colorado, 3 May 1971.

I remember my parents were . . . like, 'Oh my God': Bill Frisell, in 'Bill Frisell on Studying with Dale Bruning: I don't know if I'd really be playing now if it wasn't for him', by Jon Solomon, Denver *Westword*, 23 March 2012.

Not only did Bill's new focus on the guitar: Dale Bruning, author interview by phone, 15 December 2014.

At that time, I couldn't see anything but basically: Bill Frisell, in 'Interview with Bill Frisell', January 2018, published on Ethan Iverson's blog *Do the Math*, 1 July 2018.

I think I barely played a note; I was like the: Bill Frisell, ibid.

It was awesome . . . but as far as being able to decipher it: Bill Frisell, ibid.

It didn't click: Bill Frisell, ibid.

the father of modern jazz guitar: Pat Metheny, in 'Bill Frisell & Friends Pay Tribute to Jim Hall at Blue Note', by Bill Milkowski, *DownBeat*, July 2014.

couldn't teach someone how *to play*: Jim Hall, ibid.

breaking apart the run-of-the-mill guitar voicings: Bill Frisell, in 'Turn Down the Amp', by Brian Glasser, *Jazzwise*, May 2000.

into a fluid, wind instrument kind of thing: Bill Frisell, ibid.

Jimmy Giuffre's 'compositional approach to performing jazz': Jim Hall, in 'Jim Hall: Jazz Guitar Elegance', by Jim Ferguson and Arnie Berle, *Guitar Player*, May 1983.

It wasn't just about the guitar: Bill Frisell, in 'Bill Frisell and Jim Hall: Free Stylists', by Evan Haga, *JazzTimes*, April 2009.

[It's] kind of my philosophy about everything: Jim Hall, ibid.

Bill's a very sensitive, sort of quiet: Kenny Vaughan, author interview by phone, 1 March 2018.

My hair was really long: Bill Frisell, in 'The Unpredictable World of Bill Frisell', by Matt Resnicoff, *Guitar Player*, January 1996.

In Denver, you can't make a living: Ron Miles, in 'Splendid Isolation', by Shaun Brady, *Jazziz*, winter 2015.

Denver in the seventies was a Wonderland: Kenny Vaughan, author interview by phone, 1 March 2018.

real strong undercurrent of eclecticism: Rudy Royston, author interview by phone, 12 December 2016.

Ornette Coleman . . . 'always loved': Bill Frisell, email to Adam Levy, 12 February 2017.

I wanted to play guitar like Paul Bley played piano: Bill Frisell, ibid.

There is always one moment in childhood: Graham Greene, in *The Power and the Glory* (Vintage, 2010), p6.

we just played standards and stuff: Bill Frisell, ibid.

It wasn't right to be pretending: Bill Frisell, in 'Uncategorically Bill Frisell', by Richard Harrington, the *Washington Post*, 17 November 2006.

If you don't play yourself, you're nothing: Art Pepper, in *Straight Life, The Story of Art Pepper*, by Art and Laurie Pepper (Da Capo, 1994), p376.

5. Raised by Deer

So yeah, there was this Czech woman: Tony Scherr, author interview, Antwerp, Belgium, 16 August 2015.

We have this American expression: Ron Miles, author interview, Denver, Colorado, 4 March 2017.

I think Bill is often misunderstood: Jenny Scheinman, author interview via email, 27 April 2016.

something of a spectral presence: Jim Woodring, author interview, Seattle, 14 February 2015.

I think it's healthy, I can't imagine what: Bill Frisell, in 'Unironic', by Francis Davis, the *Atlantic*, July/August 2002.

If he couldn't play, he would just: Carole d'Inverno, author interview, Seattle, 18 February 2015.

I actually had Bill play something for me: Hal Willner, author interview, New York, 4 April 2017.

Bill is just reserved and cautious; he checks you out: Carole d'Inverno, email to author, 13 January 2021.

raised by deer: Lindsey Horner, confirmed in email to author, 16 January 2019.

Frisell wouldn't be the first performer to: the great jazz tenor saxophonist Lester Young, for example, was also noted for his taciturnity – which was sometimes, like Frisell, just as misconstrued. 'He has the well-deserved reputation of being comfortably shy, and would be content to gaze silently at his pigeon-turned feet rather than talk,' wrote Pat Harris in a *DownBeat* profile in 1949. 'Shy about everything except playing that horn.'

He's not shy. See, that's the thing: Claudia Engelhart, author interview, London, 20 October 2015.

That's what's so great about music: Joey Baron, author interview via Skype, 22 April 2016.

Music is how I express myself: Bill Frisell, author interview by phone, 18 October 2012.

some things you have to know about Frisell: Jonathan Coe, in 'Bill Frisell, He Who Hesitates . . . Er . . .', *The Wire*, July 1989.

He's a haltingly articulate speaker: Dan Ouellette, in 'Introvert Meets Extrovert', *DownBeat*, February 2000.

I find Bill to be very precise: Eyvind Kang, author interview, Seattle, 15 February 2015.

The thing is that Bill knows he has this effect: John Cumming, author interview, London, 13 October 2014. Cumming, an inspirational concert programmer and promoter, and one of the co-founders of the London Jazz Festival, died in May 2020.

the voice, say, of a man who makes his living: Tom Junod, in 'The Guy Who Always Plays the Perfect Song', (American) *GQ*, February 1997.

He talks as though he is almost but not quite: Francis Davis, in 'Unironic', the *Atlantic*, July/August 2002.

Just as he delights in dismantling: Jonathan Coe, in 'Bill Frisell, He Who Hesitates . . . Er . . .' , in *The Wire*, July 1989.

Bill holds the silence for a little longer: Martin Hayes, author interview, Cork, Ireland, 16 November 2015.

fatter and fatter: Tom Junod, in 'The Guy Who Always Plays the Perfect Song', (American) *GQ*, February 1997.

Mr Frisell, in his person and in his playing: Joseph Hooper, in 'The Axman Cometh: Bill Frisell Turns Jazz Guitar Inside Out', observer.com, 27 October 1997.

I was with Bill at the end of his time at: Hank Roberts, author interview via Skype, 11 April 2016.

the great artists, rather than just getting: Cecil Taylor, quoted in 'The Message is Music: A Conversation with Bill Frisell', by Lloyd Peterson, *Earshot Jazz* (Seattle), June 2005.

Bill is so incredibly sweet and big-hearted: Joe Henry, author interview by phone, 27 March 2018.

I've played on other things, so I know: Ron Miles, author interview, Denver, 4 March 2017.

You know, that's just him!: Jason Moran, author interview, Antwerp, Belgium, 15 August 2015.

One of the keys to Bill's music: David Breskin, author interview via Skype, 27 February 2018.

With his boyish face, round glasses: Geoffrey Himes, in 'Wide Open Spaces: Bill Frisell Finds the Jazz Vibe in Country Music's Roomy Expanse', the Baltimore *City Paper*, 10 September 2002.

One of the things that I've known about Bill: Nels Cline, author interview via Skype, 19 July 2017.

I feel a little unqualified and out of my depth: Dave Douglas, author interview via Skype, 26 August 2016.

I've had the chance to watch Bill over the years: Jim Woodring, author interview, Seattle, 14 February 2015.

He's my great high example of incredible: Bill Frisell, in 'All-American Bill', by Chris Parker, *Jazz, The Magazine*, No. 18, 1993.

I can remember soon after we first moved: Carole d'Inverno, author interview, Seattle, 18 February 2015.

The way his mind works: Carole d'Inverno, ibid.

He's superstitious about the coincidental: Jenny Scheinman, author interview via email, 27 April 2016.

I kind of hesitate to blow it up too much: Joey Baron, author interview via Skype, 22 April 2016.

There is great tension in the world: John Steinbeck, *East of Eden* (Penguin Modern Classics, 2000), chapter 13.

'social deafness' and 'low-heeled arrogance': Joe Moran, in *Shrinking Violets: A Field Guide to Shyness* (Profile Books, 2016), p4 and p63.

I hate to use this term, but there's this: Claudia Engelhart, author interview, London, 20 October 2015.

Bill will find a way to get what he wants: David Breskin, author interview via Skype, 27 February 2018.

the filthiest joke I've ever heard: Mike Gibbs, author interview via FaceTime, 3 September 2017.

I didn't write anything for a long time: Bill Frisell in 'Interview with Bill Frisell', by Ethan Iverson, posted on his *Do the Math* blog on 1 July 2018.

Oh yeah, he swears all the time: Claudia Engelhart, author interview, London, 20 October 2015.

People like to think of him as a gentle sort of soul: Rudy Royston, author interview by phone, 12 December 2016.

He holds a really quite unique balance: Joe Henry, author interview by phone, 27 March 2018.

6. Is That You?

We would play for hours and hours: Bill Frisell, email to Adam Levy, 12 February 2017.

The following day he met . . . Kermit Driscoll: Colby is a small prairie town in northwestern Kansas, 235 miles east of Denver.

That messed me up. It was bad, bad: Bill Frisell, in 'Interview with Bill Frisell', January 2018, published on Ethan Iverson's blog *Do the Math*, 1 July 2018.

light years ahead of what I could ever do: Bill Frisell, email to Adam Levy, 12 February 2017.

There really wasn't much of a lesson: Pat Metheny, author interview via email, 23 February 2017.

I couldn't believe it! There he was: Bill Frisell, in the programme notes for 'Michael Gibbs and Bill Frisell', a concert at the School of Music, University of Washington, Seattle, 14 January 2016.

In the harmony class they'd have: Bill Frisell, in 'Let's Get Lost: Touring the Harmonic Backroads with Bill Frisell', by Joe Gore, *Guitar Player*, July 1992.

When they first got to Berklee: Mike Gibbs, author interview via FaceTime, 3 September 2017.

It's one of the most aggressive things: Bill Frisell, in a Cuneiform Records press release for 'Michael Gibbs and the NDR Bigband Play a Bill Frisell Set List', June 2015.

Frisell had lucked out again: guitarist Leni Stern was taught by Damian from 1977–79 and she told me, 'Jon is one of the most magical guitar teachers I have ever seen. He was into free music, but at the same time he was a killer bebop player. And he was the most fun and fabulous and original person you could possibly imagine; he always got you thinking.'

'beautiful power' of B. B. King: Bill Frisell, in 'Farewell: Bill Frisell Remembers B. B. King', posted on JazzTimes.com, 18 May 2015.

'radical-conservative' classicism of the MJQ: Richard Cook and Brian Morton, in *The Penguin Guide to Jazz Recordings*, Ninth Edition (Penguin, 2008), p1014.

I remember going to Bill's apartment: Kermit Driscoll, author interview, Cliffside Park, New Jersey, 3 April 2017.

I remember one time we came back: Kermit Driscoll, ibid.

My ES-175 wasn't cutting it: Bill Frisell, in a Bill Frisell Facebook post, 10 July 2019.

I heard [Carlos] Santana play this incredible: Bill Frisell, in an extended version of 'A Week in Umbria with the Guitarists' Home Base of Kenny Wollesen and Tony Scherr', by Ted Panken, in *Downbeat*, October 2008 (posted on tedpanken.wordpress.com, 18 March 2014).

guitarist and vocalist Michael Gregory Jackson: Frisell saw Jackson in a duo with saxophonist and flutist Oliver Lake, and with pianist Anthony Davis and drummer Paul Maddox (who soon after changed his name to Pheeroan akLaff).

Toru 'Tiger' Okoshi: began teaching at the college in 1976; today he is professor of brass.

473

Tommy Campbell: later played with many jazz greats, including Sonny Rollins, Dizzy Gillespie and John McLaughlin.

Tiger's Baku was 'a hell of a band': Kermit Driscoll, author interview, Cliffside Park, New Jersey, 3 April 2017.

Tiger is an amazing writer, and it seemed: Leni Stern, author interview by phone, 11 September 2017.

Every other guitar player at Berklee: Mike Gibbs, author FaceTime interview, 3 September 2017.

Bill was very quiet and modest-looking: Leni Stern, author interview by phone, 11 September 2017.

Steve Houben: Houben's uncle was Jacques Pelzer, a well-known Belgian bebopper who also played alto and had been a strong influence on him. Pelzer played with and befriended Chet Baker during the trumpeter's many long stays in Europe from the late fifties until his death in Amsterdam in 1988. He also ran a pharmacy in Liège and was a popular companion and sympathetic supporter of many jazz musicians, especially from the US. Other than simply 'Jack', Pelzer was also known as 'The Pharmacist', because he dispensed drugs of all kinds.

It was very dark inside: Jean-Jacques Bloemers, author interview, Spa, Belgium, 18 August 2015.

jazz-funk with muscle: Michel Herr, author interview, Corbais, Belgium, 18 August 2015.

didn't promise, you know, nirvana, or riches: Steve Houben, author interview, Middelheim, Antwerp, Belgium, 16 August 2015.

There was nothing. Nothing. Nada: Kermit Driscoll, author interview, Cliffside Park, New Jersey, 3 April 2017.

I was attracted to him, of course: Carole d'Inverno, author interview, Seattle, 18 February 2015.

So I had to literally sit on his lap: Carole d'Inverno, ibid.

the first kind of professional real gig: Bill Frisell, in 'Bill Frisell, Infinite Set List', by Bill Milkowski, *DownBeat*, July 2017.

In these duos I was able to 'force' Bill: Eberhard Weber, author interview via email, 5 October 2017.

so terrified . . . Even travelling and staying: Bill Frisell, in 'Bill Frisell, the ECM Years', by John Kelman, posted on allaboutjazz.com, 26 April 2011.

The recording turned out to be tough: Eberhard Weber, author interview via email, 5 October 2017.

It was just a fun and informal session: Michel Herr, author interview, Corbais, Belgium, 18 August 2015.

It was a very big deal. But I think a part: Carole d'Inverno, email to author, 13 January 2021.

7. Trioism

He was sitting on the couch: Carole d'Inverno, author interview, Seattle, 18 February 2015.

The contact had come about via: Paul Motian had become friends with Pat Metheny during the previous few months, after they had toured together in a band led by the guitarist that, like Keith Jarrett's American Quartet, also included Charlie Haden and Dewey Redman. The group mostly played music from Metheny's new ECM release, the double album *80/81* (Jack DeJohnette plays drums on the record, but could not make the tour).

Bill had come a long way: Pat Metheny, author interview via email, 23 February 2017.

The following month Frisell went to Motian's apartment: the flat was on the twelfth floor of a building partly rented to musicians, artists and writers, and was described in a 1980 profile of Motian in *Modern Drummer* magazine as 'decorated with gongs, bells, maracas, plants, a piano, and a black five-piece drum set'.

I still remember, when he opened the door: Bill Frisell, in 'Interview with Bill Frisell', January 2018, published on Ethan Iverson's blog *Do the Math*, 1 July 2018.

We got along really well: Paul Motian, in 'Profile: Paul Motian', by Josef Woodard, *Jazziz*, May 1995.

Getting that call, and going over to his: Bill Frisell, in 'Bill Frisell Interview: Outtakes, Working with Paul Motian and Greg Leisz', by Barry Cleveland, on GuitarPlayer.com, 22 June 2009.

It was always this thing of, playing a gig: Bill Frisell, in 'Interview with Bill Frisell', January 2018, published on Ethan Iverson's blog *Do the Math*, 1 July 2018.

conjuring this atmosphere that you can really: Bill Frisell, in an ECM press release for *Small Town*, an album by Bill Frisell and Thomas Morgan, May 2017.

It was magical . . . Very creative. Very spontaneous: Joe Lovano, in 'Bill Frisell's Big Ocean', by Celeste Sunderland, posted on allaboutjazz.com, 14 September 2004.

Someone once said to me, 'It doesn't make any difference': Paul Motian, in 'A Fireside Chat with Paul Motian, by Fred Jung, *Jazz Weekly*, date unknown.

Paul grew up poor: David McGuirl, in a biographical introduction to *The Compositions of Paul Motian, Volumes 1 & 2* (Cynthia McGuirl, 2016 and 2018).

considered it a better option than being: Paul Motian, in 'Head to Toes', by Ben Ratliff, in *The Jazz Ear: Conversations Over Music* (Times Books, 2008), p172.

In this group Motian created a highly interactive: Barry Kernfeld (editor), *The New Grove Dictionary of Jazz*, (Oxford University Press, 2001).

Motian evolved into a drummer who could: Ethan Iverson, in 'Conception in Time', in the booklet to the six-CD ECM box set *Paul Motian*, released April 2013.

I was Bill Evans's drummer in the 1960s: Paul Motian, in a biographical introduction by David McGuirl to *The Compositions of Paul Motian, Volumes 1 & 2* (Cynthia McGuirl, 2016 and 2018).

I don't work in the States hardly at all: Paul Motian, in 'Profile: Paul Motian', by Josef Woodard, *Jazziz*, May 1995.

the geeky new kid on the block: John Cumming, author interview, London, 13 October 2014.

Spring, summer and fall – we played: Joe Lovano, author interview, Antwerp, Belgium, 13 August 2015.

We were playing one night somewhere in Italy: Paul Motian, from a transcript of a radio interview by Ted Panken on WKCR, Columbia University, New York, 7 September 2000 (posted on Panken's blog, *Today is the Question*, 25 March 2014).

For one extended moment, it just took off: Joe Lovano, author interview, Antwerp, Belgium, 13 August 2015.

That's the highest level of free group: Joshua Redman, in 'This is My Point', by Ben Ratliff, in *The Jazz Ear: Conversations Over Music* (Times Books, 2008), p138.

realised that rather than play more: Ethan Iverson, in 'Conception in Time', in the booklet to the six-CD ECM box set *Paul Motian*, released April 2013.

After many years, I realised that less is more: Paul Motian, in 'A Cultural Conversation: With Paul Motian, Master of Time, Defier of Age', by Larry Blumenfeld, the *Wall Street Journal*, 26 July 2011.

The track feels holy to me, like a kind of: Hank Shteamer, in 'Just Song: the Paul Motian Trio's "It Should've Happened a Long Time Ago"', on his blog, *Dark Forces Swing Blind Punches*, 21 January 2015.

For Bill and I to have a master musician: Joe Lovano, author interview, Antwerp, Belgium, 13 August 2015.

Motian felt close to the material: they were songs: many of these enduring American Songbook themes from the thirties and forties – 'I Got Rhythm', 'All the Things You Are', 'Just One of Those Things' – were written by artful and prolific composers such as George Gershwin, Cole Porter, Jerome Kern and Harold Arlen for Broadway, musical theatre and Hollywood films. They were Paul Motian's pop music.

Everyone has their favourite: there is even a 25,000-word doctoral dissertation – *A Study of Bill Frisell Through Paul Motian's* On Broadway *Recordings* by Travis Lewis (University of Illinois at Urbana-Champaign, 2016) – available online for those wishing to analyse Frisell's contributions further.

[the trio] do not so much play the standards: Tom Junod, in 'The Guy Who Always Plays the Perfect Song', (American) *GQ*, February 1997.

the highest musical moments: Bill Frisell, in 'Bill Frisell's Big Ocean', by Celeste Sunderland, posted on allaboutjazz.com, 14 September 2004.

One night Paul and Bill locked into this long interaction: Carole d'Inverno, author interview, Seattle, 18 February 2015.

It became an unmissable event: 'many musicians see [the trio] as a creative ideal in jazz,' wrote Ben Ratliff in *The Jazz Ear* (Times Books, 2008), p219; a year later the *New Yorker* described the triumvirate as 'one of the premier small groups of jazz' (issue of 30 August 2009).

No words for what I am feeling now: Bill Frisell, posted on his website, billfrisell.com, 22 November 2011.

8. The Rambler

None of it was exactly romantic: Carole d'Inverno, author interview, Seattle, 18 February 2015. All further quotes from Carole d'Inverno in this chapter, ibid.

New York . . . 'Fear City': The Council for Public Safety, *Welcome to Fear City: A Survival Guide for Visitors to the City of New York*, a booklet distributed at New York's airports and midtown hotels, around 1975.

In 1980 there were 1,814 murders: New York City Police Dept, as quoted in '1980 Called Worst Year of Crime in City History', by Leonard Buder, the *New York Times*, 25 February 1981. One of those crimes, on 8 December 1980, was the assassination of John Lennon.

Bob Moses was a massive turning point: Bill Frisell, in 'Interview with Bill Frisell', January 2018, published on Ethan Iverson's blog *Do the Math*, 1 July 2018.

Yeah, right away we connected: D. Sharpe had a wide and eclectic love of music, from Albert Ayler to Frank Sinatra, African drumming to all-female outsider-rockers The Shaggs. And, like Frisell, he liked to sketch and draw.

The gig didn't pay any money, like $20: Bill Frisell, in *Being Here: Conversations on Creating Music*, by Radhika Philip (self-published, 2013), p4.

Through drummer Charles Telerant: bass was provided by either Bruce Whitcomb or Dave Boonshoft, and in some ways this was a guitar power trio, plus Julian Summerhill's added effects – spoken-word poetry, vocal calls and cries, percussive piano clusters, a squeaky recorder. Summerhill later changed his name to Victor Bruce Godsey and he provides 'words and vocals' to a duo recording with Frisell, *American Blood*, released in 1994.

We played completely free as an ensemble: Julian Summerhill, in 'End of the World Sessions', in the News section on billfrisell.com, 9 November 2018.

Frisell loved Harris's warm and fluid playing: Harris had worked with two of Frisell's musical heroes, Michael Gregory Jackson and Sonny Rollins.

Stone Tiger caused quite an impact: towards the end of the band's time together, Frisell added further to Stone Tiger's go-ahead reputation by embracing, as had Pat Metheny before him, the recently developed Roland GR-300 guitar synthesiser. Luckily, the trial was short-lived.

Bill went from being, like, nobody: Kermit Driscoll, author interview, Cliffside Park, New Jersey, 3 April 2017. Driscoll also moved to New York at the beginning of 1980. The bassist had begun a relationship with Michelle Renaux, a social worker in Spa who was also a serious jazz fan, and they married in Belgium in December 1979.

Bill was wildly creative: Chris Massey, quoted in Bryan Aaker's Bill Frisell Discography at bryanaaker.net.

It was a different musical time: Eberhard Weber, author interview via email, 5 October 2017.

I was immediately attracted to Bill's playing: Jan Garbarek, author interview by phone, 9 October 2017.

the ECM boss passed on The Frisell Tape: Norwegian bassist and composer Arild Andersen had played on one of the very first ECM LPs, Jan Garbarek's *Afric Pepperbird*, and recorded with pianist Bobo Stenson and guitarist Terje Rypdal for the label.

it was to be a quartet: with English pianist John Taylor, whom Frisell knew
   through Taylor's work with Kenny Wheeler and Norma Winstone, and
   American drummer Alphonse Mouzon, whom Bill revered for his power-
   playing on classic seventies sessions with Weather Report, McCoy Tyner
   and guitarist Larry Coryell.

Eberhard Weber's next record, Later That Evening (ECM, 1982): Weber on
   bass, with a leading American quartet of Bill Frisell; Paul McCandless, one
   of the founders of 'world fusion' group Oregon, on reeds; Lyle Mays, of
   the Pat Metheny Group, on piano; and Michael DiPasqua on drums and
   percussion. It's an album that promises more than it delivers, with Frisell
   providing little more than additional atmospherics.

Paths, Prints *is by far the more successful*: the three Europeans knew each other
   of old – as well as Weber's recent work with Garbarek, Christensen had
   been an integral part of Weber's extraordinary mid-seventies Colours band
   and been playing in various Garbarek line-ups since the saxophonist was a
   teenager in Oslo in the sixties.

I will always treasure that album – thanks to Bill: Jan Garbarek, ibid.

John Coltrane's A Love Supreme *took just four*: as detailed in *A Love Supreme:
   The Creation of John Coltrane's Classic Album*, by Ashley Kahn (Granta,
   2002), pp84, 94.

It was also standard for Eicher and ECM: such a *modus operandi* probably
   didn't hurt Eicher's production costs either. Even though ECM was
   starting to enjoy the unique rewards of Keith Jarrett's *The Köln Concert* – a
   transporting live double LP released in 1975 that has gone on to become
   the best-selling solo album in jazz, and the all-time best-selling piano album
   in any genre – ECM was then, and remains today, a small independent
   label with lofty ambitions but modest budgets.

Even today it seems an extraordinary notion: that instinct is no doubt the secret
   of Eicher's maverick genius, adventuresome spirit and often winning
   strategies – the greatest risks reap the biggest rewards. All or nothing at all,
   as Sinatra once sang.

I've thought about this a lot since: Frisell says he is to blame 'for not standing up
   for myself at the time'. You can almost see the diffidence and disorientation
   in the photograph of Frisell on the back of the original LP cover – the
   goofy smile and embarrassed mien, the way he appears to be scratching
   his tilted head. In his thick-rimmed glasses and patterned woolly jumper,
   he looks more like a recently qualified chemistry tutor than the fearless
   messenger of the music of tomorrow.

If anybody was to ask me, 'What's so great': Joey Baron, author interview via
Skype, 22 April 2016.

When I first heard it, I said, 'This is my': Petra Haden, author interview,
London, 20 November 2016.

I wanted to say something big: Bill Frisell, in 'ECM's Lyrical "House Guitarist"',
by Josef Woodard, *Guitar Player*, April 1985.

I'm a commuter: I live in America: John Abercrombie, as told to the author by
John Surman in a phone interview, 26 November 2014.

I was at a loss and didn't really know what to do: Jan Garbarek, author interview
by phone, 9 October 2017.

It was a shock to me that Bill was quitting the band: Eberhard Weber, author
interview via email, 5 October 2017.

9. Counterpoint I: Hal Willner Listens to *Lookout for Hope*

This listening session took place at Willner's work studio in New York City, 4
April 2017.

various artist concept records: Willner disliked the term 'tribute album'.

There are these few people in my life: Bill Frisell, in 'Strange Weather by
Marianne Faithfull', on The Music Aficionado blog, 9 March 2016.

I mean, Hal – that was a massive shock: Bill Frisell, author interview via Skype,
26 June 2020.

10. Once Upon a Time in the East Village

The first Diamanda Galás twelve-inch single: James Reeno, in the comments
section of 'Where the Music Used to Live', a post on Alex Smith's Flaming
Pablum blog, 2 February 2015.

Instead, the participants improvised: there was a prompter with cue cards,
communication within the ensemble (and to the prompter) was by hand
signals and gestures, and the music developed freely and changed quickly.

Zorn's game pieces 'de-centred both the process': Gene Santoro, in 'John Zorn:
Quick-Change Artist Makes Good', *DownBeat*, April 1988.

'spun from many threads' Robin Holcomb: Mark Dery, in 'Recent Releases', the
New York Times, 4 November 1990.

Also present were English guitarist: others in the circle – which might have
been a better word for the wide, loose and disparate assemblage of friends

and fellow avant-garde travellers – included polymath guitarist, multi-instrumentalist and composer Elliott Sharp, and composer, turntablist, sound collagist and visual artist Christian Marclay, today best known for his twenty-four-hour video montage *The Clock*.

eclectic is far too weak a word to describe: Gene Santoro, in 'John Zorn: Quick-Change Artist Makes Good', *DownBeat*, April 1988.

I think through some kind of weird accident: Marc Ribot, in 'A Conversation with Marc Ribot and Bill Frisell', by Matthew Carlin, *Knitting Factory Knotes*, May/June 2000.

When I first started to hear about Bill: Wayne Horvitz, author interview, Seattle, 17 February 2015.

Yes, we'd heard that there was this great: Robin Holcomb, author interview, Seattle, 17 February 2015.

That whole slash-and-dice thing: Wayne Horvitz, author interview, Seattle, 17 February 2015.

In interviews with Zorn at the time: Zorn could be direct and demanding with his musicians ('I do have a reputation for being a tyrant,' he wrote in the liner notes to his 1987 album *Spillane*), and mistrustful of the media – the awkward outsider far too often, he believed, misrepresented and misunderstood (two of Zorn's song titles for the disjunctive jump-cut music he played with his thrash-punk-jazz group Naked City were 'Jazz Snob Eat Shit' and 'Perfume of a Critic's Burning Flesh').

Zorn is German for 'anger': Francis Davis, in '"Zorn" for "Anger"', the *Atlantic Monthly*, January 1991.

This was a time at the beginning of a community: John Zorn, in *Bill Frisell: A Portrait*, a documentary by Emma Franz, 2017.

a new array of sounds and techniques: Bill Frisell, in a grant application to the Shifting Foundation, 13 January 1984. The purchase of the $1,240 guitar synth (around $3,200 today) was made possible by a grant from the Shifting Foundation, a US-based not-for-profit organisation. Shifting has been awarding needs-based grants to individual musicians, writers and visual artists, and to arts organisations and environmental, humanitarian and civil liberties groups, since 1982; during its first decade John Zorn, Ronald Shannon Jackson, Tim Berne, Vernon Reid, Hank Roberts, Melvin Gibbs and Joey Baron were also among the foundation's grateful recipients. More recently Shifting has supported projects by, among others, Kris Davis, Henry Threadgill, Ches Smith, Ingrid Laubrock, Ambrose Akinmusire and Mary Halvorson, many of whom Frisell has played and recorded with.

Bill Frisell has built a little masterpiece here: Andrew Sussman, in a review of
  Rambler in *Fanfare* magazine, 1985.
'Erotico' is from Ennio Morricone's score for French director Henri Verneuil's
  1970 film *The Burglars*; 'The Big Gundown' is based on the music
  Morricone wrote for a 1966 spaghetti western of the same name by Italian
  director Sergio Sollima. Morricone was a formative influence on John
  Zorn; the Italian composer had used the electric guitar in many of his
  works, especially the Spaghetti Western soundtracks he composed in the
  1960s. Zorn was also aware that Morricone had been a key member, in the
  sixties and seventies, of Gruppo di Improvvisazione di Nuova Consonanza,
  a Rome-based experimental composers collective dedicated to exploring the
  interstices between avant-garde composition and free improvisation, as well
  as integrating elements such as noise, electronic music, guitar feedback, and
  even funk.
[It was] the first dream in his life: Robert Polito, in 'Notes on Ennio
  Morricone', in the liner notes to *The Big Gundown, John Zorn Plays the
  Music of Ennio Morricone* (Icon/Nonesuch Records, 1986).
utterly remarkable in every way: Richard Cook and Brian Morton, in *The
  Penguin Guide to Jazz Recordings*, Ninth Edition (Penguin, 2008).
Premièred at Roulette in November 1984: *Cobra* was inspired by a popular
  Second World War simulation game of that name published in 1977, and
  has been regularly staged by students and leading players of experimental
  music around the world; there have been all-women and hip-hop versions,
  and even one in which all the participants were jazz journalists.
Cobra: Zorn scholar John Brackett stated in 'Some Notes on John Zorn's
  Cobra', in *American Music* (University of Illinois Press, spring 2010): 'it
  could be argued *Cobra* has become *the* defining piece of music associated
  with the downtown scene'.
Hearing Cobra *pretty much crystallised*: Nels Cline, author interview, via Skype,
  19 July 2017.
'Godard' was released on a various-artists tribute to the director, *Godard Ça
  Vous Chante?*, on the French Nato label in 1986, and soon disappeared.
  Zorn re-released it on his own Tzadik label, paired with two other pieces, in
  1999.
'Spillane' features an ensemble of Zorn on alto and clarinet, with Frisell,
  Anthony Coleman (piano, organ, celeste) Carol Emanuel (harp), Bobby
  Previte (drums) and Jim Staley (trombone), plus David Hofstra on bass
  and tuba, Bob James on tapes and compact discs, and David Weinstein

on sampling keyboard and celeste. John Lurie and Robert Quine provide, respectively, the voice of Mickey Spillane's most famous character, detective Mike Hammer, and his conscience. The texts were written by Arto Lindsay.

America's greatest music: Wynton Marsalis, in the Introduction to *Moving to Higher Ground*, by Wynton Marsalis, with Geoffrey C Ward, pxv (Random House, 2008).

In my era I've come up between two: Wynton Marsalis, author interview, in 'Southern Blue Soul Brother Number One', *The Wire*, December 1991/ January 1992.

It's really music the way it should be: John Zorn, in 'John Zorn: Quick-Change Artist Makes Good', by Gene Santoro, *DownBeat*, April 1988.

Tradition is not worshipping ashes: this metaphor is most often attributed to Gustav Mahler; it's possible, however, that Mahler was paraphrasing another (unnamed) source, such as Thomas More or Benjamin Franklin. The aphorism has also been attributed to a speech by French politician Jean Jaurès.

A quiet, bespectacled, but musically charged: Gary Giddins, in 'Guitar Hero: Bill Frisell's Infinite Styles', the *New Yorker*, 26 January 2009.

Smash & Scatteration . . . *straddles high tech*: David Breskin, in the press release for *Smash & Scatteration* (Minor Music, 1985). It also appeared Frisell had given himself a sartorial makeover for the occasion: in back-cover photos, standing next to the snappily dressed Vernon Reid, Frisell wears a beige double-breasted suit (with collar up at the back), brightly patterned shirt and dark shades. Shorter, tidier hair; no more moustache.

The band played Outside In: a recording of that concert, long available as a bootleg and incorrectly subtitled *Bracknell Festival, England, 1988* (though, to be fair, Outside In was heir to the Bracknell Jazz weekend), was released in October 2020 on a Bandcamp page dedicated to the music of Ronald Shannon Jackson; the drummer died in October 2013, aged seventy-three.

Frisell sparks the colours of a symphonic electric storm: author, in a review of *Second Sight* by Marc Johnson's Bass Desires, *The Wire*, December 1987/ January 1988.

That awesome and under-sung Power Tools: Greg Tate, in *Burning Ambulance 5: winter 2011*, 12 December 2011.

Bill completely freaked me out: Cuong Vu, author interview, Seattle, 22 February 2015.

As Bill was playing, gradually I began: Marianne Faithfull, author interview by phone, 19 July 2016.

the story of love and obsession between: John Zorn, in the liner notes to *Filmworks 1986–1990* (Elektra Nonesuch, 1992).

Naked City was named after a 1945 book: omnivorous and polythematic Zorn may also have been inspired by the late-fifties and early-sixties pulp TV crime series *Naked City*, which was set in New York and had the concluding narration: 'There are eight million stories in the naked city. This has been one of them.'

The music was exciting and exhilarating: Joey Baron, author interview via Skype, 22 April 2016.

Naked City released five studio albums: Zorn later released a live album recorded in 1989 at the band's spiritual home, famed downtown club the Knitting Factory.

You've got to realise speed is taking over: John Zorn, in the liner notes to *Spillane* ('from the composer's notes and a conversation with Jonathan Cott; edited by David Bither'), Elektra Nonesuch, 1987.

John got us all together. Naked City was: Bill Frisell, quoted in the booklet to *Naked City: The Complete Studio Recordings* (Tzadik, 2005).

Provocation was taken a few stages further: Naked City also became noted for Zorn's selection of starkly violent and sexually explicit cover images. The use of *Corpse with Revolver*, a photograph by Weegee (Usher 'Arthur' Fellig), for the cover of the self-titled debut album proved mild in comparison with his uncompromising choice of Japanese SM, graphic manga, macabre torture and medical-archive imagery for subsequent records; it quickly ended his relationship with the Elektra Nonesuch label. It also drew criticism in some feminist and Asian American quarters.

The Zorn Marquis de Sade Paris concert: from various accounts on the thread 'John Zorn, Merzboard and more!' at offering.proboards.com.

There was this dildo that was, like: Bill Frisell, in 'United Greats of Americana', by Alan di Perna, *Guitar World*, 2011.

11. Song of Myself

It's not that this is the only thing: Mary Halvorson, author interview, Antwerp, Belgium, 13 August 2015.

It's the ones who've put together their own: Anthony Braxton, in *Reading Jazz, A Gathering of Autobiography, Reportage and Criticism from 1919 to Now*, edited by Robert Gottlieb (Bloomsbury, 1997), p327.

through metaphor: Joni Mitchell on Wayne Shorter, in 'Joni Mitchell and Cassandra Wilson, Alternate Tunings', by John Ephland, *DownBeat*,

December 1996 (also in *DownBeat, The Great Jazz Interviews*, edited by
Frank Alkyer and Ed Enright, Hal Leonard Books, 2009, p284).

An exercise in absurdity: Wayne Horvitz in 'The Sound of One Man Dreaming
– Guitarist Bill Frisell invents music without borders', by Richard Seven,
the *Seattle Times: Pacific Northwest Magazine*, 22 Apr 2001.

I mean 'sound' as it has long functioned: Ben Ratliff, in the Introduction to
Coltrane: The Story of a Sound (Picador, 2007), px.

Mr Frisell has extended the [Jim] Hall style: Jon Pareles, in 'Two Guitar Styles',
the *New York Times*, 11 May 1987.

ranging from George Harrison to Angus Young: the list of Gibson SG players
is long but also includes Cream-era Eric Clapton, Pete Townshend, Jerry
Garcia, Frank Zappa, Tony Iommi of Black Sabbath, Jerry Garcia, AC/
DC's Angus Young, Joy Division's Bernard Sumner, Johnny Marr, Thom
Yorke and Michael Kiwanuka.

like a rubber band, pretty flexible: Bill Frisell, in 'Seattle's Super Sonic', by Jude
Gold, *Guitar Player*, February 2002.

touching your finger against the edge: Dave McElfresh, in a review of the video
The Guitar Artistry of Bill Frisell, Cadence, September 1997.

That sound – was it, as other writers have: Tom Junod, in 'The Guy Who
Always Plays the Perfect Song', (American) *GQ*, February 1997.

He slides and bends pitches: Tom Moon, in 'The Language of the Guitar', the
Philadelphia Inquirer, 12 September 1999.

Bill's phrasing is so interesting, because: Dave Douglas, author interview via
Skype, 26 August 2016.

allow notes to sustain simultaneously: Bill Frisell, 'An Approach to Guitar
Fingering', in *Arcana: Musicians on Music*, edited by John Zorn (Hips
Road/Tzadik/Granary Books, 2000), pp140–144.

It takes effort to bend one note: Marc Ribot, in an introduction to a
conversation between Bill Frisell and Marc Ribot: *BOMB* magazine,
spring 2002.

Sometimes my interpretation will spring from: Bill Frisell, in 'Nonstandards Fare:
Jazz and Pop', by Geoffrey Himes, *JazzTimes*, July/August 2006.

It's not a stretch to put Bill in that category: Joe Henry, author interview by
phone, 27 March 2018.

puts a tune in its own world . . . Instead of discarding: Bill Frisell, in 'Unwitting
Iconoclast', by Mark Small, *Berklee Today*, fall 1998.

part of my bloodstream: Bill Frisell, in 'Bill Frisell's Sounds and Thoughts Flood
Forth', by Juan Rodriguez, the *Montreal Gazette*, 27 June 2013.

With his conception about melody and form: Joe Lovano, in 'Bill Frisell's Big Ocean', by Celeste Sunderland, posted on allaboutjazz.com, 14 September 2004.

The way I heard it is that it was a Saturday: Nels Cline, author interview, via Skype, 19 July 2017.

you go through the complex to get to the simple: Steve Lacy, in 'Forget Paris', by John Corbett, *DownBeat*, February 1997 (reprinted in *DownBeat – The Great Jazz Interviews*, Hal Leonard Books, 2009, p288).

expansive miniatures: Jenny Scheinman, author interview via email, 27 April 2016.

I think . . . there's a natural . . . way I have of speaking: Bill Frisell, in 'Big Think Interview with Bill Frisell', bigthink.com, posted 8 June 2010.

Put simply, he uses far fewer notes: in a similar way to how critic Ben Ratliff once described the style of saxophonist Illinois Jacquet, Frisell's sound is 'consciously anti-virtuosic'. Many jazz musicians have gravitated towards this style and perspective, whether by instinct or design; even one of the music's most famous virtuosi, Dizzy Gillespie, once said that it had taken him his whole life 'to learn what *not* to play'.

Sometimes I feel like whatever style I have: Bill Frisell, in 'Bill Frisell and John Scofield, a Meeting of Spontaneous Minds', by James Rotondi, *Guitar Player*, July 1992.

I like Charlie Parker: Bill Frisell, in 'Nonstandards Fare: Jazz and Pop', by Geoffrey Himes, *JazzTimes*, July/August 2006.

Bill's one of the few so-called jazz musicians: Joe Henry, author interview by phone, 27 March 2018.

His approach is about making exactly the right etch: Jason Moran, author interview, Antwerp, Belgium, 15 August 2015.

Bill shreds in a different way: Jason Moran, in *Bill Frisell: A Portrait*, a documentary by Emma Franz (2017).

Music is the silence between the notes: Claude Debussy; a variation of this declaration, which substitutes 'space' for 'silence', is quoted in *Turning Numbers into Knowledge: Mastering the Art of Problem Solving* (Analytics Press, 2001) by Jonathan G. Koomey, p96.

what you don't play can be more important: Thelonious Monk, in *Thelonious Monk's Advice* (1960), as transcribed by Steve Lacy, by Shaun Usher, posted on listsofnote.com, 17 February 2012.

the Thelonious Monk of the electric guitar: David Breskin, author interview via Skype, 19 February 2018. Breskin says he coined the phrase sometime in the 1980s; it was later employed most regularly by Frisell's great mentor Jim Hall.

There is a balance of powerfully oppositional: David Breskin, ibid.

I've been taking him to hear Bill since: Dave Douglas, author interview via Skype, 26 August 2016.

His music is very anchored and yet it can: Carole d'Inverno, author interview, Seattle, 18 February 2015.

When I think about Bill's sound, it's almost: Mary Halvorson, author interview, Antwerp, Belgium, 13 August 2015.

Bill builds all these forms that: Jason Moran, author interview, Antwerp, Belgium, 15 August 2015.

He's got a lot of layers: Claudia Engelhart, author interview, London, 20 October 2015.

He knows exactly what he wants out of his music: Joey Baron, in 'On the Road to Bill Frisell', by William Stephenson, *Jazziz*, May 1997.

He is so big-hearted, so invariably: Joe Henry, author interview by phone, 27 March 2018.

Wow, your bass sounds wonderful, man: a story told by Jan Garbarek, author interview by phone, 15 October 2014.

Music doesn't come from your instrument: Martin Hayes, author interview, Cork, Ireland, 16 November 2015.

Bill has this huge vision for what music: Tony Scherr, author interview, Antwerp, Belgium, 16 August 2015.

He could open a gate that not everyone: Steve Houben, author interview, Middelheim, Antwerp, Belgium, 16 August 2015.

It was beautiful, and it sounded totally like: Claudia Engelhart, author interview, London, 20 October 2015.

12. Have a Little Faith

In some ways Monica being born: Carole d'Inverno, author interview, Seattle, 18 February 2015.

It wasn't until the mid-eighties: Bill Frisell, in 'Screams and Whispers: Bill Frisell, Best CDs of the 90s', by John Ephland, *DownBeat*, January 2000.

a deep sense of love: Frisell told Jonathan Coe, in 'Bill Frisell, He Who Hesitates . . . Er . . .', *The Wire*, July 1989, 'I needed to have guys that could play in almost any style, or they could go in all kinds of different directions, and then I also needed to have people that are . . . personally, you know . . . We all love each other.'

I kept hearing about this guy Joey Baron: Bill Frisell, in 'Interview with Bill Frisell', January 2018, published on Ethan Iverson's blog *Do the Math*, 1 July 2018.

Everybody experiences it – you're around: Joey Baron, author interview via Skype, 22 April 2016.

Joey and I, we were really, really hooking up: Ethan Iverson , *Do the Math*, ibid.

a little bit of a jazz snob: Joey Baron, author interview via Skype, 22 April 2016.

I went to the gig and halfway through: Joey Baron, ibid.

He told me he was going to start a band: Hank Roberts, author interview via Skype, 11 April 2016.

I'm trying to distil all these different: Bill Frisell, in 'Bill Frisell, the New Faces: Small Hands – the Unmistakable Touch of Bill Frisell', by Andrew Jones, *Coda*, April/May 1988.

When Bill formed the band: Kermit Driscoll, author interview, Cliffside Park, New Jersey, 3 April 2017.

It was a very exciting band to be a part of: Joey Baron, author interview via Skype, 22 April 2016.

Bill was the leader, a strong leader, but: Hank Roberts, author interview via Skype, 11 April 2016.

I think his hesitation was that, Goddam: Kermit Driscoll, author interview, Cliffside Park, New Jersey, 3 April 2017.

Bill told me, he said, like, 'You either': Kermit Driscoll, ibid.

Bill would strategise. He would think: Carole d'Inverno, author interview, Seattle, 18 February 2015.

I would go hear Bill at Visiones: Dave Douglas, author interview via Skype, 26 August 2016.

suffer from a certain waywardness of focus: Richard Cook and Brian Morton, review of *Rambler* and *Lookout for Hope*, in *The Penguin Guide to Jazz Recordings*, Ninth Edition (Penguin, 2008).

a mixed bag . . . sometimes too cute: Steve Lake, review of *Lookout for Hope*, in 40 Essential Albums of the 80s, *The Wire*, December 1989/January 1990.

One reason that album, and that band: Hank Roberts, author interview via Skype, 11 April 2016.

That's one of the greatest things: Joey Baron, author interview via Skype, 22 April 2016.

As part of a new quartet brought together: Frisell had been playing regularly with Paul Motian for five years, but had never for one moment considered he might record with Paul Bley. Motian had played with Bley quite extensively during 1963–64, most notably in a celebrated trio with Gary Peacock on bass, but they had not exchanged a note since. Surman had jammed with Bley in the early seventies, in line-ups that included bassist Barre Phillips and drummer Stu Martin, but never recorded with him. Surman had never played with Frisell or Motian; he had only improvised over some of Frisell's studio recordings during the making of *In Line*, contributions that were not used or released.

We'd go in the studio and everything is ready to go: Bill Frisell, in 'Bill Frisell, Guitars & Scatterations', by John Diliberto, *DownBeat*, May 1989.

The first thing you have to note about Frisell's playing: John Surman, author interview by phone, 26 November 2014.

forcefully unemphatic . . . sense of improvisation: Steve Lake, in 'No Space Like Home', liner notes to *Fragments* by Paul Bley, released on ECM, October 1986.

It was suddenly like all this time: Bill Frisell, in 'Bill Frisell in Conversation with Curator Philip Bither', posted on walkerart.org, website of the Walker Art Center, Minneapolis, 6 February 2010. The Jim Hall/Bill Frisell duo concert took place at the Walker in 1986.

I didn't think we could get away with: Jed Eisenman, in 'Interview with Jed Eisenman', posted on Ethan Iverson's blog *Do the Math*, August 2013.

The Village Vanguard is like playing inside: Bill Frisell, quoted in *Alive at the Village Vanguard, My Life In and Out of Jazz Time*, by Lorraine Gordon, as told to Barry Singer (Hal Leonard Books, 2006).

He was just like a sponge: David Breskin, author interview via Skype, 19 February 2018.

Talk about scared . . . There was no reason: Bill Frisell, in 'ECM's Lyrical "House Guitarist"', by Josef Woodard, *Guitar Player*, April 1985.

The clip of Frisell's solo performance at the 1986 Vancouver International Jazz Festival was posted on the Facebook page of contemporary art centre and new-music venue Western Front on 1 March 2019.

This was a time when Bill was so busy: Nels Cline, author interview, via Skype, 19 July 2017.

The notion that it might have been something: Wayne Horvitz, email to author, 28 June 2020.

It's really interesting . . . I think when Bill's in the music: Carole d'Inverno, author interview, Seattle, 18 February 2015.

13. Counterpoint II: the Bad Plus Listens to *Where in the World?*

This listening session took place at the InterContinental Mark Hopkins hotel, San Francisco, 12 December 2015.

constantly searching for rules to break: the Bad Plus, from the band's website, thebadplus.com.
at the end of the twentieth century: the Bad Plus, ibid.
long-simmering internal tensions: Nate Chinen, in 'The Bad Plus Has Big News: Some Subtraction, Some Addition, for a Whole New Sum', posted on WBGO.org, 10 April 2017.
Bill Frisell's music is vitally important: Ethan Iverson, on his *Do the Math* blog, 2014.

14. Change Gonna Come

ECM's house guitarist: for example, in the headline 'ECM's Lyrical "House Guitarist"', by Josef Woodard, *Guitar Player*, April 1985.
Nonesuch, a small and struggling label: Before Hurwitz took it over Nonesuch was primarily a budget classical imprint that had expanded, somewhat randomly, into world music, early electronic music and even ragtime.
Nonesuch . . . an oasis of artistic excitement: Ed Siegel, in 'Nonesuch Lives Up to its Name', the *Boston Globe*, 12 July 1998; and *a kind of American cultural institution*: Russell Shorto, in 'The Industry Standard', the *New York Times Magazine*, 3 October 2004.
It was basically like when I left my parents: Bill Frisell, in 'Bill Frisell, the ECM Years', by John Kelman, allaboutjazz.com, 26 April 2011.
Fifteen minutes later I called him: Lee Townsend, author interview, Berkeley, California, 11 December 2015.
I stepped off the plane out onto the jetway: Bill Frisell, in 'A Ballad to Ballard', by Derk Richardson, on afar.com, 4 February 2014.
Frisell is without a doubt the single most: Paul De Barros, in 'Guitarist Bill Frisell is Smash Hit', the *Seattle Times*, 29 June 1989.
It did make the transition harder: Bill Frisell, in 'A Jazzman in Town: Bill Frisell Settles in with His New Sound', by Paul De Barros, the *Seattle Times*, 19 April 1990.
Jazz is very social music: Joe Lovano, in 'Joe Lovano's Sound of the Broad Shoulders', by Howard Mandel, in *DownBeat – The Great Jazz Interviews* (Hal Leonard Books, 2009), p261.

Some people thought we were nuts: Carole d'Inverno, author interview, Seattle, 18 February 2015.

hide out a little: Bill Frisell, in 'The Sound of One Man Dreaming – Guitarist Bill Frisell invents music without borders', by Richard Seven, the *Seattle Times: Pacific Northwest Magazine*, 22 Apr 2001.

just sit down and think: Bill Frisell, in 'Unironic', by Francis Davis, the *Atlantic*, July/August 2002.

I had all these ideas, like for different records: Bill Frisell, in 'Bill Frisell, He Who Hesitates . . . Er . . .', by Jonathan Coe, *The Wire*, July 1989.

Inspired by a sixties episode of The Twilight Zone: '*An Occurrence at Owl Creek Bridge*' was itself based on an 1891 short story of the same name, by American Civil War soldier and writer Ambrose Bierce, about a prisoner's vivid hallucinations just before his death by hanging from a railroad bridge. Of the thirty-six sections, arranged by Zorn using his file-card system, twelve were written by Frisell; twelve were improvised snippets of solos, duos or trios within the quartet; and twelve progressed through twelve different keys and twelve contrasting tempos and grooves. The music jostles and scrambles from country hoedown to dub reggae, twisted psychedelia to surf rock, slow blues to thrash metal, film noir to free jazz into a stream-of-conscious narrative intended to reflect the prisoner's gallows reverie – the subtitle of the piece was 'As I Take My Last Breath and the Noose Grows Tight, the Incredible Events of the Past Three Days Flash Before My Eyes'.

Is That You?: the photograph on the album cover is of a bashful three-year-old Frisell, pliers in hand, flies to his oversized jeans wide open to the world, taken in front of his parents' 1951 Plymouth in the driveway to their house in Krameria Street, Denver.

We took the budget that we would have: Wayne Horvitz, author interview, Seattle, 17 February 2015.

He was fascinated about how we went: Joey Baron, in 'It's Joey Baron's 56th Birthday', from *Today is the Question*, a blog by Ted Panken (originally from Panken's feature on Baron in *Jazziz* magazine in 2001).

That band was just so much fun to play: Hank Roberts, author interview via Skype, 11 April 2016.

I was kinda going through a lot of personal challenges: Hank Roberts, ibid.

Kermit's doing this weird leapfrogging: Bill Frisell, in 'No Semi, No Roadies, No Set List', by Howard Mandel, *DownBeat*, March 1992.

What's unbelievable to me about these: *DownBeat*, ibid.

Live: while the music was recorded in 1991, it was not released until four years later, in October 1995, on the instigation of Hans Wendl, who had given up managing some of Frisell's affairs to become director of the Gramavision label.

Bring the Family: the brutally confessional, melodically strong and lyrically smart John Hiatt album features a dream band of Hiatt on acoustic guitar and vocals (and piano on 'Have a Little Faith in Me'), Ry Cooder on electric guitar, Nick Lowe on bass, and Jim Keltner on drums.

I might even say that Live *is the most*: Mary Halvorson, author interview, Antwerp, Belgium, 13 August 2015.

his multiple-artist 'meditation' on the life and work of Charles Mingus: the cover title of the album is *Hal Willner Presents Weird Nightmare: Meditations on Mingus*.

There is also a jubilant version: Sousa marches were a staple of Frisell's Gold Sash Band in Denver; Frisell dedicates the record 'to my teachers, Jack Stevens and Dale Bruning'.

I've loved Dylan for almost as long as: Bill Frisell, in 'Bill Frisell: Keep Your Eyes Open', by Dennis Cook, on JamBase.com, 27 August 2009.

I had a night off on tour: Bill Frisell, quoted in the *Bill Frisell Discography*, by Bryan Aaker and Martin Lane, at bryanaaker.net.

I'm thinking that this record might help: Bill Frisell, in 'Bill Frisell: The Whole Picture', by Bill Milkowski, *JazzTimes*, May 1993.

The composers [on Have a Little Faith*] hail*: David Ake, in *Jazz Cultures* (University of California Press, 2002), p165.

I'm not trying to rewrite the songs: Bill Frisell, in 'An Uncategorizable Guitarist Returns to His Roots', by Dan Forte, *Vintage Guitar*, December 2014.

We were best friends . . . and we all: Bill Frisell, in 'Screams and Whispers: Bill Frisell, Best CDs of the 90s', by John Ephland, *DownBeat*, January 2000.

15. Counterpoint III: Justin Vernon Listens to *This Land*

This listening session took place at the Marker Hotel in Dublin, Ireland on 4 June 2017.

This Land: the cover photograph is *Railroad Station, Edwards, Mississippi* (February 1936) by Walker Evans.

this sort of Scandinavian-American-Lutheran: Justin Vernon, in 'Bon Iver's Choices', by SSkizo, on *La Blogothèque*, 21 May 2008.

A record of 'rare, quiet perfection': Laura Barton, in 'Cabin Fever', the *Guardian*, 14 May 2008.

maybe the best concert I've ever seen . . . probably my favourite record: Justin Vernon, in 'Bon Iver's Choices', by SSkizo, on *La Blogothèque*, 21 May 2008.

16. The Sounds I Saw

Everything is rhythm . . . When I first: Charles Cajori, in 'Charles Cajori, R.I.P.: The jazz inspiration of a New York painter', by Tom Reney, on NEPR.net, 7 March 2014.

trying to strike the perfect balance: Irving Sandler, in a 1961 review of Cajori's work, quoted in Reney, ibid.

In the way that he had a connection to Denver: Carole d'Inverno, author interview, Seattle, 18 February 2015.

When I met Bill, he was already doing: Carole d'Inverno, ibid.

To me, his drawings look like how his music: Tony Scherr, author interview, Antwerp, Belgium, 16 August 2015.

I can't draw, but if I didn't play music: Bill Frisell, in 'A Week In Umbria with the Guitarists' Home Base of Kenny Wollesen and Tony Scherr', by Ted Panken, *DownBeat*, October 2008.

He's trying to find things . . . that you might: Bill Frisell, in 'Music is Good: A Conversation with Bill Frisell', by Danny Barnes, *Fretboard Journal*, winter 2006.

I think our widest point of connection: Jim Woodring, author interview, Seattle, 14 February 2015.

One might say that a Bill Frisell gig: Jeff Tamarkin, in programme notes to *Bill Frisell: Up & Down the Mississippi, Traveling Highway 61*, Jazz at Lincoln Center, New York, 29–30 May 2015.

One of the things I felt very strongly: David Breskin, author interview via Skype, 27 February 2018.

The 'mirth and melancholy' [of Buster Keaton's films]: quoted in 'Reckless Introvert', by Dan Ouellette, *DownBeat*, April 1996.

The first time we did it, it was complete panic: Bill Frisell, in 'Sounds for Silence: Jazz & Silent Films', by Shaun Brady, *JazzTimes*, December 2010.

There was a Frankenstein cow: *Tales from the Far Side* was first broadcast on the CBS network as a Hallowe'en special.

The first time I saw him play live: Gary Larson, in 'The Sound of One Man Dreaming – Guitarist Bill Frisell invents music without borders', by Richard Seven, in the *Seattle Times: Pacific Northwest Magazine*, 22 Apr 2001.

493

I wasn't sure if I could play without them: Bill Frisell, in 'Reckless Introvert', by
   Dan Ouellette, *DownBeat*, April 1996.

So I thought I'd do something completely different: Frisell told me that his desire to
   form a guitar-led modern chamber group, without bass and drums, was also
   influenced by his admiration for the work of the World Saxophone Quartet –
   the free-flowing all-star ensemble of Julius Hemphill and Oliver Lake on alto,
   David Murray on tenor and Hamiet Bluiett on baritone. Around the time he
   was putting together the music and musicians for *Quartet*, Frisell was further
   deeply affected by Hemphill's death in April 1995.

La Scuola: a 1995 comedy-drama, set in a run-down technical institute on the
   outskirts of Rome, directed by Daniele Luchetti.

Much of what I do deals with opposites: Bill Frisell, in 'Reckless Introvert', by
   Dan Ouellette, *DownBeat*, April 1996.

Quartet: the cover image is *The Boy* by American Regionalist painter Thomas
   Hart Benton. A colourised 1948 lithograph showing, as the artist himself
   described, plainly, 'an Ozark boy setting out from home – to go to school
   or to find work; the folks and his horse say goodbye', the image was
   another smart choice, this time by Frisell himself – not just in its wistful
   and poignant subject matter and Midwestern setting, but in the way the
   choreography of Benton's stylised figures, arms, hands, hills, grasslands and
   clouds exhibit a strong sense of sweeping rhythm and fluid movement.

Quartet *may be his masterpiece*: Peter Watrous, in 'Critic's Choice; Variations
   on Themes of Nostalgia', the *New York Times*, 2 April 1996.

Quartet named in Elvis Costello's '500 albums essential to a happy life', *Vanity
   Fair*, November 2000.

This is an album he was born to make: in *The Penguin Guide to Jazz Recordings*,
   Ninth Edition, by Richard Cook and Brian Morton, (Penguin, 2008).

The first time I put on one of Bill's CDs: Jim Woodring, author interview,
   Seattle, 14 February 2015.

'Let's just get together and jam'; Jim Woodring, ibid.

The two artists have come to a similar place: Ben Ratliff, in 'A Visual
   Collaborator and his Accompanists', the *New York Times*, 11 June 2002.

the drawing as well as the music is now 'live': in a reciprocal exchange, Woodring
   sketched on a tablet shapes, forms and images that were projected onto a
   screen, to which Frisell and his musicians responded in real time; Woodring
   did the same with the music he heard.

That was an amazing experience: Jim Woodring, author interview, Vashon
   Island, near Seattle, Washington, 6 December 2015.

494

It's confining, in a way: Bill Frisell, in 'Bill Frisell in Conversation with Curator Philip Bither', posted on walkerart.org, website of the Walker Art Center, Minneapolis, 6 February 2010.

Just that one little extra: the soprano saxophonist Steve Lacy once said that he could learn more from a painter, actor, comedian or clown than from another musician. 'I've always been eager to collaborate with dancers, painters, poets, actors, cinema, whatever,' he told John Corbett in *DownBeat* in 1997. 'It makes the music move. Music has to be what it normally would not be. It requires something new of the music, and I like that urgency, that need to change, to adapt, to invent.'

A special kind of book: David Breskin, author interview via Skype, 27 February 2018.

The book included contributions from: there were also essays from art critic Dave Hickey and curator and gallerist Klaus Kertess, as well as a series of observations on art and art-making by Richter himself.

each piece having a 1:1 relationship: David Breskin, in 'Notes Towards Structure for Frisell', in the CD booklet for *Richter 858* by Bill Frisell (Songlines, 2005).

When I consider all the improvisers: David Breskin, in 'An Interview with David Breskin', by Lily Prillinger, in the CD booklet for *Richter 858* by Bill Frisell (Songlines, 2005).

On most of my recordings I overdub, mix: Bill Frisell, in 'An Interview with Bill Frisell by Tony Reif', in the CD booklet for *Richter 858* by Bill Frisell (Songlines, 2005).

Taciturn, eccentric and a strict disciplinarian: Disfarmer would often make his subjects wait a long time before, mostly unbeknownst to them, he would actually take their picture.

I knew nothing of Disfarmer: Bill Frisell, in the programme notes for *Musical Portraits from Heber Springs – Bill Frisell's Disfarmer Project*, the Walker Art Center, Minneapolis, 27 October 2007. The Walker co-commissioned the music.

smell the air, talk to some people: Bill Frisell, ibid.

Disfarmer: a video on the making of the music: for the March 2011 European tour of Bill Frisell's Disfarmer Project, during which this concert film was made, fiddle and tenor guitar player Carrie Rodriguez replaced Jenny Scheinman.

tragicomic romantic whodunit: from the IMDb data on *The Million Dollar Hotel*.

based on a concept story: from the film's Wikipedia page.

a catastrophe . . . Wenders's own artistic suicide: Jonathan Romney, in 'Expensive Mistake', the *New Statesman*, 1 May 2000. Romney did, however, give 'top marks' to the soundtrack, which was, perhaps unfortunately, released at the same time as the film. There are slim pickings for Frisell fans; mostly he is a hired hand supplying echoey atmospherics.

as boring as a dog's ass: Mel Gibson, reported on the film's Wikipedia page.

All Hat: Frisell, guitars and loops; Greg Leisz, steel guitars and mandolin; Jenny Scheinman, violin; Mark Graham, harmonica; Viktor Krauss, bass; Scott Amendola, drums. Produced by Lee Townsend.

in which long-forgotten, and sometimes deteriorated, imagery: from the Bio page on Bill Morrison's website, billmorrisonfilm.com.

Out of the cinematic ruins: Steve Dollar, in 'The Great Flood is Bill Morrison's latest found-footage film to focus on disaster', the *Washington Post*, 2 May 2014.

Music has always been an integral part: Morrison's work is mostly screened in cinemas, but his films have also been shown in music venues and concert halls – and in theatres, museums and art galleries.

Frisell first met Morrison in the early nineties: long before the film-maker was being given a 2014–15 mid-career retrospective at MoMA in New York, Morrison was making ends meet, and feeding his love of music, by working as a dishwasher at the Village Vanguard in New York.

The magnitude of the event: Bill Frisell, author interview by phone, 18 October 2012.

While I was just starting to write: Bill Frisell, ibid

17. Counterpoint IV: Jim Woodring Listens to *With Dave Holland and Elvin Jones*

This listening session took place at Woodring's home on Vashon Island, near Seattle, Washington, on 6 December 2015. Vashon attracts people who want to live relatively close to the city, but who seek a sense of isolation, privacy and self-determination; according to Wikipedia, 'the island is known for its strawberry festival, sheepdog trials, and high rate of unvaccinated residents' (even before the Covid-19 pandemic). It also lies on a 700-mile fault line called the Cascadia Subduction Zone, a name that could easily have sprung from Woodring's imagination, or one of his cartoons.

A children's book that really shouldn't: Christopher Porter, in '*Trosper*: Drawings/ Story by Jim Woodring', *JazzTimes*, 1 June 2002.

Talk about a big person: Bill Frisell on Dave Holland, in 'Bill Frisell, the ECM Years', by John Kelman, allaboutjazz.com, 26 April 2011.

Michael got it in his head that I should: Bill Frisell, in 'Expect the Unexpected', by Scott Nygaard, *Acoustic Guitar*, May 2002.

a kind of modern-day cowboy ballad: Francis Davis, in 'Unironic', the *Atlantic*, July/August 2002.

18. Roots

I'm a fan of your Nashville and American: Marc Ribot, in a conversation between Bill Frisell and Marc Ribot, *BOMB* magazine, spring 2002.

I was hearing these people play stuff: Bill Frisell, in 'Music is Good: A Conversation with Bill Frisell', by Danny Barnes, *Fretboard Journal*, winter 2006.

In the past few years, I've been obsessed: Bill Frisell, in 'Post-Modern America: Bill Frisell Digs into Roots Music', by Adam Levy, *Guitar Player*, September 1999.

It's a weird, exciting time for me: Bill Frisell, ibid.

I hated country music: Bill Frisell, in 'Unironic', by Francis Davis, the *Atlantic*, July/August 2002.

It was sort of like if I was going to India: Bill Frisell, in 'On the Road to Bill Frisell', by William Stephenson, *Jazziz*, May 1997.

I thought musically it was a no-brainer: Wayne Horvitz, author interview, Seattle, 17 February 2015.

were young, open, and willing to try: Bill Frisell, in an interview with Don Ayers, in 'Welcome to Klein Guitars', a post on the *Prepared Guitar* blog, 30 September 2014.

Bluegrass and jazz are very compatible: Jerry Douglas, author interview, Cork, Ireland, 26 January 2019.

There were two mostly acoustic recording sessions: the first involved Frisell, Viktor Krauss, Ron Block and Adam Steffey, in different configurations; harmonica player Pat Bergeson was added on two tracks. For the second session, again following a suggestion from Kyle Lehning, Frisell recruited Jerry Douglas.

When I heard that vibrato he would get: Chet Atkins was 'The Country Gentleman', the virtuoso guitarist whose passions ran from pop ballads to jazz improvisation, and who in the mid-fifties helped develop the more popular and contemporary 'Nashville sound'. The Louvin Brothers were a hit country and gospel duo at Nashville's Grand Ole Opry in the fifties and early sixties.

play the tune, and they would learn it: Bill Frisell, in 'Unwitting Iconoclast', by Mark Small, *Berklee Today*, fall 1998.

It feels very natural collaborating with Bill: Robin Holcomb, author interview, Seattle, 17 February 2015.

[Nashville] *tends to tread a tad too cautiously*: Simon Hopkins, review of *Nashville* in *The Wire*, August 1997.

A weak and watery collage: in *The Penguin Guide to Jazz Recordings*, Fourth Edition, by Richard Cook and Brian Morton (Penguin, 1992).

That's such a crock. He's a country & western: Dick Mace, in 'No. 1 in the Poll?', letter to *DownBeat*, in 'Chords and Discords', October 2013.

The criticism was that I was selling out: Bill Frisell, in 'The Quiet Man', by Andy Robson, *Jazzwise*, June 2002.

For me to go to Nashville, and play with guys: Bill Frisell, in *Being Here: Conversations on Creating Music*, by Radhika Philip (self-published, 2013), p15.

People want to put you in a box: Bill Frisell, in 'The Sound of One Man Dreaming – Guitarist Bill Frisell invents music without borders', by Richard Seven, in the *Seattle Times: Pacific Northwest Magazine*, 22 Apr 2001.

Bill Sr had retired as professor emeritus: during his fifty-year academic career, Frisell's father had held prominent university positions as a leading biochemist and educator, published many papers and a book on human biochemistry, and in his later years at ECU worked in diabetes research. He also played a major role in garnering for his department the university's only ever National Institutes for Health project grant.

That was the thing about Bill's father: Carole d'Inverno, author interview, Seattle, 18 February 2015.

. . . The guitarist carries his axe: extract from David Breskin's 'The Guitarist', published in *Escape Velocity* (Soft Skull Press, 2004), reproduced with permission. The full poem is available at www.davidbreskin.com/poems/escape-velocity/the-guitarist/.

Greil Marcus's famous 'invisible republic', the 'old weird America': taken from the title of Marcus's book *Invisible Republic: Bob Dylan's Basement Tapes* (Picador, 1998), re-titled *The Old, Weird America* in an updated edition of 2011.

Blind Willie Johnson – his sound 'kind of rips': Bill Frisell, in 'Music is Good: A Conversation with Bill Frisell', by Danny Barnes, in *Fretboard Journal*, Issue 4, winter 2006.

Maybelle Carter has been a big influence: Bill Frisell, in an ECM press release for *Small Town* by Bill Frisell and Thomas Morgan, May 2017.

I think I listened more to Hank Williams: Bill Frisell, in 'Solo-flex: Bill Frisell Steps into the Spotlight', by Bill Milkowski, on guitar.com, 12 December 2000.

I was fascinated with the notes and the rhythms: Bill Frisell, in a conversation between Bill Frisell and Marc Ribot, *BOMB* magazine, spring 2002.

I love looking back, but somehow, looking back: Bill Frisell, in 'Frisell on Film', by Bob Weinberg, *Jazziz*, fall 2009.

Good Dog: the album cover featured a photograph, taken by renowned music photographer Michael Wilson, of a distant smiling Frisell seated behind a friendly-looking Australian Shepherd caught running towards the camera. The good dog that inspired the title was Wesley, a pure-breed that had been given to Monica as a present when she was eleven, and that Frisell had also come to love.

Before I met Bill, I listened to a lot more: Greg Leisz, in 'Bill Frisell, Reclaiming the Elation', by Geoffrey Himes, *DownBeat*, November 2014.

It's a lot easier when it's somebody else's: Bill Frisell, in 'Bill Frisell: Jazz-Rock Guitar's Clark Kent', by Derk Richardson, on SFGate.com, 26 March, 1998.

The unlikely triumvirate recorded: it should be said that Baker, while playing rock, blues and Afrobeat with equal facility, famously always regarded himself as a jazz musician. The trio played just one live date at a jazz festival in Frankfurt, Germany, in 1995; it's on YouTube.

[In 1968] while I was still in high school: Bill Frisell, in 'Bill Frisell Remembers Ginger Baker: Nobody Sounded Like That', by Matthew Kassel, *Rolling Stone*, 7 October 2019.

It feels to me that all four musicians: Dave Okumu, author interview by phone, 24 February 2020.

favourite musicians who just happen to be: Mike Stern, in an Atlantic Jazz press release for *Play*, September 1999 (available at mikestern.org).

some of the most shocking sections [of *Naked Lunch*]: Joe Coscarelli, in 'The Dirtiest Parts of *Naked Lunch*, for Your Record Collection', the *New York Times*, 23 May 2016. A three-CD audiobook was released by Warner Bros in 1995, and buried just as quickly (it was resurrected by Willner in 2016 as *Let Me Hang You*).

'*It was intimidating . . . I was thinking*': Bill Frisell, in 'When That Happens: Bill Frisell, Elvis Costello and Burt Bacharach', by Josef Woodard, *Jazziz*, December 1999.

[They] unravel so freely. The way a phrase: Bill Frisell, in 'Introvert Meets Extrovert', by Dan Ouellette, *DownBeat*, February 2000.

Record company machinations and other forces: Josef Woodard, in 'When That Happens: Bill Frisell, Elvis Costello and Burt Bacharach', *Jazziz*, December 1999.

As a piece, the record gets boring: John Corbett, in a review of *The Sweetest Punch*, *DownBeat*, November 1999.

underneath . . . there are all these pretty: Elvis Costello, in 'When That Happens . . .', by Josef Woodard, *Jazziz*, December 1999.

A musical statement that would encompass: from a Walker Art Center press release, November 1999.

Every time you turn around: John Ephland, in 'Screams and Whispers: Bill Frisell, Best CDs of the 90s', *DownBeat*, January 2000.

It started with Nashville *and* Gone: Lee Townsend, author interview, Berkeley, California, 11 December 2015.

Frisell, at least for now, is an artist: Andy Robson, in 'The Quiet Man', *Jazzwise*, June 2002.

19. Counterpoint V: Sam Amidon Listens to *Good Dog, Happy Man*

This listening session took place at Handel's Hotel in Dublin, Ireland on 23 April 2015.

Part preservationist, part visionary: James Reed, in 'Amidon Channels Folk Traditions into Something New', the *Boston Globe*, 15 June 2013.

extracts their essence: James Reed, ibid.

[Thomas Bartlett's] *wild arrangements*: Sam Amidon, author interview/listening session, as above. Bartlett is a pianist and singer who creates his own fragile and understated music as Doveman, is a member of innovative Irish traditional group The Gloaming, and a New York-based producer who has worked with St Vincent, The National, Sufjan Stevens, Yoko Ono and many others.

It's, like, Miles Davis: Sam Amidon, in 'Versatile Sam Amidon Talks About Recording All-Terrain Folk', by Michael Hamad, the *Hartford Courant*, 13 October 2014.

Sam makes these old tunes his own: Bill Frisell, in 'Folk Tradition Meets Experimental Urge in Amidon's Music', by Jeremy D Goodwin, the *Boston Globe*, 25 October 2014.

20. Frislandia

I don't know if it matters that you call it: Nels Cline, author interview via Skype, 19 July 2017.

Essentially I'm a rock player: Marc Ribot, author interview by phone, 21 July 2017.

I think Bill is truly one of the greatest musicians: Ron Miles, author interview, Denver, 4 March 2017. In a similar way to other musicians who play jazz, Miles sometimes substitutes, as he sees it, the loaded and limited 'j' word for 'the/this music', a more all-encompassing designation.

What jazz signifies to me is the freedom: Keith Jarrett, in *And They Sang: Great Musicians Talk About Their Music*, by Studs Terkel (Granta Books, 2006), p164; interview from 1995.

'Oh, boy. [Jazz] is still the best way': Bill Frisell, in 'Unironic, by Francis Davis, the *Atlantic*, July/August 2002.

My inspiration comes from all over: Bill Frisell, in 'Jazz Album of the Year: Nashville', *DownBeat*, August 1998.

That word [jazz] has so many: Bill Frisell, author interview by phone, 18 October 2012.

There's a tradition in the music: Bill Frisell, in *Being Here: Conversations on Creating Music*, by Radhika Philip (self-published, 2013), p17.

I do think it matters that we say: Jason Moran, author interview, Antwerp, Belgium, 15 August 2015.

It's a process, a way of thinking, not a result: Pat Metheny, in 'Pat Metheny Plays with Definitions', by Don Heckman, the *Los Angeles Times*, 12 February 1998.

Music isn't a style; it's an idea: Ornette Coleman, in 'Seeking the Mystical Inside the Music', by Ben Ratliff, the *New York Times*, 22 September 2006.

The process can be applied to anything: Sonny Rollins, in 'Jazz and Country Fusion: the Searchers', by Geoffrey Himes, *JazzTimes*, December 2008. Rollins is a jazz musician who has played, alongside standard tunes from the Great American Songbook, music that has incorporated elements of, among other forms, calypso, country, Latin, R&B, funk and even disco.

I guess I don't even know what jazz is: Bill Frisell, author interview by phone, 18 October 2012.

The term jazz, in a sense: Herbie Hancock, in the documentary *Icons Among Us: Jazz in the Present Tense*, directed by Lars Larson, Michael Rivoira and Peter J. Vogt (Paradigm Studio, 2009).

So many other kinds of music have rubbed off: Francis Davis, in 'Unironic', the *Atlantic*, July/August 2002.

I find the word 'jazz' actually difficult to deal with: Vijay Iyer, in *Being Here: Conversations on Creating Music*, by Radhika Philip (self-published, 2013), pp241-242.

There are many other musicians who might: as well as those mentioned, the drummer Max Roach might also be included; the working title of his unpublished autobiography was *Jazz is a Four-Letter Word*.

I've never understood what people are: Anthony Braxton, in *DownBeat – The Great Jazz Interviews* (Hal Leonard Books, 2009), p213.

Stretch music . . . a genre-blind musical form: Christian Scott aTunde Adjuah, in the Bio on his website, christianscott.tv.

I feel as if a small victory has been made: Bill Frisell, in 'Bill Frisell: the Quiet Genius', by Lloyd N. Peterson Jr, on allaboutjazz.com, posted 24 June 2009.

Bill Frisell is always an American folk musician: Elvis Costello, in the liner notes to *The Best of Bill Frisell Vol 1: Folk Songs* (Nonesuch, 2009).

Jazz is only what you are: Louis Armstrong, epigraph in *Visions of Jazz: the First Century* by Gary Giddins (OUP, 1999).

In the early forties, so legend has it, bebop innovator: 'Charlie Parker used all the musical information that was around him at the time,' Frisell told Mark Small in *Berklee Today* in autumn 1998. 'He used to listen to Hank Williams, Stravinsky, or whatever. He was open to all that, and it came through in what he played.'

He moved Texas roustabouts, cowboys: Alfred Appel Jr, in *Jazz Modernism* (Yale University Press, 2004), p49.

Maybe other people looked down on it: Sonny Rollins, in 'Jazz and Country Fusion: the Searchers', by Geoffrey Himes, *JazzTimes*, December 2008. *Way Out West* also features one of the most famous cover images in jazz, taken by the great West Coast jazz and Hollywood photographer William Claxton, of a twenty-six-year-old Rollins wearing a suit, tie, cartridge belt, holster and ten-gallon hat against a backdrop of desert cacti and a parched cattle skull, his tenor saxophone thrust out in front of him like a Winchester.

a nickname for . . . weather-beaten, rural-sounding: Giovanni Russonello, in 'Why is a Music Genre Called Americana so Overwhelmingly White and Male?', the *Atlantic*, 1 August 2013.

The fearless and adaptable guitarist Bill Frisell: Gary Giddins, in 'Guitar Hero: Bill Frisell's Infinite Styles', the *New Yorker*, 26 January 2009.

I feel like anyone who's listening closely: Bill Frisell, in 'Q&A: Bill Frisell', by Nathan Tucker, *Portland Monthly*, 5 November 2013.

It is believed Frisland was an 'Italian fabrication': Frank Jacobs, in 'Frisland, an Italian Fabrication in the North Atlantic', on bigthink.com, posted 23 July 2010.

It seems that in the last few years: Bill Frisell, in 'The Message is Music: A Conversation with Bill Frisell', by Lloyd Peterson, *Earshot Jazz* (Seattle), June 2005.

To say that some kind of orchestral classical music: Bill Frisell, in *Being Here: Conversations on Creating Music*, by Radhika Philip (self-published, 2013), p8.

Kenny doesn't do that at all . . . He understands: Bill Frisell, in *Being Here*, by Radhika Philip, ibid, p9.

Because Bill has an incredible and amazing set of ears: Hank Roberts, author interview via Skype, 11 April 2016.

Like every other major musician: Pat Metheny, author interview via email, 23 February 2017.

I get so tired of people trying to divide: Bill Frisell, in a foreword to *Conversations with Charlie Haden*, by Josef Woodard and Charlie Haden (Silman-James Press, 2016).

polite assault on the very idea of genre: Tom Junod, in 'The Guy Who Always Plays the Perfect Song', (American) *GQ*, February 1997.

That's the magic that you find in a great musician: Eyvind Kang, author interview, Seattle, 15 February 2015.

Her playing is thirty per cent jazz: Brian Cullman, in 'Lady Soul', the *Paris Review*, 17 August 2018.

I've never had the temptation or need to: Joe Henry, author interview by phone, 27 March 2018.

The most exciting music around just now: Richard Williams, in 'Letting Rip with the Technique', *The Times*, 13 May 1989. Williams's round-up also included reviews of albums by intrepid Norwegian guitarist Terje Rypdal, ferociously experimental supergroup Last Exit, and Wayne Horvitz's postmodern sextet The President.

His impact on the landscape of creative music: Nels Cline, in *Bill Frisell: A Portrait*, a documentary by Emma Franz (2017).

I heard a million guitarists copying Bill: Mary Halvorson, author interview, Antwerp, Belgium, 13 August 2015.

21. Counterpoint VI: Martin Hayes and Dennis Cahill Listen to *The Willies*

This listening session took place at my home in Cork, Ireland, on 16 November 2015.

I'm a complete guerrilla performer: Martin Hayes, in 'Martin Hayes: "I'm a complete guerrilla performer from the side of a mountain"', by Siobhan Long, the *Irish Times*, 31 October 2017.

22. Like Dreamers Do

one of the last redoubts of Old New York: Rick Kelly, in the documentary *Carmine Street Guitars*, directed by Ron Mann, 2018.

the bones of old New York City: quoted on kellyguitars.com.

John Scofield's *'workhorse'* guitar: John Scofield, in 'John Scofield on his workhorse Ibanez and advice to his younger self', by Henry Yates, on musicradar.com, 12 May 2015.

guitarded: Frisell says he first heard the term used by John Zorn.

solo gigs as 'a mixture of terror and power': Marc Ribot, in 'A Conversation with Marc Ribot and Bill Frisell', by Matthew Carlin, *Knitting Factory Knotes*, May/June 2000.

During the concerts, I got really loose and comfortable: Bill Frisell, in 'Post-Modern America: Bill Frisell Digs into Roots Music', by Adam Levy, *Guitar Player*, September 1999.

Ghost Town: guitarist Anthony Wilson once described Frisell's acoustic-only interpretation of the Gershwin lament 'My Man's Gone Now' as 'haunting, haunting, haunting – one of the outstanding solo guitar performances of all time' ('Artist's Choice: Anthony Wilson on Bill Frisell', *JazzTimes*, 25 July 2012).

completely naked: Bill Frisell, in 'Expect the Unexpected', by Scott Nygaard, *Acoustic Guitar*, May 2002.

dreamy looping and effects-with-a-cause: Josef Woodard, in a review of *Ghost Town*, *JazzTimes*, July 2000.

The result is a guitar which has: the guitar painted by Claude Utley can be seen on the cover of *The Best of Bill Frisell Vol 1: Folk Songs*, a compilation Nonesuch released in 2009.

It's a brilliant work, a wondrous musical: Gene Santoro, in 'Visiting the Folks', *The Nation*, 16 April 2001.

The latter is significant in that Frisell and Leisz: Frisell once told Barry Cleveland in a 2009 profile for *Guitar Player*, 'I feel like Greg's filling in the other side of my brain – all the stuff that I want to be there that I can't play myself . . . Also, he's left-handed and I'm right-handed, and his birthday is exactly six months apart from mine to the day . . . It sounds crazy, but there's some kind of weird balance thing.'

I once talked to David Piltch about: Joe Henry, author interview by phone, 27 March 2018.

freaking out just thinking about it: Bill Frisell, in 'Solo-flex: Bill Frisell steps out into the spotlight', by Bill Milkowski, on guitar.com, 12 December 2000.

Elvin got the schedule mixed up: Bill Frisell, in 'Expect the Unexpected', by Scott Nygaard, *Acoustic Guitar*, May 2002.

The project . . . was more like a controlled experiment: Elvin Jones lays down his hallmark rolling polyrhythms and cascading fills, but curiously generates neither positive space nor propulsion; the drummer 'can rarely have sounded so lacklustre', wrote Cook and Morton in *The Penguin Guide to Jazz Recordings*.

I went to hear . , , Del McCoury: Bill Frisell, in 'Wide Open Spaces, Bill Frisell Finds the Jazz Vibe in Country Music's Roomy Expanse', By Geoffrey Himes, in the Baltimore *City Paper*, 10 September 2002.

He had this wealth of knowledge: Bill Frisell, in 'Let Your Fingers Do the Talking', by Richard Williams, the *Guardian*, 18 May 2002.

The record was titled, of course, The Willies: 'It's partly related to my name,' Frisell told Mike Bradley in *The Times* in 1999. 'When I was really young I didn't like being called Bill and I wished people would call me Willy.' Maybe Frisell's country inclinations are deeper than he has admitted.

I realised that jazz players have the facility: Danny Barnes, in 'At the Crossroads', by Geoffrey Himes, *No Depression*, January/February 2003.

three-way conversations between back-porch pickers: Richard Williams, in 'Let Your Fingers Do the Talking', the *Guardian*, 18 May 2002.

a combination of Louis Armstrong and Led Zeppelin: Tony Scherr, in an extended version of 'A Week in Umbria with the Guitarists' Home Base of Kenny Wollesen and Tony Scherr', by Ted Panken, in *DownBeat*, October 2008, published on Ted Panken's *Today is the Question* website.

It was incredible from the first moment: Bill Frisell, in 'Interview with Bill Frisell', by Anita Malhotra, on her *Artsmania* blog, posted 17 June 2014.

They just know everything I've ever done: Bill Frisell, in 'Expect the Unexpected',
  by Scott Nygaard, *Acoustic Guitar,* May 2002.
It's hard for a non-guitarist to get: Marc Ribot, author interview by phone, 21
  July 2017.

23. Across the Universe

Oh, you gotta hear these guys play: Bill Frisell, from a transcript of an interview
  by Banning Eyre for NPR's *AfroPop Worldwide* radio series, recorded at the
  Experience Music Project in Seattle in 2003.
The very first time I heard him play: Bill Frisell, ibid.
meant to be: Bill Frisell, ibid.
Boubacar is the Elvis of Mali: Bill Frisell, in '"Outlaw Bill" – Frisell Assembles a
  New International Musical Posse', by John Ephland, *DownBeat*, June 2003.
I felt like he gave me the key to understanding: Bill Frisell, in 'Welcome to My
  World', by Robin Denselow, the *Guardian*, 19 February 2004.
not in a bebop kind of way: Bill Frisell, in '"Outlaw Bill" – Frisell Assembles a
  New International Musical Posse', by John Ephland, *DownBeat*, June 2003.
He showed up, and he hadn't met: Bill Frisell, from a transcript of an interview
  by Banning Eyre for NPR's *AfroPop Worldwide* radio series, recorded at the
  Experience Music Project in Seattle in 2003.
The first time he was there [in the studio]: Bill Frisell, in 'Interview with Bill Frisell',
  by Frank Goodman, the *Pure Music* webzine (puremusic.com), May 2003.
I just sat there and was mesmerised: Bill Frisell, from a transcript of an interview
  by Banning Eyre for NPR's *AfroPop Worldwide* radio series, recorded at the
  Experience Music Project in Seattle in 2003.
He had heard some of my music: Bill Frisell, in 'Interview with Bill Frisell', by
  Frank Goodman, the *Pure Music* webzine (puremusic.com), May 2003.
Bill and I just had a connection immediately: Jenny Scheinman, in 'Jenny
  Scheinman on Risk, Adventure and Starting a New Band with
  Allison Miller', by Gary Fukushima, on downbeat.com, 27 June 2019.
Bill always seems to be exploring new ground: Greg Leisz, in '"Outlaw Bill" –
  Frisell Assembles a New International Musical Posse', by John Ephland,
  DownBeat, June 2003.
the soul-jazz stylings of guitarist Wes Montgomery: *Unspeakable*'s opening track is
  titled '1968', the year Montgomery died.
It was fun and rewarding, and a cool record: Kenny Wollesen, author interview,
  Antwerp, Belgium, 16 August 2015.

It's just so easy to work with Bill: Petra Haden, author interview, London, 20 November 2016.

The working quintet I had at the time: Dave Douglas, author interview via Skype, 26 August 2016.

I don't want anyone to think I'm making fun: Bill Frisell, in 'The Articulate Melodic Eloquence of Bill Frisell', by Jim Macnie, the *Phoenix Providence*, 14 June 2011.

[With Viktor] you can lean on him so hard: Bill Frisell, in 'The Far Side of Frisell', by Andy Robson, *Jazzwise*, October 2005.

For a long, long time, I had a dream about: Bill Frisell, in 'The Art of the (Frisell) Trio', by Michael D. Ayers, the *Village Voice*, 4 December 2007.

recording had been scheduled at Avatar Studios in New York: between 1996 and 2017 Power Station was known as Avatar Studios.

They hadn't really played much [together, but]: Ron Carter and Paul Motian had appeared together on Andrew Hill's *One for One*, released on Blue Note in 1975. Frisell had recorded with Carter on a pair of Joey Baron albums – 1997's *Down Home* and, two years later, *We'll Soon Find Out* – and on the bass player's own Brazilian-influenced Blue Note record *Orfeu*, from 1999.

One of my loves of Bill Frisell is how: Ron Carter, in 'Legendary Jazz Bassist Ron Carter on Playing with Bill Frisell and Paul Motian', recorded for the Artists House Music website and posted to YouTube on 4 May 2020.

Most of my own music is more of a…: Bill Frisell, in 'Off the Deep End', by Joe Charupakorn, *Premier Guitar*, June 2012.

We'd go in the studio for a day or two: 'Mr Frisell and Mr Chamberlain may be the heart and soul of Floratone,' Nate Chinen wrote in a review in the *New York Times*, 'but Mr Townsend and Mr Martine clearly make up a good chunk of its brain.' On his website, Matt Chamberlain describes *Floratone* as 'an extended process of assemblage, arrangement, and augmentation: call it composition over the long haul'.

both very clear and a little gritty: Lee Townsend, in an email to the author, 5 January 2021.

Floratone *'a laboratory experiment'*: Lee Townsend, in 'Lee Townsend: Originality and Feelings', by Nenad Georgievski, on allaboutjazz.com, posted 26 October 2007.

By the end, it was some kind of weird: Lee Townsend, in the 'Floratone EPK' (Electronic Press Kit) on Vimeo, uploaded 20 August 2012.

24. Counterpoint VII: Paul Simon Listens to *The Intercontinentals*

This listening session took place at the InterContinental Hotel, Dublin, Ireland, on 6 April 2015.

Graceland *was a bridge between cultures, genres*: Andrew Leahey, in 'Paul
  Simon, Graceland 25th Anniversary Edition', on AmericanSongwriter.com,
  posted 28 June 2012.
I learned how to collaborate with players: Paul Simon, in an interview by Tom
  Moon in the liner notes to the 2011 compilation *Paul Simon, Songwriter*
  (Sony Legacy).
Brian Eno's *'sonic landscapes'*: listed in the credits to *Surprise* (Warner Bros, 2006).
but mostly it's his sense of tone, the way: Paul Simon, in *Bill Frisell: A Portrait*, a
  documentary by Emma Franz (2017).

25. Six Hundred and Eight

The pair then edited, mixed and structured: since then, Bill and Monica have
  worked on many such projects, including videos for tracks from Frisell
  albums.
That day was incredible, because: Monica Frisell, author interview via Skype, 25
  June 2017.
It seems like the best things I do: Bill Frisell, in *Bill Frisell: A Portrait*, a
  documentary by Emma Franz (2017).
the greatest obstacle to discovery: Eric Nemeyer, quoting Dan Boorstin,
  former Librarian of Congress, in 'Interview, Bill Frisell', *Jazz Improv NY*,
  December 2007.
It's clear to me that I don't know much about anything: Bill Frisell, ibid.
Gunther Schuller's essay 'Sonny Rollins and the Challenge of Thematic
  Improvisation' appeared in the *Jazz Review*, November 1958.
because I didn't know what I was doing: Sonny Rollins, in 'Sonny Rollins,
  Improvisational Virtuoso', by Juan Rodriguez, the *Montreal Gazette*, 27
  June 2010.
The road is my home: Duke Ellington, quoted in 'Words of the Week', in *Jet*
  magazine, 2 November 1967.
You make up your mind how you want: Wayne Shorter, in 'Creativity and
  Change', by Wayne Shorter, *DownBeat*, 12 February 1968 (reprinted in
  DownBeat – The Great Jazz Interviews, Hal Leonard Books, 2009).

cradle his guitar as if he's protecting it: John Diliberto, in Bill Frisell, Guitars & Scatterations', in *DownBeat*, May 1989.

When I first saw him perform in New York: Phyllis Oyama, author interview, Berkeley, California, 11 December 2015.

He never looks ecstatic on stage: Tom Junod, in 'The Guy Who Always Plays the Perfect Song', (American) *GQ*, February 1997.

I've never really met anyone who has: Carrie Rodriguez, author interview via Skype, 13 December 2016.

I don't like sitting on a plane: Bill Frisell, in 'Music is Good: A Conversation with Bill Frisell', by Danny Barnes, *Fretboard Journal*, Issue 4, winter 2006.

That's a joke. But yes, it can be: Carole d'Inverno, author interview, Seattle, 18 February 2015.

Bill always seemed to be leaving to go: Monica Frisell, author interview via Skype, 25 June 2017.

Some partners of musicians can't deal with: Leni Stern, author interview by phone, 11 September 2017.

He doesn't hate *touring – that's all we* do: Claudia Engelhart, author interview, London, 20 October 2015.

The music can change two or three times: Tony Scherr, author interview, Antwerp, Belgium, 16 August 2015.

That's why I can't listen to the records: Claudia Engelhart, author interview, London, 20 October 2015.

Live performance offers the chance: Tom Moon, in 'The Language of the Guitar', the *Philadelphia Inquirer*, 12 September 1999.

Have you noticed at gigs that people don't: Ron Miles, author interview, Denver, 4 March 2017.

a jazz improvisation is, in a very real sense: Ted Gioia, in *How to Listen to Jazz* (Basic Books, 2016), p43.

He hears a long way into the music: Ron Miles, author interview, Denver, 4 March 2017.

When we play a song, it's like we walk: Rudy Royston, author interview by phone, 12 December 2016.

I didn't really know how free to make it: Bill Frisell, at the Village Vanguard, New York, 19 March 2017.

Bill challenges and pushes himself constantly: Claudia Engelhart, author interview, London, 20 October 2015.

He gave us a new piece to play on tour: Eyvind Kang, author interview, Seattle, 15 February 2015.

They're like my best friends: Bill Frisell, in 'Bill Frisell's Big Ocean', by Celeste Sunderland, on allaboutjazz.com, 14 September 2004.

We just play and it just works: Bill Frisell, in 'Conversation with Bill Frisell', by Mike McKinley, on stateofmindmusic.com, 20 May 2008.

In so many areas I want to go into, it's like: Bill Frisell, in 'A Week in Umbria with the Guitarists' Home Base of Kenny Wollesen and Tony Scherr', by Ted Panken, *DownBeat*, October 2008.

No one in the audience might get it: Hank Roberts, author interview via Skype, 11 April 2016.

He'd even play a bass note and then look: Kermit Driscoll, author interview, Cliffside Park, New Jersey, 3 April 2017.

listening is the most important thing in music: Duke Ellington, to Ralph Gleason in the pilot episode of Gleason's *Jazz Casuals* television show, 10 July 1960 (quoted in Ted Gioia, *How to Listen to Jazz*, Basic Books, 2016, p165).

the world's greatest listener: Duke Ellington, in *Music is My Mistress*, Doubleday, 1973, p446 (also quoted in Gioia's *How to Listen to Jazz*, p165).

Bill listens more than others, and he hears: Kenny Wollesen, author interview, Antwerp, Belgium, 16 August 2015.

You've got to go for it all the way: Bill Frisell, in 'Bill Frisell, a Shy Guitar Eclectic Stages a Quiet Revolution', by Tom Moon, *Musician* magazine, July 1989.

It was very intimate and intense: Petra Haden, author interview, London, 20 November 2016.

So Bill stopped playing . . . And he went: Claudia Engelhart, author interview, London, 20 October 2015.

Erm . . . I just can't do it; I was gonna: Bill Frisell, in 'Introduction', the opening track of Live Download #12, recorded at Meany Hall, Seattle, 16 July 2002 (available at billfrisell.com).

I remember one time we were in between: Kermit Driscoll, author interview, Cliffside Park, New Jersey, 3 April 2017.

Bill's quiet, obviously, and he can be reticent: Wayne Horvitz, author interview, Seattle, 17 February 2015.

26. Counterpoint VIII: Gavin Bryars Listens to *History, Mystery*

This listening session took place at Bryars's home in Billesdon, Leicestershire, England, on 25 September 2017.

It was what I wished I could do: Bill Frisell, in 'Bill Frisell, the ECM Years', by John Kelman, posted on allaboutjazz.com, 26 April 2011.

The different versions of 'Throughout' that were selected are on:

1. *In Line* (1983).

2. *Before We Were Born* (1989), reworked as 'Steady, Girl', with lyrics and vocals by Arto Lindsay.

3. *Live* (1995).

4. *Petra Haden and Bill Frisell* (2004).

5. *Bill Frisell Live in New York*, Live Download Series #4 (recorded 2004, released 2009), with Sam Yahel (org) and Brian Blade (dr).

6. *Not in Our Name*, Charlie Haden, Liberation Music Orchestra (2005), arrangement by Carla Bley. Frisell does not play on this recording.

7. *Hemispheres*, Jim Hall and Bill Frisell (2008).

8. *Bill Frisell Live in Chapel Hill, NC*, Live Download Series #14 (recorded 2009, released 2011), a duo with Greg Leisz on steel guitars.

9. *Bill Frisell Live in California*, Live Download Series #21 (recorded 2010, realised 2015), with Jason Moran (p) and Kenny Wollesen (dr).

10. *Play a Bill Frisell Set List*, Michael Gibbs and the NDR Bigband (2015); Frisell appears on this album.

I'll show you some of the images that accompany: Live Download #12 on Frisell's website, recorded in Seattle in 2002 with a trio of Jenny Scheinman on violin and Ron Miles on cornet, also includes video files of Jim Woodring's 'visual animations'.

27. History, Mystery

We thought Bill might need to take: Phyllis Oyama, author interview, Berkeley, California, 11 December 2015.

It was pretty intense, but being a caregiver: Bob Frisell, author interview by phone, 6/7 February 2017.

My mother's parents came to visit us in Denver: Frances was taken to a hospital in Denver and transferred back home to Catonsville, near Baltimore. She and Jane's father Benjamin moved into a 'senior living community' in Boonsboro, Maryland, where they both died – Frances in 1968 and Benjamin two years later.

[The music] happened over a long period: Bill Frisell, in 'Conversation with Bill Frisell', by Mike McKinley, on stateofmindmusic.com, 20 May 2008. The group also played some Frisell favourites, songs he had some history with – a

reworking, in three parts, of his own composition 'Monroe', as well as 'Jackie-ing' by Monk and 'Subconscious-Lee' by Lee Konitz, plus Sam Cooke's 'A Change is Gonna Come' and Boubacar Traoré's 'Baba Drame'. Interspersed were studio tracks recorded by the 858 Quartet of music Frisell had written for *Stories from the Heart of the Land*, a series on National Public Radio that explored personal connections to landscape and the natural world.

To me History, Mystery is one of Bill's: Eyvind Kang, author interview, Seattle, 15 February 2015.

that inspired me to just want to spend: Bill Frisell, in 'Bill Frisell and Jim Hall: Free Stylists', by Evan Haga, *JazzTimes*, April 2009.

I'm Bill Frisell . . . and I play the guitar: Bill Frisell, in *Solos*, a DVD co-produced by Original Spin Media and Songline/Tonefield Productions, 2009.

The film is a document of the delicate: there is a warping, looping and distorting eight-minute variation on the theme of Frisell's tune 'Boubacar', for example, that is worth the price of admission alone.

It's really a dream come true: Bill Frisell, in 'Frisell, Gibbs and the Orchestral Dream', by John Watson, posted on Watson's jazzcamera.co.uk website, 2010.

Bill's a very restless creative soul: Lee Townsend, author interview, Berkeley, California, 11 December 2015.

It wasn't like any big thing – we didn't: Bill Frisell, in 'Bill Frisell: Ramping it Up', by John Kelman, on allaboutjazz.com, posted 25 April 2011.

Ten of the sixteen tracks: and three of the tunes had dedications – 'A Worthy Endeavor' was for artist Charles Cajori; 'Better Than a Machine' for darkly brilliant American singer-songwriter Vic Chesnutt, with whom Frisell had played and recorded, and who died on Christmas Day 2009, aged forty-five; and 'Beautiful Dreamer' for schoolboy friend and Denver urban campaigner Karle Seydel, who had died in May.

The whole bass-less trio thing: Eyvind Kang, author interview, Seattle, 15 February 2015.

A lot of times people talk about my equipment: Bill Frisell, in 'Jazz: Bill Frisell', by Barry Cleveland, *Guitar Player*, September 2009.

I've got that wrench in the works: Bill Frisell, in 'Guitarist Bill Frisell Brings His Novelties from New England to Noe Valley', by Jeff Kaliss, on *San Francisco Classical Voice* (sfcv.org), posted 19 October 2010.

I just wrote, wrote, wrote, wrote music: Bill Frisell, in 'Bill Frisell and the 858 Quartet – *Sign of Life*', a promotional video produced by Normal Life Pictures for the Savoy Group, posted on Vimeo on 7 February 2011.

Maybe I'm just naïve or something: Bill Frisell, in 'Guitar Virtuoso Bill Frisell in

Residency at Vermont Studio Center', on Vermont Public Radio, interview by Mitch Wertlieb, posted on VPR.org on 26 February 2014.

Ultimately, I wouldn't describe Bill's music: Eyvind Kang, in 'Bill Frisell and the 858 Quartet – *Sign of Life*', a promotional video produced by Normal Life Pictures for the Savoy Group, posted on Vimeo on 7 February 2011.

I've been beyond overwhelmed: Bill Frisell, in 'Bill Frisell, Anything's Possible', by Eric Fine, *DownBeat*, September 2011.

I don't even know if I'd be playing guitar: Bill Frisell, in 'Bill Frisell – All We Are Saying', a promotional video produced by Normal Life Pictures for the Savoy Group, posted on Vimeo on 4 August 2011.

To go back and look at [Lennon and the Beatles]: Bill Frisell, in 'John Lennon's Music was Just Right, Eventually, for Bill Frisell', by Mark Halverson, the *Sacramento Bee*, 8 May 2014.

I am like a chameleon . . . abolished the borders: exhibition literature for *John Lennon, Unfinished Music*, at Cité de la Musique, Paris, October 2005 to June 2006 (collectionsdumusee.philharmoniedeparis.fr).

By importing unexpected sounds, the trio: David Peschek, in 'Bill Frisell Trio', a review of a concert at Usher Hall, Edinburgh, the *Guardian*, 5 November 2005.

cursed with ghastly good taste: Clive Davis, in a review of *All We Are Saying*, the *Sunday Times*, 30 October 2011.

surrender to nostalgia: 'When Musicians Surrender to Nostalgia', headline to a review of *Guitar in the Space Age!*, by David A. Graham, in the *Atlantic*, 7 October 2014.

It's true that some tracks on the album: 'There isn't a single impeachable note on the disc; even the incurably maudlin and simple "Imagine" delights,' wrote David A. Graham in the *Atlantic*. 'On the other hand, what purpose does a disc of relatively faithful covers of John Lennon tunes serve? It's not as if Lennon is an under-appreciated figure.'

You listen for five seconds and then the songs: Bill Frisell, in 'An Interview with Bill Frisell', by Donald Gibson, on his writeonmusic.com website (no post date, probably September 2011).

28. The Composer

When morning came, it blew my mind: Bill Frisell, in 'An Album Born Out of Focused Isolation', by Larry Blumenfeld, the *Wall Street Journal*, 8 July 2013.

Frisell stayed in a small guest cottage: the ranch had once been the home of

Seeley and Virginia Mudd; the couple had bequeathed the estate to the Big Sur Land Trust in 2001, with an express stipulation that the property 'be used to serve artists'.

I was looking at a donkey one day: Bill Frisell, in 'DCist Preview: Bill Frisell @ Wolf Trap', by Sriram Gopal, posted on DCist.com, 5 December 2013.

the saxophonist Charles Lloyd sought refuge: 'Big Sur was a wonderful laboratory for working on myself,' Lloyd told the *Monterey County Weekly* in 2014.

I didn't have any schedule: Bill Frisell, in 'The guitarist and man behind brand-new Big Sur, composed in 10 days at Glen Deven Ranch', by Sarah Rubin, in the *Monterey County Weekly*, 31 October 2013.

I once listened to Big Sur *as I was driving*: Phyllis Oyama, author interview, Berkeley, California, 11 December 2015.

In 2011 Frisell was approached by Hal Willner: even though Hunter S. Thompson's 7,200-word feature, with Ralph Steadman's characteristic series of grotesqueries, appeared in a short-lived American political magazine called *Scanlan's Monthly*, it is still celebrated today as the progenitor of what became known as 'gonzo journalism'. The idea to make a recording of the article had come from Michael Minzer, a spoken-word record label owner who had worked with Willner on Allen Ginsberg's *The Lion for Real*, and on recordings with William Burroughs and Terry Southern. But Hal Willner made it happen.

I've worked with Bill for so many years: Hal Willner, in 'Bill Frisell: Fear and Composing', by Geoffrey Himes, *JazzTimes*, July/August 2012.

After all that, there's a point when I start writing: Bill Frisell, ibid.

I'd read Allen Ginsberg's poetry on and off: Bill Frisell, in 'The Sound of Ginsberg's "Kaddish"', by George Robinson, in the New York *Jewish Week*, 14 February 2012.

I think that many of us guitarists tend to be: Nels Cline, author interview via Skype, 19 July 2017.

improvisation is a way of finding music that can't: Steve Lacy, in 'Forget Paris', by John Corbett, *DownBeat*, February 1997 (reprinted in *DownBeat – The Great Jazz Interviews*, Hal Leonard Books, 2009, p288).

What sets Frisell apart from other post-fusion: Gene Santoro, in a review of *Before We Were Born*, *DownBeat*, June 1989.

I don't know how that happens, but: Bill Frisell, in 'Fission', by Josef Woodard, *Jazziz*, April 1998.

I put Bill in the same category of composers: Cuong Vu, author interview, Seattle, 22 February 2015.

He is one of the truly great American composers: Dave Douglas, liner notes to
 Strange Liberation (Bluebird, 2004).
You are not the 'Great Creator' of your songs: Nick Cave, in Issue #43 of his
 online Q&A forum, *The Red Hand Files*.
They [the songs] came from out of the blue . . . they seemed to: Bob Dylan, in
 Chronicles, Volume One (Simon & Schuster, 2004), p165.
It's like fishing . . . I'm floating through: Bill Frisell, in 'Bill Frisell's Big Ocean',
 by Celeste Sunderland, on allaboutjazz.com, 14 September 2004.

29. Counterpoint IX: Van Dyke Parks Listens to *Big Sur*

This listening session took place at Van Dyke Park's home in Pasadena,
California, on 9 December 2015.

teenage symphony to God: Brian Wilson, quoted on 'The Life of Brian' page on
 brianwilson.com.
like recording with Mark Twain, Erik Satie: Vic Chesnutt, in a press release
 for *Ghetto Bells* (New West Records, 2005); both Bill Frisell and Van Dyke
 Parks play on the record.
Here's a final track; this is called 'Highway 1': Van Dyke Parks told me that he
 lived off Highway 1 in Big Sur for a couple of years; I later discovered that his
 property in Garrapata Canyon was just a few miles from the Glen Deven Ranch.

30. The Quiet American

My work is primarily focused on developing an abstract: Carole d'Inverno, in
 an 'Artist Statement', in the catalogue to *Carole d'Inverno: A Way of Saying*,
 Mercer Gallery, Rochester, New York, 2015.
Transumanza, a word . . . 'loosely translated from Italian': Tom Wachunas, in
 'Transumanza Extravaganza' posted on the *Artwach* blog, 3 January 2020.
You're crazy! It's too fast!: Bill Frisell, in 'Bill Frisell to play Speedy West at
 Portland Jazz Festival', by Paul de Barros, the *Seattle Times*, 17 February
 2012.
That Jimmy Bryant and Speedy West stuff: Bill Frisell, in 'Bill Frisell's Beach
 Blanket Guitar', by Britt Robson, the Minneapolis *Star Tribune*, 2 July 2014.
There are all these seeds that have been: Bill Frisell, in '*Guitar in the Space Age!* –
 Behind the Scenes', a promotional video for the album, posted on Vimeo
 on 10 September 2014.

Frisell gets so enraptured with the dreamy: Paul de Barros, in 'Bill Frisell's Shimmering Reverb and Nostalgic Optimism', a review of *Guitar in the Space Age!*, the *Seattle Times*, 7 October 2014.

Charles had sent me some music: Bill Frisell, author interview by phone, 3 October 2019.

It's kind of weird getting to be this age: Bill Frisell, in 'Spontaneous Combustion: Guitarist Bill Frisell Jams with Charles Lloyd', by Paul Weideman, the *Santa Fe New Mexican*, 15 November 2013.

Charles talked about growing up in Memphis: Bill Frisell, in 'Charles Lloyd's 80th Birthday Residency', by Britt Robson, the (Minneapolis) *Star Tribune*, 5 March 2018.

This record, it's deceptive: Charles Lloyd, in 'The Re-Flowering: Charles Lloyd's Second Golden Age', by David A Graham, the *Atlantic*, 1 December 2016.

In 2018 Lloyd and the Marvels released Vanished Gardens: Frisell's tapestry of connections was weaving some magic and mystery again – he had first worked with Lucinda Williams on her Hal Willner-produced 2007 album *West*. Greg Leisz's relationship with Williams stretched back even further, to one of the great albums of the nineties, *Car Wheels on a Gravel Road*. The daughter of poet Miller Williams, Lucinda was born in Louisiana and grew up in the South, and she and Lloyd formed a strong and instant bond; 'It was fated to be, because southern crossroads met,' Lloyd says in a promotional video for the album.

[There was] Wes Montgomery . . . he influenced: Charles Lloyd, in 'Charles Lloyd Comes to Palladium Next Thursday', by Kyle Long, *NUVO* (Indianapolis), 13 April 2017.

I'm stunned. I can't believe this is happening: Bill Frisell, in 'Bill Frisell Gave a Tour of His Musical Past at East High School Last Night', by Jon Solomon, Denver *Westword*, 22 January 2015.

They played a Bob Dylan song on that record: Bill Frisell, in a foreword to *Conversations with Charlie Haden*, by Josef Woodard and Charlie Haden (Silman-James Press, 2016).

The idea is to put Ornette Coleman: John Zorn, in 'Masada, John Zorn's Jazz Band', posted on Scott Maykrantz's (now defunct) omnology.com site, 9 December 2004.

I went in without any preparation: Bill Frisell, in 'Swirling in Circles', by Barry Cleveland, *Guitar Player*, October 2013.

You will never think of Bill Frisell: John Zorn, blurb for *Silent Comedy* on tzadik.com.

Inspired by early music, Debussy, the minimalism of: blurb for *John Zorn: The Gnostic Preludes* on tzadik.com.

Zorn is a great guy, totally amazing: Kenny Wollesen, author interview, Antwerp, Belgium, 16 August 2015.

musicians swim backwards up the stream: Marc Ribot, in a conversation between Bill Frisell and Marc Ribot, *BOMB* magazine, spring 2002.

The music I chose for this [album] is: Bill Frisell, in 'Bill Frisell's New Album Celebrates Movie Music', by Steve Dollar, the *Wall Street Journal*, 27 January 2016.

It's like having cataracts surgery: Bill Frisell, in 'Bill Frisell, Infinite Set List', by Bill Milkowski, *DownBeat*, July 2017.

I'm afraid I don't get much from this CD: John Corbett, in 'The Hot Box', *DownBeat*, January 2012.

a little too perfect for the NPR: David A. Graham, in 'When Musicians Surrender to Nostalgia', a review of *Guitar in the Space Age!*, the *Atlantic*, 7 October 2014.

I don't want forgettable music: Dave Sumner, in 'From Now on All Bill Frisell Decisions Get Run Past Me First', on his *Bird is the Worm* blog, 20 March 2018.

Sometimes I feel like he's just relaxing: Claudia Engelhart, author interview, London, 20 October 2015.

You can cut through the fabric of: David Breskin, author interview via Skype, 27 February 2018.

31. Counterpoint X: Gus Van Sant Listens to *When You Wish Upon a Star*

This listening session took place at Gus Van Sant's home in the Hollywood Hills, Los Angeles, on 9 December 2015.

Unusually, however, Van Sant has also found success: he has also suffered some spectacular commercial and critical flops, perhaps none more high profile than his curious, near shot-for-shot, colour remake of Alfred Hitchcock's *Psycho*, for which Frisell provided some original music.

primitive home recordings: Gus Van Sant, in a bio posted by Van Sant on Spotify.

32. Music Is

less a biography than a hangout film: John DeFore, in 'Bill Frisell, A
  Portrait: Film Review', the *Hollywood Reporter*, 20 December 2017. The
  documentary can be rented or purchased via billfrisellfilm.com.

Yeah, it was difficult . . . embarrassing: Bill Frisell, following a première of *Bill
  Frisell: A Portrait*, Austin, Texas, 13 March 2017.

He is clearly moved by watching two: there is footage of Motian, Lovano and
  Frisell playing a gentle, lyrical rendition of 'Yahllah', a Motian ballad that
  the three musicians had first played almost thirty years previously and that
  appears on *Psalm*, their debut recording together. At the end of the set
  in September 2010, Motian picks up the microphone, in the middle of
  enthusiastic applause, and exclaims, 'Hey, if you like it so much, buy a CD,
  man – give me a break!'

To me, one of the major takeaways: Emma Franz, author interview by phone,
  13 March 2018.

bipolar disorder and opioid addiction: in blurb for *Andy Irons: Kissed by God* on
  the film's website, tetongravity.com.

He's another one of these guys: Bill Frisell, in 'Bill Frisell – HARMONY (Album
  Trailer)', a promotional video posted on Vevo, 23 August 2019.

hoped one day to work up enough nerve: Bill Frisell, quoted by Francis Davis, in
  'Unironic', in the *Atlantic*, July/August 2002.

I thought, 'Oh, wait a minute, they're all vocalists': Bill Frisell, author interview
  by phone, 3 October 2019.

a quiet masterpiece, its intimate interplay: preview of Bill Frisell and Thomas
  Morgan at Jazz Standard, the *New Yorker*, 11 December 2017.

A second Andrew Cyrille Quartet CD, The News: the first album, *The
  Declaration of Musical Independence*, featured Cyrille, Frisell, bassist Ben
  Street and on keyboards composer, improviser and electronic music pioneer
  Richard Teitelbaum. For the second quartet recording Cuban-born pianist
  David Virelles replaced Teitelbaum, who was in ill health; he died, aged
  eighty, in April 2020.

It took me years and years before I even: Bill Frisell, author interview by phone,
  3 October 2019.

My plan for making this recording: Bill Frisell, in 'Conversations with
  Himself: Guitarist Bill Frisell on His New Solo Guitar Outing', by Will
  Layman, on PopMatters.com, 6 March 2018.

I brought this big pile of music and started: Bill Frisell, in 'In Conversation: The Fast-Paced Life of Bill Frisell', by Ted Panken, on Jazz in Europe, 12 July 2019 (from an interview for Qwest TV in April 2019).

It's so perfect. Everything I need: Bill Frisell, in a Sony/OKeh press release for *Music IS*, 2 March 2018.

This guy said, 'Oh yeah, I really like': Bill Frisell, in 'Bill Frisell: Made to Shine', by Nick Millevoi, *Premier Guitar*, May 2018.

Bill Frisell is the patron saint: Dan Waldman, in 'Dan Waldman (New Release "Sources & Angles")', on the *LondonJazz News* website, posted 10 August 2020.

I was just so terrified to sit there: Bill Frisell, in 'Bill Frisell: Made to Shine', by Nick Millevoi, *Premier Guitar*, May 2018.

I love the way that Bill annihilates: Don Was, in 'Bill Frisell Signs with Blue Note', a press release issued 30 July 2019.

The record includes three short new pieces: other music on *HARMONY* includes a delicate duo between Frisell and Haden on 'Lush Life'; 'There in a Dream', a song by Petra's father Charlie Haden; and 'Red River Valley', in which Frisell lays out and the arrangement is for the three voices alone. The ensemble is one of Frisell's most open and elastic – in concert the quartet also ventured down further byways such as Elizabeth Cotten's folk classic 'Freight Train' and even David Bowie's 'Space Oddity'.

openly endorse Bernie Sanders as Democratic nominee: Bill Frisell is listed in 'Artists, Musicians and Cultural Leaders Unite for Sanders', a 'Bernie 2016 Press Release', issued on p2016.org, 18 September 2015.

Well, it's not a blatant [political] thing: Bill Frisell, author interview by phone, 3 October 2019.

Well, I know I'm really lucky: Bill Frisell, author interview via Skype, 26 June 2020.

can't shake that guy off somehow: Bill Frisell on Thelonious Monk, in 'Bill Frisell – Winslow Homer – Commentary', a promotional video for *Music IS*, posted on Vevo, 6 April 2018.

Even though the selections on Valentine *hail*: J. D. Considine, in a review of 'Bill Frisell: *Valentine* (Blue Note)', *DownBeat*, August 2020.

I've been playing 'We Shall Overcome' for the last: Bill Frisell, author interview via Skype, 26 June 2020.

33. Counterpoint XI: Rhiannon Giddens Listens to *HARMONY*

This listening session took place at Rhiannon Giddens's home in Limerick, Ireland, on 21 December 2020.

systematically dismantling the myth: David Morris, in 'Rhiannon Giddens: Bluegrass in Black and White', posted on BluegrassToday.com, 26 September 2017.
dedicated to reviving and extending the tradition: Jon Pareles, in 'A Solo Spotlight for a Powerful Voice', the *New York Times*, 23 January 2015.
She has a pretty profound gift . . . I've been doing this: T Bone Burnett, ibid.
black, non-black music: Rhiannon Giddens, in 'Rhiannon Giddens and What Folk Music Means', by John Jeremiah Sullivan, the *New Yorker*, 20 May 2019.

33⅓. Becoming Bill Frisell

He appeared at the small downtown bar and club: at that time Evans was in a relatively good place, clean of a heroin addiction, and touring and recording prolifically again.
Night after night . . . I was just having these: Bill Frisell, in 'Interview: Bill Frisell', by Eric Nemeyer, *Jazz Improv NY*, December 2007.
He was out in the middle of the street: Bill Frisell, in 'Interview with Bill Frisell', by Ethan Iverson, January 2018, posted on Ethan Iverson's blog *Do the Math*, 1 July 2018.
couldn't play shit: Bill Frisell, in 'Interview: Bill Frisell', by Eric Nemeyer, *Jazz Improv NY*, December 2007.
constantly in a state of becoming: Bob Dylan, in Martin Scorsese's 2005 documentary *No Direction Home: Bob Dylan*.
you should go into every musical situation: Ry Cooder, as quoted by Bill Frisell in 'Seattle's Super Sonic', by Jude Gold, *Guitar Player*, February 2002.
When I pick it up, it doesn't feel very different: Bill Frisell, in 'Bill Frisell: Ramping it Up', by John Kelman, on allaboutjazz.com, posted 25 April 2011.
all art aspires to something it cannot achieve: Steven Poole, in a review of *Pretentiousness* by Dan Fox, the *Guardian*, 11 February 2016.
Yes, for those of us who have that kind: John Surman, author interview by phone, 26 November 2014.

dean of Colorado's folk music scene: description of Harry Tuft on his inductee
page on the Colorado Music Hall of Fame website, cmhof.org.

I grew up in Denver in the fifties: Bill Frisell, in 'Denver Folklore Center/
Swallow Hill Music', in the News section of billfrisell.com, 4 April 2019.

Discography/Tour Archive

There is a surprisingly accurate and fairly comprehensive Bill Frisell discography on Wikipedia; it lists albums as leader, the Live Download Series available through billfrisell.com, most of his work with Paul Motian and John Zorn, major collaborations, albums produced by Hal Willner, soundtracks, film and television appearances, and a good selection of recordings on which Frisell has played a significant role as sideman or guest. The completist, however, should turn to the Bill Frisell entry at discogs.com, which lists 748 (and counting) credits, including three for his illustrations and four (despite his protestation about working up 'enough nerve to sing in the shower') for vocals. An archive of tour dates stretching back to 2001 is also available at billfrisell.com.

Index

55 Grand club, New York, 121
858 Quartet, 240, 242, 249, 327, 371, 378, 379–80, 387, 390, 512n
1369 Jazz Club, Boston, 120, 180

Abercrombie, John, 91, 93, 124, 130, 409, 410
acoustic guitars, 128, 163, 171, 318, 414
Act Big Band, 95
Adams, John, 200, 247, 366, 387, 401
Adjuah, Christian Scott aTunde, 290, 502n
African American music, 18, 27, 28, 441, 445–6
African music, 84, 141, 323
Ake, David, 215
Alias, Don, 328
Allen, Geri, 108
All Hat (film), 246–7, 496n
Allison, Mose, 101
All We Are Saying . . . (Frisell album), 382–5, 406, 416, 426, 464n, 513n
Altman, Robert, 134
Aluisi, Alan, 39
Ambitious Lovers, 186, 206
Amendola, Scott, 496n
Americana, 38, 191, 194, 197, 262, 273, 277, 293–4, 336
American Composers Orchestra, 265, 275
American music: black music, 445–6; Frisell childhood, 24; Frisell contribution, 395, 401–402; Frisell enthusiasm, 259, 267; Frisell explorations, 267–8; Frisell influence, 8, 393; Giddens on, 444–5; Hayes on, 303; move to guitar, 320; Nashville/country, 260–1; Ribot on, 258; Vernon on, 223
Amidon, Sam: But This Chicken Proved Falsehearted, 280; Doveman, 500n; on Frisell's Good Dog, Happy Man, 279–85; Frisell work, 9; The Gloaming, 286; Hayes on, 307; Lily-O, 280
Andersen, Arild, 124, 125, 128, 129, 429, 478n
Andersen, Steve, 311
Anderson, Laurie, 120, 134, 236, 325, 397
Anderson, Reid, 190, 191, 192, 194–6, 198, 232

Andrew Cyrille Quartet, 353, 430; The Declaration of Musical Independence, 353; The News, 430; see also Cyrille, Andrew
Andy Irons: Kissed by God (documentary), 427
Angel Song (Wheeler album), 272–3, 302
The Animals, 'House of the Rising Sun', 27
Anthology of American Folk Music, 396
Aphex Twin, 192, 360
Appalachian folk music, 16, 267, 291, 292, 440
Appel, Alfred, Jr, 293
Apple, Fiona, 270, 318, 396
Arlen, Harold, 246, 477n
Armstrong, Louis ('Satchmo'), 67, 292–3, 295, 399, 418; 'Basin Street Blues', 293; 'Blue Yodel No. 9', 292
art: and Frisell's style, 167; and jazz, 376; and music, 228–32, 230–3, 242–3; painted guitars, 313–14; Poole on, 450; Richter project, 241; Woodring album artwork, 250–7
Art Ensemble of Chicago, 86, 290
ArtistShare label, 372
Arts at St Ann's, 233, 234
Arts Council of Great Britain, 90
Association for the Advancement of Creative Musicians (AACM), 151
The Astronauts, 'Baja', 20, 404, 409
At Close Range (film), 214
Atkins, Chet, 6, 262, 293, 497–8n
audience, 356–7
avant-garde, 47, 135, 152, 193
Avatar Studios, New York, 332, 507n

'Baba Drame' (Traoré song), 165, 324, 326, 336, 512n
Bacharach, Burt, 31, 275–6, 294, 399; Painted from Memory, 275; 'What the World Needs Now Is Love', 30, 70, 331
Bad Livers, 317
Badolato, Greg, 85
The Bad Plus, 8, 107, 190–8, 232, 291
Baez, Joan, 32
Bailey, Derek, 184, 360, 361, 467n; Solo Guitar, 361; 'The Squirrel and the Ricketty-Racketty Bridge', 361

Bailey, Philip, 28, 433
Bainbridge Island, Washington, 324
'Baja' (Hazlewood song), 20, 404, 409
Baker, Buddy, 42–3, 468n
Baker, Chet, 85, 175, 474n; *Chet Baker–Steve Houben*, 88
Baker, Ginger, 268, 272, 410, 499n; *Falling Off the Roof*, 272; *Going Back Home*, 272, 420
balalaika, 92
Balliett, Whitney, 38
banjo, 138, 150, 157, 186, 207, 235, 259, 312, 317, 321, 443
Barbican Centre, London, 317, 326, 373, 383, 425
Barnes, Danny, 232, 259, 301, 317–18, 347, 350, 381, 432, 447
Barnes, Julian, 454
Baron, Joey: Bill Frisell Band, 174–8, 181, 182, 206, 208–10, 212, 213, 217, 218, 221, 222, 233, 237; Breskin on, 67; Douglas's 'The Frisell Dream', 330; *Down Home*, 273, 507n; on Frisell, 60, 61, 71–2, 129–30, 170, 218; Frisell and Gibbs's *Collage for a Day*, 373; Frisell collaboration, 273; Frisell on, 319; Frisell's *Before We Were Born*, 206; Frisell's *Have a Little Faith*, 213; Frisell's *Is That You?* 206; Frisell's *Live*, 212; Frisell's *Lookout for Hope*, 134; Frisell's *This Land*, 219, 221, 222; Frisell's *Where in the World?* 190, 194; Frisell tours, 187; Frisell trio, 208, 358; Frisell work, 174–6; Hall quartet, 184; Hall's *Dialogues*, 372; Hoboken move, 117; Johnson album, 265, 273; Mackey's *Deal*, 274; and Morgan, 429; Naked City, 157; Robertson's *Transparency*, 153; Scherr on, 57; Shifting Foundation grant, 481n; Vernon on, 222; *We'll Soon Find Out*, 507n; and Zorn, 157–8, 176, 208
Barretto, Ray, 465n
Barry, John, 157, 415, 416, 419, 430, 431
Bartlett, Thomas, 279, 280, 282, 286, 307, 500n
Bartók, Béla, 40, 50
Basie, Count, 384
Basquiat, Jean-Michel, 274
Batiste, Jon, 290
BBC Symphony Orchestra, 373, 424–5
The Beach Boys, 20, 387; 'Surfer Girl', 20, 310, 404, 409
The Beatles: 'Across the Universe', 383, 385; 'Come Together', 383; *The Ed Sullivan Show*, 22–3, 466n; Frisell concerts, 382–3; Frisell on, 22–3, 382–5, 462n; Frisell's Lennon project, 382–4; impact of, 22–3, 24, 25, 56; 'In My Life', 165, 383; 'I Want to Hold Your Hand', 23; 'Julia', 383; 'Please, Please Me', 382; 'Revolution', 382, 383; 'Revolution 9', 136; *Sgt Pepper's*, 333; 'Strawberry Fields Forever', 380; 'You've Got to Hide Your Love Away', 383
'Beautiful Dreamer' (Foster song), 3, 34, 375, 510n
Beautiful Dreamers (Frisell album), 3, 375–6, 512n
Beautiful Dreamers trio, 3, 354, 375, 376, 387
bebop, 47, 152, 185, 293, 295
Beckett, Samuel, 168
Before We Were Born (Frisell album), 185, 202, 205–7, 260, 299, 364, 392, 511n
Belgium, 84, 85–90, 95
The Bells (film), 247
Benson, George, 5, 384
Benton, Thomas Hart, *The Boy*, 494n
Bergen, Norway, 131, 358
Bergeson, Pat, 497n
Bergman, Luke, 427, 440
Berken, Betty, 211
Berklee College of Music, Boston, 43, 45–8, 73–85, 87, 90–1, 94, 99, 106–7, 118, 121, 143, 174–5, 178, 391, 433
Bermuda Brass, 51
Berne, Tim, 5, 60, 99, 140, 143, 146, 148, 153, 174, 176, 181, 185, 479n; *Fulton Street Maul*, 153, 200; *Theoretically*, 146
Bernstein, Elmer, 415, 419; 'To Kill a Mockingbird', 422
Bernstein, Leonard, 40, 366
Bernstein, Steven, 315, 327
Berry, Chuck, 18, 33
The Best of Bill Frisell Vol 1: Folk Songs, 374, 504n
Bierce, Ambrose, 'An Occurrence at Owl Creek Bridge', 491n
big bands, 38, 43, 44, 51, 90, 95, 101, 106, 119, 146, 157
Big Brother and the Holding Company, 33
The Big Gundown (Zorn album), 148–9, 200, 415, 482n
Big Sur, 386–7, 401, 514n, 515n
Big Sur (Frisell album), 387–8, 389, 391, 396–402, 404

Bill Evans Trio, 96, 98, 101, 109; *see also* Evans, Bill

Bill Frisell: A Portrait (documentary), 67, 137, 145, 168, 299, 314, 320, 336, 343, 424–5, 518n

Bill Frisell Band: *Before We Were Born*, 205–7; end of, 217–18; first gig, 179–80; formation and members, 174, 176–82; gigs and tours, 179–80, 208, 217; *Have a Little Faith*, 212–16; Keaton film scores, 233–4; *Live*, 211–12, 217, 221–2, 491–92n; *Lookout for Hope*, 121, 181; *Night Music* TV show, 139; as quintet, 212; Roberts departure, 209–10; as sextet, 216; *This Land*, 216–17, 219–26; as trio, 210–12, 216–18, 221, 222, 233–4; *Where in the World?* 208–9

Bill Frisell, Ron Carter, Paul Motian (album), 332–3

'Billy Boy' (folk song), 213

Billy the Kid (Copland), 213

Biscotto, Laura, 149

Black, J. W., 314

Black Artists Group, 119

'Blackberry Blossom' (folk song), 318

'Black is the Colour (of My True Love's Hair)' (folk song), 42

black music, 290, 445–6, 447

Blade, Brian, 245, 276

Blakely, Chauncey, 34

Blake, William, 414

Blakey, Art, 86

Bley, Carla, 43, 96, 120, 123, 185, 328, 361, 391

Bley, Paul, 55, 76, 96, 101, 112, 182–4, 345, 375, 489n; *Fragments*, 182–3; 'Heat', 276; *The Paul Bley Quartet*, 183

Blind Blake, 267

Block, Ron, 261, 262, 497n

Bloemers, Jean-Jacques, 87

Bluebird Theater, Denver, 26, 291

bluegrass, 54, 164, 259, 261–2, 268, 292, 294, 317, 444

Blue Note jazz club, New York, 180, 332, 410, 438

Blue Note record label, 30, 151, 152, 408, 434, 438, 440

Blues Dream (Frisell album), 3, 220, 222, 276–7, 314–16, 317, 319, 374, 426, 433, 439

blues music, 24, 28, 248, 259

Bluiett, Hamiet, 494n

Blythe, Arthur, 147, 273

Boggs, Dock, 258, 267

Bolin, Tommy, 33, 55

Bollani, Stefano, 429

Bon Iver, 9, 219, 224

Boonshoft, Dave, 478n

Booth, Stanley, 453

Boston, 43, 45, 46, 48, 74, 79, 120, 179, 180, 185, 434

Boston Connection, 80–1

Bottom Line, New York, 180

Boulder, Colorado, 20, 43, 44, 54, 55, 75, 464n

bouzouki, 325, 335, 337

Bowie, David, 135, 297, 333, 420, 519n

Brackett, John, 482n

Bracknell Festival, England, 1988 bootleg, 483n

Bradfield, Polly, 142, 148

Brandes, Vera, 200

Braxton, Anthony, 79, 90, 141, 160, 290

Breskin, David: *Escape Velocity* poems, 266; on Frisell, 66–7, 73, 168, 185, 233, 417; Frisell's *Smash & Scatteration*, 154, 483n; 'The Guitarist' poem, 266–7; 'Monk of the electric guitar' phrase, 168, 486n; Power Tools, 154; Richter project, 241, 242, 243; telegram, 266, 439

Brill Building, New York, 415

Brion, Jon, 334

Bristol recording sessions, 445

Broadway, 107, 434, 477n

Bro, Jakob, 112, 381, 429

Brooklyn, New York, 115, 117, 233, 239, 240, 435–7

Brooklyn Rider, 391

Brookmeyer, Bob, 49

Brown, James, 28, 33, 34, 328

Brown, Sam, 96

Brubeck, Dave, 3, 461n

Bruning, Dale: 'Bill Music', 295; concerts, 236; on Frisell, 36, 40, 46; Frisell dedication, 492n; Frisell lessons, 36–7, 38, 40, 46, 48, 49, 51, 229, 372, 415, 492n; Frisell on, 48; guitars, 40, 71; and Hall, 47; Senate Lounge shows, 47, 448; and Smith, 466n; teaching, 467n

Brussels, 88, 93, 325

Bryant, Jimmy, 405

Bryars, Gavin: 'After the Requiem', 361, 364–5; on Frisell, 361–7; Frisell influence, 9; on Frisell's *History, Mystery*, 360–7; Frisell's

'Throughout', 123, 392; *Jesus' Blood Never Failed Me Yet*, 360, 361; and Morrison, 247; overview, 360–1; *The Sinking of the Titanic*, 360; 'The Squirrel and the Ricketty-Racketty Bridge', 361; 'Sub Rosa', 361, 362, 364

Buckley, Tim, 33, 134, 396

Bumbershoot festival, Seattle, 323

'Bumpin' on Sunset' (Montgomery song), 29, 30, 34, 83, 409

Burger, Rob, 236

The Burglars (film), 149, 482n

Burnett, T Bone, 246, 441

Burrell, Kenny, 31, 40, 237

Burroughs, William, 134, 420, 514n; *The Elvis of Letters*, 419; *Naked Lunch*, 274, 499n

Burton, Gary: Berklee College of Music, 48, 76, 77, 79, 82, 433; *Country Roads & Other Places*, 38; *Duster*, 77; and ECM/Weber, 91–2; festival judging, 38; Frisell influences, 43, 92; Frisell on, 260; Gary Burton Quartet, 31, 38, 119, 467n; Newport Jazz Festival, 31; *Tennessee Firebird*, 293; UNC/Greeley Jazz Festival, 43; Weber's *Fluid Rustle*, 92

Butterfield, Paul, 24, 32, 451

Byard, Jaki, 136

The Byrds, 25, 27, 297, 396

Byrne, David, 140, 325

Byron, Don: 'Basquiat', 274; Doris Duke award, 388; Frisell quintet/sextet, 212–14, 216; Frisell's *Have a Little Faith*, 212–14; Frisell's *The Sweetest Punch*, 276; Frisell's *This Land*, 219, 222; *Romance with the Unseen*, 274; *Tuskegee Experiments*, 212

Cabay, Guy, 95

Cage, John, 168, 360, 379

Cahill, Dennis, 381; on Frisell's *The Willies*, 301–8

Caine, Uri, 330

Cajori, Charles, 227–9, 231, 512n; *Epistrophy I and II*, 229, 431

Cajori, Florian, 227

calabash, 323, 335, 337

Camara, Sidiki, 323–4, 325, 326, 335

Campbell, Tommy, 82, 474n

Canada, 131, 186, 187, 368, 373

Cantuária, Vinicius: Frisell collaboration, 274, 325, 326, 381; Frisell concert, 326; Frisell's *The Intercontinentals*, 335; Intercontinental

Quartet, 326; *Lágrimas Mexicanas* (*Mexican Tears*), 338; *Tucuma*, 325; *Vinicius*, 325

Capra, Frank, 68

Captain Beefheart, 200, 254

Cardew, Cornelius, 360

Carmichael, Hoagy, 329

Carmine Street Guitars, New York, 309–10

Carnegie Hall, New York, 240, 265, 275, 381

Carolina Chocolate Drops, 440

Carter, A. P., 301, 313, 318, 431

Carter, 'Mother' Maybelle, 262, 267, 297

Carter, Ron: Baron's *Down Home*, 273; *Bill Frisell, Ron Carter, Paul Motian*, 332–3; and Davis, 332, 466n; double bass, 310–11; 'Eighty-One', 332; on Frisell, 332; Frisell collaboration, 5, 274, 507n; Frisell concerts, 381; Frisell guidance, 38; Frisell interest, 31; Frisell's 'Ron Carter', 315, 332; Hall duo, 332; and Montgomery, 31, 273, 465n; 'Mood', 332, 355; and Motian, 332, 507n; *Orfeu*, 507n

Carter Family, 267; 'Keep on the Sunny Side', 375; 'Wildwood Flower', 324, 326, 430

Carter Sisters, 262

Carthy, Eliza, 326

cartoons, 17, 18, 20, 231, 496n

Cash, Johnny, 3, 246, 292, 299

Cassady, Neal, 54, 465n

Castelluci, Bruno, 88

Catherine, Philip, 90

Catonsville, 16, 511n

Cave, Nick, 394

CBGB, New York, 109, 123, 180

Chadbourne, Eugene, 143

Chamberlain, Bob, 30

Chamberlain, Matt, 333, 507n

Chandelier, New York, 144, 175, 206

Change in the Air (film), 427, 432

The Chantays, 'Pipeline', 404, 409

Chapati club, Spa, Belgium, 86, 87, 89, 90, 93, 115, 174

Charles Lloyd and the Marvels, 408, 409, 434; *see also* Lloyd, Charles

Cherry, Don, 101

Chesnutt, Vic, 329, 397, 512n

Chicago, 203, 248, 266, 301

Chinen, Nate, 507n

Christensen, Jon, 125, 131, 479n

Christian, Charlie, 30, 50, 270, 421

Cité de la Musique, Paris, 382

civil rights, 10, 24, 28, 439

Clapton, Eric, 56, 269, 421, 485n

clarinet (Frisell experience), 21–2, 25, 27–8, 34, 36, 38, 43, 45, 106, 119, 162, 207, 370, 378, 436

Clark, Mike, 118, 122

Clarke, Kenny, 229

Claxton, William, 502n

Clayton College for Boys, Denver, 27

Cline, Alex, 153

Cline, Nels, 68, 122, 149–50, 165, 187, 287, 299, 309, 391, 410

Close Your Eyes (Frisell and Woodring multimedia), 240

Club Zircon, 76, 79

'Cluck Old Hen' (folk song), 305–6, 318, 380, 446

Coe, Jonathan, 61–2, 63, 64, 174, 205, 487n

Coen Brothers, 207; *O Brother, Where Art Thou?* 246

Cohen, Greg, 245

Colaiuta, Vinnie, 80

Colby, Kansas, 75, 470

Coleman, Anthony, 142, 148, 482n

Coleman, George, 466n

Coleman, Ornette: Amidon on, 281; and Bley, 183; Frisell concerts, 381; as Frisell influence, 41, 55, 56, 56, 69, 69; Frisell on, 145, 276, 297; and Hall, 49; Lloyd's *Tone Poem*, 409; on music, 289; Vu on Frisell, 393; Zorn exploration, 157, 176, 412

Coleman, Steve, 155

Collage for a Day (Frisell and Gibbs), 373–4, 424–5

Colley, Scott, 372

Collings guitars, 318

Collins, Billy, 286

Collins, Judy, 24, 32, 464n

Colorado, and music scene, 20, 32, 54

Colorado All-State Orchestra, 22

Colorado Music Hall of Fame, 433, 521n

Colorado Springs, 41, 410, 467n

Colorado State College (UNC), 38, 41–5

Colours (band), 479n

Coltrane, John: '26-2', 375; 'Impressions', 78; Iyer on jazz, 290; *A Love Supreme*, 24, 126, 155, 479n; 'Moment's Notice', 354; Monk quartet, 228; 'Naima', 270; quartet, 251; Ratliff on sound, 161; 'Resolution', 155; and Sandole, 36; Vu on Frisell, 393; Zorn on, 145

comics, 224, 238, 250, 282

Comme des Garçons, 186

commercials, 69–70, 423

composition, 64, 87–8, 138, 148, 164–5, 229, 242, 378–80, 391–5, 437

Convict 13 (Keaton film), 234, 237

Cooder, Ry, 269, 271, 281, 396, 433, 449, 492n

Cook, Richard, 92, 149, 181, 209, 238, 263–4, 505n

Cooke, Sam, 360, 384; 'A Change is Gonna Come', 163, 512n

Cooper, Victor, 10, 34

Copland, Aaron, 56, 77, 197, 217, 294, 393, 402, 422; *Billy the Kid*, 213

Corbett, John, 276, 416, 495n

Coryell, Larry, 5, 31, 260, 479n

Costello, Elvis, 9, 237–8, 292, 329; 'Deep Dead Blue', 435; *Deep Dead Blue*, 272; Frisell's *The Sweetest Punch*, 275, 276; *Painted from Memory*, 275

Cotten, Elizabeth, 'Freight Train', 519n

country music, 258, 260–4, 267–8, 288, 292–3, 303

Covid-19 pandemic, 65, 139, 430, 435–8, 441, 496n

cowboy music, 100, 213, 256, 292, 364

Cream, 32, 190, 268, 272, 420, 485n

Crouch, Stanley, 151

Cullman, Brian, 298

Cumming, John, 63, 103, 471n

Cynical Hysterie Hour, 157

Cyrille, Andrew, 5, 352–3, 356, 429; *The Declaration of Musical Independence*, 391, 518n; *Lebroba*, 430; *The News*, 430

Damian, Jon, 78–9, 151, 274, 473n

D'Aquisto guitars, 310

David, Hal, 30, 31

Davidson, Eddie, 85

Davies, Dennis Russell, 265

Davies, Ray, 406

Davis, Anthony, 200, 473n

Davis, Bea, 19

Davis, Francis, 59, 64, 145, 260, 288, 290

Davis, Jimmy, 'You Are My Sunshine', 332

Davis, Miles: Amidon on, 279, 281, 282; bands/groups, 146, 155, 465n; *Bitches Brew*, 47, 153, 254, 279, 282; *ESP*, 332; and Evans, 448; Five Points district, 54; Frisell comparison, 6; as Frisell influence, 20, 31, 43, 56, 81, 97, 332; Frisell on, 5, 164, 214, 228, 251; Frisell on jazz, 289; Frisell's *Unspeakable*, 328; and Holland, 251; *In a Silent Way*, 47, 333; and jazz, 290; *Kind of Blue*, 126; *Miles in the Sky*, 31; *Miles Smiles*, 31; musical sound, 55, 161; *My Funny Valentine*, 31; Savoy label, 375; silence, 168; 'So What', 78; and Mike Stern, 121

Davis, Skeeter, 'The End of the World', 263

Day, Doris, 'Please Don't Eat the Daisies', 423

'Days of Wine and Roses' (Mancini/Mercer song), 164, 426

Deal (Mackey concerto), 274–5

de Barros, Paul, 203, 406

Debussy, Claude, 22, 40, 157, 168, 413, 486n

Decoding Society, 154

Deep Dead Blue (Costello and Frisell album), 272

DeJohnette, Jack, 91, 326, 381, 475n

Delcol, Roland, 93

Delcour, Robert, 86, 94

Delta blues, 248

Denver, Colorado: civil rights, 28–9; Frisell early years, 10, 17–19, 20, 26; Frisell return, 51, 52; music scene, 32–3, 53–4; radio, 32; shelters, 465n

Denver Folklore Center (DFC), 23–4, 32, 51, 214, 450, 451

Denver Pop Festival, 33

Denver Symphony Orchestra, 22

Denver Youth Musicians, 21

Desmond, Paul, 9, 49

De Tora, Don, 433

DFC, *see* Denver Folklore Center

Diamond, Neil, 'Solitary Man', 415

Dickens, Hazel, 'Will Jesus Wash the Bloodstains from Your Hands', 263

digital music, 121, 331, 374

d'Inverno, Carole (wife of BF): art work, 95, 230, 377–8, 403, 439; Bainbridge Island home, 324; on Bill Frisell Band, 180; birth of Monica, 173; on Cajori, 229; death of Frisell's father, 264, 265–6; death of Frisell's mother, 368; family life, 177; first Frisell meeting, 89; on Frisell and art, 230, 231; on Frisell and family, 173; on Frisell connections, 71; Frisell courtship, 89–90; Frisell debut album, 129; on Frisell fame, 70; on Frisell's character, 59, 60, 89, 129;

on Frisell's guitars, 311, 314; on Frisell's health, 188, 189; on Frisell's parents, 35; on Frisell's sound, 169; on Frisell's touring, 131, 348–50; Frisell's *Valentine* artwork, 439; gluten allergy, 373; Guttenberg home, 116–17; Hoboken home, 116–17, 133, 173, 204, 211; jobs, 117, 118; language, 113–14; marriage, 113–15, 348; on Motian, 97, 111; New York homes, 95, 115, 428–9; road trips, 403–404; sabbatical, 425–6; Seattle home, 202, 204, 418, 428; synaesthesia, 230; *Transumanza* shows, 403; Vermont Studio Center, 377–8, 403; Waits phone call, 156

DiPasqua, Michael, 131, 479n

discography, 521n

Disfarmer (Frisell album), 244–5, 374, 405, 430, 495n

Disfarmer, Mike (Mike Meyer), 241, 243–5, 495n

Disney films, 134, 137, 302, 415

Ditmas Park, Brooklyn, 429, 437

dobro, 262, 269

documentaries, 245; *see also Bill Frisell: A Portrait*

Dodd, Jimmie, 18

Domino, Fats, 'What a Party', 430

Doris Duke Charitable Foundation award, 388, 425

Dorn, Adam, 245, 327

Douglas, Dave, 68, 162–3, 168–9, 180, 247, 330, 393; *Strange Liberation*, 68, 330, 393

Douglas, Jerry, 262, 497n

DownBeat (magazine), 4, 62, 184, 237, 263, 264, 277, 288, 345, 407, 439

downloads, 121, 331, 358, 374, 381, 383, 511n, 521n

downtown scene, 142–5, 153, 223, 482n

dreams, 1–4, 149, 232, 283, 330, 363, 409, 416; The Frisell Dream, 4, 81, 94, 96, 158, 170, 215, 270, 353, 450

Drewes, Billy, 99, 100, 103, 175, 206, 216, 219, 222, 276, 315

The Drifters, 'Save the Last Dance for Me', 431

Driscoll, Kermit: benefit concert, 381; Bill Frisell Band, 174, 177, 178–9, 206, 209, 210, 213, 217, 218, 221, 222, 233, 237; Boston Connection, 80; *Chet Baker–Steve Houben*, 88; Douglas's 'The Frisell Dream', 330; drinking and health, 178–9, 218, 381; in Europe, 85–9, 94; on Frisell, 80, 123, 218, 358; Frisell first meeting, 75–6; Frisell gigs and 'The Look', 355; Frisell on, 75–6, 319; Frisell's *Before We Were Born*, 206; Frisell's *Have a Little Faith*, 213; Frisell's *Is That You?* 206; Frisell's *Lookout for Hope*, 134; Frisell's *This Land*, 219, 221, 222; Frisell's *Where in the World?* 190, 194; Frisell tours, 187; Frisell trio, 208, 358; *Good Buddies* album, 93; marriage, 478n; Tiger's Baku, 82, 83; *Triode* album, 93

Dr John, 137, 389

drugs, 54, 88, 91

Drury, Stephen, 159

Dunn, Larry, 28, 433

Dusty Strings, Seattle, 325

Dylan, Bob: on artists, 449; birthplace, 12; Burton versions, 293; Carmine Street Guitars, 309; on composition, 394; folk music, 24, 32; folk-rock, 43; as Frisell influence, 20, 33, 43, 56, 294; Frisell on, 214, 260; 'Just Like a Woman', 214; 'Masters of War', 70, 331, 372, 409; 'My Back Pages', 410; panoramic approach, 297; 'The Times They Are a-Changin'', 35; *Walk the Line* soundtrack, 246

Eakins, Thomas, 427

Earshot Jazz Festival, Seattle, 202, 326

Earth, Wind & Fire, 28, 433

East Carolina University (ECU), 115, 265, 498n

East High School, Denver, 10, 21, 27–9, 34, 409, 433–4, 451, 465n

Eastman School of Music, 38

East/West (Frisell album), 330–1, 332

Eberhart, Tony, 25, 27

ECM (record label): Bill Frisell Band, 180; Bryars's 'After the Requiem', 361, 364; Burton recordings, 91–2; costs, 479n; Cyrille albums, 353, 430; Frisell departure, 199, 200, 201, 374; Frisell invitation, 91; Frisell on, 93, 125–6, 146, 201; Frisell's *In Line*, 126–7; Frisell's *Rambler*, 146–8; Frisell's *Small Town*, 429; Frisell work, 143, 429; Garbarek albums, 124, 126; Metheny, 475n; *A Molde Concert*, 125; Motian, 102, 104, 112, 126, 132, 476n; Weber albums, 91–2

ECU, *see* East Carolina University

Eddy, Duane, 'Rebel Rouser', 404

Edgewater Chamber Players, 51

The Ed Sullivan Show, 22, 23, 466n

Egan, Mark, 79

Eicher, Manfred: Bill Frisell Band, 180; Bley quartet, 182; and Bryars, 361; ECM albums, 126; ECM costs, 479n; ECM founding, 91; and Frisell, 92–4, 125, 199; Frisell ECM departure, 200, 201, 202, 374; Frisell on, 93, 125–6, 146, 201; Frisell's *In Line*, 126–8, 312, 361, 412; The Frisell Tape, 124, 391; Frisell work, 92, 146, 206; Garbarek tour, 132; Motian albums, 103; and Müller, 429; Weber's *Fluid Rustle*, 92, 93

Eisenman, Jed, 185

Electric Bebop Band, 110

electric guitars, 18–19, 24, 119, 163

Electricity (Frisell and Morrison project), 249

Elektra Records, 199, 205, 484n

Elizondo, Mike, 334

Ellington, Duke, 54, 77, 126, 220, 259, 274, 287, 290, 295, 344, 355, 442; 'Satin Doll', 466n

Emanuel, Carol, 148, 150, 413, 482n

Engelhart, Claudia, 61, 73, 169, 172, 211, 350, 353, 357, 358, 417

Eno, Brian, 122, 123, 245, 336

Ephland, John, 277

Epistrophy (Frisell and Morgan album), 430–1

Erskine, Peter, 155, 197

Europe: Belgium, 84, 85–90, 95; Frisell tours, 102, 104, 130–3, 187, 189, 199, 277, 324–5, 348, 434, 435; Motian tours, 102, 104, 105, 132

Evans, Bill: albums, 101; Bill Evans Trio, 96, 98, 101, 109; and Davis, 448; death of, 98; as Frisell influence, 37; Frisell meeting, 448; Frisell on, 98, 259, 448–9; and Hall, 37, 49, 50; *Intermodulation*, 37, 55, 372; and Motian, 96, 102, 108, 363; Senate Lounge shows, 47, 448, 520n; Village Vanguard, 109

Evans, Gil, 77, 101, 153

Evans, Orrin, 190

Evans, Walker, 215, 492n

Evelev, Yale, 140

The Exciters, 'Do-Wah-Diddy', 464n

Eye, Yamatsuka, 157

Faithfull, Marianne, 9, 32, 134, 137, 156; 'As Tears Go By', 438; *Strange Weather*, 137, 156

Falk, Thyra, *see* Frisell, Thyra

Fantasy Studios, Berkeley, 375, 379, 382, 387

Farlinger, Leonard, *All Hat*, 246

Farmer, Art, 37, 49, 50; *Interaction*, 55

Index

The Far Side (Larson), 7, 224, 234–6; *see also*
  Tales from the Far Side
Fender guitars: Broadcaster, 319; Frisell
  interest, 312; Jaguar, 26, 311–12, 314, 319,
  404, 465n; Jazzmaster, 314, 432; Mustang,
  24, 26, 404; Rhodes, 330; 'Rubbertellie', 78;
  Stratocaster, 122, 206, 384, 420; Telecaster,
  19, 78, 206, 258, 301, 309, 314, 319–21,
  331, 376, 377, 405, 420, 421; Telecaster
  Relic, 373
Fields, Charles, 21
Fier, Anton, 140
film music, 233, 241, 245, 415–16, 426, 477n
The Film of Her (film), 247
Finding Forrester (Van Sant film), 246, 422
Fitzgerald, Ella, 49
Five Points district, Denver, 54
Five Spot club, New York, 228
Flanders Festival, 362
Fleagle, Benjamin (maternal grandfather of
  BF), 14–15, 16, 511n
Fleagle, Frances ('Fanny', née Guthrie, maternal
  grandmother of BF), 15–16, 369, 511n
Fleagle, Margaret Jane (mother of BF), *see*
  Frisell, (Margaret) Jane
Fleagle, Matt (second cousin of BF), 14
Fleagle family name, 15, 463n
Fleck, Béla, 391
Flora Avenue Studio, Seattle, 318, 438
Floratone, 333–4, 507n; *Floratone* album, 333;
  Floratone II album, 333–4
Flute Juice, 118, 122
folk music, 20, 32, 33, 42, 54, 78, 280, 281,
  325, 440
folk-rock, 43
Foster, Al, 146, 147, 317
Foster, Stephen, 56, 375, 384, 427, 440;
  'Beautiful Dreamer', 3, 34, 375, 512n; 'Hard
  Times', 165, 250, 317, 427, 441; 'Little
  Jenny Dow', 213
Fowlkes, Curtis, 216, 217, 219, 222, 236, 276,
  315, 327, 390
Franklin, Aretha, 298; 'Chain of Fools', 164,
  208
Franz, Emma, *Bill Frisell: A Portrait*
  documentary, 67, 137, 145, 314, 320, 336,
  343, 424–5
Frederiksen, Jack, 21
free jazz, 47, 269, 281, 427
FreshGrass, 427

Friday, Gavin, 134, 381; *Each Man Kills the
  Thing He Loves*, 156
Friedel, Megan, 33
Frisell, Bill (William Richard)
  BIOGRAPHY OVERVIEW: birth, 11;
    childhood, 11–15, 16–19, 26, 35; family
    background, 11–16; marriage, 89–90, 95,
    113–16; birth of daughter, 173
  APPEARANCE: album covers, 483n, 491n;
    body language, 64; clothing, 67–8, 80, 345,
    373, 483n; facial hair, 44, 437; hair, 35–6,
    43, 45, 53, 358; 'The Look', 355; size and
    strength, 7, 60, 64, 65; in youth, 36
  BANDS: Act Big Band, 95; Bill Frisell Band,
    121, 174, 176–82, 205–10, 211–18;
    Boston Connection, 80–1; Elvis covers
    band, 118; Floratone, 333–4, 507n;
    Gnostic Trio, 413–14; Gold Sash Band,
    21–2, 34, 53, 492n; Joshua, 39, 44, 51;
    Market Street Trolley, 27; Mauve Traffic,
    87–8; Naked City, 157–9, 187; Portraits,
    51; Power Tools, 154; The Publik, 27;
    Tiger's Baku, 82–3, 84; The Weeds, 25,
    26; The Willies, 276, 317–19, 505n
  CHARACTER: ambiguity, 58–61, 197;
    articulacy, 62, 63; confidence, 197;
    determination, 49; emotional nature, 66,
    170; generosity, 195; goodness, 68–9,
    70, 123, 138–9; humility, 169; humour,
    57, 74, 197, 224, 232, 358, 359; inside
    of brain, 424–5; intelligence, 73–4;
    kindness, 170, 188; modesty, 266; 'Moose'
    nickname, 60; passive-aggressiveness, 73;
    politics and protest, 45, 70, 435, 438,
    439; sensitivity, 67; shyness, 7, 16–17, 23,
    26, 43, 49, 52, 58–61, 64, 72, 144, 345,
    359, 442; speech and language, 61–4,
    166, 356, 364; spiritual side, 182; stage
    presence, 28, 34, 345–6, 359; strangeness,
    232; strength, 123; stubbornness, 72–3,
    129; swearing, 73; voice, 63
  EDUCATION: Berklee College of Music,
    43, 45–8, 74, 77–8, 433; Colorado State
    College (UNC), 38, 41–5; East High
    School, 21, 23, 27–9; Gove Junior High
    School, 21; Teller Elementary School, 21
  GIGS/TOURS: audience, 356–7; ensembles,
    353; Europe tours, 102, 104, 130–3,
    187, 189, 199, 277, 324–5, 348, 434,
    435; Garbarek tour, 131–2, 133; Hayes

and Cahill Irish tour, 302, 304, 307; live dialogue, 356, 357–9; livestream concerts, 437–8; Motian tours, 132, 133; schedule demands, 187–8, 343–4, 346–7, 356, 359; solo gigs, 185, 186, 312, 434; tour dates archive, 519n; on touring, 347–50, 435–6; US tours, 276, 277, 347; world tours, 348, 435

HEALTH: anxiety, 188, 189; appendectomy, 98; childhood, 11–12; diet and weight, 373; drinking, 178; drugs, 44; fatigue, 187–8; hives, 187, 188; injuries, 65; Seattle move, 203, 205; smoking, 189

HOMES: Bainbridge Island, 324; Denver, 10–11; Europe, 85–9, 94, 95; Guttenberg, 116–17; Hoboken, 116–17, 133, 143, 173, 187–8, 197, 204, 211; New York, 95, 115–18, 428–9; Seattle, 202–4, 299–300, 418

INTERESTS: art, 7, 230–1, 240–1, 274, 306, 519n; cars, 20–1, 38, 46, 50, 85, 115; cartoons, 18, 20; CD collection, 299–300; cycling, 64–5; dreams, 1–2; hugging, 65–6; radio, 19, 370; road trips, 403–404; walking, 64, 65, 426

MUSIC: Americana, 294–5; and art, 230–2, 240–1, 242; balalaika, 92; banjo, 138, 150, 157, 186, 207, 259, 312, 321; body of work, 4–5; as catharsis, 59–61, 437; CD collection, 299–300; charts and scores, 353; clarinet, 21–2, 25, 27–8, 34, 36, 38, 43, 45, 106, 119, 162, 207, 370, 378, 436; composition, 64, 87–8, 138, 148, 164–5, 229, 242, 378–80, 391–5, 437; connections, 71; country music, 260, 292–3; and dreams, 1–3; drum lessons, 120; first guitars, 10, 18, 21–2, 24–5; The Frisell Tape, 123–4, 391; genre, 286–7, 295–300, 434; Grammy award, 134, 138, 328; Grammy nominations, 327, 371, 416; guitar interest, 10, 18, 19, 21–7, 30, 34, 43, 45–6, 451; guitar lessons, 36–7, 40, 41, 48–50, 318; guitars owned, 10, 18, 21–2, 24–5, 40–1, 71, 81, 309–14, 316, 318–22, 331, 436–7, 449, 451; guitar style, 64, 119, 123, 143–4, 183; guitar teaching, 51–2, 78–9, 117; improvisation, 64, 198, 229, 242, 351–2, 380, 392; jazz, 5, 7–8, 30–2, 47, 287–9, 294, 296, 298–9, 366, 399; as

life choice, 29, 41, 69; and life lessons, 449–50; listening, 355; mandolin, 321; melody, 163–5, 198, 225, 284; 'music is good', 112, 432, 447; roots, 267–8; Ruhr Triennale festival, 328–9; saxophone, 22, 34, 36, 38, 43, 162, 163; set-lists, 353; singing and vocals, 163–4, 428, 521n; solos, 64, 164, 225, 270, 351; sound and voice, 160–3, 164–71; soundworld, 130, 135, 232, 277, 353; space and silence, 166–8; style, 6–8, 25, 56, 99–100, 155, 164, 166–7; ukulele, 207, 321

ALBUMS: *All We Are Saying...*, 382–5, 406, 416, 426, 464n, 513n; *Beautiful Dreamers*, 3, 375–6, 512n; *Before We Were Born*, 185, 202, 205–7, 260, 299, 364, 392, 511n; *The Best of Bill Frisell Vol 1: Folk Songs*, 374, 504n; *Big Sur*, 387–8, 389, 391, 396–402, 404; *Bill Frisell, Ron Carter, Paul Motian*, 332–3; *Blues Dream*, 3, 220, 222, 276–7, 314–16, 317, 319, 374, 426, 433, 439; *Deep Dead Blue*, 272; discography, 521n; *Disfarmer*, 244–5, 374, 430, 495n; *East/West*, 330–1, 332; *Epistrophy*, 430–1; *Floratone* albums, 333–4; *Further East/Further West*, 331; *Ghost Town*, 246, 266, 276, 277, 312–13, 324, 412, 430, 431; *Gone, Just Like a Train*, 191, 221, 222, 238–9, 250, 256, 264, 268–9, 277, 282, 307; *Good Buddies*, 93; *Good Dog, Happy Man*, 222, 269–71, 277, 279–85, 499n; *Guitar in the Space Age!* 20, 404–407, 416, 417, 426; *HARMONY*, 434–5, 440–7, 519n; *Have a Little Faith*, 191, 212–16, 221, 261, 405; *Hemispheres*, 363, 372, 511n; *History, Mystery*, 240, 360–7, 371–2, 390; *In Line*, 126–9, 132–3, 184, 211, 312, 361–2, 392, 412, 429, 479n, 489n, 511n; *The Intercontinentals*, 326–7, 335–40; *Is That You?* 207–8, 237, 247, 260, 319, 491n; *Just So Happens*, 271; *The Kentucky Derby is Decadent and Depraved*, 138, 389–90, 404, 514n; *Lágrimas Mexicanas (Mexican Tears)*, 338; *Live*, 211–12, 217, 221–2, 491–2n, 511n; Live Download Series, 521n; *Lookout for Hope*, 121, 134–9, 181, 185, 191, 364, 429; *The Maid with the Flaxen Hair*, 411; *Motian and Frisell*, 105; *Motion Pictures*, 272; *Music IS*, 431–3,

434; *Nashville*, 221, 222, 258–64, 268, 269, 277, 288, 413, 497n; *Petra Haden and Bill Frisell*, 329–30, 511n; *Quartet*, 220, 221, 224, 234, 236–8, 262, 315, 494n; *Rambler*, 122, 146–8, 178, 180, 181, 191, 260, 272, 317; *Richter 858*, 243; *Sign of Life*, 379–80; *Silent Comedy*, 412–13, 431; *Small Town*, 429–30; *Smash & Scatteration*, 154, 483n; *Songs We Know*, 271; *The Sweetest Punch*, 275–6; *Theoretically*, 146; *This Land*, 191, 216–17, 219–26, 260, 315; *Triode*, 93–4; *Unspeakable*, 134, 138, 327–8, 378, 390, 504n; *Valentine*, 266, 391, 438–9; *When You Wish Upon a Star*, 415–17, 419–23; *Where in the World?* 190–8, 208–9, 211; *The Willies*, 231, 301–8, 318–19; *With Dave Holland and Elvin Jones*, 250–7, 316–17, 338, 374
DVDs/FILMS: *Bill Frisell: A Portrait*, 67, 137, 145, 168, 299, 314, 320, 336, 343, 424–5, 518n; *Solos*, 372–3
FILM MUSIC: *All Hat*, 246–7, 496n; *Andy Irons: Kissed by God*, 427; *Change in the Air*, 427; discography, 521n; *Finding Forrester*, 246, 419, 422; *Four Boys in a Volvo*, 423; Frisell on, 426; Keaton film scores, 7, 191, 217, 233–4, 235, 364; *The Million Dollar Hotel*, 245–6, 496n; *Psycho*, 246, 421; *Tales from the Far Side*, 234–5, 236, 237, 416, 422; *Tales from the Far Side II*, 236; *Tongzhi in Love*, 246; *Walk the Line*, 246
MULTIMEDIA: Burroughs' *Naked Lunch*, 274, 420–1; *Close Your Eyes*, 240; *Collage for a Day*, 373–4; *Electricity*, 249; Ginsberg's '*Kaddish*', 390–1, 438; *The Great Flood*, 247–9, 389, 439; *Mysterio Simpatico*, 239, 240, 358; *Probability Cloud*, 239–40; Richter project, 241–3; *Saint Joan*, 434; *Stories from the Heart of the Land*, 512n; Woodring projects, 250
SONGS: '1968', 506n; 'Again', 193, 247, 373; 'Alien Prints', 121; 'As Tears Go By', 438; 'Baba Drame', 336; 'The Beach', 129; 'Beautiful Dreamer', 3, 34, 375, 512n; 'Beautiful E', 191, 246; 'Better Than a Machine', 512n; 'The Big One', 400; 'Billy Boy', 213; 'Boubacar', 326, 512n; 'Change in the Air', 432; 'Child at Heart', 209; 'Cluck Old Hen', 305–6, 318,

380, 446; 'Coffaro's Theme', 246; 'Cold, Cold Ground', 283; 'Days of Wine and Roses', 164, 426; 'Deep Dead Blue', 435; 'Desolation Theme', 139; discography, 519n; 'Dream On', 3; 'Egg Radio', 224; 'Going to California', 398; 'Good Old People', 338; 'Greg Leisz', 315; 'Hangdog', 137; 'Hard Plains Drifter', 206, 491n; 'Hard Times', 165, 317, 427, 441; 'Hawks', 401; 'Highway 1', 401; 'Home on the Range', 293; 'Hour Glass', 391; 'I Can't Be Satisfied', 214; 'I Don't Want to Grow Up', 330; 'I Heard it Through the Grapevine', 331; 'I Know You Care', 306; 'I'm So Lonesome I Could Cry', 163, 304–5, 313, 333, 437; 'In Line', 432; 'It Should've Happened a Long Time Ago', 430; 'I Want to Go Home', 304; '*Jackie-ing*', 366; 'John Goldfarb, Please Come Home!' 413; 'Juliet of the Spirits', 103, 120, 136, 361; 'Julius Hemphill', 216, 225; 'Justice and Honor', 256; 'Just Like a Woman', 214; 'Kaddish', 438; 'Lazy Robinson', 365; 'Levees', 439; 'Like Dreamers Do', 3; 'Little Brother Bobby', 139, 181; 'Little Jenny Dow', 213; 'Live to Tell', 214; 'The Lone Ranger', 373; 'Lonesome', 443; 'Lush Life', 427, 431, 517n; 'Masters of War', 70, 331, 372; 'Melody for Jack', 181; 'Monica Jane', 182, 432; 'Monroe', 282, 512n; 'Moon River', 250, 317, 330; 'The Music of Glen Deven Ranch', 397; 'My Man's Gone Now', 313; 'No Man's Land', 207; 'Outlaws', 253, 315; 'Over the Rainbow', 246, 422; 'Poem for Eva', 246, 284–5; 'Pretty Flowers Were Made for Blooming', 222; 'Pretty Stars Were Made to Shine', 433; 'Probability Cloud', 364; '*Psycho, Pts 1 and 2*', 421; 'Rag', 207, 211, 373; 'Rambler', 275, 432–3; 'Red River Valley', 431, 519n; 'Remedios the Beauty', 181; 'Ron Carter', 315, 332, 432; 'Roscoe', 282; 'Shenandoah', 165, 271, 281, 354, 408, 426; 'Shutter, Dream', 3; 'Sing Together Like a Family', 388; 'Sittin' on Top of the World', 303; 'Small Town', 430; 'Smilin' Jones', 209; 'Some Song and Dance', 206; 'Soul Merchant', 315; 'Steady Girl', 206, 511n; 'Strange Meeting', 148, 211, 221, 251–2; 'Struggle', 366; 'Tag', 219; 'Tales from the Far Side', 416, 422; 'Tell Your Ma, Tell Your Pa', 247; 'That Was Then', 9, 222, 223; 'Think About it', 432; 'This Land', 223; 'Throughout', 123, 129–30, 206, 211, 362, 392, 511n; 'To Kill a Mockingbird', 422; 'Tractor Tavern', 317; 'Twenty Years', 237; 'Under a Golden Sky', 246; 'Unsung Heroes', 195; 'Verona', 307–8; 'Washington Post March', 213; 'The Way Home', 247; 'We Are Everywhere', 340; 'Weepy Donuts', 421; 'We Shall Overcome', 70, 435, 437, 439; 'What Do You Mean?' 94; 'What the World Needs Now Is Love', 30, 70, 331; 'When I Fall in Love', 214; 'Where Do We Go?' 439; 'Wildwood Flower', 324; 'Winslow Homer', 376; 'Winter Always Turns to Spring', 266, 439; 'A Worthy Endeavor', 512n

Frisell, Bill, Sr (Wilhelm Richard, father of BF): academic career, 12, 16, 115, 498n; and Cajoris, 227; character, 16–17; Denver move, 11; education, 13–14; family background, 12; Frisell guitar focus concerns, 45–6; Frisell on, 13, 14, 16, 264–5, 266, 369–70; Frisell's clarinet, 21; Frisell's early years, 11–14, 17, 18; Frisell's marriage, 113; marriage, 12; musical interest, 13–14, 21, 34–5, 48–9; New Jersey move, 37; painting, 17, 230, 463n; wife's mental health, 369–70; final illness, 264–5; death, 265–6, 439; grave, 371

Frisell, Bob (brother of BF), 12–13, 16–17, 21, 35–6, 113, 115, 181, 368–9

Frisell, (Margaret) Jane (née Fleagle, mother of BF): birth, 14; and Cajoris, 227; character and shyness, 16; Denver move, 11; family background, 14–16; Frisell birth, 11; Frisell guitar focus concerns, 45–6; Frisell on, 16, 368–70; on Frisell protest, 468n; on Frisell's appearance, 35, 36; Frisell's early years, 11–12, 15–16, 19, 21; Frisell's marriage, 113; Frisell's radio, 19; interests and studies, 369; marriage, 12; memoir, 11, 12; mental health, 369–70; musical interest, 16, 21, 34–5; name and birth of Monica, 173; New Jersey move, 37; poetry, 369; 'Prance in a Black Robe' essay, 466n; death of Frisell's father, 265; death, 368, 370, 390; grave, 371

Frisell, Monica Jane (daughter of BF): birth, 173, 182; cycling, 342–3; death of Frisell's

father, 264–5; death of Frisell's mother, 368; education, 238; on father, 341–2, 349; Frisell and Roberts tape, 177; Frisell collaboration, 341, 508n; Frisell on, 173, 189, 341–3; Frisell respite, 380; Frisell sabbatical, 425, 426; Frisell's custom guitar, 314; Frisell's touring, 348–9; gluten allergy, 373; on mother, 349; New York burglary, 203; New York University, 428; photography degree, 425; Portrait of US project, 403; road trips, 204; Seattle home, 202; table tennis game, 341–2; Vermont Studio Center, 341, 403–404

Frisell, Olof (Ole, paternal grandfather of BF), 12, 13, 17, 36, 71

Frisell, Thyra (née Falk, paternal grandmother of BF), 12, 13

Frisellium microorganism, 265–6

The Frisell Dream, 4, 81, 94, 96, 158, 170, 215, 270, 353, 450

The Frisell Tape, 123–4, 391

Frisland/Frislandia, 295, 299

Frith, Fred, 142, 149, 157, 421

Frost, Robert, 240

Further East/Further West (Frisell album), 331

Futterman, Steve, 7

Gabriela, 275, 326; Detrás del Sol, 275; El Viaje, 275; Viento Rojo, 275, 326

Galás, Diamanda, 148

Garbarek, Jan, 103, 124, 125–6, 131–2, 133, 477n; Afric Pepperbird, 476n; Paths, Prints, 125–6; Wayfarer, 131–2

Gary Burton Quartet, 31, 38, 119, 467n; see also Burton, Gary

genre, 6, 286–90, 293–300, 434

Gentile, Dana, 403

Genus, James, 330

Gershwin, George, 431, 477n, 504n; 'I Got Rhythm', 477n; 'My Man's Gone Now', 98

Getz, Stan, 99, 101

Ghost Town (Frisell album), 246, 266, 276, 277, 312–13, 324, 412, 430, 431

Gibbs, Melvin, 148, 154, 481n

Gibbs, Mike: bands, 82; Berklee College of Music, 77–8, 82, 83, 118, 391; big band, 90–1, 119, 146; Big Music, 153; in Bill Frisell: A Portrait documentary, 424–5; Collage for a Day, 373–4, 424–5; on Frisell, 73, 83; Frisell gigs, 90–1, 185; Frisell lessons, 77–8; Frisell on, 90, 374; Frisell reputation, 146; Frisell's style, 181; Frisell's 'Throughout', 123; The Frisell Tape, 123, 124; London Jazz Festival, 373; *Play a Bill Frisell Set List*, 511n; 'Sweet Rain', 373

Gibson guitars: 1962, 411; acoustic guitars, 171; Amidon on, 284; ES-125, 331; ES-175, 40, 55, 71, 85, 161, 310, 467n; ES-295, 40; ES-446, 316, 318; guitar technology, 19; Johnny Smith, 41, 312; L-5, 30, 310; players, 485n; SG, 81, 161, 311, 485n; Van Sant, 420

Gibson, Mel, 245, 246

Giddens, Rhiannon, 9, 440–7

Giddins, Gary, 152, 294

Gil, Gilberto, 335, 339

Gillespie, Dizzy, 36, 40, 474n, 486n

Gillis, Bob, 39, 40, 43, 44, 50, 51

Ginsberg, Allen: Frisell on, 390; '*Kaddish*', 138, 390–1, 438; *The Lion for Real*, 155–6, 514n

Gioia, Ted, 351

Giuffre, Jimmy, 37, 49, 50

Glass, Philip, 200, 247, 297, 391, 413

Glen Deven Ranch, Big Sur, 386, 387, 515n

The Gloaming, 286, 301, 500n

Gnostic Trio, 413–14; *The Gnostic Preludes: Music of Splendor*, 413–14; *Transmigration of the Magus*, 414

Godard, Jean-Luc, 150, 482n

The Godfather (film), 423

Godsey, Victor Bruce (was Julian Summerhill), 121–2, 478n

Goes, Derryl, 468n

Gold Sash Band, 21–2, 34, 53, 492n

Gómez, Eddie, 448

Gone, Just Like a Train (Frisell album), 191, 221, 222, 238–9, 250, 256, 264, 268–9, 277, 282, 307

Good Buddies (Frisell et al. album), 93

Good Dog, Happy Man (Frisell album), 222, 269–71, 277, 279–85, 499n

Goodman, Benny, 30; 'Benny's Bugle', 373

Goodrick, Mick, 76, 91, 421

Goodwin, Bill, 467n

Gordon Close's Melody Music, 51

Gordon, Lorraine, 110, 185

Gordon, Max, 110, 184, 185

Gorshin, Frank, 51

Gossard, Stone, 427

Gottlieb, Danny, 79

Gove Junior High School, 21

Govetas, Christos, 325–6, 335

Go West (Keaton film), 233, 234

Graham, David A., 417, 512n

Graham, Mark, 496n

Gramavision Records, 200, 492n

Grammy award, 134, 138, 328

Grammy nominations, 327, 371, 416

Grand Lake, 51

Grand Ole Opry, 261, 303, 498n

Granelli, Jerry, 274

Grauerholz, James, 420, 421

Great American Music Hall, San Francisco, 186

Great American Songbook, 108, 271, 427, 477n, 501n

The Great Flood (film), 247–9, 389, 439

Great Migration, 248

Greek music, 325, 337

Greeley, Colorado, 38, 43, 45, 50, 126, 448

Greeley Philharmonic Orchestra, 468n

Green, Freddie, 50, 235

Green, Grant, 31

Greene, Graham, 55

Greenville, North Carolina, 113, 114, 441

Greenwich Village, 24, 33, 37, 49, 228, 424, 441

Gretsch guitars, 19, 432

Gruppo di Improvvisazione di Nuova Consonanza, 482n

Guild guitars, 41, 411

The Guitar Artistry of Bill Frisell (video), 225, 275

Guitar club, Manhattan, 48

Guitar in the Space Age! (Frisell album), 20, 404–407, 416, 417, 426

guitars: acoustic, 128, 163, 171, 318, 414; American music, 267; archtop, 21, 23, 36, 40, 42, 310; effects, 7, 81, 122, 163, 186, 225, 283, 376–7; electric, 18–19, 24, 119, 163; fingerings, 163; Frisell and genre, 299; Frisell early interest in, 34; Frisell on, 310–12, 316, 320–2, 436–7, 449, 451; jazz guitar, 4–8, 49, 277, 281–2, 287, 298, 366; looping, 225–6, 283, 339, 376, 421; painted guitars, 313–14; Seattle music store, 165; shredding, 167–8, 196, 198, 274, 284; slide guitar, 408; solos, 225; surf music, 20; sustain, 81, 162–3, 225; women guitar players, 84; *see also under individual makes*

guitar synthesiser, 146, 148, 478n, 481n

Guthrie, Arlo, 96

Guthrie, Frances ('Fanny'), *see* Fleagle, Frances

Guthrie, Woody, 15, 32, 96; 'This Land is Your Land', 216, 435
Guttenberg, New Jersey, 116–17
Guy, Buddy, 24, 56

Haden, Charlie: Baker trio, 268, 272, 499n; Bryars concerto, 361; *Conversations with Charlie Haden*, 297, 410; death of, 410; Frisell concerts, 185, 381; Frisell on, 410; Frisell's *HARMONY*, 440; and Garbarek, 131; Jarrett trio, 410; Liberation Music Orchestra, 104; and Metheny, 475n; Motian's *On Broadway*, 108; *Not in Our Name*, 511n; 'There in a Dream', 519n
Haden, Petra: on Frisell, 130, 330, 357; Frisell's *HARMONY*, 434, 440, 519n; on Frisell's 'Throughout', 130; Frisell's *When You Wish Upon a Star*, 416, 419; HARMONY quartet, 427; *Imaginaryland*, 329; Motian's *Windmills of Your Mind*, 112; *Petra Goes to the Movies*, 416; *Petra Haden and Bill Frisell*, 329–30, 357
Hall, Jim: album features, 55; 'All Across the City', 372; and Bruning, 40, 47; Bryars on, 363; and Carter, 332; death of, 410, 425; Desmond on, 9; *Dialogues*, 273–4, 372; and Evans, 37; Frisell and Larson, 235; Frisell collaboration, 5, 161, 184, 273–4, 372, 489n; Frisell concerts, 381; Frisell duo, 184, 489n; 'Frisell Frazzle', 274; Frisell guitar lessons, 48–50, 318; as Frisell influence, 41, 47, 56, 83, 88, 100, 152, 208; Frisell meeting, 47; Frisell on, 37, 47, 49–50, 56, 119, 184, 425; Frisell's sound, 161; Gibson guitar, 40, 310; *Hemispheres*, 363, 372, 511n; *Intermodulation*, 37, 55, 372; Metheny on, 49; Metheny on Frisell, 76; 'Migration', 372; 'Monk of the guitar' phrase, 486n; Senate Lounge shows, 448; 'Simple Things', 274; and Van Eps, 398; Village Vanguard, 184, 185
Halvorson, Mary, 160, 169, 212, 299, 411, 411, 434, 481n; *The Maid with the Flaxen Hair*, 411
Hamilton, Fred, 39, 44
Hammerstein, Oscar, 112; 'All the Things You Are', 34–5, 477n
Hancock, Herbie, 47, 48, 118, 274, 289–90, 466n
Happy Logan Music, 10, 24–5
'Hard Times' (Foster song), 165, 250, 317, 427, 441

Harland, Eric, 408
HARMONY (Frisell album), 434–5, 440–7, 517n
HARMONY quartet, 427–8, 434–5, 450–1
Harris, Jerome, 122, 147, 178, 478n
Harris, Pat, 470n
Hart, Billy: *Oshumare*, 155, 272; *Rah*, 155
Hart, Linda, 409
Hassell, Jon, 200, 245
Have a Little Faith (Frisell album), 191, 212–16, 221, 261, 405
Hawkins, Coleman, 85, 101, 161
Hayes, Martin, 9, 64, 171, 286, 301–8, 381, 391
Hazlewood, Lee, 'Baja', 20, 404, 409
Helm, Chuck, 244, 405
Hemispheres (Hall and Frisell album), 363, 372, 511n
Hemphill, Julius, 5, 119, 122, 145–6, 206, 393, 494n; *Big Band*, 153; Frisell's 'Julius Hemphill', 216, 225
Hendrix, Jimi, 3, 6, 33, 91, 154, 195–7, 203, 284, 365; 'The Wind Cries Mary', 406
Henry, Joe, 66, 74, 164, 167, 170, 298, 315, 397
Herman, Bonnie, 92
Herman, Woody, 99, 468n
Herman's Hermits, 24, 419
Herr, Michel, 87, 88, 93, 95
Herrmann, Bernard, 139, 246, 415, 421
Hersch, Fred, 174; *Songs We Know*, 271
Hiatt, John, 294; *Bring the Family*, 211, 269, 492n; 'Have a Little Faith in Me', 164, 211, 492n
Hickey, Dave, 495n
The High Sign (Keaton film), 233
Hill, Andrew, *One for One*, 507n
Hillbilly Hellcats, 52
Himes, Geoffrey, 67
History, Mystery (Frisell album), 240, 360–7, 371–2, 390
Hitchcock, Alfred, *Psycho*, 246, 421, 517n
Hoboken, New Jersey, 115, 116–17, 173, 187–8, 197, 204, 211
Hofstra, Dave, 176, 206, 482n
Holcomb, Robin, 117, 142, 143, 145, 173, 202, 263, 390; *Robin Holcomb*, 153; *Todos Santos*, 186
Holcomb, Roscoe, 258, 268, 282, 314, 355
Holland, Dave, 91, 155, 171, 239, 251, 272, 316, 317; *Conference of the Birds*, 55; *With Dave Holland and Elvin Jones*, 250–7, 316, 338

Holland, Jools, 139

Hollenbeck, John, 388–9

Holly, Buddy, 18, 24

Hopkins, Fred, 147

Horner, Lindsey, 60, 153

Horovitz, Michael, 7

Horvitz, Nica, 173, 202

Horvitz, Wayne: Burroughs' *Naked Lunch*, 274; Frisell collaboration, 60, 381; Frisell friendship, 143–4; on Frisell live, 359; Frisell's *Good Dog, Happy Man*, 269, 279, 283; Frisell's *Have a Little Faith*, 214; Frisell's *Is That You?* 206; Frisell's *Nashville*, 261, 262; Frisell's sound, 160–1; Frisell's *Where in the World?* 190; health, 188, 202; Hoboken move, 117, 173; and Lowe, 318; Naked City, 157; *The President*, 153, 503n; Seattle move, 202; on *Stay Awake*, 137; and Van Sant, 246, 423; 'Weepy Donuts', 421; and Zorn, 140, 142, 145, 148

Houben, Stéphane (Steve), 85–90, 95, 102, 171, 472n; *Chet Baker–Steve Houben*, 88

Hubble, Jack, 27

Hudson, Garth, 137

Hughes, Chuck, 52

Hulej, Cindy, 309

Hurt, Mississippi John, 24, 32, 246, 451

Hurwitz, Bob, 199, 205, 212, 215, 260, 261, 277, 374

Hussain, Zakir, 381

Ibanez guitars, 310

Ibrahim, Abdullah, 281

improvisation, 64, 104, 141, 167, 192, 198, 229, 242, 262, 351, 351–2, 380, 392

In C (Riley), 286

Indian music, 47, 54, 298

In Line (Frisell album), 126–9, 132–3, 184, 211, 312, 361–2, 392, 412, 429, 479n, 489n, 511n

The Intercontinentals (Frisell album), 326–7, 335–40

Interlochen Arts Academy, Michigan, 34

Intuition (record label), 200–1

Irons, Andy, 427

Israel, 70, 368

Is That You? (Frisell album), 207–8, 237, 247, 260, 319, 491n

It Should've Happened a Long Time Ago (Motian trio album), 104, 105, 199

Iverson, Ethan, 73, 102, 105, 107, 190–4, 196–8, 391

Ives, Charles, 40, 153, 159, 177, 197, 217, 393; *Three Places in New England*, 69, 213

Iyer, Vijay, 247, 290, 388, 391

Jackson, Michael Gregory, 82, 97, 473n, 478n

Jackson, Ronald Shannon, 67, 154, 266, 481n, 483n

Jacquet, Illinois, 486n

James, Bob, 482n

Jansson, Tove, 17

Jarmusch, Jim, 310

Jarrett, Keith, 91, 96, 101, 102, 108, 128, 131, 200, 287–8, 410, 473n; *The Köln Concert*, 479n; *Somewhere Before*, 410

Jaurès, Jean, 483n

jazz: and American music, 223; Armstrong on, 292; and art, 376; Braxton on, 290; Cajori on, 228; and country music, 292–3; Francis Davis on, 290; free jazz, 47, 269, 281, 427; and Frisell, 5, 7–8, 30–2, 287–9, 294, 296, 298–9, 366, 399; Frisell on, 5, 30–2, 47, 288–9, 296; fusion, 38, 46–7, 80, 88, 93–4, 294, 307; as genre, 287–90, 298; improvisation, 351; Iyer on, 290; Lovano on, 204; Metheny on, 5, 289; Miles on, 501n; neoclassical movement, 296; and other musical styles, 5–6; Parks on, 399; *The Real Book*, 79; Rollins on, 289; smooth jazz, 296; solos, 351; traditionalism, 151–2; and Zorn, 151

Jazz at Lincoln Center, 294, 376, 410

jazz guitar, 4–8, 49, 277, 281–2, 287, 298, 366

Jazziz magazine, 263, 294

jazz studies, 38, 42, 45

Jazzwise magazine, 278

Jazz Workshop, Boston, 48, 79

'Jesse James' (folk song), 433

Jethro Tull, 54

Jewish music, 412

Jobim, Antônio Carlos, 30; 'Corcovado', 326

John Lennon, Unfinished Music (exhibition), 382, 513n

Johnson, Blind Willie, 258, 267

Johnson, Marc, 98, 99, 109, 185; *Bass Desires*, 155, 197, 199, 273; 'Crossing the Corpus Callosum', 197; *Second Sight*, 155, 197; *The Sound of Summer Running*, 265, 273

Johnson, Ray, 245

Johnson, Vinnie, 85, 93, 94

Joiner, Richard, 22
Jones, Elvin, 239, 505n; *With Dave Holland and Elvin Jones*, 250–7, 316, 338
Jones, Greg, 25
Jones, Norah, 225, 408
Jones, Percy, 122–3
Jones, Rickie Lee, 329, 381
Jones, Tom, 106
Joplin, Janis, 33
Joshua (band), 39, 44, 51
'Juliet of the Spirits', 103, 120, 136, 361
Junod, Tom, 63, 109, 161–2, 236, 346
Just So Happens (Frisell and Peacock album), 271

'*Kaddish*' (Ginsberg poem/Frisell music), 138, 390–1, 438
Kamen, Leslie, 117
Kang, Eyvind: 858 Quartet, 240, 242, 249, 327, 371, 378, 379, 380; Beautiful Dreamers trio, 3, 354, 375, 376; Burroughs' *Naked Lunch*, 274; *Close Your Eyes*, 240; *Electricity* project, 249; *Floratone* albums, 333, 334; on Frisell, 63, 298; on The Frisell Dream, 4; Frisell ensembles, 217; Frisell gigs, 171, 354; Frisell on, 270; Frisell's *Big Sur*, 387, 396; Frisell's *History, Mystery*, 360, 371, 372; Frisell's *Quartet*, 236, Frisell's *Tales from the Far Side*, 236; Frisell's *When You Wish Upon a Star*, 416, 419; on improvisation, 380; White as mentor, 272; The Willies, 317
Kawamoto, George, 19
Keaton, Buster, 7, 191, 217, 233–4, 235, 364; *Convict 13*, 234, 237; *Go West*, 233, 234; *The High Sign*, 233; *Neighbors*, 234; *One Week*, 233; *Sherlock Jr.*, 234
Kelly, Rick, 309–10
Kelman, John, 92, 454
Keltner, Jim, 238, 268–9, 270, 271, 279, 283, 492n
Kennedy, John F., 24, 466n
Kenny's Castaways club, New York, 123
Kenton, Stan, 468n
The Kentucky Derby is Decadent and Depraved (Thompson words/Frisell music), 138, 389–90, 404, 514n
Kern, Jerome, 112, 475n; 'All the Things You Are', 34–5, 477n; 'Yesterdays', 466n
Kerouac, Jack, 54, 386; *Big Sur*, 386
Kertess, Klaus, 495n
Kibbey, Bridget, 414

Kilkenny Arts Festival, 286, 295, 302, 307
King, B. B., 79, 467n
King, David (Dave), 8, 190, 191–8, 291
King, Martin Luther, 24, 28, 409, 465n
Kingston Trio, 'Jesse James', 433
The Kinks, 56; 'Tired of Waiting for You', 400, 406; 'You Really Got Me', 27
Kirk, Rahsaan Roland, 3
Klein, Steve, 209, 312
Klein guitars, 209, 224, 236, 312, 316
Klucevsek, Guy, 212, 213, 214
Knitting Factory, New York, 109, 136, 187, 260, 264, 484n
Knowles, Liz, 301
Kongshaug, Jan Erik, 126, 128
Konishi, Keiko, 159
Konitz, Lee, 49, 96, 108, 109–10, 272, 360, 381, 435; 'Subconscious-Lee', 512n
Kotche, Glenn, 391
Kramer, *The Brill Building, Book Two, Featuring Bill Frisell*, 414–15
Krantz, Wayne, 120
Kraus, Bill, 27
Krauss, Alison, 261, 262, 443
Krauss, Briggan, 327
Krauss, Viktor, 238, 244, 262, 268–9, 276, 279, 283, 330–3, 381, 496n, 497n
Kubo, Kiribo, 157

LaBarbera, Joe, 98
Lacy, Steve, 136, 165, 392, 495n
LaFaro, Scott, 101, 109
Lage, Julian, 410, 414
Lake, Oliver, 141, 200, 473n, 494n
Lake, Steve, 181, 183
Landers, Tim, 118
lang, k. d., 270, 314, 420
Lanois, Daniel, 245
Larson, Gary, 234–6; *The Far Side*, 7, 224, 234–6; on Frisell, 236; Frisell guitars, 311, 411; *Tales from the Far Side*, 234–5, 236, 237, 313, 422, 493n; *Tales from the Far Side II*, 236
LaSpina, Steve, 184
The Late Show with Stephen Colbert, 336
Latin music, 325, 335
Lead Belly (Huddie Ledbetter), 267, 301, 318
Leahey, Andrew, 335
Leave it to Beaver, 26, 465n
Lee, Harper, *To Kill a Mockingbird*, 422
Lee, Russell, 215

Lehning, Kyle, 261, 497n
Leighton, Chris, 317
Leisz, Greg: *All Hat* film music, 496n; *Disfarmer*
    project, 244; Frisell conversation, 159; Frisell
    on, 270, 408, 505n; Frisell's *Blues Dream*,
    314, 315–16; Frisell's *Good Dog, Happy Man*,
    269–70, 279, 283; Frisell's 'Greg Leisz', 315;
    Frisell's *Guitar in the Space Age!* 406; Frisell's
    The Intercontinentals, 326, 327, 335; Lennon
    music trio, 382; and Lloyd, 408; and Lucinda
    Williams, 516n; New Quartet, 325; West and
    Bryant project, 405
Lennon, John: 'Across the Universe', 383, 385;
    All We Are Saying . . . (Frisell album), 382–5;
    assassination, 477n; 'Beautiful Boy', 382;
    Byron recordings, 274; 'Come Together',
    382; Frisell concerts, 382–3; Frisell on,
    382–5, 464n; Frisell project, 382–5, 404,
    406, 426, 513n; 'Give Peace a Chance',
    384–5; 'Imagine', 384; 'In My Life', 165,
    383; 'Julia', 383, 385; 'Mother', 385;
    'Number 9 Dream', 382; 'Please, Please Me',
    382; 'Revolution', 382, 383; 'Strawberry
    Fields Forever', 380; 'Woman', 384; 'You've
    Got to Hide Your Love Away', 382
Lennon, Sean, 315
Levi's commercial, 423
Lewis, George, 151
Lewis, Mike, 224
Lewis, Travis, 477n
Liberation Music Orchestra, 104, 410
Lifetime trio, 47
Liljestrand, Eric, 328
Lindsay, Arto, 60, 142, 149, 158–9, 176, 186,
    205, 206, 274, 325, 483n
Lipowski, Al, 414
listening, 355
Live (Frisell album), 211–12, 217, 221–2,
    491–2n, 511n
Live Download Series, 381, 383, 510n, 511n,
    521n
livestream concerts, 437–8
Lloyd, Charles: Big Sur, 387, 513n; Blue Note
    label, 408, 434; Charles Lloyd Quartet,
    96, 407; on Frisell, 409; Frisell concerts,
    407–408; Frisell on, 407; Frisell work, 5,
    407–408; *I Long to See You*, 408; Marvels,
    408, 409, 434; and Motian, 96; New
    Quartet, 408; *Tone Poem*, 409; *Vanished
    Gardens*, 409, 516n

Lockwood, John, 120
Logan, 'Happy', 24–5, 464n
London Jazz Festival, 373, 471n
Lookout for Hope (Frisell album), 121, 134–9,
    181, 185, 191, 364, 429
looping, 225–6, 283, 339, 376, 421
Los Angeles Philharmonic, 274
The Lounge Lizards, 143, 319
Louvin Brothers, 262, 498n
Lovano, Joe (Joseph Salvatore): birth, 106; and
    Baron, 175; Berklee College of Music, 106,
    107; on Frisell, 165; Frisell on, 99; on jazz,
    204; jazz supergroup, 317; on Motian, 106,
    107; Motian quintet, 100; Motian sessions,
    98–100; Motian trio, 5, 104–10, 192, 363,
    518n; saxophone lessons, 106; Simon's *In
    the Blue Light*, 336; Vernon on, 224; Village
    Vanguard, 110
Lovano, Tony ('Big T'), 106, 108
Lowe, Keith, 301, 317, 318
Lowe, Nick, 492n
Lucas, Gary, 200
Luchetti, Daniele, *La Scuola*, 494n
Lull, Mike, 314, 319
Lurie, Evan, 143
Lurie, John, 200, 483n
luthiers, 207, 209, 309, 311, 314
Luxion, Dennis, 88

MacGowan, Shane, 381
Mackey, Steve, *Deal*, 274–5
Maclay, Christian, 148
Maddox, Paul (Pheeroan akLaff), 473n
Madonna, 294; 'Live to Tell', 214
Mahavishnu Orchestra, 47; *Apocalypse*, 77
Mahler, Gustav, 152, 483n
The Maid with the Flaxen Hair (Halvorson and
    Frisell), 411
Malian music, 323–4, 336, 337
Mancini, Henry, 56, 157; 'Days of Wine and
    Roses', 164, 426; 'Moon River', 250
Mandel, Johnny, 'The Shadow of Your Smile', 36
mandolin, 269, 321
Manfred Mann, 24; 'Do Wah Diddy Diddy',
    464n
Mann, Ron, 310
marching bands, 21–2, 25, 34, 53, 106, 119,
    492n
Marclay, Christian, 148, 150, 481n; *The Clock*,
    481n

Marcus, Bob, 23, 451
Marcus, Greil, 267, 498n
Mariano, Charlie, 90
Market Street Trolley, 27
Márquez, Gabriel García, 181
Marsalis, Branford, 136, 155
Marsalis, Wynton, 136, 151, 152, 336, 376
Marshall, John, 90, 91
Martin, Stu, 489n
Martine, Tucker, 236, 318, 326, 333, 431, 438, 507n
Massey, Chris, 123
Mauve Traffic, 87–8; *Oh Boy . . .*, 88
Ma, Yo-Yo, 441
Mays, Lyle, 79, 154, 479n; *Street Dreams*, 186
McCandless, Paul, 479n
McCartney, Paul, 3, 274; 'In My Life', 165, 383; 'Strawberry Fields Forever', 380
McClure, Ron, 96
McCoy, Charlie, 293
McDonald's All-American High School Band, 34
McGuirl, Cindy, *Uncle Paul's Jazz Closet*, 99
McGuirl, David, 100
McKuen, Rod, 51
McLaughlin, John, 47, 237, 421, 422, 431, 474n, 'Follow Your Heart', 313
McLaughlin, Sheila, *She Must Be Seeing Things*, 157
Meany Hall, Seattle, 358
Medeski, John, 414
Meek, Joe, 'Telstar', 405
Mehldau, Brad, 333, 381, 384
Mel Lewis Jazz Orchestra, 98
melody, 163, 164, 165, 198, 225, 284
Mercer, Johnny, 293; 'Days of Wine and Roses', 164, 426
mescaline, 44
The Mesmerist (film), 247
Metheny, Mike, *Blue Jay Sessions*, 121
Metheny, Pat: *80/81*, 475n; Berklee College of Music, 76, 79, 82, 121; *Bright Size Life*, 76; first trio, 79; on Frisell, 76, 97, 296; Frisell and Motian, 97; as Frisell influence, 76, 82, 119; Frisell work, 5; guitars, 40; guitar synthesiser, 478n; on Hall, 49; on jazz, 5, 289; Johnson album, 265, 273; and Moses, 120; and Motian, 475n; Pat Metheny Group, 79; reputation, 155; Van Sant on, 421; Village Vanguard, 185; and Weber, 91

Meyer, Mike, *see* Disfarmer, Mike
Michihiro, Sato, 186
Miles, Ron: Blue Note label, 434; Colorado Music Hall of Fame, 433; on Denver scene, 54; East High School, 27; *Floratone* albums, 333, 334; on Frisell, 58, 66, 287, 352; Frisell collaboration, 274; Frisell friendship, 465n; Frisell on, 270; Frisell quartet, 217, 236; Frisell's *Blues Dream*, 315; Frisell's *History, Mystery*, 360, 371, 511n; Frisell's *Kentucky Derby*, 390; on Frisell solos, 351; Frisell's *Quartet*, 236; Frisell's *The Sweetest Punch*, 276; *The Great Flood*, 248; on jazz, 501n; *Mysterio Simpatico*, 239, 240; *Woman's Day*, 274
Miller, Buddy, 329; *Buddy Miller Majestic Silver Strings*, 435; 'God's Wing'd Horse', 435
Miller, Mike, 55, 74, 75
The Million Dollar Hotel (film), 245–6, 246, 495n
Mingus, Charles, 134, 137, 212, 275, 329
minstrel songs, 441–2
Minzer, Michael, 514n
Mipso, 291–2
Mississippi River flood, 248
Mitchell, Joni, 160, 297, 328
Modern Jazz Quartet, 79
Molde Jazz Festival, Norway, 124–5
MoMA (Museum of Modern Art), New York, 241, 496n
Monder, Ben, 190
Monk, Thelonious: Amidon on, 281, 284; Bill Frisell Band, 177; and Coltrane, 228; *Criss-Cross*, 228; Douglas on Frisell, 393; 'Epistrophy', 164, 229, 431; Five Spot club, 228; as Frisell influence, 41, 56, 107, 191, 196, 197, 228, 392; Frisell on, 5, 164, 228, 351; Frisell on jazz, 289; Frisell parallels, 168; Frisell's *History, Mystery*, 360; Frisell's *Lookout for Hope* album, 134; Frisell style, 165; 'Hackensack', 134, 135; 'Jackie-ing', 366, 512n; Lloyd's *Tone Poem*, 409; Miles on, 287; 'Misterioso', 332; 'Monk's Mood', 108; and Motian, 96, 100, 101, 107, 108; Newport Jazz Festival, 31; 'Raise Four', 332; 'Round Midnight', 466n; silences, 165, 168; 'Skippy', 380; Vernon on, 223; Vu on Frisell, 393
Monk, Meredith, 389
Monroe, Bill, 259, 261, 268, 282, 295
Monterey Jazz Festival, 386, 387

Montgomery, Wes: Beatles music, 384; 'Bumpin' on Sunset', 29, 30, 34, 83, 409; death of, 32, 504n; as Frisell influence, 56, 83, 185, 208; Frisell on, 29–31, 32, 37, 324, 418; Frisell's *Unspeakable*, 328; as guitar influence, 203; guitars, 36, 40, 310; Hall on, 50; Lloyd on, 409; 'Solo Flight', 30; *Tequila*, 29, 30, 31, 273, 465n; *The Wes Montgomery Trio*, 31, 466n

Montreal International Jazz Festival, 407

Montreux jazz festival, 44, 45

Moon, Tom, 162, 350–1

'Moon River' (Mancini song), 250, 317, 330, 416

Moore, Scotty, 40

Moran, Jason, 66, 167–8, 169, 289, 381, 408

Moran, Joe, 16–17; *Shrinking Violets*, 72

Morell, Marty, 448

Morgan, Thomas, 112, 352, 356, 416, 419, 429–31, 438–9; *Epistrophy*, 430–1; *Small Town*, 429–30

Mori, Ikue, 142, 153, 176

Morricone, Ennio, 148–9, 415, 419, 482n; 'Erotico', 149, 482n; 'Poverty', 149

Morrison, Bill: Bryars's *The Sinking of the Titanic*, 360; *Electricity*, 249; *The Film of Her*, 247; film showings, 496n; Frisell collaboration, 247–8, 381; Frisland map, 295; *The Great Flood*, 247–9, 387; *The Mesmerist*, 247; MoMA retrospective, 496n; The Tank Center for Sonic Arts project, 249; website, 496n

Morton, Brian, 92, 149, 181, 209, 238, 263–4, 505n

Moses, Bob, 31, 76, 97, 119–20, 123, 146, 200; *When Elephants Dream of Music*, 120

Moss, David, 142

Motian, Paul: birth, 100; on apartment, 475n; The Bad Plus on, 190, 192–3, 198; Barnes eulogy, 432; *Bill Evans*, 109; *Bill Frisell, Ron Carter, Paul Motian*, 332–3; and Bley, 182, 183, 489n; Carter on, 332; childhood, 100; composition, 99, 102; *Conception Vessel*, 96, 97, 102; death of, 112, 376, 390; drum style, 100–2; Electric Bebop Band, 110; Engelhart on, 417; 'Etude', 103; Europe tours, 102, 104, 105, 131, 132, 133, 156; and Evans, 102, 108, 109; 'For the Love of Sarah', 183; on Frisell, 72; Frisell and Morgan's *Epistrophy*,
431; Frisell collaboration, 96–100, 112, 125, 205, 229, 332, 487–8n, 518n; Frisell concerts, 381; Frisell discography, 521n; Frisell gigs, 180, 185, 189, 277, 277, 363; as Frisell influence, 96, 123; Frisell meeting, 97–8; Frisell on, 96–9, 103, 110–12, 189, 269, 329, 390; Frisell on Haden, 410; Frisell phone call, 96–7; Frisell rehearsals, 98, 99; Frisell reputation, 146; Frisell's 'It Should've Happened a Long Time Ago', 430; Frisell's *Rambler*, 147–8; Frisell's stage presence, 345; Great American Songbook, 108; and Petra Haden, 329; heart surgery, 111; *I Have the Room Above Her*, 112; 'Introduction', 333; *It Should've Happened a Long Time Ago*, 104, 105, 199; *Jack of Clubs*, 104; Jarrett trio, 410; 'Lament', 104; Lovano on, 106, 107; and Metheny, 475n; *Misterioso*, 107; and Monk, 96, 100, 101, 107, 108; *Monk in Motian*, 108; and Morgan, 429; *Motian and Frisell*, 105; 'My Foolish Heart', 363; name pronunciation, 100; navy, 101; nicknames, 107; *On Broadway*, 108–9, 272; *One Time Out*, 107, 198; *Paul Motian boxset*, 476n; 'Portrait of T', 108; *Psalm*, 102–3, 126, 516n; quintet, 102, 107, 131, 192; rehearsals, 155; Ryles club, 180; songbooks, 99, 100; Soul Note records, 130; *Sound of Love*, 111; *The Story of Maryam*, 104; 'The Storyteller', 198; *Time and Time Again*, 112; tours, 376; *Tribute*, 97; trio, 5, 104–12, 192, 193, 198, 224, 363, 425, 518n; *Trioism*, 110; Vernon on, 224; Village Vanguard, 109–11; *The Windmills of Your Mind*, 112, 429; 'Yahllah', 518n; *You Took the Words Right Out of My Heart*, 111

Motion Pictures (White and Frisell album), 272

Mount Vernon, 221, 222

Mouzon, Alphonse, 124, 479n

Muhly, Nico, 279

Müller, Wulf, 387, 429

Murray, Albert, 151

Murray, David, 494n

Music City players, 260, 293

Musician (record label), 205

Music IS (Frisell album), 431–3, 434

Mwandishi, 47, 48

Mysterio Simpatico (Frisell and Woodring multimedia), 239, 240, 358

Naked City, 157–9, 176, 187, 217, 220, 260, 412, 418, 481n, 484n; *Naked City*, 217
Naked Lunch (Burroughs), 274, 499n
Nascimento, Milton, 201
Nash guitars, 413
Nashville, 203, 258, 260–1, 293, 381, 496n
Nashville (Frisell album), 221, 222, 258–64, 268, 269, 277, 288, 413, 497n
National guitars, 420
Neighbors (Keaton film), 234
Nelson, Willie, 408
Nemeyer, Eric, 343
new Americana, 294
New England folk music, 280, 281
New Jersey, 37, 96, 116–17, 118, 133, 143, 188
Newman, Randy, 134, 400
New Orleans, 147, 203, 221, 232
Newport Jazz Festival, 31, 32, 190, 196, 198, 276
New York: Bill Frisell Band, 180; Covid-19 pandemic, 435–8; downtown scene, 142–5, 153, 223, 482n; Frisell homes, 95, 115–18, 428–9; Frisell solo gigs, 186; Motian in, 101; reputation, 52–3, 116–17; and Seattle, 204
New York Guitar Festival, 247
Niehaus, Lennie, 36
Night Music (Willner TV programme), 139
Nippon Kan Theatre, Seattle, 202–3
Nitta, Keary, 34, 39, 40, 44
Nocentelli, Jack, 399
Nonesuch (record label), 199–202, 205, 212, 216–17, 234, 244, 271, 277, 318, 332, 374–5, 441, 484n, 490n, 504n
Nordine, Ken, 137, 139
Not So Fast (West and Bryant project), 405

O Brother, Where Art Thou? (film), 246
Ogerman, Claus, 463n
O'Henry Sound, Burbank, 269
OKeh label, 387, 396, 404, 419
Okoshi, Toru 'Tiger', 82, 83, 84, 116, 473n
Okumu, Dave, 273
old-time music, 267, 440, 444, 445
On Broadway (Motian albums), 108–9, 272
Once Upon a Time in America (film), 149
One Week (Keaton film), 233
online concerts, 437–8
Ono, Seigen, 186
Ono, Yoko, 142, 358, 382
Oregon (group), 479n

O'Rourke, Jim, 138
oud, 325
Ouellette, Dan, 62
Outside In festival, Crawley, 154, 483n
Oxley, Tony, 360
Oyama, Phyllis, 181, 345, 368, 388

Paco de Lucía, 6
Page, Jimmy, 421
painting, 17, 229–31, 241–3, 313–14, 367, 376, 463n
pan-Americana, 294
pandemic (Covid-19), 65, 139, 430, 435–8, 441
Panken, Ted, 81, 104, 491n
Pareles, Jon, 161, 162
Parker, Charlie, 36, 47, 52, 56, 167, 183, 290, 293, 314, 502n
Parker, Paul, 466n
Parkins, Zeena, 143
Parks, Van Dyke, 9, 329, 396–402, 515n
Partch, Harry, 137
Pastorius, Jaco, 76, 93
Pat Metheny Group, 79, 154, 155; *see also* Metheny, Pat
Patton, Big John, 148
Patton, Mike, 159, 412
Paul Bley Quartet, 182, 183–4, 276; *see also* Bley, Paul
Paul, Les, 5
Paul Motian Quintet, 102, 131; *Misterioso*, 107
Paul Motian Trio, 104–5, 107–12; *I Have the Room Above Her*, 112; *It Should've Happened a Long Time Ago*, 104, 105, 199; *Monk in Motian*, 108; *On Broadway*, 108–9, 272; *One Time Out*, 107, 198; *Time and Time Again*, 112; *Trioism*, 110; Village Vanguard, 109–11; *see also* Motian, Paul
Paul's Mall, Boston, 48, 79
Payton, Nicholas, 290
Peacock, Gary, 293, 489n; *Just So Happens*, 271
Pelzer, Jacques, 474n
Penguin Guide to Jazz Recordings, 92, 149, 181, 209, 238, 264
Penn, Clarence, 330
Peoples, Tommy, 279
Pepper, Art, *Straight Life*, 56
Pepper, Jim, 103
performance art, 159, 358
Peschek, David, 383

Peter, Paul and Mary, 214, 444, 451
Petra Haden and Bill Frisell (album), 329–30, 511n
Philharmonic Hall, Lincoln Center, 466n
Philip, Radhika, 120, 264, 288, 296
Phillips, Barre, 489n
photography, 241, 243–5
Pike, Nick, 118
Piltch, David, 314, 315, 325
'Playing for Jim Hall' tribute, 410
Pomeroy, Herb, 77, 94, 391
Pooh's Pub, Boston, 79, 82
Poole, Steven, 450
Porter, Cole, 475n; 'Just One of Those Things', 477n
Portraits (band), 51
Potter, Chris, 330, 435
Pousseur, Henri, 85
Power Station studio, New York, 181, 272, 507n
Power Tools, 345; *Strange Meeting*, 154
Prague, 94
The President sextet, 503n
Presley, Elvis, 18, 40, 118, 295
Previte, Bobby, 60, 143, 148, 150, 176, 200, 480n; *Claude's Late Morning*, 186
Pritchard, David, 467n
Probability Cloud (Frisell and Woodring multimedia), 239, 239–40
Psycho (Van Sant film), 246, 421, 517n
The Publik, 27

Quartet (Frisell album), 220, 221, 224, 234, 236–8, 262, 315, 494n
Quine, Robert, 122, 123, 149, 156, 309, 483n

R&B, 5, 10, 30, 79, 258, 296
racial interaction, 27, 28, 53
radio, 19, 32, 51, 60, 512n
Radio City studios, New York, 149, 150, 150, 151
Rainbow Studio, Oslo, 182, 183
Raitt, Bonnie, 66, 302, 381
Rambler (Frisell album), 122, 146–8, 178, 180, 181, 191, 260, 272, 317
Ratliff, Ben, 101, 160, 477n, 486n
RAT pedal, 224, 225
The Real Book, 79
Redman, Dewey, 108, 475n
Redman, Joshua, 104, 391
'Red River Valley' (folk song), 431, 519n

Red Rocks Amphitheatre, Colorado, 31, 32, 33, 54, 276, 464n
Reed, Lou, 122, 134, 309, 381, 414
Reich, Steve, 200, 247, 281, 413
Reid, Vernon, 5, 60, 149, 481n, 483n; *Smash & Scatteration*, 154
Renaux, Michelle, 478n
Rhyne, Melvin, 466n
Ribot, Marc: Carmine Street Guitars, 309; on Frisell, 163, 287, 320; Frisell conversation, 159, 258–9, 268; guitars, 319, 320; The Lounge Lizards, 143; on musicians, 415; Ruhr Triennale festival, 329; on solo gigs, 312; and Waits, 156; Willner on, 135; Willner's *Stay Awake*, 302; Wollesen work, 315; Zorn's *Masada Guitars*, 412
Richter, Gerhard, 7, 241–3, 327, 378, 495n; *Abstract Pictures, 1999 (858-1 to 8)*, 241
Richter 858 (Frisell album), 243
Riley, Gyan, 414
Riley, Terry, 413, 414; *In C*, 286
Ringler, Mike, 30, 38
Roach, Max, 502n
Robbins, Tim, 389
Roberts, Hank: 858 Quartet, 240, 242, 249, 327, 371, 378, 379, 380; and Baron, 176; Bill Frisell Band, 174, 176–7, 178, 181–2, 206, 209–10, 212; *Black Pastels*, 153; Douglas's 'The Frisell Dream', 330; *Electricity* project, 249; on Frisell, 65, 295–6; Frisell collaboration, 81–2, 174, 381; Frisell gigs and 'The Look', 355; Frisell quintet, 171; Frisell's *Before We Were Born*, 206; Frisell's *Big Sur*, 387, 396; Frisell's *HARMONY*, 440; Frisell's *History, Mystery*, 360, 371; Frisell's *Is That You?* 206; Frisell's *Lookout for Hope*, 134, 137, 428; Frisell's *Where in the World?* 190, 194; HARMONY quartet, 427–8; Shifting Foundation grant, 481n
Robertson, Herb, 176; *Transparency*, 153
'Rob Roy' building, Denver, 51
rock and roll, 48, 445, 447
rock guitar, 83, 192
rock music, 23, 48, 195
Rodgers and Hart, 'My Funny Valentine', 31
Rodgers, Jimmie, 267; 'Blue Yodel No. 9', 292
Rodriguez, Carrie, 329, 347, 381, 495n
Rogers, Fred, 379
Rogers, Kenny, 261, 333
Rogers, Reuben, 408

Rogers, Smokey, 293
Roland guitar synthesiser, 146, 478n
The Rolling Stones, 24, 25, 281
Rollins, Sonny: Amidon on, 281; bands, 147;
    and Bley, 183; 'Blue 7', 344; in Boston, 79;
    The Bridge, 55; and Campbell, 474n; on
    country music, 293; as Frisell influence, 31,
    41–2, 56, 69; Frisell on, 5, 145, 211, 259,
    260; Frisell on jazz, 289; Frisell's *Have a
    Little Faith*, 214; and Hall, 37, 49, 50; and
    Harris, 478n; 'I'm an Old Cowhand', 293;
    on jazz, 289; music styles, 501n; 'No Moe',
    211; *Saxophone Colossus*, 344; Schuller on,
    344; style, 155; 'Wagon Wheels', 293, 439;
    Way Out West, 260, 293, 439, 502n
Romney, Jonathan, 245, 496n
Ronnie Scott's jazz club, London, 379
Roots of Americana concerts, 294
Rose, Jonathan, 200
Ross, Annie, 389
Rota, Nino, 59, 103, 136, 361, 415, 419, 423;
    Amarcord, 361; *The Godfather*, 423
Roth, Ed 'Big Daddy', 20–1
Rothko, Mark, 168
Roulette club, New York, 144, 149, 176, 186
Royal Conservatory, Liège, 87
Royal Festival Hall, London, 208
Royston, Rudy: Beautiful Dreamers trio, 3, 354,
    375; Denver music scene, 54; on Frisell, 73,
    352; Frisell gigs, 354; Frisell's *Big Sur*, 387,
    396; Frisell's *Valentine*, 438–9; Frisell's *When
    You Wish Upon a Star*, 416, 419; Frisell trio,
    368, 438–9; livestream events, 438; Miles's
    Woman's Day, 274; SFJAZZ Center gig, 171
'Rubbertellie', 78
Rubinstein, Donald, 224, 274
Ruhr Triennale festival, 328–9, 397
Russell, George, 77, 101, 131
Russonello, Giovanni, 293–4
Ryles club, Boston, 100, 180
Rypdal, Terje, 124, 478n, 503n

Sade, Marquis de, 134, 158–9
Sadowsky, Roger, 206, 311
St Ann's church, Brooklyn Heights, 233, 234,
    239
Saint Joan (Shaw), 434
Salonen, Esa-Pekka, 274
Sanborn, David, 79, 274, 410; *Another Hand*,
    139

Sandburg, Carl, 63
Sanders, Bernie, 435, 519n
Sandole, Dennis, 36, 37, 40
San Francisco, 241, 427, 428
San Francisco Contemporary Music Players, 275
San Francisco Museum of Modern Art
    (SFMoMA), 241
San Francisco Sound, 33
Santana, Carlos, 6, 81
Santing, Mathilde, *Out of This Dream*, 186
Santoro, Gene, 7, 142, 315, 392
Satchmo, *see* Armstrong, Louis
Saturday Night Live, 134
Saudades Tourneen, 199
Savoy (record label), 375, 384, 387
Scheinman, Jenny: 858 Quartet, 240, 242,
    249, 327, 371, 378, 379, 380; *All Hat*
    film music, 496n; *Disfarmer* project, 244,
    495n; *Electricity* project, 249; on Frisell, 58,
    65, 71, 326–7; Frisell collaboration, 166,
    381; Frisell's *Big Sur*, 387, 396; Frisell's
    History, Mystery, 360, 371, 511n; Frisell's
    The Intercontinentals, 326–7, 335; Gabriela's
    Viento Rojo, 326; Lennon music trio, 382;
    Mysterio Simpatico, 239; SFJAZZ Center gig,
    171; Zilberman film music, 427
Scherer, Peter, 186, 206
Scherr, Tony: on Frisell, 57–8, 171, 231, 350;
    Frisell film scores, 247; Frisell on, 332,
    354; Frisell's *East/West*, 330, 331; Frisell's
    Guitar in the Space Age! 406; Frisell's *History,
    Mystery*, 360, 371; Frisell's Lennon project,
    383; Frisell's *Unspeakable*, 327; Frisell trio,
    319, 323, 327, 330, 354, 368; *The Great
    Flood*, 248
Schuller, Ed, 99, 100
Schuller, Gunther, 49, 77, 99, 344, 352
Scofield, John, 5, 155, 197, 198, 200, 237,
    273, 274, 274, 302, 310, 317, 410
La Scuola (film), 237, 494n
Seattle, 33, 202–4, 209, 235, 299, 418, 420,
    428
Seeger, Peggy, 444
Seeger, Pete, 32, 56, 256, 440; 'Where Have All
    the Flowers Gone?' 427, 435, 443–4
Senate Lounge, Denver, 47, 448
set-lists, 353
Seventh Avenue South club, New York, 119, 121
Sexmob, 315, 319, 327
Seydel, Karle, 10, 512n

Index

SFJAZZ Center, San Francisco, 171, 191, 390
SFMoMA (San Francisco Museum of Modern
    Art), 241
Shankar, Ravi, 33
Sharp, Elliott, 5, 60, 481n
Sharpe, David 'D.', 117, 120–1, 123, 180, 185,
    478n
Shaw, George Bernard, *Saint Joan*, 434
'Shenandoah' (folk song), 42, 165, 271, 279,
    281, 408, 410, 426
Shepp, Archie, 375
Sherburg, John, 39
Sherlock Jr. (Keaton film), 234
Shifting Foundation, 481n
Shioi, Luli, 150
Shorter, Wayne, 31, 47, 69, 160, 344, 434;
    'Nefertiti', 76
shredding, 167–8, 196, 198, 274, 284
Shrieve, Michael, 250, 251, 316
Shteamer, Hank, 105–6
Sign of Life (Frisell album), 379–80
silence, 64, 166, 168
Silent Comedy (Frisell album), 412–13, 431
Simon, Paul: 'America', 415; 'Cecilia', 338;
    'Everything About it is a Love Song', 338;
    on Frisell, 336–40; Frisell collaboration,
    336, 338, 381, 434; Frisell influence, 9;
    on Frisell's *The Intercontinentals*, 335–40;
    Graceland, 335; *In the Blue Light*, 336;
    The Rhythm of the Saints, 335; songs, 335;
    Surprise, 336, 338
Sims, Zoot, 101
Sinatra, Frank, 479n; 'In the Wee Small Hours
    of the Morning', 431
Siskind, Sarah: *Covered*, 224; 'Lovin's for Fools',
    224
slide guitar, 408, 423
Small Town (Frisell and Morgan album),
    429–30
Smash & Scatteration (Frisell and Reid album),
    154, 483n
Smith, Harry, 396, 397
Smith, Jimmy, 82
Smith, Johnny, 41–2, 44, 49, 52, 271, 281,
    410–11, 467–8n; 'Black is the Colour (of
    My True Love's Hair)', 411; 'Moonlight in
    Vermont', 42, 411; 'Shenandoah', 271, 281,
    410; 'Walk, Don't Run', 42, 411
Smith, Wadada Leo, 430
smooth jazz, 296

Snow, Hank, 261
social music, 290
Soft Machine, 33, 91, 123
SoHo Music Gallery, 140, 142
Sollima, Sergio, *The Big Gundown*, 482n
solo gigs, 185, 186, 312, 434
solos, 64, 164, 225, 270, 351
Solos (Frisell live DVD), 372–3
song architecture, 164–5
Songs We Know (Frisell and Hersch album), 271
Songtone company, 181, 345
Sontag, Susan, 17
Soul Merchants, 10, 34, 39
soul music, 28, 328
Soul Note (record label), 104, 107
sound, 160–1, 166
Sound Emporium, Nashville, 262
Sousa, John Philip, 492n; 'Washington Post
    March', 213
South by Southwest (SXSW), 424, 425
Southern, Terry, 514n
Spa, Belgium, 86–7, 89, 90, 174
Sparks, Tim, 412
Speed, Chris, 190
Spillane, Mickey, 150, 483n
Spotify, 438
Staley, Jim, 480n; *Mumbo Jumbo*, 153
Stanley, Dr Ralph, 67, 268
s t a r g a z e ensemble, 286
Starr, Ringo, 137, 415
*Stay Awake: Various Interpretations of Music from
    Vintage Disney Films*, 137, 139, 302, 415
Steadman, Ralph, 389, 390, 514n
Steffey, Adam, 261, 262, 497n
Steinbeck, John, 391; *East of Eden*, 72, 386
'Stella by Starlight' (Young song), 36, 49
Stenson, Bobo, 478n
Stern, Chip, 42, 122, 123, 147, 272
Stern, Leni (Magdalena Thora), 83–4, 87, 112,
    121, 315, 349, 473n; *Clairvoyant*, 154
Stern, Mike, 84, 85, 121, 274, 349; 'Frizz',
    274; *Play*, 274
Stevens, Jack, 22, 53, 492n
Stewart, Bob, 147
Sting, 335–40, 336
The Stone, New York, 431, 433
Stone Tiger, 122–3, 478n
Stories from the Heart of the Land (radio series),
    512n
Stöwsand, Thomas, 199

'Strange Meeting' (Frisell track), 148, 211, 221, 251–2
Strayhorn, Billy: 'A Flower is a Lovesome Thing', 439; 'Lush Life', 427, 431, 519n; 'Satin Doll', 466n
Street, Ben, 518n
Streisand, Barbra, 'People', 331
stretch music, 290
string bands, 292, 441, 446
string bass, 147
Studio Henry, 142
Summerhill, Julian (later Victor Bruce Godsey), 121–2, 478n
Sumner, Dave, 417
Sunny Adé, King, 140, 141
Sun Ra, 281, 375
'Surfer Girl' (Beach Boys song), 20, 310, 404, 409
surf music, 20, 30, 31, 157, 400, 404, 411, 417
Surman, John, 128, 182, 183, 450, 489n
sustain, 81, 162–3, 225
Svedberg, Theodor, 12
Swallow, Steve, 31, 120, 391, 467n
Swallow Hill Music, Denver, 450, 451
Sweden, 12, 13, 16
The Sweetest Punch (Frisell album), 275–6
synaesthesia, 230
synthesisers, 146, 148, 154, 476n, 481n
Szabó, Gábor, 409

Tagliavore, Vincent, 21, 29, 34
Talent Studio, Oslo, 125, 126, 129
Tales from the Far Side, 234–5, 236, 237, 313, 416, 422, 493n
Tales from the Far Side II, 236
Tamarkin, Jeff, 232
The Tank Center for Sonic Arts, Colorado, 249
Tardy, Greg, 240, 360, 371
Tate, Grady, 465n
Tate, Greg, 154
Taylor, Cecil, 66
Taylor, Creed, 328, 466n
Taylor, John, 124, 125, 479n
Teitelbaum, Richard, 518n
Telerant, Charles, 121
Teller Elementary School, 21
Terkel, Studs, 288
Terrell, Joseph, 292
Testa, Gianmaria, 381
Tharpe, Sister Rosetta, 246, 445

Theoretically (Berne and Frisell album), 146
Thielemans, Toots, 148
This Land (Frisell album), 191, 216–17, 219–26, 260, 315
'This Land is Your Land' (Guthrie song), 216, 435
Thomas, John, 85
Thompson, Hunter S., 134, 386; The Kentucky Derby is Decadent and Depraved, 138, 389–90, 404, 514n
Thora, Magdalena, see Stern, Leni
Threadgill, Henry, 86, 481n
'Throughout' (Frisell song), 123, 129–30, 206, 211, 362, 392, 511n
Tiger's Baku, 82–3, 84, 99
Tiselius, Arne, 12
Tone Field Productions, 202
Tongzhi in Love (film), 246
Tonstudio Bauer, Ludwigsburg, 92, 102, 104, 125
The Tornados, 'Telstar', 405
Tounkara, Djelimady, 326
tour dates archive, 521n
touring, 347–50, 353
Toussaint, Allen, 66; American Tunes, 442
Towner, Ralph, 5, 91, 124, 128, 131
Townsend, Lee: All Hat film music, 496n; Cantuária album, 325; ECM and Eicher, 199, 201–2; Floratone, 333, 334, 507n; on Frisell, 277, 375; as Frisell producer, 180, 269; Frisell relations, 277; Frisell's All We Are Saying . . ., 382, 384; Frisell's Before We Were Born, 206; Frisell's Big Sur, 387, 396; Frisell's Ghost Town, 313, 412; Frisell's Good Dog, Happy Man, 279; Frisell's HARMONY, 440; Frisell's History, Mystery, 360; Frisell's Lookout for Hope album, 134, 180–1; Frisell's The Intercontinentals, 326, 335; Frisell's This Land, 216, 219; Frisell's Valentine, 438; Frisell's When You Wish Upon a Star, 419; Frisell's The Willies, 301; Frisell's With Dave Holland and Elvin Jones (Frisell album), 250; Gabriela albums, 275; Ruhr Triennale festival, 329; SFJAZZ Center gig, 171; Songtone company, 181, 345; Tone Field Productions, 202
Tractor Tavern, Seattle, 317
Traoré, Boubacar, 323, 324, 326, 335, 360; 'Baba Drame', 165, 324, 326, 336, 512n
Triode (Frisell trio album), 93–4

Tristano, Lennie, 96, 101
Trosper (Woodring), 250
Trump, Donald, 70, 409, 438
Tsugaru-shamisen, 186
tuba, 13, 147, 207, 217
Tuft, Harry, 450, 451, 521n
Turrell, Terry, 314
Turrisi, Francesco, 442
The Twilight Zone, 139, 206, 491n
Twitty, Conway, 139
Two Harbors, Minnesota, 12, 13
Tyler, William, 434
Tyner, McCoy, 5, 79, 381, 479n
Tzadik label, 411, 414, 482n

ukulele, 207, 321
Ulmer, James Blood, 5, 147
Umbria Jazz Festival, 368
UNC/Greeley Jazz Festival, 43
Union Station, 261
University of Northern Colorado (UNC), 38,
    41–5, 51, 52, 411, 468n
Univox guitars, 36, 40, 41
Unspeakable (Frisell album), 134, 138, 327–8,
    378, 390, 506n
Upchurch, Phil, 420
Uppsala University, Sweden, 12
Upsala College, New Jersey, 369
Usher Hall, Edinburgh, 383
Utley, Claude, 313–14, 504n

Valente, Gary, 120
Valentine (Frisell album), 266, 391, 438–9
Vanbuskirk, Paul, 27
Vancouver International Jazz Festival, 186, 489n
Van Eps, George, 50, 235, 397–8
Van Gelder, Rudy, 466n
Van Halen, Eddie, 193
Van Sant, Gus: *18 Songs About Golf*, 419;
    critical response, 517n; Destroy All Blondes,
    419; *The Elvis of Letters*, 419; *Finding
    Forrester*, 246, 419, 422; *Four Boys in a Volvo*,
    423; Frisell collaboration, 9, 423; on Frisell's
    When You Wish Upon a Star, 419–23; guitars,
    420, 421–2; *Gus Van Sant*, 419; Levi's
    commercial, 423; other films, 419; *Psycho*,
    246, 421, 517n
Van Zandt, Steven, 23
Varèse, Edgard, 'Un Grand Sommeil Noir', 354
Vashon Island, 250, 496n

Vaughan, Kenny, 52, 54
Veloso, Caetano, 200, 325
The Ventures, 20, 42, 56; 'Walk, Don't Run',
    411
Vermont Studio Center (VSC), 65, 341,
    377–9, 380, 394, 403
Verneuil, Henri, *The Burglars*, 482n
Vernon, Justin, 9, 219–26, 291
Verve label, 466n
vibraphone, 43, 362
vibrato, 161, 262, 311
Vietnam war, 28, 44, 53
Viklický, Emil: *Dveře* ('*Door*'), 94; *Okno*
    ('*Window*'), 94
Village Vanguard club, New York: Bill Frisell
    Band, 180; Cajori at, 228–9; Frisell and
    Morgan duo, 429, 430–1; Frisell gigs,
    184–5, 190, 229, 277, 283, 319, 352, 356,
    424; Frisell's *East/West*, 330, 331; Frisell's first
    appearance, 161; Frisell's first visit, 37–8;
    Frisell's *Small Town*, 429; *Live at the Village
    Vanguard*, 111; livestream events, 438; Mel
    Lewis Jazz Orchestra, 98; Morrison job,
    496n; and Motian, 109–11, 363, 425, 430
Virelles, David, 518n
Visiones club, New York, 109, 180
visual arts, 7, 228–33, 240–3, 247–9, 313–14
Vitouš, Miroslav, 47
vocal quality, 163–4
VSC, *see* Vermont Studio Center
Vu, Cuong, 155, 393

Wainwright, Loudon, III, 329, 381, 396–7
Wainwright, Rufus, 381, 396
Waits, Tom, 137, 156, 315, 360; 'I Don't Want
    to Grow Up', 330; *Rain Dogs*, 156
Waldman, Dan, 433
Waldron, Mal, *Mingus Lives*, 86
Walker, T-Bone, 85
Walker Art Center, Minneapolis, 190, 192,
    220, 244, 276, 489n
Walk the Line (film), 246
Waller, Lyle, 39
Walters, John L., 153
Warner Bros Records, 199
Warwick, Dionne, 31, 276
Was, Don, 434
Waters, Muddy, 294; *Electric Mud*, 420; 'I Can't
    Be Satisfied', 214
Watrous, Peter, 237

Watson, Doc, 204

Weather Report, 47, 55, 83, 93, 155, 164, 479n

Webb, Chloe, 390

Weber, Eberhard: Colours band, 479n; and ECM, 91–3, 102, 103; *Fluid Rustle*, 92–3; on Frisell, 91, 93; Frisell collaboration, 91–3, 102, 479n; The Frisell Tape, 124, 391; Frisell tours, 124, 132–3; and Garbarek, 103, 125; Gibbs big band, 90, 91; *Later That Evening*, 125, 479n

The Weeds, 25, 26

Weegee, *Corpse with Revolver*, 484n

Weill, Kurt, 134, 156, 364

Weinstein, David, 150, 482n

Wenders, Wim, *The Million Dollar Hotel*, 245

Wendl, Hans, 199, 202, 325, 492n

Werner, Kenny, 174, 175

'We Shall Overcome' (protest song), 70, 435, 437, 439

Westerlund, Joe, 221, 222

Westerlund, Yan, 291–2

West (Frisell album), 330; *see also East/West* (Frisell album)

West, Speedy, 405; 'Reflections from the Moon', 405

Weston, Edward, 387

Wexner Center, 244, 405

Wheeler, Kenny, 90–1, 146, 272–3, 479n; *Angel Song*, 272–3, 302, 316; *Gnu High*, 91; 'Nicolette', 302

When You Wish Upon a Star (Frisell album), 415–17, 419–23

Where in the World? (Frisell album), 190–8, 208–9, 211

Whitcomb, Bruce, 478n

white culture, and black music, 446, 447

White, John, 360

White, Josh, 32

White, Michael, *Motion Pictures*, 272

Whitehead, Kevin, 294

Wieselman, Doug, 186, 206, 286, 301, 390

'Wildwood Flower' (Carter Family song), 324, 326, 430

Wilkins, Frank, 82

Williams, Hank, 268, 293, 301, 313, 318, 329, 333, 384, 431; 'I'm So Lonesome I Could Cry', 163, 304–5, 313, 333, 437

Williams, Lucinda, 9, 52, 134, 381, 409, 516n

Williams, Miller, 516n

Williams, Richard, 299, 318, 318, 503n

Williams, Tony, 47, 80, 228, 466n

The Willies (band), 231, 276, 301–8, 317–19, 446, 503n; *The Willies* album, 231, 301–8, 318–19, 446, 505n

Willner, Hal: Burroughs' *Naked Lunch*, 274, 420–1, 499n; death of, 139, 435–6, 438; experimental spirit, 333; *Finding Forrester* soundtrack, 419; on Frisell, 59; Frisell collaboration, 212, 302, 381; Frisell discography, 521n; Frisell on, 134–5, 139, 436; Frisell's 'Juliet of the Spirits', 103, 120; on Frisell's *Lookout for Hope*, 134–9; Frisell's *Unspeakable*, 327–8; Ginsberg's '*Kaddish*', 390, 438; Ginsberg's *The Lion for Real*, 155–6, 514n; Grammy award, 328; *The Kentucky Derby is Decadent and Depraved*, 138, 389–90, 404, 514n; *Let Me Hang You*, 499n; *Lost in the Stars*, 156; and Lucinda Williams, 516n; *The Million Dollar Hotel* soundtrack, 245; *Night Music* TV programme, 139; Parks on, 397, 401; *Rogue's Gallery: Pirate Ballads, Sea Songs and Chanteys*, 139; Nino Rota album, 103, 140; sampling, 328; Santing's *Out of This Dream*, 186; *Stay Awake: Various Interpretations of Music from Vintage Disney Films*, 137, 139, 302, 415; studio, 231; *Weird Nightmare: Meditations on Mingus*, 137, 212, 275, 492n

Wills, Bob, 'Basin Street Blues', 293

Wilson, Anthony, 504n

Wilson, Brian, 396, 404; *Smile*, 396

Wilson, Cassandra, 276

Wilson, Matt, *Honey and Salt*, 63

Wilson, Michael, 499n

Winstone, Norma, 92, 479n

The Wire, 61, 64, 154, 174, 181, 205, 263

With Dave Holland and Elvin Jones (Frisell album), 250–7, 316–17, 338, 374

Wollesen, Kenny: on Frisell, 4, 355–6; Frisell film scores, 247; Frisell on, 296, 354; Frisell's *Blues Dream*, 314; Frisell's *East/West*, 330; Frisell's *Guitar in the Space Age!* 406; Frisell's *History, Mystery*, 360, 371; Frisell's *Kentucky Derby*, 390; Frisell's Lennon project, 383; Frisell's *Unspeakable*, 327, 328; Frisell trio, 319, 323, 327, 328, 330, 354, 368; Gnostic Trio, 413, 414; *The Great Flood*, 248; New Quartet, 325; Yan Westerlund on, 291; and Zorn, 315, 414

women guitar players, 84

Wonder, Stevie, 55; 'I Believe', 357
Woodard, Josef, 28, 276, 313, 410;
    Conversations with Charlie Haden, 410
Woodring, Jim: album covers, 4; *Close Your
    Eyes*, 240; Frank cartoon series, 250;
    on Frisell, 58–9, 68–9, 251–7; Frisell
    collaboration, 238–40, 250, 494n; Frisell
    documentary, 343; on The Frisell Dream, 4;
    Frisell on, 231–2, 238, 256; Frisell's *Gone,
    Just Like a Train*, 238–40, 250, 256, 282;
    Frisell's *History, Mystery*, 365, 371, 511n;
    JIM magazine, 250; *Mysterio Simpatico*,
    239, 240; *Probability Cloud*, 239–40;
    Trosper, 250; Vashon Island home, 250,
    496n; on *With Dave Holland and Elvin
    Jones*, 250–7
Woodstock, 96, 136
Woolfolk, Andrew, 28, 433
World Saxophone Quartet, 494n
Wray, Link, 'Rumble', 404
Wright, Ken, 34

Yamamoto, Rick, 34
Yang, Ruby, *Tongzhi in Love*, 246
Yazgol Music, 100
Yoshi's club, California, 330, 331, 383
Young, Larry, 47
Young, Lester, 470n
Young, Neil, 134; 'One of These Days', 263
Young, Victor, 431; 'Stella by Starlight', 36, 49

Zankel Hall, New York, 240
Zappa, Frank, 32, 33, 80, 297, 297, 396, 485n
Zawinul, Joe, 47, 164
Zilberman, Yaron, 427

Zorn, John: acoustic guitar trio, 414; *Arcana*
    book, 163, 225; and Baron, 157–8, 176, 208;
    The Big Gundown, 148–9, 200, 415, 480n; on
    Bill Frisell Band, 208; Breskin on, 67; *Cobra*,
    149–50, 482n; *Cynical Hysterie Hour*, 157;
    file-card composition, 150, 491n; fingerings,
    163; on Frisell, 145; Frisell band, 176; Frisell
    collaboration, 138–46, 148–52, 157–9, 186,
    205, 212, 274, 412, 414, 482n, 491n; Frisell
    discography, 521n; Frisell gigs, 185; Frisell
    influence, 9; Frisell in New York, 174; Frisell
    meeting, 140–2; Frisell on, 140–1, 144–5,
    150, 158; Frisell's *Before We Were Born*, 206;
    Frisell's character, 60; Frisell's *Silent Comedy*,
    412–13; and genre, 297; *The Gnostic Preludes:
    Music of Splendor*, 413–14; Gnostic Trio, 413–
    14; 'Godard', 150, 482n; 'guitarded' term,
    504n; improvisation, 141; *The Maid with
    the Flaxen Hair* album, 411; *Masada Guitars*,
    412; Masada songbook, 414; and Monk,
    136; *More News for Lulu*, 152; Morricone as
    influence, 482n; on music, 152; Naked City,
    157–9, 176, 220, 412, 481n, 484n; *News for
    Lulu*, 151–2; Nonesuch records, 200; *Nove
    Cantici Per Francesco d'Assisi*, 414; panoramic
    approach, 297; *Parables*, 414; reputation, 145,
    481n; *Rodan*, 186; The Saint clubhouse, 144;
    She Must Be Seeing Things soundtrack, 157;
    Shifting Foundation grant, 481n; and Smith,
    411; SoHo Music Gallery, 140; *Spillane*,
    150–1, 200, 481n, 482n; *Spy vs Spy*, 176;
    The Stone, 431; *Teresa de Ávila*, 414; '*Track
    & Field*', 141, 142, 144; *Transmigration of the
    Magus*, 414; Tzadik label, 411, 482n; Vernon
    on, 220; *Virtue*, 414; and Wollesen, 315, 414